Date Due

JUN 21 '61			
JUL 5 '61			
JUL 26 '61			
AUG 8 '61			
OCT 14 '61			
MAY 19 '62			
JUL 12 '63			
MAY 26 '64			
MAR 11 '67			
M.H.C. LIBRARY			
MAR 20 '71			
OCT 18 '71 M.H.C. LIBRARY			
M.H.C. LIBRARY			
APR 15 '72			
DEC 15 '80 LIBRARY			
	PRINTED	IN U.S.A.	

AN INTRODUCTION TO SOCIAL PSYCHOLOGY

BY

L. L. BERNARD

Author of "INSTINCT: *A Study in Social Psychology*"

NEW YORK
HENRY HOLT AND COMPANY

COPYRIGHT, 1926,
BY
HENRY HOLT AND COMPANY

Printed July, 1926.

PRINTED IN THE
UNITED STATES OF AMERICA

PREFACE

The present *Introduction to Social Psychology* represents an attempt at a more synthetic type of treatment of the field than has ordinarily been given. It seems to the writer that the time has arrived when "schools" of social psychology may properly be regarded as obsolete and the subject as a whole may be presented systematically. In a sense social psychology overlaps a very large portion of social science and of psychology and education. In this respect it is central to all psychological and social science disciplines. This fact necessarily renders the content of social psychology voluminous. It is no longer possible to treat this subject adequately in small compass. The text-books which have so far appeared, although for the most part excellent from their several viewpoints, are nevertheless but partial treatments. So notably true is this that there exists a marked controversy as to what properly constitutes social psychology. In Part I of this volume an attempt has been made to bring this controversy into relief for the purpose of enabling the reader to see the subject as a whole.

Originally the writer intended to publish this volume in five parts to make the synthetic treatment more pronounced. But the length of the volume as thus planned was prohibitive and it was decided to change the plan somewhat. The synthetic character of the treatment has been retained, but the detailed presentation of the process of the development of personality and of self and social consciousness has been reserved for a second volume. The present volume treats the subject from the standpoint of the more objective factors which integrate the personality and its responses in a social environment. Throughout it has been the intention of the writer, not only to make the treatment complete in itself, but to keep the presentation on such a level that the volume can be used successfully as a second book in social theory, following directly upon the introductory course in sociology in departments of sociology. If the approach to the social sciences is a psychological one, the organization of this volume should make it available as an introduction to the first course in sociology, economics, politics, and more advanced courses in history and literature, in those departments which care to use it in this way. That social psychology will ultimately be regarded as a necessary introduction to the several social sciences and the literatures can scarcely be doubted. While the present volume is intended for undergraduate students, it is hoped that it may also be used profitably in more advanced courses in combination with the more extended treatment of the subjective aspects of personality development later to be published.

I wish to express my appreciation to Professors E. A. Ross and C. H. Cooley, pioneers in social psychology in this country, and to Professors Ellwood, Thomas, Vincent, and Mead, my teachers. Professor Cooley has read a portion of the text and has made valuable criticisms and suggestions. Also I wish to express my gratitude to Mrs. Elizabeth Hayes Robinson, formerly of the Child Guidance Clinic of St. Paul, Minn., who read some of the chapters critically, and to numerous writers for ideas which I have embodied in the text. Where this obligation is specific I have cited the author in the text. Where the obligation has been general only, I have contented myself with acknowledging their work in the special bibliographies at the end of each chapter and at the end of the volume.[1] A consistent effort has been made throughout the book to keep footnotes off the textual page, unless necessary for the sake of clearness. It is hoped that the bibliographies will be found to be relatively complete for the recent literature in the field. This literature is now becoming so voluminous that it is very difficult to cover the whole of it.

L. L. BERNARD.

Cornell University, January 4, 1926.

[1] I am also indebted to the *American Journal of Sociology* for permission to use in Chapter VI material from an article of my own entitled "A Classification of Environments," published in the November, 1925, issue, and to the *Psychological Review* for the use in Chapter X of material from my article entitled "Neuro-Psychic Technique," which appeared in the November, 1923, issue.

NOTE TO TEACHERS

Either of three possible methods of using this text is open to the teacher. In a brief course the present volume may prove sufficient for the needs of the student. If more reading material is required, recourse may be had to the bibliographies. Brief bibliographies, consisting for the most part of that supplementary material which is most easily available, are presented at the end of each chapter. More extended bibliographies of materials not so readily available to most classes, but frequently containing even more specialized results of research, are placed at the end of the textual material of the volume.

In other cases the teacher may prefer to use this volume in conjunction with some other text which emphasizes another aspect of the subject or a different viewpoint. Such a procedure has many advantages and, when carried out by a skillful teacher, need have few drawbacks. Those who wish to combine the psychological and sociological viewpoints may supplement with Allport's text. For greater emphasis upon instinctive and purposive factors in collective behavior, McDougall's volume will be found most useful. In supplementing special phases of the subject, Gault should be used with Parts II and III, Cooley's *Human Nature and the Social Order* with Part III, and Ellwood, Ross, Bogardus, Williams, and Cooley's *Social Organization* with Part IV. In more elementary classes Part I may be deferred until the end of the course, or omitted altogether, at the discretion of the instructor.

CONTENTS

PART I. INTRODUCTION

CHAPTER		PAGE
I.	SCIENCE AND THE ENVIRONMENT	3
II.	THE SCOPE AND RELATIONS OF SOCIAL PSYCHOLOGY	13
III.	PHASES OF THE SUBJECT	25
IV.	METHOD OF THE PRESENT TREATMENT	38

PART II. THE FOUNDATIONS OF COLLECTIVE BEHAVIOR

V.	THE ORGANIC BASES OF BEHAVIOR	51
VI.	THE ENVIRONMENTAL BASES OF BEHAVIOR	69
VII.	THE INHERITED AND ACQUIRED EQUIPMENT OF MAN	90
VIII.	BEHAVIOR PATTERNS: THEIR NATURE AND DEVELOPMENT	107
IX.	MISUSE OF THE CONCEPT OF INSTINCT	123
X.	HABIT MECHANISMS AND THE ADJUSTMENT PROCESS	142
XI.	THE FUNCTIONAL ORGANIZATION OF CONSCIOUSNESS—THE FORMS OF CONSCIOUSNESS	158
XII.	THE FUNCTIONAL ORGANIZATION OF CONSCIOUSNESS—THE OBJECTS OF CONSCIOUSNESS	172
XIII.	PATHOLOGICAL FORMS OF CONSCIOUSNESS	187
XIV.	GENERAL SETS, POWERS, AND INTELLIGENCE	206
XV.	RACE, NATIONALITY, CLASS	224
XVI.	THE ATTITUDES AND PERSONALITY	246
XVII.	SUMMARY OF PART II	262

PART III. THE INTEGRATION OF PERSONALITY IN THE PSYCHO-SOCIAL ENVIRONMENT

XVIII.	THE INTEGRATION OF PERSONALITY IN THE SOCIAL ENVIRONMENT	269

CONTENTS

CHAPTER		PAGE
XIX.	Suggestion and Personality Development	282
XX.	The Conditions of Suggestibility	300
XXI.	Imitation and Personality Development	322
XXII.	Personality Development Through the Direct Imitation of Persons	342
XXIII.	Personality Development Through the Indirect Imitation of Ideal Persons	361
XXIV.	Personality Development Through the Projective Imitation and Assimilation of Principles and Concepts	383
XXV.	Summary of Part III	403

PART IV. THE PSYCHO-SOCIAL ENVIRONMENT AND THE ORGANIZATION OF COLLECTIVE BEHAVIOR

XXVI.	Primary and Derivative Groups	411
XXVII.	Primary and Derivative Attitudes and Ideals	425
XXVIII.	Direct Contact Groups: Rational Types	438
XXIX.	Direct Contact Groups: Non-Rational Types	451
XXX.	Indirect Contact Groups and Communication	465
XXXI.	Types and Functions of Indirect Contact Groups	479
XXXII.	The Influence of Contacts upon Individual and Collective Behavior	496
XXXIII.	Collective Responses and Leadership	517
XXXIV.	The Qualities of Leaders	528
XXXV.	Non-Institutional Controls	541
XXXVI.	Institutional Controls	564
XXXVII.	Summary and Conclusions	583
	Bibliography	591
	Index	637

Part I
INTRODUCTION

CHAPTER I

SCIENCE AND THE ENVIRONMENT

THE NATURE OF SCIENCE—Science is tested and classified knowledge. It is not a matter of primary importance whether this knowledge comes from the laboratory or from some form of observation properly controlled and tested and generalized. The source of the knowledge is of secondary importance. Its accuracy is the primary consideration. It must be tested or verified to be science, that is, trustworthy knowledge. Hypotheses supported by all relative facts which are known, and not contradicted by other data or hypotheses, are also usually regarded as scientifically dependable or as science content.

To be most useful, that is, readily available, for the one who works with scientific data, it should not only be tested, but it should also be classified knowledge. Classification is the storekeeping of science. It brings each fact or principle ready to the mind of the user, as a tool to the workman. Thus both the testing and the classifying of knowledge are essential procedures in rendering science available for both the professional investigator and thinker and the intelligent layman who makes use of facts in adjusting himself immediately to his environment and in thinking out a livable theory of his world.

THE SCIENCES—CLASSIFICATION—It is generally agreed that the field of science may be segregated into certain major divisions and into various sciences, which we call collectively the sciences. The general or basic sciences, which are commonly recognized, are mathematics, physics, chemistry, biology, psychology, and social science. The subdivisions under these generic headings are of two general kinds: (1) the special sciences, such as arithmetic, geometry, algebra, etc., under mathematics, for example; or bacteriology, physiology, anatomy, neurology, botany, etc., under biology; and (2) the applied sciences. The applied sciences do not always come so regularly under any one heading as do the special sciences mentioned. They fall between two general sciences, or they may even be dependent, more or less indiscriminately, upon a number of general and special, or even other applied, sciences. Thus, astronomy is frequently regarded as an applied branch of mathematics, but it is also dependent upon physics and chemistry. Mechanics, which is more frequently considered to be an applied science, is dependent upon both mathematics and physics. Social psychology is a special science resting directly upon psychology and sociology, but indirectly also upon biology, and all of the other sciences in less degree. It also has interrelationships with other special sciences, such as educational psychology, economics, and political science, and with such applied sciences as the psychology of advertising, educational and political administration, etc.

Some writers on methodology might not regard the type of sciences represented by astronomy and mechanics as applied sciences at all, but rather as special sciences arising out of two or more general sciences, and this view is probably correct. The older special sciences mentioned above by way of illustration are all tributary to some one general science. But it is only within the limits of expectation that as the general sciences overlap, there will arise from them hybrid or multiple special sciences, as in the cases mentioned. The older special sciences apparently became integrated before the general sciences to which they logically belong were given composite or conceptual existence. But the newer special sciences were split off to cover and integrate special problems arising in human consciousness after the general sciences were established. Hence the fact that they often depend upon more than one general science. The later the special science develops the more likely it is to have specific relationships with several general sciences.

Some obviously applied sciences have already been mentioned. There are many of this type and the number is constantly growing. As our collective life becomes more complex and as the physical, biological, and social phenomena which we must take into consideration in making our adjustment processes become more numerous, we organize these new fields of knowledge into special and applied sciences. An applied science is a system or classification of knowledge arranged in such form as to make it readily and immediately available for purposes of technology. It is drawn directly out of the more generally classified and logically arranged data of the special, sometimes of the general, sciences, or it may grow up directly out of experience and experiment and observation. In this latter case it becomes an important source for the development of a special, or of a general, science, instead of being merely drawn from these more abstract sources. Perhaps the technologies have always been the primary feeders for the abstract sciences, but in our time scientific investigation, which is being pursued more and more as an immediate end in itself, is becoming increasingly the source of such tested and classified general knowledge.

THE UNITY OF THE SCIENCES—The dividing lines between the three types of sciences here mentioned are not always easily drawn. Not even the general sciences can be kept uniformly separate. For example, the distinction between physics and chemistry tends to disappear at certain points, especially where both merge in physical chemistry. In a similar way psychology and sociology tend to find a common ground in social psychology. And some social scientists are inclined to anticipate a development of these two basic sciences in which social psychology will absorb the most important content of both psychology and sociology. Some sociologists already define the subject matter of sociology as the psychic interstimulation and response of people living in society, and the author of this book knows at least one psychologist of reputation who believes that the introduction of the college student to the science of psychology should be through the doorway of social psychology.

Likewise, it is sometimes difficult to determine whether a science should be regarded as independent and general or as subsidiary and special. For example, are economics and political science special subdivisions of the general science of sociology; or are they equally general and coördinate with sociology; or are they along with sociology but subdivisions of and subordinate to a developing and emerging general *social science* on the analogy of the synthetic sciences of mathematics, physics, chemistry, or biology? Are political science and economics independent sciences at all, or are they rather applied sciences? Unquestionably both have their applied aspects and apparently the pure and applied science aspects of these sciences have not yet been clearly differentiated—at least not as clearly separated as in the case of some of the older sciences.

Finally, it is sometimes maintained that the social sciences are synthetic sciences organized primarily out of materials taken from the older and better developed sciences and from each other, with an increasing body of data and principles resulting from their own investigations. Thus sociology is supposed to be based primarily upon psychology and biology and it might therefore be considered as a special science depending upon these earlier developed sciences. Yet sociology did not originate in this way, but as an attempt to organize tested knowledge about the major field of human relationships in general. However, it would be possible for a special science to develop into the status of a general science through growth in volume and in importance as a means of adjustment. It might be contended that just this is happening to social psychology. But such a conclusion would probably be premature at this stage of its development.

THE ORIGIN OF THE SCIENCES—Such questions can be settled, or rather understood, only if we examine the method by which the sciences arose. Also, we must not forget that science is simply tested knowledge, which is all the more available for the worker if it is also classified. Any particular science, as distinguished from science in general, comes into existence with the organization of a considerable body of this tested knowledge about the statement of some problem situation. It is immaterial, as far as the particular science is concerned, whether this tested knowledge was drawn from other sciences—borrowed—or whether it was produced, so to speak, to order, through laboratory or other investigations, in an attempt to solve the specific problems outstanding. There is no exclusive ownership of scientific data, as far as the several sciences are concerned. Tested knowledge passes current in all principalities of science, and there is no customs barrier or other tax or embargo upon it. It is free to every scientist who understands its symbolism, although he may not use the form in which it is cast without permission. The form is art rather than science.

Some sciences are organized on the federal principle. As suggested above, the special sciences may arise before the related general science and only in the course of time come to be organized or synthesized into a general science. Whether this is a principle of universal application is open to question, but it certainly has been the case with mathematics, which had its beginnings in the special sciences of arithmetic, geometry, algebra, and trigonometry. Only relatively recently have we come to think of mathematics as a unit science instead of as independent sciences, which we now call mathematical. Possibly a similar movement towards federalism in the social sciences is under way. If this is the case, we shall probably adopt the generalized term *social science* to cover the conceptual unity of the various social sciences. Possibly a general social science is just now being integrated conceptually out of the special social sciences, as formerly mathematics was integrated out of arithmetic, geometry, algebra, etc. Or, as some writers seem inclined to believe, we might possibly regard sociology as in part a federal synthesis of the abstract findings of the special social sciences, even though sociology began as an independent science.

The reverse tendency, for special and applied sciences to split off from the earlier formal and more general sciences, is perhaps the more common one. We are so familiar with this process that it requires no elucidation or illustration. The relations of the sciences to each other are constantly changing, with the result that the relative importance of any science, general or special, varies from time to time. The social sciences have come into very great importance in recent decades and their significance is likely to increase rather than diminish. Social psychology in particular has obtained a noticeably increased hearing for itself, because we have begun to study human society with greater earnestness and we recognize that the most important phases of human relationships are those which involve neuro-psychic stimulation and response.

THE FUNCTION OF SCIENCE—When viewed from the standpoint of society, the function of science is adjustment. It is often said that science has no other concern than the truth, and this is unquestionably the case in so far as investigational method is concerned. No bias or prepossession should be allowed to distort technique or to color conclusions. Otherwise the cardinal principle of the definition of science—the tested quality of its data and principles—is violated.

When viewed from an androcentric standpoint, however—and science is a human product—its function is to collect the data and principles which enable man the better to control his relationship to his world. Man is the collector of tested knowledge and presumably his object in gathering facts and principles is not a purely esthetic one, but is primarily practical. Originally the practical motive was probably dominant in the individual, although mere curiosity may have played a part in the origins of science. All collections of data were relative to some problem or interest which was of great importance to the collector. In our highly complex society, however, where the investigator often lives relatively detached from the concrete and urgent elementary problems of life, it is possible for him to have only an abstract interest in his results. This detachment from the stress of life, which enables the scientist to concentrate on the method and process of investigation without being concerned as to what social effect it will ultimately have, favors the impartiality of his conclusions. Consequently we are apt to approve what we sometimes call the "pure science" attitude of the investigator.

But society as a whole is likely to demand practical results. The motives of those who endow scientific research may be merely esthetic, although they are more likely to be practical, or to be concerned with social welfare or industrial development. The problems of investigation, the foci around which the collections of data constituting science are organized, are set primarily by practical adjustment situations. The desire for knowledge for knowledge's sake, although a growing conception, usually has back of it the realization that its findings will ultimately be utilized in some practical situation.

The older or so-called natural sciences of course investigate

SCIENCE AND THE ENVIRONMENT

many subjects only indirectly related to the problems of human adjustment. The questions of the distance and composition of stars, the constitution of matter, the qualities of chemical elements, or even the causes of climatic cycles, may appear to have little immediate concern for the practical problems of life. They are more interesting as intellectual than as social problems. But there is little knowledge which does not in the last analysis have some bearing upon the problem of an intelligent organization and control of our world. The recognition of this fact is perhaps the strongest moral justification we have for our individual and social support of scientific investigation.

THE FUNCTION OF THE SOCIAL SCIENCES—It is the business of the social sciences especially to assist man in making his adjustment to his world. The social sciences deal with human relationships. But it is not with the interrelationships of people alone that the social sciences are concerned. They are interested in man's adjustment to nature or to the external and non-human world or environments. This is sometimes the adjustment of the individual to his environment, but it is more frequently the adjustment of a collection or organization of individuals to their common environment.

This sort of collective adjustment may be either an aggregate adjustment or a coöperative adjustment. The former term refers more particularly to those collective adjustments which are not primarily purposive on the part of the participating members and for which no special preparation has been made in the way of conscious organization. Even among modern civilized men we can find examples of merely aggregate adjustment on the part of people who are thrown together adventitiously, as in a storm or at an amusement place or on a journey. But even in such cases people are never wholly unprepared by their previous experiences and by traditions and customs and conventions for acting together. Consequently their responses to the common environment will soon become consciously coöperative, if the difficulties are sufficiently great to call forth mutual aid.

In a certain sense all collective human adjustment to environment is coöperative and purposive. The very fact of being born into a coöperating society and of having one's character molded by it gives each person the technique for a larger measure of coöperation, even under adventitious circumstances. Coöperative adjustment involves a certain amount of organization, which tends to become both more extensive and intensive the closer and more effective the coöperation is. Of course this organization is primarily psychic in character, and when it becomes relatively fixed and permanent we speak of it as institutional. Not all coöperation is institutional in character, but the more ephemeral types of organization tend to become institutionalized as they grow older, especially if the conditions of coöperation are not changing rapidly. Nor are all institutions self-conscious or purposively coöperative. But all modern institutions tend to become highly self-conscious and purposively coöperative, perhaps because the problem of maintaining a continuity of integration under a fairly rapid change of environmental pressures becomes increasingly difficult and can be solved only as the result of conscious effort.

It is clear, therefore, that much of this problem of adjustment of man to his environments falls within the range of social psychology and must be solved in the light of the data of this special social science. Since the content of institutions, the chief forms of coöperative collective or coadaptive adjustment, is mainly psycho-social, it is necessary constantly to make use of the data of psychology to interpret and apply the processes of adjustment. It is largely through social psychology that sociology makes its contact with psychology.

THE FACTORS IN SOCIAL ADJUSTMENT—We have spoken of the function of science, considered as an anthropomorphic and anthropocentric system, as being to aid in the adjustment of man to his environment. Also, it may be truly said, the content of the social sciences is the technique, in theory and in practice, of the adjustment processes. In order to understand adequately these adjustment processes it is necessary to analyze all of the factors and conditions of these processes. These include the inner or psychic processes in the individual, the social contact processes, the maintenance and social sustenance processes, and the social organization and control processes. And to these must be added an analysis of the environments which serve as the conditioning factors for individual and collective behavior.

In this work it will not be necessary to do more than outline the various environments and to indicate how they function as conditioners of adjustment processes. Nor shall we be further concerned with the maintenance and sustenance processes, except as they constitute an aspect of the environment. Likewise the individual psychic mechanisms are of interest to us as students of social psychology only in so far as they mediate collective adjustments or condition social or collective responses. Social psychology is concerned, however, with the analysis of the growth and exercise of psychic behavior processes in response to social stimuli, in the analysis of those contact situations which afford effective stimuli to such responses, and even in the forms of social organization and the means of social control which condition and modify those stimuli.

SCIENCE AND ENVIRONMENT—Science in general, and the social sciences in particular, are the product of the study of objects—including organisms—and their relation to their environments. The concept environment has developed particularly in the field of the biological and social sciences, but we find it also in those sciences dealing with fields of physical forces converging upon a center, as in the case of electrical phenomena. C. M. Child apparently would extend it to all phases of science. The objects and organisms may be studied as materials for direct analysis, or they may be considered in relation to other objects and groups of objects, that is, as environment for other objects or as themselves subject to the influence of environing objects or organisms.

The various social sciences are the products of the study of the relation of the various environments to man and of man to his environments. Thus economics is the tested and organized data relative to man's adjustment to his physical environment and of the exchange and productive contacts of men with each other in pursuit of this adjustment. Political administration embodies the data of the publicly supervised contacts of men, especially in the economic field, but also in other fields. Ethics is the organized data concerning the valuation of human contacts in terms of their effect upon personalities, isolated and as members of groups. Educational psychology is the study of the effect of the environments, mainly social, upon the individual behavior as determined through personal direction or training. Social psychology is the study of the influence of the environments, mainly social, upon the individual and collective behavior, or of the response of individual behavior in collective situations to all sorts of stimuli. The analysis of the organism and of its environments, and of the types of individual reaction to these environments, will be undertaken in Part II. The reactions of individuals to social situations will be considered in Part III. The collective processes themselves, which embrace both individual responses in social situations and environmental forms, are discussed in Part IV.

CHAPTER II

THE SCOPE AND RELATIONS OF SOCIAL PSYCHOLOGY

SOME DEFINITIONS—Social psychology has been differently defined by various writers. McDougall declares [1] that "Social psychology has to show how, given the native propensities and capacities of the individual human mind, all the complex mental life of societies is shaped by them and in turn reacts upon the course of their development and operation in the individual." He does not consider that the study of the "native propensities and capacities of the individual human mind" is properly a part of social psychology, but is "an indispensable preliminary to all social psychology." This definition places the emphasis less upon *what* happens to the complex mental (psycho-social) life of societies and the consciousness of individuals than upon *how* it happens.

Allport [1a] also stresses the mechanism of the consciousness and behavior of the individual acting in a social situation and is not directly concerned with what occurs in the social organization as the result or the cause of these behavior processes. He says, "Social psychology is the science which studies the behavior of the individual in so far as his behavior stimulates other individuals, or is itself a reaction to their behavior; and which describes the consciousness of the individuals in so far as it is a consciousness of social objects and social reactions." In Chapter I we classified social psychology as a special science falling between psychology and the various social sciences. Allport regards it as a subdivision of individual psychology. "Social psychology must not be placed in contradistinction to the psychology of the individual; *it is a part of the psychology of the individual,* whose behavior it studies in relation to that sector of his environment comprised by his fellows." The definition of social psychology presented

---

[1] *Introd. to Social Psychology,* Ch. I.
[1a] *Social Psychology,* Ch. I.

by J. M. Williams,[2] as "the science of the motives of people living in social relations," is not essentially different from this view on its face. But as a matter of fact Williams is very much concerned in his treatment with the social processes also, especially those of antagonism between groups and institutions. We may also be justified in saying that Williams includes unconscious along with conscious impulses in his category of motives.

Ellwood [3] claims social psychology as a subdivision of sociology, which he defines as "the science of the origin, development, structure, and functioning of groups." He maintains that "the problem of psychology is to explain the experience and behavior of the individual, while the problem of sociology is to explain the nature and the behavior of the group. As soon as interest shifts from the individual to the group, it shifts from the purely psychological to the sociological." He concludes that "Social psychology, in the sense of the psychology of group behavior, is accordingly a part of sociology. It is a *study of the psychic factors involved in the origin, development, structure, and functioning of social groups.*" He contends, however, in his *Sociology in Its Psychological Aspects,* that the chief content of sociological data is psychological. Presumably, therefore, he would regard social psychology as the chief division of sociology.

Bogardus, like McDougall, defines social psychology in terms of what it does. He says,[4] "Social psychology studies intersocial stimulation and response, social attitudes, values and personalities. It begins with the individual human beings and original human nature and traces their growth through intersocial stimulation into persons with socialized attitudes." This definition would appear to apply to all socially conditioned behavior of individuals, but there is nothing in the statement, unless it is the terms "attitudes" and "values," to indicate the large measure of emphasis upon collective behavior processes which obtains in the actual treatment of this author.

---

[2] *Principles of Social Psychology,* Ch. I.

[3] "Relations of Sociology to Social Psychology," *Jour. Abnormal Psy. and Soc. Psy.,* XIX, p. 9; also *The Psychology of Human Society,* p. 16.

[4] *Fundamentals of Social Psychology,* p. 3.

Ross' conception of social psychology is only in part similar to that of Bogardus; it is stated as follows:[5] "Social psychology, as the writer conceives it, studies the psychic planes and currents that come into existence among men in consequence of their association. It seeks to understand and account for those uniformities in feeling, belief, or volition—and hence in action —which are due to the interaction of human beings, i.e., to *social* causes." Ross is less interested in the mechanism of the behavior processes, also less concerned with the personalities which develop out of the associational or intersocial stimulation and response contacts. His chief interest is in the form of the psycho-social contacts. He deals with uniformities, or social planes and currents. The subject matter is primarily that of crowds, publics, fads, fashions, crazes, conventions, and customs, and only secondarily that of the methods of contact, such as suggestion and imitation, with which Bogardus is so largely concerned.

The broadest definition of all is that of Gault:[6] "Social psychology in its widest sense applies to a study of interactions among animals. More specifically, and as the term is usually employed, it applies to the reactions of members of the human race one to another. . . . They may or may not be accompanied by a consciousness of the social relation." Apparently, according to this definition, all interactions of men or of animals is socio-psychic. Therefore, it would seem to follow, that almost all conduct in a social situation would belong to the field of social psychology. This appears also to be essentially the viewpoint of Dunlap who declares,[7] "The psychological study of man is . . . not complete until we have investigated his groupings, and analyzed the mental factors involved therein. This study is *social psychology,* or *group psychology.*" And further, "Social psychology, therefore, deals not with a specific 'social' type of reaction alone, but with the 'social' factor in all reactions. It is interested primarily in that which is contributed to our life (i.e., to our total system of reactions), by other people. The distinction between social psychology

---

[5] *Social Psychology,* Ch. I.
[6] *Social Psychology,* Ch. I.
[7] *Social Psychology,* pp. 14-15.

and general psychology is, therefore, not an absolute one, but is largely one of emphasis. Social psychology is the study of whatever the stimuli from other persons have contributed to our conscious lives, and to the activity (whether conscious or non-conscious) which results from the conscious life."

CRITICISM AND CONSTRUCTIVE STATEMENT—If we arrange these eight leading definitions of social psychology in the order of the objectivity of the subject matter indicated by each, we find that on the face of it Ellwood's definition appears to be the most subjective, for he says that social psychology studies (1) the psychic factors involved in the social process. He means, however, to include psycho-social as well as purely psychic factors in his study. McDougall is really more subjective, for (2) he would show how the *native* psychic factors determine social life. However, he introduces the objective side in including the return influence of social life upon the psychic processes. Although Allport states his definition rather objectively in terms of behavior, he develops the theme in his book primarily in terms of the inner psychic mechanisms. Williams, on the other hand, while stating a subjective definition, presents a fairly (3) objective treatment. This is perhaps even truer of Dunlap. In fact one might even speak of his text as a treatise in sociology, although he regards it as a phase or extension of psychol-(4) ogy. Bogardus is interested not alone in the psychic mechanisms of intersocial stimulation and response, but also in the objective social and psycho-social products of this process. On the whole, his treatment seems to fall somewhat between that of Ellwood and that of Ross. Gault speaks solely in terms (6) of behavior and in practice includes the objectified psycho-social processes, such as custom and convention, fashion and craze, in his treatment. In this he is very similar to Bogardus and Ellwood, but he probably regards the objectified psycho-social content more as object, while Bogardus treats it more as process. Ross is concerned still more extensively with the object of the psycho-social, bringing in the process side primarily to explain the development or the dissolution of the object aspect.

It will be seen from this brief analysis that the definitions are not wholly in the same plane, but cut across each other in some degree. Also the wording of the definition does not always adequately indicate the content, although the departure of fact from description in this respect is perhaps not striking. There is on the whole a noticeable similarity among the several definitions. All emphasize directly or indirectly the interrelationship character of the behavior-affording stimuli and the psychic character of the response mechanisms. Some develop the theme from the standpoint of the inner psychic processes —native processes, in McDougall's definition, or the almost equally elusive desires of Dunlap—which cause the overt responses. Others develop it from the standpoint of the behavior as a whole or of the personalities which result from the interrelationships. Others still (notably Ross) are interested in the psycho-social processes, or currents and planes, which arise from this interaction and produce new interactive behavior. Only one of the writers (Allport) would seem to wish to limit the subject matter wholly to the behavior mechanisms of individuals as individuals. Although this writer would appear to neglect somewhat the social stimuli which release individual responses in a social situation and to give inadequate attention to the collective aspects of individual responses, these partial omissions are probably incident to the author's particular purpose in preparing his text book rather than characteristic of his general viewpoint.

DEFINITION AND FIELD—Definitions are of course only formal statements of relationships of the subject matter of a science. They can never be more than an outline map of the territory covered. Some scientists, not without good reason, decry their use altogether, on the ground that they tend too rigidly to delimit the field. The watchword of scientific method is expansion, and the ordinary procedure is to pursue a lead towards knowledge across the frontiers of the sciences when the chase offers to be crowned with success. Sciences, like dynamic and evolving states, are constantly shifting their boundary lines and some of them are becoming vassal to others, while the more vital ones seem to occupy the rôle of peaceful conquerors. However, their wars are ordinarily peaceful ones, waged with the weapons of the laboratory and statistical investigation and logic, and their diplomacy is as sober and as sincere as a statistical formula.

Nevertheless, there are some virtues to be attributed to definitions. The chief one, perhaps, is administrative. It gives a sort of patent right and a warrant of respectability to the worker in the field which is characterized or delimited by it. It is also in a measure the statement of the purpose of the investigation in this field. We may therefore be justified in stating as a working definition of our subject the following: Social psychology studies the behavior of individuals in a psycho-social situation. This behavior is valid subject matter for social psychology whether it conditions or is conditioned by other social behavior or responses. It is also concerned with all collective responses, that is, responses of individuals which mutually and reciprocally condition each other and those which are uniform throughout the group, regardless of what environment they arise from. Of course the chief source of stimuli of which social psychology takes cognizance is the psycho-social environment, and the chief type of behavior in which it is interested is collective behavior.

Mutual conditioning of the behavior of a man and a horse would not in any very direct or ordinary sense be subject matter for social psychology. But the conditioning of a man's behavior by a book or by a picture would properly constitute such subject matter, provided this conditioning was determined by the psycho-social content which the book or the picture carried, and not by the mere physical character of these objects. The conditioning of the behavior of two men by each other is properly taken cognizance of by social psychology only when their mutual responses are psychic, which is usually the case. A mere collision of two people, without mutual psychic adjustment, would be social but not psycho-social. If they adjust themselves to each other in some psychic way, such as by dodging, pushing or warning each other by means of gestures or vocal language, there is a psycho-social situation of a low or high degree of complexity, and this behavior is subject matter for social psychology.

PSYCHOLOGY AND SOCIAL PSYCHOLOGY—It may be inferred

from the above discussion that there is not a true psycho-social situation, cognizable by social psychology, unless there are two or more persons in contact with each other through psychic processes or one or more persons in contact with psycho-social environments by means of psychic processes. Where one person alone is in contact with a natural or a physico-social or a bio-social environmental object—not a carrier of a psycho-social object or content—the relationship is not psycho-social and therefore is not subject matter for social psychology. Psychic processes, however, are involved in such a relationship, and these are properly the subject matter of individual psychology as distinguished from social psychology.

Psychology is concerned with the behavior processes occurring in an organism whose responses are conditioned by some phase or factor occurring in any type of environment, whether natural or social; physico-social, bio-social, or psycho-social. The essential fact to be noted here is that a stimulus-response process or neural complex is set up or organized with reference to such environmental object or objects. The adjustment of the animal organism to its environment is initiated through the senses. The stimulus-response processes which originate here are either of the nature of automatic behavior patterns, sometimes instinctive, or, as in the case of man, they may consist of neural sets which may come into consciousness as perceptions or concepts, or as feelings or emotions. These cortical sets are also adjustment processes, but they are complex and are more or less delayed in functioning between stimuli and responses.

The psycho-social processes which constitute subject matter for social psychology are of course also subject matter for individual psychology, since they occur in the behavior of individuals. The fact that individuals are in interrelationship with each other, either in the definite organizations of groups or in the more adventitious forms of contact, does not prevent these psycho-social and collective processes from being also individual psychic processes. Thus those who claim social psychology as a branch of individual psychology (e.g., Allport) are in one sense justified. But from another angle—that of the social character of the stimuli, or of the social interstimulation which is necessary to secure the individual's adjustment to environment—they are not justified. From this angle it would be equally appropriate to speak of social psychology as a phase of sociology, as Ellwood does.

SOCIOLOGY AND SOCIAL PSYCHOLOGY—All sorts of contacts between persons, whether psychically mediated or merely of a biological character, between persons and impersonal elements of the psycho-social environment, or even between persons and the bio-social or the physico-social environments, are in varying degrees social. The highest forms of social contacts are of course those of a psycho-social character, such as have been under discussion above. Where men discuss peace treaties or plan and put social reform programs through legislatures, or teach the contents of the social sciences, or attend a political convention or a social reception, they are engaging in social activities which are recognized by everybody as such. Such behavior is also taken cognizance of by social psychology, and since the processes involved are psychic, they are subject matter also for psychology.

It is equally, if less obviously, true that the relationship of men to institutions, their responses to the stimulation of customs and traditions, to conventions and mores, and to printed matter and art, are also social. It is immaterial if one term in the relationship is non-human or symbolic, or even invisible, as is the case with the abstract content of the psycho-social environment, provided it is the product of human action or thinking and if it is carried or symbolized by some social environmental object or organization. Likewise, and less obviously, the individual's or the group's relation to bio-social and physico-social objects is also social, but it is not psycho-social, as in the other two types of social relationship, unless these bio-social and physico-social objects are carriers of a psycho-social content, as in the case of books or statuary, of art or memorial tablets, which symbolize psycho-social relationships. Of course these last forms of social relationship are of the lowest order of the class and consequently they are not always recognized as true social relationships. The contacts of individuals with such objects must also be psychic, if it is social; although, as was explained above, it need not be psycho-social unless the stimulus as well as the response involves some human or personality content, either concrete or symbolical. If it is not a psychic relationship it must then be bio-physical in character, as is the case where one is accidentally injured by a falling building or a bridge.

Dominance of the Psycho-Social—It is apparent from the preceding discussion that the psycho-social relationships are dominant in the human world. Whether we consider social psychology as a branch either of psychology or of sociology or of the social sciences in general, it will be perceived that it constitutes the greater division of these. This is so especially because of the vast development in the complexity of modern life, involving the multiplication of psycho-social contacts or relationships.

An interesting, although an academic, question which was hinted at earlier, might be raised in this connection. Should we regard social psychology as the subsidiary special science which has outgrown its parent sciences, or should we shift the boundary lines and, upon its reaching adulthood, make it the more inclusive or dominant science, while the other aspects of psychology and the social sciences become secondary to it? This does not seem possible, because both psychology and social science are more general in character than social psychology, and should therefore be entitled to characterization as the more general sciences.

Two Types of Emphasis—There is to-day a marked contrast in emphasis between two rival viewpoints in social psychology. One, as was pointed out above, stresses the behavior patterns in the individual nervous system as they occur in response to social stimuli or as they create objective collective response situations. The other places the emphasis upon the organization of the psycho-social environment, especially in its more formal aspect of traditions, conventions, institutions, etc. The forms of behavior emphasized in both of these viewpoints are, in the last analysis, identical with the individual behavior patterns proceeding from a social contact situation, and they in turn act as environmental pressures to produce character responses in other individuals.

These two extremes are represented by Allport and Ross.

Perhaps they are not so far apart as they appear to be at first view, but theirs are unquestionably opposite viewpoints. Between these are all sorts of intermediate points of view. How can these differences be explained? They arise naturally enough out of the limitations of the two general sciences in which these two writers were trained. The social psychologist coming to this new field by way of psychology has his attention concentrated upon the specific behavior of individuals and the neuro-psychic mechanisms which account for this behavior on the organic side. He attempts to see the whole process of social interrelationships and social adjustment in terms of the neural or symbolic processes, and the conditioned responses built upon these.

On the other hand, the social psychologist coming to the field from sociology sees the process of social adjustment in terms of the objective social interrelationships and of the uniformities under which these occur. Sociology deals primarily with people in functional relationship as unit organisms and as members of groups and only secondarily with the neuro-psychic and symbolic processes by which these adjustments of organisms and groups are mainly mediated. Conceptualized psycho-social processes, such as traditions, beliefs, conventions, mores, institutions, are abstract verbal pictures of social relationships. They are the symbols of the relationships which have been objectified and which have now become verbal or conceptual stimuli to psycho-social behavior. These symbols, although less concrete and fixed and visible, are as real as the psycho-social relationships themselves which are carried in the actual behavior of persons having contacts in groups. They are symbolical of group relationships which have been, will be, or may never be, but are potential. To the sociologist such psycho-social objects or environmental symbols and stimuli are much more important than they are to the individual psychologist; while the neuro-psychic mechanisms are relatively more important to the latter. The sociologist takes the inner mechanisms for granted, much as the psychologist takes the psycho-social environment for granted. Hence, the objective emphasis of social psychologists with sociological antecedents.

ARTIFICIAL CHARACTER OF LOGICAL OR CONCEPTUAL DIS-

TINCTIONS—The making of definitions and of classifications in this and the preceding chapter has led us rather frequently to make nominal or logical distinctions which do not exist in concrete behavior. For example, we have spoken of psycho-social and of biological and of bio-physical relationships in the social adjustment situation. These are abstracted relationships. As a matter of fact relationships of objects, whether human or inanimate, occur as wholes. The same is true of adjustments of men to such objects as books or art of any kind. We abstract out for emphasis and analysis the adjustment of the individual on a psychic basis to the psycho-social environmental content of the book. Or we emphasize the relationship of the biological organism of the man to the physical aspect of the book for purposes of analysis only. Such abstraction is a useful, if a fictitious or merely logical, process. Its value consists in the fact that it enables us the better to distribute the environmental pressures into logical systems of social or psycho-social organization. Perceiving this ideal system as something which can be made into an effective control environment we utilize our psychic and biological processes, separate only in abstraction, to make a new behavior adjustment to it. In this way we are constantly reorganizing our personalities and reconstituting our environments by the use of projected logical systems which are not yet actualized in experience. The justification for thus transcending observed facts in our theory of classification is that which must be invoked in the utilization of any hypothesis. The hypothesis is a structure built up conceptually in order to symbolize adjustment patterns that later may be reduced to concrete overt behavior. Nowadays we, in large measure, think our adjustments before we act them. In order to do this effectively and derive the obvious gain which this procedure has to offer, it is necessary to analyze all of the phases of behavior and adjustment into their logical if not actual or concrete elements.

CONCLUSIONS—We may say by way of conclusion that social psychology deals with the psycho-social processes which arise in individual and collective behavior as the result of human interrelationships on a neuro-psychic plane. It is clearly not possible to divide and isolate human conduct according to the classificatory divisions of the sciences. Life and behavior are units, otherwise they would not exist as such in concept or in action. For purposes of analysis and control we break up the unity of behavior into its logical components, and redistribute these conceptually for purposes of forming new control systems which may bring about new habits or behavior systems in individuals and in groups of individuals. But when we speak of psychic and biological planes of behavior, of our physiological or anatomical or psychological or social natures, we are not describing separate and detachable units in our personalities or organisms, but we are outlining different ways of looking at an organic whole of personality, including its behavior. Therefore, when we limit social psychology to associational or collective phenomena occurring in the psychic plane, we mean that we are isolating these aspects of phenomena from those other aspects of the same phenomena which occur in a lower biological plane. It is merely a difference in viewpoint adopted as a device for clearer thinking preliminary to more effective adjustment to our environments.

MATERIALS FOR SUPPLEMENTARY READING

Allport, F. H., *Social Psychology*, Ch. I
Baldwin, J. M., *The Individual and Society*, Chs. I, VII
Bentley, M., "A Preface to Social Psychology," *Psychological Monographs*, XXI: 1-25
Dewey, John, "The Need for Social Psychology," *Psy. Rev.*, XXIV: 266-77
Dunlap, K., *Social Psychology*, Ch. I
Ellwood, C. A., *Introduction to Social Psychology*, Ch. I
———, *The Psychology of Human Society*, Ch. I
Gault, R. H., *Social Psychology*, Ch. I
Ginsberg, M., *The Psychology of Society*, Introduction
Hunter, W. S., *General Psychology*, Pt. I, Ch. 4
Kroeber, A. L., "The Possibility of a Social Psychology," *Amer. Jour. Sociol.*, XXIII: 633-50
McDougall, W., *The Group Mind*, Ch. I
Maciver, R. M., *Community*, pp. 58-63
Ross, E. A., *Social Psychology*, Ch. I
Wallas, G., *The Great Society*, Ch. II
Warren, H. C., *Human Psychology*, Ch. I
Williams, J. M., *The Foundations of Social Science*, Bks. III, IV
———, *Our Rural Heritage*, Ch. II

CHAPTER III

PHASES OF THE SUBJECT

KINDS OF SOCIAL PSYCHOLOGY—There are essentially three types of social psychology set forth in the text books, two of which are similar in form if not in principles. These have already been indicated in a general way in the review of the several definitions included in the previous chapter. Of the two most general subdivisions of the subject, one refers to the treatment of psycho-social phenomena objectively and in the mass. This is what Ross means by the planes and currents viewpoint, which is concerned with crowds and publics, and with such phenomena as fads, fashions, crazes, conventions, customs, traditions, mores, folkways, and the like. This was formerly the type of social psychology most commonly presented in text books and class room, and it is still much emphasized, especially in the departments of sociology.

The other two types of social psychology are of the same general pattern. They are concerned with the ways in which character or personality is built up in the individual. There are two hypothetical answers to this question. One is that character or behavior patterns are integrated from within on the basis of native processes or instincts, which dominate the process of character building. This is the view of the instinctivist school of social psychology, which became so popular among the educational theorists and many sociologists upon the publication of McDougall's *Introduction to Social Psychology* in 1908. Recently this school has markedly declined in favor among students of the subject.

The third type of social psychology, second of the types which emphasize personality development, accounts for the integration of behavior patterns under the influence of environmental pressures, especially of those from the psycho-social environment. This aspect of the subject has been chiefly represented by Professor Cooley's writings. It is now the most emphasized by students of the subject. It does not deny the existence of instincts, or of other inherited behavior patterns, but it does deny that instincts dominate the process of character formation or that they determine the resulting characteristics of the individual. It maintains that the environment utilizes the inherited bases as foundations for the construction of matured and acquired behavior patterns. On the other hand, the instinctivist type of social psychology claims that the instincts themselves dominate the formation of the matured behavior patterns, although it does not deny some significance to the selective powers of environment. The development of the theory of conditioned responses as an explanation of the method by which new traits may be acquired has added much to the acceptance of this environmentalist type of social psychology.

THE PLANES AND CURRENTS SCHOOL—This type of social psychology may be said to have begun definitely with the publication of Walter Bagehot's *Physics and Politics* in 1872, although there are earlier traces of it in some of the older writers, especially those of the French Enlightenment of the eighteenth century. William Godwin, in his *Enquiry Concerning Political Justice,* also discussed many problems which may be considered as belonging to social psychology. But it was Bagehot who first evinced a clear insight into the abstract and distance contacts of publics and the traits which men develop when immersed in crowds. This viewpoint appealed strongly to those students of society who wished to see the invisible and abstract social processes as definite realities. He made such things as custom, tradition, convention, fashions, and public opinion stand out as objective facts. It was the Sophists who first learned to objectify the subjective constituent elements of these processes in such a way as to make them take on definite form. But it was Bagehot who first taught us to use these forms effectively in social analysis and constructive sociological thinking.

Gabriel Tarde followed up the same method of analysis, but more extensively, in his several books, such as *The Laws of Imitation, La Logique Sociale, L'Opposition Universelle,* etc.

He made a more systematic use of such connecting or contact categories as imitation and suggestion than did Bagehot. Whether he was influenced directly by the brilliant essayist of Lombard Street is difficult to determine, but certainly he must have felt his influence indirectly through the discussion of the time. In fact the new way of looking at subjective processes collectively as objective entities was, so to speak, in the air. The psycho-social environment was being rapidly extended and expanded and the carriers of it, especially books, newspapers, telephone and telegraph, and what Bagehot called just "talk," were multiplying with equal rapidity.

The chief American follower of Tarde has been Professor Ross, but his numerous books in this field, which include almost all of his academic works, except *The Foundations of Sociology,* have made abundant novel departures of their own. Bogardus, and to some extent J. M. Baldwin (*Social and Ethical Interpretations*), Veblen (*Theory of the Leisure Class* and *The Instinct of Workmanship*), Ellwood, and W. G. Sumner (*Folkways*), may be regarded as other outstanding American writers of this type of social psychology. Some of the better recognized European writers dealing with planes and currents of the psycho-social environment are Duprat (*La Psychologie Sociale*), Scipio Sighele, who is known especially for his *La Foule Criminelle* and *Psychologie des Sectes,* Gustav LeBon, author of numerous works of this type, but best known for his *The Crowd,* and Graham Wallas, author of *Human Nature and Politics* and *The Great Society. Public Opinion* by Walter Lippmann, an American writer, may also properly be regarded as falling largely under this classification.

The present partial lack of appreciation of this school of sociological analysis is due in the main to two causes. It is in part the victim of one of its own categories, fashion. It is no longer the fashion to deal with the larger psycho-social processes as it once was. The trend is more toward the analysis of individual reactions in a social medium. The other outstanding difficulty is that the phenomena dealt with are abstract and conceptual. They are furthermore so vast and so elusive that the temptation has been great to generalize hastily on the basis of random observations, without an adequate testing of data and conclusions. The result is that this type of social psychology has sometimes been held in partial disrepute. While this method of psycho-social analysis provides a general perspective of what goes on in human contacts in the large it does not show exactly how changes in adjustment occur in the concrete. After all the individual and not the group is the ultimate unit in social change and therefore it is necessary to know what goes on in his behavior in order to find an adequate explanation of what occurs in the group as a whole. There is apparently a sort of rhythm of explanation between individual and collective behavior analysis. When one type of analysis gets ahead the other grows in favor. Just now the analysis of individual response to social stimuli is increasing in importance.

THE INSTINCTIVIST SCHOOL—This type of writing in social psychology also goes back fairly distinctly to the eighteenth century and beyond. The writers on ethics, especially Shaftesbury, Hutcheson, Price, Hume, Adam Smith, and Kant, and the early psychologists, particularly Helvetius and Hartley, and the Scotch metaphysical psychologists, Thomas Reid and Dugald Stewart, were much concerned with the native foundations of human behavior. The eighteenth century ethicists particularly emphasized inherited or innate and intuitive conscience, sympathy, and benevolence, upon which other finished social characteristics were built. These basic elements of character were in large measure supposed to control and direct other traits. Most of the Utilitarians, especially J. S. Mill, Spencer, and Leslie Stephen, author of *The Science of Ethics,* and the psychologist Bain, also made large use of the category of innate impulses and tendencies. But the Utilitarians were also feeling their way over toward the third type of social psychology, as indeed were the ethicists of the eighteenth century.

By far the most outstanding book in this field is McDougall's *Introduction to Social Psychology.* But McDougall was preceded by William James, who, drawing from Preyer and Schneider in Germany, gave a dignity and plausibility to the instinct category which hitherto had been lacking. W. Trotter, in *Instincts of the Herd in Peace and War,* William Drever, and Graham Wallas, already mentioned in another connection, are British writers of prominence belonging to the instinctivist school. Ellwood and Bogardus in their earlier writings also inclined largely in this direction, but have since altered their position.

The writers on the new subject of educational psychology, beginning with E. A. Kirkpatrick (*Fundamentals of Child Study*) and coming down to the recent works of Starch and Pyle, and many of the writers on educational sociology, emphasize rather generally the instinctive basis and domination of finished behavior. In this they are apparently following rather closely the lead of James and McDougall. In fact it seemed for a time quite recently that the whole of social science might pay tribute to the instinct theory.

THE ENVIRONMENTALIST SCHOOL—This school also began in the seventeenth and eighteenth centuries, with the theories of the ethicists and psychologists who took into account the influence of the environment in shaping human character traits. Locke and, in less degree, Hume and Helvetius prepared the way in the study of acquired character traits for the rather systematic treatise of Godwin previously referred to. Adam Smith also made some contribution to this phase of social psychology in his *Theory of the Moral Sentiments*. J. M. Baldwin and Charles H. Cooley were the first writers of marked prominence in this country to work extensively in this direction of sociopsychological analysis, although James had preceded them by almost twenty years in his article entitled *Great Men, Great Thoughts, and the Environment,* published in 1880, in the *Atlantic Monthly*. Cooley's *Human Nature and the Social Order* was a particularly valuable introduction to this field of study. It was a very specific attempt to describe the growth of the self or personality in the child in terms of its experiences as conditioned by the environment in which it moved. This attempt was made at a time when the mechanism of the conditioned response was not yet known, at least by name.

This newer terminology has been adopted in large measure by Allport, who takes the conditioned response as the specific mechanism by which habit responses are built up in the developing personality. Allport applies this concept very extensively to the solving of all sorts of problems of training. No other concept has proved of equal value in social psychology and it promises soon to outstrip the popularity which the concept of instinct formerly enjoyed among the social psychologists. It is also entering into the field of mental hygiene, which is closely related to social psychology. William H. Burnham has included five chapters on the conditioned reflex in his work on *The Normal Mind* and most of the other sixteen chapters are largely applications of this principle.

Dewey, Mead, and Thomas should also be mentioned as writers in this field of social psychology. Wallas and Ellwood, although less characteristic of this school, should be mentioned in this connection. These writers use essentially the philosophic approach rather than the strictly technical behavioristic one in discussing the data and principles of social psychology. No one of them has made any considerable use of the conditioned response concept in accounting for the building up of habits within the psycho-social adjustment process. Dewey and Mead make an approach largely from the angle of the logic of the social sciences. Thomas is very definitely of the environmentalist school. Allport, Thomas (in his theory of the four wishes), Martin, and Wallas show traces of the psychoanalytic influence. The chief interest of Wallas is in the foundations of collective behavior. Ellwood is concerned very largely with the rational processes in learned psycho-social adjustment.

SYNTHETIC TYPES—As a matter of actual composition most of the social psychologies make various combinations of these relatively pure types. Ellwood and Wallas combine all three phases of social psychology in greater or less degree. Bogardus did the same in his earlier text book in this field, but now he emphasizes primarily the planes and currents and environmental pressures types. Gault follows the same method with even greater emphasis. Even McDougall employs environmental data at points in the second section of his *Social Psychology,* and especially in his *Group Mind.* But on the whole, McDougall, Cooley, Ross, and Allport, conform pretty closely to the different types which they represent.

The most frequent overlapping occurs between the planes

and currents and environmental pressures types. This may be due to a number of causes. In the first place, both deal with objective phenomena, although the third type of social psychology is concerned with the subjective behavior patterns which are formed under the environmental pressures. Both Cooley and Allport illustrate this fact in their treatments. Secondly, since science interests itself first of all in objective phenomena, which can be measured and if possible perceived directly through the senses, and since social psychology is in its formative period, it is to be expected that more correlations would appear between these two fields of objective behavior than between either of these and that field which concerns itself with the subjective phenomena of instinct. Finally, our modern world emphasizes largely external processes and phenomena. We have just recently come to objectify in regular collective forms the subjective phenomena which constitute traditions, conventions, mores, beliefs, customs, etc., and to conceptualize them as planes and currents instead of remaining in the realm of purely introspective phenomena. This has objectified collective behavior in a way analogous to that in which behaviorism has objectified the behavior of the individual. It has caused the perceived psycho-social environment to increase very rapidly in volume and content. Consequently the amount of material which has to be observed and interpreted has also greatly expanded, calling for systematic analyses and treatments.

The most neglected of all aspects of social psychology hitherto has been an account of the integration of behavior mechanisms arising from the environmental pressures or organizations of stimuli. Cooley and Baldwin introduced this treatment in more or less general terms, getting down to specific processes of habit formation only occasionally. But Allport, Watson, and Woodworth have attempted to give us the actual mechanisms by which the processes of acquired behavior growth take place. The development of the theory of the conditioned response makes further expansion in this direction easier. Probably the largest growth in social psychology in the near future will be in this direction.

The more recent emphasis by writers of this type is not so

much upon the steps in the development of personality in the individual as upon the processes of behavior modification and integration by which these changes occur. Also, there is perhaps less of a tendency among recent social psychologists to give an account of the more permanent integrations of personality traits than was customary among those (like Baldwin and Cooley) who were influenced by the educational psychologists of two decades ago, and more of a leaning toward the analysis of relatively immediate and temporary responses of individuals in social situations. This latter tendency, represented by Allport and Martin, is probably in some degree a response to the influence of the planes and currents school, on the one hand, and to the marked increase of such appeal from commercialized amusement and publicity interests, on the other hand.

EARLIER INTELLECTUALISM OF SOCIAL SCIENCE—The development of theories of behavior mechanisms in social psychology recently has been largely in the direction of an analysis of suggestion processes and of the unconscious patterns generally. The early accounts of psychic processes were all couched in highly intellectualistic terms. The reason for this is obvious. The first systematic studies of behavior phenomena were mainly introspective. Where the phenomena of hysteria or other psychopathic behavior were observed, they were more likely to be attributed to outside, frequently to spirit, causes than to be looked upon as distorted phases of the normal mental processes. The psychological treatises of the eighteenth and most of those of the early nineteenth century left these things out of account altogether. The result, as McDougall has so well shown, was that the social sciences and ethics of that time were hopelessly artificial, *aprioristic* and intellectualistic.

It was this one-sided intellectualism in psychological interpretation which made the Utilitarian philosophy possible. The philosophers of this school believed that society could be controlled by a properly regulated appeal to self-interest. Their assumption was that every one plans his conduct beforehand with regard for his greatest advantage. This procedure could be possible only if the human mind were capable of grasping all the details of any situation at once and of acting on them effectively. But there is neither time, nor energy, nor a sufficient body of data to make this possible. The fact is that we are constantly acting on some suggestion after incomplete analysis and with little, if any, foresight of ultimate consequences.

The same intellectualistic bias created the theory of the economic man who followed in his economic relationships the Utilitarian principle of enlightened self-interest without error or distorted prejudice. According to this concept the market place was a battle ground of wits and all exchanges tended to the mutual and maximum advantage of all the parties participating. In jurisprudence the same bias conceived of the jury as a group of twelve apostles of philosophy and of the judge as a dispenser of cold logic. Law itself was conceived as the embodiment of reason as it earlier had been regarded as the social extension of the principle of natural law. Retributive punishment was based on the tacit assumption that all crimes were acts of deliberation and emanated from a free will. In ethics the good was identified with the pleasant, and the pleasant was conceived of as the product of rational choice. The bad was the unpleasant, which afflicted the individual who failed to use his reason. The world was regarded as the product of creative reason, and human happiness was supposed to correlate with the maximum of rational guidance. Reason was itself looked upon more as an absolutistic entity than as a method of judgment, and it was scarcely conceived that reason could support the anti-social motive or justify the unworthy cause. If one were judged for his behavior it was invariably assumed by the intellectualists that he had acted from choice with a full knowledge of all of the consequences. The mystics, however, might assume that some satanic personage had dimmed his vision or warped his power of judgment. This mystical interpretation was the anthropomorphic forerunner of the modern psychological theory of the unconscious.

THREE TYPES OF ACTION—More extended and careful analyses of behavior, however, have convinced us that man is not necessarily so intellectually rigorous or logical in his choices. We may classify the types of overt action in which one may engage somewhat as follows.

1. *Action by impact,* in which the organism reacts, not to a stimulus differentially and distributively, but to some force as a mass of matter, very much as if it had no nervous organization or other inner communicating system which would enable it to redirect its initial motion into a controlled response. An example of this type of action is the bodily transference of position of a man when struck by an automobile or train. Of course most action by impact soon transforms itself into action by response to stimuli. That is, the organism rapidly gains control of itself through its nervous system and brings itself into a position or attitude more advantageous to itself. In many cases the action by impact is partly or wholly transformed into action by selective response before the activity is completed.

2. *Action on the basis of relatively automatic behavior mechanisms.* These mechanisms are of two sorts: (1) instinctive processes and (2) habitual processes. It is now believed that the degree of complexity of the inherited reaction patterns has been greatly overestimated. Apparently not a very large portion of human behavior belongs to the instinctive category, for complex activity calls for so much differentiation of response that the basic instinctive patterns are quickly changed into habitual ones. Not all habits are necessarily unconscious in their operation. Only the purely automatic ones call forth no conscious responses in the nervous mechanism. Most habitual responses occur on a relatively low level of consciousness.

3. *Action by choice* constitutes a third type of behavior. The fact of choice implies some degree of foresight and evaluation of the nature and aims of the response. Where the behavior involves foresight, this consciousness of the end becomes itself an important consideration in understanding and describing the act. We may divide the motives to conscious choices into two groups: (1) Those choices which are made on the basis of subjective appeal, that is, when the desire for pleasant feeling or the wish to escape unpleasantness is the dominant motive; and (2) those in which the choice is based

on an objective consideration of the logical merits of the behavior. Presumably the choice would here be made on the basis of some socially approved criterion of values, but the choice may be based on some metaphysically assumed obligation or relationship. Choice as here used does not imply fiatistic behavior. As a matter of fact, all behavior is the product of a conjunction of environmental pressures and the set of the organism. What we call choice is the resolution of conflicting sets and the prevision of the direction of the resulting behavior.

Of course these three major types of behavior graduate into each other and no thoroughly distinct dividing line can be drawn between any two of them. The middle group apparently comprises by far the largest number of behavior patterns, although the other two are also very significant in an inclusive account of behavior. Under the first group we should classify the more than a million more or less serious accidents which occur in this country annually. In the third group we find those phases of behavior which arise in times of conflict or of crisis. Apparently we do not make choices unless we are compelled to do so, even in a crucial situation. And the choice itself may be emotional and subjective rather than rational and objective. When possible we fall back upon the guidance of ready-made action patterns. That is, we act either from instinct (which is not very frequently the case) or from habit. In such relatively unconscious conduct we are able to save time and energy for other phases of adjustment which require more conscious resolution of conflicting impulses.

The emphasis upon unconscious behavior has come primarily from three sources. With the remarkable growth in complexity of modern life there has come about a vast increase in crowd phenomena and of those more abstract types of contacts which Ross classes under the phenomena of the public. It was perceived that the crowd and some forms of the public operate largely through suggestion and only partly on a conscious and purposive basis. Certainly the grade of choice in these types of behavior is very low. Also, as psychology came to be applied to business, in personnel management and especially in the field of advertising, a large group of unconscious behavior phenomena opened up for psychological analysis. The psychology of the newspaper presentation and of the movie, among other examples, also urged itself on our attention. From such sources materials have come which are of great value to social psychology.

The students of so-called abnormal psychology—the psychiatrists, suggestion therapists, and the psychoanalysts—also began, a generation or more ago, to uncover vast fields of unconscious or dimly conscious behavior. These phenomena had previously been explained in the terminology of the pseudo-sciences of spiritism, demonology, and other mystical interpretations, when not neglected altogether. The work of Kraepelin, Charcot, Bernheim, and Janet introduced us to the new methods of interpretation which have been so widely extended and accepted in recent years. Perhaps it is psychoanalysis which latterly has given us most data in this field. Without accepting its teachings uncritically we can say without hesitation that it has opened up many new psychic phenomena arising from sublimations and repressions and conflicts and the consequent attempts to escape from reality into a pleasanter world of imagination or of dreams. This tendency to seek flight from reality is now seen to be one of the most persistent and universal characteristics of practically all men. Art, social intercourse, play of all sorts, our ideas and ideals, even our daily hobbies in some degree afford us an opportunity to shift our attention from the active conflict situations to that of comfortable adjustment, even if only in our dreams.

HABIT VERSUS INSTINCT IN RELATIVELY AUTOMATIC BEHAVIOR—McDougall has correctly indicated the need for an escape from an artificial and overintellectualized interpretation of social processes. As we have seen, it has become increasingly clear from our analysis of the mass phenomena of the psycho-social environment and from our studies of psychopathic personalities that in a large part of our behavior we act from relatively unconscious impulses rather than from highly conscious motives of advantage to ourselves or to society. What is the nature of these impulses which dominate our behavior? McDougall says they are instinctive; that the factor in psychology which we have neglected is the original nature of man; that in order to achieve a complete picture of men in action, whether performing as individuals or as members of a group, or in any social contacts whatever, it is necessary to unravel the hidden springs of conduct which come to us by inheritance.

This theory represents the dominance of the biological viewpoint in psychology, which began to be so strong soon after 1900 and which was clearly discernible as early as the 1890's when the physiological psychologies began to appear. Before this, psychology had been dominated by metaphysics and formal logic, and if we were compelled to choose between the two methods of interpreting conduct, we should unquestionably prefer the instinct theory. But the environmentalist believes he has a more adequate substitute for both of the preceding methods of accounting for human behavior. He does not deny that the instinctivist view has great significance and explains many basic facts. He contends, however, that we live not in a world of primitive nature, but in one in which our adjustments are on an acquired or cultural basis. Therefore the impulses which give man largely an unconscious direction are habits rather than instincts. Why this rather obvious fact should not sooner have been perceived and appreciated is difficult to explain. It may have been due to the fact that the analysis of the behavior of living forms had proceeded farther than the analysis of the objective phenomena of the psycho-social environment when the instinctivist interpretations of behavior were produced. That was in the day of the dominance of the biological concepts and methodology in all science. We are now beginning to appreciate the environmentalist conception. This transition is taking effect even in the field of the biological sciences, as is so amply evidenced by the conclusions of Professors Child, Herrick, Newman, and even Jennings and C. B. Davenport.

MATERIALS FOR SUPPLEMENTARY READING

Allport, F. H., "Social Psychology," *Psy. Bul.,* XVII: 85-94
Bernard, L. L., "Recent Trends in Social Psychology," *J. S. F.,* II: 737-43
Ginsberg, M., *The Psychology of Society,* Introduction
McDougall, W., *An Introduction to Social Psychology,* Ch. I
Schaupp, Z., "A Review of Some Present Tendencies in Social Psychology," *J. A. P. S. P.,* XVII: 93-103

CHAPTER IV

METHOD OF THE PRESENT TREATMENT

SYNTHETIC TREATMENT—The present treatment of social psychology is more or less synthetic and eclectic in its plan and content. It attempts to make use of the most valid materials in all three phases of the subject as it has been presented hitherto, but it emphasizes especially the development of acquired character in the individual under social pressures or stimulus patterns. As will appear from the context, and from a previous work by the author, the ordinary presentation of the theory of inherited behavior patterns cannot be accepted in this treatise. The position is taken that environment rather than inheritance is responsible for the major portion of the adjustment traits of the individual, although there is no denial that individual differences in inherited capacities exist. The basic contention is that the social environment has now come to be so highly organized and powerful that it presents stimuli which select these inherited and other acquired responses in the individual and give predominance to those characteristics and impulses within him which are necessary for his effective adjustment to any social situation. That is, the social environment, through the selective operation of the stimuli which it presents, selects in the individual those responses which are necessary for his adequate adjustment to its own organization.

DIVISIONS—The book as written falls into four parts. The first part presents the general and special considerations which must be taken into account in grasping the significance and content of the science of social psychology. This part deals with the nature of science and scientific methods, the relations of social psychology to psychology and the social sciences, and the phases of the subject of social psychology as they have been developed and treated by various writers. These phases may properly be called the schools of social psychology. Part I is therefore an introduction to the science of social psychology, which is developed in the other three parts.

BEHAVIOR OF THE ORGANISM—Part II presents the human organism as a functioning unit in a social situation. This presentation is made on the assumption that it is necessary to understand the character of the socius before an intelligible exposition of his development and transformation under environmental pressures can be made. It is through his response to stimuli from the environment that all transformations in the social structure or organization are made. It is also through him that all social functioning occurs. In this treatment the individual or socius is not taken as a static or fixed quantum, but is regarded as a changing psycho-biological organism. First he is considered from the standpoint of his inheritance as determined by the organization of his protoplasms in the germ cells. Next, the factors in the environment which operate selectively to modify and transform these inherited structures and integrations are passed in review, with some analysis of the method by which they operate upon the psycho-biological organism through their presentation of stimuli. The remainder of Part II is concerned with a presentation and discussion of the behavior patterns and bio-psychic and neuro-psychic processes and technique which arise in the individual out of the combined operation of heredity and environment. These behavior patterns and processes are treated both analytically and developmentally. The interest here is in the types of behavior mechanisms possessed by the individual, as an aid to understanding the method by which these are organized and transformed by the social and natural pressures or stimuli to which he is subjected in our socially integrated world. Part II, therefore, is in the nature of an application of bio-psychology to social psychology proper. But, as McDougall has indicated, an analysis of the individual is so indispensable to the treatment of his behavior in a social situation that it must be presented here in order to acquaint the student adequately with the tools which he must use in dissecting the socio-psychological and psycho-social processes as such.

THE INDIVIDUAL IN RESPONSE TO HIS ENVIRONMENT—Part III presents the socio-psychological processes proper.

Part IV is concerned with the psycho-social processes, or those which operate selectively upon the individual's behavior. Part III makes the transition from the socio-psychic responses of individuals to the psycho-social organization of stimuli from the environment. It is concerned, therefore, with the method by which habits are developed in the individual as a means of enabling him to adjust his behavior to the collective behavior and to all of those environmental conditions which may be termed social. This process of adaptation of the self to the collectivity is also a process of defining and organizing the self, and likewise of constantly transforming the environment.

The process of adaptation is not merely negative, one of passive conformity to the environmental situation. It is also constructive and involves the expansion and integration of one's own personality through the acquisition of habits or acquired behavior mechanisms, and also the re-creation or reorganization of the environment, especially the social environment. But the power of any one individual unaided to transform the environment grows relatively less and the power of the social environment to transform the individual responses grows relatively greater as it becomes more strongly integrated. The transformation of the environment becomes increasingly a collective undertaking. The process of adaptation is, therefore, as Professor Cooley and others have pointed out, bipolar or reciprocal. One comes to understand himself as he understands his environment, especially his psycho-social environment. And he develops and creates self—a socialized self—through the development and integration of habits as he analyzes and, in a measure, helps to integrate and create collective forms and processes. The process of differentiating and segregating the self or personality and the environment and of objects within both categories is, as we shall see in Part III, necessary as a means of giving the individual leverage for the effective organization of his adjustment behavior. But this same process of adjustment results in new assimilative integrations of the personality and the environment, through imitation and otherwise, as will be shown in Parts III and IV. Differentiation from and reintegration with the environment go on constantly as phases of the adjustment process.

THE PSYCHO-SOCIAL ORGANIZATION—Part IV is concerned primarily with the objective or group processes which condition and organize the individual responses collectively. It outlines in moderate detail those psycho-social processes and structures which serve as the social environmental pressures and provide the stimuli which initiate and control the recognitive and imitative processes discussed in Part III. These objective psycho-social processes consist of direct and indirect contact groups, of attitudes and ideals which symbolize and project collective behavior, of institutional and non-institutional controls. As objective phenomena they are a part of the data of sociology and of the social sciences generally. But as processes affording stimuli to the individual behaving in a collective response situation they are also data for social psychology. In this second respect they bear a relationship to social psychology analogous to that of the data of the bio-psychic organism treated in Part II, which are also data for bio-psychology as well as for social psychology. It is through these data of individual behavior, treated in Part II, and the psycho-social data of social organization and control, treated in Part IV, that social psychology makes its chief liaisons with the sciences of individual psychology on the one hand and with the other social sciences on the other hand.

DEPARTURES IN THIS TEXT—It has been the purpose in this treatise to present the subject matter of social psychology as data and principles, or, as sometimes said, as pure science, rather than as application or applied science. Consequently, some readers may be concerned at the omission from the discussion of certain problems relating to the adjustment of individuals and groups which they have been accustomed to meet in the text books on this subject. It is the view of the present writer, however, that such discussions belong in separate treatises on social organization, social control, and social ethics, rather than in a treatise on the principles and data of social psychology.

In the matter of terminology also there has been some departure from previous usage. This seemed to the present writer to be unavoidable because of his emphasis upon certain themes and relationships not previously discussed in sufficient detail to call forth corresponding terminology. In the majority of cases, in all instances, in fact, in which it was possible to do so, the older terminology has been retained. Some of the ultra behaviorists (the author thinks of himself as a behaviorist) may even blame him for being so conservative in his retention of much of the terminology of the old introspective psychology. His justification is that under present conditions it appears to be necessary to clearness, and clearness should be one of the chief aims of any exposition. The chief departures from the old terminology are, therefore, mainly in the nature of additions to it. They center primarily in the adoption of the term neuro-psychic technique and the various terms differentiating the environment into its several phases. To this also may possibly be added the concrete emphasis upon a psychological and functional distinction between the inner or attitudinal (sometimes called covert or implicit) and overt aspects of behavior. An explanation of the purpose of these departures is made in each case at the point at which the variation from custom occurs. It is hoped that the results justify the usage. The term neuro-psychic technique merely emphasizes the neural (conscious or unconscious) aspects of behavior in contrast to the more complete or total overt adjustment responses, to which they are usually preliminary and preparatory. There is no attempt to draw any complete or final distinction between neuro-psychic (symbolic and internal) and neuro-muscular (total overt response) behavior. Both aspects of behavior have their neural organization, but only the latter has a well defined overt phase as distinguished from symbolic responses, and only the former normally is highly conscious and complex. Neuro-psychic behavior is a substitute for neuro-muscular behavior, and appears only in so far as the latter is being interrupted or modified.

ANTICIPATED CRITICISMS—Some psychologists may also object to the retention of a distinction between conscious and unconscious behavior. So far as the actual bio-chemical functioning of the nervous processes within the individual is concerned there is, possibly, no such distinction. All behavior mechanisms are equally definite anatomical and physiological facts whether they are conscious or unconscious. The social psychologist makes this distinction because conscious behavior mechanisms apparently can be more effectively projected into symbolic collective behavior patterns to function as means to purposive social organization and social control. Similarly there are socio-psychological and sociological justifications for distinguishing rational and irrational, social and anti-social, moral and immoral, imitative and non-imitative behavior which are not apparent in the premises to the individual psychologist who looks only to the neural and physiological mechanisms for the data of his science. Psychology, to meet the needs of social science, must look beyond mere neurological and physiological mechanisms and seek to include social or collective relationship patterns, although the neurological and physiological emphases are indispensable to the social scientists as well as to the psychologist.

It may also be necessary in this connection to forestall an erroneous interpretation. Because this volume emphasizes the development of the technique of the adjustment of the individual to his social environment from the instinctive aspects to the rational, some readers may conclude that the writer is under the impression that in our day men ordinarily and habitually use the rational adjustment procedures. There is no such illusion on his part. In writing a treatise on the general principles of a science it is necessary to describe all of the significant processes involved, but it is not incumbent upon the author —in many cases not even desirable—to attempt to estimate the extent to which the various processes are employed in practice. This is quite as true in the theory of social psychology as of chemistry. In the applied aspects of the subject, however, such estimates may very properly constitute a phase of the treatment.

ORGANISM AND ENVIRONMENT—Three other criticisms should, perhaps, be anticipated. The first is an objection to the distinction between environment and organism so frequently made in this volume. This criticism will probably be to the effect that such a segregation is impossible, since a part of the organism, even the organism as a whole, frequently serves to release response mechanisms within itself. This is, of course, true. Nor is it the intention of this book to confine the environment to stimulus-giving objects wholly outside the organism. The contention is that every response mechanism has its stimulus, inside or outside of the organism, and that stimulus-response processes indicate stimulus-giving objects which constitute environment for the reacting mechanisms. Since in a social situation the organism usually responds as a unit to its stimuli it is well to know what objects, including the organism itself and its behavior patterns, constitute its environment. Environment is simply that which offers stimuli or conditions responses.

A closely related criticism anticipated is that the social psychologist and the sociologist are interested in behavior, that they are concerned more with what people do under certain circumstances than with what constitutes an environment or an organism. This also is true. But it is not possible to anticipate behavior without knowing what stimuli are available. Watson, in his behavioristic program, states that the ultimate purpose of the science of behavior is to make it possible to predict what will be the probable response when a given stimulus is applied. Such a program involves the ascertainment of two things: the nature of the response mechanisms (the organization of the organism), and the nature of the stimuli (the organization of the environment). Psychology has already gone far in the investigation of the former. The time is more than ripe for the sociologists or others to undertake the systematic study of the latter. Hence the emphasis in this volume upon the organization of the environment (including that of the internal physiology and anatomy of the organism itself treated in Chapter VII).

A corollary to this second criticism is to be found in the contention of some social psychologists that social psychology is concerned with the behavior of groups and of individuals in groups and that what goes on within the individual's neuropsychic organization is the concern of the psychologist, not of the social psychologist. They draw an analogy from physics, saying that physics would not have been able to make progress if it had refused to investigate the behavior of masses before investigating the inner organization of the constituent atoms.

The two problems of investigation are not exactly analogous, but aside from this fact, the comparison is properly of physics and sociology rather than of physics and social psychology. It is true that sociology may be studied as the behavior of groups and of individuals in groups without raising the question directly as to the organization of the internal mechanisms. It was studied in this manner until it recognized the need of assistance from social psychology. But social psychology is not sociology. The very fact that it is a psychological as well as a social science indicates that its task is the study of the responses of the individual to his social environment. Its task is exactly this of connecting the environment (stimulus-giving objects) with the organism (response mechanisms). The function of social psychology is to tell us how we can control the behavior of individuals in the group or in any social situation, and how the individual can control the behavior of the group. This involves both an organized presentation of stimulus controls (environmental organization) and of response mechanisms (the organization of the personality). The neglect of the former aspect leaves us psychology; of the latter, sociology. In either case of neglect we have no social psychology.

THE DOMINANCE OF THE ENVIRONMENT—Still another criticism, this time from the standpoint of individual psychology, is likely to be directed against the "metaphysical" assumption of an environmental organization and control where we have only individuals behaving with reference to one another. On the one hand it will be objected that institutions and groups, considered aside from the behavior of individuals, are only metaphysical assumptions, not tangible realities capable of presenting stimuli of their own. This is true, except where such institutional and group behavior has deposited some tangible organization, symbolic or physical, which is usually the case. Where reference is made to institutional or group control in this volume the intention is always to convey the meaning that it is individuals (although mutually conditioned or "organized" individuals) or tangible structures of organization which give the stimuli to responses.

On the other hand, and in pursuance of this criticism, it will be objected that it is the individual who acts by virtue of his inner organization and that the environment has no power to compel a response. Throughout this volume the environment is referred to as dominating the formation of behavior patterns in the individual. His character is regarded as in large measure the result of the operation of social pressures. It will scarcely be necessary to explain that the author does not conceive of these pressures as operating in any physical sense. All behavior is the behavior of individuals, even when they act in collective behavior or adjustment situations. Also, the behavior of individuals, as was indicated in the preceding chapter, is organized primarily in the form of neural responses to stimuli. The preëxisting neural organization of the individual, inherited and acquired, and his other physiological and anatomical organizations function in the determination of the responses of the organism to the environmental stimuli. Normally the internal organization determines these responses, and, as Allport has so clearly shown, the drives or prepotent impulses which result from this inner organization may be said metaphorically and somewhat metaphysically to reach out for suitable stimuli to release their response mechanisms. But it is, after all, the environment which offers the stimuli, whether this environment be another part of the same organism, other organisms, or physical and symbolic structures organized outside of the individual and themselves organized or created by mankind in the past and the present. It is also true that each individual contributes to the organization of this external stimulus-giving environment, but any one individual can construct only a very infinitesimal part of it, unless his construction be in the realm of phantasy instead of fact. It is because the individual's character development depends so overwhelmingly upon the stimuli which the environment affords him before and after birth that we speak of this environment as dominating his behavior and his acquired human nature. In the long run he becomes pretty much what the environment affords him opportunity for becoming through offering him stimuli for the release of preconditioned responses and for the conditioning of new responses. Control of individual adjustment and character formation is, therefore, not physical, but psychological and social. The environmental or objective social interpretation of character control is therefore not psychologically unsound. It is, on the contrary, the only possible interpretation, for, while the social environment is in the long run created by individuals, it is constituted of their responses to environments already existing, either natural or social.

THE GENERAL POINT OF VIEW OF THIS BOOK may be stated as follows:

1. The organic or internal bases of behavior have always been determined through selection and in the long run by environmental factors or controls. But with the development of human-made or social environments there has appeared a tendency for them to become increasingly dependent upon and subordinate to the psycho-social and other highly derivative behavior controls.

2. Behavior patterns tend to evolve, both phylogenetically and ontogenetically, from the concrete, inherited, immediate, and predominantly overt types to the abstract, acquired, symbolic, and predominantly internal types.

3. Symbolic behavior and symbolic behavior controls (language) tend to evolve from the concrete and partial overt responses of the organism to the abstract and verbal or substitute overt and internal response forms.

4. Symbolic behavior tends to become increasingly important in the adjustment process:

    (1) In individual adjustment, such as delayed or modified response, where it functions as thinking;

    (2) In social adjustment, where it functions objectively as the content of science;

    (3) In communication, where it functions both directly and indirectly between people of the same time, and wholly indirectly between people of different times by means of its storage functions.

5. Individual character or behavior patterns and sets tend to become increasingly acquired or habitual as the result of the differentiation of new stimuli in the environment and the conditioning of new responses to these stimuli. By this means the world or universe constantly expands for the individual and the capacity of the individual to respond to this world increases

pari passu. Thus individual character or personality becomes richer and more intellectual, and the environment becomes increasingly elaborate and social, expanding into highly derivative forms of the social and institutional type.

6. Social organization tends to be characterized increasingly by abstract derivative and non face-to-face groups rather than by primary, concrete, and face-to-face groups. The sanctions for this increasingly abstract social organization also tend to evolve from the concrete emotional attitudes of the primary groups to the highly abstract and derivative ideals and principles which dominate the abstract derivative groups.

7. Institutional controls tend to shift from the primarily customary and traditional to the predominantly scientific.

8. Leadership, which represents the process of focusing stimuli upon individuals responding in a social situation, tends to evolve from the direct, personal, emotional type to the indirect, impersonal, and intellectual types.

9. Men learn to project their adjustments into the future and to behave telically, at first largely as individuals and later collectively. In the early stages of their social evolution men project relatively personal and immediate ends or objectives. But as their power of handling symbolic behavior mechanisms and concepts develops and abstract science is invented as the supreme symbolic system for making adjustments, the ends projected become increasingly social or impersonal and indirect or intermediary to other ends. In this way mankind may be said to attempt to control their own social evolution.

These tendencies are not regarded as inevitable or absolute metaphysical principles inherent in the organization of nature itself, but are stated as empirical or projected generalizations of observed data. They are emphasized throughout the book because it is believed that these are the psychological and sociopsychological tendencies which are most characteristic of men as distinguished from other animals and which distinguish modern society from primitive society, and that an understanding of these points is essential to an understanding of modern society.

Part II

THE FOUNDATIONS OF COLLECTIVE
BEHAVIOR

CHAPTER V

THE ORGANIC BASES OF BEHAVIOR

THE NATURE OF THE ORGANISM—The individual animal organism is the primary unit mechanism of social as well as of individual behavior. There are more complex units of collective behavior, consisting of groups and associations of all kinds, but these are always either multiples of individual organisms or some other combination, in a more or less complex ratio, of individuals. These complex and multiple units in social behavior patterns will be discussed later. In this chapter it will be our task to sketch some of the more important traits of the individual organism in so far as they are significant for the problem of social or collective behavior.

All animal organisms are constituted of protoplasms. These protoplasms are in general similar for all of the organs and tissues of the body, but they differ sufficiently in chemical composition and structure as to be distinguished functionally, at least in some measure. The most obvious distinctions in protoplasms are, perhaps, between those of the nervous system, the muscles, the glands, the osseous system, and the blood or lymph. Each of these, and each other type of protoplasm, has its own specific set of functions to perform. The psychologist is of course interested especially in the nervous system, the business of which is to be susceptible to stimuli sources in the environment and to transmit the impulses thus received and to mediate a partial or total response of the organism to its environment. The nervous system is a special protoplasmic mechanism developed in connection with the other protoplasms of the organism for the purpose of securing a more rapid and economical and accurate adjustment of the organism to its environment than would be possible without such an adjusting mechanism.

SOME CHARACTERISTICS OF PROTOPLASM—All protoplasm

possesses the quality known as irritability. It receives and retains and transmits impressions. The types of stimuli to which it is originally sensitive are sometimes stated as mechanical, chemical, thermal, electrical, or even photal. The quality of retaining impressions is the basis of organic and associative, and later of conscious, memory, which is so important a factor in orienting the organism with reference to its past as well as its present environments. Its transmissive power enables it to serve as a "telegraphic" system for turning stimuli into appropriate responses and thus secures for the organism an effective adjustment to its environment. These qualities are of course best developed in neural protoplasm, which is particularly specialized for retentive and transmissive functions.

Protoplasm is also highly metabolic, and the nerve cells are said to explode their protein under certain conditions. This high rate of metabolism of nervous protoplasm gives to it the advantage which Child so well describes in his work on *The Physiological Foundations of Behavior* when discussing gradients and dominants. Gradients are established between protoplasms of higher and lower metabolism qualities, and those with the higher metabolism assume dominance in determining the axes of organismic integration and behavior. Thus the development and responsiveness of the organism depend upon its gradients. And these, in turn, are set or determined on the one hand by the rates of metabolism of its protoplasms and on the other hand by the reception of the environmental pressures or stimuli through its sense organs.

DOMINANCE OF THE NEURAL PROTOPLASM—The nervous system, after it once appears, sets the gradients and dominates the development of the rest of the organism because of its higher rate of metabolism. Likewise, the anterior portions of the nervous system dominate the posterior portions, and therefore, once these anterior portions of the nervous system have been developed, they dominate the development of the whole organism. But just as muscular protoplasm appeared phylogenetically before nervous protoplasm, so have the anterior portions of the nervous system, especially the cerebral cortex, appeared after the posterior and lower spinal portions. Thus we may say that nervous control came after muscle control and brain control after nervous control in general, while intelligent cortical control of the organism came last of all. And now to intelligent cortical control of the organism the human species is adding control through externally stored neuro-psychic symbols, such as language and value symbols of all sorts. With the appearance of each of these new controls, it has subordinated the previously dominant controls and has assumed functional direction of the organism. The development of each of the new supreme controls, except the last, was apparently due to the appearance of a new variety or organization of protoplasm possessing a higher rate of metabolism and greater retentive and transmissive powers than the protoplasms which preceded it possessed. But the last type of control, that of the neuro-psychic storage symbols, is not protoplasmic or biological, but is psycho-social, and the coming of its dominance in molding and directing the individual organism represents the coming of the supremacy of the social factors over the organic in collective and individual behavior.

ADJUSTMENT THE FUNCTION OF NERVOUS PROTOPLASM—Protoplasm is of course living matter and before it can serve any other function it must replenish itself. The primary and almost the exclusive function of the lower forms of protoplasm appears to remain permanently that of self-maintenance or replenishment. The lower organisms, like the amœba, in which there is apparently little specialization of protoplasm, do little more than ingest food, assimilate it and excrete the indigestible portions. In addition it has some mechanisms of motion by which it comes in contact with food objects or escapes from dangerous situations. As the protoplasms of organisms become more specialized, muscles and other tissues, like the circulating medium, secretions possessing behavioristic significance, and finally neural tissues, are developed. These specialized forms of protoplasm must still maintain themselves, and even in the highly specialized nerve cells we find tissue material devoted primarily to the nutritive function. But the primary function of the specialized protoplasm ceases to be nutritive and becomes something else. That of muscular protoplasm is contraction, while the primary functions of nervous protoplasm are retention and transmission. Secondarily it dominates the direction of development or growth of the other parts of the organism, as indicated above; and tertiarily it replenishes itself. But the great primary and general function of the nervous tissues is to facilitate the adjustment of the organism to its environment.

This general quality of the irritability of protoplasm enables the organism to respond to pressures or stimuli in a differential manner instead of merely as a mass. It is this quality, extended and specialized in the various specific structures of the body—particularly of the nervous system—which differentiates the behavior of the animal organism from that of bodies of a more homogeneous sort. It enables the animal to act on the two higher planes of responses to stimuli mentioned in Chapter III, instead of being moved by direct impact.

COMPLEXITY AND ADJUSTMENT—Man is motile to a particularly high degree. This fact increases the range and completeness and effectiveness of his adjustments. Man adjusts himself more completely to his environment than any other organism, except possibly the parasites. This is because of the great degree of specialization and organization of his protoplasms, especially of his nervous system, on the one hand, and of his development of a super organic or an externalized neurosymbolic technique of control, on the other hand. His superior rate of metabolism, especially in his higher protoplasmic organizations, and the retentive and transmissive powers of his neural protoplasm, bring him in touch with an almost infinite range of stimuli, both past and present, and render him capable of responding to almost any type of environment. With his external storage symbols he is enabled to store or deposit "memories" far in excess of what his protoplasmic organization could carry and make these available for his adjustment tasks at a later date or even to preserve them in this superorganic memory for future generations.

There is a close correlation between the complexity of the organism—especially of its nervous organization—and the complexity of the adjustment which it must make to its environments. Simple organisms adjust themselves by means of relatively simple mechanisms to relatively few environmental pressures or stimuli. These pressures may be summed up under such general terms as food, sex, dangerous objects, and protective or sustaining factors in the environment. The lower life forms often react directly to a food object by enveloping it and later disgorging the indigestible portions. Frequently sex responses are in the nature of a direct discharge of reproductive cells upon an appropriate stimulus regardless of the coöperation or lack of it of an organism of the opposite sex. But as the environment to which the organism can respond becomes much more highly differentiated and the organism multiplies its organs of adjustment, especially its nervous technique and organization, the response processes also become vastly complicated and highly differentiated. The processes themselves cease to be exclusively direct and are frequently indirect, even abstract and symbolic in character. That is, much adjustment of the human organism in our complicated society takes place not merely through the protoplasmic neural mnemic and transmissive processes, but is mediated through verbal or written, symbolic language mechanisms, some of which are even of a mathematical or other super-lingual character. In such cases, of course, the adjustment of the organism to its environment is on a mental, often an intellectual, plane and is organized upon the organic protoplasmic bases out of which it has arisen.

THE NERVOUS SYSTEM—The organism can exist only if it maintains a functional adjustment to its environments. The process of living is itself a process of adjustment continually developing and changing. This adjustment the complex organism is able to maintain only by virtue of the sensitivity and differentiation of its protoplasms. The lowest organisms make their adjustments to some extent through the power of responding directly to stimuli transmitted through undifferentiated protoplasm. But the higher animals, as we have seen, make use of a highly differentiated form of protoplasm, the nervous system, for the purpose of transmitting stimuli into effective and rapid responses. The more highly developed and differentiated the organism is, and the more complex the environment to which it finds it necessary to adjust itself, the more complicated and highly organized is the nervous system which serves the function of mediating the adjustment processes. In man, this nervous system has become extremely complicated and specialized. Special sensory organs of some twenty-two separate types have developed as a phase of this mechanism which promotes a more highly functional and specialized adjustment. It is desirable that we have before us a brief description of the nervous system and its mechanisms as an aid to a clear understanding of its services in adjusting the organism to its environment.

Herrick divides the nervous system into two great branches: "the *central nervous system,* or axial nervous system, comprising the brain and spinal cord, and the *peripheral nervous system,* including the cranial and spinal nerves, their ganglia and peripheral end-organs, and the sympathetic nervous system." These two phases of the nervous mechanism dominate the adjustment of the organism to its environment, but on the whole in somewhat dissimilar ways. Parts of the central nervous system are the seat of the higher, or conscious and rational, adjustment mechanisms. Here are elaborated the verbal and other language symbols which earlier we termed super-organic and which function in the more complex and long-time or distance adjustments. It is also the seat of the conscious control of the organism, both in its development and in its adjustment. Through its consciousness and its external storage of language symbols the pressures of the environment are brought to bear upon the actual life adjustment processes of individuals.

THE RECEPTOR AND EFFECTOR SYSTEMS—The organism of course is integrated or lives and functions in environments. That is to say, it must make adjustments to other objects like and unlike itself. This adjustment is effected by means of two processes closely connected with each other functionally. These are called stimulation and response. The stimulus process is the process of making a contact with another object, or the environment, which sets up retentive and transmissive processes in the nervous system and normally leads over to the overt response. The overt response is muscular or glandular. If it is muscular it functions by moving a part or the whole of the organism directly with reference to its environment. If it is glandular it sets up some internal chemical change in the body as the direct result. In turn it tends to produce a muscular movement or adjustment as the final or indirect result of the transmission of an impulse from the point of stimulation by way of the glandular responses. The stimulation from the contact with external or internal environment (for some stimuli proceed from within the body) is made effective by means of sense organs, sometimes called end-organs. These are of many kinds, considered both as to structure and as to function. It is not necessary to describe the structure of these sense organs, since we are here concerned primarily with function. Good accounts of their structure can be found in any competent text book on neurology or psychology.[1]

THE SENSE ORGANS are divided into three great classes.

(1) Those which make contacts through the nervous system for the organism with the outside world. These may be further divided into the contact and the distance receptors. Together they are called the organs of the *exteroceptive senses*. Herrick classifies them as follows:

1. Organs of touch and pressure. These are numerous, widely distributed (both superficially and deep), and of very diverse form.
2. End-organs for sensibility to cold.
3. End-organs for sensibility to heat.
4. End-organs for pain.
5. End-organs for general chemical sensibility.
6. Organs of hearing.
7. Organs of vision.
8. Organs of smell.

The first five are contact receptor types and the last three are distance receptor types.

(2) The second group of sense organs are called the *proprioceptive* and are located in the muscles and joints and in other parts of the body. They appear to be more directly connected with the effector apparatus and function rather imme-

---

[1] The following classification of sense organs is adapted from C. J. Herrick, *The Neurological Foundations of Animal Behavior* (Henry Holt and Company, New York).

diately in the orientation of the body. They are, in Herrick's terminology,

1. End-organs of muscular sensibility.
2. End-organs of tendon sensibility.
3. End-organs of joint sensibility.
4. Organs of postural and equilibratory sensations in the labyrinth of the internal ear.

(3) The *visceral* group of receptors are those which function in the viscera or internal cavities and organs of the body and are connected with the vital processes rather than with those of external adjustment. They also function in the emotions, in so far as they are concerned with the mental life of the organism. They are (following Herrick, again) as follows:

General visceral group:

1. Organs of hunger. The stimulus is strong periodic contractions of the muscles of the stomach.
2. Organs of thirst. The stimulus is probably drying of mucous membrane of the pharynx, together with more general conditions.
3. Organs of nausea. The stimulus is probably an antiperistaltic reflex in the digestive tract.
4. Organs of respiratory sensations, suffocation, etc. Organs not well known.
5. Organs of circulatory sensations, flushing, heart panics, etc.
6. Organs of sexual sensations.
7. Organs of sensations of distention of cavities.
8. Organs of visceral pain.
9. Organs of obscure abdominal sensations associated with strong emotion, characterized (probably correctly) by the ancients by such expressions as "yearning of the bowels," etc.

Special visceral group:

10. Organs of taste.
11. Organs of smell. Smell is both a visceral and a somatic sense; its organs are both interoceptors and exteroceptors in Sherrington's sense.

ORGANIC BASES OF BEHAVIOR

The effectors, as already intimated, are the muscles and the glands. These are put into active operation through the impulses reaching them over the efferent nervous processes, which connect indirectly with the sense organs that receive the stimuli.

THE NEURONS are the nerve cells which receive stimuli and transmit impulses to the effectors. They also apparently retain impressions which serve to influence behavior at some future time. The neuron consists of three relatively distinct parts: the nucleus, which apparently serves largely the function of storing and dispensing nutriment to the cell as a whole, the dendritic filaments, and the axone. The dendritic portion of the neuron receives the stimulus as end-organ or takes over the transmitted impulses from an axone, which in turn delivers the impulse to another dendritic process or to an effector, that is, to a muscle or gland. In afferent neurons—those located at the stimulus receiving end of the behavior pattern or mechanism—the dendritic processes serve as sensory end-organs.

Nervous impulses travel in one direction only—from sense organ to effector, through dendrite, past the nucleus, to the axone in one neuron, and from the axone of that cell to the dendrites of another cell or neuron, or to the terminals of the neurons in the muscle or gland.

THE BEHAVIOR PATTERN—This discussion implies that neurons do not occur singly, and this is true in so far as higher animals are concerned. A number of neurons, usually three or more, are grouped together in a chain which connects the sense organs with the effectors. This chain of three or more neurons is called a behavior pattern, and as a pattern it may be inherited or acquired. That is, the connection of one neuron with another in the chain, or the stringing together to form a behavior medium or pattern may have occurred so early in the development of the individual organism that we are inclined to speak of it as inherited. But, on the other hand, many of these connections are not made even at birth and have to be completed weeks or months or even years afterwards. In fact, in some cases the dendritic and axonal processes are not themselves mature at the time of the birth of the organism. They attain their maturity and make structural and functional connections with each other under the pressure of physiological stimuli of some sort. The organization of behavior patterns connected up in this way may certainly be said to be acquired. A very large number of our behavior patterns, and perhaps all of those most basic to our modern civilization, are thus acquired under the influence of environmental pressures.

The neurons in such a behavior pattern, whether inherited or acquired, may in general be said to be of three kinds. The afferent or receiving neurons and the efferent or effector neurons have already been described briefly. They differ from each other primarily in their respective functions and positions and in the relative length of their dendrites and axones. Dendrites are relatively longer in the former and shorter in the latter, and just the reverse is true of the axones. They do not appear to differ very greatly if at all in chemical organization or in structure. The connecting or association neurons are located in the ganglia (including cortexes), are shorter, often have their dendritic processes highly developed, sometimes to the extent of possessing sixty or more branches, and they serve the function of transmitting the impulse from the receiving neuron to the effector neuron. There may be more than one such connecting neuron in the larger ganglia or cortexes, especially in the cerebrum. In these higher centers the multiplicity of dendritic processes and of connecting neurons probably greatly facilitates modifications and the redistribution of impulses, with the result that new behavior patterns are set up and habits are constantly being formed. It is probably in such differentiation and redifferentiation processes as these that consciousness appears in the cerebral cortex. By means of such modification and redistribution of impulses in man, the human behavior patterns may be multiplied indefinitely and the action system become complicated almost beyond estimation. This is undoubtedly the mechanism by which choice and voluntary control of conduct are effected.

THE SYNAPSE—The mechanism by which the axone of one neuron connects with the dendrites of another is called the synapse. The exact nature of this contact is not definitely known. "Some claim that there is actual fusion of the protoplasms of the neurons and passage of neurofibrils across the junction; others maintain that there is a membrane separating the neurons," says Herrick, who is inclined to accept the latter view. "At the synapse there is a contact of two dissimilar protoplasms, with resulting profound modification of the conduction at the opposed surface." There is a resistance to conduction at the synapse which prevents indiscriminate formation of behavior patterns, or rather uncorrelated and uncontrolled responses without the formation of any definite pattern whatever. It is at the synapses apparently that redifferentiation and distribution of nervous impulses occur, with the result that habits are formed and broken and reformed. And out of this modifiability comes the richness of human behavior under the pressures of manifold and changing environmental conditions or stimuli.

THE AUTONOMIC SYSTEM—Primarily within the peripheral nervous system, functions what has been called the autonomic nervous system, so much stressed recently by those who have just come to realize the great importance of the second general type of action mentioned in Chapter III—the unconscious adjustment processes. This system is concerned with the vital or lower organic adjustments of the organism, especially with those connected with nutrition, reproduction, and escape from danger. It came into existence early as a means of aiding the organism to make direct and immediate adjustments to its environment, especially adjustments of the lower and simpler types, such as those to food, sex, danger, protection, and organic well-being, as mentioned above. Because of its primary character as an adjustment mechanism, fitted to deal with the fundamental and primitive relationships between the organism and its environment, it has sometimes been called the vegetative system.

The autonomic system is the seat of the truly instinctive processes and out of these native adjustment mechanisms are developed many of the more basic organic habits which function on a low psychic level. Respiration, food getting and taking, excretion, circulation of the blood and lymph, reproduction, the activities of the glands, and similar organic processes, are so primitive and so relatively fixed, even when modified into a low level of habit for purposes of mediating slightly modified adjustments, that they require little or no conscious or subconscious oversight. This is particularly true of adjustments under primitive conditions of life. However, with the coming of civilization and greater complexity of environment and adjustment technique to correspond to the increased complexity of the organism, a rate of change in adjustment greater than that made possible by the autonomic nervous system becomes necessary. Hence the growth of the dominance of the central nervous system with its powers of conscious and unconscious or subconscious adaptation.

CORTICAL DOMINANCE IN HUMAN ADJUSTMENT—Although Kempf's contention that the autonomic or vegetative nervous system dominates the adjustment processes and uses even the higher sensory processes for its own ends may be true of the lower organisms and to some extent perhaps of the lowest types of human beings, it does not seem to hold, at least universally, for men living in civilized society. It may even be true that the higher sensory processes and the brain, which correlates the sensory functioning, grew up in the service of the autonomic or vegetative nervous apparatus. It would not do violence to our understanding of evolutionary logic to find that all animal life has been most concerned functionally with processes of nutrition, reproduction and avoidance of danger. It is only very recently, and in the life of a single species— the human—that there has been any concern about the esthetic, the moral, and the civic. Beauty, rightness, and the social values are the creation of man's self and social consciousness, which are no older than his civilization.

Eyes and ears, to say nothing of the lower exteroceptive senses, and even the cortex, possibly did come into being to serve the existence and persistence adjustments of life. But we have already seen that as each new type of protoplasm or each new organization of the neural protoplasm appeared, at first in the service of an older adjustment mechanism, and became perfected, it established new gradients and new axes of development. Thereby it became dominant in the control of the organism. In this way the human cortex came to take charge of higher organic adjustment processes and even to mold the development of the organism itself in no small degree. The cortex works primarily through its power of integration of nervous processes coming from the sense organs and from the lower centers, which it correlates and brings into coöperative functioning for the higher adjustments of the organism as a whole. Through its highly developed retentive functions it is able to integrate past neural processes—stimuli and responses—with those arising in the present. The adjustment of the organism thus secured transcends merely the present moment and is in fact more inclusive even than the life of any one man or of any one succession of men. Such long time and inclusive adjustments as these, occurring through the integrative functions of the cerebral cortex, we call rational. They are also usually conscious, but apparently they may be subconscious or unconscious.

It is in this way that the cortical organization has come to dominate the autonomic mechanisms in whose service it grew up. At an earlier date the vegetative neural processes, which had developed in the service of the existence and persistence functions of the organism, probably were similarly integrated into the autonomic system with the result that a better correlation of and dominance over the hitherto poorly integrated vital organic functions as a whole were secured.

Social Results of Cortical Dominance—As the result of the dominance of the cortical correlation or integrative system, what we sometimes call the aims of life have been greatly modified. We have introduced new interests into the living process. We have come to live in a moral and esthetic world. We no longer strive merely for the satisfaction of what we now call the animal impulses or for the satisfaction of these in purely animal ways. We have invented a new set of values which we call culture and civilization. The very senses which once served to indicate the presence of animal satisfactions or of bodily dangers have now been converted largely to the function of providing us with perceptions of those relationships which we call beauty and goodness and the fitness of things. This new outlook upon our world we sometimes call philosophical and esthetic.

The lower impulses have been transformed into the higher

with the growth of a mechanism for handling the higher perceptions and for the control of those relationships which exist between man and his environment and promote or hinder the realization of the cultural values. But the lower or animal impulses, which still strive for realization through the autonomic system, cannot be ignored. In the first place, the efficient functioning of the organism and the perpetuation of the race depend upon their normal exercise. And in the second place, if they are neglected or unduly repressed, they still have such an effective neural organization at their disposal that they are able to break through the cortically organized coating of culture and bring to the surface in us and expose to full view all of our animal and savage drives with unexpected frankness and vividness. So striking are such irruptions at times that we have a saying that civilization is but a thin veneer of culture and that if we scratch through the surface we come upon the tiger.

CORTICAL SELECTION AND SUBLIMATION—The cortically controlled culture is constantly striving through sublimations and wisely directed and measured repressions to keep the more primitive impulses regulated by the autonomic system under control and to harness them to the chariot of civilization itself. Thus man has developed art, in its various forms, as a means to symbolic and substitute expression of the cruder animal impulses. The drama gives us the battle and intrigue, the tragedy and the comedy of life in action, segregated upon the stage which merely pictures life and does not live it. Here death is but mimicry and the dagger as well as the crown is of pasteboard. We release our violent emotions upon a screen or in the pages of a vivid historical romance or problem novel, without doing much damage to others. We can be brave with our heroes and go with them to slaughter on the printed page or we can be bad with the heroines of the silver screen and no one else be the wiser or necessarily the worse for our psychic indiscretions. Even much of the love-making of youth can be corralled in the reading of poetry or in the tense agony of suspense of the movie fan. The older and more sobered spirits may even turn to philosophy and the social sciences as a form of sublimation in which they are able to see in clearer and more logical light, and withal abstracted far away from the stress of concrete reality, the meaning of things, the struggles and wishes and fears of life. In practice also we have learned to make the more rational choices. We have developed play at the expense of battle. We limit the population, though as yet imperfectly; and we do not consume to-day all of our substance, but preserve the surplus for to-morrow and use it as capital in the service of the future. The cortex is ever striving to intellectualize and acculturate man. And, if we view clearly that from which he came, we must admit that, in spite of many failures and hindrances, it has succeeded remarkably well.

DOMINANCE OF THE SOCIAL ENVIRONMENT—But with all that has been accomplished through the growth and the establishment of successive organic spheres of dominance, ending in the lodgment of supreme organic control in the cerebral cortex, an even greater result has been achieved for culture and civilization by the creation of a social environment to serve as an external control. As we shall see in the following chapter this environment is the creation of man himself and is the product of his efforts to make collectively ever more successful adjustments to his natural environments. Its most important phase is the psycho-social environment, which consists very largely of externally stored organized symbols of internal or neuro-psychic behavior processes and meanings. These symbols have the power when perceived or recognized to reinstate in the behavior of individuals those actions or thought processes which they symbolize. In addition to these, and of earlier origin in the history of the race, are certain collective behavior patterns which arise in society and come to be symbolized by such terms and phrases as customs, traditions, conventions, beliefs, public opinion, fads, fashions, and the like. These latter have no visible or tangible existence apart from the uniform or similar responses of individuals to uniform environmental or reciprocal stimuli. They exist as behavior wholly in the organisms of individuals. But the mind can project these conceptually and verbally as objective realities of collective or uniform social behavior. And among civilized people this is exactly what is done. The behavior of others thus designated serves as stimuli to condition in ourselves like responses. A third phase of this social environment which reacts back upon men through their cerebral cortexes to condition more advanced forms of behavior in them is their physical inventions and the bio-social environment below man.

The symbolic psycho-social controls in particular have become so important in our complex civilization that we store them in vast numbers in books and libraries, in art and architecture, in fact, in all the places which can serve as carriers of symbolic values. They originated as verbal or other neuropsychic symbolic content in the cortical processes of ourselves and others, and they were carried through long periods of time as gesture and vocal language symbols and used by men to stimulate one another to action, and they are still carried and used in these ways in vast numbers. But since the content of thought has become so great that it can no longer be carried exclusively in memory, these controls have been objectified in large numbers into literate symbols outside of human action and transferred to the printed page, to phonograph records, to pictures, statuary, films, curios, relics, and similar containers. Here they lie, especially in the printed page, in storage in any conceivable quantity and serve as stimuli sources to all the population for as many present and future generations as care to learn the keys (language forms) which will unlock them.

SYMBOLIC CONTROLS DOMINATE THROUGH THE CORTICAL ORGANIZATION—Even as externally stored symbols these social control phenomena do not divorce themselves completely from our organic or cortical control processes. It is only through these latter that their meaning can be perceived, and through these cortical processes all stimuli from the stored symbol complexes must flow in order to condition responses in the behavior of the organism. The cortex, through its mnemic functions, holds the keys to release the stimuli of the objectivated symbols, and finally they can operate only as they are distributed through the cortex into overt action. Yet the body of these external symbols and projected organizations has become so vast that now they practically dominate the functioning of the cortical processes in adjusting the individual organism to its world. It is another instance of the creation by the organism of some sort of extension mechanism to the point where it comes itself to dominate the whole organism which has created it. But in this case the newly created supplementary device, which has come to dominate the adjustment process, is not organic but is psycho-social. And with the coming of this new form of dominance our world ceased to be primarily organic and passed under the reign of the social.

THE LEVELS OF THE CONTROL OF BEHAVIOR—The most significant fact about the organism for the social psychologist is its behavior, and the most important type of behavior to the sociologist is what we call rational or intelligent behavior. It is probably at the level of rational behavior that the most significant changes and inventive redirections of individual and collective behavior occur. But there are other levels of behavior which also play significant parts in the control of the individual organism in a social situation. We may summarize and systematize the discussion of the earlier part of this chapter by presenting a brief account of the levels of behavior as they operate in the organism. This outline of the levels may be stated as follows:

Autonomic control levels dominant
    Interoceptive or visceral senses functioning
    Proprioceptive senses functioning
    Lower exteroceptive senses functioning
    Higher exteroceptive senses beginning to function
Cortical control levels dominant
    Exteroceptive senses functioning rationally
    Mechanical extensions of the exteroceptive senses
Verbal and symbolic levels dominant
    Storage symbols operate through the exteroceptive senses

This classification is constructed from the dual standpoint of the general type of nervous mechanism dominant in the control of the organism and of the types of sensory stimuli which are available for purposes of initiating responses of the nervous mechanisms. The arrangement of the sensory processes involved is not necessarily chronological, although there is doubtless some degree of sequence in the order here presented. The autonomic nervous control employs all types of sensory processes, and especially those of the interoceptive and proprioceptive systems. The exteroceptive senses may be divided into two orders: the lower, including the various tactual, temperature and surface pain organs, and taste, and the higher, including the senses of smell, hearing and sight. Both of these orders of sensory processes are operative while the autonomic nervous system is still dominant. But the exteroceptive senses, especially those of smell, hearing and sight, are largely contemporaneous in their growth with the growth of the brain, and when conscious cortical processes finally come to dominate the behavior of the human organism, the sensory instruments by which data for consciously directed adjustments are obtained are primarily sight and hearing.

MATERIALS FOR SUPPLEMENTARY READING

Allport, F. H., *Social Psychology*, Ch. II
Bernard, L. L., *Instinct: A Study in Social Psychology*, Ch. III
Child, C. M., "The Individual and Environment from a Physiological Viewpoint," in *The Child, the Clinic and the Court*, pp. 126-55.
——, *Physiological Foundations of Behavior*
Dunlap, K., *An Outline of Psychobiology*, Chs. III, VII, VIII
Herrick, C. J., *An Introduction to Neurology* (2d ed.), Chs. II-VII, XVI, XIX-XXI
——, *Neurological Foundations of Animal Behavior*
——, "Self-Control and Social Control," in *The Child, the Clinic and the Court*, pp. 156-77
Kroeber, A. L., "The Superorganic," *Amer. Anthrop.*, XIX: 163-213
Parmelee, M., *The Science of Human Behavior*, Chs. IX, X
Paton, S., *Human Behavior*, Chs. II, III, VIII
Robinson, E. S. and F. R., *Readings in General Psychology*, Chs. II, III
Sherrington, C. S., *The Integrative Action of the Nervous System*
Warren, H. C., *Human Psychology*, Chs. II-V
Watson, J. B., *Psychology from the Standpoint of a Behaviorist*, Chs. III, IV

CHAPTER VI

THE ENVIRONMENTAL BASES OF BEHAVIOR

THE SIGNIFICANCE OF ENVIRONMENT—In the previous chapter it was necessary to refer to the objective bases of behavior in the form of environment. Child's theory of the integration of the organism involves environmental factors as well as those of heredity. From his viewpoint the organism is integrated through its behavior and its behavior is a function of the reaction of its specific protoplasms to the environmental pressures. In this chapter it becomes necessary to analyze the environment as that set of objective factors which coöperate with the inheritance factors in the integration of behavior patterns through its determination of axes in the organism. The pressures of the environment determine the axes of the organism by which it orients itself with reference to the environment; the metabolic and the physico-chemical properties of the protoplasms determine the gradients and dominance in the organism, and all these factors together, determine the behavior. The social psychologist can therefore no more disregard the environment than he can ignore the heredity of the organism, if he expects to have an adequate understanding of the origins and controls of human behavior.

As a matter of fact, however, environment has been largely neglected by social scientists generally and particularly by the social psychologists. In the textbooks of this science the concept scarcely appears with any degree of definiteness. Where the term is used it is employed with a vague and somewhat general reference which is not at all comparable with the concreteness and highly organized character of the treatment of the concept of inheritance; although this concept also is at times handled all too vaguely. There is great need for rendering the concept of environment definite and for analyzing it into its constituent parts, in order that the social psychologist may have a clear notion of the objective as well as of the subjective factors which integrate for individual organisms their patterns of behavior.

COMPLEXITY AND DIFFERENTIATION OF ENVIRONMENTS—Environment, which is usually spoken of in the singular, is in reality a very complex set of phenomena. Environment does not function as a whole or as a unity in the determination of the behavior of organisms. Its unity, like that of habit, is conceptual rather than objective and sensory or experiential. No two persons ever come under exactly the same environmental controls. Even though they live in the same family or on the same street they will in all probability be subject to very different types of environments, because the subjective factors segregate them into different categories as far as the incidence of environments is concerned. Brothers and sisters of different ages, with different heredity and with differences in health and training, etc., react to their environments in vastly different ways. These differences in subjective control of their reactions actually segregate for them different kinds of environments; for while the physical and biological environments remain fairly constant for all people in a group, whatever may be their subjective reactions to them, the social environments are so fluid and often so intangible that two persons living in daily contact may be subject to very different environmental influences of this kind. One person may read fiction, another science; one may frequent musical concerts of a high order, another vaudeville and musical comedies; the one may attend church services and engage in civic welfare activities, the other may spend her time for social contacts at receptions, parties and in neighborhood gossip. And yet these two people may live in the same household and to the unanalytical appear to have identically the same environments.

If the psychic and social environments are highly fluid and intangible, it is equally true that not all aspects of the environment have equal objectivity. As a recent writer has said, it is not possible to determine exactly where the self ends and the environment begins. He speaks of the environment as existing in layers which may be successively peeled off as we approach that hypothetical entity which we call the self. But the self is so inextricably interwoven with the environment, is interconnected with it in so many ways, that if we are not careful we may destroy a large part of its identity by peeling off so many layers of environment that we kill the roots of the personality. For the roots of the personality are in the environment quite as much as in the heredity of the organism. In a way the more physical the environment is the more objective it may appear to be. But even our own bodies may be considered as an environment for our neural organization and the psychic behavior processes which are dependent upon the organization of neural protoplasm. The psycho-social environment is particularly closely connected with our psychic life and it is very difficult to segregate it functionally, even in a tentative way, from the self, which is so closely dependent upon it for its organization and content. These facts of the relatively unequal degrees of objectivity of phases of environment should be kept constantly in mind in the study of environmental pressures.

THE STUDY OF ENVIRONMENT IS RECENT—Although the general concept of environment is sufficiently ancient, the actual analysis of environmental factors at work in producing specific behavior is comparatively recent. Aristotle in his *Politics* made some references to the influence of geography and climate upon the location of city states and their prosperity, and his imitators repeated his generalizations. Ibn Khaldun in the fourteenth century considerably expanded this theme; and Bodin and Montesquieu in the seventeenth and eighteenth centuries of our era attempted fairly systematic treatments of the social effects of climate and geography. *The Spirit of Laws* of the last named contains a well organized, if not a particularly accurate, discussion of the subject. The nineteenth and twentieth centuries brought forth many anthropogeographers, particularly Buckle, Ratzel, and Huntington, who have elaborated in great detail these themes.

The influence of inventions, as a form of environmental pressures, has also been extensively treated by the anthropologists during the last hundred years or so, and very recently there have been some attempts to reduce this phase of the subject to something like systematic order. The environments which are here termed psycho-social were recognized with some degree of clearness by the Sophists, the social philosophers who preceded and were in some cases contemporaneous with Socrates and Plato. Some of these thinkers actually denied final determination of the right and the expedient to the gods and to natural law and declared that the proper criteria of conduct were to be found in public opinion and in custom, tradition, and convention. But it is doubtful if any other thinkers went as far in their analysis of the psycho-social environment before the nineteenth century. In the latter part of this century Bagehot, Tarde, Ross, and others of their school, began to objectify, classify and explain the intangible psychic processes which become organized in the life of groups. No previous writer had attempted to classify and describe the environments in such a way as to make the concepts extensively available for control purposes in building up patterns of individual and collective behavior.

The reasons for this neglect of environment are doubtless many, but a few of them stand out conspicuously. In the first place, the connection between environment and behavior is by no means obvious, except possibly where the grosser forms of the physical and organic environments act directly upon the organism and produce sensory results as well as changes in the tissue organization of the body. Thus many of the effects of temperature, humidity, soil, and geographic contour and surface must early have become apparent to more thoughtful observers, as they did to Aristotle, Bodin, and Montesquieu. But it is not as easy to perceive the connection between the intangible psycho-social factors in the environment and the changes which are wrought in our own personalities when we are brought in contact with them. Before we can achieve such an understanding it is necessary for us in some way to objectify these intangible or abstract psycho-social factors and to organize them into conceptual categories in the environment. This is what the Sophist philosophers of Greece in a measure learned to do; and this is also what the social psychologists in the second half of the nineteenth century, writing under the influence of the new processes of communication which had grown up as the result of the industrial revolution, elaborated in something approaching scientific clearness and detail.

On the other hand, the concept of inheritance was early defined in its simple forms, because the biological connection between parent and offspring was perfectly apparent to every one. The degree of resemblance was sufficiently marked and its occurrence so frequent that no one doubted the connection. But it is worthy of note that abstract theories of inheritance of a complex and differential pattern did not appear until the nineteenth century. The Mendelian theory, the most systematic and most generally accepted of all of these complex abstract theories of differential inheritance, did not begin to become generally known until the year 1900.

SUPERPERSONALITY AS ENVIRONMENTAL CAUSE OF BEHAVIOR—Another significant reason why environmental analysis, as an aid to the explanation of the origin of behavior traits, came late is that the approach to an explanation of social and psychic causation was through the theological concept of divine will and the metaphysical concepts of natural law and its derivatives, reason and intuition. This is really another way of saying that such causal explanations were at first concrete and only gradually evolved into an abstract analysis. The will of the gods was a synthetic and projected explanation on the analogy of individual will which man had actually experienced and observed in operation as a cause. Before the individual could grasp the concept of a collective exercise of will and a collective response, he created superpersonalities on the analogy of human personalities which he knew, and he ascribed to them a power to influence individual and social behavior greater than any power he himself possessed. The superpersonal environment was thus a projected personality environment.

NATURAL LAW AS ENVIRONMENTAL CAUSE—The concept of natural law evolved indirectly out of that of personal divinity, through a process of increasing depersonalization. At first it was the semi-animate, semi-abstract *Nous* which took the place of *Zeus* as a universal cause of things. But *Nous* long retained some of the attributes of personality, such as love, justice, order, and power. When finally the abstract concept of natural law as a set of universal rules objectified into a timeless and spaceless infinity, evolved from the half personal concept of *Nous,* it became necessary to find some method by which this intangible essence of natural law could penetrate into tangible human beings and produce their behavior. The method by which this problem was solved involved the invention of personal concepts of an individual reason and intuition and the social concept of general or political reason or law. Thus human conduct, as individual behavior and as social action and law and the various collective codes and procedures, was regarded as the extension of this principle or essence of natural law infiltrating itself into personality and collectivity by means of direct contact between these and the universal. The concept of divinity was now relegated to a position in the background, as the *deus ex machina,* which had created natural law as the systematized thought of divinity but no longer concerned itself with this law. In this way the account of causation in individual and collective behavior became metaphysical. It was directly descended from the ancient personal will explanation so closely akin to magic which had created, for purposes of the objectification and universalization of the causes of behavior, the numerous systems of mythologies or theologies. The natural law environment was, therefore, not only a projected but also a conceptualized environment.

SCIENTIFIC ANALYSIS AS A FORERUNNER OF ENVIRONMENTAL THEORY—A scientific account of the origin and organization of behavior could arise only as concrete and definite analyses and measurements were made of the relationships between classes of objective phenomena on the one hand and human beings acting individually and collectively on the other hand. Such analyses, as we have seen, were begun by such men as the Sophists, Aristotle, Ibn Khaldun, Bodin, Montesquieu, and others, and are now being rapidly perfected. The growth of scientific facts and the analysis of environmental data are closely correlated processes. Each supplements and aids the other, and each is a function of the other. This

ENVIRONMENTAL BASES

process of scientific analysis has gone far enough forward that it is now possible to offer a tentative synthesis of results in the form of a classification of the types of environments and their pressures, as an aid to an understanding of environmental controls over individual and collective behavior.

A Scientific Classification of the Environments—A general outline classification of the environments, with representative subdivisions, may be presented as follows:

I. The physical (inorganic) environments
   1. Cosmic, 2. Physico-geographic, 3. Soil, 4. Climate, 5. Inorganic resources, 6. Natural physical agencies (falling water, winds, tides, etc.), 7. Natural mechanical processes (combustion, radiation, gravity, etc.)

II. The biological or organic environments
   1. Microörganisms, 2. Insects and parasites, 3. Larger plants used for food, clothing, shelter, etc., 4. Larger animals used for food, clothing, etc., 5. Harmful relationships of larger plants and animals, 6. Ecological and symbiotic relationships of plants and animals acting indirectly upon man, 7. Prenatal environment of man, 8. Natural biological processes (reproduction, growth, decomposition, assimilation, excretion, circulation, etc.)

III. The social environments
   1. Physico-social environments
      (1) Tools, (2) Weapons, (3) Ornaments, (4) Machines, (5) Transportation systems, (6) Communication systems, (7) Household equipment, (8) Office equipment, (9) Apparatus for scientific research, etc.
   2. Bio-social environments
      A. Non-human
         (1) Domesticated plants, used for food, clothing, shelter, medicines, ornaments, (2) Domestic animals used as a source of food, (3) Domestic animals used as a source of power, (4) Medicines and perfumes of an organic character, (5) Animals used as pets and ornaments, etc.

B. Human
   (6) Human beings serving as laborers (slaves, etc.), (7) Human beings serving as ornaments, entertainers, etc., (8) Human beings rendering impersonal voluntary or professional service, (9) Regimented human groups, such as armies, workingmen, etc., (10) Men coöperating voluntarily through the use of language mechanisms.
3. Psycho-social environments
   (1) The inner behavior (attitudes, ideas, desires, etc.) of individuals with whom we come in contact, (2) The uniformities of inner behavior occurring in collective units and perceived as customs, folkways, conventions, traditions, beliefs, mores, etc., (3) Externalized language symbols used to project the above types of behavior and to condition responses in ourselves and others, (4) Those inventions, primarily physical, which perform a similar service in conditioning psychic responses, but usually with less facility and completeness.

IV. Composite or institutionalized derivative control environments (derivative combinations of the various types of environments organized for purposes of social control).
   1. General in character
      The economic, political, racial, esthetic, ethical, educational, etc., environments.
   2. Special in character
      The American, Italian, Jewish, Scandinavian, New England, Southern, Argentinean, Republican, Democratic, Catholic, Buddhist, revolutionary, conservative, feminine, masculine, etc., environments.

THE NATURAL ENVIRONMENTS—The physical (inorganic) and biological environments represent nature in practically unmodified form. These environments have been operating upon man from the period before he became human and continue to influence his behavior both individually and collectively. The operation of the natural environmental factors upon man is both direct and indirect. Examples of direct operation may

ENVIRONMENTAL BASES

be found in such matters as many of the effects of the sun's heat, of electrical disturbances, cold, the change of the seasons, degrees of humidity in the atmosphere, altitude, the action of winds, floods, rainfalls, etc., the effect of bacteria and kindred lower organisms, the influence of the mother through the prenatal period of the individual's development, etc. All of these direct forms of influence of the natural environments take effect primarily upon the protoplasmic organization of the individual by more or less direct impact and not through the method of stimulus and response, which is the common method of environmental influence upon neural protoplasm.

The indirect influences of the natural environments are vastly more numerous and more important and are exercised through the manner in which they condition the collective adjustments of man to nature. That is, climate and temperature, the seasons, humidity, altitude, the supply and character of plants and animals providing food, clothing, shelter and power, the surface configuration and topography of the geographic environment, the supply of plant food in the soil which conditions the relative plentifulness or scarcity of food, the occurrence of the metals and minerals and other inorganic resources which may be utilized by man for industrial purposes, and the presence of insects and other carriers of disease germs determine in the main the conditions under which men can live together in groups and make an effective common or coadaptive adjustment to natural and artificial environments. They set the limits in large measure to the size of populations and to the age, sex, and occupational constitution of those populations. Also, as a consequence, they indirectly determine the form of political organization, the prevalence and distribution of culture in the form of the fine arts, science, and humanitarian attitudes, the quality of religious feeling, and various other psycho-social manifestations of human behavior. Thus it is seen that the effect of the natural environments upon the psychic and psycho-social behavior of men, both individual and collective, is almost entirely indirect. Furthermore, it is probably becoming constantly more indirect as we learn to cause the natural environments as a whole to operate upon man primarily through the derivative physico-social and bio-social environments, which are the result of man's transformation of the natural environments.

THE LOWER SOCIAL ENVIRONMENTS—These are the physico-social and the bio-social environments which have arisen as part of man's technique of adjustment to the two great natural environments which originally shaped the evolution and development of all living things, including man. It is through these environments that man first came to deal indirectly rather than directly with nature, although he never lost entirely his direct contacts with the native physical (inorganic) and organic environments. The physico-social and bio-social environments are primarily environments of invention and training. Artificial shelter, clothing, and prepared foods of all kinds belong in the category of either physico-social or bio-social environments. Tools, weapons, ornaments, cities, transportation and communication systems, machines, equipment, scientific apparatus, books, ice, fire, chemical compounds, are some of the inventions of this type. Man has produced them through his inventive skill as aids in what we sometimes speak of as the control of nature, and he has produced them from the materials of nature.

On the other hand, domesticated plants and animals, human as well as non-human, improvements of biological types through breeding and training and nurture, many forms of medicines and creature comforts of man, pets and ornaments, are the products of a transformation of his organic environment on much the same basis as that in which the physical environment is transformed by man. There is, however, this partial and significant difference between the transformation of the physical environment and of the organic environment into their derivative physico-social and bio-social environments. In the former case the transformation occurs relatively completely in each generation or other short period, the concrete products having to be produced from physical nature at definite intervals as they are consumed in use. But in the case of bio-social products, especially those which arise through control of inheritance or through the institutionalization of nurture and training, the new instrument tends to persist largely of itself and to reproduce its kind either through biological mechanisms or through the continuity of custom and the consequent persistence of institutions. Thus the ability of man to invent and use oral language gives to his behavior a continuity and a quality as a phase of the bio-social environment which is not approached by the physico-social environment. The distinction here is by no means absolute, but it is significant enough to deserve mention because of its relation to the permanent physico-social and bio-social processes.

THE LOWER SOCIAL ENVIRONMENTS AND BEHAVIOR—The physico-social and bio-social environments are intimately connected with human behavior, individual and collective, in two well-marked ways. In the first place, it is human behavior that creates the inventions and gives the training, physical, biological, and psychological, which constitute the content of these two environments. The earliest inventions are of course empirical and are often accidental to such an extent that they involve little constructive or projective thinking. But even so they are the product of behavior that is of necessity neuro-psychic in content and constitute standardized forms of adjustment to environment. The higher forms of inventions—physical, social, and method—are particularly the product of projective thinking, in some cases of the most abstract type. Such inventions call into play the highest types of cortical neural organization and utilize the most abstract forms of storage symbols and content of the externalized neuro-psychic technique described in the previous chapter. In such cases man transforms his environment—sometimes his concepts of it—as an aid to adjustment to that environment by means of behavior of the most advanced type. Most inventions are co-operative and therefore involve the exercise of collective as well as of individual behavior. The same is true of training.

Not only did the inventions and training which constitute the physico-social and the bio-social environments arise out of human individual and collective behavior as a result of efforts, conscious or otherwise, to control more advantageously man's adjustment to his environment, but these inventions and training also react back upon the behavior of men in a multitude of ways which have the greatest significance for the future organization and evolution of their adjustment processes. Many inventions react upon man by direct impact in ways quite similar to those in which the natural environments operate directly upon him. Many also operate indirectly by conditioning the size and constitution of populations, the forms and effectiveness of economic organizations, the types of political and religious and other cultural and control institutions and organizations, and even the major interests and functions of men. These invention and training elements of the physico-social and bio-social environments do vastly more to condition the collective behavior of men, by setting limits to it and by giving stimuli and material for its development, than the corresponding untransformed factors of the natural environments. The conditioning effect upon collective behavior of modern transportation and communication, of power-machine industry, and of cheap food, clothing and shelter, to mention only a few illustrations, is so striking that it does not require elaboration.

THE TRANSITION TO THE PSYCHO-SOCIAL ENVIRONMENT—But besides these direct and indirect effects of the material social environments upon behavior, it is in connection with these environments that we first come into touch with the tremendous importance of the psycho-social environment for the control and differentiation of human behavior. Many of the inventions of the material social environments and much of the training of human beings, especially in language content, are carriers of psycho-social content and thus make this latter environment effective in the control of human behavior. This is especially true of books and other printed matter and of all objects of art. It is true also of the trained human being who is at once a bio-social product and a carrier of vast quantities of that language technique which is so large a constituent element of the psycho-social environment. The psycho-social environment cannot exist without carriers and these are to be found in the two lower social environments, especially in the human bio-social environment. In fact, the customs of men constitute bio-social environment, and the same may be said of conventions, mores, folkways, fads, fashions, crazes, in their external manifestations. But since it is to the psycho-social content rather than to the carriers that we respond, we ordinarily speak of customs, conventions, mores, etc., as psycho-social rather than as bio-social environment. The latter environment in its earlier forms was created gradually as the result of the accumulated neuro-psychic adjustment technique arising out of man's compulsory adaptation to physical nature. That is, he no longer adapted directly to the natural world, at least in any preponderating degree, but he adapted to it indirectly through his bio-social environment of men coöperating through the use of language in the collective forms of customs, folkways, conventions, mores, etc. This coöperating bio-social environment he built up as a buffer or protector between himself and the remorseless natural world with which in his early history he came so rudely and harshly in contact.

Originally our institutions and conventions in their overt behavior aspects grew up as phases of the bio-social environment on the basis of gesture and vocal language and overt coöperative behavior of men. They were the overt aspects of the inner habit organization or neuro-psychic technique. This was also the source of the psycho-social environment, which arose with the practice of attaching standardized or conventionalized meanings to external symbols, and especially with the invention of written language or symbols. It is in the symbolic behavior of men that the highest forms of the bio-social and the lowest forms of the psycho-social environment overlap. Just to the extent that symbolic behavior comes to exceed in importance total overt responses or behavior, as language takes the place of action in adjustment, just to that extent must the human bio-social environment be transformed into this more stable and voluminous and abstract content of the psycho-social environment. The psycho-social environment is no longer simple and concrete and transparent; it constantly becomes more abstract and general.

THE PSYCHO-SOCIAL ENVIRONMENT is the environment of inner or neuro-psychic behavior and ideas. But, since neuro-psychic processes cannot be observed directly and cannot exist without organic or inorganic carriers, we can know this environment only through its symbols. These symbols are manifest in the overt (usually symbolical overt) behavior of other men and in detached or externalized language symbols, pictorial art, sculpture, books, phonographs, etc., including even the physical inventions and trained animals, plants, etc., which have acquired the power of conditioning neuro-psychic behavior in men. Thus either the bio-social or the physico-social environments may carry this symbolic content which conditions in us psychic responses or by which we recognize meaning or psychic behavior. Even the abstract language symbols used in literature must be carried by a physical invention, such as a book, magazine, radio, phonograph, if they are not transmitted directly from one person to another. Thus the lower social environments and the psycho-social environments overlap with each other to a marked degree, just as all other environments overlap with one another.

Much of the psycho-social environmental content reaches us directly through the language behavior of individuals and we adjust to this environment in this form merely as to the psychic or language behavior of individuals. In such cases we think only of individuals and to all intents and purposes our environing world is made up of psychically behaving individuals and of environmental objects of a lower order. This is especially true of the less cultured or intellectual types. They do not think particularly of the uniformities of psychic behavior which exist in their psycho-social environment. But less frequently we see the human element of our psycho-social environment not as separate persons but as groups of persons behaving uniformly, or we may even see it as abstract collective processes or forces or tendencies in the psycho-social environment. We may speak of these as customs, folkways, conventions, traditions, beliefs, mores, fads, fashions, crazes, gossip, propaganda, public opinion, even science and religion.

The question has been raised as to whether such abstractions can really constitute psycho-social environment, since they are intangible and cannot offer stimuli directly to the senses. It is true that they cannot be perceived directly as sensory objects in the same way in which an apple or a pencil can be perceived. They are grasped conceptually rather than through concrete perception. However, the difference is only one of degree. The *gestalt* theorists have reëmphasized for us the fact that we almost never see all of the details of an object.

We ordinarily see all objects conceptually. That is, on the basis of our response to certain strategic or skeleton stimuli we integrate the perception or concept of the object as a whole. We see what we are prepared by previous experience to see. Some people can see only the behavior of individuals and this not very well, while others can see the behavior of groups of men or the collective behavior of men, even though they do not see all of the men or all of their behavior. And some few can see such collective behavior very well. Their previous integrations of perceptions of behavior enable them to project the parts of the behavior which they do not see through their senses directly and to see abstractly or conceptually the larger psycho-social processes in society. It is in this way that we have learned to apprehend customs, traditions, conventions, folkways, mores, public opinion, in fact societies, publics and all mankind. We respond to such stimuli quite as definitely as we respond to the stimulus of a single person, but more abstractly. Even the individual is an abstraction, but less so than the group. We may say, therefore, that these abstract uniformities of behavior are as much objective realities as persons, but more abstract realities. They also condition our responses quite as much when we have acquired the power of integrating them perceptually or conceptually. They are not mere metaphysical fictions as some psychologists would have us believe.

But the most important phase of the psycho-social environment in our civilization is the externalized symbolic one of newspapers, books, etc. It standardizes and stabilizes our responses and it carries a psychic content more abstract and weighty than that of individuals or collections of them.

BEHAVIOR AND THE PSYCHO-SOCIAL ENVIRONMENT—The double relationship between behavior and environment referred to above is especially well marked in connection with the psycho-social environment. It is the psychic behavior of individuals primarily which constitutes the psycho-social environment, either when externalized and stored in the form of meaning symbols and complexes of meaning symbols of the neuro-psychic technique, or when merely objectified and communicated through the symbolic behavior or language as customs, beliefs, conventions, etc. Because the psycho-social environment is built wholly out of objectified neuro-psychic behavior as meaning, it is ordinarily the most fluid of all of the environments. It is never twice the same, but is changing constantly as men think and as they develop attitudes, especially as they think and act collectively. Man has integrated and projected this environment for himself as a sort of bulwark or protection against nature and through its aid he has largely transformed nature into the derivative physico-social and bio-social environments. Science, as one of the larger, and unquestionably the most important, of the elements of the psycho-social environment, has been most useful in this process of transforming the natural environments into the derivative environments.

But the psycho-social environment in turn re-creates the behavior of man. It was this environment which largely transformed him from an element in the original natural organic environment into an element in the bio-social environment, on the biological side. It made of him a trained and domesticated animal at the same time that he as such an animal was creating the psycho-social environment out of his own neuro-psychic behavior. The two processes have always been reciprocal. But to-day the volume of the psycho-social environment, especially on the externalized side, has become so great and its refinement and differentiation and definition so specific and effective that it acts as a powerful force to create new behavior patterns in nascent or developing individuals. The race throughout its history has created the psycho-social environment, but the psycho-social environment creates exclusively and completely the complex mental and moral and social character traits of individuals. This environment which mankind, collectively, has created now dominates completely their spiritual life. Through the stimuli which it offers it molds them entirely, and if it affects men differently at different times and in different places this is because it is possessed of an almost endless variety of forms and intensities and operates upon men of vastly different capacities and characteristics.

THE COMPOSITE OR DERIVATIVE CONTROL ENVIRONMENTS are, as the title implies, made up of all of the other environments,

ENVIRONMENTAL BASES

with the psycho-social invariably in the ascendancy. This is the environment which actually functions in our social organization. The other environments, when considered as wholes, are more or less abstractions. Their constituent elements never are assembled in one place and at one time in all their completeness, but it is possible to think of them as synthetic wholes arising out of the multiplicity of our experiences and observations. But the composite or derivative control environment, either general or special, represents an actual organization of selected aspects of the other environments which are recognized as having more or less concrete, as well as conceptual, integration, although no one of these environments in its entirety ever operates upon an individual or upon groups. Thus if we consider a national environment, such as the Irish People, or the economic or industrial environment, or the Christian Church as an environment, we can readily conceive each of these as objective and concretely integrated facts. Each does possess a considerable degree of objective unity of organization, and yet no one person subject to the environment is equally affected by all aspects of it. Nor are any two people affected by nominally the same environment in the same ways. Even here different ones of these composite control environments affect the individual or the group with different degrees of concreteness and inclusiveness.

DEGREES OF DEFINITENESS OF ORGANIZATION—It is through these environments that society becomes organized, that is, becomes most truly and completely a society or a group of societies and associations. This social organization possesses all degrees of definiteness and concreteness. It may, at one extreme, have the indefiniteness of organization of the "nationality" or the "race," which is a more or less loosely assembled group of concepts of customs, traditions, mores and folkways, and institutions, changing slowly and possessing no definite internal unity, but a certain vague conceptual unity. At the other extreme, it may possess the definite unity of a highly organized association performing a specific function, such as the W.C.T.U., or the Republican party, the Baptist Church, or a local civic improvement club, or a bank. Even in these illustrations of associations different degrees of objective and conceptual unity are observable.

INSTITUTIONS—In between these two extremes are to be found all sorts of gradations, most outstanding of which perhaps are what we ordinarily call institutions. Institutions are themselves highly composite environmental phenomena, the component elements of which possess varying degrees of definiteness and unity. In any institution will be found a certain number of definite associations. Possibly the institution itself may have the nominal or actual character of an association, as in the case of some religious denomination or a political party. Alongside of the more or less definitely organized associations in institutions will be found many other elements, such as traditions and customs, mores and folkways. These various elements of such an institutional environment function together as a variable and inconstant unity. The nature of an institution changes slowly, as its content changes, and its life history is long, but not eternal.

COMPOSITE CHARACTER—Elements from all of the environments may be assembled in the derivative control environments, and such is usually the case. Some of the more limited and definitely organized associations may lack elements from the natural environments, but all other environments will be represented. In the more general derivative control environments, including the social institutions, all elements are present. But in all cases the psycho-social environment is dominant in the composite or derivative control environments. The very existence of control, with a certain degree of consciousness of the nature and functions of the control environment, implies this fact. Here we find the two-fold or reciprocal relationship of behavior and environment most completely illustrated. Constantly the behavior of individuals and groups is molding and reshaping the character of the derivative control institution, and this institution is in turn molding the character of constituent individuals and groups and associations. Often this interchange of behavior pressures is highly conscious and purposive on the part of individuals subject to the environment. But whether conscious or unconscious in its operation, it is in such behavior relations that we find the chief subject matter of social psychology and it is out of the study of such relationships between behavior and environment that the science of social psychology grew.

INDIVIDUAL AND COLLECTIVE BEHAVIOR DISTINGUISHED—Frequently it has been necessary in the preceding pages to use the terms individual and collective or social behavior. The meaning of these terms should now be clear. Individual behavior is the response of the integrated organism to stimuli from its environment. The nature of this integration and the part which environment plays in it were elaborated in the preceding chapter and will be discussed in some of its details in the following. Collective behavior, on the other hand, is the occurrence of identical or similar responses in several individuals at the same time and place or in response to the same or similar stimuli, or of unlike responses which have a reciprocal or supplementary relationship to each other.

COLLECTIVE BEHAVIOR AND UNIFORMITY OF RESPONSE—Such identity or similarity of responses may arise from identity of inner organization of individuals or from their being conditioned by identical or similar stimuli. In practice of course it usually proceeds from both of these conditions. Where people respond in this similar manner we speak of them collectively as groups, whether they have face-to-face contacts or are connected only by stimuli operating at a distance.

Modern life has developed so many communicating agencies that it is possible, almost inevitable, that vast numbers of people should be subjected to the same or similar stimuli and that their behavior should take on a highly uniform character. In relatively settled or static periods and societies the derivative control environments, especially the institutional environments, assume such a highly uniform character that almost all behavior seems to possess a collective aspect at the same time that it is individual. So true is this that the individual may stand out from the group scarcely at all. In more dynamic times and societies, individual behavior is less uniform in character, because of the rapid change in stimuli and of their unequal incidence at different places. But it may still be collective behavior because it is reciprocal or supplementary or both. But on the whole, due to the universalization of communication apparatus, modern society approaches in its wider behavior processes the highly uniform character which obtained in the primitive primary group, organized and perpetuated under the sway of custom and tradition and convention and relatively untouched by the dynamic force of science or revolutionizing experience. This wider uniformity of modern response is not due so much to the sway of custom and tradition as to the universality of modes and content of communication, that is, to convention in the large. It must not be supposed, however, that the uniformity of our complex civilization is as specific and simple as that of primitive groups. Although communication makes possible the wider spread of stimuli, the responses to these stimuli are more various within certain general limits.

COLLECTIVE BEHAVIOR AND DISSIMILARITY OF RESPONSES —A more highly complex type of collective behavior is that which is not composed of the uniform or similar responses of several individuals to the same or similar stimuli, but is in the nature of interlocking reciprocal responses of the members of a group to one another or of supplementary responses of different individuals to the same or concurrent stimuli. It is the reciprocal and supplementary character of such responses which integrates into a group or society the organisms which make these responses. Of course reciprocal responses must also be coöperative or supplementary rather than conflicting if the group or society is to remain integrated. A large portion of the collective behavior of modern societies is of this reciprocal and supplementary, but differential, character. The reason for this is that modern societies are too complex and too rapidly changing to permit of complete dominance by any one stimulus or for responses to be of uniform character in minor details, although there may be relative uniformity in the larger patterns of behavior. The greater the variety of different types of plants growing on any unit of area the larger the total number of plants that area will accommodate. Similarly, societies can become increasingly complex in their behavior only by differentiating the content of that behavior increasingly. But all of these differences in behavior must be integrated into a larger functional unity by having a common objective in adjustment, such as that of survival, or conquest, or production, or any other end. Coöperation in solving common problems does not necessarily imply uniformity of behavior in detail. But it must involve supplementation and integration in keeping with the larger values and pressures.

ALL BEHAVIOR IS OF COURSE INDIVIDUAL, for response must occur through the integrated organism. And practically all behavior, whether individual or collective, is social. Even individual behavior is nearly always response to stimuli from a social environment or is conditioned by such stimuli or by responses of other individuals or by collective behavior which serve as stimuli. It is possible to think of groups or societies as organisms, and the experimental biologist Child takes this viewpoint, already made familiar in a different connection by some of the leading sociologists of the nineteenth century. In such a case we might conceivably speak of collective behavior as an indivisible or irreducible form of response to environmental stimuli, and some might be inclined to regard this as the true social behavior. But closer examination shows us that after all the unity in the behavior reduces itself to similarity and supplementariness of the responses of the constituent or individual members of the groups. The group itself is both the product of this uniformity of response to similar or reciprocal and concatenated stimuli from the environments and is one of the environmental conditions which tend to uniformize and coördinate the stimuli which operate on individuals within the group. The group or society is therefore both effect and cause of response.

MATERIALS FOR SUPPLEMENTARY READING

Bernard, L. L., "A Classification of Environments," *A. J. S.*, XXXI: 318-32
———, *Instinct: A Study in Social Psychology,* Chs. V, VI
Case, C. M., *Outlines of Introductory Sociology,* Ch. VI
Dewey, J., *Democracy and Education,* Ch. II
Ellwood, C. A., *The Psychology of Human Society,* Chs. V, VI, XIV, XV
Goldenweiser, A. A., *Early Civilization,* 292-301
Keller, A. G., *Societal Evolution,* VII-X
Ross, E. A., *Principles of Sociology,* Ch. VII
Thomas, F., *The Environmental Basis of Society*
Wallas, G., *The Great Society,* Ch. IV
Wissler, C., *Man and Culture*
Williams, J. M., *Our Rural Heritage,* Ch. IV

CHAPTER VII

THE INHERITED AND ACQUIRED EQUIPMENT OF MAN

HEREDITY—*The Somatic Cells*—The inherited equipment of the organism is usually spoken of as its heredity in contradistinction to its acquired nature, which is regarded as the more immediate and direct result of environmental pressures. Biologists are now generally accustomed to think of the inheritance as determined in the chromosomes of the reproductive cells. Any trait or quality which is added to the organism from any other source or through any other channel may be regarded as acquired. This viewpoint represents the Mendelian theory of inheritance, which is dominant among the biological theories of heredity. This process of inheritance through the chromosome content of the reproductive cells may be illustrated by the diagram on the following page.

The diagram is, of course, merely symbolic, and represents the union of the two parental reproductive cells (M and F) to form the offspring cell (O). Each human, like any other, individual begins life as a single cell. This initial cell multiplies through fission into a vast number of cells. These derivative cells are of two general kinds, somatic and reproductive. The somatic cells differentiate into the various organs and tissues of the body, totaling approximately 26,500,000,000,000 in the human adult. The development of the individual somatic organism parallels very largely the development of the type in the race. Thus the digestive and circulatory tissues are followed by the growth of a skeletal system, muscles and glands, and a nervous apparatus. The nervous system, like the other parts of the body, is not matured until several years after the birth of the organism, and perhaps it is still immature at the point of natural death.

The reproductive cells are differentiated from the somatic cells during the first two or three days after the formation of the new cell body or offspring. These also multiply by fission. Unlike the somatic cells, which have their greatest period of

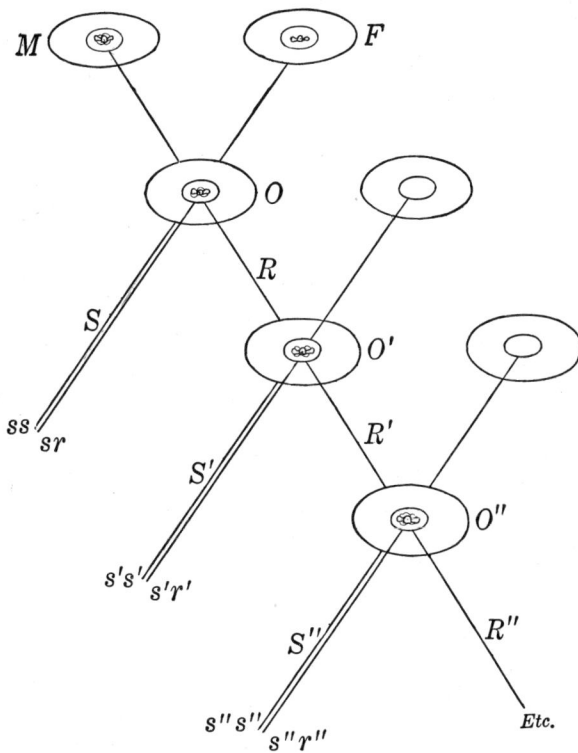

EXPLANATION OF THE DIAGRAM: M and F represent symbolically the male and female reproductive cells respectively combining to produce a new or offspring cell; they include both cytoplasm and nucleus with chromosome content, as indicated. O represents the offspring cells, O', O", etc., being successive generations. S, S', S" represent the somatic organisms which develop by fission and integration from the original offspring cell. R, R', R" represent the production of reproductive cells from the maturing offspring. These are used for the production of new offspring. The letters ss, s' s', s" s" represent the cytoplasmic determination of the somatic organization of new organisms, while sr, s'r', s"r" represent the chromosome determination of these same organisms. Note that lines of chromosome determination are indicated by direct extension to the nucleus, while lines of cytoplasmic determination are indicated by extension to the cytoplasm only. No attempt is made here to represent diagrammatically determination by external environmental factors.

normal multiplication during the first twenty years of life or less, with only minor divisions or multiplications thereafter, the male reproductive cells do not reach a very active stage of multiplication until the age of puberty is reached in the early or middle 'teens. They probably have their most prolific period of multiplication in the late 'teens and early twenties and gradually decline in activity thereafter, but in most cases in the male they do not cease to multiply until advanced old age. The number of male reproductive cells generated (approximately 340,000,000,000) vastly exceeds that of the female for obvious reasons. It is said that the new-born female contains from 36,000 to 200,000 ova, which number has been reduced to 30,000 or fewer at puberty, and of which not more than 400 become mature and capable of fertilization by the male reproductive cells. The relative rates of multiplication of the male reproductive cells at different age periods doubtless has much to do with the organization of the emotional and other behavior patterns of the male at different stages of his development.

DETERMINATION OF THE INHERITANCE—If the inheritance of the new organism is determined by the union of the chromosomes of the parent reproductive cells, there must be some point at which this inheritance determination is completed. Obviously this is the point of fertilization. Parts of the chromosomes and of the cytoplasm of the parent cells enter into the structure of the new offspring cell and determine its initial character. This in turn is modified within limits by environmental pressures. After the point of fertilization the offspring cell has no further contact with the parental reproductive cells. Consequently it is not able to receive further chromosome determination. The subsequent contacts which it has with the somatic organization of the mother during the nine months before birth and with the organisms, directly and indirectly, of both parents after birth are in the nature of environmental pressures rather than of inheritance determiners.

The inheritance of the organism is, therefore, completed at the point of fertilization, with the result that any traits developed subsequent to this point, unless predetermined in the heredity, are of environmental origin. This is a fact which it is very important to remember, because there is still much confusion about the nature and extent of the individual inheritance. The old, pre-Mendelian view of inheritance was that any traits which the child possessed at the period of birth had been received through the inheritance mechanism. It is not surprising that many persons, including not a few with biological training—usually acquired before the Mendelian theory became well known after 1900—still do their thinking about inheritance from this untenable viewpoint. They have not yet adjusted themselves to the newer facts of biological science. Much, therefore, which formerly has been called inheritance is in reality only the product of the pre-natal environment.

THE METHOD OF ENVIRONMENTAL DETERMINATION—Child, who has made recent contributions in biology of great significance to social psychology, rejects the preformistic conception of the organism which holds that heredity presents it fully formed and ready for action like a machine especially constructed to do its work. Such a viewpoint fails to take account of the facts either of physiology or of sociology, that is, of the relationship of the organism to either its internal or its external environments. "Actually the organism is not at any stage a closed system. . . . Reaction to environment is occurring at all stages of development, though of course the kinds and complexity of reaction differ at different stages according to the mechanisms present. Moreover, such behavior or reaction is itself a factor in development and therefore in the construction of the behavior mechanisms of later stages. The behavior of the various developmental stages as well as the specific hereditary constitution of the protoplasm is a factor in determining the behavior of the fully developed organism."[1] And this modification of behavior patterns by the behavior of the new organism in response to environment begins as soon as the new organism itself enters upon the life process. It is the failure to appreciate this fact which has prevented the biologists and psychologists of the predeterministic or preformistic type from appreciating adequately the importance of environment in determining human traits.

[1] This and other quotations in this chapter are taken from C. M. Child's *Physiological Foundations of Behavior*, Chs. I-IV.

The character of the behavior of the organism is determined by the character of the organism itself. The organism is a complex integration of functioning protoplasms of varying constitution and rates of metabolism. These protoplasms are fundamentally fixed in type by inheritance, although their physiology, and consequently their internal functioning, may be modified to some extent by internal chemical environment. Heredity in the protoplasms determines the general characteristics of the organism. "The organismic mechanisms arise on the basis of the hereditary substratum and . . . this determines that the organism shall be a certain species or variety of fern, elm, snail, fish, or ape. From this viewpoint the problem of behavior involves the whole problem of evolution as well as that of inheritance." The organism is a physico-chemical unity, and its primary physiological pattern is the action system which is the basis of its unity. This pattern, as before said, is constantly undergoing reformation as a result of reaction to the environment. "The organism may, in fact, be defined as a pattern of relation to environment appearing in protoplasm. . . . Organismic pattern then appears to be a behavior pattern in a protoplasm," while life itself, the greatest of the complexes of behavior, "is the behavior of protoplasmic systems in relation to an external world." The potentialities of the pattern, inherited and acquired, can be realized only through the action of external or environmental factors. Consequently, we may say that inheritance initiates the behavior process, but only in its simplest and most general terms; while environment gives formation and determination increasingly to the specific content of behavior, both in the individual and in the human race.

As the functional relationships between organisms and environments become more highly differentiated and the necessity for rapid changes in these relationships becomes greater in the higher types, less of behavior is determined by heredity and more by environment. The lower animals, especially the insects, which have a short life period and live throughout this period in relatively uniform environments, require but little flexibility in their behavior. They can make their adjustments to a relatively constant environment on the basis of instinctive mechanisms or inherited organizations of behavior patterns in neural protoplasms. But in the higher animals, especially in man, whose life period covers all the seasons, hence a wide range of temperatures, and whose great motility brings him in contact with numerous diverse environments in rapid succession, instinct or fixed inherited organizations of protoplasm are no longer adequate to guide behavior, and a vast range of habits or acquired integrations of protoplasmic patterns has been developed. Man has, in fact, created for himself inventions, he has domesticated plant and animal types, and he has objectified behavior meanings in the form of symbol complexes, all of which constitute new environments to direct and organize his behavior. The flexibility and incompleteness of the neural organization of the cerebral cortex make possible adjustment to these new environments on the basis of habit in the higher mammals and man.

MODIFICATION OF BEHAVIOR PATTERNS—This modification of behavior and the formation of acquired behavior patterns to replace and to elaborate the inherited or previously acquired patterns occur in two ways. In the first instance the internal organization of the protoplasms is itself modified as a result of functional contact with the environment. This is particularly true in the higher organisms, and preëminently so in the case of man, where so large a portion of the neurons are incompletely developed and unconnected synaptically until many months or even years after the initial development of the organism. This fact of cortical flexibility in the higher organisms makes it possible to reorganize patterns in the neural protoplasm with great ease and to an extent of complexity not appreciated before the rise of modern neurology and physiology. These changing neural patterns also produce modifications of overt behavior through their neuro-muscular and neuro-glandular or efferent responses. The net result of such modifiability is that the countless number of new things we learn—mental or psychic skills—and of the new things we learn to do—neuro-muscular skills—are added as acquired characteristics to the accomplishments (themselves partly acquired) characteristic of the lower animals. In our modern civilized world, and perhaps among all peoples, however low in the cultural scale they may be, the acquired characteristics, mental and neuro-muscular, far outnumber and outrank in importance for adjustment purposes those which are inherited or instinctive.

The second way in which this modification of behavior patterns occurs is more indirect. The reaction of the changing organism upon the environment constantly modifies the environment itself. This fact was earlier illustrated in pointing out how the social environments are created out of the natural physical and biological external environments and out of the internal physiological and neural processes through their modification. As Child aptly remarks, "Most organisms would cease to exist in a very short time if it were impossible for them to alter their environment by mechanical action upon it." The modified environment reacts back upon the behavior organization and integration of the organism and produces further changes in it. The result is that the organism changes coordinately and more or less in conformity with the changes in the environment. This interaction between the organism and its behavior and the environment goes on indefinitely, augmented by independent changes in the individual (such as mutations, metabolism, etc.) and the environment (such as population growth, changes in climate and soil resources, which are not wholly independent of organismic influences). The resulting changes in environment and in the behavior of individual organisms are practically unlimited in extent and complexity.

WHERE THE CHANGES OCCUR—The final result in man is that behavior is completely transformed, although the general and original protoplasmic structures largely keep their form. The structure of the non-neural protoplasms remains much the same throughout life, except for a progressive physico-chemical integration which excludes to a large degree variational adjustment and therefore leads ultimately to fixity and death of the organism. Even the organization of the nervous protoplasms tends in this general direction, but only after the higher centers have undergone countless changes in organization and reorganization of behavior patterns. At first there is a lack of organization of behavior patterns in the neural protoplasm of the higher levels. Under the influence of changing environmental pressures this organization is effected in great complexity and in a multiplicity of forms. The higher life is developed as habits and these are modified endlessly and quite freely to suit the demands of a constantly changing environment, until the old age of the non-neural tissues, and even to some extent of the neural tissues themselves, narrows the limits and effectiveness of these variations in behavior.

We have spoken in this section primarily of the modification of behavior patterns rather than of the modification of organs and tissues of non-neural protoplasms, for the social psychologist is interested in behavior. Non-neural protoplasms are not so easily modified by environmental pressures as are the neural protoplasms, because the former react in a primarily mechanical and direct manner to environmental pressures, while the latter respond primarily in an indirect and excitatory manner to environmental stimuli. In this second type of reaction, the excitatory, "the energy transfer between the external world and protoplasm serves merely as the initiating factor in bringing about energy changes which themselves depend upon the configuration of the system acted upon." The stimulus or initiating factor merely liberates energy from the system. It is in this excitation-response system of neural protoplasm that we find the greatest flexibility of behavior patterns. It is here that conscious memory and intelligence function as the highest forms of organismic control. Of course the higher and cortical centers of neural organizations illustrate the principles of the excitation-response system better than the lower centers, for it is in the former that we find the greatest degree of complexity and flexibility of response.

THE ACQUIRED TRAITS—It is not easy to distinguish acquired and inherited characteristics. The general formulas that the inherited traits are determined by the union of the chromosomes of the parental reproductive cells to form the new offspring cell, and that the acquired traits are determined by environmental pressures, do not reveal to us the actual mechanisms by which the two types of traits appear in the processes of growth. The process of fertilization and the genesis of the inheritance traits in the new individual have been frequently described by the geneticists and the reader is referred to that source for such information, if he does not already possess it. But the building up of the acquired traits, especially in the prenatal stage of development, has not been so well described. The recent work of Child (1924) already quoted and of Herrick (1924) also referred to, and of their collaborators, has done most to open up this process of the growth of the organism in its initial stages under environmental pressures. Also the recent investigations of the embryologists have given us many data on the determination of specific traits in the prenatal stage.

STAGES OF DEVELOPMENT—*Postnatal*—The best results from the standpoint of an estimate of the contribution of environmental pressures to individual traits may be obtained if we divide the developmental process into three stages. These stages may be outlined as follows:

[1. Preconceptual stage]
2. Prenatal stage
3. Postnatal stage

The first is bracketed, because it is not an actual stage of individual development but is preliminary to the other two stages, which are actual. Some writers add a natal stage to take account of those events which occur during the birth process. Practically all types of traits, except those which come to the child directly from the mother through the blood stream, may be acquired in the postnatal stage of development. Some of these even may be acquired during the nursing period through her milk. Thus the various germ diseases, the organic and functional diseases, the neuroses and psychoses, the results of nutrition in its various normal and abnormal aspects, modifications of the organism due to direct impact with the environment, such as wounds, distortions, and malformations, the effects of temperature and of chemical substances, and the various skills, physiological and psychical, which come to us as the result of the pressures of our psycho-social, bio-social and physico-social environments, are acquired by us in this postnatal stage of development. The traits are too numerous to specify individually and we must content ourselves at this point with a mere enumeration of their general classes or types.

HUMAN EQUIPMENT

In the prenatal stage of development the number of characteristics which may be acquired is much more limited because the volume and kinds of the environment which operate in this stage are much less outstanding. The classes of traits which may be acquired in this stage may be outlined as follows:

1. Traumatisms and malformations or deformities due to injury to the offspring in utero. This category also includes injuries due to abortions resulting from physical violence.

2. Infections. The most important of these is syphilis, from which it is said approximately fifty percent of the stillbirths result. Other infections, such as typhoid and typhus fever, tuberculosis and various other skin and blood diseases, affect the child either through the mother's blood stream or at parturition.

3. Toxic conditions due to such chemical poisons as lead, phosphorus and alcohol and the poisonous ethers reaching the child through the mother. Such poisons often are induced as the result of the occupation of the mother. These may cause aborted or generally and specifically defective offspring.

4. Toxic conditions arising within the metabolism of the mother from such causes as infections, undernutrition or malnutrition, excessive fatigue or strain, and affecting the child through some modification of its metabolism, causing it to be born weak or defective or even dead, or to be aborted.

5. The hormones developed in the ductless glands of the mother often affect the tissues of the unborn child through the blood stream from the mother. Normal endocrines probably predispose the child towards normal development, while abnormal endocrines produce defective development and capacities in the child. For example, an endocrine disease in the mother, such as goiter, may appear in the child at birth through this means of transmission. Possibly also the vitamins from foods consumed by the mother may in some way affect the development of the child.

It is very probable that much disease formerly regarded as inherited and many of the physiological and anatomical conditions which predispose to feeble-mindedness and other forms of mental and emotional defect in childhood originate by acquisition through the prenatal environmental channels here indicated. If this is true it will necessitate a change of viewpoint among the educational sociologists and psychopathologists regarding the origin and social treatment of mental defectiveness.

PRECONCEPTUAL INFLUENCES—Obviously the offspring organism cannot acquire traits in the preconceptual stage of development, because the organism does not yet exist. But anything which can happen to the cytoplasm of the parental reproductive cells may produce an effect upon the new organism at or after the point of fertilization. Anything occurring to the chromosomes in the nucleus of the parent cells would probably affect the heredity or prevent fertilization altogether through destruction of the chromosome content. But the cytoplasm of the parent reproductive cells is environment for the new offspring cells because parts of the cytoplasm of the parent cells enter into the somatic organization of the offspring organism. The cytoplasm of reproductive cells has been known to be infected or to develop toxic conditions or to undergo tissue modification under the influence of the environing somatic structure or body of the parents who carried the reproductive cells. In this way environmental pressures even from a preconceptual environment are able to reach the offspring. Apparently such environmental influences are comparatively limited and the effects upon the offspring are primarily of the nature of lesions, infections and toxic conditions due to specific germs or to poisons. Also, anything of appropriate character which can be carried to the point of fertilization along with or in the environment of the reproductive cell has a chance of influencing the development of the offspring body in the same manner.

CULTURE THE PRODUCT OF THE POSTNATAL STAGE—It will be clear from the preceding analysis of the types of acquired traits receivable from environmental pressures in the various stages of development that from neither the prenatal nor the preconceptual sources do we acquire those specific mental traits and intellectual skills which collectively we call culture. No ideas or other complex mental, moral, and social traits are acquired in these stages of development. Such characteristics are the product of the postnatal environments. They are initiated primarily by the pressures of the psycho-social environment. The other social environments also play some part more or less directly in this connection, and the natural environments condition man in such ways that they influence the acquisition of culture indirectly. Especially is this true where the climate, the supply of fauna and flora, and of natural resources influence the degree and kinds of culture through the effects they have upon human behavior and the accumulation of a surplus of wealth over the bare necessities of existence which enables the culture development to be financed or promoted.

The reason why the specific mental, moral, and social traits cannot be acquired under preconceptual and prenatal conditions is that such acquisitions must come through the use of the higher exteroceptive senses, which, as was pointed out in a previous chapter, are the foundations of all intellectual development. These senses are not operative in preconceptual and prenatal stages. Certain physiological and neurological conditions, however, can be brought about through the operation of the prenatal and preconceptual environmental pressures outlined above which will predispose indirectly toward or against the acquisition of various intellectual skills and moral and social attitudes and values.

ENVIRONMENTAL VERSUS HEREDITARY TRANSMISSION OF TRAITS—There is considerable controversy regarding the relative importance of heredity and environment in the determination of behavior patterns of individual organisms. The extremists on both sides appear to be loath to grant any considerable weight to the contentions of the opposing view. It is not the purpose of this volume to enter into this controversy, but to state the facts on both sides when they are pertinent to the discussion of the mechanisms of behavior as they function in organisms and are determined or modified by environments. It is axiomatic that both heredity and environment play their parts in determining behavior. The one serves as the initial basis, while the other determines for the most part the differential development of behavior.

Heredity is racial. That is, it generally occurs in successive generations of individual organisms in direct line of biological descent. So likewise do acquired characteristics occur. The essential distinction, therefore, between the inherited and the acquired traits is not in the occurrence of the characteristics in successive generations but in the method of their transmission. As we have already seen, the transmission of inherited traits is commonly accounted for as by means of the chromosomes. Transmission of acquired traits, however, occurs through some more external process, such as through the cytoplasm of the reproductive cells, through the environing mother during the prenatal development of the child, or through the organisms and behavior of parents, playfellows, teachers, or any other persons or "carriers" of infections, toxins, ideas, behavior symbols, or what not, with which one comes in physiological or sensory contact in his postnatal development. The psycho-social environment is perhaps the most potent and voluminous carrier through which acquired characteristics are transmitted in our modern world. Traits carried by this environment are of course not physical or biological directly, but are mental, moral, and social characteristics or attitudes which are capable of being transmitted by the intangible symbolic structures of the psycho-social environment. The composite or derivative control environments, which organize the psycho-social and other social as well as the underived environments around some process of social organization and construction, and which appear to us ordinarily as institutions, can of course carry all classes and kinds of characteristics, not merely the mental, moral, and social.

THEORY OF THE INHERITANCE OF ACQUIRED CHARACTERISTICS—The importance of environment as a source of structure and of behavior has been observed even in the midst of those periods when the theory of inheritance had most vogue. This fact gave rise to attempts to assimilate the two viewpoints. The most important of these attempts is to be found in the theory of the inheritance of acquired characters, which was approved by Lamarck and Darwin and their followers and was later questioned by the school of Weismann. In its history it has invented many ingenious theories of the method of the transmission of acquired characters, including Darwin's doctrine of pangenesis and Semon's theory of the Mneme.

It still has its adherents, some of the most noted of whom are Dr. Paul Kammerer of Vienna and Professor Guyer of the University of Wisconsin.

The evidence however seems scarcely convincing. Dr. Kammerer finds his best illustrations among very low and simple organisms where it is doubtful if inheritance through gametes is established and where apparently the transmission which he calls hereditary takes place through external tissues and therefore comes under the category of environmental. The same criticism in general may be made of other work in support of the inheritance of acquired characteristics. Transmission of acquired traits seems to be carried from one generation to another through the blood or the endocrines or some other tissue rather than through the chromosomes, hence is not inheritance in the Mendelian sense. If it does take place through the chromosomes it is probably in those cases where the physico-chemical content of the matured tissue or characteristic is identical in kind with the substance which enters into the chromosome segments.

Certainly there is no evidence that mental, moral, and social traits can be carried through the chromosomes and thus become a part of true inheritance. True inheritance is always of structures or of organization of structures. It is inheritance of biological materials; there can be no inheritance of ideas or of moral and social attitudes and values which have no constant relation to structure, but vary freely according to time and place and value to the organism concerned. As far as the psychologist and the social psychologist are concerned the theory of the inheritance of acquired characteristics appears to have little or nothing to offer as an explanation of the appearance and modification of behavior patterns. These sciences, as well as sociology, must look rather to Child's theory of the integration of the organism through the functioning of its behavior patterns in relation to environmental pressures and to other similar theories of environmental determination.

The Source of Inherited Traits—There has also been considerable discussion as to the source of inherited traits in the first instance, if they were not induced in the heredity through use. What causes variations and mutations in the inheritance? It is fairly easy to account for variations in structure and behavior which are obviously the product of environment and persist only a single generation or are carried from one generation to the next by means of the same external mechanisms by which they can be transferred from one individual to another in the same generation. The transmission here is environmental. But unquestionably changes or variations also occur in the chromosomes which persist through successive generations, and appear in the somatic organization as inherited traits. These often appear in the type suddenly as mutations. From what source do they come? There are various theories as to their origin which cannot be elaborated here, such as that they are the result of conditions of temperature, of nutrition, of forced development, of the penetration of hormones and even of toxins and of formative substances into the nucleus where the chromosomes are segregated as far as possible from somatic interference. All of these theories, it will be seen, trace the variation or mutation in heredity back to an environmental source or cause. It should also be noted that in no case, unless in that of the last hypothesis mentioned, would the inherited trait produced by a change in the chromosomes be the same as the environing factor or condition (which may or may not be an acquired somatic characteristic) which produced the modification of the chromosomes. These theories of the origin of true inheritance traits, even if correct, can not offer much in support of the doctrine of the inheritance of acquired characteristics.

ENVIRONMENTAL SELECTION OF TRAITS—The most commonly accepted theory of environmental determination of inherited traits is that of natural and artificial selection. This theory holds that many biological characteristics appear "spontaneously" in the chromosomes—although the true explanation of the apparent spontaneity may be that suggested in the preceding paragraph—and that those traits which aid the organism in making effective adjustments to its environment are the ones which survive and reproduce themselves, because the carrier organism survives and reproduces. This is essentially the old doctrine of the survival of the fittest, which was formulated by Darwin to explain why certain types survived the struggle for existence in nature.

To this process of natural selection we have added artificial selection, which consciously or unconsciously throws the weight of advantage, through social aid, upon the side of the socially favored. This artificial selection may result in great improvements of types, and also in degeneration, according as the selection is wisely or unwisely directed from a social standpoint. Artificial selection, especially in the form of eugenic control, is one of the great social problems of our age.

Such selection of traits for inheritance is obviously the product primarily of environmental pressures and when artificial it is the result mainly of the pressure of the psycho-social environment. The characteristics selected in the inheritance are, of course, biological. They occur apparently for the most part in the non-neural protoplasms and affect the organization of the higher or cortical neurons indirectly rather than directly.

The behavior patterns which concern the social psychologist most intimately are rarely produced as the result of natural or artificial selection of inheritance, although the acquired behavior patterns organized under the direct or indirect pressures of the environments may be significantly conditioned by selected inheritance traits or structures. The social psychologist is interested not so much in structural traits as in the neuro-psychic and neuro-muscular mechanisms resulting and the social significance of behavior which proceeds from the structural conditions.

MATERIALS FOR SUPPLEMENTARY READING

Baldwin, J. M., *Social and Ethical Interpretations*, Ch. II
Bernard, L. L., "The Significance of Environment as a Social Factor," *Pub. Amer. Sociological Soc.*, XVI: 84-112
———, *Instinct: A Study in Social Psychology*, Chs. XI, XII
Boas, F., "Growth and Development, Bodily and Mental, as Determined by Heredity and by Social Environment," in *The Child, the Clinic and the Court*, pp. 178-88
Bogardus, E. S., *Fundamentals of Social Psychology*, Ch. I
Burnham, W., *The Normal Mind*, Ch. XVIII

Child, C. M., "The Individual and Environment from a Physiological Viewpoint," in *The Child, the Clinic and the Court*, pp. 126-55
———, *Physiological Foundations of Environment*
Conklin, E. G., *Heredity and Environment*
Davies, G. R., *Social Environment*, Ch. IV
Dunlap, K., *Social Psychology*, Ch. VI
Feldman, W. M., *The Principles of Anti-natal and Post-natal Child Physiology, Pure and Applied*
Gault, R. H., *Social Psychology*, Ch. IV
Ward, L. F., *Applied Sociology*, pp. 95-110 and Part II

CHAPTER VIII

BEHAVIOR PATTERNS: THEIR NATURE AND DEVELOPMENT

BEHAVIOR THE CONCERN OF SOCIAL PSYCHOLOGY—Social psychology is interested directly and primarily in human behavior in a social situation. It may concern itself with the inner mechanisms of responses to social stimuli, or it may focus its attention upon collective response to similar or identical or to mutual or supplementary stimuli. In the one case it leans towards psychology and in the other it rests upon sociology. Both interests are legitimate to the field of social psychology and in both cases its theme is human behavior.

THE UNITS OF BEHAVIOR—In either case it is concerned with the individual or neural patterns of response, and in the latter case it must consider the collective patterns of response. In this chapter we shall review the fundamental and general individual or neural (primarily neuro-muscular) patterns of response. In later chapters we will consider the more specific and derivative (primarily neuro-psychic) individual patterns of adjustment.

The units of behavior discussed in this chapter are random movements, reflexes, instincts, and tropisms. It has been the custom of some social psychologists to consider all more complex forms of behavior as constructed rather mechanically from preëxisting instinct patterns by a process of assembling. This atomic conception has been almost as strongly marked with reference to behavior as it has been in regard to matter. As a matter of fact the complex patterns of acquired behavior are integrated originally and in the main from much simpler and in part from less definite units of behavior than the instincts, namely, reflexes and random movements and impulses.

TROPISMS—There are two views regarding the nature of tropisms.[1] Jennings and others consider the tropism to be "any

[1] See C. J. Herrick, *Neurological Foundations of Animal Behavior*.

reaction in which orientation of the body or of direction of movement with respect to the external factor occurs, whether by trial and error or otherwise." This definition, however, does not distinguish the tropism essentially from habit, or for that matter from any other type of behavior. It is decidedly too broad and to accept it would be essentially to make tropic behavior synonymous with all behavior whatever. Loeb's view of the tropism, that it is a forced movement or orientation of the organism dependent upon its general symmetry or the symmetry of the orientation mechanism, appears to be the better one. Tropisms are also generally regarded as determined by inherited structure and mechanisms. According to the symmetry view of Loeb, animals walk forward in approximately a straight line or the moths fly into the flame because of their bilateral symmetry and the bifocal nature of their vision. Asymmetrical animals also have tropic responses in some variation of the normal curve of behavior from that of the symmetrical ones, according to the kind and degree of variation from symmetry which they possess. The more or less spiral movement of the paramecium serves as an illustration of this variation.

Loeb has isolated a considerable number of types of tropic response. He speaks of heliotropism, or forced orientation due to light; galvanotropism, relating to the influence of an electric current; geotropism, which he thinks has some of its best illustrations in the growth behavior of plants; stereotropism; chemotropism; and thermotropism. Animals may of course be negatively as well as positively tropic and certain organic or physico-chemical changes within the organism may so modify the capacity of the organism to respond to stimuli that the negative form may be changed into the positive form of tropism, or vice versa.

Tropisms, according to Loeb, may occur in both plants and animals. Likewise they are to be found in animals without nervous systems as well as in those possessing differentiated nervous systems. In the former case the tropism must function on the basis of excitation gradients developed in the non-neural protoplasm or on the basis of temporary axes established in the undifferentiated nervous processes. Where reflex arcs and patterns have been established in a nervous system these necessarily serve in the process of forced orientation. Responses will of necessity occur on the basis of existing behavior patterns where stimuli can be effective through them. Doubtless most tropisms do occur on the basis of reflexes, and possibly of instincts, which serve as mechanisms of response.

TROPISMS AND HUMAN BEHAVIOR—Whether we conceive of tropisms as playing any considerable part in the behavior of the highest animals and man does not depend on whether we limit them to inherited behavior patterns, as is sometimes supposed. If we conceive of tropisms as including all forced or rigidly determined behavior arising out of the symmetry of the organism, and based on acquired as well as on inherited patterns and structure, tropistic response among human beings would normally cover as wide a range of behavior as among other animals. Man performs acquired as well as instinctive activities according to the general limitations of his structure quite the same as other animals. He moves straight forward towards an object, faces it, hears with both ears, sees with both eyes, and orients himself accordingly. The only difference is that he may learn fairly easily to vary such symmetrical responses when he finds it to his advantage to do so.

It is impossible to characterize tropisms strictly on the basis of the inheritance or non-inheritance of their constituent behavior mechanisms. The tropism is not a stimulus-response process in the same sense that reflexes and instincts are. It makes use of stimulus-response mechanisms, but the essential fact about it is that it is response *in a certain direction,* on the basis of whatever neural or other mechanisms are essential to it, determined by the symmetry or specific degrees of asymmetry of the organism and its sensory equipment. In the degree, therefore, to which this structural symmetry is hereditary the tropism will itself be determined by inheritance. But the behavior mechanisms which set the tropism into action may be either inherited or acquired. They are not a part of the tropism proper, but a means to its operation. The essential thing about the tropism is the forced orientation, not the content of the neural mechanism operating within it.

On this basis it seems justifiable to regard tropistic behavior as being equally as characteristic of man as of other animals. But the opportunity, and perhaps the necessity, for modifying tropistic responses by acquired behavior is doubtless much greater in the case of man, who is primarily a habit-forming animal. A child crawling toward the light or a man taking the shortest path between two points or approaching a fire in cold weather will serve to illustrate the persistence of tropistic response in the human type. On the other hand, man has doubtless lost the capacity to respond tropically to various chemical stimuli. And it is certain that in the present complex world he inhibits many tendencies to spontaneous and direct response to stimuli which in a less sophisticated world would not be inhibited. The tropism is merely the general form of the movement of the organism as a whole as determined by the animal's structure. The random movement, reflex, instinct, and habit are the specific mechanisms by which the animal responds tropically.

RANDOM MOVEMENTS AND IMPULSES may be regarded as raw materials for larger integrated behavior patterns. They are termed random because as movements and impulses they do not appear to be directed to any particular adjustment end. They seem to arise out of the excess general energy of the organism and its specific drives and to be determined structurally more or less by its metabolism on the one hand and by the general conformation of the various protoplasmic systems or organs and tissue structures on the other. For example, the structure of the somatic organization as a whole, the bones, joints, and the placement of muscles, as well as the existence of predetermined neural connections, set the limits of such random movements as kicking, turning the head, wriggling the toes, moving the arms and fingers, and even such vocal acts as crying, sighing, shrieking, and early monosyllabic expressions. These types of behavior are not entirely random, for they are clearly delimited by such structural characteristics of the organism as those mentioned. And yet they are in no sense truly adaptive, because they occur as an expression of the inner forces of metabolism rather than as an effort or predisposition to do some particular thing. Random behavior is, of course, a characteristic of early childhood and does not normally appear to any considerable extent in older children or in adults. If it does occur in the latter it is a sign of temporary nervousness or of chronic neural disorganization and is distinctly pathological. Normally random behavior of all kinds, except possibly in part that of the higher cortical processes, should become integrated and transformed into definite and economical patterns as the individual reaches the age when one ordinarily makes an effective adjustment to his environments.

While random behavior is not purposive and is not functional or adaptive in any specific sense, it is not without a general function. It is the raw material out of which habits are to a large extent built. The specific methods by which random behavior is organized into adaptive and purposive habits or acquired behavior will be presented in the discussion of the processes and methods of imitation. But it is possible at the present time to indicate the general method by which the integration of random behavior into definite or purposive behavior occurs. The child in moving his head or hands or in kicking in a random way brings parts of his body into contact with objects and establishes useful stimulus-response processes which thereupon are repeated, at first with little or no awareness of their significance, but later frequently in a highly purposive way. In this manner the child learns to reach out for objects which have given it satisfaction and to appropriate them, or it acquires the definite coördinations of crawling and walking. In a similar way, it develops the random cry or shriek and other random articulations into a more or less rich language content, because it observes that certain types of cries and sounds bring desirable results. The early life of the child is a period of strenuous practice in evolving all sorts of definitely coördinated movements and vocal expressions out of the raw material of random behavior as a means to a favorable adjustment to its environment. The child comes into the world relatively helpless and would be unable to survive without the aid of others, but it is equipped with a random behavior capital which it gradually develops through practice until under normal conditions it becomes a well integrated and relatively self-sufficing individual, but always of course in a social world.

REFLEXES—Another behavior unit of a simple character is the reflex which occurs in animals with nervous systems. The reflex arc is a highly specialized mechanism of the stimulus-response type. That is, a definite stimulus such as a pin prick or the dryness of the eyeball produces a definite and predictable response, in these instances in the form of withdrawal or of winking. It is a purely unconscious behavior process and is in no sense purposive, although it is highly adaptive and regulatory in character. We speak of simple reflex arcs, but as a matter of fact such do not ordinarily function in isolation. Nearly always they integrate with other reflexes or with other behavior patterns in the organism.

The origin of reflexes in the organism has been most clearly described by Child.[1] The reflex arc and integrations of reflex behavior in an organism are products of the trend of development of that organism. "They are consequences and expressions of all that has gone before. The receptor and effector connections of each reflex arc, the interrelations of different arcs, whatever their adaptive evolutionary significance, must all have a physiological basis in the developmental processes and are evidently outgrowths of the general organismic pattern. In fact, the physiological continuity in the individual between the physiological or metabolic gradient and the reflex arc is evident. The physiological gradient is the general physiological foundation on which the reflex arc develops. If we consider development in its functional, rather than in its structural aspects, it appears that the gradient is the primitive and generalized excitation arc out of which the various reflex arcs develop by specialization of function and differentiation of structure. In short, the physiology of development of the reflex arc has its starting point in the excitability of protoplasm, the differential action of environmental factors upon it and the resulting physiological gradient or gradients. . . . From the physiological viewpoint, then, the reflex arcs and the reflex behavior of any particular organism, like other character-

[1] See his *Physiological Foundations of Behavior*.

istics of the individual, are determined by this primary behavior and from the viewpoint of heredity, by the hereditary constitution of the protoplasm. Here, as elsewhere, heredity determines the possibilities in each case and behavior in the broad sense determines the realization of possibilities in each individual."

THE FUNCTION OF THE REFLEX would therefore appear to be to give some sort of stability to the behavior of the organism in a standardized environmental situation. This is the function also of the axial gradient which arises within the protoplasmic systems of the organism and which precedes the organization of the more definite and fixed reflex arcs and their combinations. Organisms must be able to respond repeatedly in the same way to the same or similar environments, or they will suffer disintegration and destruction. Continuity of life is, at least in the lower and simpler forms, dependent upon continuity of behavior patterns. Consequently permanent gradients and reflex arcs and behavior systems arise to insure this integrity and continuity of the organism and of its type.

But variability in behavior is also necessary to survival, particularly in the higher and more complex organisms which are compelled to make rapid and frequent changes in their adjustments to changing and complex environments. This flexibility is sometimes secured, at least in the less specialized lower organisms, by modifying the protoplasmic gradient, but in complex types it can also be secured by building up new integrations of acquired reflex arcs and systems. In this way the reflexes are merged into acquired or habit behavior mechanisms often of a more complex constitution. Where, as in the case of man, the requisite modifiability of behavior mechanisms cannot be obtained on the basis of acquired combinations of reflex arcs, a greater degree of flexibility of neural organization appears in the cerebral cortex in the form of unconnected and modifiable synapses out of which new and highly diverse and variable control patterns or habits are integrated to supplement the modified and reintegrated reflex patterns on a lower level. Such possibilities of modification of behavior are especially necessary in the highly complex and changing social environments of man. The human animal could not possibly respond to all of the necessary stimuli arising out of his social environments on a purely reflex basis or on the basis of recombinations of his reflexes. His reflexes are valuable to him mainly in that they give him economical and unconscious mechanisms for taking care of the routine and simpler affairs of adjustment, chiefly the physiological ones, while he handles the more complex and pressing adjustment problems through the organization of acquired patterns in the cortical neurons. Even these cortical patterns may be reduced to routine uniformity and relegated to the unconscious. There they mediate adjustments in much the same manner as the original reflexes, when they can be sufficiently standardized and stereotyped, that is, where the adjustment to the environment which they mediate can remain sufficiently constant to make this fixity of type and unconscious functioning possible.

THE RELATION OF REFLEXES TO RANDOM MOVEMENTS—A question may be raised as to the relationship between random behavior and reflexes. It is not always easy to distinguish the two categories, but in general we may say that random behavior is less specific and less adaptive than reflexes, which are both highly specific and adaptive. However, random behavior often includes or makes use of reflexes, and in some cases perhaps it approaches pretty closely to the reflex in character. No random movement is entirely random or uncontrolled. Nor, perhaps, is any reflex absolutely invariable. Both random movements and reflexes serve as raw materials for the building of habit mechanisms, but the acquired behavior built out of reflexes is necessarily more limited in scope and more predetermined than that arising out of the raw materials of the random movements, because the latter are themselves less fixed and more freely modified in the habit building process.

INSTINCTS differ from reflexes primarily in their greater degree of complexity. Like reflexes they are definite and apparently inherited stimulus-response or neural behavior mechanisms, by means of which a specific stimulus produces a specific and definite response. They also normally operate without the exercise of consciousness. If consciousness appears in the behavior processes it is because the original or inherited behavior pattern has been modified or is being interfered with in the adjustment situation. The fact that we find a consciousness of the end or of the process involved in the operation of most so-called instinct mechanisms is not to be regarded as proof that instincts, unlike reflexes, have a conscious element in their constitution, but that in our human and complex social world adjustment to a rapidly changing environmental complex is not possible on the rigid basis of unmodified instinct. Very few instincts remain intact in the human adult. The modifying pressures of environment are too insistent. The simpler reflexes may keep their original form, but even they are constantly reorganized into new acquired combination patterns or habits, as was pointed out above. The instinct is itself just such a combination or organization of reflexes. But this organization has been determined by biological selection and is therefore fixed in the inheritance instead of being determined directly by environment, and therefore acquired.

Such inherited organizations of reflexes into instincts are in the form either of complexes and sets or of chains. An instinct composed of a chain of reflexes may be illustrated by the swallowing instinct, where the completion of one reflex sets in operation another, until the total act of swallowing is completed. An instinct composed of a complex or constellation of reflexes may be illustrated by digestion, where the presence of food in the viscera sets up a number of reflexes more or less simultaneously rather than in series. Instincts composed of chains of reflexes and of constellations of reflexes differ essentially only in the relative degree of consecutiveness with which the reflexes come into operation.

INSTINCTS ARE NOT PURPOSIVE, but like reflexes they are adaptive. They serve a definite function in the adjustment process. Like the reflexes they constitute a method of standardizing and economizing the behavior of organisms in adjusting to fairly permanent and constant environmental conditions. In this way they aid in preserving the integrity of the organism under stable environmental conditions, and prevent its destruction by random responses to stimuli. They also render adjustments more economical of energy and of time. But even less able are the instincts to withstand the rapidity and irregularity of change which modern complex and highly differentiated social environments bring to bear upon the human organism as the result of its intellectual development and the consequent accumulation of culture which it has created and symbolized and objectified. Since instincts are larger and more complex units of fixed behavior the necessity for breaking them up into constituent units is all the greater under these conditions. As a result not many complex animal instincts survive in the human type. Those that remain relatively intact control the comparatively fixed physiological functions connected with eating, breathing, digestion, circulation, excretion, reproduction, and other vegetative processes. Even these functions are subjected to increasing degrees of acquired control under modern environmental conditions. We modify our tastes and our foods, we injure our digestions and "doctor" them up again, we acquire diseases of the circulatory system, our food and lack of exercise induce constipation and other kindred disorders, and so on indefinitely. In the sphere of the somatic adjustments of the organism as a whole to its environments, the original processes have been even more extensively modified, with the result that few instincts appear as units in our somatic behavior. Habits and acquired behavior of the sort described under the discussion of reflexes have taken their place.

AN ERRONEOUS VIEW OF INSTINCT—Some writers persist in speaking of these modified behavior processes as instinctive or inherited. Such usage, as is shown elsewhere, is of course untenable. Instincts must be defined in terms of their structure, since it is the biological structure only which is inherited. We cannot inherit ideas, values, or the ends of adjustment behavior processes, because these are conceptual and not structural facts. Yet those who speak of the modified behavior patterns as instinctive frequently do so because they define the instinct in terms of its function rather than of its structure. This is a metaphysical rather than a scientific usage and has no basis in fact. To speak of instincts as teleological or purposive is unwarranted. If the instinct is not a conscious behavior pattern, neither can it involve within its own organization any foresight of ends. Nor can it control its own organization and functioning in the interest of these ends. If the teleological concept of instinct also involves a moral or a prudential judgment regarding the worth or value of the behavior, by the same token it is impossible to attribute this moral or prudential quality to the instincts. Such judgments are based on acquired knowledge regarding consequences and relationships and thus grow out of the experience of the individual or the collective experience of mankind which is transmitted culturally to the individual. Such complex forms of consciousness, arising out of relatively modern situations which have not had an opportunity to select attitudes and responses into the individual organism, cannot be a part of man's instinctive equipment. The metaphysical and unscientific character of the teleological view of instinct becomes easily apparent once we analyze it.

DISINTEGRATION AND ADAPTATION OF INSTINCTS IN MAN—Some of the instincts themselves have apparently disintegrated in man under the pressures of the new environments and man's heredity has correspondingly changed. Or, perhaps we should say, following the general line of argument of Child, that certain of the behavior patterns which seem to be congenital and have therefore commonly been called instincts have failed to develop in the human protoplasms in the course of the growth of the organism because the environments no longer call them into existence. Whether we speak from the standpoint of the disintegration of instinctive behavior patterns in the inheritance or from that of the failure of specific behavior patterns to develop in the protoplasm under the influence of environmental pressures, it is quite clear that the human infant is helpless in a world where the young of the lower types of organisms are able to survive of their own initiative. The "instincts" which would enable it to go in search of food and to appropriate it and to escape from danger are lacking. The explanation of this fact is that the human infant is born into and is adjusted to a human and social environment, while the offspring of the lower animals are born into and adjust themselves to the natural environments. The human mother and the various social agencies and institutions through their ministrations to the child take the place of the "instincts" which it lacks or has failed to develop because its environment did not offer it the proper stimulus. If we take the view that the heredity of the child has been changed, we have here a clear case of the disintegration or breaking down of instinctive behavior patterns into their constituent reflexes under the pressures of a changed environment. This environment no longer calls for such behavior patterns, but builds its own patterns out of the constituent elements of the now vestigial instincts as a means of securing a more efficient and economical adjustment of the organism to its environment.

We find a similar marked change in the method of adaptation to environment in connection with what we call the delayed instincts, such as those of sex. These behavior patterns are not matured until the human offspring approaches maturity in the remainder of his structures and behavior mechanisms. In the meantime his social environments, especially the psychosocial, have built up in him those habitual and acquired attitudes regarding sex which are conventional in his social milieu. The result is that the maturing of the sex instincts comes after his behavior patterns in this field are already relatively fixed, with the consequence that the sex activity of the lower animal type is largely inhibited or diverted into substitute channels as sublimations or perversions. In this case environment has been beforehand with nature and has already built up its own system of behavior which the tardily maturing instincts ordinarily are not able to overturn or set aside.

ACQUIRED BEHAVIOR PATTERNS—The conclusion which apparently we are compelled to draw from these facts is that the significance of instinctive behavior for man has been vastly overestimated. Instincts, like reflexes, undoubtedly have served a useful function in the adjustment processes of lower animal types, especially in the case of the simpler responses under relatively constant environmental conditions. But as environment became more complex and fluid or flexible for higher types of animals, and as the complexity of both organism and environment grew up and changed together, instincts no longer served adequately the higher functions of adjustment. They hindered rather than aided the coördinated and concomitant changes in environment and organism. It became necessary to discard them, or to reduce them to their constituent reflexes or to inhibit their development and functioning, as was the case with the delayed instincts. The reflexes could, in large measure, still remain, because their greater simplicity made it possible for them to be organized into new and acquired composite patterns by environmental pressures or selection. Thus habits have largely supplanted the instincts and the independent or isolated reflexes as human behavior patterns. Modern culture and civilization are built primarily, if not wholly, out of acquired behavior patterns. Civilization itself has sometimes rightly been termed a complex of acquired characteristics.

The Source of Acquired Behavior Patterns—The acquired behavior patterns, which are dominant in modern human behavior, do not arise out of nothing. They are developed from underlying behavior patterns which can be organized into habits and habit complexes by the environmental pressures. These underlying patterns, as we have seen, are random movements, reflexes, instincts, and other simpler antecedent habits. How the inherited behavior patterns are organized into acquired patterns was shown in a general way in connection with the antecedent discussion of each of the underlying types of behavior patterns. The modern derivative control environments, especially the formative institutions which are organized within these composite or derivative control environments, are vast social mechanisms with the specific function of seizing upon the inherited behavior patterns through the selective stimuli which they offer the organism and of organizing these patterns of behavior into more inclusive derivative acquired behavior complexes or sets to dominate the behavior of individual organisms in social situations. It is always the organism which acts, or reacts, but this behavior is always on the basis of a stimulus or a set of stimuli which is to the organism the environment. This is true even when one part of the organism or its behavior is stimulus to the behavior of another part or the whole of the organism. Thus acquired behavior complexes are integrated within the individual organism and are, properly speaking, individual habits. But they also function in collective situations and are therefore a part of the data of sociology and social psychology. Because they are organized in individuals by the pressures of a social environment they occur in essentially the same form or in similar forms in the various members of groups, with the result that in the aggregate they constitute collective or social behavior. Habits, acquired under the pressures of social environments, especially under the dominance of the psycho-social environment, are preëminently social, not only in their origin, but also in their collective modes of expression and in the social effects which they produce when themselves operating in the rôle of environment.

THE METHOD OF ACQUIRING HABITS is that known as the conditioning of responses. It has long been known that old responses may be adjusted to new stimuli and that new responses may be integrated and adapted to old stimuli. Pavlow demonstrated the mechanism experimentally. He showed that by ringing a bell at the same time that meat was shown to a dog, the dog would come in time to respond with a flow of saliva to the sound of the bell even when the meat was not present. Here was an old instinctive response occurring through association upon the presentation of a stimulus not originally biologically adequate. This is the simplest or positive method of conditioning a response. It is also a simple form of habit acquisition. A simple negative method of conditioning responses is to modify the response by a process of substitution of one response for another, as in the case of a rat learning the maze. Protopathic stimuli or blind alleys cause the rat to modify its responses, either by selecting a substitute response pattern for the one already in use, or by making a combination of old response patterns. These combination responses are made up of the original and acquired behavior patterns referred to in the previous section. Both positive and negative conditioning of responses may become highly complex and result in the acquisition of compound habits or responses. This may be called the abbreviated or abstract and symbolic method of conditioning responses. But always the acquired response is a conditioned response. It is never made out of nothing, but is always a modification or a combination of some behavior pattern or set which existed before.

The process of conditioning responses or the integration of new habits begins in the earliest days of infancy, probably even before birth, and continues throughout life. But it is especially active for most people in the earliest years of their lives, that is, before they get their adjustment to their worlds. It apparently begins postnatally in the act of nursing and of crying and develops from one movement and vocalization to another. Random movements and vocalizations are especially valuable material out of which to integrate new composite or variational responses, but reflexes, and even instincts, must not be neglected in an account of the formation of habits. The fact that the original behavior patterns of man are so simple and rudimentary facilitates greatly the process by which he acquires new habits by means of the mechanism of the conditioned response. This simplicity of his inherited patterns is closely correlated with his neural flexibility or synaptic incompleteness. Animals with greater fixity of neural connections and with correspondingly more complete response patterns are relatively less capable of learning new habits, that is, of conditioning new responses to their environmental stimuli.

ACQUIRED NON-OVERT BEHAVIOR PATTERNS—Acquired behavior patterns are not merely overt, or neuro-muscular, response systems. Behavior is also psychic, or neuro-psychic, in character. Perhaps we should say that the behavior merges at one extreme into the almost purely cortical, with a minimum of overt or symbolical activity, just as at the other extreme it is almost wholly muscular and glandular with a minimum of cortical and conscious direction. Or, perhaps it is wholly automatic, mediated entirely through the lower neural centers. Those acquired behavior patterns which have a large and visible element of overt or striated muscular adjustment in them and which are integrated clearly with reference to the overt adjustments of the organism to its environment we ordinarily call habitual. This is the popular understanding of the term habit. But there are also neuro-psychic habits or organizations and integrations of symbolic behavior or inner adjustment patterns which have not yet been realized in complete overt expression. They are preliminary to the complete overt or neuro-muscular adaptation of the organism to its environment. In their conscious aspects they consist of a survey, perhaps in terms of words, of the possibilities of such adjustment and a weighing or evaluation of the significance of various contemplated or projected behavior patterns for adjustment purposes. These are attitudinal or neuro-psychic behavior patterns and involve a minimum of muscular activity. When speaking in terms of consciousness they might perhaps better be called value complexes instead of merely habit complexes, although they are as truly acquired as any overt behavior patterns. Merely for purposes of distinction this term value complex will be used frequently in this book.

The term habit itself is here employed, not to indicate an acquired behavior pattern which has become so fixed by repeated functioning as to be relatively automatic, although this appears to be the popular usage. It is used rather in the technical sense of an acquired behavior pattern, regardless of whether it has functioned only once or many times.

MATERIALS FOR SUPPLEMENTARY READING

Allport, F. H., *Social Psychology,* Ch. III
Bernard, L. L., *Instinct: A Study in Social Psychology,* Chs. IV, V
Bogardus, E. S., *Fundamentals of Social Psychology,* Chs. I, IV
Burnham, W. H., *The Normal Mind,* Chs. III-VII, XII, XIII
Dewey, J., *Human Nature and Conduct,* Part I, Sec. I; Part II, Sec. II
Ellwood, C. A., *The Psychology of Human Society,* Chs. III, IX
Gault, R. H., *Social Psychology,* Ch. III
Herrick, C. J., *An Introduction to Neurology,* Ch. IV
Jennings, H. S., *Behavior of the Lower Organisms*
Kantor, J. R., *Principles of Psychology,* Ch. XV
Loeb, J., *Forced Movements, Tropisms, and Animal Conduct*
Norsworthy and Whitley, *Psychology of Childhood,* Ch. XI
Park and Burgess, *Introduction to the Science of Sociology,* pp. 73-94
Paton, S., *Human Behavior,* Ch. VII, IX
Watson, J. B., *Behavior, an Introduction to Comparative Psychology,* Chs IV-VIII
———, *Psychology from the Standpoint of a Behaviorist,* Ch. VII, VIII
Woodworth, R. S., *Psychology, a Study of Mental Life,* Chs. V, VI, VII

CHAPTER IX

MISUSE OF THE CONCEPT OF INSTINCT

WIDESPREAD USE OF THE TERM INSTINCT—Since the eighteenth century, when there was a strong attempt to understand the mechanisms by which human behavior actually occurred as well as to understand the environmental forces which produced behavior, there has been a good deal of emphasis upon the concept of instinct among the psychologists and ethicists. The concepts of conscience, sympathy, benevolence, and of other supposedly native impulses and behavior sets, were then already beginning to lose prestige. The nineteenth century saw these reputed causes of behavior pass out of legitimate social psychology as innate motives to conduct, although they remained as class terms for certain types of acquired dispositions. The demand was for more specific units of original behavior patterns, and the term instinct came largely to take the place of, and in some cases to include, the older projected entities which we have enumerated. At first the term instinct was itself used quite generally and loosely, as we have seen. Recognized specific instincts were few, but the general principle of instinct, or inborn behavior trait, was quite frequently invoked. Gradually the number of specific instincts increased, until late in the nineteenth and early in the twentieth centuries it became overwhelmingly large.

ORIGINS OF THE CONCEPT—The reason for the invention of a vast number of specific instincts was the insistent demand of a number of newly integrated sciences, applied and theoretical, for a detailed explanation of human behavior. Psychology, having made connections with physiology and neurology about this time, was supposed to be able to speak authoritatively on the matter. The social and mental sciences had at the close of the nineteenth century a flowering which was even more remarkable than that of the physical sciences a century and a half earlier and of the biological sciences in the middle of the nineteenth century. Education was evolving from an art into a science, and it was making connections with the new and independent science of psychology through two overlapping theoretical sciences, educational psychology and child psychology. Sociology had also come to demand for itself a scientific status in the study of institutions and groups. Social psychology, overlapping both psychology and sociology, was attempting to generalize individual behavior into collective behavior. Even economics and political science, and to a faint degree history, were beginning to look beneath the visible plane of conscious and purposive behavior in the market place and the political arena for the hidden motives and powers which their students began to suspect after all had made history and still continued to rule the world. Religion was beginning, as an intellectual discipline, to break with authoritarian dogmas and theories and to seek for the explanation of its doctrines in human personality and environmental conditions. Ethics was passing out of the status of an absolutistic doctrine into a theory of relativity in evaluating concepts of right and wrong.

The findings of biology and psychology and sociology were being invoked by all of these new trends. The search, in so far as it turned to an analysis of human nature instead of environment, was for more specific elements of behavior which could account for the relative fluidity and unfinality of behavior which were now perceived to be dominant in individual character and in human affairs. The principle of the reflex arc had been discovered and it had been elaborated into complex patterns of behavior. The organization of the nervous system and the complicated sensory structures began to be fairly well known. Behavior was no longer a mystical infiltration into the organism from the divine or metaphysical entities which ruled the human world from outside. An independent, self-existing natural law became one of the myths to be added to the more concrete traditions of the pagan gods. Reason and intuition, conscience, the soul, the virtues and the vices, formerly regarded as entities residing in the individual to whom they had come as emanations from the mystical natural law or from divinity, were now perceived to be analytical and synthetic verbal concepts symbolic of the nervous functioning arising out of the normal stimulus-response mechanisms by means of which the organism made its adjustments to its environment.

FIXITY OF BEHAVIOR NOT A PROOF OF ITS INSTINCTIVE CHARACTER—Introspection and objective observation easily disclosed the fact that many, perhaps most, of these stimulus-response processes or behavior patterns occurred in relatively fixed forms. People were observed to act in much the same way in similar situations over and over again. It was also noticeable that it was frequently very difficult to change the behavior pattern even when new stimuli were applied. This relative fixity of behavior, especially in what were called the fundamental relationships of life, was a matter of age-old observation. And since biology, which dealt primarily with the inherited mechanisms of the lower animal types, was the fashion of thought in the latter half of the nineteenth century, an inheritance explanation of the relative constancy of human behavior became the accepted theory. The behavior patterns were studied. Reflexes and random movements were neglected by the mental and social scientists as relatively unimportant, because they were too simple to loom large in adult collective behavior which was first studied by them. Tropisms had not yet been described or had but little vogue. The complex behavior patterns which were observed to function day by day, in both individual and collective adjustment situations, were seized upon and emphasized. Under the influence of biology, and in the absence of any account of an acquired origin—for the elements of the learning process were relatively unknown—their inheritance as units was assumed.

Since the beginning of the twentieth century we have gone much further in the analysis of the habit forming process. We have been able to show that it is an absurdity to claim true instinctive character for most of the complex behavior patterns, especially for those which mediate the rapidly changing adjustments of the organism as a whole to complex changing environments. This analysis has shown them to be acquired behavior patterns, or habit complexes. These acquired behavior patterns are also integrated in the neuro-protoplasm under the influence of the environmental pressures, just as are the other more fixed behavior patterns. But their integration occurs in the more flexible neuro-protoplasmic elements of the higher brain centers, and therefore they are more easily changed. Not all students of social psychology, and of the other sciences and arts which depend upon psychology and sociology, have yet come to make these distinctions or to see their importance. Many of them still cling to the old notion that all or practically all of the relatively fixed behavior patterns are inherited or instinctive, although this attitude of mind is rapidly disappearing from social psychology. The following paragraphs will serve to illustrate its error.

EXAMPLES OF THE MISUSE OF THE CONCEPT OF INSTINCT —We have defined an instinct as a specific response to a specific stimulus, the neural pattern or structure mediating the response being inherited. If the pattern—that is, the neural connections—is not inherited, then the behavior pattern is acquired and not instinctive, however definite and specific it may be. In the examples which follow these simple facts defining the nature of instinct will be seen to be violated.

LITERARY USAGE—The most inaccurate or unscientific employment of the term instinct is the literary one so frequently found in poetry or other elegant writing. The very common terms "instinct with beauty," "instinct with music," "instinct with spirit," or "instinct with truth" are examples of this. But this usage is found among serious as well as esthetic writers. One author says that matter is instinct with eternal energy. Marett tells us that the savage considers white animals, birds of night, monkeys, mice, frogs, crabs, snakes, and lizards to be instinct with a dreadful divinity. The historian Marvin speaks of "a view instinct with reverence for all existence." Benjamin Kidd has affirmed that "the labor movement in the west is becoming consciously instinct with the principle of universal war." Another writer tells us that "Everywhere this world and life are instinct with service." Washington Gladden found that "nature is instinct with reason," and another religious writer declares that "the message of the church has always been instinct with a power of social renewal." The term as here used does not necessarily imply a behavior pattern or any hereditary connection, but is more or less a figurative usage.

Confusion with Automatic, Unpremeditated, Vague, and Impulsive Behavior—One of the most frequent misuses of the term instinct or of its derivatives, "instinctive" and "instinctively," is to employ it to cover almost any behavior which is unconscious or automatic or unpremeditated or vague or impulsive. A few examples will illustrate this improper usage. Forel says that "woman has an instinctive admiration for men of high intellect and lofty sentiments." A. W. Small tells us that a certain program is "instinctively adopted, after a fashion, by every man who tries to deal with concrete social questions." A writer on housing reform insists that the method which the average citizen "instinctively adopts is to get up a petition of thousands of names in favor of his measure and send it to the legislature." If instincts are embedded in the race inheritance, as is claimed, this would indeed be an unexpected instinct, since interest in housing reform is very recent. A writer on international affairs states that "the Italian people have an instinctive affection for the people of Britain," although he does not explain to us the inherited basis of it. Jane Addams says that bad men were instinctively afraid of Lincoln. LeBon, the social psychologist and French publicist, even goes so far as to speak of "instinctive agreements among all its (the nation's) members on all great questions." Such agreements, if they existed, would necessitate a highly flexible and complicated inheritance mechanism indeed. Another writer comments on "the instinctive alliance of the woman suffrage movement with the uncertain and dangerous elements in our political life." Nietzsche says that the "will of the spirit . . . instinctively aims at appearance and superficiality." Small and Vincent's declaration that amenities become instinctive when they are insisted upon in early life would seem to make the instinctive (inherited) mechanism itself acquired. Likewise, E. T. Devine says, "Those especially who find their approach to the problems of social work through the doorway of economics have been trained . . . to ask instinctively two questions: Have we the money, or the resources, to do what we see requires to be done?"

Such examples might easily be multiplied many fold from the literature even of the social and psychological sciences, but it is not necessary. It must be clear from the context that the persons who are responsible for these illustrations were not speaking of inherited behavior at all, but misused the term instinct to cover learned attitudes although they may have believed they were dealing with inheritance.

COMPLEX HABITS MISTAKEN FOR INSTINCTS—In the case of supposed highly specific and definite, although complex, instincts we find the same tendency among writers who should be on their guard against such errors to confuse the acquired with the inherited. One writer speaks of the "instinct of the desire to liberate the Christian subjects of the Sultan." Professor Ross avers that "Christianity was born with the imperishable instinct to impregnate the meanest man with its soul," an expression which includes a rare collection of anthropomorphisms. A psychoanalyst thinks there is an instinct to mummify the corpse, also to photograph it. A novelist speaks of an instinct in one of his characters to offer himself as a sop to conventional honor. A writer on play and education has found an instinct for engaging the groceryman in conversation while a companion makes off with the bananas. The same writer knows of an instinct "for escaping down dark alleys and over roofs and by the exercise of many wiles." In the accompanying instance—"On the day that these decisions are announced from Paris, the instinct of every Turk will be to kill a Christian"—the instinct seems to be highly correlated with the human calendar as well as with persons. In this case, cited by Ross—"the instinct of an angry community to refuse coöperation"—the instinct appears to be a collective rather than an individual behavior pattern, an assumption which is scarcely tenable. The "instinct that prescribes the robbing of cellars and greenhouses" must be of relatively recent origin. According to another writer there was "an instinct to substitute for slavery a condition of serfdom," which gives a new and non-economic interpretation to at least one aspect of history. "A business man's instinct for organization and administration" would also appear to have more of the acquired than of the inherited in it. The "instinct of the life of the underworld of finance," of which Benjamin Kidd speaks, is both indefinite and doubtful. An "instinct for paying propositions" should be of the greatest value to a financier.

In the world of culture as well as of economics there seems to be the same misapprehension about instincts. For example, *The Nation* declares that "Lamb had a fine instinct for apocalyptic passages." Less exalted, but equally improbable, is the "instinct of the girl to pat and arrange her hair" which has been isolated by an educational sociologist. Illustrations of this sort might be vastly multiplied. But it should be clear from these instances that the writers of these passages really have in mind the results of training and have fallen into the prevalent error already mentioned of mistaking habits for instincts because they are relatively definite and constant in their operation.

CLASSIFICATIONS OF INSTINCTS—The absurdity of classifying the behavior patterns which have just been reviewed as instincts is sufficiently evident without further comment. But when one comes to make a classification of supposedly true instincts the problem of discrimination becomes more difficult. What are the instincts which actually do exist and operate in directing human behavior or enter into composite acquired behavior complexes? Various Utopians and social theorists with unilateral explanations of social conditions and problems often recognize only a single dominant instinct, with possibly a few subordinate or supporting instincts thrown in for good measure. Thus the so-called instincts of acquisitiveness, constructiveness, gregariousness, sex, fear, play, nutrition, etc., have at various times and under various circumstances served as the key to all human behavior. Freud, the psychoanalyst, recognizes only two fundamental instincts, sex and self-preservation, which he believes determine all human conduct. To these Jung and his followers add the herd instinct. McDougall, in his *Social Psychology,* lists twelve such instincts, of which the first seven may be called primary and the others secondary. They are fear, repulsion, pugnacity, curiosity, self-abasement, self-assertion, parental, reproduction, gregariousness, emulation, acquisitiveness, hunger. To these he adds some general dispositions, which he does not call instincts, viz., sympathy, suggestion, play, and imitation. He does not even maintain that these general tendencies or dispositions are wholly or primarily inherited.

SOME SAMPLES—The number of classifications offered by various writers is almost without limit, and some of these classifications are very long.

Professor William McDougall, in his *Outline of Psychology*, lists and describes thirteen major and seven minor instincts as follows:

Major instincts	Acquisitive
Parental or Protective	Constructive
Combat	Appeal
Curiosity	*Minor instincts*
Food-seeking or Hunting	Laughter
Repulsion	Scratching
Escape	Sneezing
Gregarious	Coughing
Self-assertion	Defecating
Submission	Urinating
Mating or Pairing	Falling asleep (?)

S. S. Colvin [1] lists thirty instincts in the approximate order of their supposed development, as follows:

Fear	Hunting
Anger	Predation
Sympathy	Migration
Affection	Love of adventure and the unknown
Play	
Imitation	Superstition
Curiosity	Sex love
Acquisitiveness	Vanity
Constructiveness	Coquetry
Self-assertion (leadership)	Modesty
Self-abasement	Love of nature
Rivalry	Love of solitude
Envy	Esthetic ⎫
Jealousy	Religious ⎬ Emotions
Pugnacity	Moral ⎭
Clannishness	

[1] *The Learning Process.*

CONCEPT OF INSTINCT 131

R. C. Givler [2] attempts a classification of instincts from the functional standpoint, making use primarily of the concept of tropic response. He finds both primary (four in number) and derivative instincts. His list of the latter includes only the more important as he understands them. It should also be remarked that he regards any automatic response pattern as an instinct, whether it is inherited or acquired.

Primary instincts	Curiosity
Chemotaxis	Self-abasement or Subjection
Thermotaxis	Self-assertion or Self-display
Heliotaxis	Pugnacity
Barotaxis	Reproductive and Parental
Derivative instincts	Sympathy
Flight	Suggestibility
Repulsion	Imitation

William James [3] presented a carefully selected list of fifty-two supposedly legitimate instincts, while Thorndike [4] appears to have literally hundreds.

Woodworth (*Psychology*) seems to accept at least 110.

Many of the psychologists and others writing on instincts group their approved instincts into general classes. Thus Colvin and Bagley [5] list 25 instincts under the following general headings: Adaptive, individualistic, sex and parental, social, and religious and esthetic. E. A. Kirkpatrick [6] accepts 30 instincts which he arranges under the headings: Individualistic or self-preservative, parental, group or social, adaptive, regulative, and resultant or miscellaneous. H. C. Warren [7] has only 26 instincts, which he classifies generally as nutritive, reproductive, defensive, aggressive, and social. Woodworth's 110 instincts are arranged under the three general headings of responses to organic needs, responses to other persons, and play

---

[2] Givler, R. C., *Psychology, the Science of Human Behavior.*
[3] *Principles of Psychology.*
[4] *Original Nature of Man.*
[5] Colvin, S. S. and Bagley, W. C., *Human Behavior: a First Book in Psychology for Teachers.*
[6] *Fundamentals of Child Study.*
[7] *Human Psychology.*

instincts. Watson (*Behavior*) has 11 general headings or classes, as follows: (1) Structural characteristics, action systems, etc., (2) obtaining food, (3) shelter, (4) rest, sleep, play, etc., (5) sex, (6) defense and attack, (7) special forms of instinct, (8) vocalization, (9) unclassified and non-adaptive but complex and complete acts, (10) unclassified and non-adaptive reflexes, (11) individual peculiarities in response.

A STATISTICAL ANALYSIS of the usage of instincts in 5684 cases taken from various types of literature, but mainly from the social sciences, by the author seems to show that the so-called instincts distribute themselves under 22 distinct headings and a group called miscellaneous as follows:

Types	No. Cases	Types	No. Cases
Altruistic	119	Migratory and climatic	64
Anti-social	185	Play	168
Disgust or repulsion	74	Recessive and repose	36
Economic	281	Religious	83
Esthetic	152	Retaliative	96
Ethical	48	Self-abasement	139
Family	413	Self-assertive	806
Fear and flight	287	Self-display	107
Food	228	Sex	853
Gregarious or social	697	Workmanship	266
Intellectual	262	Miscellaneous	229
Imitative	91		

The presentation of this list does not mean that the writer accepts them as true instincts or complex inherited behavior patterns. The list merely represents the usage accepted as a whole or in part by approximately five hundred writers, mainly from the mental and social sciences. The numbers after the titles represent the frequency with which the type was found to occur.

The large number of classifications here presented or indicated is for the purpose of providing data for the student to analyze and make comparisons of usages.[8]

[8] For more extended classifications see the author's *Instinct: A Study in Social Psychology*, Chs. VII-IX and XVI; also E. L. Thorndike's *Original Nature of Man*.

CRITICISM OF THE CURRENT USAGE OF THE CONCEPT OF INSTINCT—Some criticisms of the current usage of the concept of instinct have doubtless already occurred to the reader. One is that there is no sort of agreement in regard to what are the true instincts. Some of the terms, such as acquisition, fighting, sexual love, gregariousness, self-assertion, self-abasement, appear repeatedly in the classifications, but an even larger number of so-called instincts can be found occasionally in a large number of classifications. Sometimes, also, a term which is used as a single specific instinct in one classification may be used to characterize a whole group or class of so-called specific instincts in another classification. An instinct must have original or inherited unity as a behavior pattern or it is not an instinct. A mere group of instincts, a concept, or a classificatory title cannot be an instinct. Such is not a concrete behavior pattern at all, for it does not exist except as a conceptual or abstract meaning term. It never appears in an adjustment situation as a unitary process of behavior. It is in effect only a list of concrete behavior patterns, which may or may not appear together at any one time or in some one individual organism.

This same criticism applies also to most of the so-called specific instincts in the classifications cited. Thus such terms as fighting, gregariousness, self-assertion, self-abasement, acquisition, play, imitation, and the like are not single and definite behavior patterns. They are class terms for hundreds and thousands of concrete behavior mechanisms which are grouped together in action or in conceptual thinking because of their general similarity of function. There are almost numberless ways of fighting, playing, imitating, or of having gregarious contacts with one's fellows. Each one of these may be a unit behavior pattern and therefore entitled to be called an instinct, if it is inherited. But the whole list of activities having a common conceptual or classificatory name never occur in action together, that is, they never function as a unit behavior process, as would be necessary if they were true instincts. They occur in consciousness only by a short-cut process of symbolic integration and condensation. That is, the whole neuro-muscular organization which would be necessary to the effective overt expression of such a complex so-called instinct does not appear as the basis of the verbal concept which is used to symbolize the group of potential behavior processes included in the reputed instinct. It would probably not be possible for all of such behavior processes to come into consciousness at once in sufficient detail to enable them to go into action. It certainly would not be possible for all of the behavior patterns symbolized by one of these terms, miscalled an instinct, to go into overt action at the same time. What we are dealing with in such cases is, therefore, not behavior patterns in the neuro-muscular protoplasmic systems of the organism, but merely a collective or class symbol of many such concrete behavior patterns which never occur together or as a single overt behavior unit. And an instinct must be a unitary behavior pattern or it is not an instinct.

INSTINCTS ARE STRUCTURAL, NOT CONCEPTUAL—An instinct is a biological fact and it is a unit character, or it does not exist. It is structural. It is not possible to inherit an abstraction. The activity, which ordinarily by a species of metonymy is miscalled the instinct, is of course not inherited. The actual instinct which is inherited is the unit organization of the neurons, the physiological and neurological bases of which lie back of and give form to the activity or resulting behavior. The behavior is the visible manifestation of the structural neural organization which is not visible, because it is rooted in an inner neural organization. The behavior is the response of this neuro-muscular organization of the organism to environmental pressures. Only the structural organization can be inherited and therefore be an instinct.

A TRUE CLASSIFICATION OF THE INSTINCTS would be a description of these various neural mechanisms. But such a description is of course impossible in the present state of our knowledge about the distribution and organization of neural processes. As a consequence we are compelled to use the less accurate method of classifying instincts in terms of their overt manifestations, that is, in terms of their stimuli and responses. Thorndike [9] has listed four such methods of classification as follows:

[9] *Original Nature of Man.*

1. By the functions which the tendencies perform
2. By the responses which are their end-terms
3. By the situations which are their first terms
4. By their origins or affinities in development

It is clear of course that there is no relationship of identity between the adjustment-function of a behavior pattern and its structure. The one is a psycho-social fact, is apprehended conceptually, and has objective existence only in consciousness. While the other is a matter of organic relationship and is developed in the protoplasm. Several very diverse structures or behavior patterns may have the same adjustment function, while the same behavior pattern may at different times or in different situations perform antagonistic adjustment functions. The structure may be inherited, while the function never can be, since it is organized only conceptually or symbolically as a method of evaluating the adjustment which is made to environment. Neither is there a complete correlation between responses and stimuli, on the one hand, and the behavior patterns or neural organizations, on the other hand, which produce the one and are the result of the other. Consequently these methods of classifying instincts are of but little value.

EXAMPLES OF CONCEPTUAL TERMS MISTAKEN FOR INSTINCTS—Finally, these complex functional or value terms which are miscalled instincts, not only lack the structural unity of instincts, but they are not even inherited units. In each of these complexes of potential activity or behavior represented by such class terms as fighting, the maternal instinct, gregariousness, play, and the like, the acquired elements far outnumber the inherited. Take, for example, the so-called maternal instinct. There is no one activity or set of activities which the instinctivists have in mind when they speak of this "instinct." In different situations and on various occasions the imputed content of this so-called instinct may vary as widely as affection for the child, nursing it, spanking it to make it behave, caressing it, taking it to a baby clinic, getting it off to school, starting it in a profession, and thousands of other things. Of all of the possible activities and attitudes which the mother may manifest toward the child only a few are really inherited, and these are among the simplest of the whole number. They may possibly be represented by such acts as pressing the child to the breast, yielding it milk when it nurses, responding to its presence in the arms by clasping or pressure, and possibly kissing and emotional and mental disturbance when it cries or laughs.

But such acts as these are not sufficient to care for a helpless human infant. The real care of the child, that which enables it to survive and develop into a normal and well adjusted organic and social personality, must be learned. The behavior patterns for such care are acquired by observation and imitation of others in play, by reading books and hearing lectures on the subject, and by the experience of caring for a child. Thus the maternal instinct, which is supposed to account for our behavior in caring for children and to constitute the content of this behavior, turns out to be no instinct at all, is not even a unitary habit process, but is a classificatory concept covering many potential acts which never occur together or in unity. This so-called instinct is an abstract and acquired value term or complex rather than a concrete act. It exists actually as a symbol or as a meaning complex of symbols, but not as overt behavior or action. Consequently it cannot be an instinct. Moreover, the analysis and criticism which have been applied to the term maternal instinct may also be applied with like validity to practically all of the other complex "instincts" in the classifications here cited.

Do Instincts Exist in Man?—It may be asked, therefore, if there are any instincts. This question has been raised and sometimes it has been answered in the negative. It seems proper, however, to affirm the existence of instincts, but to deny that they are as numerous or as important relatively in the adjustment processes of man as in the lower animals. As said before, the human instincts which remain intact are concerned primarily with the vegetative or strictly vital processes, rather than with the wider adjustments of the organism to its environment. The latter, and especially those adjustments which we call cultural, are mediated by acquired behavior patterns. If we make a rigid distinction between reflexes and instincts on the basis of the relative complexity of the behavior pattern, then it may be said that there are very few true instincts left intact in the human organism. But there is no definite dividing line between reflexes and instincts on the grounds of complexity, or on any other basis of distinction, and the tendency appears to be to make the term instinct inclusive of that of reflex. From this viewpoint it may be said that we have a great many very simple instincts. But the important fact to note is that the value complexes which for the most part constitute the content of the current classifications of instincts are not instincts, but are acquired complexes and behavior patterns or systems.

Do Instincts Dominate the Formation of Habits?—It has been claimed by some of the instinctivists that even if we admit that many or most of the so-called instincts are acquired behavior patterns or value complexes, nevertheless the latter are organized under the dominance of the instincts which they include in their structural organization. The contention is that even the acquired behavior patterns and complexes are not composed wholly of non-instinctive elements, but that they include inherited as well as acquired processes. This unquestionably is true. All, or practically all, of the acquired adjustment patterns are built up on the basis of the reflexes, instincts, and random impulses, as described in the previous chapter. In many cases, with the partial exception of the delayed instincts, the acquired pattern is organized about some instinctive pattern, sometimes to reënforce it and at other times to transform and sublimate or to repress it. The fact is that as the higher social and institutional environments multiply and increase in volume they come increasingly to dominate our behavior. They select our responses out of all the behavior units at our disposal and organize the suitable elements into new and acquired complexes which constitute the content of what we call civilized behavior. If we turn again to the analysis of the so-called maternal instinct, we shall find that the attitudes and practices which the modern mother develops towards her children are not determined by the relatively unimportant instinctive elements which we discovered in the total behavior. These may at times reënforce acquired tendencies, but often they motivate the mother in the opposite direction to that which is enjoined upon her by her scientific training. Her behavior towards her child is dictated primarily by the social environment which brings to bear upon her the collective practices of the members of her group. These she imitates and practices herself, even when they are contrary to her instinctive urges. It is not the good mother who yields to her native impulses and amuses the baby when it cries or gives it the food it desires or spoils it for the sake of the satisfaction of her own emotions. The good mother does what the child specialists tell her, even at the cost of repressing or sublimating her inherited maternal impulses.

ENVIRONMENTAL DOMINANCE—And so it is with much or most of our modern civilization. Civilization is itself in large part a system of sublimations and repressions. We do not give our pugnacious, sexual, gustatory, fear, and gregarious impulses free rein. On the contrary we build up innumerable controls over them in order that we may not destroy the fabric of culture by a "return to nature" through a blind following of our impulses. If we eat without restraint we are liable to organic diseases and we lack sufficient incentive and initiative to do the work of society. If we do not learn to control our anger impulses society becomes a state of war instead of peace. Unbridled sex activity means overpopulation and poverty and degradation for large portions of mankind. Even unrestrained gregariousness results in an excess of entertainment and amusement and too little useful productive effort. The best method of control of these inherited impulses where they exist, as well as of their acquired modifications, is by what we call sublimation. This involves the turning of the impulses into derivative and substitute channels, as in the creation of art and the making and doing of useful things in the service of a derived ideal. If we employ the method of repression, which has sometimes been practiced and preached by the more puritanical factions and philosophies, there is always the danger that the thin veneer of culture may be broken through and that there will be an irresponsible release of the repressed impulses in a "return to nature" or to "barbarism." Our formative institutions, including those of education and religion, are always busy with this problem of the most effective control systems and gradually, with the aid of social psychology and the social sciences, they should be able to devise a system which will bend the native impulses to the service of the best abstract ideals of a cultural civilization. Thus environment, rather than instinct, now shapes our behavior in the main. Environment even utilizes instinct in the service of its own collective mechanisms and values or ideals.

GENERAL LIMITATIONS DUE TO INHERITANCE—The argument as here presented is sometimes confusing to students of behavior. That it is not instinct but habit in the form of the psycho-social environment which in the main dominates and gives uniformity to behavior may be accepted by them, but they are not able to admit that inheritance exercises no influence over behavior. They are likely to feel that a criticism of the crude instinct hypothesis is an attack upon all forms of inheritance determination of behavior.

There is an inheritance basis for behavior, but it is largely negative and exists for the most part in the non-neural protoplasms. The general characteristics of man's anatomy and physiology constitute the main inherited bases of human behavior. They function as conditions and limitations upon the development of behavior patterns in the neuro-muscular systems. All men have approximately the same general conditions and limitations of behavior of this type. For example, we cannot form the habit of flying, because we have no wings. We cannot inhabit the bottom of the sea because our lungs are not so constructed as to enable us to do this. We cannot receive the stimuli of the radio broadcasting apparatus without special receiving apparatus, because the inherited structure of our auditory organs is not adequate for the purpose. In short, the limits within which all behavior must take place are determined by our inherited non-neural as well as neural structures. But the specific character or form which this behavior takes is in large degree determined by environment. These general imitations and facilitations due to inherited structures and physiological processes, as well as to acquired modifications of them, will be discussed in a subsequent chapter.

These limitations are perhaps more important than we sometimes realize, because they are so fixed and inflexible, while the neural structures are relatively flexible and modifiable. We can build up, under environmental pressures, new neural patterns of behavior, especially in the cerebral cortex, but we cannot modify in any great degree our fundamental anatomy and physiology. Consequently the control which we seek to exercise over our behavior through the production of new neural integrations and organizations is frequently vetoed by the relative fixity of our non-neural inheritance.

PHYSIOLOGICAL NEED NOT INSTINCT—Other limitations and conditions of our behavior, structurally less specific, but largely inherited, are due to the physiological makeup of our organisms. Thus the taking of food, breathing, sleeping, and the performance of certain other functions are inevitable if life is to be preserved. The need for the performance of these functions is not the same as the mechanisms by which they are done and should be separated from them. The mechanisms of performance may be either inherited or acquired. The necessity for the performance, by whatever mechanism, is fundamentally determined in the hereditary constitution of the protoplasms, although the extent and time and conditions of the performance of the functions may be greatly modified by the environmental pressures which shape their patterns of behavior. In a somewhat similar, but less insistent way, thinking, the general character of our emotions, temperament, and the like are determined by our physiology, but their individual expressions of patterns are largely determined by environment. This fact is made apparent in a later chapter.

This, however, does not justify us in speaking of any of these general types of behavior as instincts. An instinct is a specific stimulus-response pattern, a neural structure. Such is not the case with the physiological necessity of eating, breathing, sleeping, thinking, or experiencing emotion. These are general physiological conditions basic to specific behavior. The locomotive cannot go without fuel, but the mechanism by which it operates is a different matter. Likewise the instinct or acquired behavior pattern by which we act is different from the physiological condition which demands food or sleep in order to provide the metabolic or other transformations which render the subsequent behavior possible. The confusion of the physiological need with the instinct is a very common error and may be said to be basic to one of the prevalent misuses of instinct. It is one which will disappear when our thinking on this subject becomes somewhat clearer.

MATERIALS FOR SUPPLEMENTARY READING

Allport, F. H., *Social Psychology,* Ch. III
Bernard, L. L., *Instinct: A Study in Social Psychology,* Chs. VII-XX
Dewey, J., *Human Nature and Conduct,* Part II, Section I
Ellwood, C. A., *The Psychology of Human Society,* Ch. IX
Josey, C. C., *The Social Philosophy of Instinct*

CHAPTER X

HABIT MECHANISMS AND THE ADJUSTMENT PROCESS

THE PURPOSE OF THIS CHAPTER is to show: first, how individual adjustment patterns have evolved phylogenetically and ontogenetically from the preconscious instinctive types, in which the behavior is predominantly overt with a minimum of internal dominance, to the intellectual and rational and distinctively human modes, in which the behavior is predominantly internal and symbolical, with a minimum of immediate overt response; and, secondly, how these higher modes of inner or symbolical behavior have been conditioned to storage symbols which can serve as releases for inner or overt responses for a very long period of time, with the result that useful or insistent types of social organization and social control are preserved. By this means we shall be able to accomplish two objects. First, we shall review and state in definite order the main facts regarding the evolution of behavior which has been covered in the preceding chapters from the standpoint of the general problems of adjustment. Second, it will be possible to illustrate very clearly the growing importance of environment, especially of the symbolic and projected psycho-social environment, in the control of individual and collective behavior through the conditioning of responses by stimuli.

The transition from the dominance of inherited to acquired technique is of course most apparent in the case of man, where the latter type of control is overwhelmingly important; but it is also to be observed in the lower forms, especially those nearest to man. This development of the environmental dominance can be traced through two aspects: first, the progressive integration of acquired adjustment patterns, and, second, the progressive analysis and evaluation of behavior in adjustment situations from the primitive sensory and affective processes to the highly intellectual methods of discrimination and measurement of the adjustment values of this behavior. In this chapter we shall consider only the former of these two aspects. The latter will be discussed in the two following chapters. In both of these aspects of progressive integration of adjustment patterns, we are, of course, concerned primarily with habits.

THE FUNCTION OF HABIT—Habit is, as we have seen, an acquired mechanism employed in mediating a more effective and selective adjustment of the organism to its environment. It appears when inherited mechanisms can no longer secure sufficiently accurate, rapid, and differentiated adjustment of the organism to a radically and rapidly changing environment without changing the form and structure of the organism. Those animals which live in a relatively constant medium, especially the sea animals, or the insects which so generally have but a limited habitat and live but a season or through only a part of it, have little need of habit forming powers. Insects which live longer than one season and thus may be said to have a varied climatic environment, or those which change from the air to the earth or vice versa, usually change their form as a method of instinctive or inherited adjustment to a changing environment. Where there is no adequate inherited equipment for the mediation of adaptive adjustments, habit modifications must arise. At what stage of development they first appear it is scarcely possible to say. Jennings finds them operating very low down among living forms. In lower animals they are seen doubtless as relatively simple recombinations of primitive tropisms and reflex patterns. In fact, the earliest acquired or habit modifications of responses are of just this nature, relatively formal and simple recombinations of elemental inherited response patterns.

OVERT ADJUSTMENT MECHANISMS ACQUIRED THROUGH TRIAL AND ERROR—As intimated in Chapter VIII, habits are either overt (neuro-muscular) or internal and symbolic (neuro-psychic). The earlier habits are overt in character. That is, they involve an external readjustment of the organism on the basis of trial and error. An inner, or neural, adjustment is of course also involved, but it is secondary. There is an absence of cortical dominance in this early form of habit integration. Ordinarily the simple acquired overt adaptive readjustment neither originates nor ends primarily in the neural processes. Its inception comes from the presentation of unusual stimuli to the end organs of the nervous system with the result that new adjustments must be formed, at first by the trial and error method. In such a case the neural stimulus-response patterns act primarily or exclusively as transmitters, not as transformers, of the impulse. The organization of the environment determines in the main, through the successive stimuli presented, the organization of the response, aided by whatever neural patterns, instinctive or acquired, there are for making responses to such stimuli. Where such patterns are lacking new ones must be conditioned or integrated. The response occurs overtly and immediately, and usually as the act of the organism as a whole, instead of being transformed or redirected by previously organized sets within. Effective transformations and redirection from within can operate only if acquired neural dispositions or sets have been built up in considerable volume through the modification of instinctive patterns as the result of previous trial and error or overt adjustment processes. Among animals this transformation never occurs to any appreciable extent. It is primarily a human achievement. The animal acts; it does not think. Or, if we hold with the behaviorists that all adjustment behavior is thinking, we must say that the animal in this stage of habit formation is thinking in terms of relatively uninhibited overt responses, or trial and error thinking, instead of in terms of internally controlled adjustments, or verbal thinking. This internal control is acquired slowly and painfully only at the end of the trial and error process.

AMONG MEN TRIAL AND ERROR ADJUSTMENT BECOMES INTERNAL AND SYMBOLIC—*The Function of Language Symbols*—In the case of man, however—at least in the case of individuals whose inner behavior processes have been previously conditioned to the symbolic overt partial responses called language—total overt response adjustment behavior is not normally consummated on the overt trial and error basis. The adjustment is worked out internally and symbolically on the basis of an integration of the internal behavior mechanisms conditioned by the symbolic, usually verbal responses. This internal behavior is conditioned by the overt partial and substitute responses which we call language. Such language may be gesture or speech. Each overt partial or substitute response which arises in connection with the interruption or delay of total overt adjustment responses symbolizes the total overt response which is blocked or inhibited, that is, which attempts or tends to occur in overt behavior but fails to do so or is inhibited by the inner behavior mechanisms or by some stimulus from the environment. In the course of the evolution of human behavior, words and the combinations of words become the most important and condensed and abstract of all of the symbolic overt behavior conditioners of internal or conscious behavior. These symbolic, usually verbal, partial or substitute responses can be set up in much more rapid succession than the total overt trial and error responses could possibly occur. They immediately bring about appropriate organized internal substitute behavior. As a result the trial and error process of adjustment goes on internally instead of overtly, until finally there is a successful issue, or until the inner behavior mechanisms cease to inhibit each other and are organized supplementarily.

How Preëxisting Language Forms Aid in This Process—It is not ordinarily necessary for human beings to invent their own language symbols, and lower animals probably cannot, at least not to any appreciable extent. Human beings are born into a world with a language already made. Together with each object or stimulus presented to the child for his response the name of the object is also presented. For example, when he is handed a ball the word "ball" is also spoken by some one and he conditions the name of the object to the sight of the object, to the touch of it, or to the act of reaching for it or crawling to it and taking possession of it. In like manner he learns in time the language sets or forms which correspond to going for the ball, bouncing the ball, buying a ball, and all other forms of behavior with reference to any object whatever. Thereafter, if he desires the ball or other object it will not always be necessary for him to go for it himself. He may use the words descriptive of the ball together with other words, or even gestures, indicating the transfer of the ball from another person or place to himself. Thus as the result of saying "Ball" and pointing to it, or by saying "Give-ball," or "Give me (or baby) ball," some one may bring him the ball. Young children very early learn to get things, especially food and playthings, in this way by the use of words and gestures without getting them for themselves.

It is only a step beyond this process to the use of language as a method of deciding between two or more conflicting impulses without actually acting out both or all of them overtly, or on an overt trial and error basis. All of us, perhaps, have observed young children, when confronted by such a problem, make a gesture first in the direction of one trial response and then in another. Sometimes adults do the same thing, as if unable to make up their minds which direction to take or which object to pick up, which dress or hat to put on, etc. The young child also frequently "talks" the thing out with himself in the form of vocal gestures instead of larger body gestures. He says, "I will do this," or, "No, I will do *this;*" or "I want this," then changes his mind and says, "I want *that,*" etc. In such cases he is merely transferring his adaptive responses from the complete overt trial and error to the symbolic or language trial and error basis of gestures or words. Later on he will make such a complete substitution of symbolic responses for total overt ones in selecting the final or most desirable response that he can settle the whole matter internally or neuro-psychically, without having recourse either to gestures or to words. That is, he can "think" out his adjustment in the ordinary meaning of that term. His speech has become subvocal. And this is the case with adults in most instances, but not in all.

Words not only make possible an internal solution of immediate adjustment problems. They also serve to facilitate objective thinking. If one's verbal symbols are accurately conditioned to objects and their behavior, he can perform experiments symbolically, in terms of words, rather than actually and come to very much the same conclusion as though he had performed them overtly. Science is a method of getting accurate symbols, through laboratory or statistical methods of conditioning, in order to make possible the symbolic manipulation of the world. In physics and chemistry the symbols are quantitative and highly accurate. The architect does not have to fill the stadium to the point of collapse in order to know how strong to make it. He has formulas of tensions and strains and can work out the required strength symbolically.

The Gains from This Method—Thus, in cases of internal trial and error adjustment a reorganization of the internal activity or neuro-psychic technique is substituted for the immediate overt or external adjustment. Apparently the reason for this is that impulses to overt behavior so crowd upon each other under the pressures of a complex environment, or that the past behavior patterns integrated in the neural mechanisms have become so numerous, that it is no longer possible for all of the released impulses to go over into overt response simultaneously or consecutively. There is neither time nor energy for all of the responses to take place on an overt trial and error basis. The net result of such elimination of the overt trial response is, as we have just seen, that trial and error or trial and success in adaptation is transferred from overt to internal or symbolic behavior. The multitude of errors in conduct to which premature overt response would commit us are in the main avoided by means of first working out the adjustment internally in substitute neuro-psychic technique, which in its highest form is verbal or rational thought. Thus there is a very great advantage to the organism, from the standpoints of flexibility, rapidity, and accuracy of adjustment, as well as of economy of time and energy, in transferring adaptive habit technique largely from the overt to the inner sphere. It becomes neuro-psychic adjustment technique, instead of immediately muscular and glandular adaptation.

The Superiority of Verbal Symbols as Conditioners of Inner Behavior—Obviously when the overt symbolic or substitute responses which condition the inner adjustment mechanisms are verbal they occur in much more rapid succession than if they are in the nature of movements of the larger body muscles, or gestures. Likewise, the inner trial and error adaptation can be much more comprehensive, not only because the greater rapidity of the process permits more trials to be made, but also because verbal symbols are much more condensed and inclusive. They are also more precise. Word symbols are more likely than other overt symbols to have highly developed or abstract conscious meaning value. Meaning is the consciousness, not only of the symbol which conditions the consciousness, but of the symbol as representative of the interrupted response which it symbolizes. The refinement of meaning in words, therefore, represents a refinement of their conditioning of inner behavior. Because of all of the characteristics of verbal symbols as conditioners of inner behavior, the inner adjustments which they condition are ordinarily far superior to those conditioned by any other overt symbolic mechanism or language form.

Words, especially written words, also possess other great advantages over gestures and other symbolic conditioners of inner behavior in making preliminary adjustments. They are mobile, can be stored almost anywhere, preserved indefinitely, and they are capable of almost unlimited abstraction. Consequently, they function more frequently than all other overt symbolic responses combined in conditioning internal trial and error integrations of behavior in highly literate people. This fact, incidentally, gives the literate a great advantage over the illiterate and preliterate, provided their words are symbolic of real experiences. Primarily because we carry such a large store of words in our memories and because they have been conditioned or filled with meaning by all sorts of previous experiences, almost any sort of blocking of overt adjustment processes releases an abundance of them in either our vocal or subvocal speech. The resultant conditioning of our inner adjustment behavior we call thinking, as we indicated above. This is what we mean when we say that the intelligent or trained man thinks out his adjustments before he acts them overtly or on a trial and error basis. Communication, it will readily be seen, is merely a method by which symbols of the types here mentioned, usually verbal, occurring as partial or substitute overt responses in one person condition directly internal behavior and indirectly overt behavior in another person.

THINKING IS ESSENTIALLY HABITUAL OR ACQUIRED IN CHARACTER, although it may have an underlying groundwork of instinctive behavior patterns. Reflex or instinctive behavior is not conscious. All forms of mental experience appear with the interruption or modification of instinctive or acquired behavior patterns or responses, leading to a readaptation of the organism to its environment. Thinking is merely the highest or most flexible or verbal form of the adjustment process on the basis of internal neuro-psychic technique. In thinking, which is our name for symbolic response or substitute internal neural organization, subjective or individual habit adaptation reaches its greatest flexibility. It is thus that internal habit adjustment develops its great power of selection of adaptive responses. The organism does not respond overtly to the external stimulus until first a satisfactory organization and reorganization of behavior patterns have taken place within. Neurologically speaking, all important interferences of neuro-psychic impulses or behavior patterns have been resolved into single unitary tendencies to response which are now free to go over into overt behavior adjustment responses, so far as the actor knows, without prejudice to the effectiveness of his adjustment. We say that we think out our plan of action before we proceed. That is, we are conscious, at least in part, of the inner impulses and tendencies to action which are inhibited and of the synthetic or dominating one which finally is released from the internal inhibitions for overt expression or action. We may even say that we will it, by which we mean, in the language of neuro-psychic technique, that we are conscious of the dominant urge or impulse of the behavior pattern, viewed in the light of the response, which is freed from inhibitions and goes into overt action. Habit has become so flexible and so rational in the conscious aspect of its organization that it selects an adaptive adjustment, which we call intelligent, to the insistent and overwhelming environment.

THE FORMS OF LANGUAGE—The highest form of actual habit, therefore, is the internal neuro-psychic type, which is the most flexible in organization and which consequently offers the largest possibilities of selective and intelligent adaptive adjustment of the organism to its ever present and insistent multifold environment. We know this inner neuro-psychic habit organization objectively, especially in others, primarily through its conditioning language symbols as speech or gesture and pantomime, and only secondarily as total overt response. While the ultimate end of all thinking may be said to be action of a character appropriate to achieve the ends disclosed by the thinking process, a more immediate and preparatory—in many cases, a substitute—end or objective is communication of these ideas. The internal organization of acquired or habit processes cannot go on indefinitely in any mind without exercising the discharge as well as the receiving processes of the neuro-psychic mechanism. The forms of behavior which may be regarded as language and which serve as mechanisms for thinking and for the communication of thought or behavior patterns are total overt, partial overt, and substitute overt responses. The first is not ordinarily thought of as language. Gestures were originally partial overt responses. Merely beginning the act was sufficient to indicate what the completed act would be and thus to enable the remainder of the trial and error adjustment to be taken care of internally. The most effective substitute overt responses for purposes of thinking are vocal.

SPEECH AS PRELIMINARY ADJUSTMENT—In this way speech becomes a preliminary or preparatory adjustment process, corresponding to the internal neural and thought aspect which it symbolizes. Just as the internal or neuro-psychic organization is the indispensable first phase of any delayed overt response of an organism of a higher type, so may the second or overt phase be either total overt response or speech. In the highest or human type, it is more frequently speech than body expression, for the reasons of economy and effectiveness already mentioned, and because thinking usually occurs in a social situation and requires communication.

Among the most cultivated types of men, especially among professional thinkers, the preparatory and preliminary character of speech in the adjustment process may be so unapparent that it is not observed. Thus the philosopher may appear to think and speak or write merely for the purpose of thinking, speaking, or writing. Such would seem to be a case of "art for art's sake." But this is an illusion due to the fact that the preliminaries have developed to such huge proportions comparatively that the ultimate purpose in overt adjustment is lost sight of for the time being. In some cases this situation becomes pathological. Especially is this true where the litterateur, the artist, the logician, or the metaphysician piles up his technique or expresses himself merely for his own esthetic satisfaction without expectation of or desire for effective overt adjustment. His interests and activities become inverted and stand as a subjective substitute for overt or objective adjustment. Historically the scholastics and the ascetics have illustrated this tendency, as in some degree did the inverted philosophy of the Stoics. Hamlet is supposed to have suffered from this difficulty. And modern legislatures, with their investigating committees and debates intended only to investigate and debate, approach dangerously near to this classification on a collective basis. But ordinarily and under proper limitations and guidance, thought and the communication of that thought are valuable preliminaries to effective and rapid overt adjustment of the organism as a whole to its environment, paradoxical as it may seem.

Speech is also a means to communication on the basis of symbols representing the compression or foreshortening of total bodily response in adjustment on a large scale. It is much more economical as a means of communication than total bodily response or even than gesture. Substitute overt responses, even more than partial ones, appear to have originated primarily as means of communication, and secondarily as mechanisms of thinking or internal adjustment. Thus speech succeeds both pantomime and gesture as a means of communication as soon as adequate vocal symbols to represent total bodily response or overt behavior have been invented and have become generally understood. The mind recognizes speech as it recognizes total or partial overt responses. Speech is substituted for total overt response as a means of communication because it is more rapid, more intimately adaptive, more highly differentiated, and, therefore, more discriminative.

Written language performs the same general functions as spoken language, but in many respects even more effectively. With its advent the eye comes to be employed for a new purpose, that of perceiving abstract meaning symbols, a function which formerly belonged especially to the ear. Corresponding changes in neuro-psychic organization and association must be set up. Written language, furthermore, is capable of performing many preliminary or preparatory adjustment services which spoken language cannot render. Spoken language greatly increases the possibility of the coöperative or coadaptive adjustment of men to their environment, by enabling them to communicate their aims and formulate common procedure or technique. It also makes possible the assembling of technique which is of very great value in the adjustment process. The transmission of culture and technique by word of mouth is the second most sacred and honored process among primitive men. The most respected is the establishment and control of relationships between man and the supernatural. Spoken language, however, works only at short range. Speech must be relayed through other organisms, other minds or neuropsychic technique, if it is to travel great distances or to descend beyond a single generation—hence the great relative advantage of written language in all but the most limited range of contacts. At great distances, only the written or printed word can carry the message intact and uncorrupted by the neuro-psychic media through which the spoken word must pass. Written language is superior to the spoken, both because of the greater volume which it is able to transmit and because of the greater accuracy with which the content is conveyed.

EXTERNAL STORAGE OF SYMBOLS—With the advent of written language, and even before to some slight extent language symbols began to be organized and stored outside of the individual's behavior patterns and consciousness. This process of external storage of neuro-psychic symbols has increased to such an extent that now by far the greater portion of the stimuli or releases of acquired behavior patterns lies outside of the symbolic behavior of any one individual. It is not alone the verbal symbols and meaning complexes printed in books, newspapers, and magazines, and occurring in written documents that constitute the content of stored language symbols possessing the power of releasing neuro-psychic technique or symbolic behavior in another. These are the most important forms, but any external meaning symbol which is sufficiently standardized and effective as a stimulus to release or reinstate behavior patterns also comes under this category. Thus the various forms of art, such as painting, sculpture, musical compositions, photography or even movie films, and various carriers of symbols, such as pottery, jewelry, archeological material, and architecture, become depositories of stored meaning content or symbolic stimuli for the release of inner habit mechanisms and of overt adjustment responses.

It is only by means of this external storage of language symbols with the power to reinstate and release symbolic and overt responses in others that we have been able to achieve civilization. Non-writing peoples have not been able to advance beyond the status of barbarism. Their wise men could not carry in their brains a sufficient volume of accurate inner habit mechanisms representing external technic processes to enable them to advance greatly in the arts and in the rational interpretation of nature and society.

THE STAIRWAY OF HABIT TECHNIQUE—The evolution of the behavior controls has now been traced briefly, and it must be apparent that there has been an increase in the flexibility of the behavior patterns from the period of the dominance of instinct to the period of the dominance of externally stored language symbols over human behavior. Along with this increasing flexibility of behavior patterns has also gone a greater degree of selectiveness in the adjustment process, so that the adaptation of the organism becomes increasingly more specialized and individualized. This development from the fixity of instinct to the flexibility of habit, making possible an intelligent adjustment of man to his environment on the basis of a rational manipulation of stored language symbols, may be represented in the diagram on the following page. Man has achieved his cultural civilization literally by means of a stairway of habit adjustment technique.

INCREASING VOLUME OF EXTERNAL STORAGE AND THE EXPERT—The aggregate advantage of external storage of verbal language symbols is tremendous. It enables us to build up a body of technic adjustment processes almost without limit. No discovery, no knowledge which can be of use to man need be lost. There is no impossible burden of keeping the whole of the content in mind. It is safely stored and may await utilization for a hundred years, or any length of time,

Lower animal life	Higher animal life	Age of human savagery	Age of barbarism	Age of lower civilization	Age of higher civilization
					Age of records and of science. The psycho-social environment perfected.
				Subvocal language habits important. Written language becomes dominant.	Subvocal language habits important. Written language becomes dominant.
			Vocal language dominant. Neuro-psychic technique develops rapidly. Social control through tradition.	Vocal language dominant. Neuro-psychic technique develops rapidly. Social control through tradition.	Vocal language dominant. Neuro-psychic technique develops rapidly. Social control through tradition.
		Symbolic habit response dominant. Vocal language begins.	Symbolic habit response dominant. Vocal language begins.	Symbolic habit response dominant. Vocal language begins.	Symbolic habit response dominant. Vocal language begins.
	Overt habit response dominant.	Overt habit response dominant.	Overt habit response dominant.	Overt habit response dominant.	Overt habit response dominant.
Instinctive response dominant.	Instinctive response dominant.	Instinctive response dominant.	Instinctive response dominant.	Instinctive response dominant.	Instinctive response dominant.

Note: Read upward

and at the end of the period be as available and as intact as at the beginning. The only limitation that may be placed to the accumulation of this stored language symbolism is that which is set by the limits of storage—which are as yet remote—and by the powers of the human mind to master the keys which will unlock the storage houses of this stored language content. We no longer attempt to teach people collectively all of this externally stored knowledge, nor even any one person any considerable portion of it. Long ago we began to conten ourselves with teaching the key sciences or disciplines which would unlock the treasure houses. Now we teach any one person with any degree of profundity only one or two of these, although it is still our ideal to give everybody some knowledge of each of the basic sciences and arts which serve as keys to the greater whole which lies in storage. We have not yet reached that degree of specialization in learning which the social insects have achieved in function.

The most immediate consequence of this limitation upon the size of the field of knowledge which any one can cover is that we are forced to make collective use of the expert. In the future, society must be ruled by or through the expert, and for the correlation of the work of the experts we must devise some social or administrative mechanism; for no one man can carry in his actual neuro-psychic habit patterns all of the knowledge which is necessary to perform this function. Nor can all men together do it, except by the aid of some social mechanism or device. For example, in the matter of legislation we have found it necessary to provide the legislative expert with legislative reference libraries, expert bill drafters, scientific advice and information from social workers, manufacturers, farmers, etc. Lobbyists formerly did this work poorly and not always in a very public spirited manner. We are now beginning to attempt it scientifically and impartially.

The problem of organizing a proper system of educational controls becomes, therefore, after the problem of the discovery of adjustment technique and data, the most important psychosocial problem. In fact, the problem of education is itself the problem of perfecting the proper organization of neuro-psychic adjustment technique within the individuals and of inventing the proper storage symbols and meaning complexes as psychosocial and institutional environments for individuals in society. Whether it be formal education through the schools or the informal education which arises from human contacts, the press, art, and all other sources, its task is to bring the proper stimuli to behavior to bear upon the individual and to organize these stimuli in such ways as to secure the most effective collective adjustment responses.

AVOIDING A CLOSED SYSTEM—As we come more and more

under the domination of the written aspect of the psycho-social environment, which is itself created as the result of the functioning of our neuro-psychic technique in adjustment situations, and as this body of externally stored meaning symbols becomes constantly greater, and as it imposes itself increasingly upon us as ready made behavior patterns, there is danger that our world will in large measure lose its flexibility and become a closed system, as formerly was the case under the dominance of tradition. This danger has been imminent many times in the past. The educational system itself is peculiarly apt to become a routine method of imposing the external storage content upon new individuals without allowing for individual needs or for flexibility of adjustment. Education is at such times primarily a carrier, not a creator of adjustment technique. Especially the custom-ridden institutions, which vouchsafe more attention to tradition than to science, tend to ossify the educational mechanism and transform society into a non-progressive closed system of psycho-social controls. As the volume of the psycho-social environment becomes greater and its power to mold behavior more compulsory this danger will increase.

The remedy lies primarily in making science, rather than tradition, the guiding spirit of education. With the ideal of discovery and the experimental attitude toward social adjustment dominant in our outlook, and in fact the chief elements in our social creed, we should be able to escape the closed system in social or collective life as well as in philosophy. Along with this we need also to keep open all avenues of knowledge. The fundamental or basic principles of all sciences would ideally be a part of the education of every individual. Holding all the keys of knowledge he should be able, with a greater degree of certainty, to find his own best adjustment, even in a highly complex and bewildering world.

MATERIALS FOR SUPPLEMENTARY READING

Allport, F. H., *Social Psychology*, Chs. VIII, IX
Baldwin, J. M., *Mental Development in the Child and the Race*, Ch. XIV
———, *Social and Ethical Interpretations*, pp. 137-48
Bernard, L. L., *Instinct: A Study in Social Psychology*, Ch. VI

Case, C. M., *Outlines of Introductory Sociology,* Ch. XII
Dewey, J., *Human Nature and Conduct,* Part I, Sec. I, Part III, Sec. I
Edman, I., *Human Traits and Their Significance,* Ch. X
Judd, C. H., *Psychology,* Ch. X
Meyer, M. F., *The Psychology of the Other One,* Ch. XIV
Robinson and Robinson, *Readings in General Psychology,* Ch. XV
Stern, W., *Psychology of Early Childhood,* Part III
Watson, J. B., *Behavior, An Introduction to Comparative Psychology,* Ch. X
——, *Psychology from the Standpoint of a Behaviorist,* Ch. IX

CHAPTER XI

THE FUNCTIONAL ORGANIZATION OF CONSCIOUSNESS—THE FORMS OF CONSCIOUSNESS

So far we have been dealing primarily with behavior from the standpoint of the types of stimulus-response or structural processes involved. In this and the following chapter we shall consider conscious behavior in the individual from the standpoint of the application of these data to the problem of effective adjustment of the individual to his environment. It is important for social psychology to include a discussion of the functional aspects of consciousness because the conscious control of social organization and adjustment is through the projection of social and public relationships which are later legislated or administered into practice. This method by which we create conceptually and projectively the collective adjustment process is of increasing importance.

THE FACULTY CONCEPT GIVES WAY TO THE FUNCTIONAL BEHAVIOR CONCEPT OF MENTAL PROCESSES—In an earlier psychology the abstracted processes of feeling, cognition, and will were supposed to be concrete and specific attributes or qualities of personalities. They were looked upon by the psychologists of this older time as "faculties" which were as objective and as specific as instincts, conscience, the soul, or any of the other so-called faculties, were believed to be. The old faculty psychology has now given way to the newer behavioristic psychology, but some of these old terms persist, largely perhaps because they are convenient synthetic or conceptual symbols for viewing highly flexible and differential processes collective or entire. We now know that such processes as feeling, willing and knowing are not distinct and biologically integrated powers or faculties, somewhere localized in a part of the brain or body. They are abstractions covering a multitude of variable and more or less conscious behavior patterns directed towards as many separate objects and arising from an equally wide range of stimuli, but possessing in common a similarity of function or of purpose or aim, although not necessarily of form. Even consciousness itself is now interpreted in terms of behavior. We shall not enter here into a detailed analysis of the forms of consciousness. That is the work of psychology proper. We are concerned particularly with certain functional integrations of consciousness, which we shall explain briefly.

FEELING is not perceptual, like the other forms of consciousness. It probably represents the lowest functional integration of consciousness, developed as a crude method of subjectively evaluating an activity before the organism was able to perceive objects definitely or grasp in any intellectual way the significance of its relation to its environment. Feeling is merely the tone of neurally mediated behavior processes when they rise into consciousness, regardless of the cognitive quality of those processes. Its original function seems to have been to put a stop to behavior unfavorable (unpleasant) to the organism and to continue favorable (pleasant) behavior. Max Meyer has explained acceptably the neural structure back of these two tones of feeling. Pleasant feeling tone exists whenever all or practically all of the behavior and perceptual patterns of the organism are being integrated toward a single unit response or a group or chain of coöperative responses. Thus at dinner the olfactory sensations, the sight of the meal well served, the taste of the food cooked in the way we like, conversation replete with friendliness and good will, all combine to produce a pleasant mealtime. There are no conflicts. All of our behavior processes supplement one another. On the other hand, if the food is scorched, the service slovenly, and the conversation discordant, and if some one calls up over the telephone to announce bad news, our dinner is likely to be spoiled. The behavior impulses interfere with one another. There is a blocking of behavior instead of its facilitation. Consequently we may give up altogether the attempt to dine and do something else which is not thus inhibited. Thus pleasantness seems to arise in behavior which is facilitated and unpleasantness in behavior which is blocked.

Whether the feeling tone can control behavior or is itself the result of the type of response, is still a moot question. One functional fact, however, stands out clearly as a result of this explanation. The character of the feeling tone has no inherent relation to the individual welfare or the social and moral quality of the behavior. Any sort of behavior, however disastrous to the organism or to society in the long run, may be pleasant if it can be carried through without interruption. Thus the use of narcotics and gossip are generally pleasant for the time being. The increasing complexity and rapidly changing character of our environments and the growth of acquired dispositions in the adjusting organism render it impossible any longer to make wise decisions regarding our behavior wholly on the basis of our feelings, although in a simpler world where there were fewer acquired attitudes this may have been fairly possible. Farther down in the animal scale feeling is probably the only conscious criterion available except that of pain. Pain, which is a sensation, must of course be distinguished from unpleasantness, which is a feeling tone.

EMOTION is a functional type of consciousness which is frequently used interchangeably with feeling. This confusion of the two is due to the fact that emotion is the lowest form of objectivating functional consciousness, just as feeling is probably the lowest form of functional consciousness altogether. Consequently there is always a large element of feeling in emotional consciousness, especially of the simpler and more primary forms of emotion. But there is a very important distinction between the two. Feeling does not localize or objectivate the stimulus. It is entirely subjective and does not take into account the objective relation of the organism to its environment. It merely indicates an open (facilitated) or a closed (blocked) behavior disposition or set of the organism. But in emotion there are perceptions of the stimulus and there is, as a consequence, some degree of recognition in the animal of its relation to its environment. This constitutes emotion a higher type of functional consciousness for purposes of adjustment.

FORMS OF CONSCIOUSNESS 161

Composite Nature of Emotion—Psychological analysis indicates that emotion is a composite type of consciousness. It is made up on the one hand of feeling tones and on the other hand of sensations, perceptions, and conceptual organizations of perceptions. Thus in all emotions there is some degree of reference to or recognition of objects in the environment to which the organism is making adjustments and there is feeling tone arising out of this adjustment situation according as the behavior is facilitated or blocked in the organization of the stimulus response processes. There can be only two clear feeling tones, pleasantness and unpleasantness, and combinations of these. But there may be as many emotions as we have perceptions or recognitions of our adjustment relation to environment. Thus the cognitive factors are the chief differentiating elements in emotions.

The Primary Emotions—Those emotions which have strong feeling tones and relatively primitive cognitive elements, consisting of organic sensations and of the simpler perceptions we call the primary emotions. Thus in anger, love, hate, fear, etc., there is a great deal of visceral sensory consciousness and a few simple, not always very clear, perceptions of the object to which our organic (visceral and skeletal) responses have been conditioned. It is a truism, for example, that people in love do not judge the object of their affections with clearness and discrimination. Anger is said to be blind and hate unreasoning. Likewise objects of fear are nearly always greatly distorted in our perceptions, frequently looming much larger in our vision or other perceptual apprehensions than they really are. In fact, all sorts of highly emotional perceptions and judgments are largely untrustworthy because of this tendency to unclearness and distortion. We always discount the amateur fisherman's account of his catch, the new car owner's valuation of his vehicle, the Easter girl's appraisal of her "stunningness," and the newly wed housewife's characterization of her new home as "simply perfect" or "just a dream."

The Derivative Emotions—Those emotions, on the other hand, in which the cognitive element is clearly perceptual or even conceptual are much better guides to adjustment. They are derivative rather than primary emotions, and in their higher forms they are called intellectual emotions and sentiments. Sentiments are emotional attitudes toward some object which we recognize as friendly and helpful or unfriendly and harmful. Thus we have sentiments of affection for our parents, of loyalty to our friends, of patriotism towards our country, of devotion toward or faith in our religion. Likewise we speak of the sentiments of aversion, of disloyalty, of distrust, dislike, etc., in conflict situations. An intellectual emotion is one in which the cognitive element is relatively abstract and the feeling tone is the result of this intellectual adjustment to the object of our attention and not of any gross organic adjustment. Thus we experience intellectual emotions in the appreciation of literature, pictures, and music, and even in the contemplation of the work of a great scientist, reformer, or other person of genius. Enthusiasm is a term which we apply to our emotional feeling or attitude of identification of self with the efforts, aims, or idealism of the other person or a cause. Ideals are among the most intellectual phases of emotion. The central content of an ideal is a cognitive plan or organization for some sort of worthy achievement by and for ourselves or others. About this center there is organized a feeling tone content or sanction. Thus ideals come under the general classification of sentiments, but they are highly intellectualized sentiments.

COGNITION has already been referred to in our discussion in the preceding sections of this chapter. It is the objectivating aspect of our consciousness. Its bases are the sensory mechanisms previously described, which are integrated into perceptions and concepts. Thus the most elementary forms of cognitive consciousness which we can isolate are perceptions, and these are further integrated selectively into conceptual forms. We perceive objects, but we conceive types or classes of objects. In thus apprehending types or classes we may select either a concrete "typical" representative to serve as the basis of our recognition of the type, such as "Uncle Sam," or "John Bull," or "La Belle France," or we may make a composite picture, even a word picture, of the class. In fact most concepts are verbal. Statistics is one of the most accurate and most abstract methods of following the latter procedure.

Here we deal with the average or the mean. In our less orderly and mathematical thinking we do the same thing in a more general and off-hand manner by saying or thinking, "In the long run" or "In general," etc., such a thing is true or happens. Such methods of generalizing enable us to see a much wider range of facts than is possible through direct sensory perception. It also enables us to relate things at a distance in space and time with things in the present and now. The further extension of this principle of conceptualization or abstraction leads us to the generalization of formulas, principles, scientific laws, and the whole field of science itself.

Unquestionably of all of the functional organizations of consciousness the cognitive is the most important for men. In its various forms it enables them to objectivate their environments and to see themselves in adjustment relations with the environments. As a result of this insight men are able in large measure to control their environments and to make adjustments which we call progressive. In fact the whole structure of our civilization came out of the exercise of the cognitive functioning of conscious processes. We shall now consider a few of the cognitive processes which are most frequently used in making conscious adjustments to our environments or responses to definitely perceived stimuli.

Reason or the rationality processes, like feelings, imply nothing as to the nature or content of the behavior processes to which we impute rationality. It is the conscious processes of adjustment which we ordinarily think of as rational or as irrational, but even in the subconsciousness, processes analogous to the rational and conscious ones may go on with so much effectiveness that they are sometimes termed rational. Rational is merely a general term used to indicate that under the circumstances the behavior is to be expected rather than unexpected, or that the responses are the ones ordinarily and conventionally conditioned to the stimuli which we recognize as existing. Therefore, behavior may be called rational when it is "expected" behavior, whether conscious or otherwise. The function of reason can be exercised quite as well with respect to the consciousness which arises from one stimulus or ends in one response as from another stimulus or in another response. But both in overt action and in inner behavior or thinking there is no necessary correspondence between the content of the behavior, or its source or objective, and the form of the correlation of stimulus and response here emphasized. That is, anything may seem reasonable if such conduct is familiar to us, or if our responses have been effectively conditioned to the stimuli in the manner prevalent. The essence of rationality is the existence of an agreement between the actual and the expected occurrence in behavior as the result of the conditioning of responses by stimuli. If the response which is traditionally or logically associated with or conditioned by a stimulus is forthcoming in behavior we say the behavior is rational. Reason is the process of inner behavior by which we make the response, either in the overt form of action or as a verbal response, correspond in an expected way to the stimulus.

Logic as a formal discipline is the verbal statement of traditionally or otherwise expected correspondences between stimuli and responses. The tendency of logic is to reduce its statements of the expectedness of the response to standardized statements of principles and to quantitative or mathematical form. In this way logic protects itself against undue change in meaning or conditioning by accepting the established evidences of the senses and by utilizing statements of relationships both quantitative and qualitative, which have become in a measure axiomatic. Thus we have both qualitative and quantitative logic, or the logic of verbal values and principles and of formulas and equations. Logic, as distinguished from rational overt behavior, is an inner or symbolic discipline. Logic has nothing to do with the determination of the validity of the facts or conditionings of responses with which it deals. It is merely the mechanism of discovering relationships of responses conditioned to the same or related stimuli or environmental facts.

Judgment is merely the conscious process by which we summarize or otherwise state the correlation or conditioning of stimulus and response in behavior. If the conditioning is an expected or conventional one, or can be justified hypothetically on the grounds of an acceptable quantitative or qualitative ar-alysis, we term the verbal announcement of the correlation or expectedness a rational judgment or conclusion. But if it violates the accepted canons of expectancy we condemn the judgment as irrational. And here again we do not expect to find any inherent relationship between the subject matter, source, aim, or the function of the behavior under consideration and the character of the judgment. Judgment is the process of exercising the reason as described above within the limits of fact or expectancy to which we are accustomed or conditioned. It operates on the basis of accepted facts and does not seek to create new facts.

Investigation is the method by which we expand the range of our conditioned responses to environmental stimuli. Every new fact which we discover with regard to ourselves or our environment means in the last analysis a revision of our behavior or new conditionings of responses. It is in this way that we systematically reorganize our environment and revise our adjustment to it.

Invention is the highest form of cognitive consciousness. All conceptual thinking is inventive, because it is a method of projecting or conditioning new meaning through the abstract and verbal integration of old meanings. But we ordinarily apply the term invention to the integration of something more complex and frequently more tangible than ordinary conceptual thinking.

Types of Inventions—Thus we have physical inventions, as in the case of a primitive club or a modern toothpick or a Hoe printing press. There are also social inventions, such as a primitive ceremony or a modern state or system of education. Finally, there are method inventions, which consist of the concepts, principles, formulas, scientific laws, and the like, which we have already discussed. In all of these cases, overt and symbolical responses have been reconditioned in new and previously unknown combinations, with the consequence that something appears as the result of or in this new behavior which previously did not exist. The physical inventions, and to some extent the social, appear as the result of this newly conditioned or reconditioned behavior. The social inventions occur as the result of the new behavior of the inventor and in the behavior of those who act out the invention. The method invention occurs in the behavior of the inventor, especially in his inner or symbolic behavior. The method invention is a symbolic invention and its function is to assist in the making of more complex physical and social inventions.

We may distinguish two degrees of abstractness in inventions. Those inventions which appear as the result of conditioning new responses directly in the presence of concrete objective stimuli are properly called empirical inventions. That is, they appear as the relatively direct result of immediate experiences of needs for readjustment to our environment. Empirical inventions may thus be so concrete and so immediately conditioned that they are accidental. For example, the first use of a stick as a club (as an extension of the arm), or of a stone as a hammer (to give weight and hardness to the fist) was probably purely an accident. The hollowing of a log for a boat may have been at first an accident, as the result of burning, and later a purposive act in the presence of the stimulus of actual need. Empirical inventions are still made, some of them by accident, but the most important inventions for modern civilization are not empirical, even when accidental, but highly abstract and synthetic in character. The conditioning of the new responses which constitute or produce the invention in such cases is both symbolic and indirect. The inventor does not merely elaborate an old object or practice by observing that he can make an improvement in it empirically here and there in response to a pressing and immediate need.

The great modern inventions like radio transmission, printing presses, synthetic chemical products, scientific laws and systems of science, were constructed first of all verbally or symbolically. That is, the inventor conditioned his psychic responses in a complex manner to a vast number of data and as a result produced a new integration or system of data which could in turn be used as a means to much more efficient adjustment to environment. Thus the invention of a great bridge occurs first in the form of a complex integration of physical formulas all organized into a functional unity by the adjustment function which the bridge is to serve. Likewise, TNT was integrated in the form of chemical formulas before i was made in the laboratory. The bridge, which first appeared as an integration of formulas was next transformed into blue prints with specifications, and finally into a physical structure. The invention of a new school system goes through analogous processes. First there is an integration of principles and data from psychology, sociology, hygiene, etc. Next, these are transformed into a code, a formal statement, treatise, resolutions, or other written form which corresponds to the specifications and are finally put into practice by an administrative organization.

By such abstract and indirect inventive methods as these we are able to transform our environments and our adjustment to our environments both radically and rapidly. This is the supreme functional service of cognitive thinking to modern civilization.

WILL—Finally, will is not, as some have supposed, any more a directive faculty of the brain or mind than is judgment or reason. Will merely represents the final direction which a dominant impulse to behavior takes. Where there are several conflicting impulses in consciousness contending for mastery in the cortical mechanisms we are likely to be conscious of the struggle of each one. Usually each impulse presents itself to our consciousness either in such vague emotional forms as desire, or uneasiness and strain, or in the more definitely intellectual forms of what we call reason, that is, verbal consciousness of objectives which are recognized as more or less conventional expectancies of relationship between stimulus and response, or as rational. The relative claims of each set of conflicting factors is likely to be passed in more or less conscious review if the subject is self-conscious about the situation, and when finally one set of impulses becomes dominant over the others the result is looked upon as an act of conscious choice or, as we say, of will. Our consciousness of the dominant impulse is transformed into a recognition of the greater reasonableness or expediency or practicality of the behavior which finally becomes dominant and obtains overt expression, and thus we mistake the consciousness of the greater strength of this impulse for the cause of its successful issue. Such an erroneous conclusion is a method of putting the cart before the horse, as the saying is, which arises from the confusion of conscious effect with unconscious cause, one of the most common errors of the old introspective psychology.

FREE WILL—This confusion is responsible for the erroneous metaphysical doctrine of free will. This theory assumes that there is some underived entity or faculty in the personality, called will, which arbitrarily decides a course of behavior. We have just seen that such is not the case. Not even the consciousness of motivation is the cause, but it is a part of the resolution of the conflict of motivations which is taking place and is therefore itself a part of the resulting internal behavior preliminary to the final or overt stages of adjustment response. The real causes of the act lie back of the consciousness of strain or conflicting motives and impulses, partly in the observable stimuli operating through the senses, but more particularly in the neural sets and organization of the personality which have themselves been acquired and built up primarily under the influence of previous stimuli and environmental pressures. In part the personality is also the product of inheritance, as well as of environmental pressures and acquired integrations or sets of behavior. But whether the personality, as the chief cause of the behavior which our self-consciousness presents as willed, is the product of heredity or environment, it is itself "caused," and the so-called willed act is caused in a normal and perfectly natural way. There is nothing mystical or metaphysical or supernatural about will, and it is no more and no less free than any other causal event in our experience. It should also be noted that the consciousness of will in ourselves appears only in connection with self-consciousness and is closely coördinate with this phase of personality.

DEGREES OF EASE OF THE APPREHENSION OF TYPES OF BEHAVIOR—Professor Ross has pointed out an important distinction with reference to the differences of ease with which we apprehend different phases of the behavior of others. We grasp the meaning of action or overt behavior by others with the greatest facility and we understand the significance of their expression of emotions with the next greatest ease, while their ideas are much more difficult to apprehend than either of the other two types of behavior. The reasons for these differences

FORMS OF CONSCIOUSNESS 169

in ease of apprehension are easy to understand. We perceive best what comes most directly within the range of our senses. Overt behavior in others is immediately and clearly within the range of the sense of sight, and to some extent also of hearing. While the emotions are deep seated within the consciousness, and therefore not directly perceptible by the senses, they nevertheless have their overt or symbolic expression aspects, which are easily seen by the eye or heard by the ear, or in other ways detected, as in some cases by odor.

Ideas, on the other hand, can with difficulty be detected by viewing the surface expression of the thinker. There are no instinctive, or very definitely standardized acquired, organic expression symbols for ideas. Those ideas that go over into overt behavior may be inferred from that behavior, but it is never possible for the observer to judge whether all of the idea content has become overt in behavior. Ideas must be communicated primarily by means of words, which are more abstract than other language symbols. Consequently it is more difficult for one's responses to be successfully conditioned to ideas, expressed through concepts and even formulas and principles, than it is for them to be conditioned to emotional and overt behavior symbols.

The significance of these facts regarding the relative ease of communicating these three forms of behavior for psycho-social organization and control is very great. It explains why fiction is more interesting and more often read than books of abstract facts, and why books of travel or adventure appeal more than books of science. It also serves to indicate the reason why superficial social contacts, or "social life," so-called, appeal more to the young, and frequently to those advanced in years, than do the more sober and intellectual contacts. The sentimental nearly always have the edge on the intellectual, a fact which is partly to be explained by the greater power of the organic drives as contrasted with the acquired intellectual ones, as well as on the grounds of difference in ease of perception. The chief themes in literature, on the stage (including the movies), and in life, are sex, fear, and successful action in the pursuit of an end. Here strong organic drives and training combine with ease of perception to make these themes dominant in our interests. Love and melodrama, or in cheaper stage performances just sex display and the exhibition of motion (dancing and gymnastics), hold the boards. Usually, by common consent, a more or less moralized population will insist that these themes be sublimated and somewhat conventionalized, but in an age like ours, where there is a strong reaction towards primitive frankness and the deification of the natural impulses in behavior, even this phase of idealism is largely dispensed with.

WHY PROGRESS IS DIFFICULT—Consequently, it is always difficult to carry forward the task of civilization. Social progress demands that we rise above our crude primitive impulses, our instincts, and lower traditional values, and make our adjustments on the basis of abstract values or ideas. The great moral and social values of our civilization are abstract and can be carried only through abstract verbal communication. We can perceive them in others and imitate them into our own behavior only through this abstract verbal process of communication. The lower values, often anti-social in our acquired civilization, are however much more easily communicated, because they can be expressed in relatively simple and easily understood overt behavior and emotional symbolism. Our lower selves and the lower social values are therefore at a great advantage in their competition with our higher selves and the higher intellectual and moral values. Consequently progress is uphill work and we are never quite certain that civilization can continue to maintain its lead over savagery and barbarism. Without the aid of numerous institutional organizations, such as education and religion and government, which are devoted to the support of the higher intellectual and moral values, we should most probably sink back quickly into a lower order of culture. This eternal struggle between the higher and lower values in man's own personality and in his culture has been symbolized dramatically in the theological tradition and dogma of the struggle between the powers of evil and of good, or darkness and of light, as portrayed in the great moral epics of practically all lands and peoples of a fair degree of culture dealing with the fall and the ascent of man.

MATERIALS FOR SUPPLEMENTARY READING

Allport, F. H., *Social Psychology,* Ch. IV
Baldwin, J. M., *Social and Ethical Interpretations,* Ch. VIII
Bernard, L. L., *Instinct: A Study in Social Psychology,* Chs. XVIII, XIX
——, "Invention and Social Progress," *Amer. Jour. Sociol.,* XXIX: 1-33
Bogardus, E. S., *Fundamentals of Social Psychology,* Ch. II
Dewey, J., *How We Think*
——, *Human Nature and Conduct,* Part II, Sec. II, Part III, Secs. II-IV
Edman, I., *Human Traits and Their Significance,* Ch. III
Ellwood, C. A., *The Psychology of Human Society,* Ch. VII
Herrick, C. J., *An Introduction to Neurology* (2d ed.), Ch. XVIII
Köhler, W., *The Mentality of Apes,* Chs. I-VI, VIII
McDougall, W., *An Introduction to Social Psychology,* Chs. V, VI, IX
Miller, I. E., *The Psychology of Thinking*
Ross, E. A., *Principles of Sociology,* Chs. XXIII, XXIV, LIV
Stern, W., *Psychology of Early Childhood,* Parts IV, V, VII, VIII
Wallas, G., *The Great Society,* Chs. VII, X, XI-XIII
Watson, J. B., *Psychology from the Standpoint of a Behaviorist,* Ch. VI
Woodworth, R. S., *Psychology, a Study of Mental Life,* Chs. VII, IX, XVII-XX

CHAPTER XII

THE FUNCTIONAL ORGANIZATION OF CONSCIOUSNESS—THE OBJECTS OF CONSCIOUSNESS

CLASSIFICATION—Professor Cooley has spoken of three types of consciousness—self, social, and public. We shall use these same categories, with others, but vary the application somewhat, keeping in mind the fact that consciousness is always subjective, and that even social consciousness and public consciousness are the consciousness experienced by individuals with reference to others and to the public as a whole, and not consciousness experienced by a group or by a public. The objects of consciousness may be classified in outline as follows:

I. Self-consciousness.
　1. Of the organic and overt behavior selves.
　2. Of the inner (symbolical or attitudinal) self.
II. Physical Consciousness.
　1. Of self to physical objects—the sensory qualities of physical objects.
　2. Of physical objects to other physical objects—the data of the sciences of physics, chemistry, and perhaps biology.
III. Social Consciousness.
　1. Of the relation of self to others.
　2. Of the relation of others to others.
IV. Public Consciousness.
　1. The normative relation of self to others.
　2. The normative relation of others to others, or the objective problem of what our social organization should be.
V. Collective Consciousness.
　1. Non-normative collective attitudes, etc.
　2. Public opinion, or normative collective attitudes.

OBJECTS OF CONSCIOUSNESS

The Forms of the Classification—The general analysis and classification of the environments have already been presented in a previous chapter. Also, the general analysis of personality begun in the discussion of behavior patterns will be continued in the following four chapters. These two fields of data are basic to all social science and in the subsequent divisions of this book we shall elaborate and apply those aspects which are foundational to social psychology. The significance of physical consciousness for social psychology is slight and mainly indirect, although it is greater for some of the other social sciences. The data of social psychology fall primarily within the field of social consciousness. Hence the expansion of this category into two main subsidiary classifications, public and collective consciousness. In most of the classifications of the objective types of consciousness one phase of the consciousness has been stated as that of the relationship of self to the external objects involved. The other form of consciousness is that of the relation of the objects, persons, groups, institutions, and other phenomena to one another.

This is because it is possible to approach the study of these more objective and abstract relationships only by means of first studying our perceptual and conceptual relations or responses to them. As was said above, self-consciousness and social consciousness develop out of the necessity we are under of distinguishing for control purposes our own organism from its environment. Likewise we find it necessary to separate our environments into various units and relationships, a process which we begin when we learn to distinguish self from various more or less separate units in our environment. The term "others" in this classification of course includes not only individuals but all types of organizations of individuals and extensions and elaborations of personalities. Although our physical and social relationships begin in very concrete forms they may become very abstract and those physical and social relationships which are wholly objective or external to us may become particularly abstract to our consciousness, especially when they are apprehended only through symbols.

The forms of public consciousness are merely the more normative aspects of general social consciousness. Collective consciousness is not, like the other aspects of social consciousness, the consciousness of one, but of many individuals, with reference to the same or related phenomena. It is what is sometimes called the social mind and an important phase of it is public opinion.

SELF-CONSCIOUSNESS is what the individual perceives or thinks regarding himself. It is his method of seeing himself as an object, of perceiving himself as a behavior unit reacting upon other similar units and groups of behavior units. In its lower and simpler forms it is primarily the consciousness arising from contact with parts of his own body as stimuli sources as distinguished from that which arises from the stimulation of external objects. Thus the child learns to outline himself in regard to form, size, and weight by getting different tactual and kinesthetic experiences when he manipulates his own body or parts or extensions of it from those he experiences when he manipulates objects which are not attached to it.

The main sensory distinctions which enable the child to differentiate his organism from other objects in his immediate environment are the kinesthetic and those arising from pain, heat and cold, touch, and somewhat later from sight and hearing organs. He soon makes a distinction between the double sensations he gets from his own body and the single sensory experiences he receives from other objects. Also the associations which he makes between the consciousness of intention in performing an act and the response of parts of his body to that will or intention are of a different sort from the associations which arise when objects not a part of his body respond to his intentions. The latter response requires an intermediate action of some part of his own body, such as manipulation by the hands or feet, while the former is executed directly through the nervous system without the use of intermediate or supplementary overt behavior controls.

The child, of course, has no such understanding as this of the philosophy of the development of his consciousness of his organic and overt behavior self. Neither, for that matter, have most adults. But it is in some such way as this that the child comes in time to recognize the parts of his body as different from those objects which are not parts of his own organism.

OBJECTS OF CONSCIOUSNESS

The different parts of the organic self or organism are correlated in his consciousness through the association of simultaneous and coördinate responses of the different parts of the organism. Thus he comes to integrate as a single unit this correlated consciousness of self, and self-consciousness in the large appears.

The sensory and perceptual self-consciousness of the child is not, of course, equally vivid with respect to all parts of his organism. He is not at first aware of any of the internal mechanisms which enable him to live and to make adjustments to his environment. Ordinarily he learns of these, not through sensory experiences in connection with his own body, but through the descriptions of observations made on the bodies of other persons conveyed to him verbally or pictorially. This extension of the range of organic and overt behavior self-consciousness to include the inner parts of the organism also comes at a much later period than that involving the more external parts of the body which are perceived through direct sensory observation. Since the internal mechanisms and structures are apprehended by most of us indirectly through verbal and photographic media, rather than directly through the sensory mechanisms, this type of knowledge of self might perhaps better be called self-awareness than self-consciousness, strictly speaking. Even the external parts of the body are not all perceived with equal completeness and clearness of definition. Those parts which are most active in making the adjustment to environment, such as the hands and feet, and the face, in case the child is taught to make his toilet before a mirror, are most clearly defined in the sensory and perceptual self-consciousness. The rear parts of the body may be included consciously as a part of the self much later than the front parts, because they cannot easily be seen, even with the aid of a mirror. They can, of course, be felt. Consequently they are never wholly absent from the child's corporate feeling of self. The story is told of a boy who never could be taught to comb the back part of his head until he had been shown a reflection of it in a mirror. Until then it was not sufficiently a factor in his self-consciousness to secure attention along with other parts of his organism.

EXTENSION OF SELF-CONSCIOUSNESS TO EXTERNAL OBJECTS—The consciousness or awareness of self on the sensory and perceptual plane very early extends beyond the consciousness of the bare body to include those objects which are closely associated with the body, although the child, like the adult, distinguishes between his body self and his accessory or possessions self, which might also be called his secondary organic self. Of all external objects, his clothes and other ornaments partake most intimately of his self-conscious sensory and perceptual self. He thinks of himself only in connection with his clothes and his playthings and the ornaments he wears. If these should be removed after he has become thoroughly adjusted or conditioned to them there would be so great a disturbance of the functioning of the consciousness of self that his adjustments to his environment would be greatly altered and, in some cases even, effectively disintegrated. This inclusion of dress and other intimate possessions in the consciousness of self is equally, possibly more, characteristic of older people than of children. It extends even beyond merely immediate possessions to other persons who have relatively permanent and important relationships with us, and to all sorts of contacts which we make with our environment. The phrase "I am a part of all I have met," might well be transformed for our purposes into, "All things I have met are a part of me." Of course the more distant the external objects or the less frequent or intense our contacts with them, the less, other things being equal, they are a part of us. The very way in which we wear our clothes or ornaments, or the manner in which we care for our bodies or arrange our hair, even, enters into the composition of our perceptual self-consciousness.

ATTITUDINAL OR INNER SELF-CONSCIOUSNESS is that which develops in delayed adjustment situations. It is under such conditions of delayed response that we develop attitudes instead of acting immediately and overtly. These attitudes are conditioned closely to our language symbols or partial and substitute overt responses which, as we saw in Chapter X, appear in delayed adjustment situations. The content of this attitudinal self-consciousness is very large and diverse in a complexly organized society, because it represents our striving for adjust ment to this environment. Consequently it consists of feelings, emotions, judgments, valuations of all sorts. These will be discussed in considerable detail in this and the following chapters in so far as they have significance for communication and social contacts. Even the various forms of social consciousness are made up largely of attitudinal self-consciousness. An important aspect of self-consciousness is the self we see reflected in the attitudes of others toward us, or, as Cooley calls it, the looking glass self.

SOCIAL CONSCIOUSNESS, we are told by Professor Cooley and others, grows up as the other pole of self-consciousness. Both self and social consciousness develop in social situations and they are merely complementary aspects of the same process by which the individual gains at the same time a functional definition of himself and makes an analysis and synthesis of his environment which enables him as a personality to adjust himself to it or to mold it to himself. Both self and social consciousness arise out of the process by which the organism finds its relationship to the rest of the world. Consciousness is an internal behavior process for defining objects, including self and others as well as things. It functions as an aid to the control of relationships and to the organization of these into larger projective wholes. It also helps to split up improperly functioning units of behavior into manageable elements and to rearrange them in more adequately functioning systems. Self and social consciousness arise together out of this process of definition and adjustment, and they differ primarily according to whether self or others and public relationships are the major objects of definition and conscious adjustment control. But even this distinction is not absolute.

TWO PHASES OF SOCIAL CONSCIOUSNESS—Social consciousness, like self-consciousness, has two aspects. In the simpler and more concrete of these two forms, the consciousness is directed toward the relation of self to others or of others to self. In the more abstract form of social consciousness the attention is upon the relationship of others to others. It is this first form of social consciousness which has the closest relationships with self-consciousness, especially with the second type of self-consciousness. It is in fact not always easy to distinguish social consciousness on this plane from self-consciousness with a definite adjustment reference. The chief basis of distinction, however, lies here as elsewhere in the determination of the direction or of the object of consciousness. If attention is focussed primarily upon the self in considering the relationship between others and self we may speak of the type of consciousness as self-consciousness, although social consciousness is involved. But if the attention is primarily upon the other person or persons or relationship we may usually consider our understanding or appreciation of the relationship to be social consciousness, although clearly self-consciousness as well as social consciousness is involved in such a case.

Social consciousness in the other sense, however, of our awareness of relationships between two or more people or groups, in which we do not directly participate, does not necessarily involve self-consciousness in any immediate sense at all. It is, indeed, true that we cannot become aware of these purely objective relationships in any but the most superficial sense except by a process of more or less consciously putting ourselves in the places of the other persons who are experiencing the relationship. We are able to interpret their words or gestures or other forms of behavior only in the degree to which we have engaged in the same or similar behavior and have developed definite forms or contents of self-consciousness in performing such behavior. We interpret the meaning of such objective forms of social conduct only by means of projecting our own behavior or experiences into the other persons who are now behaving more or less as we have done. When, for instance, one small boy observes two other small boys in certain characteristic relations with each other and declares they are fighting, or playing a game, perhaps himself becomes highly excited about their behavior and wishes to participate in their activities, he is able to get the meaning of their behavior and experience the emotional impulse to participate only because he has previously had the same experience or similar experiences. If he had not had similar experiences their behavior would be no more significant to him emotionally or intellectually than the activities of two very complicated machines. In fact the thing which renders his con

OBJECTS OF CONSCIOUSNESS 179

sciousness of the behavior of the other boys' behavior social instead of merely physical is the fact that he can interpret their behavior in terms of his own previous behavior, overt and internal or emotional and intellectual.

UNDERSTANDING THE WORLD AT A DISTANCE—Since we cannot actually perceive through our senses more than a very small fraction of this second or objective type of social behavior, our fullest awareness of it depends primarily upon the use of language symbols, by which it is conveyed to us through newspapers, books, conversation, radio, and upon picture symbols, such as photographs, paintings, sculpture, movie films, etc., which present the objective forms of social behavior in less abstract forms directly to our eyes. The degree of our familiarity with such symbols for communicating objective behavior will determine in large measure the extent to which we are able to be in contact with the external social world. Such contacts, especially those which employ verbal language symbols, are decidedly abstract and could function only in a highly developed cultural civilization. We are able through the use of pictures and printed descriptions to come in contact with the most remote areas of social contacts and—in so far as we are able to assimilate their behavior to our own experiences— to become cognizant of the significance and meaning of these relationships even in the most dissimilar types of cultures. In this way we gradually acquire the power of viewing ever wider reaches of the world of social behavior. Early peoples were confined in their understanding of the social world very largely to those relationships which were typical of their own groups. They lacked a knowledge of other languages through which they could understand the cultures carried by those languages, and they had no books to describe alien practices. They lacked almost wholly the comparative outlook or viewpoint. But gradually, with the development of verbal symbols to condition their perceptions and aid in interpretation, we have pushed out the borders of our intellectual and social worlds beyond the merely political ones. And even now the world as a whole is becoming, through our increased powers of understanding and interpretation, in large measure a social unity.

PUBLIC CONSCIOUSNESS is, of course, a phase of social consciousness. It is to be distinguished from ordinary social consciousness in that it is the normative aspect of the latter, that is, the abstract evaluative phase of the consciousness of the relationship of individuals and groups in society. It may appear to some that it is superfluous to distinguish public consciousness from social consciousness. The only justification for doing so is that most social consciousness is descriptive rather than evaluative and normative. The larger part of our consciousness of our relations to others and of our awareness of the relations of others to others consists merely of perceptions or conceptualizations of the facts of such relationships. We view the social world largely as a passing show, not particularly concerning ourselves about whether it should be different or how it could be changed. If we develop some interest in the possibility and the desirability of a different social order as a whole—which is rarely the case with most people—or in the desirability of changing some particular situation which impinges particularly upon ourselves, this interest is in most cases quite superficial and fleeting. Most of our contacts with the social world are either routine occupational contacts or those of amusement seeking. We are ordinarily more receptive or passive in both of these than we are active with the intention of producing change, especially far-reaching public changes. The concern of most people in the public social order and in the public welfare is decidedly limited in comprehensiveness and in persistence, as well as in depth of understanding and analysis. Therefore, for the sake of emphasizing a phase of evaluative consciousness which should become more effective with the development of the social sciences and more persistent with the increasing habit of analysis of our social environment and institutions, it seems wise to segregate the normative aspect of social consciousness and to establish for it a new category as public consciousness.

Two Aspects of Public Consciousness—In public consciousness also we discover two phases. In one of these we find that self-consciousness plays a considerable part and in the other we have mainly a detached or objectified consciousness of social relationships. In other words, the two phases of public consciousness correspond to the two phases of social consciousness, and they include the relations of self to others and of others to others. The former type of public consciousness is involved when the concern is with reference to the obligations of self to society or to other individuals in a social situation, or of their obligations to us as a phase of the proper functioning of the social system. In this phase of public consciousness, self-consciousness looms large and is sometimes in the ascendancy over public consciousness itself. This is a much more concrete phase of public consciousness than the other, which deals with obligations of the members and organizations of society in the abstract. But it can never be as concrete as non-normative social consciousness of this same general phase, because even the most concrete and trivial aspects of our relations to each other, such as occur in connection with ephemeral pleasure functions, social entertainments, etc., are included in non-normative social consciousness of the first type, while in public consciousness of the first type there must always be an abstract aspect because of the fact that the question of what should be is always an issue. This question cannot be raised in any fundamental sense except on the basis of abstract values and value concepts.

Public consciousness of the second type involves the highest degree of abstractions. It calls for the abstract formulas of social sciences, and likewise of all the antecedent sciences, as a means to measuring the degrees and kinds of responsibilities and obligations of individuals and organizations in society. In its perfected form it makes the most extensive possible use of abstract storage symbols and of the experience of the race and the results of experiments and refined observations of a mathematico-statistical sort in order to establish norms of measurement of obligations and relationships.

ILLUSTRATIONS OF THE OPERATION OF SOME PHASES OF FUNCTIONAL CONSCIOUSNESS—*Self-consciousness*—Illustrations of the first type of self-consciousness in literature are to be found in accounts of emotional experiences in viewing nature, or in undergoing hardships in travel or on other expeditions, or in accounts of one's adventures with wild animals, experiences with foods, housing conditions, accommodations in hotels, the organic contacts of friendship, love-making, fighting, etc., when the narration is in the first person. Inevitably in such narratives there will be intermingled also the more abstract aspects of self-consciousness, as well as phases of social consciousness, and possibly of public or normative social consciousness also. Such a book as *Robinson Crusoe* contains much material of the character of the first aspect of self-consciousness, and also much of the second aspect.

Such autobiographies as those of Herbert Spencer or Charles Darwin, or *The Education of Henry Adams,* serve well to illustrate the second aspect of self-consciousness. Men of great intelligence and of wide philosophic interests who write their own lives are likely to devote a minimum of space to the sensory and perceptual aspects of self, particularly of the organic and overt behavior self, and are certain to give considerable attention to the abstract and conceptual relationships of self to the environment, including or emphasizing such relationships with others. They live ordinarily in a world of ideas more than in a world of things, and their contacts with others are primarily on the basis of abstract idea values rather than on the more concrete basis of things. Consequently their accounts of themselves are couched mainly in terms of the former rather than of the latter.

Examples of social consciousness in literature are numerous. All narratives in the first person, recording conversations and other behavior between the narrator and other persons, either in fiction or in factual writing, illustrate social consciousness of the first type, as well as self-consciousness. In most such writing the social consciousness is probably dominant over self-consciousness, although the latter is always in the background as a basis of interpretation. Examples of the second type of non-normative social consciousness are to be found in the great mass of fiction writing which records supposed conversations and other contacts between characters of the story. Much of the news of newspapers is of this type, although it frequently extends over into some degree and quality of public consciousness. Also travel books, histories, descriptions of primitive peoples, including most of the content of anthropology, and a large part of the subject matter of geography represent more serious, and possibly more accurately descriptive, phases of the second type of social consciousness. Sometimes this material in the descriptive social sciences becomes highly abstract, and not infrequently it is material for social consciousness rather than an account of social consciousness as such.

Public consciousness finds its best illustrations in the treatises on ethics and on political, economic, and social institutions and organizations, although it is also to be found in orations on public questions, in sermons, in newspaper editorials, in special articles and sometimes in the news itself. It also occurs in all types of serious magazines and periodicals, in public lectures, in the propaganda literature of public welfare organizations and agencies. Here also it is necessary to distinguish between public consciousness and material for public consciousness, because most of the content of such books and articles is stated impersonally rather than conversationally and is objectified into storage categories and symbolic meaning complexes. In such cases it is not only the objectified public consciousness of the author and of those who have read his book approvingly, but it is also material for the public consciousness of many more who may read it in the future. This is especially true of the content of text books in the social sciences dealing with the problems of public policy rather than with the descriptive facts of social organization and contacts.

PUBLIC OPINION AND COLLECTIVE CONSCIOUSNESS—Public opinion is sometimes confused with public consciousness. Such a confusion, however, is unjustifiable, although there is a strong functional relationship between the two. Public consciousness is always the consciousness of an individual with regard to public relationships, while public opinion is the normative aspect of collective consciousness, more or less clearly defined, with regard to any type of objects whatever. Consequently the consciousness content of public opinion may concern itself with the collective aspect of any of the several types of either self-consciousness, social consciousness, or public consciousness, or it may even be a normative collective manifestation of consciousness directed toward non-personal and non-social objects. The essential characteristic of public opinion is that it shall be collective and normative, that is, that a number of individuals in the same group shall think or act as if they thought the same or closely similar or complementary things. It matters very little what they think as long as they think it together and with conviction. It is opinion, not merely non-normative consciousness. Collective consciousness itself refers merely to any consciousness whatever of the members of a group or public provided it possesses some degree of unity or organization. It may be normative (public opinion) or non-normative. Its content may be either self, social, or public consciousness, or even physical consciousness (the consciousness of physical objects).

GRADES AND QUALITIES OF PUBLIC OPINION—There are of course grades and qualities in public opinion, and the highest type from the standpoint of its influence on public policy is that which is constituted primarily of public consciousness. Most writers on social psychology apparently have this type of consciousness content of public opinion in mind when they discuss the nature of public opinion, and this fact probably accounts for the frequent confusion of the two categories. A public opinion constituted of self-consciousness is the rarest form of collective consciousness, rarer even than a public opinion directed towards physical or other non-human objects, but it exists. Groups of very similar individuals of an egotistical bent may come together in a mutual admiration society, exchanging compliments and agreeing on mutual worth, where the primary purpose of each participant individual is to enhance his own self-feeling, even at the expense of exchanging felicitations with others. Groups engaged in mutual condolence and groups of worshipers intent upon saving their own souls may also come under this category. Many social gatherings, as well as art and discussion clubs, have much of this character, and perhaps almost all associations have something of this element in them. Collective consciousness of the non-normative type, however, may have a considerable element of self-consciousness content in it. This fact may be illustrated by the everyday gossip of people which largely centers around the personalities of the gossipers' selves in relation to others. Non-normative social consciousness frequently enters into collective consciousness. Most of the daily news of the newspaper fairly represents this type. But when social consciousness becomes public opinion in passing into the category of collective consciousness, it also becomes public consciousness. There can be no public opinion made up of social consciousness of the non-normative kind, because public opinion is the normative aspect of collective consciousness and the normative aspect of social consciousness is public consciousness. The term public opinion has a suggestion of the normative in it which does much to justify superficially the confusion which is so often to be found between public opinion and public consciousness.

It must not be supposed that the content of public opinion, as distinguished from collective consciousness in general, is limited wholly to public consciousness although it is predominantly of such character. Public opinion, as distinguished from less attitudinal and less normative collective consciousness, can exist with reference to other objects than the public. There can be convictions collectively held regarding a theory of light or of evolution, quite as well as toward a theory of the classification of races or the nature of the mentality of the members of any particular race, or regarding the proper policy of dealing with alien races or immigrant peoples, for example. The term collective consciousness is, as before said, inclusive of that of public opinion. The two are not mutually exclusive, but the latter bears much the same relation to the former as the term public consciousness bears to that of social consciousness. The application and organization of these categories will be discussed in subsequent chapters.

MATERIALS FOR SUPPLEMENTARY READING

Allport, F. H., *Social Psychology,* Ch. XIII
Baldwin, J. M., *Social and Ethical Interpretations,* Ch. I
Burnham, W. H., *The Normal Mind,* Ch. II
Bogardus, E. S., *Fundamentals of Social Psychology,* Ch. III
Cooley, C. H., *Human Nature and the Social Order,* Chs. III-VI
——, *Social Organization,* Chs. I, II, XII, XIII
——, *Social Process,* Ch. XXXI
Dewey, J., *Human Nature and Conduct,* Part III, Sections VI, VIII
Edman, I., *Human Traits and Their Significance,* Ch. XI
Gault, R. H., *Social Psychology,* Ch. II

Giddings, F. H., *The Principles of Sociology,* Part II, Ch. II
Ginsberg, M., *The Psychology of Society,* Chs. IV, V
Groves, E. R., *Personality and Social Adjustment,* Ch. IX
Judd, C. H., *Psychology,* Ch. XIII
McDougall, W., *An Introduction to Social Psychology,* Chs. VII, VIII
Ross, E. A., *Social Psychology,* Ch. VIII
Stern, W., *Psychology of Early Childhood,* Ch. XXXIV

CHAPTER XIII

PATHOLOGICAL FORMS OF CONSCIOUSNESS

THE UNCONSCIOUS—The older writers on psychology, even until nearly the end of the nineteenth century, spoke and wrote of all human behavior as if it were highly conscious and the product of an active and self-conscious will. Recent analyses of behavior have shown us that such a view is erroneous. The studies made by the social psychologists of the group and suggestion-imitation schools, and the investigations of the French students of hysteria and hypnotism, and more recently the work of the psychoanalysts, have done most to dispense with an overintellectualistic interpretation of behavior. These and other studies have shown us that stimulus-response processes occur and that complete and apparently logical sequences of behavior are carried through in individuals without their having retained any conscious memory of the things they did. This unconscious behavior may be very complicated and long continued, or it may constitute only parts or fragments of a continuous series of behavior processes which is in the main definitely conscious and is later subject to recall. Every one has had the experience of going some place and arriving without remembering the process of getting there. Old and familiar landmarks evidently gave our unconsciousness the cue and we proceeded "mechanically," as we say, while our focally conscious processes were occupied with something else. The arrival at our destination stopped the mechanical process by making it necessary for us to orient ourselves anew to other objects. Other instances are the reading of a page of a book without understanding it, doing the housework or driving a car on a quiet street, or running the fingers through the hair while conversing with a friend or thinking about something else quite different from what he is saying.

What is it that takes care of our behavior in this mechanical way when our attention, at least our focally conscious attention, is elsewhere? It has been variously called the unconscious, the subconscious, the co-conscious, the peripheral and the subliminal consciousness by different writers. Any one of these terms would perhaps be reasonably adequate for our needs, for all of them mean much the same thing. Each term is accepted by some one of standing in the field of psychology and each is equally condemned on some ground or other. The two terms which have the greatest currency at the present time are the subconscious and the unconscious. The latter is perhaps the more inclusive term, because it embraces all behavior which does not come into focal consciousness. The former term, however, applies only to that behavior which, although definitely mediated by neural mechanisms of the higher brain centers, is kept out of focal consciousness by some method of displacement, as in the case of habits which have become practically automatic, or by means of the "censorship" emphasized by the psychoanalysts.

There are those, of course, who deny that there is any such thing as an unconscious psychic process, although they probably would not deny the existence of unconscious behavior. Wohlgemuth, for example, defines the psychic process as a conscious process and then proceeds to show that it is impossible for a conscious process to be unconscious. Many neuropsychic mechanisms, however, are not conscious, and many others which are but dimly conscious are not focally conscious. These latter, or non-focal conscious neuro-psychic processes, do not become focal in the attention. They are, consequently, to all intents and purposes unconscious processes and are usually classified as such. Later on one may with effort occasionally bring such a dimly conscious process of behavior into focal consciousness through memory recall by means of introspection, showing that it really was in consciousness or at least in the neuro-psychic organization, although at the time not in the focus of attention. It is of course possible that all unconscious neuro-psychic behavior processes are really of this dimly conscious or non-focal character. Without quarreling over these distinctions we may adopt the usual terminology for

PATHOLOGICAL BEHAVIOR

behavior which does not occupy the attention and pass briefly in review the various types of unconscious and subconscious behavior and estimate their significance for the adjustment of the organism to its social or other environments.

TYPES OF UNCONSCIOUS BEHAVIOR—Reflexes and instincts, of course, belong in the category of unconscious behavior. The neural processes involved operate mainly at sub-cortical levels and are fixed in the organic mechanisms before birth, and apparently are determined by the hereditary character of the protoplasm. They come into consciousness only through their transformation or modification into habit patterns which are controlled through cortical extensions. They have vast significance for both individual and social behavior; but this significance is greatest for a relatively fixed adjustment to environmental conditions which have persisted in pretty much the same form from very early, perhaps in most cases from pre-human, times. Consequently they are of minor significance for adjustments to recent and strictly social types of environments, in some cases even antagonistic to them. The instincts and other inherited unconscious behavior mechanisms do not adjust us to the psycho-social or the institutionalized derivative control environments, because these environments are constantly changing.

Initial adjustments to a definitely new type of social environment, or even to a natural environment, are usually conscious. The radically different type of behavior required for such an adjustment brings the neural mechanisms under cortical supervision. But not all new environmental situations are radically different from the old. They usually have much of their content in common with the old, or they operate in closely analogous ways. Consequently, many acquired behavior patterns, developed in adjustment to new environmental situations, apparently come into existence with a minimum of consciousness. Only when the new situation is sufficiently different from the old that we *recognize* it as new may it be said that the new behavior pattern is adopted consciously. In many other cases we make an adjustment to a new or a partially new situation consciously, and after it has become standardized and relatively automatic it drops out of consciousness or becomes a part of the *unconscious* in behavior. A very large amount, perhaps the larger portion, of our behavior in definitely social situations, that is, in adjustment to the psycho-social and derivative control environments, is of this character. Consequently this phase of the unconscious is of great importance socially. It enables the higher (conscious or cortical) types of behavior control to initiate an adjustment to the changing and maturing environment and then to pass it on to the supervision of a lower (unconscious) type of adjustment control.

REPRESSION—Another form of the unconscious or of the subconsciousness is that sometimes called repression. Repressed consciousness is unlike the instinctive behavior which fails to rise into consciousness or that in which the modification of the old behavior is so slight that it never quite enters into the focus of attention. Also it is unlike the habitual behavior which recedes from conscious attention as soon as the neural mechanism has been reduced to an economical and automatic pattern. The inner mechanism of this type of behavior is on a conscious level, but because it disturbs the functional organization of our dominant consciousness or behavior we refuse to admit it to the focus of attention. Usually we prevent the repressed inner behavior mechanisms from going over into overt behavior. But if this cannot be done we are likely to forget this behavior or to minimize its importance, just as we exclude or attempt to exclude from our consciousness the desire for such behavior. The neurological explanation of this exclusion or censorship of the unwelcome or unpleasant from consciousness and overt behavior, or at least from memory, is apparently that blocking of behavior processes which earlier we found accompanies, or causes, unpleasant feeling tones in consciousness. The unpleasant behavior is unsuccessful behavior or that behavior which occurs with difficulty. It is not the unpleasantness which blocks or censors it, as popular language has it, but the blocking or conflict itself causes the unpleasantness, and likewise puts a stop to the behavior itself, either as it occurs in the first instance or as it seeks to reproduce itself in memory. Behavior which was not originally unpleasant may easily become so in the recall because its unpleasant consequences or associations may become much more patent as increasing perspective allows of more comparison of behavior values. As a consequence it sometimes occurs that the memory of an act may be blocked when the act itself was facilitated and pleasant.

THE SO-CALLED CENSORSHIP—In the words of the psychoanalysts, however, our dominant consciousness censors the idea or desire and the memory of the deed, if it occurs. This phraseology, although in common use, is merely an anthropomorphism based upon the old metaphysics of a free will. The explanation must be made in neurological and behavioristic instead of in fiatistic terms. This so-called censorship or refusal of our dominant conscious organization to attend to the variant or interrupting consciousness may be so complete and successful that the dominantly conscious self does not recognize the existence of the unassimilated behavior impulses and processes. Not infrequently it requires the artificial synthesis of hypnosis or psychoanalysis to bring the two phases of conscious behavior within the purview of each other.

Instances of this sort are familiar enough. We forget the names of people we dislike or that dislike us. We do not remember without an effort, if at all, circumstances or events in which we have appeared to a disadvantage. And if we do suddenly come upon such an event in the random exercise of our memories we meet it with a start and dismiss it from consciousness as soon as we are able. For most of us, our memories represent a fairly consistent selection of those events which enhance our positive self-feeling and encourage us to further attempts at successful adjustment. The mistakes and discreditable events are crowded out or minimized or explained away for the sake of the picture, which we make as nearly perfect as possible.

RATIONALIZATION—This process of building up an ideal reconstruction of past behavior we call rationalization. If our memories are not thus selective it is an indication that there is something pathological or ineffective in our personalities and in their power to make future adjustments. Our lives may have mistakes, but there is no reason why our ideals of ourselves—which project into the past as well as into the future—should be defective. They may be as completely rounded out and as perfect as we choose to make them. And if we are not mere sentimentalists, that is, desirers instead of doers, if we actually try to put our rationalized ideals of self into practice and face the difficulties of adjustment instead of taking refuge in daydreams or phantasy regarding self, the more perfect the ideals the better for our conduct. Thus rationalization, which is capable of being a potent instrument of self-deception, may also be a great aid to a constructive orientation of character. It is destructive to any one's morale to see himself in the worst possible light, except for temporary therapeutic purposes, which in religious terminology we characterize as repentance or remorse. But, also in religious terminology, repentance should lead to conversion or the determination to behave differently.

DISTORTION OF VIEWS OF PERSONALITIES AND NATIONALITIES—The same sort of selective and idealizing process which we apply to ourselves we also apply to others who command our favor. Thus our chosen heroes of history are gradually stripped of their unworthy or anti-social qualities and of their inadequacies of character and achievement, and in place of these imperfections we clothe them in a selection of those qualities which we approve. In early times, before the more accurate written records of history had supplanted easily molded and distorted traditions, the great men were deified by this process of creating a folk tradition about their characters and achievements. Now that the written records prevent us from manufacturing history to suit our desires we merely select and gild those events in the lives of our heroes which are most pleasing to us. However, myth-making is not entirely dead even in our day, as stories similar to that of Washington and the cherry tree will bear witness.

What we do in this positive way of creating good characters for ourselves and others we also accomplish in a negative manner by creating disreputable personalities for those of whom history has disapproved. Having set the adverse folk evaluation upon them we fail to recall their good qualities until they may actually be lost to record. We create as much of a devil in the one case as of a saint or hero in the other.

Sometimes we apply these two processes of selection o

traits to whole nations. This occurs more frequently, or at least with greater emphasis, in war time, when we conceive of the allied peoples as generous and brave and as motivated by only the highest considerations, while the enemy peoples are looked upon as cowardly, despicable, grasping and cruel. Much the same psychology of selection applies also with reference to classes, especially if class lines are closely drawn over some highly conscious interest. We are sufficiently familiar with the distortions of the capitalists in the cartoons published in the socialist journals and the widely current belief of many of the well to do that those who are poor are either feeble-minded, criminal, or otherwise defective in character.

The disadvantages of such distortions of personality, individually or collectively considered, are perhaps obvious enough. In the case of self-distortion the chief danger is that it so often prevents us from facing reality. We bring ourselves to live in a highly selected dream world. We imagine ourselves to be motivated by considerations which are much more lofty and acceptable to the public than the ones which actually do move us. By such distortion we may lose that intimacy of touch with ourselves which would enable us to forestall failure or disaster by recognizing our weaknesses and the environmental circumstances which are peculiarly liable to offer too great temptations to us. Thus the novice in the use of alcoholics or of drugs is rarely aware of his own weakness in overcoming the growing habit until he is hopelessly lost. The young man who allows social pleasures to interfere with a career ordinarily does not do so deliberately, but constantly underestimates the drain which his pleasures make upon his time and energies and overestimates his professional success and prospects, until his clients or patients or other supporters have lost confidence in his poise and judgment. Perhaps most cases in which young women drift into prostitution are of much the same character. In their pursuit of expensive clothes, or of entertainment, or of other pleasures, they minimize the dangers or their weaknesses and overemphasize their powers of self-control. Very few people possess the faculty of looking at themselves dispassionately and objectively and of recognizing frankly their actual motives in behavior. Even when they do understand themselves, only too often the result is that they suffer from deterioration of character instead of building up compensatory safeguards. The strong personality is one which can not only face self but can correct self by modifying character traits in the direction of strength.

The difficulties of personality distortion in the wider or collective relationships are that we tend to distort the meaning of history and the true worth of historic personalities, on the one hand, and that we deprive ourselves of the most effective instruments of orientation with reference to our contemporaries, on the other hand. In connection with the second case, it is often apparent that international peace or interclass adjustments are hindered by a failure to see our rivals as they are. One of the most commonly cited causes of war is the adverse public opinion, the fears, and the hatreds, which grow up between peoples and are not infrequently fanned by interested persons who understand well this tendency of people, when subject to fear or other strong emotions, to distort the traits and motives of their antagonists. The favorite psychological method of adjusting class disputes is to bring the class leaders together in conference, not only to agree upon administrative details, but also to acquaint them with the essential humanness of their opponents or rivals.

COMPENSATORY MECHANISMS—Alfred Adler, the psychoanalyst, has given striking emphasis to a fact which has long been known, that people who suffer from some defect tend normally to throw their developmental energies in the direction of repairing the difficulty or of overcoming the defect, until it disappears. In many cases the defective organ or process or trait or complex of traits is rendered superior to those which were not originally regarded as inferior. This principle is well known to the surgeons who ordinarily expect to see the tissues of a surgical wound heal and knit together until the healed tissues are as strong or stronger than they were before the operation. We are told that Demosthenes was originally a stammerer and could not express himself clearly in public, but that he practiced speaking to audiences until he became a great orator. It is a common experience for very timid people, who feel that they are unable to do this thing or that, to force themselves to go through with tasks until they overcome their timidity and acquire facility in the dreaded activities. Perhaps most of us have made more progress in overcoming our weaknesses and in going forward to build up positive skills in the direction of these compensations than we have in developing our natural gifts and capacities. The psychology of this compensatory process is relatively simple. Our social contacts render us highly conscious of our defects and inadequacies. This strong fixing of the attention upon the defect either produces in us a strong feeling of inferiority which prevents us from trying to overcome its cause, the defect, or it produces by contra-suggestion a strong impulse to remedy the situation. Since the fixing of attention upon a problem is the necessary prerequisite to its solution, the stimulus of public disapproval or commiseration is usually necessary to secure such active compensatory behavior as will remedy the defect.

The Abnormal Aspect of Compensation—Normally the remedial compensatory behavior aims at and succeeds in removing the cause of the defect or the defect itself. If this cannot be done, it attempts to build up substitute powers and technique, which is truly remedial compensation. But there is also a pathological side to compensation of very great individual and social significance. The minor aspect of this is to be found in those cases where real defects are compensated for by means of sham technique or accomplishments. Thus the public speaker or the social leader often substitutes tricks of language, adroit and perhaps unconscious appeals to prejudice, inflection of voice or tone, or showy dress and lavishness of expenditure for genuine worth. Ignorance has proverbially been hidden by profuseness of verbiage. The person who lacks ability or training sufficient to be productive himself often seeks to associate with others who have this ability, not really that he may acquire it, but that he may appear to others to possess it, or feel as if he possessed it because he identifies himself vicariously with the group of capables. The charlatan succeeds by the use of fine sounding phrases and by the display of "personality." Personality itself is only too often made up of mannerisms and "correct" clothes or verbiage, which are easily seen or heard.

Another very frequent method of compensating for an inferiority feeling is to indulge in invidious criticisms of others. Such criticism may succeed in raising one's relative standard by lowering that of others, or it may result merely in a sort of subjective heightening of one's own ego by causing him to feel that he is superior to the one criticized. Such compensations are negative rather than constructive. Truly valuable compensation for defect should be positive and constructive.

OVERCOMPENSATION FOR INFERIORITY FEELING—One particular form of the attempt at compensation is most interesting and on the whole rather pathetic. Many individuals who have developed inferiority complexes, either because they were defective in some physical or mental attribute, or because they belong to some proscribed race, creed, or faction, often attempt to compensate their repressed personalities by adopting an attitude of strong self-assertion or the show of greater wisdom or goodness, or of more wealth or power, than they possess. Thus the newly rich are needlessly lavish with their wealth, while they feel ill at ease even in the eyes of domestics and porters. The ignorant often use large words ridiculously, pronounce them ludicrously, and discuss topics out of their depth with an empty bombastic phraseology which betrays their lack of genuine knowledge. Women have often been blamed for their unwillingness to abide by the rules of the game as they come into a new world of freedom—clinging to privileges along with their acquired rights. Negroes with some education are often said by some southern people to be spoiled and "mean" because their intellectual achievements and associations have made their inferior position seem unbearable to them and they develop resentment and unconventional self-assertion as a consequence. Jews, especially the self-made type, have in common with many non-Jews of a similar type, a degree of self-assertiveness which appears to many to be a biological quality. As a matter of fact it is merely overcompensation for an inferiority feeling which their social position makes it practically impossible for them to escape. In the course of time this attempt of traditionally inferior classes and peoples to compensate for their depressed social position develops in them a technique and alertness by means of which they may become

PATHOLOGICAL BEHAVIOR

dominant in a civilization. If we wait long enough the last may become first.

PHANTASY—But the more seriously abnormal distortions of personality which are developed as compensations for inadequacy are purely subjective and are to be found in the subject's own consciousness. Unable to compensate for weakness by achievement of objective adjustments or by improvement of his subjective qualities and capacities, he builds up an internal world of phantasy. These phantasies misrepresent the situation to him, in somewhat the same way as that described earlier in the chapter, except that in those cases the individual selects the favorable traits of his personality and disregards the unfavorable ones. He lives in a world which is real as far as it goes; it is merely incomplete. In the type of cases we are presenting here the unadjusted or unadjustable subject goes beyond the stage of distorting his world merely by selection and distorts it by creating unrealities. He imagines things, creates as phantasies things which do not exist. The two types of distortions are not absolutely dissimilar, nor are they unconnected, but their results may be very different. In its milder phases this distortion of self and of environment takes the form of daydreaming, which is practically universal. Those things and powers which we long for and do not possess we compensate for in a small way, especially when the strenuous work of the day is over, by making believe or playing "as if." Even the child, who indulges this mild form of phantasy more than the adult, because as yet the world of reality has not so completely ossified about him, is not often deceived as to the distinction between fact and fancy here. Some children to be sure cannot be perfectly certain whether the thing they imagine is real or only make-believe, and sometimes the apparent falsehoods they tell are the result of a semi-belief in the reality of their daydreams. But, at its best, this type of distortion is merely compensatory selection of our best traits and a forgetting of the worst, with the result that they may aid us materially in bringing our character to an idealistic plane of values.

THE FORMS OF PHANTASY—Various devices are used to give form or body to this compensatory distortion through phantasy. Daydreaming is a form which can be carried on by the compensator alone, and it has the advantage that it can be indulged in practically anywhere and under all circumstances, and there are no limitations to the imaginary achievements or good fortune of the subject. Story-telling is another form closely related to dreaming. In fact it differs mainly from the latter in that it requires listeners—an actual as well as an imaginary social situation. And because it does involve listeners it ordinarily must pay more attention to probability. It is said that Samuel Richardson and Walter Scott learned to write novels and romances from early practice in successful story-telling with playmates as auditors. The production of written fiction is probably in most cases in part a compensatory distortion of reality for the writer as well as for the reader. But in most cases, at least in our day, fiction is written for the market, that is, it provides daydreaming material in packages for those who lack the skill or other qualifications to produce as good a product for themselves. The production of poetry and painting, and perhaps some of the other fine arts, is carried on quite as much for the purpose of compensating the self for hard reality as for the similar satisfaction of others. Artists of all types are always in some sense dreamers. Our interest in the theater and the movies, and likewise to a considerable extent in ordinary social intercourse of the superficial and artificial sort called "society," has this same function of compensatory distortion of reality. Lying is a more serious form of compensatory distortion, although any form of such distortion may have its serious consequences. Lying varies in its form from deliberate distortion for personal advantage to scarcely recognized distortion for the sake of producing harmony in an ideal situation created in the imagination apart from objective reality.

SCHIZOPHRENIC DISTORTIONS—The most pathological of all compensatory distortions of reality are those we ordinarily speak of as schizophrenic distortions. Radical distortions more or less of this character are dementia præcox and paranoia. Originally these psychoses were regarded as the products of physiological disorders, and it is possible that physiological causes not infrequently are contributing factors. But they are more likely to be indirectly operating factors. The consciousness of organ inferiority or of functional incapacity may so discourage the subject that he resorts to the creation of phantasies as a means of compensating for his failures in adjustment to the demands of his environment. In the case of dementia præcox the individual, either because of mental or physical incapacity or because of some emotional distortion or blocking due to any cause whatever, or possibly merely because of the lack of sufficient positive motivation, gives up the struggle for real and objective compensation by building up substitute powers, and turns to phantasy or self-deception as a means of escape from the world of reality which makes greater demands upon him than he is able to meet. In the milder cases it is little more than exaggerated daydreaming. But in the highly developed instances the subject may lose practically all powers of apprehending the meaning and significance of the external world, even to the point of having to be fed and cared for like a child. He may not understand the words which are spoken to him, or at least he may be unable to react to them in any normal way. He may continue indefinitely in silence or repeat constantly some autistic phrase or perform some act which has symbolic significance for him. In such extreme cases there appears to be a truly schizophrenic condition, for tests seem to show that what goes on in the external world is recorded in internal behavior mechanisms, but that these mechanisms are not sufficiently focal to dominate the behavior of the organism. Stimuli which connect up with the compensatory or distorted complexes will, however, produce responses. And in some cases the normal or original mechanisms of behavior can be reached by adequate meaning stimuli and for the time being be rendered dominant. But in extreme cases this dominance of the normal can rarely if ever be rendered permanent. The retreat into a world of compensatory unreality has gone too far and the compensatory mechanisms have become too highly symbolic to be effectively analyzed and discharged by the patient. For this reason dementia præcox when extreme is regarded as incurable.

DEMENTIA PRÆCOX AND PARANOIA COMPARED—Dementia præcox is compensatory distortion through inversion or subjective adjustment. It creates phantasies to take the place of measurable objective realities. The subject imagines that he is some one or something, or that he is doing something which is not true in fact. He distorts the external world, to be sure, but above all he distorts his relationship to the external world. Many of his adjustments to environment are symbolical. That is, a phrase or a movement or a gesture may come to mean to him and to be substituted for a whole complex or series of activities or satisfactions. This symbolic gesture or phrase may be repeated indefinitely as the means of establishing the relationship or of securing the satisfaction which he desires and which the real objective world has denied to him.

Paranoia is also a compensatory adjustment mechanism. The emphasis in the compensatory adjustment in this psychosis is upon external objects, which are looked upon as preventing the desired satisfactions or achievements. In dementia præcox the adjustment is achieved, but wholly in the imagination. In paranoia its achievement is recognized as lacking and the explanation offered for the failure is not the inadequacy or defect of the subject, but the ill will of persons or of the gods or of the general order of things, fate, society, our institutions, etc. Both involve in some degree the exercise of phantasy, but the former directs the phantasy inward and the latter directs it outward. In both cases the distortion of reality seems to aim at ignoring the inadequacy of the subject's personality and an escape from the sense of inferiority. Sometimes it is necessary, in order to escape effectively from the galling sense of inferiority, to destroy the unfriendly persons or objects which prevent adjustment. For this reason paranoia is regarded as a decidedly homicidal psychosis, while dementia præcox is much more recessive and negative.

CONFLICT AND THE DISTORTION OF PERSONALITY—THE FREUDIAN HYPOTHESIS—Any sort of social inhibition or repression of events in consciousness tends to give rise to conflicts with consequent attempts to overcome the difficulty or a compensatory distortion of consciousness and personality. Some of the minor and more serious instances of such conflicts and their results have already been treated in this chapter. It is difficult to conceive of more striking or pathological types of cases than those called dementia præcox and paranoia. Various attempts have been made to explain the causes and mechanisms of conflict. The Freudians, who have had a considerable vogue during the past decade or two, originally attributed practically all conflicts to sex repressions. They said that the sex impulse is the strongest and most universal of all organic drives and that it is at the same time the one most universally censored and regulated by society and our own consciences, which are a reflection of social pressures. Consequently every child and every adult has smothered down into his subconsciousness or his unconscious mechanisms those desires and impulses for sex satisfaction to which society and his own conscience will not permit him to give expression. At times of strain, or when the resistance is for some other reason of health or environmental pressure inadequate, or when the inhibitions are weakened, these repressed tendencies evade their censors and escape into effective behavior. Sometimes the escape is into direct and normal, that is, the ordinary or conventional modes of overt expression. According to this theory, marriage gives a normal opportunity for the removal of repression and escape from the censor.

THE "ESCAPE FROM THE CENSOR"—But in many cases, where a normal escape is not possible, the restiveness of the impulses or drives becomes so great that they escape by the censor in disguise. That is, they come forth as a symbolic form of behavior. One of the most harmless of these symbolic escapes is in dreams. Here the dreamer may do what he likes without fear of censure because he knows that it is not a real situation, or because he has clothed himself and other violators of the social conventions with masks which effectually hide their identity from the censor and frequently from himself. As it were, he stands on the side observing himself in disguise performing the forbidden behavior and thus escapes the reprimand of his conscience or social mentor. But many other escapes from the vigilance of the censor are not so harmless as those in dreams. There may be a development of symptoms which are symbolic of the behavior he desires, although they may have no visual resemblance to that behavior. The subject may become ill in order to have the attention of a loved one of the opposite sex or to go to the hospital and be under the care of a doctor or a nurse. Fainting may, apparently, under certain circumstances come under this classification of symbolic symptoms or neuroses and serve as an escape from reality. Or one may develop or ape those personality traits which belong to a loved one or which will attract that person's attention. Thus schoolgirls and schoolboys who have "crushes" on their teachers often develop the most ridiculous mannerisms as attempts at the imitation of behavior traits in the objects of their adoration. The neurotic symptoms may also function negatively, as where some one develops incapacity to walk or speak or even total functional paralysis to prevent detested contacts with a person of the opposite sex or to escape from some hated task. These substitute or symbolic symptoms are called neuroses. Of the reality of their existence there can be no doubt. They are of extremely frequent occurrence, at least a milder forms of social indispositions and disabilities, and they represent attempts at escapes from conflicts and repression which have become intolerable.

CONFLICTS AND REPRESSIONS OF VARIOUS ORIGINS—The principle of conflict between the unconscious impulses (which should include acquired impulses as well as the unconventional instinctive ones) and the conscious values obtained from our social adjustment, or between two unconscious disposition aiming at the mastery of the personality, with consequent repression and censorship, appears to be sound. But to attribute all conflicts and resulting neurotic escapes from social supervision to sex repression is sheer nonsense. Repressions and inhibitions may occur in any field of interest. Many people become ill and make themselves burdens to others throughout life or as long as they will bear the burden, because of the wish to avoid work. The mother of one of my students retired gracefully from the art of housekeeping by means of paralysis when her daughter entered the university, to which she was opposed and regained complete health when her daughter went to work in a department store. There was no indication that the mother's neurosis was a case of conscious deception. Habitual inattention frequently arises and reaches the degree of functional deafness among children of nervous and nagging par ents. Pseudo feeble-mindedness may arise as the result of a marked distaste for school studies in the lower grades. Cases of neuroses of a non-sexual origin might be multiplied without limit.

DIVISION OF PERSONALITY—In very extreme cases, where the conflict cannot be resolved by any of the devices of constructive compensation, of compensation by distortion of reality, or by that process of distortion which is ordinarily called simply neurosis, the personality may seek an escape from the situation by an actual division of the personality or schizophrenia proper. The several warring interests develop behavior sets of considerable complexity, each capable of independent conscious existence, and struggle for the control or domination of the organism as a whole. Apparently, the split in personality ordinarily occurs in the more extreme cases by the organization of the repressed consciousness into an independently functioning consciousness. Since this subsidiary consciousness is censored or repressed by the dominant consciousness the latter is apparently unaware of the existence of the newly arising personality. But the new personality, which has struggled for recognition and has striven to avoid detection, is itself aware of the dominant personality. Dr. Morton Prince's case of Miss Beauchamp and Sally illustrates these facts well. In the course of time the subordinate personality may come to be dominant or it may be content with acquiring functional control of the organism from time to time. But perhaps in the vast majority of cases it never becomes the master of the organism for more than a fleeting instant, as in absent-mindedness or temporary forgetfulness, if at all.

Extreme cases of divided personality, where one clear-cut personality alternates with the other in the control of the organism, are apparently quite rare. However, we may well be convinced that in its milder forms division of personality is very frequent. Inability to turn readily from one train of thought to another, differences in moral attitudes of the same people in different circumstances, the releases which we observe the behavior of people to undergo when they escape from the routine of their work or of family or institutional obligations, all of those multitudes of evidences of the existence of ethical dualism and of so-called hypocrisy and lack of good faith, would appear to offer strong evidence in support of this contention.

SOCIAL SIGNIFICANCE OF PATHOLOGICAL TYPES OF CONSCIOUSNESS—Although all of the types of consciousness which have been discussed in this chapter are in greater or less degree pathological, they nevertheless have great social significance. This significance is little if at all constructive, but it is nevertheless profound in its negative aspects. With the poor control which we at present have developed, and will for a long period of time continue to have, over environmental factors there is bound to be a great deal of social and individual maladjustment in our society. These pathological types of consciousness or of conscious behavior are, of course, not inherited, although inherited defects may in some cases help to predispose towards such forms of maladjustment of personality. They are environmentally induced in the main and to cure or control them it is necessary to look to the control of the environmental pressures as the means.

We have just begun to develop the principles of mental and social hygiene and to apply them to the problems of an intelligent social control. The result is that we still have a vast volume of neuroses and psychoses of all sorts which interfere with the efficient functioning of our institutions. Thus the significance of the pathological types of consciousness is seen to be a negative one and it will diminish only as we learn to understand and detect neuroses and psychoses in individuals and further learn how to locate and remove those environmental conditions which give rise to repressions and conflict and the inevitable attempts at distorted compensations. Many of the worst cases of individual maladjustment are cases of induced neuroses resulting from unnecessary repressions, which could have been avoided by means of wise guidance of impulses through substitution or sublimation. Also many of the most serious mistakes in social policy have arisen from the dominance of those with neurotic or psychotic dispositions in positions of crucial importance in our social organization. Equally urgent with the need for intelligence tests is that for tests of emotional and moral-social normality and stability

Gradually we are developing the sciences of mental and social hygiene on the one hand and the sciences of environmental organization and control on the other hand to meet these needs.

In the three chapters which follow we shall discuss in detail the organization of personality.

MATERIALS FOR SUPPLEMENTARY READING

Beers, C. W., *The Mind That Found Itself*
Bernard, L. L., "The Psychoanalysts' Theory of the Conflict-Neurosis," *Amer. Jour. Psy.*, XXXIV: 511-30
Groves, E. R., *Personality and Social Adjustment*, Chs. XV-XVIII
Hamilton, G. V., *An Introduction to Objective Psychopathology*
Hart, B., *The Psychology of Insanity*
Healy, W., *Honesty*, Chs. IX-XI
——, *Mental Conflicts and Misconduct*
Judd, C. H., *Psychology*, Ch. XIV
MacCurdy, J. T., *Problems in Dynamic Psychology*
Norsworthy, N., and Whitley, M. T., *Psychology of Childhood*, Ch. XVI
Prince, M., *The Dissociation of a Personality*
Stern, W., *Psychology of Early Childhood*, Pt. VI, and Chs. XXXIII, XXXV
Varendonck, J., *The Psychology of Day-Dreams*
Watts, F., *Abnormal Psychology and Education*, Ch. III
White, W. A., *Mechanisms of Character Formation*, Chs. XI, XII
Wohlgemuth, A., *A Critical Examination of Psychoanalysis*

CHAPTER XIV

GENERAL SETS, POWERS, AND INTELLIGENCE

GENERAL ORGANIC STRUCTURES—The behavior of the organism is determined by the total organization of its protoplasms in reaction with the environment. In the human organism the protoplasmic systems are very complex. The nervous system alone has cells running into the billions. The neurons of the cerebral cortex are said to number approximately 9,000,000,000. The muscles are much less numerous, but these are composed of perhaps a larger number of separate cells than constitute the nervous organization. The osseous tissues and the various secretions and lymphs also disclose a vast physical and chemical complexity. While each organism of the same species is built according to the same general type and therefore possesses much the same powers and is sufficiently similar in the form of its protoplasmic organization to be readily recognized as a member of that species, there are always distinct differences of organization within the general patterns. We have a saying that no two blades of grass are alike. Also people are similar, but not identical. They are different because they behave differently and because they look different and measure up to different specifications. And these ways of being different go back in the last analysis to individual differences in protoplasmic structure and organization.

We have already seen that such individual protoplasmic differences are not wholly, perhaps not even primarily, hereditary, but are produced largely as the effect of differentiation under environmental pressures. Protoplasmic structure and organization are constantly integrating along more or less individual patterns under the pressures of environment, which are in some degree different for every individual. Only the general structure of the organism, which characterizes it a a member of a particular species, is primarily the result of inheritance of the protoplasmic constitution instead of the product of environmental pressures. And even the species type is only approximate. No individual member can be said to be wholly typical of the species. That is, the term species is an abstraction, symbolic of a synthetic conceptual organization of similar traits. There is no inheritance of a type, but inheritance plays a part in the production of individuals who together by a process of logical or abstract synthesis and comparison are conceived to constitute collectively a distinct species. But even here there is sometimes difficulty in distinguishing species at the border lines.

THE FOUR GREAT HUMAN STRUCTURAL ORGANIZATIONS—As indicated above, differences in structure are of as many kinds as there are types and uses of protoplasm on the one hand, and as there are occasions for individual differentiation of protoplasm by functional adjustments to environmental pressures on the other hand. Both heredity and environment play their rôles in producing organic and collective similarities, or types, and differences. The most obvious of the differences in protoplasmic organization which influence the behavior of individuals and modify or help to mold the social or collective patterns are the general structures of the organism. They are perhaps in many ways the least important, although in other ways very important indeed. Four of these structural facts are foundational to all human collective or social organization and are therefore of the utmost importance in explaining man's supreme position, not only in the animal kingdom, but as the organizer of the vast system of collective behavior patterns which we term civilization as well. These four basic structural factors are his highly complex and structurally differentiated nervous system, his hands, the upright position, and his vocal apparatus.

His upright position gives the dominant part of his organism, his head, a better altitude for directing the behavior of the lower parts of the organism and provides a better orientation for the exercise of the exteroceptive senses, except smell and possibly taste. It also frees the hands from the primary function of locomotion and enables them to specialize in tactual sensory and manipulative contacts. The evolution of the hands into the chief tactual sense organs makes it possible also for them to become the chief adjustment organs of the body on the response side. Man manipulates his environment as does no other animal, because his hands are free and their form permits of easy manipulation, and the location of highly differentiated sense organs in the fingers and palms permits of a close connection between stimulus and response in manipulation. The vocal apparatus enables man to develop verbal communication symbols which far surpass the non-verbal gestures and facial expressions in complexity, volume, and precision of meaning. An intellectual content to communication was scarcely possible before verbal language developed. The transference of vocal verbal symbols to written form brings the manipulative hand into the service of communication and greatly expands the service of language to collective behavior. Collective behavior is dependent primarily upon the language symbols, which in turn are rendered possible only by the vocal apparatus and the writing hand. Civilization, or collective behavior in its highest and most intellectual forms, dominated by cortical organization, is dependent primarily upon the volume and accuracy and permanency of written records.

The high brain organization of man, especially the acquired cortical mechanisms which control the symbolizing processes and interpret conceptually the stored symbolic meaning complexes, makes possible the efficiency of manual and vocal differentiation and renders effective the better orientation of sight and hearing through the upright position. Man's collective behavior, or the organization of his social life, is thus dependent ultimately upon the inner organization of the cerebral cortex which is so responsive to all sorts of environmental pressures, especially those of the psycho-social environment which operate upon it primarily through the mechanisms of vocal and written symbols. This fact affords another illustration of Child's principle that the appearence of a new dominant organization in the protoplasmic system establishes a new gradient and a new system of behavior patterns. The general structural organization—upright body, hands, vocal apparatus complex and highly differentiated nervous system—work through the mechanism of the cerebral cortex and are controlled by them. And the cerebral cortex is itself now largely dominated by the stored symbolic content of the psycho-social environment.

OTHER GENERAL ORGANIC MECHANISMS, such as the length of hands, the joints, muscles and tendons, the eating, respiratory, digestive, circulatory, excretory, and reproductive systems, also influence behavior profoundly, but in relatively fixed ways. They serve as conditions and limitations to the functioning of behavior patterns set up in the neural protoplasm and, especially in man, in the flexible cortical system. They do not initiate new adjustment patterns, as does the cortical system. They are, in fact, relatively fixed elements in the old adjustment system of the organism. Any derangement of their functioning, due to disease or other unwonted environmental pressures, may seriously interfere with the adjustment patterns worked out in the highly flexible cortical organization. Because of this fact the cortex, with the aid of external stored mechanisms, has developed elaborate supplementary acquired social adjustment mechanisms intended to keep the functioning of the lower organic mechanisms as efficient and regular as possible. Among these are the techniques of medicine, hygiene, sanitation, recreation, etc. The cerebral cortex responding to stimuli from without, must take the initiative in making new adjustment patterns demanded by a changing environment and in providing for the regular functioning of the old ones, including the organic mechanisms, because of the highly flexible and responsive character of its neural organization.

INTELLIGENCE—Since the cerebral cortex is supreme in the organization and control of the higher forms of behavior, and since the functioning of this cortex is expressed evaluatively in what we call intelligence, it is necessary to examine to some extent the nature and conditions of intelligence. Intelligence is, of course, a synthetic or abstract term used to symbolize the effectiveness of adjustments made through cerebral functioning and control. Intelligence is the most significant of all of the individual powers serving the adjustment of the organism to its environment. It is a very complex system of phenomena, embracing all sorts of adjustment capacities and techniques. It cannot be measured by facility in verbal symbols only, as some of the systems of mental tests would seem to imply.

The ability to form verbal concepts and to communicate these to others through language mechanisms is very important, but there are other aspects to intelligence also. Ability to make manual adjustments through the creation of transforming inventions, the capacity to do skilled artistic work, to play the rôle of the leader or to perform well and accurately the task assigned one, or even to formulate high and proper ideals of individual and collective behavior—social inventions—and to put these in practice, are other manifestations of intelligence which are also important. A good plumber, a good scholar, a skilled organist, an efficient legislator, and an able scientist must all be intelligent, although the forms and patterns which their several intelligences take may be very different.

But it should be noted that as all of the techniques of these and other skilled performers become more highly developed and scientific and quantitative in their procedure, more and more of the verbal or symbolic element comes into all intelligence processes. As invention, or constructive manipulation of the various environments, advances from the merely accidental and empirical to the abstract and symbolical level, where the adjustment process or invention is planned in detail before it is executed, the verbal element in thinking becomes dominant. This is true whether the invention is of the physical, social, or method type. Even the plumber cannot meet new situations without the use of the symbolic or verbal element. The artist is "creative" or "expressive" in the degree to which he can symbolize his situation and the adjustment which his environment demands. The scientist and the social reformer or leader create new worlds of adjustment technique by means of the manipulation of symbolic or verbal mechanisms. We should expect this growing dominance of the verbal and abstract element in intelligence in keeping with the increasing functioning of the cortical processes in control over adjustment.

LEADING FORMS OF INTELLIGENCE RELATED—The usual contrast between types of intelligence is between the ability to do things with one's hands or body, that is, to make the proper organic adjustments with relation to the form, distance, weight, color, etc., of objects and to do things with one's mind, that is, to use the abstracting or symbolic verbal mechanisms for the construction of mental pictures and symbols of things later to be done with the hands and body. The correlation between these two types of abilities or intelligence is very close and the differences are largely or wholly the result of differences of training in manual and abstract mental operations. In fact, there appear to be limits beyond which one cannot go in developing skill in one direction without having had at least initial practice in the other. At least, this is particularly true in the case of the development of verbal and abstract skills.

Intelligence is not necessarily conscious, although the higher forms of intelligence are very likely to be so. Intelligence is a character or complex of characters imputed to the organism functioning effectively in an adjustment process. The association of intelligence and consciousness in the popular mind is due to the fact that they are so frequently found together.

FACTORS BASIC TO INTELLIGENCE—Woodworth has attempted to summarize the factors which are basic to intelligence. The first of these he calls *retentiveness*. Intelligence involves the use of past experience—"not for instinctive reactions, but for previously learned reactions. Though the Binet tests attempt to steer clear of specific school knowledge, they do depend upon knowledge and skill picked up by the child in the course of his ordinary experience. They depend on the ability to learn and remember." But intelligence is not best indicated by sheer power of memory. There must be power to apply what one learns and retains to other problems which arise. The one whose intelligence is being examined "has to see the point of the problem now set him, and to adapt what he has learned to this novel situation." This ability is what the mental tests attempt to measure. Therefore, Woodworth includes *responsiveness to relationships* as a second general factor in intelligence. Certain moral or impulsive factors are also of importance. There must be *persistence*. Otherwise there will not be sufficient *attention* to fix the matter in hand and enable the subject to build up an effective attitude towards it. Without persistence the adjustment to the situation is never sufficiently complete to be adequately functional, and we pronounce the flighty or inattentive person unintelligent because he appears to be incapable of mastering a situation or of carrying anything through. But if the person is too persistent is stubborn, his adjustment is also likely to be defective. He attempts to do things he cannot accomplish, or he retains an attitude after the occasion for it has gone by. He may be quite as much out of line with reality as the person who cannot stick with a proposition or a situation until he masters it. We say of such a person that he is not intelligent enough to know when he has had enough or when to let go of the situation or when he has extracted the meat from the pie. Hence a certain degree of *submissiveness* is necessary to intelligent behavior. Perhaps, as some moralists do, we should speak of it as *humility,* for, it is said the truly great and wise are also humble. Still another factor in intelligence is *curiosity*. Without this quality of behavior there can be no attention, hence no analysis and no adequate orientation in behavior. A condition of intelligence is undoubtedly constant *alertness* to new situations, to be able to sense new problems, to understand them, and then to solve them. This last involves the factor of persistence.

All of these factors in intelligence are of course abstract value terms. They are not concrete behavior patterns, but they are synthetic attitudes toward concrete behavior patterns which count much for effectiveness—another synonym for intelligence—in adjustment.

DRIVES AND INTELLIGENCE—While the foregoing factors most of them mentioned by Woodworth, may be said to cover satisfactorily the background of intelligence, many psychologists also use the term drive conspicuously in this connection. Another term employed with closely related meaning is motivation. Drive and motivation are among the most essential factors in stimulating the organism to intelligent behavior. Many times the chief distinction between an intelligent and an unintelligent child or adult lies in the degrees of incentive which activate them. Without drive, which is in large measure an organic, if not an inherited, trait, the child is not capable

ble of acquiring intelligence skills. Without motivation, which is primarily social rather than organic in its inception, the child will not acquire intelligence, however great may be his capacity for doing so. Motivation is largely dependent upon the postnatal environment, especially the psycho-social environment. Drive is basically an organic fact, and bears a close relationship to what Allport terms the prepotent impulses.

The drive does not depend upon an independent mechanism of its own, but makes use of all of the behavior mechanisms, instinctive or acquired, which the organism possesses. Habits function in the expression of drives quite as much, if not more than, reflexes and instincts. Without such pattern organization the drive can scarcely be said to exist or find expression. The organization itself constitutes an important aspect or constituent element of the drive. The underlying organic condition which makes the drive effective is probably chemical, especially the physiology of the neurons and of the endocrines. It is not wholly unlike that physiology which is basic to temperament. In fact, drive might be considered as a phase of temperament. Both drive and temperament are closely related to intelligence. The major organic drives are intimately connected with the organic needs or dispositions of the organism, such as food, water, sleep, and sex expression. We may also speak of drives in connection with social contacts and security, and even clearly acquired interests of any sort, such as religious, intellectual, moral, or for play, the success of the group. But these latter drives are built up in the habit mechanisms rather than in the original organic constitution. The organic drives also build up a large number of supplementary stimulus-response patterns which predispose us to aim not merely at food, sleep, and sex, but also at food and sex satisfactions of certain qualities, and at sleep under certain conditions.

In order to satisfy to the best advantage these inherited and acquired dispositions of the organisms, intelligent behavior is developed. Originally this behavior is merely the restlessness which comes from an unsatisfied organic need or appetite and is not intelligent. But this restlessness, like random movements, is later organized or transformed into adaptive behavior which serves to adjust the organism to those environmental conditions which will satisfy its needs. This adaptive behavior which grows out of the original restlessness is at first the product of trial and success, but it finally becomes in man projective or previsional. It is in this last form that it may be said to be truly intelligent. Civilized men plan collectively for the satisfaction of their individual and collective needs. In this way they satisfy their drives in the most intelligent way possible, with the aid of science and those institutions which make scientific knowledge available. The coöperative or collective situation of mutual stimulation gives men the motivation through the stimulation of rivalry which is necessary for the satisfaction of their drives. The coöperative social system not only gives the individual mechanisms for the satisfaction of his desires, but it also gives him incentive or motivation to seek their satisfaction.

MENTAL TESTS—Various methods of testing the behavior qualities of individuals, especially intelligence, emotionality, personality, etc., have been devised. The ones that have been perfected with the greatest degree of accuracy are the intelligence tests. These were first given prominence by Binet, a French psychologist, and later modified by various educational psychologists. Terman's adaptations are most used in the United States. The original aim of the tests was merely to pick out those children who were suspected of mental defect in order that they might be referred to the physician for further examination. Further refinements and applications in the tests have come with their continued use.

The intention of the testers is not to limit the tests merely to knowledge or facility gained by formal instruction. Accordingly text book knowledge is carefully avoided and tasks are set in "information and skill picked up by the child from his elders and playmates in the ordinary experience of life." Also the tests are as widely distributed over the whole field of easily accessible experience as possible. The reason for these precautions is that tests are likely to approach more closely to the substratum of organic inheritance by taking those experiences which have a chance to come to every child and on this basis find out what the child has been able to achieve. But of course this attempt to get back of individual differences in training and opportunity for training is only partly successful. As Watts says, "the fact cannot be denied that they favor children to whom a superior social status or education has given a greater range of knowledge as well as a more facile understanding of language with increased capacity for its use." Attempts have been made to overcome this difficulty by the use of the Yerkes point-scale tests, and the performance tests which test manual and sensory instead of language skills. But even here experience and training count, and it does not appear that differences in training can ever be eliminated sufficiently to enable the tests to reveal inherited capacity exclusively or fully. Even if it were possible to eliminate differences in acquisitions of knowledge there would still be the problem of locating differences in acquired organic mechanisms or conditioning factors, both prenatal and postnatal. This difficulty would seem to be at present quite insuperable.

The Alpha tests of the U. S. Army are perhaps the most up-to-date intelligence tests and it has been claimed for them that they actually do get back of educational acquirement and training to inborn intelligence, or to the inherited capacity to acquire intelligence skills. Yet it has been shown that even these tests discriminate against certain types of persons. They, too, apparently have not eliminated the differential factor of cultured homes and intellectual associations such as may be had in school. It has also been charged that they discriminate against women because some of these tests call for arithmetical training, and that they discriminate against manual as contrasted with clerical workers because they demand an accurate knowledge of the meaning of certain words that do not commonly occur in everyday vocabularies, such as adventitious, equivocal, lugubrious, maudlin, encomium, abstruse, recondite. Such defects might also work strongly against rural populations in more isolated geographic sections.

Is INTELLIGENCE INHERITED?—If intelligence depends upon such general and diverse synthetic factors as those mentioned above, can we say that it is inherited? Most of the intelligence testers are inclined to hold that it is a matter of inheritance. Their chief argument in support of this position is that the intelligence quotient remains essentially the same throughout life, the inference being that if intelligence were not inherited it would either improve or deteriorate under the influence of favorable or unfavorable environmental pressures. The fact that the dull child must also perforce become a man or woman of less than average achievement appears to them to be conclusive proof of their contention.

INTELLIGENCE MEASURED IN TERMS OF ACQUIRED SKILLS—Two things, however, seem to have been overlooked or underestimated in making this contention. The first is the fact that intelligence is measured in terms of acquired mental or manual skills. Mental tests are based upon the acquired knowledge of the individual tested, for native or natural capacity is an abstraction, and capacity of any sort can be observed and tested only through the skills which one has shown himself able to acquire. But the test is not so much of what one is able to acquire as of what he has acquired under the environmental conditions in which he has been placed. The testers themselves admit this. Woodworth states it clearly when he says, "The intelligence of an individual at any age depends on what he has learned previously." Intelligence therefore consists of acquired skills and is measured in terms of these skills. All of us are born without these skills. Some develop them with great difficulty or not at all, while others acquire them under favorable environmental conditions, with comparative ease. What is it that determines whether or not the child born without the skills which constitute his intelligence will be able to acquire them? Most of these determining factors are perhaps organic and are subjective to the individual, but others are environmental and objective. Both of these condition is the individual certain patterns for the discharge of energy which determine in large degree the kind and quality of future development in behavior.

It is extremely difficult to determine whether the organic limitations upon the development of intelligence are inherited or acquired. It is sometimes assumed that inherited capacity and organic capacity are the same. Such, of course, is not the case, for inherited capacity may be lowered by acquired organic modifications of the protoplasmic structures by disease, or

POWERS AND INTELLIGENCE 217

other agencies. The analysis in Chapter VII showing how toxins, infections, hormones, and traumatisms may affect the development of the child in the prenatal period should render us extremely hesitant about assuming off-hand that all native defects are also inherited. We cannot be sure, for example, that even the small brains of idiots or the defective functioning of neural mechanisms in the dullard, who may nevertheless possess a normal sized brain, are not due to some toxic condition which has prevented the normal development of neural or other tissue. Nor is it clear that some prenatal physico-chemical condition has not disturbed the endocrine balance or the chemistry of the neurons in such a way that the nervous system never can function properly. Some chronic defect in the nutrition of the cells or of neuro-muscular tonus may prevent the normal development of responses or of sensitivity to stimuli.

It is clear that the intelligence tests measure acquired skills developed on an inherited substratum. The former quantum may always be represented as a smaller circle within a larger one, for probably no one ever achieves all of the behavior patterns of which he is organically capable. Nor does he develop the degree of efficiency in the use of these patterns which might be attained under the most favorable circumstances. Thus the tests, even if they functioned perfectly, could not reveal native intelligence as fully and as accurately as acquired intelligence and skill. It is obviously not possible, however, for the tests to reveal a greater intelligence than there is inherited capacity for.

There is here no intention to deny the possibility of the inheritance of these underlying conditions which inhibit the development of those neuro-psychic skills constituting what we call intelligence. It should, however, be admitted that such inheritance is not proved. The fact that defects in intelligence run in families and that they occur according to certain typical statistical curves which characterize Mendelian inheritance is not conclusive proof of the inheritance of the underlying organic conditions of intelligence. We should expect environmentally induced traits to run in families also, for families constitute relatively segregated environments. Also, the curves for environmental transmission are essentially the same as those for transmission by biological inheritance. As has been intimated, nothing can be proved in this respect by statistics. Statistics merely counts cases, and does not determine causes. As yet the subject must be regarded as an open question to be settled later, as knowledge accumulates on both sides.

EARLY ORIGIN OF FUNDAMENTAL DISPOSITIONS—The other matter which has been neglected by those who hold that intelligence is inherited is that the organism gets its fundamental acquired sets and powers early. It is in the first months and years of infancy that the human brain is freest from dominant and perfected behavior patterns. But rapidly these acquired patterns and dispositions are organized under the dominance of environment, and the general attitudes and powers of the child become relatively fixed. The child probably makes more fundamental and basic pattern adjustments in his first two to six years than in all the rest of his life. He acquires those rather intangible, but nevertheless very effective, emotional and attitudinal sets which later dominate the range and powers of his contacts with others, and which determine whether he is to be aggressive and self-confident and a leader with initiative or whether he is to have an inferiority complex and is to be timid, unexpressive, and easily dominated. Also his major interests are likely to be fixed in this period. He develops aversions and likes, and a whole host of conventional attitudes. All of these are likely to remain fairly constant in their fundamental aspects throughout life, although he may compensate superficially for some of them. Changes of attitude made subsequently are not likely to go very deep into fundamental character. This is as true of the organic sets or dispositions acquired in infancy, such as food preferences, posture, sensory adjustments, speed in response, etc., as it is of the emotional and psychic ones. In many cases, because of fear or some other complex, the young child builds up such definite inhibitions upon expression that he develops what Burnham has aptly called pseudo feeble-mindedness. To all appearances the child is feeble-minded and will actually become so permanently unless the cause of the repression or conflict can be discovered and removed clinically.

The conditions which determine the intelligence quotient are doubtless primarily organic, although by no means entirely so. Also most of these organic conditions are apparently fixed before or soon after birth, either in the inheritance or by such prenatal and postnatal environmental factors as have been mentioned here. But it is by no means inconceivable that a postnatal environment, especially in his earlier years, may induce those organic or emotional and psychic dispositions in the child, which give a permanent set to his personality and fix or limit his power to learn in certain directions. In fact there appear to be excellent reasons for believing that such is the case. All of us undoubtedly receive permanent organic and emotional and intellectual biases in our early years which we never fully overcome. Indeed, it is not abnormal for us to do so. It is part of the process of our character determination, for childhood is the period in which character is most easily and deeply fixed.

ALL INTELLIGENCE SPECIAL—SPECIAL TESTS—Since intelligence tests measure acquired knowledge and skills it is not possible for any usable test to be so extensive and inclusive that it would cover all possible experience. Therefore all intelligence tests are discriminatory. There is no such thing as general native or inherited intelligence, except in the sense of an unrealized abstraction. All intelligence is special to the type of experience and interests of the subject. Consequently any general test, however nearly perfect, can only approximate in its results an average level of the subject's intellectual abilities. It is necessary to devise numerous special tests in addition to this preliminary general test to determine specific abilities along different lines in which inheritance or training and experience may have equipped the subject. From the results of the various special tests it may then, as Watts suggests, be possible to construct an "intellectual index" of an individual to be used as a more dependable indication of his "general" capacity. But in the meantime we do well to use the prevailing tests for what they are worth, not forgetting that they measure only *within* the limits of inherited capacity and not the whole of that capacity, that no method has been devised for eliminating the differential influence of environment, and that the accuracy of the tests in determining the general level or average of intelligence of any individual is only approximate, with numerous chances for error.

SPECIAL ABILITIES—An interesting phase of intelligence is that of highly developed special abilities. Many kinds of these have been recorded, such as exceptional ability to do the simpler mathematical processes, in the performance of unusual feats of memory, in color analysis and matching, for finding one's way, with tools and in understanding machinery, in language, in the writing of verses, in rhythm and in dancing, in playing or recalling and reproducing music once heard, etc. Phenomenal stories are told of "prodigies" who are able to perform feats of one kind or another and thereby to astonish the crowd. Often this special ability is wholly out of proportion to the other abilities of its possessor. The biologist S. J. Holmes gives some examples of special aptitudes. He says, "Blind Tom who possessed a phenomenal aptitude for playing any piece of music he may have heard was practically an imbecile. Often these 'idiot savants' possess remarkable memory, as in the case of the boy described by Langdon Down, who could repeat verbatim pages from a book that he had once read. Some of the mathematical prodigies are otherwise mentally defective. Heron reports a boy, nearly an idiot, who when given a man's age could calculate quickly the number of minutes he had lived. Another boy could multiply any three figures with any three others almost as rapidly as they were written, although he was of a very low grade of mentality." But this association of a low level of intelligence in general with a special ability is apparently the exception rather than the rule. Abilities of all types in the individual tend to correlate rather than otherwise, unless some are developed through training to the neglect of others. And this last is probably what had happened in most of the cases just cited.

How can such unusual traits or capacities be accounted for? Are they inherited or acquired? Formerly, of course, like all other peculiarities or pathological traits, they were explained as the product of inheritance. We are not so certain now. The normal special abilities, such as facility in music or in some other relatively concrete performance, tend to run in families

[1] *The Trend of the Race,* p. 29

POWERS AND INTELLIGENCE 221

but this is as much to be expected on the basis of an explanation by environment as by inheritance. Apparently those special abilities which are not concrete and easily observed, and therefore easily imitated, do not run by families to the same extent as do the more concrete ones. This fact is a point in favor of the theory of the environmental origin and transmission of special abilities. Neither do they appear according to any definite Mendelian ratio.

UNDERLYING INHERITED STRUCTURES—No doubt there are frequently inherited structures which aid in the acquisition of special abilities. There could be no special development of ability at piano playing without flexible wrists and hands and long fingers, and these may be inherited. Musical ability of any kind is not possible without that particular nervous structure in the inner ear which renders acute pitch discrimination possible. And singers must have vocal cords and throat and mouth cavities of certain types if they are to be remarkably superior. It is possible even that the occurrence of an unusually large supply of neurons of a particular physico-chemical quality in certain regions of the brain may facilitate the development of powers, especially of memory associations, in those regions. But this raises the question of the localization of particular functions in definite regions of the brain, a question which is still undecided.

But the inheritance of these underlying structures, if it could in all cases be established, would not prove the inheritance of special abilities. While the special abilities could not be developed without the underlying structures, the existence of the structure by no means guarantees the development of the ability. In any case the ability, which we know as a special technique, or skill, is always acquired, whatever its underlying biological bases. It should also be realized that special abilities are not so remarkable and unusual as they appear to the popular mind. Only those special abilities which we meet infrequently seem so astonishing and so difficult to account for. All of us use every day just as remarkable skills and think nothing of this fact, or do not even realize it, because they are of such frequent occurrence. Our use of a language, the ability to read or write, the habit of finding our way about the streets of a great city with which we are familiar, with a minimum of conscious attention, the art of crossing a busy corner, the society woman's social technique, the gambler's ability to play his hand, the professional athlete's mastery of his game, the business man's habit of reading letters at a glance, or of the vaudeville mystery man's "tricks," or for that matter the mere ability to walk or talk, are quite as remarkable from the standpoint of technique as the unusual skills achieved by the "prodigies" at whom we marvel.

ALTERNATIVE EXPLANATIONS—The fact that the performer can give no account of how he acquired the skill is not significant with regard to the rival claims of heredity and environment as causes. The same is true of many of the more commonly distributed skills. A bias in the direction of counting things, due to the fixation of some hysterical trend or merely to the random selection of a play interest in early childhood would suffice to account for the phenomenal adders, subtracters, multipliers, etc. Accountants often trained themselves to similar expertness on purpose before the days of calculating machines. It is to be noted that many of the musicians who "play any tune they have heard" are blind. The sense of hearing has been stimulated to compensate for the lost sense of sight. In many cases the unusual special ability has been developed on the basis of a lead or interest in attention developed by accident and thereafter persisted in because of lack of interference. The fact that many of the "prodigies" have not developed intelligence equally or even normally in other direction would tend to show that their mental life had been isolated and introverted, and there subjected to the development of more or less hysterical fixations. Studies of these types might reveal hysterical biases and possibly in many or all cases show that their subnormal intelligence in other directions was not the result of inheritance but of those environmental and organic conditions which produce what Burnham has called pseudo-feeble-mindedness.

These rarer and more sensational types of special abilities which have caught the attention of the psychologists are not of very great significance for our collective life. But the more common special abilities or skills have the greatest significance for society. Civilization advances through the development of a high grade of skill along these more functional or useful, and therefore more common, lines. The art of a Paderewski or of a Rachmaninoff is even more phenomenal than that of a Blind Tom and at least as difficult to attain, but it surprises us less because we understand the technique of its attainment. The ability to count and measure electrons is much more remarkable than that of multiplying three numbers by three other numbers rapidly, and we know that the former technique was acquired. So may the latter be acquired by the accountant in a perfectly normal manner. It is only when we find an apparently imbecile boy performing such feats that we are astonished. We need to know more about hysteria and fixations and the working of the subnormal mind in personalities isolated by their defect to supplement our theories of inheritance, if we are to understand better the occurrence of unusual abilities.

MATERIALS FOR SUPPLEMENTARY READING

Bagley, W. C., "Educational Determinism; or Democracy and the I.Q.," *School and Soc.*, XV: 373-84
——, "Intelligence Tests," *School and Soc.*, XVII: 329-30
Baldwin, J. M., *Social and Ethical Interpretations*, Ch. VII
Bawden, H. H., "The Evolution of Behavior," *Psy. Rev.*, XXVI: 247-76
Bernard, L. L., *Instinct: A Study in Social Psychology*, pp. 430-38
Burnham, W. H., *The Normal Mind*, Ch. XVIII
Colvin, S. S., "The Use of Intelligence Tests," *Educational Review*, LXII: 134-48
Edman, I., *Human Traits and Their Significance*, Ch. IV
Ellwood, C. A., *The Psychology of Human Society*, Ch. X
Gault, R. H., *Social Psychology*, Ch. IV, and pp. 305-12
Kretschmer, E., *Physique and Character*, Part I
Paton, S., *Human Behavior*, Ch. III
Watts, F., *Abnormal Psychology and Education*, pp. 152-70
Woodworth, R. S., *Psychology, a Study of Mental Life*, Chs. XI, XII
Yoakum and Yerkes, *Army Mental Tests*

CHAPTER XV

RACE, NATIONALITY, CLASS

In the preceding chapter those inherited and acquired general traits and sets which characterize the individual as an organism functioning in a psycho-social situation were reviewed and analyzed. In the present chapter the conclusions arrived at in the preceding chapter will be applied to an examination of some of the major and outstanding groupings of mankind. To what extent do races, the sexes, nationalities, and social classes differ in intelligence and to what are the differences due? The answer to the first of these two questions is best secured by examining the results of the mental tests already introduced in the preceding chapter.

TESTS AND RACE—The attempt has been made to apply the mental tests not only to individuals but also to groups or classes of individuals in order to secure a comparative rating of these groups or classes with reference to each other. This application has been made especially with respect to racial groups, the sexes, and occupational groups. The method as applied to racial groups is that of selecting typical individuals from a race and measuring their intelligence by means of approved tests. Then it is possible to compare the index of one race with that of another. Such method is subject to all the advantages and disadvantages of testing outlined in the preceding chapter. If a sufficiently large number of representative and well distributed individuals is selected from the racial group it may be possible to secure an approximation to the average of intelligence of the group, but the intelligence thus measured is only the acquired intelligence within the limits of inherited capacity and not the inherited capacity itself. The degree to which the actual indices of intelligence measured for a racial group approximates to the actual inherited capacity will depend on the environmental factors of home training, cultural contacts, motivation, opportunity, etc., available to the members of the group.

RACE TRAITS—The supposed race traits may be divided into two general groups—the physiological and anatomical, on the one hand, and the psychological and social, on the other hand. If we should attempt to list these traits we should place under the former category such items as color of skin, hair, and eyes, hair texture, the shape and distribution of hair over the body, head shape, and in a minor sense size, form of face, lips, and nose, stature, position of eyes, odor, and possibly certain differences in the endocrines and in the structure of the brain, although this last matter has not been definitely settled. Under the psychological and social characteristics which we ordinarily associate with races we might include various qualities and degrees of such characteristics or attitudes and complexes as education, morals, religion, superstition, scientific appreciation, mysticism, practical outlook, recessive or aggressive disposition, the various temperaments, commercial or philosophic bent, absolutistic or democratic governmental institutions, etc.

As between these two types of characteristics a marked difference is noticeable. Both types vary greatly in occurrence within any so-called race. Also the latter type changes readily in the individual, while the former type changes only or primarily through selection of the inheritance. The psychological and social traits can be made to conform very readily and within very short periods of time to the psycho-social environment in which the members of the race are placed. This is especially true of the younger members of a race. To transplant them from one culture to another while still in infancy renders it certain that they will assimilate the culture into which they are translated, if they are actually and fully immersed in it. This may also happen in less degree to older persons, whose habits or acquired dispositions are more firmly set. But the anatomical and physiological traits are modified within the same individual only with the greatest difficulty. Possibly the endocrine balance may be altered by changing to a new physico-chemical environment or by the adoption of new habits of living, which is equivalent to changing the social environment. Of course disease and conditions of labor, of nutrition, and of climatic pressures may modify the functioning and structure of organs and tissues. And the cortical organization is always modifiable under proper environmental pressures. Skin color is also subject to modification under the influence of the sun's rays, humidity, etc. Some of the more stable somatic characteristics, such as head shape and stature, appear also to be modified in the second generation under the influence of changed conditions of nutrition and possibly of climate, if we accept the results of Boas' studies.

But in spite of these partial exceptions it appears that the fundamental biological structures in man, with the exception of the cerebral cortical processes, are relatively fixed. The anatomical and physiological traits appear to breed true to type in a very large number of cases, while so far as we know the complex mental, moral and social traits do not breed true to type at all, but are wholly acquired from whatever environment is dominant for that race or group. Accordingly we are accustomed to speak of the former as race traits and of the latter as cultural traits. Sometimes we refer to the one as biological and to the other as social. The *fact* of race *is* biological, but the *concept* of race is sociological. That is, the conceptual organization of the biological traits into a collective racial unit is sociological, not biological.

WHITE AND COLORED—Race comparisons on an academic basis in this country usually make use of the data regarding Negroes and Whites, and sometimes of Indians. There seems to be no question but that the average levels of intelligence shown by Negroes is anywhere from one to three years below that of Whites of the same chronological age. The army tests in the recent war showed very few Negroes in A and B grades while twelve percent of the typical Whites belonged to these grades. However, in the lowest passing grade (D—) there were seven times as many Negroes as Whites. The statistics as summarized by Gault are as follows:

Classes	Number of Cases	D—	D	C—	C	C+	B	A
Whites, Groups I, II, III.	93,973	7.0	17.1	23.8	25.0	12.0	8.0	4.
Negroes Group IV.	18,891	49.0	29.7	12.9	5.7	2.0	0.6	0.

RACE, NATIONALITY, CLASS

The groups of Whites and Negroes were comparable as to composition.

The results of experiments by Dr. Pyle [1] are interesting in this connection. He gave a series of tests to a group of grade school Negro children in Missouri and compared the results with those obtained from the same tests given to white children. The absolute superiority in technique of the Whites over the Negroes indicated by the army tests is clearly confirmed by Dr. Pyle's data, as shown in the following table comparing the relative efficiency of the two races in the several tests made. Columns (4) and (7) also indicate the degree to which the Negro children approached the white children in the various tests.

	Boys			Girls		
(1)	(2)	(3)	(4)	(5)	(6)	(7)
Type of Tests	White score	Negro score	Percent which negro score is of white [2]	White score	Negro score	Percent which negro score is of white [2]
Rote Memory	34.8	24.6	68.5	36.1	28.3	76.6
Substitution	28.7	13.6	44.0	33.0	15.1	42.6
Logical Memory	24.4	19.7	80.3	25.3	20.1	78.4
Manthanometer [3]	16.6	12.96	78.2	17.5	13.0	73.8

[1] Dr. Pyle's data, taken from his *Nature and Development of Learning Capacity*, Warwick and York, Inc., 1925, are used extensively in this chapter for purposes of economy of space. They cover at one and the same time differences of race, sex, age, and geographic distribution. They are also reasonably typical and carefully induced.

[2] Averaged on the basis of the percentage scored at each age from eight to sixteen.

[3] Dr. Pyle describes the Manthanometer test as "A study of the development of a complicated form of sensori-motor learning. . . . The subject must keep in mind some rather complicated instructions. He must keep doing several simultaneous processes. The experiment requires in a rather high degree what is commonly called attention or concentration. In my opinion this experiment measures not only general learning capacity but a specific type of ability, the type required in operating complex machinery. . . . A person capable of carrying on only one process at a time does not succeed well at this experiment."

These results are difficult to explain by a theory of inherited racial inferiority, since the negro children apparently were better relative to white children in the difficult tests than in the simple ones.

In tests given under the direction of Dr. Pyle by Mrs. Lappin to five hundred Indian boys and girls, the average score of Indian boys approaches most nearly to that of white boys in logical memory tests (80.1 percent), next in concrete rote memory tests (72.8 percent), third in substitution tests (60. percent), fourth in abstract rote memory tests (60.8 percent), fifth in word building tests (44.5 percent), sixth in analogy tests (34.6 percent), and seventh in free association tests (28. percent). The order in which the average scores of Indian girls approach those of white girls is, concrete rote memory (70.2 percent), abstract rote memory (65.9 percent), logical memory (63.5 percent), substitution (57.1 percent), word building (42.2 percent), analogues (30.6 percent), and free association (30.5 percent).

HEREDITY AND ENVIRONMENT IN RACE—The following table compiled from Dr. Pyle's data shows the order of the relative efficiency in the several tests of both negro and white children to be largely similar. The order of efficiency is the same for both boys and girls in each race.

Negro	White
Rote Memory	Rote Memory
Logical Memory	Substitution
Substitution	Logical Memory
Manthanometer	Manthanometer

The relative efficiency of negro and Indian children of both sexes in the several tests as compared with the efficiency of white children was shown in the preceding section. In the opinion of the present writer Dr. Pyle's data indicate that negro and Indian boys do least well as compared with the Whites in the more academic test, in which presumably they have least practice, and best in those tests in which their general experience with the adjustment problems of life tends

RACE, NATIONALITY, CLASS

count most. Making due allowance for differences in training and traditions of girls as compared with boys, the same statement appears to hold for negro and Indian girls.

Miss Strong's results [4] also appear to justify such a conclusion. She found from a comparison of city white children, mill children (white) and colored children, that the white mill children were more closely related to the negro children than to the city white children in two out of three types of results. Of those children that were more than one year retarded in school work she found only 5.4 percent of the city white children, 18.3 percent of the mill children, and 25.6 percent of the colored children. Of those more than one year above normal, 10.4 percent of the city white children, and of the other two classes none. Of those who were doing normal work, 84.2 percent of the city white children belonged to this class, 81.6 percent of the mill children, and 74.4 percent of the negro children.

Other facts which appear to support the hypothesis that so-called racial differences in intelligence are due largely to environmental influences upon opportunity to acquire the mental and manual and sensory skills required by the tests are to be found in the fact that the grading of Italians and Negroes corresponded much more closely than did that of the Negroes and Whites as a whole. The same is true of the Negroes and Indians who seem to vary from each other in relation to their cultural opportunities rather than on a basis of absolute race differences. Also, the northern Negro tests to much better advantage than the southern Negro. Of course it may be urged that in the last two instances there is a selection on the basis of inherited ability—that the Indians of greatest ability are selected for culture and the brighter Negroes go north while the naturally dull ones stay in the south—and to some extent this contention must be true. But it is also interesting to note that 19 percent of the southern Negroes included in the army tests had received no schooling, while only seven percent of the northern Negroes had suffered a like disadvantage.

In regard to the environmental disadvantage of the Negro,

[4] "Three Hundred Fifty White and Colored Children Measured by the Binet-Simon Measuring Scale of Intelligence," *Ped. Sem.*, Vol. XXII, pp. 1-8.

Long, an educated member of the race, makes some pertinent remarks: "One who has first-hand acquaintance with the environment of the average negro child—separated from the culture of the community in which he lives; reared in a home without books, without stimulating conversation, in the most undesirable location; *kept* in a schoolroom under a teacher who, perchance, has finished the fifth or sixth grade; and plied with religious beliefs that are but one step removed from crass superstition, beliefs shot through with the other worldliness of the Dark Ages—understands, or fancies that he understands a very potent reason why the army scores for Negroes were not high and could not in the nature of things have been otherwise."[5]

ITALIANS AND NATIVE AMERICANS—Very similar results have been found to hold for a comparison of Italians and native Americans. The conclusions of Miss Margaret Mead, who studied children of similar social background in a New Jersey town, serve to illustrate this fact. Her conclusions follow: "The Italians are definitely inferior to the American if judged by test showing alone. Therefore, if grading and promotion were to be governed by test results the Italian would be placed clearly at a disadvantage in competing with the American children in these schools.

"The scores of the Italians have been shown to be influenced by the factors of language, as demonstrated by the classification according to language spoken at home; by the length of time the parent has been in this country, this factor being somewhat interwoven with the language factor; and by the social status of the parent.

"This would indicate that

"Intelligence-test scores of foreign children, particularly group tests involving the use of language, are subject vitiation by the above-mentioned factors.

"Classification of foreign children, in schools where they have to compete with American children, on the basis of group intelligence-test findings alone, is not a just evaluation of the child's innate capacity."[6]

[5] Long, E. H., "Race and Mental Tests," *Opportunity*, Vol. I, p. 28.
[6] Quoted by M. J. Herskovitz, "Brains and the Immigrant," *Nation* (N. Y.), CXX, p. 140.

In these cases language differences appear to have been the chief cause of disparity in test results. The influence of the language difficulty may be further illustrated by the following table drawn from Miss Mead's studies.

Language Spoken in the Home	Number	Index of Brightness
Italian	82	65.00
Italian and some English	100	70.00
English and some Italian	64	73.90
English	23	72.93

It is not possible now to settle finally the question of relative inherited race superiority and inferiority. But it may be well to note that psychologists and sociologists are inclined to attribute differences in intelligence between the races more to cultural transmission or "social heredity" than to chromosome transmission or biological heredity. However, there may well be minor differences in intelligence due to inheritance. If it can be shown, as some anthropologists believe, that racial differences depend largely on inherited differences in endocrine supply and distribution, this difference in endocrines might conceivably reflect itself in intelligence levels, although we have at present little or no direct evidence to support such a theory. If differences in neural structure could also be established between the members of any two races this fact might lead to the same general conclusion. But endocrine differences might be expected more easily to lead to differences in emotional attitude and expression. Whether the different emotional attitudes of various races can be traced to such a cause or whether they are dependent upon different conditions of living and different customs and traditions we cannot now say. Southern peoples are more expressive of their emotions, are of a more active temperament, gesticulate and exclaim more than northern peoples. But this may be the result of their constant outdoor life which leads to much association and interstimulation and to the constant need for adjustment. Their religion also seems to be less intellectual and more ritualistic, and they also have more illiteracy. Perhaps their more general habit of submitting to autocratic government in spite of their impulsive dispositions may also go back to the matter of education, or the lack of it.

MENTAL DEFECT AND RACE—Certainly we find more mental defect in the so-called inferior races. Odum found in Philadelphia that Negroes showed 6.3 percent feeble-mindedness among school children as against 3.9 percent for the Whites. Of course feeble-mindedness is an individual trait and not in any sense a race trait as such. For that matter, perhaps none of the traits which we call racial are anything but individual traits which we assimilate or impute variously to the several so-called races because of their more frequent occurrence among some peoples than among others. That is why earlier in this chapter it was pointed out that the so-called race traits are biological, but the so-called races are sociological concepts rather than biological facts. We group together, conceptually, those individual traits which by prepossession or from observed juxtaposition we feel properly belong together and call them in this collective conceptual synthesis a race. Feeble-mindedness is found more frequently correlated with dark skins and kinky hair and other "Negro" characteristics than with the "White" characteristics. But we know of no inherent biological affinity of feeble-mindedness for the one set of traits as against the other. Yet this inherited affinity would have to exist if feeble-mindedness was a part of the race heredity of the Negro, instead of being merely a matter of statistical distribution on the basis of social selection.

The reasons for the more frequent occurrence of feeble-mindedness among the inferior races seem to be primarily social. Isolated rural environments and standards of living and achievement generally do not readily eliminate feeble-mindedness. Even among the Whites there is twice as high a rate of feeble-mindedness in the less intellectually competitive rural districts as in the cities. Negroes lived in a rural environment before coming to America and they have continued to do so since their arrival here. And the larger part of the negro population now living in cities was born and brought up in rural communities, while the white population has a much longer urban history. Negroes also undergo more physical stress before and after birth. Infections are more numerous, malnutrition and undernutrition, toxins, drug addictions, bad housing conditions, sanitation, and the opportunity for the practice of normal hygiene, all show up less favorably for the Negroes than for the Whites and tell upon their general biological organization and predispose them towards retardation and acquired feeble-mindedness. If we add to these more physiological influences of environment the fact that the Negroes have less cultural opportunity it is not surprising that they show up to a disadvantage in intelligence tests, regardless of the question of biological race differences as such.

VARIATIONS WITH AGE—It was also observed by Odum that negro children of the earlier ages showed a closer correspondence to white levels in intellectual tests than did the older negro children. Some writers attribute this increasing disparity with increasing age to organic changes occurring in the Negro due to inheritance. There may possibly be some such changes, of which we do not know, but it seems safer to attribute this relative lowering of intelligence with the approach of maturity, where it exists, to acquired general changes of an organic and mental sort. The older children among Negroes are taken from school and put to work earlier than white children, they are less regular in school attendance, their recreation is less well supervised and therefore less normal, they form bad physiological and mental habits, they develop inferiority complexes and therefore feel less motivation to study, with the result, possibly, that they even develop pseudo feeble-mindedness in the more extreme cases. Their opportunities for study at home and for restful sleep are also poorer than for white children, and their nutrition and hygiene are inferior. Such handicaps may be even more important than those of inheritance, racial or individual, in lowering the intellectual levels of negro children by comparison with Whites.

Dr. Pyle's results in the matter of the relative intelligence showings for Negroes and Whites at different age periods are interesting. His tests were performed upon school children. This eliminates the selective factor working adversely with reference to negro children in age period comparisons for the population as a whole due to the circumstance that negro children are more frequently forced out of school by economic or other circumstances not necessarily connected with their learning capacity. On the other hand it selects somewhat in favor of the brighter negro children of more advanced age groups in mixed schools, where those of lowest intelligence would be eliminated in the lower grades, in comparative tests with the white children. But Dr. Pyle's tests were made upon children in segregated schools. Hence this comparative elimination in favor of the average intelligence of the negro children of the upper ages would obtain but slightly if at all. His figures, showing the average relative percentage scores of negro school children in comparison with white school children (taken as 100 percent efficient), are as follows:

Ages	10	11	12	13	14	15
Negro boys	59	52	65	69	74	80
Negro girls	63	65	68	71	73	76

Apparently bringing the negro child out of the home environment into the school environment improves his intelligence showing more rapidly than the same transition improves the intelligence showing of the white child. If other things were equal this would tend to indicate that the white child is of inferior natural ability. But other things are not equal. The explanation of this better relative showing of the negro child is apparently to be found in an environmental situation—the fact that the superiority of the Negro's school environment over his home environment is more marked than that of the white child's school environment over his home environment. Certainly we should scarcely be justified in predicating feeble-mindedness as a racial trait of a group which apparently shows a relative acceleration of learning in the years up to fifteen, although as an individual trait defective mentality, neuroses, and other personality distortions probably occur more frequently among Negroes and other depressed races than among Whites.

RACE AN ABSTRACTION, NOT A CONCRETE OBJECTIVE FACT —What has been said by way of comparison of Negroes and Whites might be affirmed, with suitable modifications according to the circumstances, of any two races. These two races have been utilized for illustration of the general principles regarding race differences because there are more data available regarding them. We should be very careful about speaking of inherited racial differences, especially in the mental sphere. There is more justification for speaking of inherited race differences in connection with purely biological traits. But even here it is a question as to whether we are dealing with individual or racial traits. Race is, after all, primarily an abstract synthetic concept, a class term, used to symbolize a conceptual synthesis of a great many characteristics which we more or less arbitrarily agree to call collectively by some specific race name. Its unity is merely an abstraction existing as a statistical mean or average in our own minds, without concrete objective reality. There is no one person in a so-called race who is wholly typical of our abstract and synthetic concept of that race. Nor do we find any conclusive unity or identity of traits in the various members of a so-called race. Always the extremes of traits within a race show greater differences than do the means of any two races. Also there are large numbers of a people whom it is impossible to classify definitely and scientifically within one race as against another, except on arbitrary grounds. Thus we classify in this country as Negro any person known to have traces of Negro "blood," even though only a small proportion of his inheritance may have come from Negro ancestry. Race is therefore primarily an abstract statistical concept, based on averages of certain isolable traits, and not a concrete biological and psychological fact. It is a collective or social concept. But it is not wholly divorced from concrete biological traits. In fact the statistical average is built up around a synthesis of concrete biological traits. These constitute the basis of race distinctions. Recognized as such, race is an effective social symbol by means of which we control human relationships and compel collective adjustments on a wide scale. As an abstract or conceptual social phenomenon race is very real. So also is race prejudice, which is a psycho-social phenomenon growing out of our abstract synthetic concept of race and reënforced by it. Not all realities are biological and concrete. Some are abstract and social. And the latter may be as powerful for control purposes as the former. But we should not confuse an abstract conceptual social fact with a concrete biological one in our thinking.

URBAN AND RURAL CHILDREN COMPARED—The retardation in the development of rural children is shown by the experiments by Dr. P. E. Collings under Dr. Pyle's direction. The table gives the efficiency of rural as compared with urban children according to the substitution test.

Age	8	9	10	11	12	13	14	Ave.
Boys	60	65	68	81	82	98	95	78
Girls	56	61	76	80	97	97	100	81

Dr. Pyle summarizes his conclusions as follows:

"One interesting fact which the table shows is that at age eight the rural children are but little over half as efficient as are city children and that as they grow older they approach nearer and nearer to the efficiency of city children. . . .

"It seems to me that the legitimate explanation for the facts is as follows: (1) The country children show up more poorly partly because they really have poorer learning capacity than do city children and partly because of poorer training. The young rural children get very little attention in school. When given an experiment, they do not so readily understand what is expected of them, and do not know so well how to take hold of tasks given them, because they have not had much practice that would prepare them for such things.

"(2) In the later years, the rural children come nearer to the city children partly because they have gained somewhat, relatively, by training, and partly because in rural communities more dull children drop out of school than is the case in the city."

Pressey and Thomas obtained similar results: "A group of unselected country children rate about a year and a half in mental age below city children." But they also found that "the children in a good farming district average above children in a poor farming district. Like Collings and Pyle, they find the evidence from such tests less trustworthy for country than for urban children. They urge "that the usual type of intelligence tests does not give adequate measures of the ability of country children; performance tests and materials more relative to their environment are needed."

OCCUPATIONAL DIFFERENCES—The tests reveal differences in mental efficiency according to occupational classes. Dr. Hornell Hart has summarized these data as follows. "In the three cities in which are located the Universities of Ohio, Indiana and Wisconsin, studies have severally been made by psychologists from those universities to determine the comparative abilities of the children of men of different occupational levels. In each of the three studies the children of professional men average by far the highest in mental-test ability, the children of business men next highest, skilled workmen's children next and the children of unskilled laborers lower than any of the above three occupational groups." [7] His tabular data follow:

Occupation	Indiana Study	Columbus Study	Madison Study
Professional	83	1.42	114
Business	66	1.26	104
Skilled Trades	47	1.22	97
Unskilled Labor	39	.83	89
Farming	27	...	94
Number Tested	1,206	228	2,782

For purposes of comparison, the following table showing the "distribution of intelligence of school children by occupation of parents in the Isle of Wight" [8] is cited.

[7] Hart, Hornell, "Occupational Differential Fecundity," *Scientific Monthly*, XIX: 527-32.
[8] Taken by permission from Hector MacDonald, "The Social Distribution of Intelligence in the Isle of Wight," *British Journal of Psychology*, XVI: 123-29.

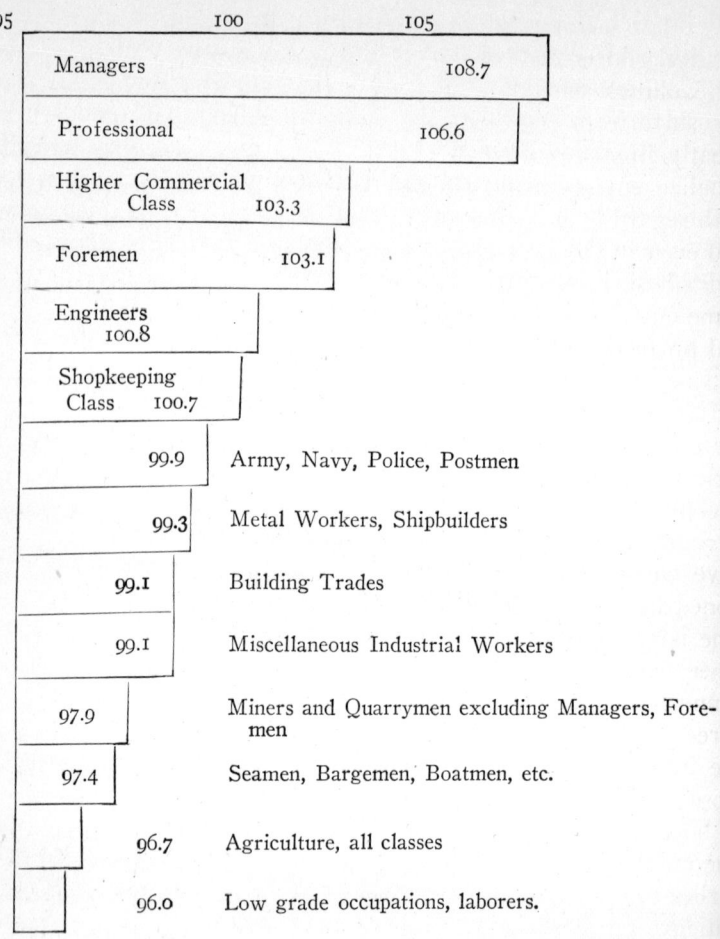

CONCLUSIONS REGARDING GEOGRAPHIC AND OCCUPATIONAL DIFFERENCES—The results of tests here cited are fairly typical of a large body of data now available. They show clearly that rural children test below urban children and the children of manual laborers (to which class farmers in the main belong) below those of professional and business men. The explanations are still largely matters of inference. But we are probably safe in saying that the more strenuous competition of professional and business life selects a higher grade of native ability than do the manual occupations. But there are undoubtdly other factors also, one of which is difference in language facility. After making due allowance for selective elimination Dr. Collings' data show that, as in the case of negro children, the shift from the home environment to that of the school greatly improves their relative rating. The school tends to equalize environments which previously were very dissimilar with regard to language facility, cultural contacts and interests, and even in the matter of general morale and habits of mental and physical accuracy, hygiene, etc.[9] Similar contrasts in some environments exist with respect to laboring and business and professional classes in the city.

SEX DIFFERENCES—The data used by Dr. Pyle also show differences in efficiency between the sexes, as is indicated in the comparative tables above. In most forms of learning the girls showed most improvement in the years before eleven or twelve, and the boys after that age period. This variation was attributed to differences in physiological maturity. It may also have had something to do with differences in interests sanctioned by the community and by tradition for the two sexes. The boys were generally behind the girls until after puberty, when the boys appeared to catch up and forge ahead. In this connection the important environmental fact should be remembered, that, according to custom and economic circumstances, the intellectually competitive career of most girls ends at the close of puberty and the close of their school days, while that of boys begins at this period. Girls compete with boys and with one another for intellectual and social standing mainly in their earlier years. Boys are often impatient of their school work in anticipation of the real "battle of life" which is to come later. The statement that the "superiority of girls is greater in mechanical, motor forms of learning than in the forms of learning involving reasoning" is to be expected in the light of the training and problems encountered by the two sexes. Dr. Helen P. Thompson (Wooley) found in her laboratory experiments that women had better memories and were more rapid in associative thinking, while men were more ingenious. Men

---

[9] The author speaks advisedly regarding contrasts in home environments. A cultural and standard of living survey of a township in the same county was made under his direction by Dr. Collings.

were also more socially minded and women more interested i[n]
religious matters. She concluded that the original mental di[f]-
ferences between the sexes were slight. Others have pointe[d]
out that men are more interested in events and things an[d]
women in persons and emotions, also that women appear [to]
have a bent for domesticity and children while men seem [to]
prefer business and professional contacts and to do better [in]
them. Few would claim that these variations are due direct[ly]
to heredity, but the differences in physiology and anatomy [of]
the two sexes doubtless coöperate with differences in traditio[n]
and custom in determining the two sexes in the acquisition [of]
their interests and skills. There appears to be no clear eviden[ce]
that the native intellectual capacity of the two sexes diffe[rs]
materially.

NATIONALITY—Nationality would scarcely be regarded as [a]
biological fact, although there are biological elements include[d]
in it. It is primarily a social category. The members of [a]
nationality are not necessarily all of the same race, althoug[h]
there is some tendency in this direction, since consciousness [of]
race similarity is one of the strongest subjective bonds bindi[ng]
a people together. They do not need to be of the same regio[n]
geographically, although a nationality originates in a particul[ar]
geographic region. The Jews afford an example of a nation[al]-
ity which has remained strongly unified spiritually although t[he]
members are scattered throughout the world. Some write[rs]
among them Jews, are doubtful whether the Jewish people ca[n]
be characterized as of a single race. Yet they think of the[m]-
selves as a single people closely bound together by unbreakab[le]
ties, especially of religion and culture.

THE ELEMENTS OF NATIONALITY—The essential and indi[s]-
pensable elements of nationality therefore are social. The chi[ef]
of these elements are a common language, a common cultu[re]
including a common history through at least part of the[ir]
career, common traditions, customs, conventions, religion, e[tc.]
And over and above all this there should be a collective co[n]-
sciousness of their similarities in the respects mentioned. Th[at]
is, each one should be vividly aware that other members of h[is]
national group are like himself and that they have experienc[es]
and interests in common with him. Without this consciou[s]

RACE, NATIONALITY, CLASS

less of kind, the psycho-social elements in the nationality may themselves dissolve and disappear under the influence of conflicting pressures from other psycho-social and institutional environments, if these are not regulated or controlled. Each nationality has its own forms of characteristic institutions, its own religion or version of a common religion, its legends, beliefs, rites and rituals, its mores and folkways, its own customs and traditions. These may vary in details in different parts of the world, if the nationality lacks geographic unity, but they retain their identity or similarity in their larger and more fundamental aspects.

THE UNITY OF NATIONALITY—This unity of nationality comes through the integration of the same or similar behavior patterns in the cerebral cortexes of all the members of the nationality. These common cortical behavior patterns are induced through the psycho-social pressures of communication and the common access of all members to the stored symbols and meaning complexes of the common psycho-social environment. Those very elements mentioned above, which are the visible signs of a common nationality, are also in large part the psycho-social environmental factors which produce the cortical and conscious, or subconscious, similarity and awareness of similarity which constitute the content of their nationality. Of course this cortical basis of national unity is organic, but it is superinduced by the environment and is highly flexible and not inherited. Race similarity, where it exists, is the only hereditary basis of national unity. But consciousness of race, with its usual correlate of race prejudice, may be a very strong factor in maintaining a nationality and the common feeling of support for it.

CLASSES—What has been said about the behavior of nationalities holds very largely also with respect to classes. Classes are ordinarily smaller groups, usually possessing some degree of self-consciousness, within larger social groupings such as nationalities, states, or other larger classes. Classes are usually integrated objectively around some one interest or aim, or consciousness of similarity of purpose, or defensive interest which seems very important to those allying themselves with the class behavior and partaking of the collective or class consciousness. Nationalities which are integrated on a defensive basis or because of the recognition of common interests are also classes. We also speak of classes in a purely objective sense, where group self-consciousness or consciousness of collective interests can scarcely be said to exist, as when for example we distinguish laboring classes in general from clerical classes.

BASES OF CLASS INTEGRATION—In our modern society the common interest is very likely to be basically economic, although it may appear, when viewed more superficially, to be primarily political, cultural, religious, esthetic, feministic, or otherwise. Similarity of race and of nationality is not necessary to class unity, but it is very helpful because of the strength of this appeal. Nor is it necessary that the members of the same class shall have the same psycho-social and institutional consciousness and alliances, such as membership in the same religious organizations, lodges, political parties, or adherence to the same customs and rituals, or credence in like beliefs and traditions. But unity in all of these matters helpful as a secondary factor in welding classes together. Thus it is evident that the necessary organic and psychic bases of class integration are even more flexible and more fully acquired than are those of nationality or race.

The more fundamental factors integrating individuals in class groups are primarily environmental, although some are biological or organic. The environmental pressures have their extensions into the subjective response mechanisms of the organism. The integration of a class, whatever the environmental pressures involved is mediated through the cerebral cortical processes. Class alignments may easily change or disintegrate under appropriate environmental stimuli, whereupon the cortical behavior patterns which constitute their subjective aspect also disintegrate or are transformed into other patterns which function to integrate the collective overt behavior other classes. Examples of these environmental integrating factors are raw materials for production which predispose towards certain types of occupations in certain regions, the physico-social environments of machines and technology, and the psycho-social and institutional environments which pred

RACE, NATIONALITY, CLASS 243

pose or mold people into certain class affiliations and alignments. There are also sometimes rather general correlations of the structural organization of the organisms of the members of classes, such as similarities of physique and of muscular development in some laboring classes, or of hands or other organs in artistic classes, and of sex traits when people divide into classes along sex lines, or of race traits when the division is made in this direction. But such correlations are very uncertain and incomplete and fluctuating and ordinarily of secondary importance. The exceptions almost or quite invalidate the rule in most cases.

INHERITED AND ACQUIRED FACTORS IN CLASS—Such general structural traits may or may not be acquired. There may also be some tendency for classes to segregate along lines of inherited capacity and acquired intelligence skills, as was indicated above with reference to occupational groups. The test ratings of the members of various manual laboring classes is inferior to that of business and professional classes. The so-called intellectual classes show a decidedly higher test level of intelligence than the other classes. But we should be careful about attributing the whole of such record differences of intelligence among classes to inheritance. Undoubtedly some of this is due to the character of the tests applied and perhaps more of it to differences in the environments and opportunities to which people are subjected. Some of these environments stimulate the development of intellectual skills more than others. The biological inheritance theory of class differences on the intellectual side can point logically only to a theory of caste organization of society.

SPECIAL CLASSES—We should, perhaps, include in this chapter some mention of certain maladjusted classes which have primarily an objective existence, and whose members possess little consciousness of common interests or awareness of similarity to each other.[10] Therefore the subjective organization of such classes is very meager. This is especially true of the various classes of mental defectives. Whatever class integration they have is forced upon them as a result of the

[10] Some writers would prefer to speak of classes which lack consciousness of common interests or of similarity of members as groups.

attitudes of the remainder of the population who recogni[ze]
their defect, and as a result of whatever primitive means [or]
mechanisms of coöperation they develop when herded togeth[er]
by the pressures of their environment. Their defects preve[nt]
them from developing a high degree of class consciousness a[nd]
corresponding neural organization of patterns of collective b[e-]
havior as a subjective basis of class integration.

On the other hand the members of dependent and delinque[nt]
classes, and other maladjusted classes relatively normal me[n-]
tally, have more awareness of their similarity and are to so[me]
degree conscious of a community of interests. As a cons[e-]
quence they develop certain cortical behavior mechanis[ms]
which constitute an organic and psychic basis of class uni[ty.]
They may even organize themselves coöperatively for purpos[es]
of mutual aid or for mutual defense and the protection of co[m-]
mon interests. Criminal classes are more likely to take a[g-]
gressive class measures of this sort than are dependent class[es]
although they are usually greatly handicapped by the necess[ity]
of working under cover.

ORGANIC BASIS OF MALADJUSTED CLASSES OR GROUPS—[It]
may be said of all of these special classes or groups here me[n-]
tioned that their members are likely to have a large organic
structural basis for their class integration of which they ha[ve]
little or no adequate awareness. This common structural bas[is]
which is more or less typical for each class, consists of th[e]
defects, intellectual, emotional, physiological, and anatomic[al,]
both inherited and acquired. Even if the members of a cl[ass]
do not recognize these traits as the basis of classification, oth[er]
people do. The fact of their existence imposes upon th[eir]
possessors more or less common types of responses wh[ich]
render the members functionally as well as organically simi[lar]
along many lines.

ACQUIRED AND ABSTRACT CHARACTER OF THESE WI[DER]
GROUPINGS—It must be evident from the preceding discuss[ion]
that the characteristics of social units or collectivities, such [as]
have been analyzed here, are primarily acquired, although th[ey]
have individual inherited bases. These characteristics are [of]
course always based on the behavior patterns of individu[als.]
But a collectivity may also be said to have abstract or conc[rete]

al characteristics of its own, as distinguished (but not separate) from the more concrete ones of its members. This is particularly true where the members are able to analyze their behavior elements and to relate them up symbolically and abstractly into synthetic concepts. The unity of races, nationalities, classes, and other non-face-to-face groups, is conceptual as it relates to consciousness. And it is abstract and general rather than concrete and specific in the totality of its relationships, although it is made up of concrete specific relationships and behavior patterns. This aspect of the subject will be further developed in Part IV.

MATERIALS FOR SUPPLEMENTARY READING

Boas, F., *The Mind of Primitive Man*
Bushee, F. A., *Principles of Sociology*, Ch. XVI
Case, C. M., *Outlines of Introductory Sociology*, Ch. V
Dunlap, K., *Social Psychology*, Ch. II
Edman, I., *Human Traits and Their Significance*, Ch. IX
Ellwood, C. A., *The Psychology of Human Society*, pp. 45-50
Finot, J., *Race Prejudice*
Fishberg, M., *The Jews*
Gault, R. H., *Social Psychology*, Chs. V, X
Ginsberg, M., *The Psychology of Society*, Ch. VI
Goldenweiser, A. A., *Early Civilization*, Pt. III
Miller, K., *Race Adjustment*
Odum, H. W., *Social and Mental Traits of the Negro*
Park and Burgess, *Introduction to the Science of Sociology*, pp. 616-67 !
Pillsbury, W. B., *The Psychology of Nationalism and Internationalism*, Chs. I, II
Pyle, W. H., *Nature and Development of Learning Capacity*
Reuter, E. B., *The Mulatto in the United States*
Thomas, W. I., and Znanieki, F., *The Polish Peasant*
Thompson, H. B., *The Mental Traits of Sex*

CHAPTER XVI

THE ATTITUDES AND PERSONALITY

ATTITUDES AND ADJUSTMENT—We have had occasion
number of times to speak of attitudes, but have not hither
discussed this phase of behavior. The category of attitudes
a broad one and covers all aspects of the behavior of t[he]
organism in partially effective adjustments. An attitude
essentially an incompleted or potential adjustment behavi[or]
process. It is the set of the organism toward the object [or]
situation to which an adjustment is called for. When the a[d]
justment is made the attitude disappears, except in so far as [it]
is retained in memory or in the habitual set of the organis[m.]
Attitudes are strong or weak in inverse proportion to t[he]
amount of the adjustment which remains unexecuted, and [in]
direct ratio to the strength of the drives behind the adjustme[nt]
behavior. Attitudes arise only in an adjustment situation a[nd]
they may be regarded primarily as preparation for the adju[st]
ment which is in its initial stages and is to be completed. [As]
that adjustment proceeds the behavior is transformed fro[m]
attitudinal or preparatory into true or successful adjustme[nt]
behavior. However, the attitude persists while the adjustme[nt]
is in process, and the attitude is often regarded as more cha[r]
acteristic of the actual adjustment behavior than of the pr[ep]
aration for that behavior. As a matter of fact the attitude [is]
characterized by both preparation and execution, for the tw[o]
processes are continuous. But if behavior occurred witho[ut]
interruption or blocking we should think but little of attitud[e]
and speak primarily of adjustment. Thus, attitude and adju[st]
ment are usually continuous processes, and the one arises with
the other.

THE NATURE OF ATTITUDES—Attitudes may be either ove[rt]
or inner and psychic. The muscular or body attitudes are ve[ry]
familiar to all of us, both through observation and experien[ce.]

ATTITUDES AND PERSONALITY

We know what it is to take an attitude of defense against a blow or against crowding, to have an attitude of assistance, or of readiness to grasp an object, etc. The muscular tensions which develop in a situation of readiness for play, fighting, or vocational behavior are among the strongest of our kinesthetic sensory experiences and play a very large part in the consciousness of childhood, of the athlete, actor, laborer, etc., in fact of any one who is acquiring a skill. It is through the "feel" of these tensions that one comes to control his technic behavior and acquire skills or technique. We perceive our own body attitudes largely kinesthetically, those of others mainly visually.

Likewise we are familiar with emotional and intellectual attitudes. We have attitudes of sympathy for those in distress, of anger toward those who frustrate our aims, of intellectual eagerness or weariness toward some problem which has arisen. Our emotional attitudes are perceived by us largely through our kinesthetic and subvocal responses but we perceive these attitudes in others by observing their overt signs and expressions visually and auditorily. When we solve our problems or dismiss them, or when the distress of the other person who has aroused our sympathies is relieved, our attitudes of eagerness, or weariness, or sympathy disappear, just as our muscular attitudes of defense against attack are transformed into some other type of behavior as soon as there is no longer any threat of attack. Although the execution of the action for which the attitude was a preparation is a continuation of the attitude itself, the behavior which follows is not identical with that of the attitude. If it were we should never get beyond the stage of preparation in our behavior. And in a sense this is true, for the completion of one act ordinarily puts us in an attitude of preparation for another act. Our behavior itself is continuous, and what is completion of one phase of behavior in an adjustment situation is at the same time preparation for another phase. The problem and the process of adjustment are always with us. Life itself is adjustment. Consequently, attitude and adjustment are not distinguishable except by a process of analysis. Attitudes are omnipresent in behavior.

Attitudes are for the most part acquired behavior patterns

having been built up out of our experiences in characteristic situations. But there are inherited or instinctive elements in attitudes as in all other types of behavior. It may even transpire that the inherited elements are sometimes dominant, especially in the case of fundamental organic needs. Attitudes serve as conditioning stimuli as well as conditioned responses and vice versa. In their simplest form they are symbolized overtly merely by emotional expressions and rudimentary gesture and vocal language. But in their more developed forms they constitute our conscious desires, valuations, and ideals and all of the normative aspects of our social consciousness or behavior. In such form they find overt or symbolic expression in highly integrated and complex language forms. Thus the attitudinal behavior which is symbolized by the partial and substitute overt responses is ordinarily inner or neuro-psychic behavior. All inner or neuro-psychic behavior, in so far as it represents delayed or modified or potential overt adjustment response, is attitudinal behavior. But it can be known by and communicated to another only through its overt symbolic responses. The attitude is partial or symbolic behavior preparatory to overt adjustment and is transformed into true overt adjustment behavior as the adjustment proceeds.

THE ATTITUDES AND SOCIAL PSYCHOLOGY—Social psychology is concerned with the analysis of attitudes primarily because its function is to interpret those stimulus-response interrelationships between people in groups and between people and the material or tangible and symbolic aspects of institutions by means of which they communicate. Furthermore, a large part of the psycho-social environment consists of the attitudes of people. We grow up in social contact situations and develop our own behavior or personalities in the degree to which we are able to respond to, or, as Cooley would say, identify ourselves with, the behavior or personalities of others. This mutual stimulus-response or intercommunication relationship in society is predominantly psychic. That is, it is carried on mainly by means of symbols. Contacts in modern society are overwhelmingly by means of the interpretation of symbols. Symbolic expression is attitudinal expression. It is the function of social psychology to interpret this symbolic or atttudinal behavior and to give an account of the methods by which it is integrated and the processes by which its meaning is communicated. It is because of this function of social psychology that it has recently devoted so much of its attention to language, which embraces the chief forms of attitudinal or symbolic behavior.

This study of attitudes or the communication of inner behavior from one person to another takes on two aspects. One is the analysis and classification of the attitudes. Some of the older writers on social psychology appear to have considered this the most important aspect of the subject matter. This is, of course, a relatively static phase of social psychology. It is indeed important to be able to recognize the significant types of attitudes in an adjustment situation where it is necessary to guide or divert responses. The orator, actor, salesman, advertiser especially, must be acquainted with the language of attitudes if he wishes to gauge successfully and control adequately his efforts. The study of attitudes is also important from the dynamic aspect. The social and educational psychologists desire to know how the attitudes are built up and what environmental pressures—educational and social—to bring to bear upon individuals and groups of individuals to build up the desired response mechanisms. This is the problem of conditioning responses in others through the control of stimuli. It is also the problem of imitation and suggestion.

The subsequent parts of this volume are concerned with these two aspects of attitudes. In Part III the theme is the methods of conditioning our responses to the attitudinal behavior of others and thus building up in ourselves effective forms of personality through suggestion and imitation. In Part IV we shall discuss kinds of attitudes and the conditions under which they are integrated. After discussing briefly some of the typical attitudes and the relatively permanent attitudinal sets of the organism in the remainder of this chapter we shall turn to the development of these themes.

TYPICAL ATTITUDES are very numerous and of great diversity of form and emotional quality. There have been many attempts to classify them. One classification, that of primary and derivative attitudes and ideals, is presented in some detail in a subsequent chapter. Other classifications may be presented very briefly here. As pointed out in Chapter IX, the old classifications of abstract or general so-called instincts were in reality classifications of acquired attitudes which undertook to name and evaluate classes or general types of behavior. Thus the so-called instincts of pugnacity, maternal care, self-assertion, self-abasement, self-preservation, gregariousness, criminality, altruism, and scores of others, are but general classes of concrete forms of behavior which we have learned to think of together or conceptually. It is because people had learned to conceptualize or generalize concrete forms of behavior into types that earlier psychologists mistook them for inherited unit patterns of behavior or instincts. In a similar way the ethicists have spoken and written about the virtues. Goodness, kindness, sympathy, charity, benevolence, truthfulness, honor, loyalty, and all of the other general or abstract virtues are but class terms used to evaluate and classify a vast array of behavior forms which possess similar emotional and adjustment value. Such classifications are devices to secure economy of attention so that we can dispense with the necessity of naming all of the concrete cases and substitute therefor concepts which summarize the whole on the basis of typical representatives or a synthetic view, or some other conceptualized device, as discussed in Chapter XI.

We may also speak of attitudes from the standpoint of their relative prevalence. Thomas has attempted to reduce all attitudinal behavior to four basic types, which he calls wishes. These are (1) the desire for new experience, (2) the desire for security, (3) the desire for recognition, and (4) the desire for response. Small, following in part the lead of Ratzenhofer, has sought to state the springs of human behavior in terms of interests and has given six, as follows: health, wealth, sociability, knowledge, beauty, and rightness. Classifications of this sort are legion. They have been made by psychologists, educationists, ethicists, sociologists, economists, in fact by all classes of social thinkers, as a means of looking the almost impossibly large complex of human behavior into some sort of perspective. But they are always classes, or concepts, never the concrete attitudes as they actually appear in human behavior.

They are our abstract words for such behavior in the large, not that behavior. If we desire to descend to the concrete attitudes as such and list them we shall find it an endless task. But there are some relatively concrete attitudes which are especially prominent and fairly constantly in our attention. Some of these are affection, dislike, tenderness, heedlessness, envy, rivalry, competition, sympathy, ambition, truthfulness, deceit, domination, submission, coöperation, etc. But even these relatively concrete attitudes are by no means constant in form. They vary markedly according to the place, time, the personalities of those who exercise them and other circumstances.

THE PERMANENT ATTITUDES—So far we have discussed the attitude as preparation for an adjustment which arises out of an immediate situation. We should also speak of attitudes in connection with persistent habits of preparedness for recurrent situations or of attack in making adjustments to them. Those problems and situations which recur frequently or persist throughout a large portion or the whole of one's life necessarily develop in the organism concerned a constant readiness for the expected stimulus. Regular modes of behavior or of response to these fairly constant stimuli arise in the organism. These attitudes become permanent parts of the organism's behavior equipment. In their abnormal manifestations the preparatory attitudes may become so dominant that they actually inhibit the consummation of the adjustments for which they are the preparation, as in the case of people who are always talking about what they are going to do but never do it. Here the preparation or attitude becomes a substitute for the final behavior. This result is caused by the overemphasis of the attitudes through too great concentration of environmental pressures upon the organism in the adjustment process. In their normal aspects these permanent sets of induced attitudes are generally known as temperament, disposition, character, and personality. Because of their permanence and relative fixity of form they have in the past frequently been regarded as instinctive. We shall turn now to an examination of their nature.

TEMPERAMENT—Temperament is the name of one of those general background conditions or relatively permanent sets of attitudes which influence behavior; or, perhaps we should say, it is the characteristic form or direction which behavior takes under certain organic and neuro-psychic conditions. It belongs in the general category of attitudinal sets which we have just discussed. There is no absolute agreement about the nature of temperament, but practically all writers recognize its existence, at least as an abstraction, although they differ in their characterizations of it. Some of the definitions which the present writer has collected from various sources run as follows: "Result of the physiological condition of the body as shown in the behavior . . . a person with a sluggish liver will be habitually morbid." "Temperament is physical and mental behavior which results from physiological conditions." "Result of the functioning of the organs of the body . . . as affected by both external and internal conditions." "Peculiarities of physical and mental constitution of individuals." "Their inborn traits and those traits of circulatory, secretive, and other non-neural organs which have an effect on the conscious activities of individuals." "The characteristic manner in which a person reacts to a stimulus." "Tendency to act or behave in a certain way when in a given environment." "That quality of our physical organization which affects our manner of acting, feeling, and thinking." "Those inborn traits which manifest themselves in outward behavior."

Most of these definitions express the view that temperament is behavior rather than structure, but all trace this behavior back to organic structure. Only one places the explanation in the environment, and even here of course the organic constitution is assumed. It furthermore appears that the behavior is characteristic of the person who possesses the temperament, that is, the peculiarity of his behavior constitutes his temperament. Of course one's temperament is not definitely fixed, but is rather a fluid thing, changing as outward circumstances and inner organization change. Perhaps the brief definition, "the characteristic manner in which a person reacts to a stimulus," is as good and as accurate as any other definition of temperament.

ORGANIC BASES OF TEMPERAMENTS—If this characteristic reaction to a stimulus is primarily the result of organic condition, what in particular are the organic conditions which are responsible for temperamental behavior patterns? McDougall has one of the best brief treatments of this question. He says, "The temperamental factors may conveniently be grouped in two principal classes—on the one hand, the influences exerted on the nervous system and through it, on mental process by the functioning of the bodily organs; on the other hand, general functional peculiarities of the nervous tissues."

One of the most important organic factors in temperament is probably the functioning of the endocrines or secretions of the ductless glands. Both McDougall and Woodworth rank this factor very prominently. The latter says, "The excitable individual might be one with over-active adrenals. And . . . the strenuous individual might be one with an unusually active thyroid gland. . . . There are several other glands that possibly affect behavior in somewhat similar ways, so that it is not improbable, though still rather hypothetical, that chemical substances, produced in these glands, and carried by the blood to the brain and muscles, have much to do with the elusive traits that we class under temperament and personality." Phlegmatic behavior also seems to be due in some cases to underactivity of the thyroid gland and some writers on the endocrines claim to find an aggressive intellectual curiosity connected with high pituitary activity. The instincts no doubt have their influence upon temperament, but in most cases they probably stabilize it rather than differentiate it. Diseases, especially the organic diseases, are important factors, for it is necessary for the organism to make permanent adjustments in behavior to chronic pathological conditions of the organism. Toxins and general bodily and muscular or nervous tone also exert their shares in determining characteristic types of behavior in the individual. Among the influences coming from the nervous organization, McDougall cites native differences of excitability, rapidity of response and transmission of nervous impulse, and differences in respect to fatigability and rapidity of recuperation. These are all physico-chemical qualities, and are doubtless influenced by the general physico-chemical organization of the organism as a whole, as well as by the special organic conditions already mentioned.

The neural organization basis of temperament is perhaps equally important with the other organic bases here discussed. These are the habitual psychic sets of the organism and need not be discussed in detail at this point, since a large part of the present volume is given over to the consideration of them.

CLASSIFICATION OF TEMPERAMENTS—There have been many attempts to classify the temperaments, although there is no more agreement here than in the matter of definition. The classification most generally mentioned comes down from an early unscientific physiology and psychology and includes the terms sanguine, choleric, phlegmatic, and melancholic, to which we often add nervous. In addition to these characteristic terms, indicating corresponding behavior of the individual, the present author has collected the following terms indicating types of behavior or temperament: feminine, masculine, cheerful, happy, sweet, morbid, gloomy, sour, secretive, dainty, precise, lazy, slow, indifferent, dull, stupid, calm, average, restless, ambitious, active, quick, alert, brilliant, emotional, sympathetic, frank. Obviously some of these terms overlap, just as temperamental types overlap, and some may object that in certain cases they indicate disposition or character rather than temperament.

DISPOSITION AND CHARACTER—It is doubtful if any definite distinctions can be drawn between temperament and disposition and character. McDougall believes that such a distinction should be made and he defines disposition as "the sum of all the innate dispositions or instincts with their specific impulses or tendencies." "Character, on the other hand," he thinks, "is the sum of acquired tendencies built upon the native basis of disposition and temperament." He also regards temperament as inborn, in spite of the fact that he finds that it is influenced by diseases and toxins. As examples of dispositions he mentions irascible, tender, and timid. To the present writer these distinctions regarding temperament, disposition, and character seem largely artificial. However, we might properly distinguish character from temperament and disposition by attributing to the former a moral and mental bent

ATTITUDES AND PERSONALITY

which does not necessarily inhere in the two latter. Also, we might perhaps further distinguish disposition from temperament on the ground that the latter is more active than the former—that temperament is disposition in action. No one of these sets or processes is entirely inherited. Acquired elements enter freely into all of them. This is true of both the neural and non-neural protoplasmic organizations which condition the behavior. The acquired elements are perhaps particularly prominent in character because it contains so many adjustment mechanisms in the higher cortical centers.

PERSONALITY—Personality is another of the general background conditions closely related to temperament, disposition, and character. It also is largely composed of attitudinal sets. In fact, it includes all of these other behavior systems and all other traits of the individual. It is the general term describing all conceivable aspects of the individual behavior, and it corresponds to the collective term society, which includes all aspects of collective behavior. All of one's qualities, moral, intellectual, emotional, active and passive, are to be grouped under the general head of personality. Personality includes anything which can function in an attitude or in action. It is the functioning self or selves, for personality is ever changing as condition and situation, as organism and environment, change. Just as the self is largely a social product, that is, as the social self is more important in the personality than the physical self, so personality is primarily, but not wholly, a social fact and product. Inheritance exerts its influence basically, and the acquired organic processes operate alongside of the mental, in building up the personality, especially through temperament and disposition. But character is at least as important in personality as are temperament and disposition, and character is very largely psychical. Allport defines personality as the individual's characteristic reactions to social stimuli, and the quality of his adaptation to the social features of his environment." The similarity of this definition to that adopted for temperament will be noted. It differs primarily in being somewhat more inclusive. As Allport says, personality is a result of social behavior, and also a cause. It is the individual's persistent or longtime behavior in a social situation.

ALLPORT'S ANALYSIS OF PERSONALITY—Allport has an extensive analysis of the traits of personality, perhaps the most satisfactory in the literature of social psychology. His outline follows:[1]

1. Intelligence
    Problem-solving Ability
    Memory and Learning Ability
    Perceptual Ability
    Constructive Imagination
    Special Abilities
    Soundness of Judgment
    General Adaptability

2. Motility
    Hyperkinesis—Hypokinesis
    Impulsion—Inhibition (Control)
    Tenacity
    Skill
    Style

3. Temperament
    Emotional Frequency and Change
    Emotional Breadth
    Emotional Strength
    Characteristic Mood
    Emotional Attitude

4. Self-expression
    Drive
    Compensation
    Extroversion—Introversion
    Insight
    Ascendance—Submission
    Expansion—Reclusion

5. Sociality
    Susceptibility to Social Stimulation
    Socialization—Self-seeking (Aggressive). Social Participation
    Character

[1] For a complete description see his *Social Psychology*, pp. 104-12 (Houghton Mifflin Company, Boston).

It will be seen from this list of traits that Allport includes elements which we have not mentioned by name, although we have implied them in other terminology. It will be observed also that he makes temperament more exclusively emotional than is customary with most writers. This usage has at least one advantage in its favor. It sets temperament off more definitely from the general and inclusive fact of personality.

INHERITED AND ACQUIRED ELEMENTS IN PERSONALITY—Perhaps we should raise the question as to the relative importance of inherited and acquired elements in personality. Like the self, its more static synonym, it is predominantly acquired. Its behavior aspect is determined chiefly by environmental pressures acting upon the protoplasmic constitution of the organism. But these environmental pressures take effect primarily upon the neuro-protoplasm of the cerebral cortex. Hence the chief induced organic mechanisms of the personality are cortical and highly flexible. Personality is chiefly mental, moral, and social, and is made up very largely of traits of these types. It is not easy to distinguish between the inherited and acquired neuro-protoplasmic organization of the organic side of the personality, because many, perhaps most, of the relatively constant behavior patterns in the personality are acquired patterns which are, so to speak, "stored" in the neuro-protoplasm as habit mechanisms. Accordingly, when we speak of behavior as determined by environment we must include past environment operating through the "stored" habit mechanisms as well as immediate environment acting upon the personality in the immediate present.

There has been a number of attempts to test or measure personality and character traits, references to which are made in the bibliography at the end of this chapter.

MATERIAL EXTENSIONS OF PERSONALITY—Personality is by no means wholly within the organism, but it also embraces such external attachments and appendages as become assimilated to and are utilized by the self. Thus one's clothes, books, ornaments, even his living quarters and possessions—both in the concrete and in the abstract sense of "wealth"—become by induction parts of his personality. This is true both subjectively and objectively, or as viewed in the behavior of ourselves as well as of others. Every one has observed how such an article of clothing as a hat, or a pair of spectacles, or a cane may frequently seem to be the dominant characteristic about some other person. It may even happen that such "equipment" as these articles of furnishings may so condition and dominate the behavior of the person possessing them that they determine in large measure the growth of his personality. This is particularly true of such possessions as wealth, families, a home, an office, or other things and obligations to which we must constantly adjust our behavior. A change in one's possessions not infrequently induces a change in his personality in conformity therewith. Such external material facts as property and such psycho-social facts as conventions constantly mold the personalities of people in society into much the same general forms and thus produce the phenomena of uniform personalities and collective behavior of the uniform type.

THE EXTROVERT PERSONALITY—One interesting classification of personalities from the functional standpoint is that of extrovert and introvert, according as their behavior is directed outwards or inwards. An extrovert personality is one in which there is a minimum of conflict or reflection upon the propriety and significance of the overt behavior, of self-criticism, and introspection. Such personalities belong to men of action, to those who act first and then reflect about it afterwards or not at all. We call them forceful personalities. They are most fit for rôles in a world of conflict and strife where forcefulness of attack and brute egoism are most effective in getting results. Such men and women are not necessarily intentionally selfish. On the contrary they may be very generous on the level of naïve and non-reflective sympathy, but they are not remarkable for their understanding of the motives of others when these are in opposition to their own interest. Tolerance and the capacity to make ready compromises are not among their chief virtues. They drive straight toward their goals, and if they succeed, they are apt to turn as readily to the subsequent tasks which their success brings them. They are as little likely to pause to gloat over victory or enjoy refined forms of vengeance and torture as they are to study the ethics of their methods or the social values of their aims. They are irectly from the impulses that well up within them; they peak before they think; they love and hate whole-heartedly, nd if they have occasion for either rewards or punishment ney administer both with little ceremony, but with thorough onviction. They make better soldiers, promoters, political :aders, thugs, husbands, and surgeons than they do philosphers, statesmen, investigators, lovers, and physicians. They atch inspirations without much intellectual application or nalysis and carry them through because they possess the selfssurance which secures for them abundance of followers, as ong as their efforts are crowned with success.

THE INTROVERT PERSONALITY—The detailed work of the 'orld, however, is likely to be done by the introvert type. It the introvert who develops the habit of careful analysis as e result of painstaking self-study. He is ever ready to queson his own motives, to raise the question as to the rightfulss of his conduct, to weigh this method of procedure over gainst that, and perhaps in the end to defer the execution of l plans "until the matter has had time to settle in his mind." o many he appears—as indeed he may be—a person overirdened with hesitancy and conflicts and fears. He moves owly and consciously, and not infrequently winds himself p in such a mass of red tape that he is practically incapable f any forward motion. This perhaps explains why great niversities are so poorly administered, for if they are conolled by scholars, who are likely to be introvert in temperaent, they run heavily to overhead organization and too little instruction and investigation. If they are ruled by exoverts they are likely to pick their faculties for "personaly" rather than for scholarship and powers of intellectual alysis.[2] The introvert is ordinarily better equipped by temrament to follow than to lead. He is capable of inexustible research and definition and can oil (or clog) the

[2] In 1925 a prominent psychiatrist gave expression in a public address to e opinion that it is not alone the poor and the obviously maladjusted who ould be examined for conflicts and complexes which tend to vitiate their rk. He added that he believed many of the troubles of administrators e due to such causes and that university presidents and deans especially ould undergo some sort of emotional tests as part of the proof of their mpetency to control men in delicate personal and professional relationips.

machinery of action with a vast quantity of facts. No cou[n]try can have a successful existence without large numbers [of] men of his type. Yet others are better able to appreciate a[nd] to use their products for constructive programs of adjustme[nt] than they. They are the power behind the throne, whi[ch] speaks out from cloister and study and research laborator[y.] Their reward is relatively meager, both in worldly goods a[nd] in praise, but they find their chief satisfactions in neither, b[ut] in the perfection of the system in which they are workin[g,] that is, in wrapping their cocoon about themselves.

THE CASE OF THE AVERAGE MAN—Such a classification [is] more interesting as a practical functional view than for [its] strict scientific accuracy. As here presented the types appe[ar] at their extremes. Actual men and women ordinarily find the[ir] rôles somewhere between the extremes. All of us, perha[ps,] have something of each type of character or personality [in] our make up. The classification itself is, like all classificatio[ns,] more or less artificial and schematic, to which the actual fac[ts] approximate as best they may. Classifications are made p[ri]marily for the purpose of securing perspective of concre[te] cases, not because they accurately describe those constitue[nt] individual instances. People are not always and under [all] circumstances equally extrovert or introvert. Most you[ng] people begin by being extrovert and if life represses the[m] and puts them on the defensive—makes logicians of them i[n]stead of generals—they become introvert, unless, as so[me] criminals do, they rebel against the social organization a[nd] refuse to be self-disciplined. Others who get an early sta[rt] in introversion and become hesitant and reflective sometim[es] consciously or otherwise cultivate the opposite habit of mi[nd] and by a process of constructive compensation build up e[x]trovert personalities. It has been claimed that such w[as] the mental history of Theodore Roosevelt. Others still, pe[r]ceiving the rewards gained by the successful extrovert, sim[u]late his qualities and develop secondary traits of self-asserti[on,] overbearingness, and ruthlessness. Such men can usually [be] distinguished from the genuine members of the type. Lik[e]wise, men who are not fitted for the student life, but who la[ck] the energy or the courage required for the extrovert caree[r]

ATTITUDES AND PERSONALITY

frequently drift into the learned or sacerdotal pursuits and play at the technique of the more introvert careers.

Some functional psychologists and psychoanalysts look upon these two types of personality or temperament as inherited. All complexes of attitudes so complete as to constitute character are of course primarily acquired. However, the inherited organic constitution may do much to predispose one to either the extrovert or introvert character. Robust people with strong native or acquired drives are likely to become extrovert, and the less robust and those with weak organic drives are likely to develop introversion. But there is no invariable rule to this effect.

MATERIALS FOR SUPPLEMENTARY READING

Allport, F. H., *Social Psychology,* Chs. V, VI, XIII
Burnham, W. H., *The Normal Mind,* Ch. X
Downey, J., *The Will-Temperament and Its Testing*
Edman, I., *Human Traits and Their Significance,* Ch. VIII
Hollingworth, H. L., *Judging Human Character*
Jastrow, J., *Character and Temperament*
Kretschmer, E., *Physique and Character,* Part II
McDougall, W., *An Introduction to Social Psychology,* pp. 116-120
Peters, C. C., *Human Conduct,* Chs. XII, XVIII-XXIII
Robinson and Robinson, *Readings in General Psychology,* Ch. XX
Stratton, G. M., *Anger: Its Religious and Moral Significance*
Thomas, W. I., *The Unadjusted Girl*
Watson, J. B., *Psychology from the Standpoint of a Behaviorist,* Ch. XI
Watts, F., *Abnormal Psychology and Education,* pp. 207-15
Williams, J. M., *Our Rural Heritage,* Chs. V-XX
Woodworth, R. S., *Psychology, a Study of Mental Life,* Ch. XXI

CHAPTER XVII

SUMMARY OF PART II

In Part II an attempt has been made to present the necessary facts regarding the human organism viewed as a complex organization of inherited and acquired behavior mechanisms, responding to typical environments. The method then followed was to present, first, the organization of the various types of protoplasms and to show how they became integrated under environmental pressures; and, secondly, to show how they determine the future behavior of the organism as a whole in response to the environmental pressures or stimuli which condition them. Since the neural protoplasm is the most important of the protoplasms for integrating and determining organic behavior, special attention was next given to the development of neural mechanisms as conductors and distributors of impulses initiated by environmental stimuli and a methods of securing appropriate responses to environment pressures. The pursuit of this subject made it necessary show how the dominance of the cerebral cortex in integrating the behavior patterns of the organism is finally lost to the dominance of externally stored meaning symbols and complexes of symbols which constitute externalized or stored neuro-psychic technique or culture. This technique operate back through the cerebral cortex in which it arose and thus as psycho-social environment, controls the major part of the behavior of civilized man. Finally, since in modern life behavior is dominated primarily by the psycho-social and derivative control environments, and since these environments are reflected in the individual consciousness, from which they arose, it was necessary to present an analysis of some of the major forms of consciousness to make clear the method by which the psycho-social environment is organized and in turn operates upon the human organism, and how the individual

SUMMARY OF PART II

personality responds functionally to that environment. The forms and functions of the unconscious and the subconscious and the co-conscious behavior mechanisms were discussed for the same reasons. In connection with the treatment of the individual's behavior in a social situation, which was the theme of Part II, an outline of the structure and functioning of the environments was also presented. The environments constitute the social and natural conditioning factors to which the human organism responds in integrating and repeating its behavior patterns.

The method of development followed in Part II, therefore, was to proceed from the description of the structure and functioning of the purely biological to an account of the psychological or bio-psychological aspects of the organism and its behavior. An attempt was made at all points to show how these processes are conditioned by the environments which operate upon the organism. It is perhaps not necessary to caution the reader at this point to remember that the author does not consider the individual and the environment as entirely separate and distinct facts. They are in fact more or less interchangeable data. Not only are all organisms actual or potential environment for all other organisms, but parts of our own behavior serve as stimuli for our own other responses. Also, it is impossible to determine at what point the personality ends and its extensions, such as clothing, ornaments, physical extensions of the sense organs, verbal symbols, and other persons with whom we associate and the organizations to which we belong, become external to the self. And the most important of our environments, the psycho-social, is made up of the neuro-psychic behavior patterns and their symbolic extensions. This content is constantly interchanging from what is subjective to what is objective to the individual, and back again.

In Part II the treatment has been mainly analytical and in cross section. In Part III the purpose will be to discover the manner in which the behavior which we outlined in Part II develops or is integrated in the individual under the selective influence of environmental stimuli. This part will therefore be concerned primarily with the dynamic aspects of behavior and

will be synthetic as well as analytical in character. We sh[all]
attempt to trace this development or integration of behav[ior]
patterns from the earliest and simplest forms of adjustm[ent]
mechanisms up to the most complex and abstract. In the ea[rly]
forms of behavior the response is primarily overt, direct, a[nd]
immediate. In the forms developed later the immediate [re-]
sponses are more frequently internal or neuro-psychic. Th[e]
later complex and largely conscious integrations of behav[ior]
patterns are normally preparatory to total overt adjustm[ent]
responses by which the organism adapts itself to its envir[on-]
ment. But overt neuro-muscular response by each individ[ual]
organism is not necessarily the sole or chief end of so[cial]
adjustment. Overt response of any particular type may [be]
inhibited in the individual organism through a long per[iod]
of time, even for a number of years, in order that the adju[st-]
ment of the individual or the collective adaptive response [of]
the group to its environment may be all the more effecti[ve.]
Such suspended individual overt response could of course oc[cur]
only after the higher forms of neuro-psychic technique, [in-]
cluding those of external storage, had been developed.

In developing Part II in its more specifically physiolog[ical]
aspects the work and findings of Professor C. M. Child and [his]
coworkers in experimental biology were followed. In p[re-]
senting the integration and organization of the neural me[ch-]
anisms and systems the lead of Professor C. J. Herrick [was]
adopted. It has seemed to the present writer that these li[nes]
of experimentation and analysis have most to offer as a[id]
to the development of a behavioristic social psychology. Th[ese]
men and their coworkers are, with the possible exception [of]
the late Professor Conn, the first among the biologists [to]
recognize adequately the rôle of environment in integra[ting]
behavior patterns in the organism. The sociologist and [the]
social psychologist, working from the standpoint of the [in-]
tegration of the higher conscious, and largely purposive, [be-]
havior systems of the organism have for a much longer pe[riod]
recognized the significance of environmental pressures [and]
stimuli as conditioning factors. But it is only recently [that]
even the sociologist has begun to formulate a theory and [to]
make an analysis of the environments which will enable [him]

SUMMARY OF PART II

adopt relatively refined methods in the study of these higher processes of behavior integration in organisms, individually and collectively. It is now possible, as it was not before, for the physiologist and the biologist, and especially for the neurologist and the social psychologist, to find a common meeting ground upon which they can render mutual aid to each other through the utilization of this category of environmental dominance or selection. The biological sciences will have most to offer in the matter of mapping out behavior patterns, while the social and mental sciences, working with their environmental data relative to the types of pressures or the distribution of stimuli will be able to give a wider background to the biologists seeking the causes and conditions of the differentiation of higher behavior patterns.

Although the problem of Part III will be the development and growth of specific behavior patterns arising within the individual as he functions in the adjustment situation, no attempt will be made to go back of the postnatal stage of the development of the organism. In Part II the factors operating prenatally to differentiate the physiological and neural structures are presented briefly in order that the reader might understand how largely the general conditions of the adaptation of the organism to its environment might be set through acquired structure and function, pathological as well as normal, even before birth. But to attempt to give a detailed account of the development and integration of neural patterns before birth would go beyond the limits of social psychology into the fields of neurology and embryology and duplicate poorly the work which has been done so brilliantly by Child, Herrick, and others. Also, the field of social psychology lies almost exclusively in the period of the postnatal behavior of individuals.

Part III

THE INTEGRATION OF PERSONALITY IN
THE PSYCHO-SOCIAL ENVIRONMENT

CHAPTER XVIII

THE INTEGRATION OF PERSONALITY IN THE SOCIAL ENVIRONMENT

THE PROBLEM STATED—In Part III we shall undertake to indicate those objective processes by which the personality of the individual born into a social world with highly developed language mechanisms is integrated. We need not at this point necessarily inquire into the nature of the neuro-psychic mechanisms by which we differentiate ourselves from our environments and by which we become aware of our own behavior and that of others. Our problem is to discover and analyze the objective methods by which the individual integrates his personality and the sources from which he receives the stimuli which set up the responses which bring about the integration. The sources of his stimuli are, of course, his social environment. The objective methods which he employs are suggestion and imitation.

In assigning to suggestion and imitation this important function of integrating the personality there is, of course, no intention of treating these objective processes as underived entities, as was too frequently the practice among the Tardean social psychologists. They are not entities or ultimate socio-psychological processes at all. They are merely objective or conceptual terms used to describe the two outstanding forms which the conditioning of responses of the individual to stimuli in his social environment takes. There is nothing mystical or compulsory in either suggestion or imitation. Both are only class terms for a great many concrete instances of the conditioning of responses. From the purely psychological standpoint such terms probably have little or no value. But from the more objective standpoint of the social sciences, which must of necessity deal with conceptual and collective processes, they are practically indispensable.

All phases of the social environment offer stimuli for the conditioning of responses, especially responses by suggestion. But the chief sources of stimuli are of course the psycho-social environment. Imitative conditioning of responses must always be by the behavior of some concrete person or by the symbols of such behavior which serve as stimuli. We do not imitate institutions, although we may imitate the behavior of persons in institutions. Consequently, for purposes of the integration of personality through imitation the bio-social environment is essential. There must be models to imitate, and these are bio-social persons as well as psycho-social symbols. On the other hand, any sort of object which has become the effective substitute stimulus to conditioned responses may serve as the cue to suggested behavior. Suggestion and imitation merely name categories of conditioned responses.

THE RECIPROCAL PROCESS—The individual and the social environment, especially the psycho-social environment, are constantly creating each other. But the process of creation is very different in the two cases. Each individual adds only an infinitesimal part to the environmental whole. For the most part, or in most cases, his contribution is with respect to mere details and influences only those in his immediate circle. Individually he rarely transforms to any appreciable degree the great social environmental complex which we call culture or civilization. And yet the persistent and consecutive impacts of millions and billions of individuals upon the social environmental complex gradually transform it and render it somewhat different from generation to generation, and from age to age. Thus the social environmental complex is the result of growth. It has not always been of such magnitude. the days of primitive man, before writing had been developed even before there were voluminous and well organized traditions, and before the physical inventions had passed beyond the most rudimentary empirical stage, the social environment was relatively meager and relatively easily changed, when there was sufficient dynamic leverage in the behavior of individuals to transform it. But the personalities of men also were relatively poor and meager, with the result that they were able individuals to exert much less transforming pressure upon environment than is possible to-day.

But the aggregate effect of their dynamic efforts was perhaps comparatively greater then than now, for we read of languages changing their form and verbal contents rapidly, sometimes so swiftly as to become unrecognizable within a period of twenty years. Religious practices and beliefs might also be transformed over night by fiat of chieftan or king, when one set of divinities was proved inferior to another in some important service to a people. Even as late as the Middle Egyptian period, recently made vivid to us by the discovery of the tomb of Tut-Ankh-Amen, religions changed back and forth somewhat dizzily with the accession of new Pharaohs. But now the social environmental complex has become so extremely voluminous and it is so set in written and printed documents and so hemmed in with property and other social obligations, so verified and approved as utilitarian by scientific tests, that it changes but slowly. Not even very great men can do much to modify it as a whole. Now and then some exceptional inventive genius or group of such geniuses attacks it at its economic foundations and produces in it dynamic currents which leaven it throughout, by means of such a transforming process as the Industrial Revolution, for example. Great thinkers—philosophers or scientists—sometimes produce new philosophies of individual and collective behavior which cause a gradual transformation of the social environmental fabric and give us new stereotyped attitudes, ideals, and organizations. Such a change has perhaps been effected through the growth of the social sciences in the last century or so. But in the main such transformations as these in the social environmental complex are no longer the product of single individuals, but of many individuals working coöperatively upon the same problems. The social world is now too vast and intricate to be mastered by a single individual. It overwhelms, masters him, and he can return to it but a partial reaction which sets in motion here and there a current which adds something to the social whole. Yet no response of the individual, however slight, is without effect upon the social environments which control him and those who come after him, although this individual effect will generally be almost imperceptible and local.

THE SOCIAL ENVIRONMENT AS OBJECTIFIED BEHAVIOR—Of course this social environment is not wholly external to man, however much our language may sometimes have seemed to imply this. The psycho-social environment, in the form of traditions, customs, beliefs, conventions, folkways, mores, philosophy, science, and the like, is carried about by individuals, as well as by books and other inanimate carriers of symbols. The farther back we go in the history of mankind the larger the portion of the psycho-social environment we find actually existing in the immediate behavior of individuals. While for most purposes we may not speak of the behavior of any particular individual as his own environment, the behavior of other individuals, even though it should be very similar or identical behavior, is environment to him. It is capable of exerting upon him pressures in the form of stimuli and controls which condition his responses and make his personality what it is. But with the passage of time and the accumulation of culture, especially objectified and externally stored culture, larger and larger proportions of the social environment have come to be outside of any individual or individuals. The physical inventions, which were at first largely direct extensions of man's organic personality, and which are now frequently highly indirect extensions of the personality, and the social inventions, which were and are also extensions of man's psychic as well as of his organic personality, and the method inventions, which are in our day extremely abstract and indirect extensions of his psychic personality, have all together come to constitute a vast collective extension of the individual personality and a transformation of nature and self into objective social environments—physico-social, bio-social, and psycho-social. These are together man and nature extended and transformed. But they are more than that. By reason of their relative permanence and ever growing volume, their immanence and persistence, they are man's creators. They take the individual as he comes into the world, even before he arrives in the outer world of action, and mold him by means of the stimuli they offer him after patterns, according to types, from which he cannot escape.

The Sources of Individual Personality—But the individual is not wholly created by this social environment, at least not in any one generation. His general biological structure, form, and organization are derived from the inherited patterns in the protoplasm. That these have been selected in the inheritance in the long run or phylogenetically by the natural environment, and in some degree by the social environments, there can be no doubt. But the less general elements of his structure, much of the specific neural organization, especially in the cerebral cortex, and some of his physiology, and less of his anatomy, are selected and determined in each generation largely by the pressures and stimuli of the social environments. This molding process is going on continuously. It is greatest in infancy, childhood, and youth, but it is never absent as long as the personality remains a unit. Our beliefs, attitudes, habits, behavior generally, are molded primarily by the psychosocial environment which, as was shown above, now remains relatively intact from generation to generation. Thus the individual has his personality made for him by the social environment and his personality remains much the same throughout life because of the persistence of habits or sets and gradients. But what is perhaps equally important is the fact that our personalities are closely similar to those of previous generations, as similar in fact as our social environments are to theirs. This fact is very important for the continuity of civilization.

Types of Behavior and the Integration of Personality—But we must not suppose that the flexible or acquired aspects of our personalities, those portions to which we commonly applied the term character, are imposed upon us as mechanically as an impression made by a seal upon wax. The social pressures do not operate in this way. As we saw in one of the introductory chapters, behavior belongs roughly to three classes. These are reaction to material environment by impact, non-purposive or relatively unconscious response on the basis of an internal or neuro-psychic mechanism, and conscious purposive response on the basis also of the neuro-psychic mechanism involving choice or decision. The first type of behavior involves little or no internal adjustment and transformation of behavior patterns and consequently it has as little effect upon the integration of personality. It is this type of behavior which would most accurately compare with impressions on wax, although such behavior does not leave traces either so lasting or so profound. Personality building responses belong to the other two types of behavior, and of these response by choice is obviously of the higher type if not of the larger volume. But even here the method by which environment influences the individual is not that of direct mechanical pressures. It works by the method of stimulus and response. Personality building is a process of personality integration in ourselves and in others under the influence of sensory stimuli, which are gradually organized into higher and more abstract recognition processes. Such integration becomes effective for social and ethical behavior of an economical and efficient type in so far as valuable and suitable responses become conditioned to appropriate stimuli.

METHODS OF INTEGRATING THE PERSONALITY—We have already explained in Chapter VIII how the human personality is integrated through the process of conditioning old responses to new or substitute stimuli and of integrating new and more complex responses out of the random movements, reflexes, instincts, and previously integrated habits, or through both processes together. This is in the aggregate the process of integrating new habits or acquired responses to new environmental stimuli or situations. It is a method of learning to adapt ourselves to new conditions, at least to conditions which are new to us, if not to society as a whole. From our very earliest hours this is an assisted or social process. The mother or nurse who manipulates the child presents constantly to him new stimuli which condition old responses and, by providing a multitude of stimuli simultaneously and in organized form, integrates complex responses or habits in the manner just described. In this way the child soon learns to integrate his random and non-functional responses into definitely coördinated functional responses. In a similar manner he develops coördinated and definite speech forms out of his random vocalizations. He learns, in other words, to use his body as a coordinated whole, to move about, to manipulate objects, and to manipulate himself as a means to manipulating external objects. All this is a part of the process of integrating his physical or organic personality.

But he also learns to use language to ask for things, to give commands, to state relationships, to express emotions, to think. In this way he develops attitudes towards things, including himself and other persons, without actually performing the behavior organically or in complete overt adjustment. He substitutes symbols for completed overt behavior, and thus in large part meaning takes the place of action. It is this meaning which he conveys to others through his language symbols, which they also understand, instead of acting out his impulses or attitudes in complete overt behavior before them. One of the main functions of language is to convey meaning or attitudes and intentions or desires as a means to securing the cooperation—positive or negative—of others in fulfilling our wishes. In this way, through the understanding of language symbols, we develop our inner or attitudinal personalities.

SIGNIFICANCE OF THE CONDITIONED RESPONSE—From the brief treatment of the conditioned response in Chapter VIII an important conclusion for social science can be drawn with reference to the functioning of environment. The conditioning process is always accomplished through the manipulation and functioning of stimuli. No acquired response is ever self-conditioned. Since stimuli are in all cases environmental in origin, the extreme importance of environment in conditioning responses is immediately obvious. It is this fact which leads us to the view that the conditioned responses or habit mechanisms are environmentally induced or conditioned behavior patterns which are stored within the individual's neural organization.

It will also readily be seen that all we have learned from experimental evidence about the conditioned response has long been known in a vague and non-scientific sort of way by intelligent thinkers about behavior. Scientists are always extending the scope of knowledge and rendering it more detailed through further analysis. In psychology this has been done by applying the concept of the conditioned response to the explanation of the development of acquired behavior as a means to the adaptation of the organism to its environment. In one way, it does little more than name a process already known, and still falls short of giving us a complete account of the actual mechanics of the process of acquiring habit adjustments. We must, therefore, avoid making a fetish of the concept of the conditioned response and of ending our investigations into the habit building process with the adoption of this term, as some of the psychologists apparently do.

SIGNIFICANCE FOR THE PROBLEM OF SOCIAL CONTROL—The ease with which responses, both overt and internal or attitudinal, may be conditioned and the extent to which the conditioning may occur (there is almost no limitation to the process) render the conditioning mechanism of the greatest importance for individual and collective behavior. No other socio-psychic process which we know anything about is perhaps of so great importance. It is the ever ready mechanism by means of which a constant fluidity and flexibility are introduced into social life and institutions. Not only may stimuli, or environmental pressures, which are similar to each other in form or in functioning, or which are related to each other genetically or causally, vary the causation of individual or collective behavior by replacing other associated stimuli, but even the most unlike and antagonistic stimuli may condition one another by mere contiguity in time or place, and thus change the moral and social implications of behavior completely. By means of such a shift of effective stimuli a person may be transformed from a good citizen to a criminal or from a loyal spouse or lover to the most inconstant sort of individual, and this change may occur without any act of choice, or indeed any clear understanding of the significance of the change on the part of the changing personality.

On the other hand, the responses, considered from the standpoint of concrete overt behavior mechanisms, may remain much the same or even identical with previous ones, but morally and socially they may have changed character altogether because of a change in the behavior values. The abstract or abbreviated conditioning of psychic responses makes it possible to bring into existence new types of value response

INTEGRATION OF PERSONALITY

without changing the old positive and negative overt responses. Thus overt behavior may easily and does constantly acquire new social and moral significance. It is because of this fact that it becomes necessary in modern life, where the environments are so complex and highly social and moral in their significance or consequences for us, to regulate the character and extent of stimuli. Especially is it necessary to control rigorously the commercial application of stimuli as environmental pressures for the purpose of providing amusement for private profit. It is not alone the traditional economic relationships that we need to control in the interest of society, but equally as much the exploitation of the psychic behavior which largely ends in itself as psychic satisfaction or pleasure and amusement.

IMITATION AND PERSONALITY LEVELS—But we not only convey our meaning to others through language; we also use language as a means of interpreting the behavior of others and of making their behavior a part of our own. This is what we call imitation. Strictly speaking verbal language is not prerequisite to imitation. Köhler has shown that chimpanzees imitate without the use of language. It is necessary only to perceive clearly the form of the act in order to repeat or imitate it ourselves. We cannot imitate anything which we do not perceive clearly. But we can imitate overt behavior, which we saw in Chapter XI is relatively easily perceived, more readily than we can imitate or copy symbolic or attitudinal behavior. But, as was shown in Chapter XII, we can perceive in a social or personality or human behavior sense only what we have ourselves in some measure experienced. Consequently, all imitation has to await a corresponding integration of our own personalities.

This is why very young children do not imitate. They have not experienced sufficient personality integration to enable them to perceive the behavior of others in terms of their own behavior mechanisms or to assimilate the behavior of the other person to their own consciousness. After they have achieved sufficient personality integration—either overt or inner, that is, organic or attitudinal—they may proceed to imitate on the level of the personality integration which they have achieved. Consequently, thereafter their rate of personality integration is rendered much more rapid. The rate is especially increased when the child reaches the plane of symbolic or attitudinal personality integration. He is then a language using animal and can imitate another on the basis of his perceptions of the meaning of the other person as expressed in his symbolic or language behavior. It is no longer necessary for the child to see his model make complete overt adjustments in order to imitate him. He can reproduce in himself the same attitudes by perceiving the symbols of the attitudes of the other person, and these attitudes may even go over into total adjustment responses in the imitator without the same overt behavior ever having occurred in the model. In fact the object imitated may even be the symbolic or language content of a book, which could not behave in this overt manner. Thus while the child begins by imitating the complete overt behavior of another on the organic personality level, the chief content of his imitation soon comes to be symbolic imitation or imitation through language symbols.

SUGGESTED RESPONSES ARE CONDITIONED ON ANY LEVEL —The largest part of our personality content, therefore, is integrated through the vicarious process or method of imitation. We take over through conditioning by analogy the personality content which others have already integrated. In this way we may extend our own personalities indefinitely. But, as was stated earlier, our human bio-social or personality environment also conditions in us responses which are not imitative. It is not necessary for us to perceive the character or meaning of the behavior of another which serves as stimuli to condition in us new reponses. In fact the stimuli which condition these new responses are not necessarily personal ones at all; they may be any sort of object to which we have learned to react or to which we have been conditioned to respond. But personality stimuli offer us much more complex and therefore much more effective controls for the integration of socially effective responses of a non-imitative character in ourselves than do non-personality objects. These non-imitative responses, when they have become automatic, are usually referred to as suggested responses. Automatic imitated respon es are also called suggested responses. The automatic character of the suggested response probably accounts for the fact that suggestion is ordinarily considered to be of a lower order psychologically than imitation. The suggested response also appears earlier in the behavior of the individual, and it will be discussed earlier in Part III of this volume. The initial conditioning of the suggested response differs in no wise from that of any other response whatever. The distinguishing quality of the suggested response is the completeness of the conditioning which renders the response automatic and relatively immediate upon the perception of the stimulus or the cue.

DIRECT AND INDIRECT, OVERT AND SYMBOLIC, IMITATION —We do not imitate society as a whole, except by a process of abstraction and indirection. Concrete imitation is always of persons, or of specific aspects of the behavior of persons. And these are persons and activities which we can hear or see. They are recognizable directly by one or more of the senses and we do not have to depend upon the abstract or indirect symbolical method of perceiving and recognizing their behavior. This sort of imitation we may call direct overt imitation in contrast with that which we call abstract or indirect symbolic imitation.

The person who is imitated may be called a model, because his behavior is copied. Models are both immediate and remote and the imitation of them is direct and indirect, but concrete models are always imitated directly or through the medium of some other model who is to us the direct object of imitation. We do not always come in direct contact with the great personality models of our own time, much less with those of previous times. We perhaps have seen or known but few of the personalities who have done most to shape our own characters through the process of imitation. We can imitate only those who have imitated them or who have imitated others in a series of imitations which leads back ultimately to those personalities who have served as models for a considerable portion of mankind. This also is a form of indirect imitation, and it is concrete rather than abstract or symbolic. We do not always know who originally served as model for any particular type of personality imitation. Few know who invented the type of handshake or the form of salutation, or the dance which the perform. They imitated it from some undistinguished perso near by who had in turn imitated it in an equally anonymou manner. But some of the great original models, such as ou standing religious teachers, the military heroes, the movi stars, and the popular leaders of politics, business, fashion, an thought, in our own times, are known to us. We may eve recognize that, although we have imitated directly an inter mediate personality or their symbolic extensions we are copyin the overt behavior of others indirectly. Thus the stimulus t imitate may travel over long distances, or through a va period of time, and reach us indirectly through the mediu of many personalities, but where imitation is based upon dire contact with and analysis of a personality we always imita some one who is known to us.

Direct, concrete, overt imitation is, as we said above, t first type experienced by the child. Indirect symbolic or a stract imitation comes later and its highest form, that imitating abstract meanings in books and treatises, comes on after the child has already integrated a large personality co tent through more concrete and direct methods of imitatic Because of this fact we shall present the actual processes personality integration through imitation in Chapters XXI XXIV in the order of increasing abstractness. Chapter XX will deal with the concrete direct imitation of personalitie Chapter XXIII with the indirect imitation of concrete pe sonalities; and Chapter XXIV with symbolic imitation of no personal values. But before taking up these themes we sh investigate more thoroughly the nature of suggestion and im tation in the following three chapters.

MATERIALS FOR SUPPLEMENTARY READING

Allport, F. H., *Social Psychology*, pp. 239-242
Baldwin, J. M., *Social and Ethical Interpretations*, Part I
Burnham, W. H., *The Normal Mind*, Chs. VII-IX, XI
Cooley, C. H., *Human Nature and the Social Order*, Chs. II-VI
——, *Social Organization*, Part I
Dewey, J., *Democracy and Education*, pp. 40-47
Follett, M. P., *Creative Experience*, Ch. IV

Healy, W., *Honesty,* Ch. II
Paton, S., *Human Behavior,* Ch. V
Ross, E. A., *Social Control,* Chs. XXI, XXII
——, *Social Psychology,* Chs. VIII, XVI
Woodworth, R. S., *Psychology, A Study of Mental Life,* Ch. XIII

CHAPTER XIX

SUGGESTION AND PERSONALITY DEVELOPMENT

DEFINITIONS—Suggestion exists when any relatively uncritical and immediate response occurs to a stimulus by means of behavior mechanisms which have already been prepared. A suggested response is conditioned ordinarily to a symbol or cue and not to the perception of a total situation, although the term suggestion is also sometimes used to indicate the skillful organization and presentation by another person of stimuli which will compel or induce logically or emotionally the response desired. Since it is a concept adopted for the description of phenomena of a social character, its use is ordinarily limited to behavior in social situations, and especially to behavior in response to symbolic or cue stimuli coming from another person. The cue itself may be either a concrete perceptual or an abstract stimulus. In any case the stimulus is in the nature of an object, act, or symbol which is ordinarily perceived concretely and immediately.

A suggested response may be either imitative or nonimitative, according as it does or does not reproduce the behavior which originally served as the stimulus and which the symbolic or foreshortened cue now represents. If the response has been conditioned to a total stimulus situation which it does not reproduce or resemble, or if it has been conditioned to a symbolic stimulus merely by association of stimuli it is not imitative. In such a case it is even possible for the response to resemble the behavior of another, some part of which behavior serves as the cue to the response, without its being an imitated response. Such resemblance between the behavior of the two persons is accidental, and is likely to be confused with true imitation.

SUGGESTED AND RATIONAL BEHAVIOR DISTINGUISHED—

SUGGESTION AND PERSONALITY

The suggested response may occur consciously or unconsciously. As a matter of fact most suggested behavior, in the sense in which we are here considering it, is only partly conscious. The greater the degree of the interruption of the suggested behavior, the more conscious the response is, and the more critical or analytical we are of it. Hence the less immediate and more rational the response is, the less truly suggested is the behavior. Purely suggested behavior would be wholly unconscious, or at least unpremeditated and immediate. But there are all degrees of modification of the suggested response from that which is purely automatic and is conditioned to an abbreviated or symbolic cue to that which is in the nature of a rational response. The characteristic of suggested behavior is that it approaches the automatic, while rational behavior is ordinarily highly conscious and is controlled by abstract psychic mechanisms. In suggestion the stimulus situation is ordinarily reduced to a symbolic cue, while in rational behavior the stimulus situation may take on a succession of forms, sometimes even contradictory, and be highly differentiated and spread out over a considerable period of time. Also the suggested response, in its purest form, comes almost immediately after the stimulus is given. Delay in the response means either that thought is entering in to elaborate the response on a more or less critical or rational basis or that there is some hidden unconscious conflict which will not allow the impulses normally arising from the stimulus to go over into immediate action.

Suggestion occurs in the realm of ideas and attitudes or neuro-psychic behavior as well as in that of overt behavior, but the purest forms of suggestion go over immediately into overt responses. Psychic responses to suggestion are never rational in character, for by becoming rational they would cease to have the characteristics of suggested behavior, such as immediacy, automaticity, and unconsciousness. Suggested psychic responses are stereotyped responses, such as conventional beliefs, emotions, desires, opinions, and expressions of polite intercourse. The mechanism for the psychic response is already present, and all that is necessary to put the mechanism into effect is to present the appropriate cue or abbreviated stimulus. The essential characteristic of suggestion is that the stimulus, usually in the form of a cue or a symbol of the total stimulus is conditioned definitely to the response, with the result that the conditioned response occurs immediately upon the occurrence of the stimulus or cue.

THREE ASPECTS OF SUGGESTION—Suggestion, as Allport says, may be considered from three standpoints. In the first place, it may be treated as the building up in the individual of those stimulus-response mechanisms which predispose him to behave in particular ways. Such dispositions to activity are usually organized around more or less native drives or prepotent impulses, such as those concerned with food, sex, fear, gregariousness, and the like. However, behavior dispositions of unusual strength may also be organized around acquired tendencies or habits, such as political beliefs, religious loyalties, gardening, golf, reading, or even our food, friendship, esthetic and courtship preferences, or any other activity or attitude. It is possible, if enough attention is given to the matter, to organize a disposition to behavior of any sort which functions with the automaticity and readiness of a suggested response.

The second and most common use of the term suggestion is to consider it as the "signal (social stimulus) which releases the attitude already established." Objectively we know the situation by observing the immediate and complete response in people when certain cues or stimuli are presented to them. When people are highly suggestible or strongly conditioned to any particular stimulus we say they are "quick on the trigger," meaning by the "trigger" their disposition to respond. The thing which pulls the trigger is the stimulus or cue. Subjectively we may recognize the stimulus as something highly desirable or towards which we are very antagonistic. Even if we have no positive attitude of seeking or avoiding the stimulus, we cannot be emotionally indifferent to it. It excites us.

The third sense in which we use the term suggestion is to indicate a stimulus which increases or augments a response to a releasing or suggesting stimulus or cue already operating. This intensification of response is sought by advertisers and propagandists generally. This third aspect of suggestion closely allied in form to the first, but comes farther along in the behavior process. All three aspects are essential to the complete definition of suggestion, but we ordinarily have in mind primarily the second aspect of suggestion, or the highly automatic and relatively immediate response to a preconditioned stimulus. The first aspect is not essentially different from any other type of conditioning of response. In such a sense, any stimulus could be said to "suggest" its conditioned response. The same may be said of the third form. The second usage is preferable because it defines suggestion in terms of its most essential characteristics, the strength of the conditioning, the automaticity and the relative immediacy of the response.

INSTINCTIVE AND ACQUIRED ELEMENTS IN SUGGESTION—Considered from the standpoint of the behavior pattern, suggested behavior is always a conditioned response, unless we may assume that there is an instinctive connection between particular responses and corresponding stimuli. We find many cases in which reflex or instinctive processes are set off automatically by suggestion. But it is not an instinctive release which serves as the suggestion cue. Thus the pin prick causes an automatic, although not a well controlled or coördinated, movement of the body. Light causes the eyes to wink, at least within a short period after birth. The patellar reflex, swallowing, sneezing, coughing, vomiting, etc., all seem to be definite instinctive or reflex responses to definite and specific stimuli. Yet we would scarcely call any of these reflex responses suggested unless they have been conditioned by association to some cue or stimulus which did not originally have the power to release them. And this, of course, frequently occurs, as in the case of yawning. It is the perception of some one else, or even ourselves, performing the act which releases the instinctive mechanism. Or it may be some other stimulus of a non-personal and non-behavior sort, not originally adequate to release the response, which has become an adequate cue to the act through the process of conditioning. In the case where the perception of the other person performing the act becomes the effective cue we have suggestion imitation; in other cases, merely suggestion. The usage appears to be to reserve the term suggestion or suggested behavior for those automatic and immediate responses, whether instinctive or acquired, which have been conditioned to particular specific stimuli or cues by association rather than by inheritance.

ABBREVIATED OR SYMBOLIC CONDITIONING OF THE RESPONSE IN SUGGESTED BEHAVIOR—The response may or may not have some similarity to the stimulus. If it is similar to it the chances are strong that the response was at one time consciously imitative, and that it has now been transformed into suggested behavior by becoming relatively automatic and perhaps by dispensing with the necessity for a perception or recognition of the total behavior stimulus. In such cases of substitution of suggestion imitation for conscious or rational imitation, some conspicuous portion of the total behavior stimulus will ordinarily be singled out to serve as a cue and will condition the response as a whole to itself. This specific portion of the original complete stimulus is now sufficient to produce the total response. Perhaps in the organism's attempt to economize attention no more than this particular selected portion of the stimulus is any longer perceived or recognized. Yet, in real life, such an isolated or selected portion of the original stimulus-giving behavior is not likely to operate alone, unless it be artificially isolated by the subject's attention. In most cases the original total behavior stimulus continues to function and to the uncritical or unanalytical observer it appears to be necessary to set off the response. Therefore, even if the observer has made the delimitation of the stimulus which we have set forth above, he is likely to mistake such a response for a conscious act of imitation.

This is as true of psychic as of overt responses in suggestion imitation. For example, the mere sight of a certain book or picture or the oral or visual presentation of its title, may be sufficient to set up the habitual or stereotyped line of thinking which we have previously established through abstract imitation of it. It is not necessary actually to reread the book in order to recall the contents which have become conditioned to the title or to the image of the book through their constant association with these symbols. Much also that we do of a similar nature when in the presence of others, although it was originally consciously imitated behavior, is no longer such

SUGGESTION AND PERSONALITY 287

We have the mechanisms of response already fixed or stereotyped and it is merely necessary to receive the selected conditioning stimulus of the presence of the other person or of the perception of some article belonging to him or associated with him to put the behavior in operation. Thus the mere presence of people in a crowd looking toward the top of a building will cause us to look up, expecting to see a man climbing the wall or smoke issuing from the windows. A picture of people at a football game in the attitude of cheering or singing will call up in the inner or attitudinal behavior of the subject the words of a cheer or of a song, which may or may not be the one which these people are shouting or singing. Acting under the influence of the selected stimulus or cue he responds with the behavior pattern which is preconditioned in him. Such a response is still truly imitative, but it is suggestion imitation, and is not rational or even necessarily conscious imitation. However, non-imitative suggested behavior operates by the same partial or substitute mechanism.

STEREOTYPING THE SYMBOLS CONDITIONING SUGGESTED RESPONSES—Thus the stimulus which sets off a suggested response is nearly always a symbol which has come by substitution or by selective elimination to condition the original response. In the type of cases just described, where suggestion imitation behavior is substituted for conscious imitation behavior, selection of an outstanding portion of the original total behavior stimulus by means of elimination is the method ordinarily used. The effective stimulus is here a selected partial stimulus. But in many, perhaps in most, other cases the stimulus is a complete substitution, depending wholly upon similarity or association in time or spacial contiguity for its chance to condition the original response. In such cases there may be no recognizable similarity of the stimulus to the response which is conditioned to it. In fact the stimulus or cue may not even be a part of the behavior of another person. This substitute conditioning of the response occurs especially in connection with language symbols. Any word or phrase or gesture or facial or other expression may become associated with any response and thereafter call forth the response by suggestion, although it may have nothing to do with the situation in which the behavior was originally learned or imitated. Thus the word "eventually" has come to have the power of suggesting Gold Medal flour to millions of people. Likewise such conditioning symbols as commands, prohibitions, words or gestures denoting things, qualities, action, etc., must at some time in human history have come to be associated with behavior which they conditioned for the first time in this manner. Consequently in the life of each child they are made, as a part of his training, to condition his behavior through such arbitrary association. Words and gestures as language symbols are also associated with our ideas and attitudes in exactly the same manner and become capable of calling up any sentiment, belief, judgment or train of thought which has become stereotyped and has been conditioned to these stimuli. This is in fact the method of the origin of language and shows how meaning is conveyed through language from one generation or age to another. This fact will explain why certain stock phrases, shibboleths, proverbs, and the like are so effective in gaining the desired response through advertising, propaganda literature, newspapers, the oratorical efforts of revivalists, political spell-binders, and the like.

THE CONTINUITY OF MEANING AND STEREOTYPED SYMBOLS—A very large portion of the symbols which serve as suggestion stimuli for the release of conditioned responses are of this long time stereotyped character. That is, they remain the same or almost the same from year to year and from generation to generation. Each child does not create them for himself, but acquires them or learns them from others. They are a part of his social heritage. This is true not only of words and phrases and sentences and systems of knowledge, such as sciences and philosophies, but it is also true of those symbolized personal and social values which condition our behavior with reference to men, groups, and things. It is as true of emotional as of intellectual symbols. The esthetic values in art are transmitted from one generation to another and from one individual or group to other units of the same character. Although we do not always fully realize it, pictures, statuary, music, ritual, poetry, have meanings which are dependent primarily upon this continuity in transmission, just as is the case with meaning which reposes in intellectual symbols. The meaning of art and of science is not a function of the symbols which represent or condition them to us, but it resides in the persons whose responses, overt and internal or attitudinal, are conditioned to the symbols. The symbols are merely the communicative media which carry the meaning from one person to another through the process of conditioning by association. Once the chain of conditioned responses is broken by omitting a generation of men thus conditioned to respond psychically and overtly to these symbols, their meaning is gone. Such has actually happened at times in history, where whole systems of symbols, like the languages and the writing and culture of the Hittites and the Philistines and the Minoans have been lost because the chain of conditioned responses which preserved the meaning of their writings was broken. As yet no one has been able to recondition his responses to these symbols in the same way in which these ancient peoples had conditioned theirs and thus to interpret their meaning. Consequently their cultures are to us sealed books and their symbols have lost completely their original power of suggestion.

CONTRASUGGESTION—In contrasuggestion, in suggestion by negation, and in partial suggestion and inference, the same principle of the conditioning of responses by cues or symbols obtains. Contrasuggestion is a pathological phenomenon arising ordinarily in people who are attempting to compensate for a feeling of inferiority. Believing, however unconsciously or subconsciously, in the necessity of self-assertion as a method of hiding a weakness of personality, they develop the habit of responding with the directly opposite form of behavior from that which is indicated to most people by the symbol or cue which they receive. Such tendencies to contrasuggested behavior are particularly likely to develop in too much hectored children, henpecked husbands, and overdominated wives, also in employes who feel that they have been mistreated. Occasionally voters, too long maneuvered by a political boss or a machine which they have come to mistrust, develop the habit of voting by opposites. The writer has heard a number of people say, apparently with more seriousness than humor, that they determined how they would vote by ascertaining whom certain newspapers would support and then deciding to cast their

ballots for the opposing candidates. Sometimes people decid[e]
questions of policy in a very similar manner by putting them[-]
selves in opposition to the choices or advice of particular re[-]
ligious or propaganda organizations which they fear or dislike[.]

SUGGESTION BY NEGATION is particularly effective when em[-]
ployed with discretion. It is a form of contrasuggestion use[d]
for the purpose of emphasis. The method is to state the op[-]
posite of what one means and of what he intends others t[o]
understand he means, in such a way as to leave no doubt a[s]
to his own belief or attitude. This can be done in such [a]
manner as to ridicule the view which the speaker opposes. It[s]
most common and striking forms are sarcasm and irony. Fo[r]
example, some one may say of a man in public life, "He i[s]
a very public-spirited man." The answer to this statement[,]
meant to suggest skepticism or ridicule, might be, "Oh, with[-]
out doubt!" with an inflection on "doubt." Or the ridicul[e]
might be made more intense by saying, "What wonderful dis[-]
cernment of motives! I had never suspected it, really." Mar[k]
Antony's famous expression that Cæsar's enemies were "a[ll]
all honorable men," made with an implied sneer, was well ca[l-]
culated to suggest just the opposite belief in his hearers. An[-]
other way of suggesting the opposite of the thing stated o[r]
indicated is to give the statement a pathetic turn which carrie[s]
ethical doubt or may even imply that to believe the opposite [is]
too terrible to be entertained. Such an effect may be pro[-]
duced by answering the first statement recorded above, t[o]
the effect that the public man has a public spirit, by sayin[g]
hesitatingly, "Y-e-s, one would suppose so," or "One cer[-]
tainly would not wish to believe otherwise," or "Whom ca[n]
we trust if not him? Let us believe in him as long as we can."
Iago made striking use of this negative form of suggestio[n]
in inciting Othello to suspicion of Desdemona. Skilled polit[-]
ical orators and partisan newspapers are frequently past mas[-]
ters of this technique. Mr. Dooley has shown us some goo[d]
examples of its use in a telling, humorous, rather than in [a]
biting, sarcastic, manner.

PARTIAL SUGGESTION is often employed in connection wit[h]
negative suggestion. In fact, some of our examples in the pre[-]
ceding paragraph illustrate both types of suggestion. Partia[l]

Suggestion is especially effective where the suggester wishes to give the appearance of exercising care and restraint in pronouncing a judgment. He may seem to be uncertain himself. In such a case he is likely to state the argument both for and against the proposition, possibly with more emphasis upon the side to which he inclines than upon the other side. This method may be used to suggest a condemnation of the views held by another whom it is not expedient to oppose obviously, or to support one's own views which one does not feel it safe to state openly and frankly. Affirming the viewpoint of the other side, perhaps with an air of suppressed doubt, and then stating the opposite, as if in all fairness, as others might be expected to see it, will often plant the seeds of doubt in the mind of another person who never before knew there was more than one side to the question, to sprout there and later to bear fruit. This can be done all the more easily with people who are highly suggestible. Thus one may say of the supposedly public-spirited politician referred to above, "Yes, he has always given his best energies to the service of the people" (following with examples). Then it may be added, "But while we understand this," etc., or, to be a little more strenuous in the suggestion, "Yet it must be admitted that he has never satisfied his enemies regarding . . . (certain deals)," or "It certainly is to be regretted that he never cleared up that —— affair. Although his friends will stand by him, it will never cease to be something of a blemish on the reputation of a man of wonderful power and achievement, and may in the end spoil his place in history."

If the words of praise can be aside from the point as urged by the one who is the object of suggestion, as in the last statement above, where his personal success rather than his public service is commended, and the words of implied criticism are directed toward the issue under discussion, the partial suggestion is more effective. An example of supporting one's own cause by partial suggestion may be cited as follows: "Yes, I know I was to blame in the situation and I won't try to make any excuse. I only wish I had understood the danger better," or: "I realize there is nothing to be said in his favor, yet I feel sure that he is good at heart and if he could have had better training and a happy home this thing would not have happened." The advantage of such a method lies largely in the fact that the opponent is conciliated by agreement and the suggestion in favor of the other side is introduced under cover of a benevolent emotion or attitude.

WIT AND HUMOR are also forms of suggestion. When a newly associated verbal stimulus unexpectedly releases an idea or emotion which is taboo we speak of the expression as witty. The inhibition or censorship is covertly removed without the removal being made obvious. "Brevity is the soul of wit" because the witty cue or expression must be merely suggestive. It must not be detailed or it may cross the line of social acceptability. Humor is not so much the releasing of an inhibited response in all cases, as the releasing of an unexpected or incongruous and illogical one by suggestion. Humor, like wit, must be trenchant and brief. If one attempts to explain the point of a joke it loses its cogency. The response is no longer unexpected or suggestive and it ceases to be funny. Mellow humor, so-called, is characterized by sentimentality. A situation which gives us an opportunity to feel superior to another is likely to be considered funny. Situations in which we can make fun of people, or see them in positions of outraged dignity, are funny because they release responses which are usually inhibited but satisfying to us. Humor of this type resembles, in a measure, the nature of wit. One's sense of humor depends upon the type of response which is released or suggested. Thus we speak of coarse and refined humor, rough and gentle, malevolent and kindly humor, etc. What appears humorous to one depends to a large degree upon his training. Wit also may be sharp and biting, spicy, keen, scintillating, etc. Wit and humor may use any of the forms of suggestion described above.

AUTO-SUGGESTION is a process by which something in the subject—a memory or other complex or set or derivative sensory process—sets off responses, overt or psychic, without the apparent intervention of peripheral stimuli. Or, if there are peripheral stimuli, they are merely incidental to or in the nature of releases for the internal sets or drives. Of course all suggestion is in a certain sense auto-suggestion, because the essence of suggestion is in the fact that the response occurs on the basis of an inner impulsive mechanism which is released by a mere cue or symbol. In ordinary suggestion this cue operates from the outside, while in auto-suggestion so-called the cue exists in the inner or neuro-psychic behavior. Sometimes the internal releases are isolated and merely touch off a particular kind of overt or psychic response which terminates when it has run its course, without repetition. In other cases the process of auto-suggestion is circular or serial. In cases of circular auto-suggestion the response to the internal release mechanism or cue reinstates the stimulus or release in the psychic mechanism, while in the serial type the response either acts as the release to another conditioned response or sets up such a release mechanism for another response. Auto-suggestion, at least in its milder and non-pathological forms of circular responses, is a frequent form of behavior. Some overt or symbolical act or some memory apparently unconnected with any immediate external stimulus or condition suddenly calls forth an exclamation or an overt response or a train of thought. In the last case the train of thought may go on indefinitely through a chain process of auto-suggestion, one thought or image releasing another, as in reverie, until one has reviewed a considerable portion of his past history or has built a multitude of castles in Spain. Much thinking of a functional sort, aiming at external adjustment, consists largely of auto-suggestion, although of course not wholly of such.

In overt behavior also auto-suggestion operates to a considerable extent by the chain method. Some internal stimulus or cue, such as a memory image, perception, or idea, or some overt response or symbolic act of the person, releases an exclamation or a movement, which in turn releases another movement, or perhaps a conversation with one's self. Such a conversation or even response of movements to other movements may go on for some considerable time without ceasing or coming under the dominance of external control stimuli. Autonomous conversations in particular are likely to occur in certain people, particularly in pathological cases. The verbal and sentence forms are of course largely stereotyped, as indeed the overt muscular responses are also. They are conversations or responses which have been learned and practiced so often that each successive expression or movement is strongly conditioned to the one which preceded it. In abnormal cases such series of language or motor behavior are fairly frequent and once started or released they will continue automatically until the conditioned series is completed, unless terminated by a conflicting external or internal stimulus or set of stimuli or some other psychic complex.

It is the same or much the same with circular response in auto-suggestion. Pathological persons often repeat a word or phrase or a train of imagery or a series of overt behavior over and over again, the last word or act having become the release for the initial stage in the series. In cases of dementia præcox this process sometimes appears to go on almost endlessly or ceaselessly. The normal child or adult may also repeat words or phrases as if for enjoyment for minutes or even an hour at a time when in a solitary situation. Most audible conversation with one's self seems to be largely automatic and stereotyped and of this circular or serial type or of both types combined.

AUTO-SUGGESTION AND HETERO-SUGGESTION COMPARED—It is difficult sometimes to distinguish auto-suggestion from hetero-suggestion; for, although no external stimulus or release may be observed by the subject or by another, there may still be such a release. Ideas and images scarcely arise spontaneously in the mind. They, like all other types of behavior, are conditioned to some sort of antecedent stimulus or process, internal or external. Sometimes this antecedent stimulus of release may be in the sensory-motor system or it may arise in the metabolic process itself. Or it may come from without in the form of some imperceptible, or almost imperceptible, stimulus from the clothing, the wind, temperature of the room, the light, the rustle of a curtain or a paper, a gleam of color, a word spoken or printed, even the recurrence of the same time of day or night, or week or year, or anything else seemingly trivial. Such slight stimuli have their power of release, not in their volume or intensity, but in the fact that the behavior responses have been previously conditioned to them. The seeming complete automaticity is therefore illusional, for i

SUGGESTION AND PERSONALITY

most, perhaps all, cases of auto-suggestion there is some external stimulus, or at least internal organic stimulus, however slight, which sets up the process. However, the major part of the suggestion may still be auto-suggestion, for the train of thought or action which goes on probably depends more upon its inner organization and conditioning for its completeness or automaticity than upon the initial external or internal stimulus which releases it. But this internal conditioned mechanism for release by suggestion depends primarily or wholly upon past experience and practice and is therefore social and external in its origin. Consequently we may say that auto-suggestion is as much a social or collective process as is any other form of suggestion, but less directly so.

DIRECT AND INDIRECT SUGGESTION differ primarily in the extent to which the ultimate stimulus is recognized as the source of our suggested behavior and the purpose of the manipulator of the suggestion is perceived. In direct suggestion the manipulator relies upon the strength of the conditioning of the response to the stimulus and does not hesitate to bring himself out clearly into the foreground and issue commands or statements which he expects the other person or persons to accept and act upon. This method of suggestion is most effective when used by people who have prestige with the subject. Thus parents, teachers, ministers and priests, officials, employers, and others with authority or who are our recognized superiors, can afford to employ direct suggestion and may secure effective results from its use. They save time and energy simply by giving directions or commands or making descriptive and positive statements. But even when used by persons in authority this method of suggestion must be employed with tact and consideration for others. If the directly suggested person gets the impression that he is being manipulated contrary to his advantage and for the selfish purposes of another person, or if he feels that the suggestions are given harshly and without sympathy, or that they are commandments merely and not "suggestions," or advice, as that term is sometimes understood by induction, they are likely to lose their moral effect, although they may continue to be obeyed as a matter of policy. Many a parent has lost his or her moral prestige with a child by employing direct suggestion too baldly and with too much show of authority. Employers and superintendents or foremen are more often hated because of the brutal directness and unsympathetic character of their suggestions or commands to laborers than for being hard taskmasters.

SUPERIORITY OF INDIRECT SUGGESTION—Indirect suggestion is usually better in every way except for the lack of economy of time and energy involved in using it and sometimes in the lack of clearness of the instructions. Sometimes there is even a saving of time and energy in the long run as the result of the use of indirect suggestion. Ministers perhaps should always employ it and teachers usually, parents and employers at least frequently. The public lecturer and the newspaper and periodical almost invariably make use of indirect suggestion. Its method is merely that of selecting by chance or intention some type of stimulus which calls forth the desired response in the subject without revealing the motive, or perhaps even the source, or the identity of the suggester. Thus one may say to a child who objects to taking his medicine that the medicine looks like honey, or some other substance which appeals to the child. Perhaps even this method is too direct and likely to lead to suspicion or detection of ulterior motives on the part of the suggester. It may be better to ask the child what he thinks it looks like before offering it or if *he* doesn't think it looks like honey. Or it may sometimes be advisable for some one else to sample the substance and declare it tastes very much like honey. The child's eating responses are sufficiently closely conditioned to the stimulus of honey that he will take the medicine unless he suspects the purpose or content of the indirect suggestion.

METHODS AND EXAMPLES OF INDIRECT SUGGESTION—Indirect suggestions are best made by means of an incidental appeal to the appetites or interests and close associations of the subject. Indeed, no indirect suggestion can be very effective unless thus made. An indirect appeal to vanity is almost invariably successful. People will decide as if of their own initiative to do almost anything if the suggester has succeeded in conditioning the response to the stimulus of his approval their personal appearance or conduct. The best way for love or married people to make up after quarrels is for the offender, or at least the one who must assume the rôle of the offender, to become enraptured with the attractiveness of the other or to speak appreciatively of her many virtues, skillfully conditioning the desired response to the imputed qualities, which will readily be accepted and approved by the subject. This method does not always work so well with marital parties as with lovers, because the element of suspicion of motives or the lack of novelty of the device may have entered into the equation. Tom Sawyer's method of getting his fence whitewashed is a classic example of the employment of the method of indirect suggestion. The political orator's flattery of the reputed wisdom of the people, which he has skillfully associated with the response of voting for his candidate, affords another excellent illustration. The successful insurance salesman or book agent is a master of indirect suggestion. He tells you of all the élite who are his patrons and of the large amount of insurance they carry through his company or of the fine bindings they have purchased.

Dangers of Indirect Suggestion—But indirect suggestion is not without its faults and dangers. It can be employed for socially bad as well as for socially good ends even more effectively than direct suggestion. Direct suggestion brings the moral issue more clearly into view and if a choice is permitted more opportunity is provided for a rational decision on the merits of the proposition. The act or belief desired by the suggester is called by its own name and it is not hidden behind a simile or a compliment. But in the case of indirect suggestion the chief art is to cover up or lessen the direct adjustment significance of the response and to condition it to a movie or an attitude which is really extrinsic to the situation. One is induced to take medicine because it tastes or looks like honey, not because it cures an ill. Another yields to a lover because he thinks she is beautiful. A third votes for a bad candidate because he has been told that he (the voter) is a patriotic American Citizen. A fourth purchases insurance of an agent because he is told that a railway president did likewise. There is always the danger that a decision may be a wrong one when made for extrinsic reasons. Certainly it is not good moral training to be coddled and teased into doing things only on the basis of a personal selfish appeal to vanity or to the sense of approbation of superiors or to personal pleasure. It is better for one's moral fiber and self-respect especially for his social and ethical outlook, to face propositions on their own merits. Perhaps there has been too much indirect suggestion used to control the younger generation. It is possible that they have come to feel that they must be wheedled into meeting their obligations to themselves and society. It sometimes looks as if they felt they were doing others a favor in living up to the best social and personal ideals. It is a difficult question to decide in any particular case, whether to use direct or indirect suggestion.

INNUENDO is a complex sort of suggestion which may make use of indirect, partial, or negative suggestion, or of any combination of these types. Its purpose is to convey a meaning which is not explicitly stated. It is sometimes also called insinuation. Some one wishes a window closed. He remarks that there is quite a draft or that it is becoming chilly in the room. This is sometimes called "hinting." If another person present can "take the hint" that person may close the window. Or it may be that some one wishes to be left alone or left with a third person. The suggestion may be conveyed in some relatively indirect or partial manner. An article of value may have been lost and some one present may be suspected of having taken it. Remarks employing indirect or negative suggestion may be made which are intended to convey the fact to the suspected person that he is under suspicion. This would be called innuendo or insinuation. Innuendo, insinuation, hinting, are very frequently used, sometimes because the suggester does not feel sufficiently confident of his impressions to make a direct statement, and sometimes because it would seem to the suggester to be impolite to deal frankly and "brutally" with the object personality involved. Thus politeness as a system is built largely upon suggestion. Sometimes innuendo is used as a method for the detection of guilt. The person who is suspected, realizing that he is under suspicion, betrays himself by his perturbation. However, the emotional response in such case may easily be mistaken. Innuendo is a relatively poor

SUGGESTION AND PERSONALITY

detective method. A more subtle method of arriving at the same result is the use of the word association test made familiar in this country some years ago by Professor Münsterberg in his book, *On the Witness Stand.*

Most people with a considerable development of self-feeling resent being subjected to innuendo or being the object of hints and insinuations. There is a strong trend in our present-day civilization, at least where democracy is best developed, to deal directly and frankly with others. Excessive politeness, which has been called a system of covert lying, is less valued than it was formerly. Among equals and in a situation where good will and good fellowship exist, such indirections as those here described are not necessary to oil the machinery of intercourse. They are more likely to block it. Apparently those civilizations, peoples, and classes in which there is least equality and safety and where status is least related to merit and service are the ones in which artificial politeness and indirection are most highly developed.

MATERIALS FOR SUPPLEMENTARY READING

Allport, F. H., *Social Psychology,* pp. 242-258
Baldwin, J. M., *Mental Development in the Child and the Race,* Ch. VI
Baudouin, C., *Suggestion and Auto-Suggestion*
Bogardus, E. S., *Fundamentals of Social Psychology,* Chs. VII, XI
Cooley, C. H., *Human Nature and the Social Order,* Ch. II
Follett, M. P., *Creative Experience,* Ch. III
Gault, R. H., *Social Psychology,* Ch. VI
Lumley, F. E., *Means of Social Control*
McDougall, W., *An Introduction to Social Psychology,* pp. 96-102
Martin, E. D., *The Behavior of Crowds*
Park and Burgess, *Introduction to the Science of Sociology,* pp. 408-420
Patrick, G. T. W., *The Psychology of Relaxation,* Chs. III, IV
Ross, E. A., *Social Control,* Chs. IX, XXIII
Sidis, B., *The Psychology of Suggestion*
Stern, W., *Psychology of Early Childhood,* Ch. XXXII

CHAPTER XX

THE CONDITIONS OF SUGGESTIBILITY

After what has been said in the previous chapter about the kinds of suggestion, the meaning of suggestibility will be sufficiently clear. One is suggestible in the degree to which (1) he has ready made stimulus-response mechanisms which are effectively conditioned to definite stimuli, (2) in the degree to which interrupting and inhibiting stimulus-response mechanisms or psychic behavior patterns are absent, and (3) the immediacy and unreflectiveness with which the response follows the stimulus. This is a general statement of the conditions of suggestibility or of the effectiveness of the conditioning of stimuli to suggested responses. These conditions may be stated in more detail under two general headings: the external and internal conditions of suggestibility. The external conditions will be discussed first. Conditions (1) and (3) have already been considered.

THE EXTERNAL CONDITIONS OF SUGGESTIBILITY—It is not enough to state the internal conditions favorable to the effectiveness of suggestion in the purely negative manner of freedom from the outside interference which tends to stimulate internal conflicts. There are also certain positive external conditions which increase suggestion.

Monotony and rhythm—The two types which are most closely associated with the negative condition just stated are monotony and rhythm in the stimulus. Monotony of sound, in speaking or reading, invariability of the form or position of a visual object, repetition of caresses, continuous motion, all tend to favor concentration of the attention or relaxation of the attention altogether. This brings about a condition of temporary dissociation of the psychic processes which is very favorable to that undue dominance over behavior of some one stimulus which we call suggestion. Rhythm is either monotony regularly interrupted, a regularly recurring series of stimuli-

monotonous variation,—or the regular recurrence of the same number of units of stimuli variously organized. Examples of the first of these types of rhythm are the flapping of a loose chain on the wheel of an automobile, repetition of a note in the same key in vocal practice, the recurrence of some visual irregularity, such as a nut, on a uniformly revolving wheel, the actual stimulation of knots made at equal distances on a rope or string passed through the hand at a uniform speed. Examples of the second type of rhythm, which is more complex, are walking, breathing, the sound of another person breathing, riding, the recurrence of the scale or of parts of the scale in musical practice. This is perhaps the most frequent form of rhythm in nature. The third type may be illustrated by a symphony (which is a very complex type of rhythm) or any other form of musical composition, most dancing, diurnal activities as a whole, riding several times around a scenic railway, or watching a moving picture program repeat itself (the last two constitute a combination of types two and three). Quite obviously not all of these examples of rhythm would contribute equally, if at all, to suggestion. If the rhythm involves a repetition of a startling stimulus, such as a loud or harsh sound, or a pain sensation, or a shock, concentration and dissociation will be prevented. Also, there must not be so much change or variation in the units of types two and three as to interfere with dissociation, and the recurring stimuli must be sufficiently close together to establish a clearly evident repetition or monotony according to expectancy.

Duration and repetition of the stimulus are other important external conditions of suggestibility. But they are more important in establishing a strongly conditioned relationship between a stimulus and a response than they are in releasing the response. Ordinarily any considerable duration of stimulus is not necessary to the release of a response which is already thoroughly conditioned to that stimulus. Duration usually means repetition of the stimulus, and this repetition is especially important in all situations where a well fixed habit is to be broken, that is, where a response is to be conditioned away from an old stimulus which is acceptable and attached to a new one which is not particularly grateful to our apprehension. Such conditioning through duration and repetition of course goes on at unconscious as well as at conscious levels of psychic behavior. Duration and repetition are made use of in all "educational" campaigns, such as political or religious propaganda, the advertising of commercial products, reform movements, and formal education or training itself. Persistence wins the convert to any cause. "At first we endure, then we tolerate, and next we embrace," is another way of saying that we condition a favorable response through constant operation of some stimulus which formerly was ineffective.

Volume of stimuli is closely allied in method and results to duration and repetition. The latter attributes in fact, when taken consecutively, constitute volume. The propagandist and the advertiser and the proselytizer know well the uses of volume. What one hears or sees or tastes constantly, if it is at all tolerable, becomes essential to one's comfort. Thus men learn to use narcotics and intoxicants, develop habits of labor, or fall into the dissipations of vice. Volume of suggestion works negatively as well as positively. It cuts off former stimuli from operation and concentrates attention upon new ones which thereby are afforded a clear field for the conditioning of responses. There is no particular reason why we should eat K's cornflakes instead of A's, except that we see them advertised more persistently and with greater frequency. If we hear of nothing but the lost condition of our soul we will eventually save it according to the method prescribed by the particular religious propaganda which we have the good fortune to hear. We are Protestants or Catholics, Jews or Christians, Republicans or Democrats, not because each system of belief or interests is superior to all the rest—a contradiction in itself—but because the volume of suggestion in that direction has been overwhelming. We establish our conditioning of response almost unconsciously (some people erroneously say, instinctively) and thereafter we respond readily to Protestant, Catholic, Jewish, Christian, Republican, or Democratic stimuli, according as we have been conditioned to respond. If the other side challenges us, we learn, that is, condition, arguments with which to confound them. Since they have done the same, and since the whole argument is a contest of suggestion instead of

CONDITIONS OF SUGGESTIBILITY 303

reason, neither side wins, unless one side is more suggestible, or there is greater vitality or volume or prestige on the one side than the other. Volume is perhaps not so exclusively limited to the conditioning of responses as are duration and repetition. The greater the volume the greater, within limits, is the opportunity for the suggesting or conditioning stimuli to be effective, that is, to cross the threshold of stimulation.

Prestige in the stimulating object, usually a personality, group of personalities, or a theory or a system of thought, or belief, conditions a strong readiness to respond to this object. This readiness is due to the fact that the responses of the subject are conditioned strongly through previous experience by certain attributes or powers possessed by the object. Thus prestige as an external factor means simply power to give suggestion and relates primarily to the power of the object to release a ready made response and secondarily to its power to condition such a response to itself as stimulus. Prestige is the prime external essential condition of suggestibility. If it exists, volume, duration and repetition are not necessary in order to make the suggestion effective. Prestige is effective conditioning plus a strong affective evaluation of the stimulus. There are many qualities in the object which, because they have already conditioned favorable responses, give to the object suggestive power. Some of the most important of these may be mentioned. Superiority in strength, intellectual ability, management, cunning, etc., are especially likely to have conditioned in us responses of acquiescence and subordination. The same is true of any other signs of power which are concrete and objective and which may therefore readily be apprehended. Those in authority over us, such as parents, guardians, officials, or those in positions of public trust or strategy, such as bankers, teachers, ministers, usually have conditioned in us attitudes of respect and partial subordination, even before we have come to recognize the fact. Other qualities, separate from or overlapping the above, which give prestige to their possessors for the same or similar reasons as were mentioned above, are age, experience, wealth, learning, birth, moral integrity, success, religious sanctity, piety, authority, relative length of establishment, splendor and show, reputation for power, intelligence, mystery, self-confidence, inscrutability, dramatic capacity, strong emotions, personal reserve, uniqueness, antiquity modernity, universality, numbers, logicality, specialization membership in the élite, beauty, awesomeness, sanity, sanctity Men and institutions or organizations and propaganda possessing these attributes can secure followers and hold them as long as they preserve their qualities. For the most part our allegiances, personal and social, are not so much based on principles or rational choice as they are suggested or conditioned by the qualities in leaders here mentioned. We respond largely automatically and immediately to those who possess such stimuli in their personalities or in the social organization, and we rationalize our behavior into principles later on. Such people are leaders, and institutions with such qualities are almost certain to dominate society. Such qualities or persons possess prestige because we recognize them as sources or conveyors of satisfactions. A favorable response to them is associated with pleasant feeling which gives us our affective or emotionally sanctioning attitude toward them.

THE INTERNAL CONDITIONS OF SUGGESTIBILITY are both negative and positive. The positive condition is, as has already been stated, the existence of a strongly conditioned association between stimuli and response mechanisms. The negative internal condition is the absence of any conflicting or inhibiting psychic processes or competing stimulus-response mechanisms. This absence of inhibiting mechanisms may arise either from the fact that such competing tendencies or psychic behavior organizations have never been introduced into the psychic personality or from the fact that dissociation of conditioned overt response or inner behavior processes has been effected. These two negative conditions are very similar, except that the former is simpler and more negative than the latter. In such cases the mind or inner behavior organization has never been filled with inhibiting dispositions, with the result that there is little chance for inner conflicts or interruptions to occur. In the second case the development of conflicting conditioned responses may have occurred, but the conflict is prevented by isolating the inner behavior mechanisms either by means of concentrating the attention upon certain stimuli to the exclusion of others o by developing some internal control over psychic content which leads to dissociation of inner mechanisms, such as occurs typically in auto-suggestion. This inner control is probably effected by fixing the attention upon some external or, more frequently, psychic or mnemic symbol or cue which organizes the psychic and overt responses in the desired manner as preconditioned. Thus concentration of the attention upon external involuntary stimuli or voluntary fixation upon an external object, as in crystal gazing, or upon an internal symbol, as in automatic trance, is essential to that degree of dissociation of psychic processes which renders one readily suggestible in a unilateral direction.

Where one is suggestible to a large number of stimuli at the same time we say he is excited. He is as truly suggestible or suggested in this as in other cases of suggestion where the behavior is more direct and unified, but since we have associated the term suggestion with a fairly well integrated and isolated type of response which excludes other types we do not speak of response by general excitement as suggested behavior. Of course, excitement may also be due to conflicts in imitation or of some other form of stimulation. The more intense and concentrated or isolated the relatively automatic and uncritical conditioned responses are, the purer and more profound the type of suggestion, according to conventional usage.

THE UNFILLED MIND AS A CONDITION OF SUGGESTIBILITY —The unfilled mind operates as a favorable factor in suggestibility in a great many types of cases. But it can thus operate only if there are certain behavior mechanisms in the mind which are effectively conditioned to stimuli. This condition is likely always to exist, even in those of the lowest intelligence quotient or with the least training. Because all animals, human or otherwise, have certain natural drives or prepotent dispositions, such as the need for food, and the desire for sex satisfaction—to which they soon add other and acquired drives for at least shelter, protection from enemies, and possibly for association with their kind, as a minimum requirement for existence—certain habits of response grow up to supplement whatever instinctive behavior processes there may be for the effective realization of such drives. These responses, native and acquired, become conditioned to appropriate stimuli an[d] render the subject suggestible to these stimuli which call fo[r] the satisfaction of his native and acquired interests by what[-] ever means he has learned or inherited. What we really mea[n] when we speak of a mind unfilled by inhibiting behavior mech[-] anisms is that the higher and more socialized, esthetic and eth[-] ical, behavior patterns which we find in cultivated or civilize[d] man have not yet been, or cannot be, added to our behavio[r] complexes to serve as restraints upon the relatively irration[al] satisfaction of our wants and desires under the dominance o[f] suggestion. Certain classes of animals and human beings a[re] particularly suggestible because of this fact.

The animals below man are highly suggestible in the direc[-] tion of their instinctive and simple acquired interests or need[s.] Only the most rigorous training or substitute conditioning o[f] responses can prevent the hungry dog from eating his master['s] food when his back is turned. Male work horses are mad[e] into geldings because it is difficult or impossible otherwise [to] train them not to respond to sex stimuli from females. B[ut] a dog carefully trained to point, or to hunt only certain type[s] of game, will usually hold that training unless stimulated b[y] his master (to whose suggestions he responds preferentially) [to] break it. Monkeys and apes are highly suggestible along ce[r-] tain limited natural lines, as is the case with some other an[i-] mals, and they will hold careful training for a considerab[le] period of time. They, together with elephants and dogs an[d] horses, can be conditioned to respond with a very large num[-] ber of simple learned behavior mechanisms to appropriate c[ues] or symbolic stimuli which have become conditioning facto[rs] through association. These responses, however, are all in th[e] field of suggestion. They are not able to imitate, except in th[e] case of apes who do so in a rudimentary manner, because the[y] cannot easily perceive or recognize the total behavior stimulu[s.] Suggestion is of a lower order of adaptive control than imit[a-] tion.

Feeble-minded persons, like lower animals, are highly sug[-] gestible in line with their fundamental drives, but find it ve[ry] difficult or impossible to condition their responses effectively [to] cultural or social stimuli of a high order, especially when considerable degree of intelligence is involved. The higher grades of the feeble-minded can be successfully conditioned to stimuli to sympathetic response, acquiescence and loyalty and tenderness of a high degree of concentration in simple relationships, and are thus made highly suggestible to some of the finest simple emotional values in our culture. But, without constant reënforcement of the suggestion through the presence of the stimulus or even some supplementary stimulus, the cultural and more complex and abstract acquired conditionings give way before the more nearly instinctive and appetitive. Sometimes the lapse from the artificial to the natural control in this respect is very striking and even shocking, as in cases where carefully regimented morons suddenly yield to the stimulus to commit some sex delinquency or some act of violence in anger. Because the feeble-minded are relatively so wanting in inhibiting psychic behavior mechanisms, especially of the intellectual or rational type, they are highly suggestible in those directions in which they have built up conditioned responses and in the direction of their native drives. They pour their energies without reserve into any line of activities which they have learned to perform, but they are fickle and can be suggested with surprising facility into other, even contradictory, types of behavior, in which they are equally violent and excessive. We are accustomed to say that the feeble-minded have strong emotions, but weak characters. The trouble is that they are not able to build up sufficient rational or intellectual content for their psychic personalities and consequently develop little power of inhibition of contrary suggestion. They may not even have the intelligence to perceive the illogicality of their own behavior, or if they have they are unable to inhibit suggestions and control their conduct. The feeble-minded often suffer acute remorse, if they have been conditioned by ethical stimuli, but the remorse is easily wiped out of consciousness by the appearance of some other suggestion. It does not become a permanent mode of response.

The young, like the feeble-minded and lower animals, are highly suggestible in the direction of their relatively few preconditioned responses. But unlike the feeble-minded and animals, they can build up a rational psychic content or rival con-

ditioned responses, which inhibit the more appetitive response
to suggestion. The conditioning of rival responses is in effect
a process of rendering the subject responsive to new and
more cultural or more highly socialized stimuli to which he
was not before subject or sensitive. This process of acquiring
a sensitivity to a broader range of stimuli which serve to condition
responses away from the more appetitive stimuli and
thus to sublimate and intellectualize and socialize behavior is
in the broadest sense, the process of education, whether it be
in schools or elsewhere. Childhood is the period preëminently
of heterosuggestibility. Home and school and playgroup give
him conditioning stimuli of great volume in a continuous
stream, until the new associations of stimuli and responses take
the place of the old. Here also the adults with whom he comes
in contact have such prestige as no other persons probably ever
will possess. Consequently their suggestions or stimuli—the
commands, wishes, preferences, which he perceives—take effect
with great force upon the behavior of the child. As the
child's experience grows he begins to develop rational imitation
at the expense of suggestion and he may even develop a
considerable degree of original thinking. But as age advances
and as life becomes more highly stereotyped for him, in those
ways indicated in the following chapter, he begins again to act
on the basis of suggestion and probably ends his natural life
period with as large a proportion of his behavior controlled by
auto-suggestion or the repetition of his own responses as
childhood was controlled by hetero-suggestion.

The uneducated and those inexperienced in the problems of
life adjustment are much like children both in their lack of the
development of susceptibility to rival stimuli of a cultural character
to condition or inhibit their prepotent or previously conditioned
responses and in their capacity to develop a high degree
of susceptibility under proper circumstances. The same
is also true of *backward races and peoples.* In fact, there is a
very close social analogy between the backward peoples or
races, whether they come from isolated districts in the midst
of a highly cultivated civilization, as from mountainous regions,
or from the slums of great cities, or from larger geographical
units of isolation in the midst of a world civilization.

the types of stimuli to which the untutored mountaineer and the south sea islander will react are not essentially different from those to which the denizen of the slum responds, although the latter may have developed more variety and faddism in the method of his response. All alike may be conditioned to new cultural stimuli and given new responses under proper conditions of training. These people are easily suggestible in the direction of their previous habits of acting and thinking, but is very difficult to suggest to them behavior contrary to their experience, even when the suggestion comes from some one with much prestige. The backwoodsman may be sold "green goods" or a "gold brick" or be conditioned to an intolerance of the theory of evolution; the savage may be convinced that the civilized man has a wonderful magic superior to his own; and the slum dweller may accept the statement that farmers "pick" potatoes and "dig" cabbages without question. But it is not possible to "put over" on the first any "nonsense" about methods of trapping "varmints"; or the second, with regard to stalking game; or the last, about the location of "moonshine joints" or the economic condition of the poor.

Men and women of culture are also highly suggestible, by skilled manipulators, in those fields in which they lack experience or scientific data with which to check stimuli. Insurance agents, book agents, and other persistent salesmen, usually find women easier prey than men, and a pretty woman can sell some men almost anything in spite of their experience with agents. In the one case, the woman's responses are conditioned to the glowing words of idealism and day-dreamy promises, which her experience or knowledge is not able to contradict. Living a more or less repressed and inexperienced life, she consequently responds to the stimuli of hope or to the suggestion that all the other women of intelligence and fashion have purchased the article, instead of to the actual merits of the object which is before her. In the second case, the average man responds by previous conditioning to the artfully manipulated sex stimuli, while he thinks he is rationally considering the value of the books or other articles. Thus in reality women sell sex appeal while the men frequently buy this stimulus and pay for books they never open. It is not possible, however, under normal stimuli conditions, to suggest a social false step to a well-trained woman of fashion or the purchase of worthless oil stock or submerged real estate to a keen business man. In their own fields men and women are "hard boiled," unless their responses are conditioned by analogy and unconsciously to stimuli that release other responses which are ordinarily censored and kept in the background. This is what happens in the case of the man buying books for which he has no use because the saleswoman appealed to his unconscious admiration for a pretty woman while his critical financial judgment was in temporary abeyance. On the whole, it may be said that women of good intelligence are more likely to be suggested contrary to reason where a matter of lack of experience is involved. Both men and women are likely to be suggested contrary to interest where the suggester can make a covert and unrecognized appeal by conditioning a substitute stimulus which operates strongly in the subconsciousness of the one being manipulated, but is carefully kept out of the argument.

DISSOCIATION of stimulus-response processes facilitates suggestion by removing competing response mechanisms which may be conditioned as a whole or in part to the same stimuli and by eliminating or making of no effect rival stimuli which condition effective responses. The manner of the operation of dissociation has already been shown with sufficient clearness. The competing psychic processes do not cease to exist in dissociation. They are still in the nervous system, but dormant because not stimulated to active response, either through inhibitions, or lack of stimuli. Various subjective conditions organic and psychic, facilitate this dissociation. People with abnormal psychological traits, the hystericals and psychopaths generally, dissociate their psychic behavior mechanisms more easily than the psychically normal individuals. Hysteria and all types of schizophrenia, from absent-mindedness to actual division of personality and chronic functional amnesia, are cases of dissociation. But temporary and intermittent dissociation, resulting in "queer" and sometimes contradictory behavior, is probably more frequent than the layman suspects. Practically all people vary considerably in the degree and type of their suggestibility according to environmental circum-

CONDITIONS OF SUGGESTIBILITY 311

stances and organic and mental condition. During illness, or when the body's resistance is lowered through fatigue or strain, or during any great emotional stress, one is much more suggestible than at other times, because these conditions facilitate dissociation and render the connection between conditioned response and stimulus more readily open. Some of the typical subjective conditions producing dissociation and therefore facilitating suggestion will be explained in the following paragraphs.

FATIGUE, FASTING, INTOXICATION, and like conditions have a tendency to raise the threshold of stimulation because of their toxic effects upon the nervous system. This probably causes the weaker synaptic connections to cease functioning, thereby dissociating the behavior patterns of the weaker from the stronger impulses. The impulses which are strongest are likely, other things being equal, to be those dispositions in which the stimulus-response organizations have the largest number of instinctive connections, or in which the acquired connections have been made most effective through conditioning. Some habits frequently practiced become in this way as firmly rooted as the instincts themselves. In fact all of the behavior complexes, including those which contain strong instinctive elements, are habitual or acquired. Through the raising of the threshold of stimulation, due to fatigue, fasting, intoxication, or any sort of tissue poisoning or interference with the synapses, the weaker impulses, which are usually the more cultural and the more recent, drop out of operation, and leave the stronger impulses operative and easily subject to uninterrupted suggestion. The diagram on page 312 serves to illustrate this principle.

ABNORMAL ASPECTS OF THIS TYPE OF SUGGESTION—It is under such conditions as these that much of the unconventional, brutal and apparently inexplicable conduct of otherwise conventional people occurs. People are more frequently irritable when fatigued or ill or intoxicated than at other times, and they will respond to stimulation with violence as they would not if their more rational and cultural complexes were functioning as inhibitory mechanisms. It is often said that when drunk or tired one's true nature shows up, and this is in large measure correct, for the usual cultural inhibitions are then re-

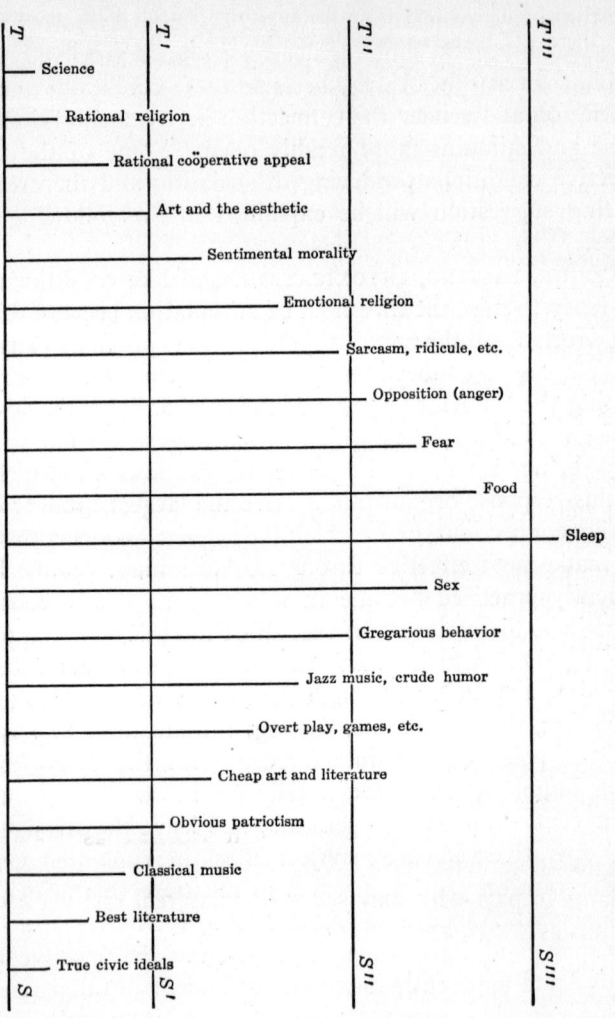

The base line, TS, represents the hypothetical and theoretical norm threshold of stimulation, at which all of the behavior complexes represented by perpendicular lines are susceptible of stimulation or release by appropriate stimuli. The height of the perpendicular lines indicates the synaptic or impulsive strength of these several complexes for which they stand. fatigue or other toxic producing conditions occur the threshold of stimulation is raised to T'S'. The result is that the weaker or cultural impulses can no longer be stimulated or pass through the synapses and they drop

CONDITIONS OF SUGGESTIBILITY

as inhibiting factors. If the threshold is not raised too greatly and if the dissociation of the cultural from the appetitive stimuli is not too thoroughgoing, there will be no remarkable change in the character of the type of suggestion to which one is subject. But if the threshold of stimulation is raised, say to $T''S''$, the dissociation of behavior patterns is very marked, practically all of the cultural inhibiting processes having disappeared, with the result that the more appetitive behavior complexes remain in possession of the organism. The organism may become quiescent or "go to sleep" in extreme cases (when the threshold has been raised to $T'''S'''$), or it may, if properly stimulated, seek the satisfaction of one or more of the other dominant drives. No attempt has been made to include all of the interests or impulses of the organism in this chart.

moved. If it is not the true nature, it is at least the deepest rooted nature which is thus made apparent. Intoxicated people commit more sex delinquencies and acts of violence, and evidence less control generally, including indulgence in undignified conduct and buffoonery, than people who are not intoxicated. It is not, however, always easy here to distinguish between cause and effect. Possibly intoxication is in part the result, as well as the cause, of inadequate inhibitory controls. People who have fasted are in a sense toxic, through the lack of adequate replenishment of broken down tissues and elimination of waste matter. Because of this fact, and because there are lacking adequate chemical stimuli or metabolism for the nervous processes, the threshold of stimulation is raised or the synaptic connections of the weaker behavior sets cease to operate effectively, and inhibition of suggestion in the direction of dominant interests or impulses is lessened.

This will explain why religious beliefs are much more evident to those who have fasted than to the fleshly. It also explains in part why they see visions as real objects and have phantasies which are counterparts of their waking meditations. Delirium in fever appears under conditions of marked autointoxication and slight inhibition of dominant impulses. In all of these cases of the raising of the threshold of stimulation and the consequent dissociation of behavior complexes, it is the more firmly fixed or deeply rooted interests which are susceptible to suggestion. These are not necessarily the more nearly instinctive complexes. They may be wholly acquired interests, as in the case of religion, which is fostered by suggestion. People also develop phobias of various sorts which show up during intoxication or extreme fatigue or hunger, and especially in deliriums from fevers or in delirium tremens. Other people are "hipped" on politics, art, or in fact, on anything. Any interest whatever may become the dominant set in one's character, showing up with surprising susceptibility to suggestion under proper conditions for suggestibility.

FIXED IDEAS, MANIAS, AND PHOBIAS—When this dissociation is for any cause relatively permanent and the subject is rendered particularly and constantly suggestible along the line of a dominant interest we speak of fixed ideas or manias. These may range in intensity all the way from mild peculiarities, foibles, hobbies, nuisances, and the like, up to distinct and recognized types of insanities. The causes of such dissociation and consequent suggestibility are not merely fatigue, fasting, intoxication, narcosis, and autointoxication. These are normally temporary and transient. But occasionally they assume relatively permanent forms, as in the case of chronic neurasthenia or chronic toxemia from drug addiction or glandular infections, such as goiter. In such cases the inhibiting cultural or rational interests may disappear practically completely and leave the affected person the victim of fear hallucinations, or subject to unrelieved and uninterrupted suggestions of any preconditioned type whatever. In their extreme form these conditioned susceptibilities to suggestion render the subject psychotic and true insanities develop. The condition of radical dissociation known as hysteria may grow out of such organic conditions, or it may develop as a functional type of schizophrenia due to the subject's inability to handle difficult adjustment situations. Hysteria and radical schizophrenia, or true dissociated personality, show the greatest degrees of suggestibility along these lines.

The hysterical person is suggestible along the lines of the major conditionings of his responses to the degree of being unable to see any situation in true perspective or in a rational light. In the dissociated personality suggestion masses wholly along certain lines and cleavages, with the result that the conditioning of responses to stimuli across those cleavages cannot take place at all. The illusions of dementia præcox and paranoia, and of similar or other functional personality dis

CONDITIONS OF SUGGESTIBILITY

tortions, are due primarily to dissociation of behavior complexes which leaves the dominant set or system of conditioned responses uninhibited by the opposite or corrective tendencies. In psychoanalytic literature these dissociated corrective processes are said to be censored. As a consequence suggestion is uninterrupted and all-powerful in the direction of the psychotic imagery.

PREJUDICES AND OTHER MILD FORMS OF FIXED IDEAS—These are relatively extreme cases of suggestibility due to dissociation. They are recognized everywhere as being abnormal and sometimes require highly specialized and insistent treatment. But there are many milder forms which for the most part escape any but the most casual notice by laymen. We dismiss them ordinarily with the explanation that the subject is "queer." Dr. Samuel Johnson, it is said, could not pass a lamp post without yielding to the suggestion to touch it. Old maids are supposed each night to look under their beds to discover a man in hiding. It is recorded that Bulwer-Lytton could not write well except in evening clothes. The flow of ideas of another writer is said to be conditioned to the use of a goose quill pen. These habits of response are in fact not different in kind from many other mild types of suggestibility which we do not regard as queer or unconventional. The conventions of chivalry belong in this class, some of which still remain. Within our own memories the near approach of a lady acquaintance irresistibly conditioned the lifting of the hat and bowing by the male. Even now no one can resist, at parting from a reception, however boresome, the temptation to say, "It has been a delightful evening, Mrs. ——."

Somewhat more radical is the dissociation in the case of what we call prejudices. A prejudice arises from the strong conditioning of certain psychic behavior or attitudes to certain corresponding stimuli and the dissociation of inhibiting tendencies, with the result that the inhibiting processes are not adequate to break these conditionings. As a consequence the prejudiced person has a fixed idea or is radically suggestible in the direction of his belief or allegiance. Such prejudices are particularly liable to form in connection with religion, politics, sex matters, one's kin or property, art, or any other objects which call from us strong emotional responses. It is very difficult to be rational and objective, or unprejudiced about things which are close to us or for which we have made sacrifices or which we have molded to our own liking, that is, things to which our responses have become strongly conditioned. We are strongly suggestible in favor of our friends, family, party, creed, property, and the like, and just as strongly suggestible against our enemies and the friends, families, and property of our rivals. A "good" Republican or Democrat will believe almost anything he reads or hears in favor of his own party or in opposition to the rival parties. It is only recently that we have persuaded ourselves not to consign the adherents of rival religious creeds to the flames in the world to come or as surely to expect to meet all of those who profess our own faith, regardless of their morals, in the realms of bliss. Prejudices from which no one is free, are the result of a mild form of dissociation. Nevertheless they cause a vast amount of distortion of functional adjustment in our world.

HYPNOTISM is an artificially produced dissociation so complete as to render the isolated and remaining behavior pattern extremely suggestible. Although the dissociation connected with hypnotism occurs in the mind of the subject it usually requires the coöperation or direction of some external agency to be effected. Self-hypnosis does occur, as in the trance, but ordinarily there is involved both an operator and a subject in hypnotic phenomena. The "operator" may be passive, such as a bright object, the sound of the ticking of a clock, upon which the attention of the subject becomes fixed mechanically. But such spontaneous fixation upon a passive object, with resulting dissociation, is not ordinarily sufficiently complete to produce hypnosis, unless there has previously been a repeated experience of hypnosis through the agency of a director employing this object, and thus conditioning the hypnotic response to the stimulus. The director serves the double function of assisting the subject in selecting an object of attention and of keeping the attention centered on the object until dissociation occurs and of directing suggestive stimuli after the subject is dissociated or hypnotized. This second function of the director or operator is very important. In self-hypnosis or automatic hypnosis the direction of suggestion will either come from dominant unconscious sets within or will arise from random occurrences or impacts from without. For most persons such direction of suggestion is not very effective. It will be seen, however, that the psychic mechanism of self-hypnotism with direction of suggestion from internal sets or complexes is very similar to that of certain psychotic states, such as illusions and hallucinations in dementia præcox and paranoia, and the phobias. In the latter there is a permanent dissociation not unlike that in hypnosis in respect to its completeness. The result is that in psychotic cases the subject is rarely or never free from the dominance of the internal sets, whose responses are conditioned to almost all types of stimuli of which he takes cognizance. This internal dominance twists the stimuli into interpreted phenomena which support his own mental derangement or illusions.

THE CONDITIONS OF SUCCESS IN HYPNOSIS—The prestige of the operator has much to do with his success in securing concentration upon objects and consequent dissociation, also in securing the ready acceptance of his suggestions by the subject. But there is always a limit to what suggestions the subject will accept, and this limit is fixed by a number of factors in addition to the prestige of the operator. Some of these are the completeness of the dissociation, the mental level of the subject, his poise, the circumstances and surroundings under which hypnosis occurs, the familiarity and acceptability of the suggested behavior to the subject. Subjects can be suggested only towards behavior with which they are reasonably familiar. This fact follows from the nature of the mechanism of suggestion already explained. It is necessary that the response shall have been previously conditioned by the stimuli which are manipulated by the operator before they can take effect with such celerity and momentum and so without modification of the process as to warrant the application of the term suggestion to the behavior process. Likewise, unless the behavior suggested has the approval of the subject or at least is sufficiently indifferent as not to cause shock, its suggestion will meet opposition and criticism or produce conflict rather than secure acceptance. For example, it is rarely possible to suggest effectively to any one in hypnosis to shoot another person, even his enemy, or to commit any other serious crime. Such suggestions may produce sufficient inner conflict as to remove the dissociation and "wake up" the subject. Only the feeble-minded or hysterical or morally perverted (those who already have mechanisms or desires for such behavior) are likely to be suggested in such directions during hypnosis. Neither can one ordinarily be suggested to commit suicide in a hypnotic condition.

It is not necessary for the subject to be convinced of the truth of what he is told by the operator or of the entire reasonableness of what he is commanded to do. Dissociation is of varying degrees of completeness in different subjects, and some cannot be sufficiently dissociated as to produce true hypnosis. But the condition of hypnosis is one of suspension of judgment rather than of positive judgment in favor of the statements and commands of the operator. If the dissociation is profound the lapse of critical judgment is also profound and the subject will do within limits whatever he is told, even if it is unconventional. But in milder forms or degrees of dissociation the performer often is vaguely aware of the incongruity of the situation or of the statements and commands. He accepts them or performs them in somewhat the same spirit that he plays a game. He sees no reason why he should not. Indeed he does not reach a positive judgment that they are untrue or ridiculous. Another feature of hypnosis is that the dissociation often releases the inhibitions over certain tendencies to response or drives which are now more easily suggested than formerly. Thus tears and acts of sentiment, sex impulses (if not of such a character as to be deeply shocking), mild fears, interest in satisfaction of the appetites, are more easily suggested in hypnosis than out of it. Cultural inhibitions are to a certain extent removed and the subject goes back towards a more or less primitive type of personality.

SIGNIFICANCE OF THE VARIOUS TYPES OF SUGGESTION—These various types of suggestion have various degrees of significance in collective adjustment situations. In those types which depend upon negative dissociation, or where the associations have not yet been or cannot be organized as inhibitio processes, the significance for adjustment is fairly patent. The suggestion is relatively direct and copious. Children, the uneducated, primitive peoples, those of isolated experience and lower mentality, are in many or most respects easily suggested. They become rational personalities by virtue of developing more associations which serve as inhibitions upon random or manipulated suggestions. Suggestion due to fatigue, fasting, toxic conditions, intoxication, or drug addiction, is fairly frequent in the lives of many people and probably determines a considerable part of social behavior, particularly in domestic situations and in crowds. While suggestion due to fixed ideas or chronic dissociation is operative, at least in an extreme manner, upon relatively few people, it not infrequently plays a considerable rôle in human affairs because of its violence and the dogmatic character of the beliefs and behavior of those who are victims of such suggestion. Prejudices are especially prevalent and are very largely determinative of human relationships. Their bad effects socially and individually can scarcely be overestimated. Hypnosis is mainly an artificial condition and occurs primarily in situations where the subject and operator have little chance to influence collective relationships generally. But there are undoubtedly many milder cases of hypnotic dissociation occurring under the conscious or unconscious direction of some dominating personality or as self-hypnosis. These probably determine collective relationships to a vast extent. Such mild hypnotic suggestion phenomena are probably operative in mobs, in strong friendships, in conjugal relationships and infatuations, and in various other relationships in life. In this mild form they are not necessarily harmful, but may be of positive use in organizing behavior on a fairly automatic basis and in thus conserving energy and in regularizing conduct.

It will be seen from our discussion of the conditions of suggestibility that these various types of suggestion are not wholly separate and distinct. They merge into one another imperceptibly. It is only when we select outstanding cases in isolation that they appear as wholly distinct types. Perhaps more than one relative type is operative in practically every situation involving suggestibility.

THE UBIQUITOUSNESS OF SUGGESTION—Suggestion operates in almost every sphere and aspect of life. It is a short cut method of controlling effectively conditioned behavior. It is in itself quite devoid of moral character and may be used indifferently for ethical, non-ethical, or anti-ethical ends. It is frequently said that rationally directed conduct is of a higher type socially than suggested behavior. This is of course true, but it is not possible to be self or socially conscious about everything. Short cut controls in behavior are inevitable. The greater volume of suggestion occurs in the direction of every day contacts, as was pointed out in the previous chapter, where it is ordinarily unmanipulated by some supervising agency. But there is also a vast amount of manipulated suggestion. This comes especially through the family, the school, the church, politics, the stage, the newspaper and periodical, and advertising. The newspaper, through its news articles, editorials, and advertisements, does much to control public opinion. Commercial advertisements to a large extent determine consumption, at least with reference to brands and styles, if not with regard to the contents and quality of the articles themselves.

Through the home, school, church, movie, theater, radio, and newspaper and press generally, we are told what to think or believe in almost all relationships in life. Sometimes the suggestion is direct and sometimes it is indirect, according to the degree of resistance which the person or public offers to the suggestion. The control of propaganda suggestion for proper social ends has become one of the serious problems of our day and must be attained by some method or other if society is not to be increasingly manipulated for selfish or partisan purposes. Controlled by suggestion we probably shall be, but this control should be for legitimate social purposes. It is not the function of this work on the principles of social psychology to go into details regarding either the methods of suggestion employed in concrete cases or types or the methods of controlling such propaganda. This belongs to the applications of social psychology, especially to the subjects of social organization, social control, and social ethics.

MATERIALS FOR SUPPLEMENTARY READING

Davenport, F. M., *Primitive Traits in Religious Revivals*
Gault, R. H., *Social Psychology*, Ch. VI
Hocking, W. E., *Morale and Its Enemies*
Hollingworth, H. L., *Advertising and Selling*
Kitson, H. D., *The Mind of the Buyer*
Leopold, L., *Prestige: A Psychological Study of Social Estimates*
McDougall, W., *An Introduction to Social Psychology*, pp. 96-102
Moll, A., *Hypnotism*
Patrick, G. T. W., *The Psychology of Relaxation*
Ross, E. A., *Social Control*, Chs. XIII, XIV
——, *Social Psychology*, Ch. II
Sidis, B., *The Psychology of Suggestion*
Starch, D., *Principles of Advertising*
Stratton, G. M., *Experimental Psychology and Its Bearing upon Culture*, Ch. XI
Sumner, W. G., *Folkways*, Ch. V, pp. 22-24

CHAPTER XXI

IMITATION AND PERSONALITY DEVELOPMENT

THE CONTROVERSY REGARDING THE TERM—Imitation wa[s] a term much used and, some recent social psychologists believe misapplied by the older writers in social psychology. It was t[o] the objective school of social psychology what sympathy an[d] instinct were to the subjective schools. To some of the olde[r] writers, imitation meant simply the doing what others did, [or] repetition of behavior. They were absorbed wholly in the ex ternal aspects of the act and apparently it did not occur t[o] them to inquire into the inner or neuro-psychic mechanism [of] the imitative process. Others who did see this necessity sai[d] we imitate because we have an instinct to copy the behavior [of] others. Those who could find no such instinctive mechanism— for indeed there is none—substituted sympathy or sympathet[ic] induction, or some other near-instinctive process, as a verb[al] explanation of imitative behavior. Some of the more rece[nt] writers have found the term imitation so vague and general th[at] they would dispense with it altogether. As a collective be havior concept, however, it still has value for the social ps[y]chologist and for the social sciences generally.

THE NATURE OF IMITATION—Much that is ordinarily calle[d] imitation is in reality suggestion. The two processes overl[ap] to a considerable extent, but suggestion is largely an indepen[d]ent process, and is, as we have seen, antecedent to imitatio[n]. Imitation is the doing what the other person does because th[e] perception of his behavior sets up in the imitator the same [or] similar responses to those which serve as stimuli. The imitate[d] behavior may be either a total overt response or symbolic b[e]havior. It is not possible to imitate or copy the behavior [of] another unless that behavior has been conditioned as a respon[se] organization in the imitator to the behavior of the one imitate[d].

of some one behaving as he does, as stimulus. The initiative in conditioning these imitative responses may be taken by either the imitator or the model who is imitated. Where one behaves as another behaves without the perceived behavior of the other person acting as the effective conditioning stimulus he is merely responding to the same or to a similar or associated stimulus. Dashiell, reviewing Humphrey, summarizes the process as follows: "Imitation is not to be conceived as instinctive or innate, but as an acquired reaction. Specifically, it involves a conditioned reflex the secondary stimulus of which is similar to the reaction. This secondary stimulus may originate either in the same or in another organism, so that imitation may be of self or of another. A child suffers pain, cries, hears himself crying and the last becomes the stimulus to further crying; cattle are fear-stricken, run in stampede, after which the sight of a running fellow serves as incidental stimulus for flight. Imitative units tend to become combined with themselves and integrated to form larger and larger wholes of imitative conduct; chiseling, hammering, etc., to carpentering."[1]

The Mechanism of Imitation—Thus imitation is a social category within the field of the conditioned response. We may distinguish two general types of imitation, with four subtypes, as follows:

I. *Suggestion Imitation.*

1. Automatic or suggestion imitation proper occurs when the response of the imitator has been previously so effectively conditioned to the perception of this same behavior in another as stimulus that the imitator responds immediately and practically automatically to the perceived stimulus. Ordinarily the perception of the behavior of the other person comes in the course of time to be reduced to an automatic cue or symbol which sets off the imitative response without detailed consciousness of the relationship between the stimulus-giving person and the one who responds. Thus one removes his hat automatically upon perceiving another do the same or himself looks to the top of a building when he perceives a crowd looking in this direction, although the original stimuli producing these responses in others are not perceptible to the imitator.

Psychological Bulletin.

Such imitation may also include the release of circular responses already conditioned in us upon the perception of the same behavior in another. Frequently we smile, or yawn, laugh, cough, become restless, tap on the arm of a chair, when we see others do these things. In the same way we become irritable or excited, scold, talk loudly, when others do. These are circular responses common to every one under certain conditions. We have the patterns of them so well developed that the perception of another doing the same thing has the power to initiate automatically the response in us.

2. Accidental imitation is a term which refers primarily to the circumstances of conditioning the response. Allport gives an excellent example. "One day while the writer's baby was visiting, the hostess observed him wave his hand aimlessly up and down. She at once drew his attention and waved his hand, at the same time crying 'bye-bye.' The affair interested him greatly, and thereafter he would react either to the sight of a waving hand or to the sound of 'bye-bye' by waving his hand." Possibly the case cited by McDougall of the child sticking out his lips imitatively had a similar origin. These are simple forms of imitation and fall under the category of suggestion imitation. Other forms of imitation are purposive and more complex on the side of the conditioning process.

II. *Purposive Imitation.*

3. Imitation by trial and error conditioning is perhaps the more common of these, especially among the young. The motivating factor here is the desire to copy the behavior of the other person, because of his prestige, the convenience or profit which will result to us, or from some other motive of advantage to ourselves. Prestige, to whatever it is due, is unquestionably one of the strongest, if not the strongest, of motives to purposive imitation. In such a case, if the mechanism does not already exist for performing the act, it will have to be integrated. The conditioning here is of the negative type. We recognize the objective as desirable. We must learn to perform the behavior which will attain the desired objective. The motivating desire may be practically anything. The imitator selects as his model one who seems to him to typify the thing he desires to be and analyzes the model's behavior

IMITATION AND PERSONALITY

nd makes it his own. Such perceptual analysis of another's behavior and conditioning of one's own like responses to it as stimulus is not purely of the crude trial and error type, as in the case of the rat seeking food in the maze, although there are practically always some trial and error elements in it. The human child and adult can perceive behavior projectively and symbolically, consequently they hit upon the behavior mechanisms of their models much more quickly by the use of their inventive intelligence.

4. Projective imitation proper occurs, therefore, when the imitator creates in himself a new behavior pattern similar to that of the model by the use of internal or abbreviated trial and error instead of by overt trial and error, although the latter form of behavior may occur also. The perceptual analysis of the behavior of the other which the subject desires to imitate is accomplished on the basis of the inner or symbolic (attitudinal or verbal) responses of the model. This is the method which we have previously called abbreviated or abstract and symbolical conditioning or responses to abstract or symbolic stimuli.

THE RECOGNITIVE BASIS OF PURPOSIVE IMITATION—In the last two types of imitation it is necessary for the imitator to perceive the behavior of the model in considerable detail in order to reproduce it. It is the inability of the subject to make his perceptual or conceptual analysis adequately on a neuropsychic or symbolic basis which results in the trial and error element in the third type of imitation. The difference between the two types is determined primarily by the different degrees of development of personality levels achieved by the subjects, as was pointed out in Chapter XVIII. Lower animals and young children use trial and error method largely, although Köhler seems to have shown that chimpanzees make use of the fourth method to a slight extent. The greater ease with which concrete visible movements and simple sounds can be imitated by the child and the great difficulty with which he imitates anything abstract are easily explainable in the light of these facts. He has already made the movements and sounds in kind or in closely similar forms. He has accordingly learned to perceive these forms of behavior in himself. It is all the easier therefore for him to perceive them in another and to imitate them as a means to an end. When he has developed the same degree of skill in perceiving attitudes or symbolic behavior in himself it becomes equally easy to recognize them in another and to imitate the symbolic and abstract as well as the overt and concrete behavior of his model. It is not necessary that the behavior of the model should be copied slavishly. It may be elaborated and modified to fit the imitator's own particular needs, circumstances, or personality. This is the inventive side of imitation par excellence, although the very act of integrating the behavior of another perceptually and projectively is to some extent inventive.

SOME ILLUSTRATIONS—The inability to imitate projectively what is not perceived may be illustrated by the child's attempt to read the newspaper or a book as his father does. He gets himself into the proper position, perhaps even crossing his legs and leaning back in his little chair. Then he picks up the paper and holds it in the same relative position as that in which his father holds it. He scrutinizes his father from time to time to make sure that all the details are correct, although he may not see that he holds the paper upside down. This important detail of the correct holding of the paper he cannot imitate because he cannot perceive that there is a top and a bottom side or, if he is told there is, he cannot perceive what constitute these relative positions. Later, when he can perceive from the pictures or the print the correct position in this respect, he adds this detail to his imitative behavior. He also wishes to imitate the reading, but is unable to recognize the words. However, he has been able to perceive and recognize in some degree the sounds which his father makes, although he has not connected them with verbal symbols on the printed page. Consequently he makes sounds in imitation of his father's vocalization in reading, or he moves his lips as he sees his father's lips moving, although in each case he cannot perceive or imitate the meaning. This inability to perceive and recognize the complete behavior stimulus in the father and to imitate or copy it in his own behavior further illustrates the greater ease with which we recognize and imitate overt behavior and emotional expression than intellectual content or ideas through

IMITATION AND PERSONALITY

their symbols. I have also observed a child of less than two years imitating so closely the sounds of a huckster that one would almost believe that he recognized the actual words, although of course he did not understand anything the huckster said. He merely recognized with a considerable degree of accuracy the sounds and tones.

The cases just given illustrate largely trial and error imitation. An illustration of projective imitation by direct observation is that of a child learning to perform an act of skill by observing carefully and analytically another perform it. If the child has had sufficient similar experience previously, that is, if his previous development of behavior patterns gives him perceptual mechanisms which are adequate to grasp all of the details, he will be able to perform the act himself from observation with a considerable degree of accuracy and without practice. All of us have had the experience of "trying our hand" with a new game after observing its performance by another in great detail, and perhaps have been surprised at our success. We had a sufficient number of behavior mechanisms which could be adapted by analogy to this game so that we could start out at once to play it without first learning it by the trial and error method.

Illustrations of projective learning by the aid of verbal symbols as mechanisms of perceptual response are to be found in cases of children's learning to perform acts of skill partly by observing their teacher and partly by listening to his verbal descriptions. A still more thoroughgoing illustration is that of a child's learning how to do a thing wholly from listening to a verbal description. This is a much more difficult method of imitating, as the agricultural extension workers recognized when they substituted demonstration for lectures as a method of teaching farmers how to raise better crops.

In none of these types of imitation is it possible to imitate projectively without having behavior and perceptual patterns sufficiently similar to those of the model that his behavior can be perceived and copied by the subject. In the case of symbolic projective imitation there must also be a similarity of language equipment or conditioning.

THE NEURAL BASIS OF IMITATION IS MAINLY ACQUIRED—

We can imitate only behavior which we can perceive analytically or recognize in detail, and only the behavior we ourselves have approximate mechanisms for performing, overtly or internally. These mechanisms or stimulus-response patterns may be instinctive or acquired. There are probably very few instinctive stimulus-response mechanisms sufficiently complete to serve as patterns for imitating behavior in others in detail. Consequently, most mechanisms for such imitation have been acquired or built up through previous adjustment to environmental pressures. The infant does not imitate complex behavior until it has had time to integrate a sufficient number of stimulus-response mechanisms to enable it to perceive a fairly complex process of behavior in another. The same mechanism which mediates the response also serves as the basis for perception. The perception of the behavior of the model, by becoming the content of the neuro-psychic mechanisms of the imitator, becomes the initial stage or stimulus of the inner overt response which we call objectively the act of imitation. Perceiving is in such a case really psychic imitation, although we may recognize it as such in another only when we see the overt response. However, in psychic imitation, which we can recognize in ourselves only introspectively, and in others through certain partial and substitute responses called language symbols, the imitative inner response may be as complete of its kind as is overt imitation. In imitation of the overt response the similarity of the stimulus and the response in behavior concretely perceptible. In imitation of the psychic behavior the similarity is recognized conceptually. Both overt and psychic responses are imitative only if the stimulating behavior copied in the response. In the first two types of imitation called suggestion imitation conscious perception of the stimulus activity may be reduced to a minimum because of the automatization of the process.

If instinctive neuro-psychic mechanisms served to any considerable extent as a basis for imitation the child would begin his copying of the behavior of others as soon as he was born. The power to imitate projectively grows steadily with the increased experience of the child and adult, but this power may not be exercised so exclusively after the period of intellectual maturity is reached, because for most people life becomes largely a matter of routine or self-imitation after maturity and those for whom it does not become routine usually pride themselves on making independent judgments of their own. But such so-called independent judgments are necessarily nearly always camouflaged or abstractly conditioned imitative responses.

WHY WE IMITATE—It is easy to understand how the earlier social psychologists might confuse suggestion imitation with instinctive behavior. In such cases the response has become so stereotyped and so strongly conditioned to its stimulus that it occurs as directly and unconsciously upon the presentation of the stimulus as an instinct. If we did not know the circumstances of the conditioning, we should easily fall into the error of supposing it to be instinctive. However, completer analysis discloses the mechanism to be not different from other acquired automatic responses except that the response is like the behavior which serves as the stimulus. We need no instinct hypothesis to explain it.

In the case of purposive imitation the problem of why we imitate is more complex. In such cases the mechanism is usually not already completely present, but it must be acquired. Why do we integrate these particular behavior patterns? That is, why do we imitate only certain types of behavior and not others? In such cases imitation is a means to an end, and we take over the behavior of our model because that particular type of behavior will attain the end. Köhler's illustration of the chimpanzee's imitation is a case in point. Food was hung from the ceiling of the cage, and a stool placed in the corner. The hungry ape jumped and jumped in a vain effort to secure the food. It did not occur to him to use the stool. Köhler then entered the cage, placed a stool under the food, stood on the stool, and touched the food. When he left, after pushing the stool away, the animal immediately repeated Köhler's behavior and procured the food. Imitation was in this case the means to an end.

In human life the end may be the desire for social approbation, or to be like some one who attracts us, who has power or efficiency, who is admired or imitated by other people, in fact to be like any one who possesses prestige. The elements which constitute prestige have already been analyzed in the preceding chapter. Another important motive for imitation is the desire for new experiences. The child is full of energy, but he does not always have well integrated patterns of behavior through which to discharge his energy. As a result he looks to those about him for patterns which will release his urges in interesting ways. In childhood the models are concrete personalities, later on they are more abstract. The evolution in models is discussed in the following three chapters.

When the initiative for imitation comes from the model himself, the imitated behavior is forced upon the individual. In such cases he cannot help himself. Thus the child is obliged to imitate the manners and general etiquette of his elders under penalty of physical punishment. Later on conventional and customary and traditional responses are strongly conditioned in him and deviations are punished psychically or socially. Even the most independent minded bow to the sway of these controls in minor matters, if for no other reason than to escape notice and greater annoyance. They imitate because they are obliged to do so.

ABSTRACT SYMBOLIC OR PSYCHIC IMITATION—We imitate the psychic or attitudinal behavior of persons, either by perceiving and recognizing their symbolic behavior responses, or by recognizing the externalized symbolic expression of the psychic or attitudinal behavior in books, etc. The one form of attitudinal or symbolic imitation we may term personal and the other nonpersonal. Both are indirect forms of imitation as compared with the direct imitation of overt behavior in another.

PERSONAL PSYCHIC IMITATION—We may copy indirectly the conscious or unconscious symbolic behavior of others so far as we are able to perceive the symbols of these processes and condition our own attitudinal or psychic behavior to them. An example of the imitation of attitudinal behavior is thinking or feeling as others think or feel about politics, religion, as marriage, or any other social process, because we have recognized this psychic or attitudinal content through its symbolic expressions. Abstract psychic imitation especially, and as types of psychic imitation usually, involve the recognition of verbal language symbols as a means to the recognition of the psychic or attitudinal content of the behavior of another and the incorporation of this same psychic content into ourselves. We might in fact speak of psychic imitation as language imitation. However, in the imitation of the more primary emotions, the language is usually that of facial expression, gesture, and the like, rather than verbal language. This form of psychic imitation, the copying of the psychic attitudes, emotions, beliefs, opinions, etc., of others, is still the imitation of personality, although it is indirect, or through the medium of language or expression symbols.

NONPERSONAL SYMBOLIC OR PSYCHIC IMITATION occurs when we copy the attitudes, beliefs, opinions, principles, etc., of people through the medium of their literature, art, and other symbolic objectifications of their behavior. We imitate in this type the thoughts of persons as expressed by those persons, not directly to ourselves, but through the medium of books or other externalized communication media. To be sure the difference between this method of psychic imitation through written words, art, and other abstract extensions of personality, and the imitation of spoken words or verbal symbols of inner or attitudinal behavior of concrete persons is only one of degree, not wholly of kind. It is only a more highly indirect form of the imitation of psychic behavior than is the imitation of spoken words or visible emotional expressions and gestures. Both are in the last analysis indirect or abstract and symbolic forms of imitation. It is in this connection that the greatest device of civilization, the storage of externalized neuro-psychic technique, finds its highest degree of usefulness. In the reading of books and the absorption or the rational imitation of their symbolized contents into our own psychic behavior, and later possibly into our overt adjustment behavior, by a process of projection and elaboration of symbolic content, we are fulfilling all the conditions of projective elaboration or invention quite as fully and as effectively as if we were imitating the behavior of concrete personalities. Thus it is possible to imitate abstractly and indirectly the inner or overt behavior of a person at a great distance or long after his organic personality has ceased to exist.

This is the sort of immortality for which George Eliot expressed a desire in her verses on the "choir invisible." The importance of nonpersonal symbolic imitation is sufficiently obvious if we remember that the larger part of the adjustment technique of science in the modern world is preserved and transmitted through the medium of books and periodicals.

ABSTRACT AND CONCRETE IMITATION CONTRASTED—Although abstract psychic or symbolic imitation is of greater importance in the maintenance and dispersion of high standards of culture and conduct and consequently in the promotion of social progress, the direct and concrete imitation of overt behavior is much the easier form. As Ross has so interestingly pointed out, we are always in danger of passing up the significant models and of selecting the unimportant or positively bad ones, of imitating the superficial at the expense of the fundamental. This has always been so, but it is probably less true now, in spite of many appearances to the contrary, than it was formerly. It would probably be even less true to-day if the superficial and the unworthy were not so universally commercialized and so assiduously advertised.

Many barbarian and early civilization types of education emphasizing the form more than the substance, as this stage of culture so often did and does, begin by having the youth memorize the words long before they are taught their meaning. Some religions teach their ritual to the masses but induct them into the philosophy or meaning content but slowly and sparingly. All of us are guilty of imitating the superficial traits of those who have prestige with us much more effectively than their fundamental qualities. Thus we take on their mannerisms of speech and social intercourse, copy their minor vices believing them to be virtues, imitate their manner of dress, social and recreational habits, and the like, although we may not be able to attain to their professional or other efficiency, because we have not yet analyzed or recognized accurately that more abstract phase of their behavior.

Thus the boy who is growing up and wishes to be like a man copies the superficial traits, such as smoking, swaggering, swearing, story-telling, and perhaps gambling, drinking and other vices, of the young men around town. These traits a more easily perceived than the routine and more abstract efficiency traits of business and professional men. He copies on the assumption that if he acts like his elders, who are his superiors, in the things which he understands about them he will have adult characteristics. Later on, when he has learned to recognize the more fundamental traits of adult efficiency and to understand the true reasons for adult prestige, he revises his objectives in projective imitation to include the more abstract values. At least, most boys do this sooner or later; but some apparently never learn to recognize and imitate the more abstract qualities in behavior. Women are going through much the same process of selecting and revising their objectives in imitation in this day of their emancipation. For them also the behavior of men has much more prestige than their own traditional behavior. But the male traits which they have so far learned to recognize and value as objects of imitation have been largely superficial. The amount of drinking, smoking, and other vices among women has greatly increased since they have been taking men—especially the young men around town—as their models. But many other women also have learned to imitate the efficiency and solidity of professional and business men and the leaders of scientific thinking.

One of the most important functions of the schools, in a national educational system, as well as of the home and other formative institutions, is to aid the youth in perceiving and recognizing the meaning of behavior patterns which it is important that he should copy in his own behavior.

IMITATION AS VICARIOUS INTEGRATION OF PERSONALITY—Projective imitation is a form of vicarious personality integration. By means of this process of imitation we use the personality materials of others in building up our own personalities. However, it is not possible to take over their personality or behavior achievements bodily and without the necessity on our own part of going through the process of self-development. We cannot filch from others the personality achievements which they have attained and make them our own without first having laid the foundation for such a transference or projection into ourselves by our own previous experiences. We can imitate only what we have inner or attitudinal behavior patterns for or can understand by analogy and symbolic elaboration. This does not, of course, mean that we can imitate only that in others which we have previously done or experienced with completeness ourselves. If this were so, there would be no gain for the individual through imitation and all imitation would be of the automatic or copying by suggestion type. Here, as elsewhere, it is possible to see our own behavior processes in new relationships or organizations with the aid of the other person's behavior as model. By learning to recognize the full content of the superior personality of another we can integrate in ourselves similar behavior patterns out of the old but less effectively organized behavior patterns previously integrated in ourselves. It is not necessary that we copy the behavior of others entirely, or that we perceive beforehand the ultimate responses of the imitated behavior. It is sufficient if the perception of the behavior of another, entire or in part, starts us on a similar type of response and personality development. Once begun the completion of the activity will be taken care of by trial and error or projectively, according as we learn to analyze the models who condition our responses. Thus, every imitated behavior process, especially if it possesses any degree of complexity or is carried on over any considerable period of time, is likely to be modified and to diverge considerably from the behavior pattern which is imitated. This fact is of value from an adjustment standpoint, since it affords a much greater chance for flexibility of adaptation to environment and in fact for the modification of environmental pressures themselves than would be possible if all imitation were in the nature of an exact and precise copy.

The value of vicarious personality integration through imitation is very great in spite of the limitations here mentioned. It is not unlimited in its possibilities, for it cannot take place without previous preparation. But the fact of the existence of a model as a constellation of stimuli serves as a strong social pressure to induce the less experienced to develop their behavior in a similar manner and to a like or greater extent. Furthermore, the flexibility of the process enables people to vary their imitated responses to suit the demands of their own environments. The existence of the model as a stimulus to the development of a rich personality content through imitation is also very important for the preservation of social or cultural achievements. Those who have already built up in themselves the personality values of civilization through copying them from others, or through conditioning original traits of their own, now serve as stimuli to the younger generations to develop in themselves these same traits. From no other source could they receive as adequately these social stimuli. By the very act of projectively elaborating or recognizing these traits which already exist in another we establish the first or inner phase of the same behavior response in ourselves. Thus others stimulate us to make new personality integrations with reference to them and in this way we can enrich our own characters by imitating them. While it is true that we cannot imitate projectively what we cannot perceive, nevertheless we can learn to perceive the behavior of another person quite as well as any other object, and this recognition of the behavior of another may go on together with the imitative or elaborative process within ourselves. This fact explains why we are not dependent entirely upon previous experience for imitation, important as it is, but may imitate in part behavior which we have never experienced as such before.

Vicarious Integration of Personality as a Source of Collective Behavior—Another great social advantage arising from vicarious personality integration is that it is one of the chief sources of relatively uniform collective behavior. It is perhaps the chief source of those uniformities in society which make people sufficiently alike to live together with a minimum of friction and misunderstanding. Because of the diversity of contacts of the modern man, due to his high mobility and the great development of means of communication, he is brought in touch with a great many models representing all types of behavior. This enables him to make his own character highly cosmopolitan and to embody in it a selection of the best of everything. This multiplication of effective models undoubtedly accounts in large measure for the great degree of unity extending over wide areas which characterizes the modern world. At the same time the models presented for imitation are so numerous that some degree of selection is necessary. This fact saves us from wooden uniformity and en ables us to build up types of personality which are best suite to our particular adjustment needs without at the same tim coming in conflict with the mores and folkways as wholes.

Imitation also makes the present largely uniform with th past and thus preserves for us the achievements in knowledg and technique of those who have gone before us. Withou this temporal uniformity secured through imitation of the ol and intellectually mature by the young and intellectually imma ture, each individual would be compelled to work out his ad justments for himself and social progress would proceed, in s far as it was possible at all, only through biological selectior The chief, if not the only, present means of social progres now operative is social selection and environmental transmis sion. This method has become highly effective. Language which symbolizes the accumulated achievements of civilizatior is the chief instrument of vicarious personality developmer through projective imitation and consequently the chief aid t social progress. It also makes possible the preservative an formative institutions and the storage of externalized neuro psychic technique through which the most significant forms o vicarious personality development take place.

ORIGINAL AND IMITATIVE THINKING CONTRASTED—Nev forms of psychic behavior come in two ways: either throug abstract imitation, facilitated by reading, attendance upon lec tures, conversations, etc.; or through independent or origina conditioning of responses of our own without the aid of imita tion. Relatively few people do much of the latter. The scien tists in their laboratories, the observers of nature, and thos reflectively inclined are most prolific in the integration of nev abstract ideas or concepts. The golden age for such thinkin among the laity seems to be in the late 'teens and early twenties after abstract thinking has been stimulated by abstract sym bolic imitation and before the circumstances of occupation an age and interest have stereotyped the psychic behavior of peo ple. The professional thinker, however, may continue thinkin abstractly and imitating elaboratively the ideas of others with high degree of efficiency throughout life. Mechanical and so cial inventions, which have given most people more leisure an freedom from economic and subsistence fears, together with more training in both original and vicarious conditioning of symbolic responses, have done much in recent times to stimulate independent abstract thinking. This is true in the face of the statement by a recent writer to the effect that not more than one person in a thousand ever thinks an original thought. At least, they may now rethink the important thoughts of others. And the success or failure of democracy, and perhaps of civilization, depends on the extent to which they do this.

THE RHYTHMS OF IMITATION—There are crescendos and diminuendos in the imitative process corresponding to each type of behavior. The earliest imitated responses are of the overt type and they are dependent upon the presence of previously formed instinctive or acquired behavior patterns of a similar character. The child also learns early to recognize emotional expressions in others and to copy these projectively into his own behavior. Accompanying these imitated overt expressions are psychic attitudes which constitute his first achievement in the imitation of the psychic behavior of others in himself. This early imitation of emotional attitudes is of course in the nature of the elaboration of the child's own previous emotional experiences which have grown out of his contacts with his personality environment. As the experience of the child grows and as an ever wider range of neuro-muscular and neuro-psychic behavior patterns develops out of his original and imitative adjustment experiences, he is able to elaborate imitatively in himself both types of the behavior of others in ever greater detail. Thus, through imitation and independent experimental perceptual analysis, he comes normally to possess a considerable degree of skill in making differential neuro-muscular adaptations to his environment. These adaptive behavior patterns are in the nature of manual skills of all sorts and athletic skills, such as swimming, running, throwing objects at a mark, rowing, boxing, wrestling, and the like. They also sooner or later include some of the skills of the manual worker and the artisan, and of the professional man. In a similar manner, ordinarily, he develops considerable skill in emotional expression and in the attitudinal consciousness of the emotions.

Thus the imitation of overt action and emotional expressio[n] types of behavior grows rapidly from the second year or earlie[r] into the early 'teens, when it begins to occupy less the cente[r] of the stage. Imitation of the internal or psychic behavior o[f] others, beginning with the emotional attitudes and, expandin[g] to include ideas, and especially descriptive knowledge conten[t,] becomes important long before the child reaches the 'teens an[d] continues dominant throughout the greater part of them. H[e] learns to imitate the ideas of others through the process [of] analyzing their verbal symbols and the elaborative projectio[n] or integration of their meaning content into his own persona[l]ity. At first the intellectual content, as distinguished from th[e] more definitely emotional content, of his psychic behavior [or] inner personality is primarily of the descriptive type. Th[e] child learns about all sorts of things—plants, animals, geogr[a]phy, people, industries, transportation equipment, etc.—fro[m] direct observation and from spoken and written verbal or sym[-] bolic descriptions by others. Later he learns also to mak[e] abstract generalizations about these things and also to elabora[te] in his psychic or symbolic and attitudinal self the like general[i]zations of others. In this way he transforms his world fro[m] a concrete descriptive one into an abstract conceptual on[e,] just as earlier he had progressed from a world of overt b[e]havior experience to one of emotional attitudes,[1] and thence [to] the world of new and entrancing descriptive knowledge exper[i]ences, with which emotional attitudes were still closely an[d] largely intertwined. The knowledge of nature and of th[e] works of man which the child acquires so industriously and a[b]sorbingly from around about his sixth or seventh year throug[h] his early 'teens, or even later, is tied up closely with stron[g] emotional attitudes of appreciation. He is not likely to come [to] live in an abstract and relatively unemotional world until h[is] late 'teens or even twenties or later. Of course many neve[r] escape domination by their emotional experiences, either b[e]cause they have not been brought sufficiently constantly an[d] closely in contact with other personalities whose inner behavio[r] is of the abstract and rational type, or because they are n[ot]

[1] As a matter of fact these three phases of development are practical[ly] contemporaneous.

capable through native ability and early experience of developing abstract judgments.

Abstract or indirect symbolic imitation, thus beginning in the early 'teens or before, develops from this period until some time in the twenties or thirties, or even later, when the behavior mechanisms of the individual tend to become stereotyped. The period at which personality is stereotyped varies in different people according to their circumstances, education, vocation, and the adjustment demands of all types made upon them. In some people there is never any considerable development of abstract and indirect symbolic imitation, and even psychic imitation of the more concrete or descriptive knowledge types may be greatly limited. Such people tend to become stereotyped in their behavior sooner than others. People with low intelligence quotients also become fixed in their behavior routines quite early.

IMITATION VARIES WITH CLASSES—The same, in less degree, is true of all persons with slight literate interests, such as is the case with most hand workers, small tradesmen, many housewives, poor farmers, and other people following mechanical occupations or with poor intellectual training. Also people who incur family obligations on small incomes and thus feel strongly the constant grind of maintaining an existence, clerical workers who owe heavy obligations of conformity to the ideas of their employers, salesmen who must not offend the trade, members of organizations with prescribed codes and creeds, and soldiers, are especially liable to drop into repetitive routine or to stereotype their imitative behavior into mere response by suggestion. But the behavior of practically all people tends to become stereotyped sooner or later, if for no other reason than because of the increasing demands of occupation for all of their time and energies and because with increasing age there is less energy available for an experimental attitude toward life. Only the professional thinkers and people of leisure can hope to keep a high degree of freedom from stereotyped mental behavior, and most of these tend to fall into regular habits of thinking or opinions which prevent the acquisition of new ideas. Some one has said that practically all of the great ideas come to one before the age of thirty or forty and that achievements after this age are primarily in the nature of elaborating our old ideas.

SUMMARY AND CONCLUSIONS—Imitation is a social process by which our perception of the behavior of another conditions or initiates in us like responses. In individual psychology there is no need of the category imitation, for the mechanism can be explained wholly in terms of perception and the conditioning of responses. In the social sciences it is useful as an important abbreviated method of describing a type of collective behavior. If the imitation is in the nature of a direct and total copying of the behavior of the other person without modification or elaboration it occurs on the level of suggestion. If involves modification or elaboration of the subject's behavior is purposive or even projective imitation, as distinguished from suggestion. This imitative response cannot occur unless we have previously entertained similar experiences. But ordinarily our experiences have been only partly the same. Consequently most such imitation is purposive and projective and involves the elaboration or reconstruction of our own behavior, overt or internal. The greater the degree of elaboration of the responses, and the more internal or conscious these mechanisms are, the more rational and abstract the imitative process becomes. This process of elaborating the imitative behavior process may proceed to the extent that it involves but little pure imitation. In such cases we ordinarily term it simply rational or original behavior. In order that the elaboration of one's own behavior through the projective analysis and integration of the behavior of another shall be imitation it is necessary that the other person's behavior be copied in some perceptible degree. The occurrence of a response on the part of one person to the stimulus of the behavior of another does not in itself constitute imitative behavior. To be imitative it must be response in kind.

Imitation does not begin immediately after birth, because there are no adequate behavior bases for imitative responses. The infant has to begin his adaptive responses on an original basis. Later, when he has learned to analyze and understand other personalities, he can avail himself of their experience and make many of his adjustments vicariously by means itation. As he matures, imitation becomes increasingly important as a method of making his adjustments to his social world. The most important forms of imitative adjustment are those by abstract or indirect and projective imitation. Projective imitation enables the subject to expand his adjustments through elaboration, and indirect or symbolic imitation permits him to take over the condensed and abstracted or generalized experiences of others through externalized and stored language symbols and to apply them to his own adjustment needs. The simplest and most direct form of imitation occurs when the behavior of the imitated or object person becomes merely a cue (or is perceived as such) which sets off an automatic imitative response without elaboration. This we call suggestion imitation. As we have seen, not all responses by suggestion are imitative. This automaticity of response is usually the result of considerable practice, although it is possible for example, primarily instinctive responses, like yawning, coughing, crying, smiling, frowning, etc., to become accurately conditioned early in infancy and thus to occur on the basis of suggestion. So many imitated responses become automatic in later life that adults behave very largely on the basis of suggestion. This is particularly true of stereotyped personalities.

MATERIALS FOR SUPPLEMENTARY READING

Allport, F. H., *Social Psychology*, pp. 242-258
Baldwin, J. M., *Mental Development in the Child and the Race*, Chs. IX-XII
——, *Social and Ethical Interpretations*, Ch. XIII
Bogardus, E. S., *Fundamentals of Social Psychology*, Ch. XII
Ellwood, C. A., *The Psychology of Human Society*, Ch. XI
Follett, M. P., *Creative Experience*, Chs. I, II
Humphrey, G., "Imitation and the Conditioned Reflex," *Ped. Sem.*, XXVIII: 1-21
King, I., *The Psychology of Child Development*, Ch. X
Köhler, W., "Intelligence in Apes," *Ped. Sem.*, XXXII: 674-690
——, *The Mentality of Apes*, Ch. VII
McDougall, W., *An Introduction to Social Psychology*, pp. 102-107, 325-345
Park and Burgess, *Introduction to the Science of Sociology*, pp. 390-407
Peterson, J., "Imitation and Mental Adjustment," *J. Ab. Psy. and Soc. Psy.*, XVII: 1-15
Ross, E. A., *Social Psychology*, Chs. XII-XVI
Shinn, M. W., *Biography of a Baby*, Ch. IX

CHAPTER XXII

PERSONALITY DEVELOPMENT THROUGH THE DIRECT IMITATION OF PERSONS

THE MOTHER MODEL—The first model which the young child copies in his personality integrating process is ordinarily his mother. But he is not able to imitate her behavior until he has proceeded far enough in personality integration to be able to recognize her behavior perceptually. Imitation is not the first form of response conditioning, but develops after all major types of perception have come into use. The child does not at first grasp the personality of his mother as a whole. Her personality operates as environmental pressures upon him but his perception or recognition of it is at first vague, undifferentiated, and ill defined. Those aspects of her behavior with which he first comes most directly in contact are the ones which he learns first to imitate, because these are the first which he can perceive and recognize effectively. This is why the young child imitates first of all the mother's expressions and attitudes towards himself. He copies her acts of affection, such as caressing with his hands, kissing, pressing his cheek against the mother's cheek, cooing in response to her cooing, smiling and even a little later responding to signs of fear and anxiety, the expression of anger, defiance, general emotional disturbances, such as nervousness, and the like, when the mother exhibits these before him. He adopts her tone of voice, form of expression, gestures, even carriage, and attitudes of sincerity or insincerity, her benevolence, devices of lying or evasion, social graces or the lack of them, as soon as he can recognize them. He becomes a stronger advocate of conventional practices or "good manners" in eating, dress, social intercourse, and the like, than his own mother if she conditions strongly such responses in him. It is not uncommon to observe a child adding its own advice and admonition to that of the mother

DIRECT IMITATION OF PERSONS

holding the older children, who are beginning to differentiate their responses according to choice, down to their conventional obligations around the home.

WHAT THE YOUNG CHILD DOES AND DOES NOT IMITATE IN HIS MOTHER—All of these imitative responses develop in season. That is to say, they cannot take place until the child has learned to perceive any particular form of behavior with sufficient completeness to permit his copying it in detail and as a unit. The unvarying rule of the growth of the child's personality building by imitation is to expand always in the direction of greater and wider experience. This is of course not a set resolution on the part of the child. He is not even aware of the fact that he is following such a course. He is merely recognizing and copying. But if he is a normal and healthy child his expansion and deepening of experience and personality never cease and are pushed forward relentlessly, unless he meets with some involuntary check from his environment, until he has mined out and appropriated those qualities of character and personality in his mother which he is able to grasp. But of course the child in his earlier years is not able to grasp the more abstract aspects of behavior of the mother. He recognizes and copies her expressions of affection, her moods, every-day language, attitudes and elementary forms of social behavior or polite intercourse. These are copied in play or purposively. Even her occupational activities are imitated in play and, among the children of the poor, soon for utilitarian adjustment ends also.

The child is by his third or fourth year a simplified miniature of the mother. If the child is a daughter, she has the same tastes in clothes, the same company manners, and the same social prejudices, judgments, technique, virtues and absurdities. The expression "little woman" or "little man" which we so often apply in jest to the child of this age is by no means undeserved. But what the child does not perceive and imitate is the deeper and more abstract element of the mother's personality. Intimations of it may reach him from time to time, but he does not grasp it with sufficient detail to imitate it as a whole. It is too abstract for him to recognize as yet. Not until he is adult and has himself had the responsi-

bilities of a family, has had to undertake the character train
ing of children and the burdens of maintaining a home, wil
he realize fully the inner significance of strained facial expres
sion, silent or ill-suppressed grief, the far-away look, the tire
voice, and the abstracted answers which in his early childhoo
puzzled him. Most men and women understand best and valu
most their mothers and fathers when they themselves have un
dertaken the responsibilities of family life and have come t
see what they involve. Only then can they complete their un
derstanding of those traits of behavior which they imperfectl
recognized in childhood.

The Importance of the Mother Model—It is perhap
better that this should be so, for the child cannot perceive every
thing and be all things at once. Each step in the developmer
of his personality, when properly organized and economicall
controlled, lays the foundation in understanding for the nex
Some types of understanding, if they should come prematurel
would only retard and discourage, perhaps even produce
cynical disposition, the most to be feared of all types of pe
sonality integration in childhood. But there are other typ
of recognition which should be kept from the child perma
nently, while yet a child, if possible. It is of the utmost in
portance that the mother should not display before the chi
any form of behavior which is not wholly normal and mora
Displays of temper, the use of bad language, any letting dow
in self-control, unkind attitudes or practices towards anima
or human beings, untruthfulness, slovenliness, wastefulnes
vices of all sorts, especially unkindness and insincerity towa
the child himself, are certain to produce in him the psych
mechanisms for the same behavior and to lead to his imitati
of such conduct, unless he is protected by much stronger stim
from better models. But even then conflicts arise which a
highly detrimental to his personality.

During the first four or five years of the child's life he pe
ceives and learns to imitate the basic patterns of social an
moral behavior, and unless his models are kept intact and no
mal the adverse effects upon personality building will be li
long. What is here said of the importance of the mother
constituting a proper model for imitation by the child appl

likewise to all others who come in contact with him during his most formative years. But normally no other person has opportunities of influencing the moral and social growth of the child equal to those of the mother. As the years pass and as his personality becomes more and more integrated and fixed, the relative importance of any one model declines, but there never comes a time when those interested in the control of character can afford to disregard models entirely. These facts should serve to call attention to the supreme importance of training for motherhood, not only in the elements of the organic care of the child, but also in regard to his moral, social, and mental education or training.

THE FATHER AND MOTHER MODELS CONTRASTED—The father also serves as a model for the imitation of the child. This second model begins to condition responses in kind or otherwise soon after the mother comes to serve in this manner, but the volume of imitation of the father is slight until long after the child has imitated the mother's behavior extensively. The reason for this is that ordinarily the father is away from home during most of the child's waking hours. This is of course truer of the city father than of the rural, but even in the country the father is away at his farm duties and is not so closely copied as is the mother, who is constantly with the child. The later development of extensive imitation of the father has some rather marked effects upon the differences in the behavior which the child copies from father and mother in building up his personality content. In keeping with the principle that the child imitates first those attitudes and that behavior which are manifested toward himself, it follows that among the first things the child learns from the mother is the enjoyment and expression of affection. This is one of the first attitudes which she takes toward the child. Also, it is she who feeds and cares for the child, makes him comfortable, and stimulates his sensitive zones, thus calling forth in him those expressions of pleasure which we see indicated by the smile, laughter, and cooing. In this way the sight of the mother, the sound of her voice, or any other indication of her presence, comes to condition all of the pleasurable or comfortable experiences of the child. This conditioning, made at a time when there is little interference content or conflict in the child's mind, is very strong, if the mother is devoted and expressive and careful of her child. This conditioning lasts throughout life and the mother always remains the symbol of tenderness, refuge, care, and comfort. The term mother itself symbolizes in our culture this quality of care and tenderness.

ADVANTAGES AND DISADVANTAGES OF THE FATHER IN PERSONALITY FORMING CONTACTS WITH THE CHILD—The father, who does not perform these services and functions for the child, must always be at a disadvantage as compared with the mother in the affections of the child. Even though the child comes to look upon him with the greatest respect and to consider him as a person of almost superhuman powers, and learns to go to him for help in difficult situations, there is rarely ever the same sort of intimate understanding and affection between father and child that there is between mother and child. The contacts are essentially different in the two cases. The contacts of the father with the young child are usually more abstract. He holds it less, if at all. Some mothers for hygienic and disciplinary reasons very foolishly do not wish the father to handle the child. But in view of the moral and emotional associations which are established by such close contacts with the father, it might be wise to sacrifice something of discipline to the valuable conditioning of responses in the child to stimuli in the father, and vice versa. The father is understood and valued by the child more for his strength, activity, and generalship of an obvious sort than for his emotional expressions and the immediate organic comforts which he brings to the child. He picks the child up, handles it in an exciting and exhilarating manner, with the result that to the child he seems to possess almost unlimited strength. The very roughness of the father, attached as it is to safety and affection, gives the child a thrill which is more or less of a relief from the cloying tenderness of the mother.

And when the child is able to visit the father at his office or to go with him among the busy and complex places of industry and business, he comes to associate his father with the marvelous and entrancing outside world. Thus the distinction between the father and the mother is further emphasized. Th latter is associated with the home and with the gentler virtues and the quieter and more restful aspects of life. By the time the child is able to go with his father into the outer world he has largely recognized and imitated the more concrete content of the mother's world. This environment has become more or less commonplace to him and it no longer affords him new stimuli for recognition and imitation on a sufficiently large and complex scale. He has already learned to react to it by automatic suggestion, rather than by eager response and with a challenge to new adventures. But the very nature of the father's habits, his departure daily into a distant and mysterious world, the fact that he has contacts with other men and does things but poorly understood by the child, lends the flavor of romance to his father which far outdistances any variety or newness of appeal which his mother can offer him. It is not that he does not any longer love his mother. He is more attached emotionally to his mother than to his father and in all probability always will be. But in the irresistible search for new experiences which stimulate the expansion and development of his personality his father is now able to play the larger rôle.

The Necessity of Turning to the Father as Model—Many mothers cannot understand this turning of the child at a certain stage of development to the father. They feel hurt and jealous, believing that they have lost the child's affection. It is a perfectly natural and necessary step. If the child is not always to be a child his personality must expand and it must develop new and wider adjustments to the technique of living a collectively conditioned life. The father is the natural avenue through which the child reaches this fascinating outside complex world of things, of machines, of business and governmental relationships. It is a wise father who understands his function at this period and responds to the desires of his child to expand his contacts through him. And it is a wise mother who does not stand in the way of this expansion of personality in the child. The tendency of the child to follow the father when he goes away to work or the child's requests for a story about what he does during the day, or to be told a story about when he (the father) was a little boy, should be accepted eagerly by the father as an invitation to induct him into the wider experiences of life and to establish connections of a permanent and intimate character with his child. All of this behavior material which the child can comprehend from the father's stories of his own childhood or of his everyday experiences is assimilated or imitated into the personality of the child and becomes material for future adjustment behavior and judgments of his own.

The child also imitates the visible behavior of the father in so far as he has opportunity to observe and understand it. He walks and stands like the strong father whom he admires. He copies his language and his more energetic expressions with much satisfaction, including even his swear words, if any are used before him. He is even likely to assume an air toward his mother such as his father has, tender, nonchalant, superior, aggressive, even unkind and contemptuous, according as the father's may be. This is true of course only in so far as the child approves of his father. So great is his tenderness for an affectionate mother that a father unkind to his mother, especially if he is also unkind to the child, may greatly antagonize the child and drive him into a closer and more sympathetic, almost pathological, relationship with the mother. Such a situation is very unfortunate for the child, because it creates in his emotions a fundamental conflict which may always cloud his psychic development and it also deprives the child of his father's guidance in making normal contacts with the outside world. Where the father's habits are such as to unfit him to be the child's guide in understanding the outside world, the situation is equally or more unfortunate. For the same results are produced if the child is antagonized by the father and the imitations of the child are corrupted and distorted if he does not separate himself from his father.

SHOULD THE MOTHER SEEK TO RETAIN HER DOMINANCE AS A MODEL?—It has sometimes been suggested that the mother could retain her dominance over the personality development of the child if she were less of a home person and went out into the world and brought back stimuli such as the father brings to condition the developing behavior response of the child. This is perhaps in some degree true. But there

DIRECT IMITATION OF PERSONS 349

are serious difficulties to be overcome before such a program of mother dominance can be made fully effective. If the mother's contacts with the outside world are as full and as deep as those of the father she will have to enter into outside occupations as seriously and as devotedly as does the father. If she does this it will isolate her largely from the child in home connections and will thus prevent his tenderer and more intimate social and moral character responses from being conditioned to the mother's behavior. The question is, whether she does not lose more than she gains by following such a policy. If the mother is qualified to rear a child—and she probably should not have one if she is not—it can scarcely be regarded as desirable for her to turn over to another, who is in all probability less qualified for the function of serving as a model to the imitations of the child in those years when he is conditioning his responses to the most intimate moral and social values of life—affection, loyalty, sympathy, kindness, truthfulness, in fact all of the primary virtues and attitudes which are at the basis of strong character. It may, however, be desirable after these character traits have been conditioned in the child, for the mother to seek wider outside contacts, especially if her own spiritual welfare depends on so doing. Such contacts may serve both to enrich her own personality and to stimulate the personality growth of the child. However, any mother who takes upon herself the serious responsibility of bringing a child into the world should not shirk the greater responsibility of seeing that it has the best possible model for intimate personality development and imitation. Such functions cannot be lightly turned over to another, unless that person is especially well qualified. In any case the mother is likely in after years to pay for her freedom from the care of the child in its infancy with a diminished affection in its adulthood, because she did not condition in it permanent and deeply set affective responses to her personality. It is, however, wise for the mother to retain some interest in her husband, and also in friends, after the birth of a child, not only for the sake of recourse in the case of the death of the child, but as a means of keeping her attitude toward the child more or less objective and thus to avoid spoiling the child.

Too great show of affection is often as harmful as too little, fostering as it does in the child abnormal attitudes toward the parent.

The fact that the child grows beyond any model for imitation should not be a source of regret. It is the inevitable result of the development of the personality of the child. He is himself as yet unspecialized and must master all types of behavior. Parents and others with whom he comes in contact and whom he uses as models for imitation are likely to be highly specialized in their behavior. Hence the child takes from each of them what he can perceive and copy, mines them out with reference to their personality contributions, as it were, and then passes on to some other model there to perform the same or similar functions. All this the child does relentlessly, with the unconcern of youth and ignorance. Youth is tenderhearted where it understands, but the heartaches of parents, friends, and often of lovers, it does not as yet fully comprehend, because it has not had the experience. The impulses to new integrations or experiences, to live to the full, are irresistible, as irresistible as is the metabolism which underlies them.

THE UNAVAILABILITY AND INCOMPLETENESS OF THE FATHER MODEL—Yet the child does not mine out through imitation the whole of the personality content of any one model before he seeks to come under the influence of another. He takes only what he can perceive or understand. Just as we saw that the child did not grasp or copy into himself or herself all of the personality content of the mother, so likewise does he fail to grasp the full significance of the life of the father. He can as yet understand and imitate only the more superficial qualities of the father. The more abstract qualities, which are really the fundamental bases of his character, the child for the time being misses. Hence he turns elsewhere for his inspiration in personality development, perhaps later to return to an adequate appreciation of what his father is and does.

The serious and abstract life of the father, his intricate business or professional interests, the child is never able to grasp fully while yet a child. In that period of the first five years, when most of the child's basic attitudes are fixed, he is unable to see his father except through the eyes of romance. He is something of an adventurer with news from a strange land and strange scenes, a dispenser of bounty, a hero. But even the father pales as a producer of romance, just as the mother failed earlier as an avenue to new experiences. Unable to grasp the truly wonderful but abstract elements in the personality of his father—his intellectual grasp of his work-a-day world, his functional relationships to business and professions and people, the hundred strands of destiny which he holds constantly in his hands and with which he guides men and events —more remarkable than the fanciful and concrete ones which the child conjures up about him, he turns to less abstract and more obvious personalities to provide him with romance and to lead him into new adventures where he can follow.

OUTSIDE ADULT MODELS—The postman, with his messages and envelopes from mysterious persons at perception-defying distances; the delivery man who seems to own and dispense according to some unknown and unusual system all the world's goods; the fireman who races about the streets in wonderful machines and rings a gong as the child himself would delight to do, climbs ladders, wears a slicker and a funny hat and has command of the water hose; the policeman, the stern minion and maker of the law, "who'll get you if you aren't good," and who can put you in jail; the street car conductor and motorman who make the street car go and take your nickels and carry you into previously unknown regions; the engineer and conductor and porter who own the "chu-chu" trains and let good people ride in them; the vegetable huckster, with his heaps of things he gives to mother; the taxicab driver who joy rides continuously and to whom people give fabulous sums, and who'll run over you if you don't watch out"; and the wonderful, wonderful clothes with red bands and brass buttons which some of these romantic people wear—these people with much more wonderful experiences than his desk-driven father has—next claim his admiration and approval and provide him with models to imitate. He acts the part of all of them in turn in so far as he understands them. Through this perception and mimicry he learns much of the objective world in

its simpler and more obvious forms. Thus he gathers an un
derstanding of the more concrete aspects of the transportation
system, the police, and local trade and commerce. It is a
much as he is able at first to understand. The girl child ha
slightly different models. The feminine models correspondin,
to the uniformed males are relatively few in number. Nurses
dancers, and the like, are perhaps the most common. All o
her models hold her closer to the type of her mother.

From adults in general—neighbors, friends of his parents
chance acquaintances, men and women he sees on the street, i
stores, everywhere—the child learns that the world is mad
pretty much after a pattern. Not that he generalizes this fac
into a sentence or a formula. That would be too abstract fo
his early years. But one may learn things without ever pu
ting them into words, or at least into abstract ideas. He hea
other men and women tell about their families, friends, inter
ests, purchases, trips, recreations, visits, work, as they tal
with his parents. He finds that other men are fathers an
other women mothers. He is likely to call all men daddies an
all women mothers, whether they have children or not. He in
evitably, through the process of conditioning by analogy an
similarity, classifies people in whatever relationships he know
through experience. To him the world is a world of familie
and homes and fathers who go to work, of mothers who tal
care of their children, look after the house or apartment, atten
teas and card parties, or go to shows, and who entertain. T
these are added children of three classes: those of an age an
experience similar to his own, babies who are helpless and kno
nothing and for whose powers he has a great contempt, a
though possibly an equal affection, and big brothers and si
ters who know everything and eat and do everything and ow
everything about the house. In this world he lives and grov
in depth and breadth, imitating as much of it as he unde
stands and approves and can, building it into his own persona
ity, until he goes to school.

IN THE SCHOOL he comes in contact with another class o
adults, one he has not known before. These are people who
special function it is to guide him in his understanding ar
imitations. They bring to him his first systematic analysis ar

synthesis of objects. They also induct him into the mysterious art of understanding abstractions and symbols. The Sunday School usually precedes the public or parochial school. Here he studies personalities in the main, following their adventures in various concrete relationships of life, and now and then he steps aside to consider the abstract merits of their conduct and aims. He learns his moral lessons from studying typical cases of behavior in action. Often in early childhood, the Sunday School lessons are beyond his powers of recognition, but he goes largely because the other children are there, or because of the prizes or from loyalty to his teacher, who is a sort of foster mother to him, or because of her praises. The kindergarten and the graded school use somewhat more concrete methods of instruction with him and provide him with models for imitation and assimilation which he can understand. He handles objects, analyzes movements, learns accuracy of measurement, and attains control over things, in the kindergarten. In his readers he encounters stories dealing with concrete social relationships much like those he has had at home or on the playground, and these stories help to deepen his personality impressions. Later he comes to deal with abstract questions and relations as such, in questions of conduct, numbers, and the like.

The school systematizes the personality building process. The teacher is a guide and a mentor, a critic, and a taskmaster, or a leader, as the case may be. His allegiance to her may be great, but it is not likely to offer as much of the romantic as did the postman, fireman, policeman, and the uniformed brotherhood as a whole. These integrated for him a limited world of concrete realities. School leads him into a world where, in spite of all efforts to the contrary, system and analysis turn romance into something not far removed from toil. The problem of making the school interesting is that of making the connection between it and the actual world of people as he has learned to know it as close as possible. But abstractions and generalizations cannot be wholly avoided, if the school is to perform its functions of preparing for and inducting him into a broader world of experiences.

BROTHERS AND SISTERS AS MODELS—In order to follow up

the development of the child's personality building on the bas[is] of adults as models, we have passed by another phase of analysis and perception and imitation to which we will now return. If the child has older brothers and sisters they have begun to serve him as models for imitation almost as soon as his mother and father have performed that function. As soon as he is able to play with them they become dominant models of one class. They are so much nearer him in age and in recency and vividness of experience that he can understand them much better than he can older people, like his parents and their friends. They talk the same language, have the same desires, hopes, fears, disappointments, powers, limitations, only in slightly greater or less degree. They also have the same or very similar moral and intellectual development and standards. Hence, after he has made a preliminary adjustment to them, there [is] no one so capable of teaching the young child as an older brother or sister who is not too much older. The degree of sympathy and understanding which develops between well brought-up children is simply remarkable. The attachment of the younger for the older amounts at times almost to idolatry. There is nothing more striking than the attachment, even literal adoration, manifested by a child of two for another more a[c]tive child of four or five. It equals, although it is of a different kind, that which the child has for a good mother. And it [is] interesting to note that almost invariably the attachment of the younger child for the older is greater than that of the older for the younger. This is perhaps in part because the response[s] of the younger become more exclusively conditioned to the older than those of the older to the younger, but it is especially due to the fact that the world of new experiences opened to the younger child by this relationship is vastly greater th[an] that made available to the older. In cases where the older ch[ild] has had the major responsibility of training the younger, th[e] situation may be reversed.

PLAYMATES AS MODELS—The child without older brothe[rs] and sisters is ordinarily at a considerable disadvantage in t[he] matter of possessing models easy to understand and imita[te]. He is also at a disadvantage in the matter of making collecti[ve] or social adjustments to his world. In both of these respe[cts] must substitute in so far as possible other children on the playground for the missing brothers and sisters. The play group performs one of the most valuable socializing functions in the life of the child. It is not enough for the child to make his adjustments to his father and mother and to other older people. The relationship here is not wholly a mutual one. The differences in strength, intelligence, skill, experience, in fact, in all of the arts of life, are so great that the child is compelled to take a dependent attitude, just as the older people assume protective attitudes. But even the attitude of dependence carries with it a secondary attitude of exploitation which is made possible by the secondary attitude of tolerance which accompanies the attitude of protection in the older people. Thus the child brought up among his elders too frequently lacks initiative in constructive matters, is lazy, and is unduly artful for his age. He has not always learned the lesson of fair play or of coöperating and seeking reward on a basis of merit only. When such "spoiled" children come to associate with other children they frequently discover themselves to be nuisances and incur ill will instead of friendly approval. They wish to have their own way and will often "queer" things rather than coöperate or follow other leadership. The play group is excellent for purposes of discipline. It teaches every child to consider the equal rights of others, to work in harness and to coöperate, and to value the opinions and good will of his equals. It makes of the average child a democrat instead of a tyrant. Nowhere else can he easily find models of a democratic relationship to imitate. The play group, even more than the home, or at least the modern home with its small number of children, is the true prototype of the larger society.

DIFFERENCES IN IMITATIVE RESPONSES OF BOYS AND GIRLS

What has been said so far about the personality development of the child applies almost equally to the boy and the girl. But soon after the stage of development at which the child enters school and takes part in a play group drawn not from his immediate neighbors' families, but from the community as a whole, a divergence begins to appear in the personality development of the boy and the girl. In fact there are signs of this difference earlier. The girl is more likely to cling to the mother model more firmly and for a longer period than the boy. This is probably the result of both a conscious and an unconscious direction by the mother herself. All conventional pressures influence her to the emphasis of feminine models in her mother, playmates, and teachers. As a consequence the girl never takes the same degree of romantic interest in the father's exploits and she does not attempt to imitate him in so many details as does her brother. Nor does she seek after the adventures of the uniformed gentry with the same romantic intensity as the boy of her own age. They appeal to her also, but they do not equally tempt her away from the domicile into an unknown and venturesome world. She is already being domesticated and acquiring the "feminine virtues." She is interested in her clothes and the forms of social intercourse. She "plays doll." She dislikes the roughness of boys and their untidiness. She is consciously or unconsciously modeling herself after the ideal of "the little lady," which her mother and other adult women have expressed to her verbally or otherwise. She is even now being groomed for some man's choice, after she has passed many years of apprenticeship in making herself an object of desire by the male sex. Of course there are exceptions to the typical distinctions between boys and girls, and in this day of the leveling of sex distinctions the exceptions are more numerous than ever before. But they are not likely ever to disappear wholly. Where the general rule is violated it is more likely to produce the "tomboy" than the "sissy." This fact probably indicates that the distinction between the two sexes as it now exists is largely the result of the repression of the active tendencies of the girls.

THE GANG—The boy, having largely mined out the conventional personality values of the ordinary play group, is now ready for a further adventure in specialization. His world

---

[1] Boys "play doll" also, but to a lesser extent. One day recently on my way to meet a class I observed an interesting illustration of this difference of interests in girls and boys. Two little children, a boy and a girl, about six years of age were on the sidewalk with a small new wagon, sufficiently large for either one to ride in. The boy had been drawing it and the girl was arranging her doll in it. The girl said, "It is a nice baby carriage." The boy said, "But it is our lumber wagon, too," pleadingly. "Yes," answered the little girl diplomatically, and continued to arrange the doll carefully.

again becoming too narrow. His contacts with mother, father, brothers and sisters, teachers and playfellows, and public functionaries generally, have become largely stereotyped. He responds to them more by suggestion than by conscious and purposive imitation. His world lacks enterprise and adventure; it has grown stale. Accordingly, in his never ending youthful struggle for new experiences, he joins with a few more choice spirits in a gang. He may or he may not know that he is joining a gang. The result is much the same, except that here the leadership of the gang is strong and its separation from the old play group is well marked, his consciousness of gang specialization is more vivid. The boys may use the term gang or club, and they may even have some form of initiation, together with other gang ceremonies of admission. The purposes of the gang may even be specified and a constitution be prepared and leaders elected. In such cases it is a club. But most gangs are much more spontaneous in their origin and more random in their purposes and procedure. Whatever the formalities and the statement of ends, the one big unconscious aim of the gang is to enable the members to secure new experiences, to have adventures. They are attempting to widen the boundaries of their world, geographically, intellectually, morally, and socially. Leaders appear more or less spontaneously and each one finds the place for which nature and previous experience have fitted him.

Girls also form gangs, but ordinarily with different types of behavior in view. Their gangs are more in the nature of social cliques and are competitive with other gangs. There are boys' gangs of this sort also, especially fraternities, but they are less frequent than those organized by girls. The girls' gangs do not ordinarily run toward daring and spectacular action, although they may embrace athletic activities. The boys' gangs, in their search for adventure, not infrequently cross the borderline of morality and lawfulness. This is the worst aspect of gang life among boys and serves to emphasize the need of some sort of direction or collective control. This need of guidance in the gang life of boys is now recognized and leaders of boys' and girls' clubs, gang leaders, playground directors and play leaders of a trained and responsible sort are being provided. If such leadership is not too officious and is yet efficient, the developing child can secure almost as wide an experience as when the boys and girls are left to their own uncontrolled interests, and certainly their experiences are likely to be more valuable socially when under proper leadership or direction. The boy scouts and girl scouts, campfire girls, athletic clubs, and other similar clubs, when led by people with broad social and civic outlook, can give most valuable training in collective adjustment behavior, and not without sufficiently exciting adventures.

QUALITIES OF THE GANG LEADER—The leader of the gang is a person of prestige, whether he be a particularly able and experienced boy of a similar age and kind or an older club leader trained and practiced in the function of leadership. At first this leader is likely to command the boy's enthusiastic allegiance. For one or two seasons this leader is king and his followers may find no essential error or weakness in him. The almost absolute dominance of a quick witted, athletic, daring leader over the other members is sometimes most astonishing. The trained club leader provided by a social agency can rarely, if ever, secure such complete acquiescence and homage from a group of boys. Among girls, the situation is likely to be somewhat different. They have been brought up more to use older persons as models and to imitate the domestic, or at least the feminine, virtues. But boys early escape from the home to find their adjustments on the playgrounds or elsewhere in a life of action. They choose as leaders boys who can fight better, plan better, think faster, and execute more effectively than other boys. Their experiences are not sufficiently broad or deep to lead them to raise many questions as to the ethical or social values of their leader's proposals and conduct. They have not yet gone far in the lessons of public and ethical analysis, which are in the main general and abstract in character. What they require of a leader is first of all that he be efficient in planning and in execution. Social and ethical niceties can be adjusted later. They want action and they demand self-confidence in their leader. If this is forthcoming they will usually follow him to the limit and stand by him through thick and thin. But he must never be "yellow." T

DIRECT IMITATION OF PERSONS

s unforgivable. Next after this, he should not be slow witted; although this is under certain circumstances pardonable.

WHAT COMES AFTER THE GANG—The gang or club life of he boy and girl mark the last stage in their experimental contact adaptation or direct imitation of personal models. After his they begin the serious business of life, allying themselves vith some occupational interest or becoming responsible for omes, unless indeed they enter college or travel or pursue a fe of leisure. In their occupational connections they continue he process of imitating models and of building up personality ontent with which to meet collective adjustment situations. But their models are predetermined for them by the limits of heir business or professional life and they are no longer free o vary these models to suit their personal interests or whims nd the desire for an ever widening general experience. Life nevitably becomes largely stereotyped and the personality elements which they must acquire are in the main predetermined. instead of turning to an occupational alliance they go to college or adopt a life of social leisure they continue in much the me type of experimental imitation which they pursued in the ay group and in the club or gang. But at college at least me of the boys' models are intellectual and abstract, while the life of social leisure the selection of models is hedged out largely by convention. In the former case there is little ance to develop individuality in personality by direct imitaon, and in the latter there is almost no chance to escape relaively complete conventionalization. This does not mean that individuality of personality development necessarily ceases the middle or late 'teens, but that if it continues it must me largely—if not wholly—through indirect imitation of odels. This type of imitation will be the subject of the next apter.

MATERIALS FOR SUPPLEMENTARY READING

dams, J., *The Spirit of Youth and the City Streets*, Ch. III
ser, F. G., "Chums: A Study in Youthful Friendships," *Ped. Sem.*, IX: 221-237
vey, J., "The School as a Means of Developing Social Consciousness and Social Ideals in Children," *Jour. Soc. Forces*, I: 513-517
ris, H. J., *Girls' Clubs*

Forbush, W. B., *The Boy Problem*
Frear, C., "Imitation," *Ped. Sem.,* IV: 382-386
Hall, G. S., "The Story of a Sandpile," *Scribners,* June, 1888
Healy, W., *Honesty,* Chs. III, IV, VI
MacCunn, J., *The Making of Character,* Part II, Ch. XXXV
Puffer, J. A., *The Boy and His Gang*
Rasmussen, W., *Child Psychology,* Vol. I, Ch. XV
Sharp, F. C., *Education for Character,* Chs. I-XI
Stoner, W. S., *Natural Education,* Ch. II
Swift, E. J., *Youth and the Race,* Ch. VII
Taylor, M., "The Child in the Home," *Mental Hygiene,* VI: 746-772

CHAPTER XXIII

PERSONALITY DEVELOPMENT THROUGH THE INDIRECT IMITATION OF IDEAL PERSONS

THE INADEQUACY OF ACTUAL MODELS—In the preceding chapter we discussed the imitation of concrete actual persons serving as models for the building up of personality in the child. These models are the people with whom he comes in contact in his everyday life and activity. He himself becomes a socialized adjusted human being through his growth in understanding of them. He isolates their traits and copies them into his own personality in so far as he understands them and to the extent that they fit his needs. We saw that the child advances from one model to another in his unconscious search for new experiences by which to grow in personality content and adjustment to his environment. For the most part this growth is good, especially if there is proper collective supervision in providing him with models and if he is properly guided in the organization of his imitation processes. Much naturally depends upon whether the child is provided with a good and intelligent mother, father, brothers and sisters, playmates, teachers, and associates on the playground and in clubs and gangs.

But in spite of all the efforts that may be made for the proper selection of models and for the guidance of the child in his imitation of these, there will inevitably come a time, if he continues to grow in personality, when the actual people he knows will no longer suffice in all respects as models for him to imitate. They lose their novelty. They cease to offer him a sufficient amount of new and compelling experience. Their imperfections become all too manifest even to the child. He is disillusioned with respect to his immediate world. He yearns for something more absolute and flawless of its kind, whether good or bad. The limitations of the mother and father as all-sufficing models become apparent when the delivery man, fireman, policeman, taxicab driver, and others come on the scene with their different types of activity, informal personalities, and romantic appeal. Even older brothers and sisters, whom at first he so greatly admires, finally lose their fascination. The teachers and other intellectual and moral leaders or models to a considerable extent bore him, and their abstractions do not appear so very real to his mind which is striving after the concrete and immediately practical and the concretely romantic content of life.

WHY GANGS AND CLUBS DECAY—Even the peerless leader of the gang in the course of time loses much or all of his charm, if the child follower continues to grow. The leader himself may tire of the game and relax in his inventiveness or become unable to inspire in others those illusions of romance which he can no longer inspire in himself. Perhaps some other boy, a later comer, takes from him the leadership or he turns to other interests. What is worse, he and his followers, in order to keep up their flagging spirits and find new adventures embark in ever more exciting and ethically questionable enterprises. Criminals as well as good citizens come out of boys' gangs, and girls' clubs may train in sex delinquency as well as in the domestic virtues. But sooner or later every leader must fall from his pedestal, giving way to some one else who has more of the enthusiasm of illusion and the thirst for experience which have not in a measure been exhausted. The gang or club itself may be disintegrated because too many of the members go away to school or seek some other field for the exploitation of their energies. If the gang continues on into adulthood it is likely to lose its constructive experience-giving function and to become either formal or boresome or to be perverted to some secondary function, good or bad, like a civic organization, a card or poker club, a drinking club, an athletic or musical club, etc. The main business of life now ceases to be the gaining of random and assimilable experiences and becomes a serious occupational or homemaking interest. Clubs can be of only secondary or residual, perhaps recreational, importance. The normal thing for boys' and girls' clubs to do, when they have ceased to perform the great random experience-giving functions, is to die and give place to other forms of personality building agencies.

IDEAL MODELS IN CHILDHOOD—With the decay of prestige of the actual models due to their experience-giving insufficiency, ideal models tend normally to take their place. This substitution does not in practice await the final disillusionment which comes with the decay or disintegration of the gang organization. It is rather one of the chief causes contributing to this dissolution. It begins to function, under normal conditions of opportunity and stimulation, as soon as disappointment with actual living models has accumulated sufficient volume, provided the child has access to a story-teller or can read. His disillusionment with the real need not even be verbally formulated to be effective. When the mother shows herself to be irritable or does not provide the expected pleasurable experiences without the after-taste of penalty, or when the father is seen not to be all wise or all powerful, and is discovered as even capable of being unkind, the child begins to imagine or wish for other parents who have not these defects of character. Or he may believe that the parents of his playmates are perfect in all of these respects, because he sees them only when they are on their good behavior and are making particular efforts to be nice to him as a guest. He may even wish that he was their little boy. This is perhaps his first excursion into the world of wish projection or day-dreaming as it concerns the creation of ideal personalities. If he does not build up within himself antagonism and resentment as a result of this disillusionment and compensation in wish projection, he may copy in himself a type of response which is unconsciously modeled after the ideal personalities which he sets up or imagines other parents to be, rather than after the actual ones. Many a disillusioned little boy or girl has grown in moral idealism and sweetness of character as the result of finding that others did not measure up to his or her belief in them. But many other children on the other hand have developed resentment and antagonism because of their disillusionment and have organized in themselves mean and spiteful attitudes, untruthfulness and unkindness, or even cruelty, as a result. They become child cynics. The only way to avoid cynicism at any age, when the models of imitation and personality building fail—and fai they must in some degree, sooner or later—is to have substi tute models ready at hand. If these substitute models are actua personages they will possess the advantages of concreteness and give conviction and a sense of reality. But ideal or imaginar personalities will also serve the purpose.

EARLY IDEAL PERSONALITIES AS MODELS—The ideal per sonalities which serve as personality building models are ordi narily not wholly unreal. In some cases, however, they ar mere fancies or wish creations. From the earliest times whe man's imagination began to revolt against or regret the im perfections of the visible world, he has created supernatura beings to compensate in their power, goodness, kindness, o justice for the absence of such qualities in the actual men o the visible world. Perhaps the most effective personalities o this type for children have been fairies. Fairies are usuall conceived as kindly, lovely, transcending all limitations of natu ral powers, able to transform themselves and others at will int any form or to transport those they favor to any place, accord ing to their convenience. Nothing could be more delightful t childhood, which has not yet been sufficiently mastered by th physical and personal worlds as to bear with patience the limitations upon conduct or their actual prohibitions upon th will. To children the concept of God is essentially that of great good fairy. Santa Claus is another fairy who enable them to transcend reality.

Grateful as are unreal personalities to the child imaginatio their gifts can no more last than can the imputed but unre perfections of parents, playmates, and teachers. Sooner o later the test of actuality will come and the child will kno that Santa Claus and the fairies do not exist and that he mu turn elsewhere for the moral support which he needs, if in deed he can secure it at all. Yet, so long as they survive his imagination, they may contribute something to his chara ter development. Since he projects into them those traits o personality which he misses most in his actual world he there! elaborates models for his own imitation which, if he respond cause him to grow in depth and breadth of character. But th dangers arising from disillusionment here are the same as those already mentioned in connection with the failure of the parent ideals. The child is of all people the most addicted to idealism, although of a relatively concrete sort. He fights against a recognition of the world as it is and he creates every device he is able to, in order to escape from that bitter reality, or rather to perpetuate the protective mother and father attitude which he knew in infancy. To fail completely at any point would be fatal to his idealism and power of resistance. Consequently, when one illusion is smashed or weakened, he turns hopefully and with the enthusiasm so characteristic of childhood and youth to another.

OTHER TYPES OF STORIES PROVIDING IDEAL MODELS—One of the most valuable supplementary sources of constructive illusion in early childhood is the type of stories told him about good boys and girls and kind parents and friends. These are mainly in the nature of fables or fictitious stories, but they have the advantage of involving nothing of the unreality of the fairy stories. If they are not real, they are at least realizable, and to the child they carry all the semblances of reality. It is doubtful whether the encouragement of childish phantasies regarding such unreal supernatural beings as fairies is ever justifiable. While some of their imputed characteristics are capable of imitation by the actual child, tradition has assigned to them other powers which are so wholly unrealizable that it is a question if the child's future disillusionment with regard to them is not too great and disruptive to be compensated by any good which may arise. But the stories of good boys and girls and men and women dispense with these impossible elements and, if the characters are not so good as to produce an inferiority feeling in the child or so good-goody as to arouse his contempt, they may be made valuable vehicles for valid personality integration through his imitation of these projected models. It is interesting to note that even adults often have not lost their feeling of reality for the behavior recounted in these stories told at the parents' knees or read in the story books.

Another kind of moralizing story, which purports to give an account of the behavior and conversations and sentiments of animals or even of flowers, are even more pernicious, if possible, than those of fairies. The use of animals in this respect may have been legitimate in the past when Æsop wrote his fables. But now, when we want people to see animals as they are, as animal psychology shows them to be, such use is not advisable. It tends to foster sentimental attitudes toward animals, and as a consequence movements like the anti-vivisection agitation. Not even the child takes the fairies with complete seriousness, at least in all cases, for he has not seen them. But the animals he does know and they will continue to be in his environment long after he has learned that the absurd things he has heard about them are not true. Consequently, the task of breaking the old conditioned responses and reconditioning new ones on the basis of fact is more difficult in the case of the animals which are present as stimuli than in that of the fairies who are not present. The only possible justification for such stories is that they are the vehicles for useful lessons, but this is not a valid justification, since there are other and sounder vehicles available.

IDEALIZING DISTANT PERSONALITIES—The stories of good boys and girls and men and women constitute a form of the idealization of distant personalities, for the persons of the stories are never represented as present. But these stories are not about real persons. Consequently they are liable to lack, as the fairy tales may also lack, something of the power to give a sense of reality, at least to more matter-of-fact children. Biography and history fortunately come to the rescue about the time that the fairy stories and the tales of the good boys and girls have completed their major contributions. History cannot of course be read as the philosophy of history or even as collective behavior of a more or less abstract type at this stage of development. It must be the history of personalities in action. People must stand out as individuals or in small groups such as those which have come within the observation and experience of the child. As yet, states, codes, traditions, constitutions, revolutions, nationalities, popular movements, and the like, are no more to him than so many names, and frequently he has not heard the terms. But he does know people in personal relationships and he has seen them behaving in a limited range of collective relationships.

History must, therefore, be presented to him as the actions, motions, and simple ideas or thoughts of these men. The discovery of America, for instance, is an expedition by Columbus and his companions in three ships across the Atlantic Ocean, undertaken with the permission and aid of the queen of Spain. The child can understand the dangers from storms, the fears of the men, the fortitude and determination of Columbus, the surprise of the natives, the interest of the Castilian court in the returned voyagers and their captives. The subject matter is to him primarily a moral lesson, dealing with the personality traits and emotions of concrete individuals. Of the struggle for national supremacy, commerce, religious proselytism and the like, he knows nothing as yet. These are abstractions which he will be able to integrate only later, when his experience with abstract ideas is much greater. But these concrete persons, with their persistence and warmth of character, these heroes of history, fire him and become to him effective models. He longs to be like them. And, if conditions are favorable, he succeeds in some degree.

An Illustration—As an illustration of the tendency to see the heroes of history in the most idealistic light possible we may take almost any historical personage. No American sees George Washington or the signers of the Declaration of Independence or the Patriots of the Revolutionary Army as ordinary men. In the process of idealization, of which we spoke earlier, they have lost their shortcomings and imperfections and have become men of great idealism and probity and consecration of purpose with respect to a great cause. It is very difficult to think of them as men with selfish interests and as behaving in petty ways like ordinary human beings. In this way also one is apt to think about the founders of his religion, or of his political party, or the members of his family, unless he has been disillusioned. What happens in regard to the idealization of the leaders or concrete actors in history also occurs with reference to the processes or movements, as we call them, of history. If we are Protestant we see with difficulty evil or error in the leaders and the causes and the management of the Reformation. Catholics are as slow to recognize anything to criticize in the Mother Church. Republicans,

368 INTEGRATION OF PERSONALITY

Democrats, and all other parties, see their party history as a succession of events which were always for the best. Our country has invariably been right and our religious leaders consecrated. Of such is the idealistic nature of patriotism. When this idealization takes the form of picturing men and movements in history as better than they were it has much justification and least harm for the process of character building in the individual. It provides a better model to imitate and in some degree, for the present at least, spares the imitator the necessity of cynicism. But the difficulty lies primarily in the fact that such false or mistaken idealization prevents the individual from seeing things as they are and from adjusting himself to reality as such. The more abstract understanding and imitation of history will be considered in the following chapter.

BIOGRAPHICAL PERSONALITIES AS MODELS—As we have seen in connection with the previous discussion of the value of historical personages as models for imitation, biography is particularly valuable as a source of models in the form of ideal personalities. The biography professedly centers the narrative upon the individual rather than upon the abstract event or process which becomes central in the case of history. This gives to biography the maximum advantage in the matter of displaying concrete personality models. It also has a great advantage over any other method of presenting ideal personality models, because it affords a sense of reality which cannot ordinarily be experienced from fiction or art. The biography is here referred to as presenting an ideal personality as a model for imitation because of the tendency already mentioned to isolate and overemphasize good and bad qualities in those we like or dislike and recognize as identified with us in interests or as opposed to our interests and personalities. Washington is not the only person whom history has given more than his due. All the great and honored characters have benefited from such selective admiration. Nor is any one of the evil characters of history so bad as the passage of time has made him appear to be. But the greater number of these men and women were at heart actually as fine as we have seen them and perhaps they would have been even better and finer if they could have lived up to their own conceptions of what they wished to be and do.

Those interested in the character education and training of childhood and youth could not do better, at one stage of the process, than provide them with a well selected and edited series of biographies of great men and women, which would thus furnish a well graded series of models for their imitation as a means to character building. Perhaps the series of biographies should consist of fifty or one hundred titles and these should be read from about the fourth grade through the second year of high school, or possibly even beyond this period. It is at about the beginning of the fourth grade that the child is sufficiently prepared by previous reading and experience to understand and assimilate all aspects of a fairly simple life history. Up to that time he should find his ideal personality models in stories of good and efficient boys and girls and men and women which do not represent their lives as wholes but which select out those episodes and adjustments which are particularly valuable for teaching the lesson which the child needs to learn and for furnishing him a stimulus to imitate which will extend his personality development in the proper direction for the time being. To attempt a life history as a whole before this time would probably tax the sustained interest of the child beyond its capacity. These selected stories may be of real or imaginary persons. There is no especial disadvantage in using fiction if the imaginary persons in the stories act naturally. Ordinarily youths beyond the second or fourth years of the high school would not derive the same proportion of benefit from reading biographies as models as in earlier years, for they are then equipped for the more socialized function of appreciating collective processes or movements in history and they should have the impulse to identify themselves with these collective movements. Consequently, the reading of history and the descriptive social sciences should form the basis of their personality building interests and adjustment training during the high school period. However, this latter type of reading should begin in some elementary form far down in the grades. The reading of biography and history and the descriptive social sciences, and finally of the abstract social sciences, should supplement each other in the order here mentioned, each new form of reading gradually growing in importance in comparison with the one immediately preceding it.

THE GRADING OF BIOGRAPHIES—The biographies should be carefully graded and arranged in several classes, possibly somewhat as follows: explorers and men of action, great national heroes, soldiers and sailors of the type who defended the country rather than those who engaged in conquests, should come first. Such personalities as Columbus, the Cabots, Vasco da Gama, George Washington, Sir Walter Raleigh, Captain Cook, and Sun Yat Sen, might be utilized for this earlier section of the series. After these perhaps the great physical inventors should be included because their results, like those of the preceding type, can be grasped concretely by children even of younger years. Among these might be found such names as those of Edison, Alexander Graham Bell, Robert Fulton, George Stephenson, Marconi, Cyrus Field, Eli Whitney, and others whose productions have the romantic appeal of having helped to transform our world. Captains of industry, railroad builders, etc., with their relatively concrete and spectacular achievements might well follow these. Next, perhaps should come the statesmen who have identified themselves conspicuously with their country's welfare during great crises. Cromwell, Lincoln, R. E. Lee, Thomas Jefferson, John Adams, Andrew Jackson, Theodore Roosevelt, Woodrow Wilson, would serve in part for this group. A fifth group might properly include the lives of men and women who have devoted themselves to great concrete reforms, such as the abolition of slavery, the improvement of working conditions, the great sanitarians who have made war on disease, those who have fought the battles of civilization against vice and crime. Possibly this group should come before the preceding one, if sufficiently simple and concrete reform activities were selected. Next a group of great scientists, who have made contributions of the first importance to the older and simpler sciences. These could be followed by the moral philosophers, and these in turn by the social scientists. Perhaps other groups should be included to supplement these. In each group there should be five or ten biographies, in order to give the child volume as well as variety of contacts with several types of ideal personalities.

The grading of the works apparently should be according to two principles. First, those biographies which deal with the simplest and most concrete materials should come first, both in the series, and in the several groups. Second, the groups themselves should be arranged in the series in the order of both the relative ease of understanding and of the psychological and moral fitness of the topics for the several ages at which they would be read. It was the intention to arrange the groups suggested above on this double basis, for the two criteria of psychological adaptability and moral and social fitness will usually coincide. Within each group the same criterion of grading should be employed. In this way a series of fifty or one hundred volumes of biography may be arranged in such a manner that each succeeding volume will make somewhat greater demands upon the child's or youth's intellectual capacity and at the same time give him more stimulating material for an adventure in vicarious elaboration or character building by imitation. Not only will he be developing personality content and ideals from the reading of such a graded series, but he may also by this means supplement effectively his other and more formal studies and his everyday activities. He may learn history, science, ethics, politics, economics, sociology, and other subjects in a concrete way while he is developing his own personality and learning to apply what he learns from reading about others to his own problems of adjustment. Each successive class and volume in the series will, if properly written and graded, lead a little further in abstract analysis and synthesis.

Of course these biographies should be written with this special educational purpose in mind and edited in such a way as to fit to the greatest extent possible the powers and needs of the child and youth. Such editing may involve a certain amount of selection of data for presentation and therefore of idealization of the characters of the men and women selected for this purpose. But all biographies are subject to such selection, whether it is done consciously or unconsciously, and it will do no harm in such a series as is here proposed unless the selection and elimination are carried to the point of willful distortion and sentimental prevarication.

AUTOBIOGRAPHY is in many ways more vivid and compelling than biography, but ordinarily it could not be used for the purposes here indicated. Only living men could write for such a series and even they would probably not be able to write successfully from the viewpoint of the series. But autobiography might very well be used as a basis for critical reading and discussion late in the high school period and even in the first year of college. In such cases the student should be encouraged to react freely and constructively, as well as abstractly, to the model before him.

The reading of biography and autobiography, as well as of history and the social sciences, is valuable for character building and character renewal at all ages after sufficient maturity has been reached that such materials can be understood. Biography and autobiography especially have in them a dynamic power which is well calculated to quicken the impulses to self perfection and social or collective adjustment. They should be made a regular part of the reading of every one throughout life because of their therapeutic and prophylactic effect.

FICTIONAL CHARACTERS AS MODELS FOR IMITATION AND SUGGESTION STIMULI—While biography is the preferable source of models for personality imitation, because of the conviction of reality and the relative feasibility of copying, which it offers, fiction can present the greater variety of types. Any type of personality whatever can be created by the fiction writer and it is certain to be used consciously or unconsciously (usually the latter) as a model by the readers of novels and romances generally. Much or most of this fiction is deliberately created with reference to the expected market demand. No a great many successful writers produce solely from the inner urge to create or to objectify what is in them. Even when they do so, what is in them is generally in large degree a reflection of popular wishes and prejudices. The fact that most fiction is produced for a market therefore means that there is a great demand for the sort of characters that are produced in fiction. This demand is, to be sure, largely uncon cious on the part of the readers of fiction. They go to fiction to find the adventure and express the desires which imitations of their powers or conventional repressions prevent them from realizing in their own actual lives. Even if they live at times as the novels describe, they nevertheless resort to the novels either for more adventure and expression of that same sort, or for the sake of seeing themselves mirrored in the authors' eyes or to see themselves objectified, or finally in order that they may receive further stimulation and confirmation in organizing personality of this type. Such seeking need not be conscious, and indeed it will usually be denied altogether, the seeker offering some other relatively meaningless explanation of his interest in fiction, such as that he wishes to be amused. But amusement is as much related to the functional aspects of life as any other activity in the adjustment process, if we can only analyze the relationship.

FICTION AS A RELEASE FOR WISHES—What is said here about the tendency to go to fiction for the purpose of finding expression of unrealized impulses, thus resulting in the building up of similar personality content through imitation, applies to both social and anti-social models and to the building of approved social and of anti-social characters. Perhaps nothing of the concrete, impulse-driving, wish-releasing fiction which is read is without some effect upon the personalities of those who read it. The images are so concrete and the emotional quality of the situations and of the language is so powerful that it is almost certain to condition responses in mind by similarity or analogy. Fiction belongs to that type of writing which, as Ross has pointed out and as we have emphasized above, is most easily grasped and responded to, because its subject matter is almost wholly overt behavior or action and the expression of emotion. All that enters into the neuro-psychic mechanisms, whether as concrete behavior material of the sort dealt in by fiction or of a more abstract symbolic kind, is raw material for the future behavior of the reader. It may lie dormant as raw material for action and be used at any time. The more concrete it is and the more easily it is conditioned to stimuli to which the organism is susceptible and the fact that fiction is sought or chosen by the reader shows that there is such ready facility of conditioning here) the more likely this content stored in the neuro-psychic mech anisms is to go over into overt responses or into postulate and presuppositions of thinking, when the proper stimulu occurs. It becomes response material for suggestion and easily released into action upon the occurrence of the proper conditioned stimuli. The characters of fiction are so easi conditioned to our previous experience that often they scarcel need to be imitated. They may merely be conditioned for sug gested responses.

SERIOUS FICTION COMPARED—But other more abstra types of fiction may appeal to us, because they open up ne avenues of thought and present new problems for intellectu solution. Our response to this type of characters and situ tions is more likely to be that of rational imitation, for he there is a real problem of character building. Such fictic more nearly approximates to case material in ethics or socio ogy. The works of Sinclair Lewis illustrate this type of fi tion. But comparatively few people read fiction of this kin because it makes greater demands upon their attention tha they are prepared to give. The popular works in fiction a little more than large masses of stimuli well adapted to touc off our ready made responses of an overt behavior type, at least to give us vicarious images of such responses, especial those of sex, action, fear, love, hate, and other strong em tions and adventurous aptitudes. The average novel or pla is ordinarily popular in the degree to which it serves as make-believe release to that behavior, overt and emotion; which we are not able to indulge ourselves in publicly in ord nary life. Its chief function, therefore, is that of the vicario release of wish mechanisms and its chief method of releasi these is that of suggestion.

SOCIAL AND ANTI-SOCIAL EFFECTS OF FICTION—Cons quently, fiction is capable of much that is anti-social as w as constructively social in its influence upon character buil ing. It not only releases responses already conditioned such stimuli as the fiction offers, but it establishes new ass ciations of stimuli to responses which might not otherwise stimulated into action. And, thirdly, it also performs the offi of suggestion, it reinforces responses already habituated or in process. Fiction can be used to aid a good cause or it may prostitute itself to the lowest types of behavior. This is often done under the hypocritical—sometimes mistaken—plea of devotion to art. Such solicitude for the freedom of art not infrequently develops into a commercial motive. The greatest danger from fiction and in fact from all art lies in its commercialization. In such commercialization the content of art is often little more than effective releases to powerful impulses, some good and some bad, skillfully organized. This is, in fact, true of all art. But if fiction is not commercialized there is greater likelihood that only stimuli for good responses will be presented or that those for anti-social responses will be presented in such a way as in large measure to neutralize their power.

All that has here been said concerning characters in fiction applies equally if not more strongly to characters in moving pictures. The mannerisms, gestures, manner of dress, etc., of the popular movie queen or hero are reproduced by millions of girls and boys daily throughout the country. The very fact that their behavior is recognized through concrete perception of pictorial representations on the screen while fiction must be apprehended through abstract word symbols, makes the power of the movie in suggesting responses much greater than that of fiction. In their concreteness of imagery largely lies their strength. It is interesting to note, however, that movies which reënforce pictorial suggestion with verbal explanations and condensations are most successful. This is explained on the principle that the reënforcement of one type of sensory perception by another is always telling.

ART AS A MEANS OF SUGGESTION—What has been said of fiction may be predicated of other forms of art, with such modifications of statement as are required by the differences of form which the arts take. The fine arts are either helpful or harmful to social ideals and character, according as they are used for constructive social or anti-social purposes. The fine arts offer us models for rational imitation, but popular art belongs primarily in the field of suggestion, where our responses are already largely conditioned to their stimuli.

Art is one of the great major fields of suggestion, and in this respect it differs greatly from science. Art must above all things be suggestive. It must "release the imagination," we say. In other words, it must be a skillful organization of esthetic stimuli which can call forth a vast number of vaguely defined and emotional responses. Art is a form of emotional catharsis and a method of sublimation. It can be so only to the degree to which it is suggestive. Only when the esthetic stimuli of the fine arts condition effective responses in us do they acquire meaning for us; and the more responses these abbreviated stimuli can call forth, the more meaning the art has for us. In brief, the more suggestive the esthetic stimulus, the more effective it is as art. The responses which the conventional artistic stimuli produce are limited and circumscribed by laws, rules, habits, and customs. To the man with an untutored ear, Beethoven is accepted as great art, not because it is suggestive to him, but because of the authority of critics. Jazz may seem greater art to him. To the sophisticated musician, however, the works of Beethoven are a never ending source of suggested responses, and jazz has only a crude and insipid emotional significance.

We usually judge art according to the type of responses it suggests. If these are vulgar, we rule it out of the category of legitimate art entirely. Matthew Arnold gave as among the criteria of true poetry, high purpose and sublimity. Legitimate art must suggest social responses. Greek and Gothic architecture, truly great poetry and prose, music, painting, dancing, statuary, drama,—all the fine arts, in fact—are agencies of social control by virtue of their power of suggestion. They perform a great social function as such. Legitimate art exalts because it affords stimuli for social behavior. It is inspirational in the most fundamental meaning of the term.

ART AND SCIENCE CONTRASTED—Science, on the other hand, must never be merely vaguely suggestive. It must leave no room for doubt. Both the stimulus and the response must always be sharply and clearly defined. Otherwise confusion results; responses differ each time the experiment is performed or the observation is made, and no generalizations will remain constant. The artist and the scientist in describing or representing the same facts frequently produce widely different results. The sun, moon, stars, planets, nebulæ, etc., gave rise to a system of mythology to the early Greeks, who were in the artistic stage of thinking. To the scientists, they are definite, impersonal organizations of elements and forces. The only abbreviation of stimuli permissible in science is in the form of language symbols, which tend to become definite and quantitative; and these must be standardized, as we have seen, to produce universally identical responses. Art may use any form of abbreviation it wishes, provided it is adequate to produce a stimulating response. The greater the diversity, the less the standardization of the response, the more successful it is as recreative art. The swift and skillful method of art is often contrasted with the pedestrian and labored method of science. The artist who "sees truths intuitively" in his childish conceit often laughs at the scientist who plods along diligently examining the minutest details.

THE EDUCATIVE SIGNIFICANCE OF ART—Nevertheless, the educative value of art has been overestimated. It is an easy means of transmitting personality values and of inciting to social adaptation within the range of its possibilities, but the kind of values and the types of personalities which it can represent are relatively simple and emotional rather than complex or abstract and intellectual. The symbolism of art is comparatively concrete. In the non-literary types of art it has almost the significance of gesture representation and the picturization of the facial expression of the emotions. This is true in pictures of groups and portraits and of sculpture, which are apprehended visually. Dancing, which employs the kinesthetic as well as the visual senses, is gesture, not merely its representation. Music employs emotional holophrastic symbols, which are primarily to be interpreted by each one according to his own mood or experience. In the literary arts where verbal symbols are used, the words are nearly always concrete. Nouns and verbs and adjectives and adverbs are more frequent and of a more sensuous quality than in scientific or philosophic language. The imagery evoked by the hearing or reading of literary art is mainly concrete and overt rather than abstract and verbal. Only in the higher forms of literary art, such a philosophic poetry and drama and essays, which are obviousl philosophic material, does the abstract element play any con siderable rôle; and even these do not dispense with concret imagery. Only the meaning is abstract, not the behavior sym bols through which the meaning is expressed. Even essays, i they are true literary art as this term is usually understood, ar built around the description or hypothecation of relatively con crete behavior, and not based on the abstract logic of principle as is the case with philosophy and science, properly speaking

ART IS RELATIVELY PRIMITIVE—As a consequence th types of models which may be set up by art for imitation ar almost as concrete as those which one meets in actual huma intercourse. For this reason art is within the mental reac of a vast number of imitators. It requires but little trainin in perception to grasp the meaning of the kinesthetic and visu arts, and only slightly more to respond to the emotional urge of music. The literary arts, however, can be understood onl as one masters the language, and verbal symbols are alway in a measure abstract. The use of concrete nouns and othe sensuous verbal material, many figures of speech, rhythm, etc however, keeps lyric poetry pretty close to the plane of musi The poetry of Walt Whitman and some of the modern fre verse poets introduced a more abstract and intellectual el ment into poetry, although much free verse is a sort of phras punning not unlike the simpler word punning and is cons quently a very low and unintellectual type of art. Orator although sometimes used to carry weighty intellectual conten is in its ordinary form designed to appeal to the emotions rath than to the intellect and is closely allied to poetry in its in agery and technique.

Children can get much personality building material fro the simpler forms of art before they develop the power o appreciating the more abstract literary forms of art and phil sophic and scientific writing. The use of art as a means indirect imitation is a bridge between the direct imitation o people and the indirect imitation or embodiment of charact and social adjustment values expressed through intellectu symbols. Art belongs primarily to childhood and to the chil hood of the race. If it continues to be the chief cultural interest of adults in a mature civilization it is so because either these adults are on a low cultural level (intellectually, not necessarily emotionally) or they are pursuing art from recreational motives rather than as a means to personality building. This somewhat archaic significance of art in a highly developed civilization is illustrated by the fact that the types which are meant for adult appreciation are more largely traditional than are science or philosophy. Only the unusual or more or less freakish "modernist" types of art have broken with the primitive themes and technique of traditional art and have attempted to become intellectual. But they do not attract large numbers of followers. Children's art keeps up to date because it is definitely functional as a means of personality development.

ART AND CENSORSHIP—This archaic character of art shows up particularly in the sex, fighting, fear, food, and various other types of appetitive appeal which are still emphasized. Because its imagery is concrete it does not often get far away from nature, and sometimes its idealism is more esthetic than ethical in character. The fundamental appetites find easier expression in the concrete symbolism of art than does ethical idealism, of which the symbolism is comparatively abstract. This fact tempts to the economic exploitation of the simpler, and sometimes even the anti-social, models and appeals in art. It is because of this fact that censorship or some other form of control in art publication has been demanded by those who have keener ethical appreciation. While often this censorship has been demanded on the basis of partisan or biased motives and is therefore not always scientific as urged, there is no reason to suppose that a completely laissez-faire policy can be tolerated in art any more than in industry and commerce, finance, government, or elsewhere. But the control of art should probably be confined to its publication rather than to its individual production. The same sort of need of control has always been recognized in connection with philosophic and scientific writing. However, control is less necessary here, because usually those who are able to understand a philosophic or scientific composition are also capable of criticizing it. If every one were given a sound set of standards by which he could criticize art, there would be less need for external censorship. If every one, in short, were able to judge intelligently the anti-social manifestations in art would tend to die of inanition. Also the scientific and philosophic types of literary production are intellectual and do not ordinarily release strong impulses to overt behavior, while art is emotional and has strong impulsive force. Being intellectual, science and philosophy are subject to logical analysis. Therefore the best control for them would probably be to require that they should be logically consistent with the facts which they propose to interpret.

ART AS STIMULI FOR RECREATION—We have already spoken of the recreational value or significance of art. It is recreational because of its high suggestive power. It releases a great variety of responses readily. These responses may be highly fixed and conventional or they may be random and analogical and vaguely emotional, thus leading to a variety of new experiences. We usually think of the artist as preferring this type of behavior, disliking to be tied down to sameness of experience or even to set values in conduct. The artistic temperament is said to be impatient of restraint and responsibility. But this attitude is not characteristic of the great artist in all phases of his behavior, for he must be responsible for definiteness of procedure in his technique and for lofty conceptions in his themes, if he is truly great. But there is undoubtedly a strong tendency in almost every one to escape from too much reality or sense of responsibility through daydreaming or by letting things take care of themselves, through the enjoyment of phantasy or fantastic themes in art, and the like. The soulful love story, wild west fiction, melodrama, and sex appeal in art generally, represent persistent, if very crude and simple, attempts to get away from reality in life. There is another motive in art, that of relaxing and letting things take their course, as in crying or laughing, which perhaps has not been sufficiently recognized. Some of the anarchic music of recent times, much of jazz and free verse, and of some "modernist" discordant art, is apparently of this type. It is truly pathological, as is hysterical crying or laughter, but, like them, is a negative form of catharsis in the midst of an overwrought and too complex world of environmental pressures.

SUMMARY—The description of models for the development of personality through imitation given in this and the preceding chapters has been, of necessity, an ideal or generalized one. No child actually does develop through all of these stages of model imitation in a uniform manner. Many, in fact, never get beyond direct and immediate personality imitation. Many skip various types of models. Others imitate one or two types to the exclusion of all others. But, in general, the order of development is one of (1) direct personality imitation, or the personal contact stage, (2) the indirect or ideal personality imitation stage which we might call the artistic stage, and finally (3) the imitation of abstract models, or the scientific stage. This last step is radically different from the preceding ones. Relatively few people ever attain to it. Most people stop in personality growth at earlier stages of imitation, and thereafter rely on habit or self-imitation for future adjustments. But since the abstracted or scientific model is of increasing importance, it is necessary that we study the social function it performs and its relation to the other types of models. This we shall do in the next chapter.

The pathological forms of development in personality building have not been taken up in this study. So-called Œdipus complexes, Electra complexes, inferiority complexes, distorted compensations, repressions and conflicts of all types, etc., while of great importance in certain cases, are not the normal and usual course of events, at least in the exaggerated forms which these names indicate. It should be remembered, however, that these pathological manifestations are but extreme types of normal behavior, and that normal development includes them in mild degree.

MATERIALS FOR SUPPLEMENTARY READING

Addams, J., *The Spirit of Youth and the City Streets,* Ch. IV
Colby, E., "The Essence of Autobiography," *Open Court,* XXXVII: 483-487
Froebel, F., *Education of Man,* pp. 305-309

Geiger, J. R., "The Effects of the Motion Picture on the Mind and Morals of the Young," *International Jour. Ethics*, XXXIV:69-83
Griggs, E. H., *Moral Education*, Chs. XXI-XXIII
Luckey, G. W. A., *Essentials of Child Study*, Ch. XXIX
MacCunn, J., *The Making of Character*, Part II, Ch. X
McMillan, M., *Early Childhood*, Ch. VII
Münsterberg, H., *The Photoplay: A Psychological Study*
Poffenberger, A. T., "Motion Pictures and Crime," *Sci. Mo.*, XII: 336-33
Sharp, F. C., *Education for Character*, Chs. XIV, XV
Stoner, W. S., *Natural Education*, Ch. VII

CHAPTER XXIV

PERSONALITY DEVELOPMENT THROUGH THE PROJECTIVE IMITATION AND ASSIMILATION OF PRINCIPLES AND CONCEPTS

LIMITATIONS UPON DIRECT PERSONALITY IMITATION—Useful as personality imitation is in the personality building process it has certain limitations which prevent it from being the sole method by which we get our adjustment to society. Its concreteness and directness are entirely in its favor. The fact that models are always present in direct personality imitation is also decidedly important, especially for the young. However, here also is to be found one of the chief objections to direct personality imitation as an exclusive method of personality development. The type of model which one finds through actual contact may easily be inferior to the type which one may discover in literature and the other fine arts. That is why in literate countries the education of the child by direct imitation of adjacent models is very early supplemented by literary and artistic instruction. The literary model, especially such as is provided in well selected and properly prepared biographies, is much superior to the adjacent models with whom most children can have contact. The model in fiction may be even more perfect, but it is likely to be inferior in the sense of reality which it gives. Also, the use of real and idealized personalities, selected from biography and fiction, offers a greater range and variety of models. Finally, these ideal personalities can be employed as the need for them arises. They can be taken up or left off, multiplied and intensified or diminished in their influence upon the individual in ways which are not so easily possible for real and adjacent personalities. Altogether, although not for all purposes or in all connections, the ideal personality is superior to the actual personality as a model for personality imitation. But since the newborn infant and the child during the first years of his life cannot read or understand stories of model behavior he must begin his personality imitation from actual people who are within the range of his senses.

LIMITATIONS UPON THE USE OF HISTORIC MODELS—Even the ideal personalities are not adequate as models for the completest development of personality elaboration. If they are taken from history they are subject to the limitations of actual growth and development. No man is perfect in character, and much less is he equally perfect in all the aspects of his character development. Yet, in biography his story must be told as a whole. Whatever imperfections or irregularities there are in his personality to unfit him for service as a perfect model for imitation can be, and usually are, removed by the selective action of an admiring public or biographer. But, besides being sometimes a questionable procedure, this selection may leave the character somewhat negative at points instead of well rounded and aggressive. Another, and perhaps a greater, difficulty in ideal personality imitation arises from the fact that historical or distant personality, however adequate it may have been for meeting the adjustment demands of its own time and circumstances, may not equally well serve as a model for the same purposes in our time or under our circumstances. For instance, we would scarcely be justified in selecting George Washington as a model in making all of our adjustments to life in our day, however adequate his behavior was for his day and needs and for those with whom he had relationship. Some of his views would seem very foreign to us. We perhaps should be more democratic, less inclined to tolerate slavery, more skeptical of the use of alcoholic liquors, although no more honest in financial matters, nor more patriotic. Each generation and each environment must develop in large measure their own types of personality and their own models for imitation. But the great historical models, by a certain amount of correction and supplementation and elaboration in the process of imitation, can be used as models to the greatest advantage to ourselves.

LITERARY AND OTHER MODELS MUST BE SUPPLEMENTED

By Abstract Principles—This difficulty as to time and place applies with less cogency to current literary or artistic models. Our artists, if they are persons of true inspiration, can create models wholly in touch with the spirit of the age, or even measurably in advance of it. And if we can free ourselves from the menace of the commercialization of art and literature and in some way compensate for the feeling of unreality which attaches to fictional art of any sort, models of this type should almost perfectly serve our purposes, in so far as personality models can serve that end. Literature and art creations of the past and of other lands, however, are open to much the same criticisms as are biographical personalities. They picture types more or less out of touch with our own needs. This fact becomes especially apparent when we are asked to imitate the personalities which secured a strong emotional or religious sanction in earlier ages. Much of the backwardness of China during the past thousand or more years has been due to the imitation of the thoughts and precepts of great philosophers who were of the utmost value in their day, but whose words in new times come to be more or less in the nature of chains of custom and tradition binding their followers on a Procrustean bed of conformity. Yet, on the other hand, the imitation of their conduct and the acceptance of their wisdom in many of its aspects gave great strength to character and stability to their collective behavior.

We should not discard the imitation of historical personalities and the assimilation of the values of past art and literature, but we should learn to modify the imitation process by the utilization of logically and scientifically determined principles. We should study the collective behavior of society and generalize from it abstract principles of conduct, and learn to assimilate our conduct to these collective ideas in addition to the imitation of personalities. For this purpose we need to study history and contemporary society, as well as biography and fiction and art.

Integrating and Idealizing Collective Behavior as Models and Stimuli—History as personalities acting develops gradually into collective behavior in which the concrete deeds of particular men tend to merge into abstract processes

or movements which seem to occur more or less in general
It is not that men drop out or cease to function, but that many
men acting coöperatively lose their separateness when viewed
objectively and merge their personalities into events. When
the child advances to the stage of development that he can see
history in this way, the trees are giving way to the forest,
metaphorically speaking. In early childhood he is so near to
men that he cannot get the perspective of mankind, because the
men themselves intervene. But as he grows older and objectifies and symbolizes his experiences more, or detaches himself from his contacts for the sake of a better analysis, he at
the same time learns to see men collectively and to see their
deeds more or less abstractly and somewhat symbolically. This
is the personification of collective behavior to which we referred earlier. He probably no longer visualizes primarily the
progress of armed hosts across Persian plains in picturing
the conquests of Alexander, or sees the founders of our government sitting in Independence Hall, although such visualization does occur and is important for a concrete understanding
of the historical events. But he learns to think of these and
similar things largely in terms of symbols or verbally. To be
sure the symbolic representation of history is never far removed from the concrete imagery of it in the mind of the
child and youth. But there is a gradual development away
from the separate and relatively concrete imagery of men acting as individuals over to the more abstract pictures of men
acting in groups or coöperatively, and finally to the point of
view of seeing history in terms of verbal symbols and as
occurring in abstract or logical processes. At this last stage,
which probably rarely comes before the 'teens and is not well
developed until the middle or late 'teens, the boy and girl have
come to see integrated sections of the behavior of mankind
instead of the isolated, or even the collective, behavior of individual men. This abstracting of the processes of history,
and in a certain degree their depersonalization, is effected as
a method of comprehending more of history at a single glance
than can be grasped when it is viewed in all its personal
details.

ADVANTAGES AND DISADVANTAGES OF HISTORICAL A

straction—In learning to view history in this collective or even abstract manner there are both advantages and disadvantages. It is the only way in which a perspective of the whole of human history, or even of any large sections of it, can be obtained. If one attempted to image all of the concrete acts of behavior of all of the men participating in human events he would never be able to encompass intellectually even a small portion of history. The synthetic and abstract integration of historical processes, by which they are conditioned to symbols and thus unified in consciousness, is necessary as a means of comprehending and comparing the whole. In this way the student gradually learns to concentrate the essence of historical behavior until at last he can see it in perspective. Such abstraction and condensation have their uses for purposes of comparing and measuring social processes, but they are the work of the scientist rather than of the child.

The great disadvantage of abstraction in history is that it removes the concrete imagery of the details which serve as strong stimuli to arouse lagging impulses to imitation. Even the imagery of collective behavior in history, which is semi-symbolic in character, has not the driving power as model which inheres in the concrete deeds of individual men, who can be seen in all the vividness of the emotional expression which accompanies their behavior and who can be idealized into a degree of perfection which renders them the most desirable models for imitation. Imagery dealing with collectivities must dispense with the dynamic and exciting quality of emotional expression to just that degree in which it dispenses with personality, and this may be in any degree from the most concrete to the most abstract representation of historical events.

THE URGE FOR IDENTIFICATION WITH HISTORICAL MOVEMENTS—The desire of the youth to identify himself with the movements of history continues to be strong, even after the concrete personalities are in considerable degree merged into the collective historical process. This desire is maintained as the result of conditioning his responses to the symbols and part symbols through which the concrete historical events are abstracted and integrated. He grasps the process of collective behavior, in the past as well as in the present, as was shown in a preceding chapter, and this understanding and recognition of others behaving collectively is in large degree the result of having previously recognized or perceived his own participation in the behavior of the group. In this way all group or collective behavior has some power, either directly or by analogy, to condition his sympathetic and overt responses and thus to impel him to act in a similar manner or to merge himself in the collective movement or process in the way in which his symbolization of the process of history, or of contemporary affairs, has merged and consolidated other personalities and their behavior.

The normal urge of the child, in reading history, is to be like the great heroes of history, to act as they have acted, to be the subject of their grand emotions and the emulator of their great deeds. That of the youth is to identify himself with, to merge himself in, the great cause, to be a part of the movement. The difference of interest and motivation is dependent upon a growth in the personality of the youth himself. With this growth of his power to understand human events collectively and abstractly, his own self and social consciousness have become increasingly abstracted and he as a concrete highly individual personality begins to merge himself into the collective whole. Consequently his desires for imitation and self-realization are correspondingly transformed from the individual to the collective goals.

GENERALIZATION AND PROJECTION AS METHODS OF PERSONALITY DEVELOPMENT AND SOCIALIZATION—THE NATURE OF GENERALIZATION—This analysis of historical collective behavior and the recognition of our proper function in connection with it occurs in the form of a generalization of the concrete relationships involved. From the study and the integration of history and of contemporary society into processes movements we come to view people acting collectively and our own or another person's behavior over a considerable period of time as a unit. Since we cannot image the whole of such behavior in detail it is necessary to abstract or foreshorten it and to state it symbolically. If this symbolical and foreshortened statement of individual and collective behavior carried to the point of condensation at which it becomes highly abstract and wholly symbolical, instead of concretely descriptive, we call this statement a generalization. By generalization we mean simply that we have compressed a vast number of concrete types of behavior into a few all-inclusive verbal symbols of those responses and stimuli and of the conditioned relationships existing between them. The generalization must contain not only the symbolic condensation of the concrete stimuli and responses, but also the symbolical statement of the relationship existing between these two types of symbols as analogous and equivalent to the conditioned relationships which exist or existed between the original concrete constituent stimuli and responses. In other words, a true generalization must be a logical symbolic statement of relationships and of the objects related. We saw in an earlier chapter that the essence of logic is the statement of the expected or stereotyped relationship between stimulus and response.

RELATIVE DEGREES OF GENERALIZATION IN SCIENCE, PHILOSOPHY, AND ART—In concrete descriptive art or science the statement of the relationship between stimulus and response is a mere perceptual description of what happens as perceived more or less directly through the senses. But in the more abstract forms of art, philosophy, and science, where there is no longer time for a complete or even very considerable detailed description of stimuli and responses and of their relationships and these have to be symbolized as described above, the logical statement of relationship is transferred to the symbols of stimuli and responses. Thus symbols of stimuli become logically or verbally associated with symbols of responses, or we might say that response symbols are conditioned by or stand for stimuli symbols and this relationship must be described or indicated in any production of art or science. This statement is logic in the conventional sense. And the kind of logic which obtains depends upon the kind of relationship expressed between the two types of symbols. A quantitative generalized statement increasingly characterizes science; a qualitative statement belongs ordinarily to philosophy and the higher forms of art; while a very vague statement, or no definite generalization, of relationships puts the integration of the symbolized processes into the category of the more emotional arts or even the field of irrational behavior. Science and philosophy and the higher forms of art, which are literary rather than pictorial and plastic, can make use of verbal symbols only, and science adopts even highly specialized verbal symbols for its highly quantitative logical statements. The non-literary arts use other symbols of stimuli and responses, such as holophrases in music and analogues of the gesture and emotional expression in painting and sculpture. In architecture still forms of visual representation are employed which are even lower in abstracting power than those symbols used in painting and sculpture.

THE TENDENCY TOWARD ABSTRACT GENERALIZATION IN THE ARTS—No great degree of abstract symbolization has yet been obtained in the non-literary arts of painting and sculpture, although the recent modernist movement in art is definitely in this direction. Formal design has always stereotyped natural models, but only in simpler forms. The representation of bodies in cubist or other geometrical patterns and the tendency to symbolize and stereotype the organs and parts of the body instead of painting or sculpturing them realistically appears to be a movement, purposive or otherwise, in the direction of abstracting and generalizing communication through art. The body so represented ceases to be some particular body and becomes any body under typical circumstances. That is, the circumstances which condition the personality rather than the personality itself tend to be symbolized in such art. In the same way landscape painting gets farther away from the particularistic and photographic and is abstracted or generalized into types by means of symbolic or stereotyped symbols. In music also there has been this movement away from the reproduction of concrete specific tones heard in nature to symbolic tones and phrases which generalize emotional attitudes. Thus the holophrases are broken up in a measure and the old method of allowing each one to read whatever meaning he pleased in the rendition as he heard it is giving way to training in the technique of recognizing the conventionalized symbols, with the result that all who understand the new conventionalized language of music will respond to much the same thing.

[...]ch intellectualizing or abstracting and generalizing of the [lan]guage of music there is no longer the opportunity to revel [fr]eely in the vague and random suggestive power of natural [to]nes harmoniously and melodiously organized. In fact no [on]e without training in the conventional language of classical [mu]sic can recognize its intended meaning any more than any [on]e untrained in the language of science or philosophy or of [lite]rary art could understand those productions without special [tra]ining. By such processes of abstraction and conventionali[za]tion and generalization of symbols, literacy threatens to be [int]roduced into all forms of art as a preliminary to its appre[cia]tion, just as it has already been introduced into the literary [art]s, philosophy or metaphysics, and science.

The generalization, therefore, is an organization of the sym[bo]ls of stimuli and responses with a stated or indicated rela[tio]nship between the symbols of the stimuli and those of the [res]ponses. Art of the concrete kind, that which has not yet [ha]d its language abstracted and stereotyped into general or syn[the]tic symbols, does not generalize relationships. It only de[scr]ibes them by more or less direct reproductions or descrip[tiv]e symbolizations of the original experiences, as in the repre[sen]tation of figures in attitudes towards each other in sculp[tur]e, painting, and the drama, or in the reproduction of sounds, [ton]es, and pitch in music. The newer or modernistic tenden[cie]s in art, if realized, may make such generalization possible. [In] music there is more opportunity for generalization than in [pai]nting, sculpture, and possibly dramatic representation.

[I]n literary art this generalization has advanced to a very [con]siderable degree, especially in the allegorical poetry and the [nov]el and in the morality plays which served the function of [pre]senting general social and ethical truths before the day of [pop]ular philosophic and scientific writing. In such literary [gen]eralization through art the concrete personalities and social [rel]ations were, of course, retained, but these personalities were [ster]eotyped and given general values, so that their behavior [had] a collective or social and general ethical significance which [is l]argely or wholly wanting in most modern fiction, drama, [and] poetry. Such literature was allegorical rather than con[cret]ely descriptive in character. Even as late as Fielding's

Tom Jones, the characters were named according to their personality types. Bunyan's *Pilgrim's Progress* was written intentionally for allegorical or character teaching purposes, and the characters are named on purpose to symbolize their virtues or vices. In fact they are little more than virtues and vices speaking and acting out their parts as in the old morality plays.

THE REACTION AGAINST ABSTRACT GENERALIZATION IN THE LITERARY ARTS—The depersonalization and demoralization of literary art in recent times, the return to concrete and specific representation instead of the general and allegorical, has occurred primarily because other methods of teaching abstract lessons have been developed as the result of an increasing literacy. Literary art has, as a consequence, retired from the function of moralizing to occupy itself almost wholly with the esthetic and to serve the function of affording amusement and recreation. Whether it will again move back in the other direction, as we have shown the pre-literary forms of art, at least in the hands of the more philosophic artists, are now tending to do, is doubtful. Perhaps the reason why literary art dropped the moralizing function and retired almost wholly into the esthetic and recreative, is that it has come to be so highly commercialized in the last few centuries with the growth of literacy in the population at large and has been reduced almost wholly to the function of providing amusement rather than instruction. An analogous reaction against abstract generalizing tendencies in music is to be found in the more recent substitution of jazz for classical music. Jazz music is commercialized and serves the function of amusement and recreation. In minor ways vaguely suggestive free verse and the vivid emphasis of color in painting (as distinguished from stereotyped conventionalized forms of these arts) represent the same anti-generalizing tendencies.

THE PREËMINENCE OF SCIENCE AND PHILOSOPHY AS METHODS OF GENERALIZING BEHAVIOR—The completer symbolization and abstraction of behavior processes in philosophy and science render them much better equipped for purposes of generalizing behavior than is literary art or any of the other more primitive forms of art. Personalities and concrete collective relationships still remain as the center of interest literary art, especially in fiction and the drama. But in philosophy and science they are incidental and illustrative, if they remain at all. For the most part they drop out and abstract symbols condensing behavior replace them as their representatives. It is the logic of these symbols which constitutes the generalized content of philosophy and science. The use of the generalization is to be found in its capacity to summarize or condense a vast number of concrete personalities and individual or collective behavior relationships under its symbolical formulation or logical language organization. These symbolical generalizations can be used in the control of actual concrete behavior organization and in the building up of the individual's character and in assisting him to find his place in the social organization by a process of retranslation of the abstract condensed behavior symbols back into concrete responses. In logic this process is known as deduction. The function of the individual instance—in this case, the functioning of the concrete personality or of the collective organization or group—is deduced from the abstract statement as a whole. The collective generalization is normally integrated through induction, unless it is a corollary of a more inclusive generalization. But the location of the concrete instance is found by deduction. The several sciences are systems of such inductive integrations of concrete phenomena which have been symbolized. The social sciences are integrations of those symbolized behavior phenomena which apply to human association.

The Projection of Generalizations into the Future for Purposes of Control—The social generalization is integrated from a study of the data of history or of contemporary society. It symbolizes and synthesizes the past and the present. It can become useful for the control of behavior in the future only by a process of projection. In so far as possible we plot tendencies and discount present relationships in the light of these projected tendencies. By accumulating data with regard to tendencies we are able frequently to predict pretty accurately the future situation in any field of phenomena with which we are closely familiar and in which changes are not irregular. We are the more able to do this in direct proportion to our familiarity with the field and the degree to which we have formulated abstract generalizations in it. The method of projection is essentially, with the exception of making the allowances here indicated, simply that of changing our viewpoint from the past to the future. In astronomy we have attained such facility in generalizing relationships and tendencies that we can predict the movements of solar bodies for millennia of years ahead. Our power of projecting human phenomena is as yet much less complete.

Projective Generalizations by the Artist and Scientist Compared—It is the scientist who pushes his understanding by analysis and synthesis far out into the realm of the unknown and brings new worlds of facts into view and measures them for us, that is, conditions our responses to them in a definite and dependable way. When the poet or the Utopian prophesies a new world or grasps a truth far in advance of existing scientific verification, he is working projectively in exactly the same manner as the scientist, but much less accurately and dependably. The one, we say, is inspired, while the other is employing rational methods of projective thinking. But if we should count the number of failures of projections which are made in the form of artistic inspiration, instead of remembering only the successful prophecies, as is our habit, we should in all probability think less of the inspirational method than some of us do. Science anchors us to our world with conditioned responses which are accurate and capable of being repeated indefinitely, at least until our environing conditions change. It does not carry us so far on the wings of the morning, but our travel through lower altitudes is safer, and in the end we go farther and are able to inhabit or possess the continents of thought and behavior which we discover.

However, the higher and more abstract phases of scientific generalization are not wholly unlike the methods of artistic inspiration. All imagination, artistic or scientific, is essentially of the same pattern. The differences are primarily in the accuracy and minuteness of procedure and in the degree to which our progress in making judgments, that is, in the reconditioning of abstract and abbreviated responses to symbolic stimuli, is checked up and verified. Art, like science, extends from the concrete and perceptual into the abstract and conceptual. The

stract and esoteric forms of art deal almost wholly with the
resentation of abstract symbolic stimuli, which are to call
orth abbreviated, mainly internal conscious and subconscious,
sponses in the individual. These internal responses or con-
pts may later be translated back through the series of condi-
oned responses into overt adjustment behavior in a concrete
cial situation. Science also consists in the presentation of
ostract symbolic stimuli whose function it is to release re-
onses of an abbreviated and internal character, which may
timately in the same way be translated back into overt ad-
stment responses. But the release of responses by the art
mbols is frequently by means of vague analogy, with the
sult that the adjustments made on such a basis, either in
eory (that is, in the organization of thought) or in overt
tal adjustment responses, are not so dependable nor so fruit-
l of practical results as are those released by carefully meas-
ed scientific symbolic stimuli. The method of the one is
latively impressionistic and qualitative; that of the other is
rmally highly quantitative. But when science ventures into
alms of reconditioning abstract or abbreviated psychic re-
onses to newly symbolized stimuli complexes, it also, like
t, suffers from the lack of perfectly accurate definition or
stract recognition of stimuli. As a result, science, in these
rther speculative outreaches of generalization, often ventures
o unverified conclusions or prophecies not unlike those of
e poet. In this respect science becomes a higher and more
stract phase of speculative art or philosophy.

THE RELATIONS OF SCIENCE AND PHILOSOPHY AS METHODS
    GENERALIZING SOCIAL BEHAVIOR—Science in this phase
  generalization is really a phase of philosophy, as it was
iginally, or metaphysics. Philosophy is a higher form of
erary art, attempting always to reach out in the organization
  symbolic stimuli to condition abstract or hypothetical
ought responses beyond the reach of scientific verification by
antitative measurement. It represents the attempt of man
 grasp the meaning of his world in advance of his power to
easure it and analyze it quantitatively. He uses art in its
stract forms for the same purpose, although originally art,
e all forms of representation, was used for purposes of re-

call rather than of projection. Concrete art restores senso[r] experience, perceptions, emotions. But abstract art helps [to] project behavior into the future or the unknown and th[us] widens the limits of our world and deepens the developme[nt] of our characters. In its lighter forms, especially in poet[ry] and prophecy (which is never very far removed from the e[x]altation of poetry), and in the drama, which is sometimes pr[o]phetic, the projection of art into new integrations of exper[i]ence is likely to be recognized as largely fanciful. Hence t[he] coming of an abstract philosophy as the supreme method [of] projective art in the human attempt to subject written a[nd] spoken artistic discourse to the strictest rules of measureme[nt] or of logic known to the artist-thinker. We may, therefor[e] define philosophy as logically corrected or tested literary a[rt] just as science is philosophy or metaphysics tested and co[r]rected by quantitative measurement or mathematical logi[c]. Science verifies or rejects the hypotheses of its own or le[ss] rigorous thinkers by applying definite measurements to t[he] conditioned relationships between the stimuli (symbolic or co[n]crete) and the responses (abstract and psychic or overt).

Philosophy is always occupying this middle ground betwe[en] art and science, taking suggestions from both and evacuati[ng] intellectual territory to science as rapidly as the latter is a[ble] to develop new measuring apparatus and methods with whi[ch] to test the dependability and accuracy of the predicated re[la]tionships between stimuli and conditioned responses. Wh[at] was largely the territory of philosophy in the time of Socrat[es] and Plato and Aristotle is now mainly the province of scien[ce]. At that time there was not much science because there were b[ut] few methods and means of quantitative measurement and ge[n]eralization. What methods of measurement there were in e[x]istence were applicable primarily to the physical sciences, wh[at] we now call physics, astronomy, land measurement, and t[he] like. The biological, psychological, and social sciences we[re] almost wholly philosophic in character. The methods of me[as]urement and generalization used in these, and indeed large[ly] in the realm of the physical or natural philosophies as we[ll] were those of descriptive or qualitative logic. Socrates a[nd] Plato called it the dialectic method. Aristotle improved up[on] by systematizing it into the syllogism. The only other testing method available was that of concrete verification by observation of sensory phenomena. Such verification was largely at random and was hopelessly inaccurate in all except the simplest phenomena. And even in matters connected with these the direct and unchecked evidences of the senses could not always be trusted, as we know from our present-day studies of the psychology of testimony. To rectify this last difficulty Roger Bacon attempted to defend and extend laboratory or experimental procedure, as a method of checking up on the evidences of the senses and general speculation or "intuition." Yet even he believed that the chief source of truth was in speculative thinking or intuition, the philosophic method. It was not until the nineteenth century that statistical methods, in the hands of Quételet, Le Play, and others, reached that point of development which permitted the utilization of quantitative checks or tests in the generalizing of complex and abstract phenomena.

THE RELATIONS OF PHILOSOPHY AND ART AS METHODS OF GENERALIZING BEHAVIOR—Before the coming of philosophy as a method of projecting generalizations of collective behavior, art had attempted to perform this function. The epic poetry of Homer and the odes of other poets and the Greek drama, such as the more highly perfected works of Æschylus, Sophocles, Euripides, and Aristophanes, and even the literary historical works of Thucydides, Herodotus, and Xenophon, are good examples of the utilization of the higher forms of literary art for purposes of presenting abstract situations and principles of behavior for the imitation of the youth and citizens or to inspire the mergence of the self in the collective behavior or movements thus held up to praise. Those who have regarded the Greek civilization as the highest yet reached by man have been chiefly literary men. They are correct in their judgment in one respect. The Greeks did succeed in making the most highly perfected presentation of the great problems of human existence in the form of literary art, especially the drama. But they are in error in not recognizing that presentations of those problems involving much more detailed insight and accurate measurement of the factors concerned have since been made in scientific and philosophic form. Such semi-abstract and semi-philosophic literary presentations of th[e] great moral and social issues for public consideration and em[u]lation are still to be found in the more abstract forms of o[ur] artistic literature, but they have never again attained the d[e]gree of perfection which they reached among the Greeks. Th[is] fact is not due to a decline in the powers of the human intelle[ct] as many writers have supposed, but to an improvement [in] language integration or communication. Philosophy learn[ed] to do the same tasks better than art immediately after t[he] Periclean age, and since that day philosophy has largely tak[en] the place of art in the performance of the function of gener[al]izing human behavior concepts for purposes of social contr[ol]. Philosophy, which reigned supreme in this respect througho[ut] late ancient and mediæval times, has since the eighteenth ce[n]tury been giving way to the method of science. Out of th[is] change to the scientific method of testing and reconditioni[ng] and generalizing behavior in collective and social situatio[ns] have come the social sciences which are now so rapidly d[e]veloping.

THE EFFECT OF THE DISPLACEMENT OF PHILOSOPHY [BY] SCIENCE UPON SOCIAL AND ETHICAL STANDARDS—Many b[e]wail this giving way of philosophy before the social scienc[es] as a method of dealing with social adjustment problems a[nd] believe that it indicates a weakening of sincerity and idealis[m]. They forget that with the work of the physical and chemi[cal] experimentalists of the sixteenth, seventeenth, and eighteen[th] centuries, and of the biological and psychological experimente[rs] of the nineteenth century, metaphysics was driven out of t[he] territory which is now occupied by the sciences of physi[cs], chemistry, biology, and psychology. In each instance of d[is]placement the same cry of the decay of morals and religio[n], of sincerity and idealism, was raised. The philosophers a[nd] theologians did not realize that these very systems of valu[es] were being strengthened by the substitution of accurate met[h]ods of measuring such values for the old inaccurate a[nd] traditional methods. The struggle of philosophy and theolo[gy] against the scientific norms and methods in biology and ps[y]chology has come down to our day, and now their fight [is] against sociology and social psychology. But as these subje[cts] adopt scientific methods and tests they will vindicate themselves because of the superior results which they will offer in the fields of character building and progressive social organization.

THE ATTITUDE OF THE SCHOOLS TOWARDS THE NEWER EMPHASIS UPON SCIENTIFIC SOCIAL GENERALIZATION—The schools and the universities, however, are still organized largely from the older educational viewpoints in so far as the inclusion of material for character training in their curricula is concerned. The subject of artistic literature, in the form of poetry, the novel, and the drama, still receives more attention and detailed exposition than the social and ethical sciences. The social sciences, except in the form of history, which is now only in transition from an art to a science content, are given very little attention in schools below the grade of universities. And that portion of the social sciences which is most fully treated in the universities is the part which aids in the establishment or conduct of commercial enterprises and the practical administration of governmental units. The part of social science which can be of use in the direct processes of character formation and in directing the coöperation of the individual with the collective organization of society is still largely, but not wholly, neglected even in the higher institutions of learning. On the other hand, artistic literature and history and language occupy from three-fifths to three-fourths of the time in our high schools and perhaps half of the time of students in the universities. Whole courses are given over to the interpretation of the artistic writings of one man or to the interpretation of the types of literary production in a limited period of a single people's history. The political history of peoples, presented largely as literary narrative with little or no attempt to trace the development of scientific methods or the growth of individual or social values in the control of civilization, still receives voluminous treatment by periods or movements. Yet it is rare to find such presentations of the social or other sciences by brief epochs or by individual thinkers or movements. As yet the universities do not find money, nor students the time, for the encouragement of such detailed analyses. The students themselves are more interested in the vague suggestion materials of the literary and artistic subjects, where relatively uncontrolled imagination can still play at will and where the emotions have a chance for exercise, than they are in the more rigorous logical and quantitative analyses and critical examination of the abstract concepts and generalizations of the sciences. Also, those who administer the universities and the schools are themselves often so little acquainted with the development of the scientific trends that they are not aware to what extent the scientific procedures are supplanting those of art and philosophy.

The Legitimate Functions of Art and Philosophy in the Curricula—This does not mean, of course, that there will not always be a legitimate place in life and in our educational instruction for both art and philosophy. Art has a great recreational and cathartic value, especially for the normal release of the emotions; and man is by nature an emotional as well as an intellectual being. The old function of art as a means to individual development and collective adjustment has been largely supplanted by newer controls, but not entirely so. It can still do for childhood, in its crude and vague suggestive way and in the stimulation of the individual in copying emotional and other less intellectual forms of behavior, what it earlier did for the human race before the advent of philosophy and science. It is also an important method of conveying suggestion and of presenting objects for imitation and assimilation to people who have not yet learned to respond to the more exact and more intellectual language of science. Very illuminating from this angle is the amount of use made in our day of pictures and stories and dramatics for children. Undoubtedly children secure much valuable training in character development and in orientation to the world through these channels of art. It is to be regretted that the art thus employed should not make better use of sound psychological and ethical principles than it sometimes does. Also, the greater concreteness and simplicity of art as a vehicle for the instruction of children should not blind us to the importance of using the simpler materials of science whenever we can, because they are so much more accurate and their values are so much more easily tested. At least we may always apply the principles of science in testing the values of art in the education of children. And in this direction much progress is now being made.

The strong partiality of large numbers of adults for the artistic and philosophical over the scientific presentation of generalizations of behavior is due partly to their preference for amusement and recreation and "the interesting" to more positive and serious self-improvement through learning. Recreation and amusement fall primarily in the field of suggestion, which is the province peculiarly of art. The large range of relatively vague and random responses which art permits can always give vicarious adventures to people, and the relatively emotional content of the responses called forth by art stimuli makes it easily possible for them to find a form of art or an art theme which will give them a chance to release their own pent-up emotional impulses. This is the essence of amusement.

THE VALUE OF ART AND PHILOSOPHY FOR GENERALIZING EVERYDAY ADJUSTMENT RELATIONSHIPS—But the appeal of art and philosophy to the masses of mankind is also based on more serious considerations than those of recreation and a chance for emotional catharsis. They are valued because they are the most effective media for personality integration and collective adjustment which their advocates understand. Many art societies and art collectors find, aside from recreational hobbies, genuine moral and social inspiration in pictures, plays, novels, poetry, and philosophy, which they study or hear discussed. The very large number of art and literary study clubs and of various philosophic societies, including the mystical Hindu and various New Thought cults, constitute an overwhelming testimonial to the serious moral purpose of men and women, as well as to the poverty of their intellectual development. The existence of these organizations also testifies sadly enough to the large number of adults who have not yet grasped the methods and importance of scientific generalization for a better and farther reaching adjustment to the problems of life. But now there is happening to the masses what earlier occurred with respect to the scholars. They are beginning to grasp this superiority of science as an adjustment aid, and they are utilizing science more and more, partly in their schools, frequently by reading books on scientific themes, and also by the organization of societies and clubs and the publication of journals for the discussion of their adjustment problems in a scientific manner.

MATERIALS FOR SUPPLEMENTARY READING

Addams, J., *The Spirit of Youth and the City Streets,* Chs. V, VI
Case, C. M., *Outlines of Introductory Sociology,* Ch. XIX
Cope, H. F., *Education for Democracy*
Dewey, J., *Human Nature and Conduct,* Part III, Section VII
——, *Moral Principles in Education,* Ch. IV
Griggs, E. H., *Moral Education,* Ch. XX
Hall, G. S., "The Pedagogy of History," *Ped. Sem.,* XII: 339-349
MacCunn, J., *The Making of Character,* Part II, Chs. IX, XI, XII, Part III
Ross, E. A., *Social Control,* Chs. XXIV-XXVII
Sharp, F. C., *Education for Character,* Chs. XII-XIV
Yarros, V. S, "Ethics in Modern Fiction," *Int. Jour. Ethics,* XXIX: 39-47

CHAPTER XXV

SUMMARY OF PART III

Part III has been essentially a continuation and an application of Part II. The principles of habit integration worked out in Part II were here developed and applied to the general problem of personality development in the child and adult. The term personality building or development was used in Part III because the psychological problem before us was to find out how the infant born into the world with an incomplete behavior equipment of instinctive mechanisms acquires a sufficiently complete set of behavior patterns to enable him to make the necessary adjustments to his environment as he finds it and as it develops around him. This process of developing in himself, in response to the environmental stimuli to which he reacts, behavior sets or adjustment mechanisms is also the process of personality building. An equipment thus attained for the control of behavior in a social situation or for making adjustments to environment is personality.

The whole perceptual or recognitive process is preliminary and accessory to the completion of personality development. Every recognition of relationship of self to environmental pressures or stimuli, each orientation of the organism with reference to stimuli, builds up within the organism response mechanisms which become a part of the personality content. For personality is behavior and potential behavior, or readiness to respond to stimuli and the inhibitions upon response.

One may be conscious or unconscious of his responses and inhibitions in the adjustment situation. The unconscious or vaguely conscious adjustments probably predominate. But consciousness of one's adjustment behavior undoubtedly strengthens one's control over the process of adjustment itself. Likewise, consciousness of one's adjustment capacities, attitudes, values, beliefs—recognitions of the inner self—greatly integrates personality by rendering it self-conscious or under the direct supervision of an analysis of the adjustment process. If later these adjustments lapse into the unconscious it is ordinarily because no conflict has arisen to interrupt their automatic functioning or to transform them.

Personality is built up through all of the processes of recognition because all of them contribute to the integration of behavior patterns and the establishment of gradients in the neuropsychic and the neuro-muscular protoplasmic systems. But the chief sources of personality development are those forms of recognition which we call projective and vicarious, or imitative. It is not necessary to know we have a personality trait or complex of such traits in order to possess personality. Every adjustment we make to environment, overt or inner, muscular and neural, conscious or unconscious, contributes to our personality content. All of our recognitions, direct and original, or indirect and vicarious, of the overt or of the psychic or symbolic personality, constitute so much of a contribution to the personality or behavior control organization.

But we live in a very complex world and our behavior sets which in the aggregate we call personality, must also be complex and highly developed, even highly self-conscious at points in order to give us the greatest degree of control over ourselves and others in an adjustment situation and in that complex of adjustment situations which we call life. No one person could possibly make by his own unaided efforts, all of the analyses and behavior integrations which are necessary for successful adjustment in this complex modern world. It is necessary that each one shall profit from the experience of others and take over their behavior patterns by imitation. In this way achievement in adjustment and in personality integration becomes coöperative or collective.

The second and third chapters in Part III dealt with the mechanisms, conditions, and consequences of suggestion, both as a form of imitation and as an independent method of conditioning and releasing responses. We found that, as a form of imitation, suggestion is irrational and capable of much less elaboration of personality content than rational and conscious imitation. Also, suggestion is frequently the result of the

SUMMARY OF PART III

stereotyping of the imitated response and a high degree of effectiveness in conditioning the response to a highly selected partial stimulus or cue. In other cases suggestion is merely a method of ready release of any strongly conditioned response by the presentation of the stimulus, usually in the form of a highly selected cue or shibboleth, or other stereotyped and conventionalized symbol. Altogether suggestion, either as imitation or as an independently conditioned stimulus-response mechanism, plays a considerable part in our behavior. In the next chapter we discussed the mechanisms, types, and results of imitation in personality building and adjustment making. We found that the larger part of what we are and of the adjustments which we make is the product of this process of vicarious recognition, or imitation.

The next three chapters of Part III outlined the actual steps by which the child and adult develop in themselves, primarily through imitation, those behavior integrations which we call personality. The treatment here is primarily from the standpoint of the types of models used for the purpose of vicarious development through imitation. We found that the young child imitates first of all the concrete behavior of the persons in his immediate environment. The law of his growth in personality development is that of progress in imitation from the more simple and concrete to the more complex and abstract models, or at least of behavior patterns in the models. The child is ever striving to expand the scope of his personality and to encompass more intricate and far-reaching types of adjustment. Thus he begins with his parents, brothers and sisters, and playmates, as models, and progresses through the whole range of actual personalities with whom he comes in contact. From each of these he takes what he is capable of perceiving or understanding, and when they no longer afford him sufficient stimulus, he passes on to a wider field of models for vicarious personality development.

Thus, generally before he reaches his 'teens and early adolescence, he has developed well established habits of drawing his personality material from ideal personalities. This process began much earlier through the instrumentality of behavior stories told him by parents, older children, and teachers.

It now makes use of biography and fiction, and finally of the more concrete and descriptive aspects of history. This also is personality imitation, but it is imitation of ideal personalities. He prefers ideal personalities as models, because they are not subject to the same limitations of achievement and the same imperfections as actual and proximate personalities. The great mass of the population perhaps still does not get much beyond this stage of personality development through imitation.

The third stage of vicarious integration is the most important for a proper development of personality content and adjustment mechanisms in the modern world where so many of our most important contacts are indirect and abstract. This third stage of the imitation process consists of the imitation of abstract qualities and principles and is indirect rather than direct in character. The models are primarily those found in art, particularly in literary art, in philosophy, and in science, especially in the social sciences. This is the imitation or assimilation of abstract generalizations, as a method of making short cut and more inclusive adaptations to the social world as a whole. These generalizations of behavior appear to some extent in the more concrete forms of art, but especially in literature, and more particularly in philosophic and scientific literatures.

These latter types of literature have been developed primarily for the purpose of communicating a generalized or conceptual symbolization of human behavior to those who can assimilate it, that is, who can embody it conceptually and symbolically in their inner behavior mechanisms and retranslate it into concrete overt responses. This is the most important of all of the stages of imitation and out of it comes the most highly concentrated development of personality or orientation mechanisms. As yet, only a small portion of the population has developed this method of imitation beyond the most rudimentary stages. It is the problem of our educational system and agencies, formal and informal, to realize the importance of abstract imitation and to stimulate a universal exercise of it.

This final chapter of Part III brings us to the first two chapters in Part IV, which are concerned with the growing abstractness and indirectness of contacts in society and the in creasing abstractness of our formulation of ideals and aims. Part IV will deal with the organization of the stimuli-giving environments which dominate or condition the processes of personality integration in the individual and the collective integration of response. In Part III we studied the psycho-social environment as it presents itself to the child in the form of models for imitation and the responses which the child makes to these models. In Part IV the viewpoint is different. We shall study the psycho-social environment from the standpoint of its objective organization and control mechanisms.

Part IV

THE PSYCHO-SOCIAL ENVIRONMENT AND THE ORGANIZATION OF COLLECTIVE BEHAVIOR

CHAPTER XXVI

PRIMARY AND DERIVATIVE GROUPS

Introductory—We have now completed the discussion of the processes and technique by which personality is built up in the individual and by which this socialized individual secures his adjustments to his environing world. We shall now turn, in this last major division of this book, to a brief consideration of those psycho-social and bio-social organizations which constitute the general setting in which the individual develops and which determine the direction of his development. These conditions are his environments. Without some knowledge of the ways in which these environments operate upon the individual we cannot understand adequately why the individual responds as he does, why certain models are offered as stimuli, and why certain types of personality rather than others are selected. However, Part IV will not consist of an analysis of the social environments as such, but rather of the ways in which they exercise their controls. Nor shall we attempt a complete analysis of their functioning. Such an analysis belongs rather to the applications of social psychology to the problems of social organization and social control than to the outline principles of the science of social psychology itself. We shall deal in this fourth major division primarily with groups, communication, leadership, and institutional and non-institutional controls as they bear upon the socialization of the individual and the determination of his collective behavior. These determinants are themselves forms of collective behavior which are antecedent to the socialization of the individual or the molding of him into participation in collective behavior.

In this chapter we shall deal with the development of group integrations from their primary to their derivative forms. A primary group may be defined as a face-to-face organization in which the personality or behavior of the individual is selected from his earliest years, while a derivative group is either a face-to-face or an indirect contact organization of individuals and includes all group forms which have been elaborated from the original primary groups. This distinction is of fundamental significance in the process of personality integration.

PRIMARY GROUPS—Professor Cooley has shown very clearly how primary group contacts produce primary ideals or attitudes. The concept of the primary group is a very useful one in social psychology. Primary groups are face-to-face organizations of individual responses on the basis of very elementary or primitive impulses or sets of impulses, native or acquired in human nature.[1] These groups condition the individual's responses from his earliest days. The behavior itself is likely to be relatively simple, although under modern complex environmental conditions it may become very complex and even abstract, in its derivative manifestations. The most primary of all groups is perhaps the family. After this come the play group, the neighborhood, school, church, occupational and other groups, in increasing degrees of derivativeness. These primary groups are the first with which the new born and developing child has direct and conscious contact, as described in Part III. His contacts with most of the less primary groups are indirect rather than direct. That is, he comes in contact with nonface-to-face derivative groups only indirectly, through his distance contacts with their members, while he has direct or face-to-face contacts with all of the members of his primary groups. Not only are the primary groups the first ones which shape the personality of the modern child by direct contacts, but they are also groups which come down from the remotest antiquity; or at least, they are modifications of primitive groups of the same general character.

The family and the neighborhood and play groups have existed in some form or other from the earliest periods of social organization of any sort among men. The school and church and occupational groups are modern derivations from the early general community group, in which the functions of religion

---

[1] For Professor Cooley's definition of the primary group, see Clow, F. R. "Cooley's Doctrine of Primary Groups," *American Journal of Sociology*, Vol. XXV, p. 327.

education, and occupation were not clearly differentiated. The community of early times was less abstract and complex than it is among us, and all of these modern derivative functions were performed pretty much by the group as a whole in the rudimentary and less specialized manner characteristic of that time. Or, if there were persons specialized to take the lead in the performance of these religious training and occupational functions, the whole group participated and the functions of the followers were but little specialized. Each lay person had much the same relation to the community activities as the others. The main divisions of classes along lay lines in the primary community group depended upon functions and was with regard to age and sex.

Personality Integration a Function of the Primary Group—The primary group, whatever its form or type, has always had the function of molding the personality of the young and of controlling the behavior of the old. Thus the primary group was, and still is, a sort of educational and administrative organization at one and the same time. We of modern times, who have come to depend largely upon the less personal group controls of a more or less abstract and derivative character, cannot easily realize the degree to which the earlier primary groups determined personality and conduct. Those types of family organization which are most nearly patriarchal still surviving among us in certain races and creeds perhaps afford our best illustrations of this fact. But supplementary to the family as a closely knit personality forming and administrative group was the clan and later came the phratry and the tribe. The clan was so typical of the function of the primary group here discussed that we still speak of this sort of closeness of personal character molding and control as clannishness.

The most typical early form of the family as distinct from the clan was the patriarchal. This family in its heyday of development had the power of life and death and enslavement over all of its members. There was no appeal from its power and it molded the personalities and prescribed the collective and individual behavior of each member. Elders, especially males, were the official models of all younger members, just as the chiefs and other persons of authority were the models in the community group, whether clan, phratry, or tribe.

This power of the family has greatly diminished in our day. The first to be set free, psychologically and legally, were the adult males. The women also gained freedom little by little, until in the nineteenth and twentieth centuries they are perhaps freer in some respects than the males from responsibilities and obligations to the family group. The children have also gradually come out from under the control of the family until now it is a serious problem whether the family group is able to exercise sufficient psychological, economic, and legal pressures upon the developing child to give him a proper respect for and adherence to the traditions and customs of the greater society in which he lives.

THE PRIMARY GROUP AND DISCIPLINE—The great contributions of these early primary groups, especially of community, family, and play groups, to the socialization of the individual were three in number. First and most immediate, perhaps, was that of discipline. These groups set the models for the young to copy and compelled them to conform. This meant that any aberrant tendencies and selfish motives were repressed. Coöperation was the great lesson learned and it was enforced ruthlessly in practice wherever it was necessary to the survival of the group. There was, to be sure, much individual choice. In many cases, for example, one could elect or refuse to go on a war or hunting expedition, but if the person so choosing was conceived to be acting contrary to the interests of the group he would be strongly stigmatized and possibly expelled or outlawed. Conformity and coöperation were just as compulsory in the early patriarchal family, because it was an economic unit and failure to coöperate would have been disastrous. This coöperative discipline was necessary primarily for economic and protective reasons. Discipline is still an important function of the primary group, but it is now more difficult to enforce, partly because derivative group organizations have done much to disintegrate the powers of the primary groups and partly because the derivative groups have in some measure taken over the function of discipline.

THE PRESERVATIVE AND TRANSMISSIVE FUNCTION OF THE

DERIVATIVE GROUPS

PRIMARY GROUP—A second function of the old primary groups was that of preserving the useful technique and wisdom of the past. The chief capital of the primitive groups was in this knowledge of technique of production, of the control of the good and evil spirits, of the hunt, or war, and the like. In days before there were books or clay tablets or parchments or papyri in which to record the important cultural technique in detail it was necessary to preserve the forms and content of knowledge intact and without serious modification by oral transmission. Hence there grew up a much greater emphasis upon the formal side of knowledge and technique than we can conceive of as necessary among us, where we trust to reference books, formulas, and libraries for the accurate preservation of important processes. Out of this enforcement of accuracy of form in part grew ritual, most of which has now lost its meaning to us, although the form may continue as an esthetic or magical practice. Custom and tradition and convention were sanctified. Even now when such precautions are no longer necessary for our welfare, these forms still persist, as does the habit of fearing change, and we find it difficult to secure sufficient innovation to take care of needed progress.

Of course this fear of losing the valuable community technique is not the only cause of ritualization and the fixing of customs and traditions. The very fact that set habits tend to organize around themselves a protective envelope of feeling, which becomes unpleasant with any sort of interruption, has much to do with keeping things as they are. But it is also to be observed that people who have nothing to fear from change usually find less dissatisfaction in it and may even develop a sort of habit of change which is in itself pleasant and exciting, and sometimes disintegrating to character. We must still pay a great deal of attention to past ways of doing things, and doubtless we always shall. The primary group is now relatively much less important as a preserver and transmitter of useful culture than it formerly was. These functions are now performed primarily by indirect communicating media, such as books and journals, and by libraries. The abstract and derivative social organization has largely taken the place of the old primary groups in this respect.

THE PRIMARY GROUP AND PRODUCTION—The third compelling function of primary group life was that it made each one a producer. By being forced psychologically and socially to copy some one else as a model and to conform to those patterns emphasized in the primary group, one became a producer or worker in the group without realizing that he was performing a vital function. He found his adjustment unconsciously, as it were, and largely through play. In primary groups, and especially in the closely knit ones of primitive society, the play activities of children were much more functional and in the nature of the imitation of their elders. It is not until society comes to be organized on a derivative group basis that play ceases to be so functional socially or occupationally and becomes more artificial, being made up of carefully planned and organized games which perhaps train the child in general cooperation and in self-discipline and in the exploitation of his powers, but do not initiate him into the socially productive processes. While the primitive child learned the major arts of life, such as hunting and fighting, directly from the group through play, the modern child makes similar occupational and functional adjustments primarily through formal training agencies, such as the school.

This change comes about because occupation ceases to be to the same extent a general community matter and is largely withdrawn from community view and therefore there is no less in the way of models for play imitation by the young than formerly. Also the occupational processes have become more specialized as a result of the derivative organization of modern society. The consequence of this fact for play is that the occupational and other adjustment processes are more difficult to imitate in play by the young. The old and original primary groups no longer teach occupations to any considerable extent except perhaps housekeeping and agriculture; and even training for these occupations is going largely into the schools of one sort or another.

THE DECAY OF PRIMARY GROUP CONTACTS—The old primary groups are no longer performing their functions of personality integration and adjustment of the individual to society with the same degree of facility and completeness

DERIVATIVE GROUPS 417

formerly. The reason for this is that the old primary groups are no longer the centers of so large a proportion of the most important activities of men. Only the most minor industries, except agriculture, now center in the family; and recreation and amusements have been largely transferred from the primary play group for all except the very young to commercialized amusement organizations. The child can no longer get adequate samples of the collective life in which he is to participate from the home and neighborhood and community, because the most important collective activities center outside of these original units of social organization and are more abstractly organized than these relatively concrete primary groups can organize them. The old neighborhood and community no longer exist intact outside of rural life, and even there they are being broken up or merged into larger and more abstract units by the automobile, interurban freight and passenger transportation, the rural free delivery, newer forms of economic organization and technique, such as agricultural coöperation, and the advancement of science, invention, and industrial organization generally.

The family also shows serious indications either of dissolving or of being reorganized on a more flexible basis and with more functional contacts with and extensions into large and more derivative social units and processes. The different members of the home, except on farms, probably have no occupational interest in common. All of them may work in different parts of the city. The industries in which they labor most likely have an abstract overhead organization which is neither visible as a whole to the participant worker nor resident in his community. If the work is technical and specialized, the worker can learn his occupation only through the channels of apprenticeship or of the trade school. Thus the individual's contacts with industry, both through training and through participation in the productive processes, are becoming increasingly abstract. Citizenship and community life contacts are becoming equally abstract, both in the training for their exercise and in their performance.

THE DOMINANCE OF THE DERIVATIVE GROUPS—The meaning of all of this is that the derivative group is growing into dominance as a molding and controlling mechanism over the primary group. The contacts are indirect or distance contacts to a greater extent, and the type of communication is largely or mainly by symbols transmitted indirectly from person to person through abstract communication media, and is therefore predominantly intellectual and abstract, although not necessarily so. There are all degrees of primariness and derivativeness in groups, from the most primary, the family, to the least primary, such as the international scientific and governmental or trade societies. The following list of groups, by no means complete, in which there is an attempt at arrangement on the basis of the transition from the most to the least primary groups, will serve to illustrate the principle of increasing derivativeness of group organization and of social contacts here set forth.

Family group
Play group
Neighborhood group
Sunday school
Local school group
Gangs
Boys' and girls' clubs
Church clubs, societies, etc.
Literary societies
Local church groups or congregations
High school fraternities and sororities
High school class organizations
Local social sets or cliques
Local athletic clubs
Y.M.C.A. and Y.W.C.A.
Local markets
Local occupational groups
Local political groups
Trade union locals
Local business groups and associations
Local coöperative societies
Local professional groups
Local benefit societies
Local art societies
Local scientific or cultural societies or clubs

DERIVATIVE GROUPS

Debating societies
Local lodges
Community

Local district coöperative societies
Local protective societies
County
County organizations
District coöperative societies
District political groups (congressional, judicial, etc.)
State
State-wide organizations
Specific newspaper reading publics
Radio publics
Movie publics
Fiction reading publics
Denominational groups
Educational groups or associations
National fraternal orders and lodges
Political parties
National scientific and cultural groups
National markets
National industrial groups
National welfare workers' groups
National coöperative organizations
National artists' groups
General newspaper reading publics
Social classes
Sex groups
Age groups
International markets
International political groups
International cultural groups
International industrial groups
Major religious divisions
Nationalities
Races
The world as a whole

Although these groups are listed in the general order of their increasing derivativeness, it must be apparent that it is not possible to draw such a dividing line with complete precision at all points. A group may be more primary or more deriva-

tive than another in some respects and less so in other re
gards. For the purpose of illustrating the tendency of th
derivative groups to grow in numbers and as centers of domi
nant organizations at the expense of the primary groups it
not necessary to make such close distinctions. The genera
fact can be illustrated sufficiently well by the partial list her
presented. Each group below the neighborhood has some ele
ments of a derivative organization character in it, and eve
the play and neighborhood groups are not entirely and alway
original face-to-face groups, although they are usually and i
the main such. The line drawn after the community is ir
tended to indicate that at this point groups cease to have th
face-to-face character, although they have long since ceased
be primary.

CAUSES OF THE GROWTH OF DERIVATIVE GROUPS OR SOCIA
ORGANIZATION ON AN INDIRECT CONTACT BASIS—The growt
in importance of the derivative groups has come about be
cause of the improvement and complication of the techniqu
of men's coadaptive adjustments to nature and to each othe
and the consequent expansion and abstraction of human con
tacts. When men possessed little or no technique of adjus
ment except the direct exercise of those instruments whic
nature gave them, they lived very close to nature and in sma
groups, for only in small groups could they gain their su
tenance from nature. But the growth of productive techniqu
complicated the production process and increased its efficienc
Larger groups appeared and the problem of distribution aros
especially after division of labor appeared and indirect as we
as direct contributions to the productive process became poss
ble. Training in the principles of production and distribu
tion became necessary, and accessory processes, such as con
munication, transportation, the invention of productive in
struments, the maintenance of exchange and credit system
the growth of publicity and propaganda, and the like, appeare
to complicate the factors generating group contacts. T
human instruments in all of these processes became mo
widely scattered and contacts between them became of necessi
more abstract and symbolical. Overhead organizations whic
arose to coördinate and make effectively purposive their b

DERIVATIVE GROUPS

behavior were likewise of necessity abstract and indirect in their organization.

In this way group organizations arose and split off in somewhat the manner indicated in the list above. The school came as a modification and partial synthesis of the earlier and more primary groups mentioned. It and other face-to-face contact groups, such as local occupational groups, political or other assemblies, local coöperative societies, clubs, churches, fraternal orders, and the like, are not primary in the strictest sense of the word. They are derived, but their derivation is not acutely marked, for most of their contacts are still of a face-to-face type. All of these and others like them retain many or most of the characteristics of the more primary groups, such as localness, early and direct participation by the members, as in other more primary groups. But all of these partially or wholly derivative local groups are affiliated with overhead or directive organizations which are derivative in a high degree. Examples of these are the state and national educational associations, church hierarchies, councils and governing boards of various types, national officers or councils of fraternal orders, etc. The development of these more abstract and indirectly communicating derivative groups has been in the nature of an overflow of functions from the local groups and the extension of fellowship or participation with increase in numbers to include those who live at greater distances. There has also come the necessity of some sort of coördination of local group activities as the technique of wider and indirect adjustments has developed, as collective behavior has become more complex, and as the contacts themselves have extended further afield.

Even the old primary community groups have expanded and developed various stages of overhead or control groups of increasing abstractness. Thus has appeared historically the tribe and nation on an ethnic basis and the county, kingdom, empire, and various international organizations, on a civil or political basis. Business also has grown out of the simple communal modes of production and distribution until its many tiers of overhead organization rise into vast and complicated abstract corporations or derivative groups, some of which are international. Even the family has its normal extensions int[o] the school, the settlement, the day nursery, the supervise[d] playground, and its pathological or semi-pathological exter[n]sions into the family welfare association, associated charitie[s,] various clinics, etc. Most abstract of all are the scientific asso[-]ciations, dealing almost wholly with conceptual symbol[s] which serve as a means of evolving and disseminating the tec[h]nique by means of which derivative social organizations of a[ll] sorts can be perfected.

THE NECESSITY FOR DERIVATIVE GROUPS—Contacts i[n] modern life have come to be at such long range and so i[n]direct in character that derivative groups have become [a] necessity. They dominate our social organization, just as th[e] primary, close or direct contact groups of primitive me[n] dominated the social life of that time. Important as the pr[i]mary groups are in the molding of character of the membe[rs] of groups and in training individuals for their functions [in] the social complex of behavior, the derivative groups are eve[n] more important.

The fact that the derivative groups are not directly appr[e]hensible by the senses and that their nature and functions mu[st] be appreciated through rational processes of inference and i[n]duction does not detract from their significance. As gre[at] overhead abstract organizations, having their plan of integr[a]tion codified in the form of a constitution or charter or som[e] similar legal document, or at least operating on the basis [of] a common or group or public "opinion," they work with [an] exactness and a continuity of policy which is at least as mark[ed] as that of face-to-face groups whose "purpose" or mod[us] operandi may change as the whims of the members chang[e.] Also the power of the derivative groups, especially of the gre[at] abstract and relatively constant ones, such as the state, i[n]dustrial, religious, educational, and scientific associations, [is] very great. As a consequence they dominate the prima[ry] groups from which they were originally derived.

The derivative groups grew up as extensions of the prima[ry] groups in order to regulate those contacts and functions whi[ch] had transcended the limits of the primary groups and the[se] functions were at first subject to the direction of the prima[ry] groups. This fact is illustrated by the early practice of for[m] ing confederacies out of smaller established political groups instead of at once welding them into a strong national or other overhead and independent organization. The confederacy was given only as much power as was necessary to perform the functions which had outgrown the smaller and more concrete group organizations, and sometimes even adequate powers for these functions were denied. But gradually, with the increasing complexity of social life, these wider functions became more important, perhaps more numerous, than the narrower ones. Consequently the overhead or derivative organizations were granted or assumed greater and greater powers, until they came to dominate the smaller and more primary groups. This movement was first observable in political groups. But the same thing has happened more recently in industry and finance, and it is now occurring with respect to the family and the community. It is not possible to check it, nor is it desirable to do so. But it is important, for purposes of social justice, to make sure that the powers of the great abstract and derivative groups shall be organized and employed for the good of all of the members instead of for the advantage of only a few who happen to be serving as directors.

METHODS OF INDIRECT CONTACTS IN DERIVATIVE GROUPS —The methods of contacts in the highly derivative groups are very different from those in the more primary groups. In the latter they are direct. That is, the behavior of the person giving the stimulus to another member of the group may be perceived and integrated perceptually by the receiver of the stimulus. The stimuli may come in the form of touch, temperature, some chemical substance, movement, spoken or written symbols, and they may be apprehended through any one or more of the senses. But in the case of indirect transmission of stimuli between members of the derivative groups the giver of the stimulus is not ordinarily in direct sensory contact with the receiver of the stimulus. Consequently communication is by means of stored symbols, and intermediary carriers must be utilized to transmit them. The derivative groups could not function effectively, could not even be formed, until these carriers had been developed.

The earliest carriers of indirect contact stimuli were adapted from the carriers of tradition and custom, by means of which the more abstract cultural content of earlier groups was preserved for the later ones. Thus the medicine man and seer, and later the minstrel and traveler, were concrete personal carriers of distance contacts. Apostles and missionaries came later to perform a similar function, and we have modern analogues in the persons of preachers, lecturers, and propagandist speakers of all sorts. Early and recent art, but early more than recent for reasons stated in a previous chapter, have also been the means of making these indirect or derivative contacts. The modern theater, movie, and radio have extended and transformed some of these transmissive functions of the minstrel propagandist, and artist.

The greatest of all of the means for the indirect transmission of contacts are the abstract storage symbols of an intellectual character. These came late, but they have been of the very greatest importance. Books, newspapers, magazines, have extended the voice of the propagandist and have multiplied infinitely the messages of people at a distance. Not infrequently men and women speak to hundreds of millions of people, occasionally to practically the whole literate population of the earth through these agencies. Their power to create uniformity of behavior and of purpose among large sections of mankind cannot well be overestimated. It is not strange, therefore, that with such aids the derivative groups have been able to grow to almost unlimited size and largely to displace or transform and dominate the primary groups.

MATERIALS FOR SUPPLEMENTARY READING

Bogardus, E. S., *Fundamentals of Social Psychology*, Chs. XIX, XX
Cooley, C. H., *Social Organization*, Ch. III
Dunlap, K., *Social Psychology*, Ch. V
Ellwood, C. A., *The Psychology of Human Society*, Chs. IV, XVI
Follett, M. P., *The New State*
Lindeman, E. C., *The Community*, Ch. V
McDougall, W., *The Group Mind*, Ch. VIII
Maciver, R. M., *Community*, Ch. II
Ross, E. A., *Principles of Sociology*, Chs. XXXII, XXXVI, XLVIII, XLI
Steiner, J. F., *Community Organization*, Ch. II
Wieman, H. N., "Personal and Impersonal Groups," *Int. Jour. of Ethics*
   XXXI: 381-393
Williams, J. M., *Our Rural Heritage*, Ch. III

CHAPTER XXVII

PRIMARY AND DERIVATIVE ATTITUDES AND IDEALS

The shift in emphasis from primary to derivative group control which we have just described has had a marked influence upon the personality building process, not only in the actual mechanism of imitating models, but also in the content of the personality itself. The change in social organization has produced a corresponding change in the ideals and attitudes necessary for adequate adjustment within it. This development of derivative attitudes and ideals will be the subject matter of this chapter.

THE NATURE OF ATTITUDES AND IDEALS—Attitudes and ideals grow up in the inner or symbolic behavior of individuals as a result of their functioning in groups. These attitudes and ideals are the inner aspects of behavior corresponding to incompletely expressed or partially inhibited overt behavior. There is more or less consciousness of relationships and of objectives involved, even in the case of primary or emotional attitudes, and this consciousness is tinged with desire or a sense of obligation, however dim the desire or the sense of obligation may be. Desire in its simplest form is a condition of readiness for some inhibited behavior which it is dimly or clearly perceived will bring about a removal of the inhibiting factors. The simpler form of the sense of obligation is negative and consists of more or less well recognized impulses or ideals which tend to inhibit some behavior which is recognized should not take place.

The more clearly conscious desires or wishes consist in the projection of overt behavior which is inhibited from completion by some factors which may or may not be clearly recognized. A well-defined sense of obligation is the recognition of certain considerations or motives which either should further a type of inhibited behavior or which should inhibit or strengthen a process of behavior projected or actually undergoing execution. These better defined and more highly conscious forms of desires and the sense of obligation are ideals rather than primary or simple attitudes. The main distinction between an ideal and a primary emotional attitude lies in the greater degree of intellectualization of the former which is in reality a specialized subdivision of the latter. All ideals may be said to have a moral aspect also, and this is true of all attitudes which have developed sufficient mental content to recognize a fitness of relationship between subject and object, that is, some degree of the sense of obligation.

THE PRIMARY ATTITUDES develop in the primary group. They are essentially emotional appraisals of the functional relationship between individuals in a group, or possibly even of an individual to the group as a whole. The sense of obligation or of desire may also form a part of the attitude, as stated above, and the attitude may rise to the status of an ideal, even in the primary group. This latter possibility will be realized if there is sufficient intellectual analysis of relationships and of obligations or if the desire sufficiently objectifies means and ends. The simplest primary attitudes are probably hedonic seeking of a pleasure giving object and aversion for unpleasant objects. Out of these, as a result of social conditions, grow love, tenderness, devotion, trust, loyalty, the feeling for truthfulness, and the desire to give and receive fair play, etc., on the one hand; and hate, brusqueness, dislike, distrust, disloyalty, deceit, and cunning or trickery, on the other hand.

All of these are relatively primary attitudes before they are ideals, for we learn to practice them and to have a feeling for them, that is, to recognize them in a semi-intellectual or in an emotional manner before we can objectify them as comprehensive adjustment patterns, and thus set them up as objectives to be attained in our own conduct, or in that of others. When we can analyze them and objectify them as ends they become ideals. This process of increasing recognition, intellectualization, and objectification of attitudes and ideals follows, of course, the evolution of the integration of personality traits and of symbols which was discussed earlier. The attitude is recognized through an integration of perceptual-emotional experiences when in contact with objects, usually personal, and when we have come to recognize in some degree the relationship of those objects to ourselves and of ourselves to them. The ideal arises in the projective stage of personality integration, when we are able to set up fairly complex types and processes of behavior as ends.

DERIVATIVE IDEALS are of course primarily intellectual and abstract. They arise in connection with the recognition of distance contacts, which also involves a recognition of the meaning of the symbols by means of which the indirect contacts are effected. Here the attitudes—the wider and more inclusive term—are cast in the form of ideals. That is, they are intellectualized and abstracted. They consist of a statement or recognition of the types of social organization and relationships which should exist. Abstract or derivative ideals are expressed almost exclusively in terms of the social organization which it is recognized would produce the desired individual responses and adjustments, or the social organization which we feel should obtain, usually with ourselves as central in the situation. It is because of this close connection between the statement of the ideal and the type of social organization viewed as an objective that we say the ideal is the product of the group contacts in which it develops. It is the projection of a plan of adjustment of self or of another to the environment. This is, of course, also true of ideals and attitudes formed in connection with primary group contacts as in the derivative.

Both primary and derivative attitudes and ideals represent projections of contact relationships. In the one case these projected contacts or adjustments are concrete and mainly emotional. In the other case they are abstract and largely intellectual. The derivative ideals are simply the primary attitudes and ideals expanded and intellectualized in such ways as to enable them to picture or project wider and more abstract relationships. Thus attitudes of personal love and hate, or of trust and distrust, of loyalty and disloyalty, of truthfulness and deceit, come in their derivative form to be ideals for the promotion of local group or national or even international welfare or destruction, of confidence in or distrust of the good sense and honorable intentions of governments, business enterprises, religions, or even the masses of mankind. We may also seek in a similar way to support or to betray the aims of states, business enterprises, and classes or masses. We may, when in positions of trust or power, that is, in situations where we have many and effective abstract or indirect contacts with people in many places, act in good faith for the promotion of an abstract or symbolical understanding of relationships, or we may attempt to pervert the sources and content of news, books, propaganda, etc. The highest and most abstract ideal of truthfulness is that which motivates the scientist in his meticulous endeavor to verify each fact and to test rigorously all of his conclusions. But there is also a high degree of loyalty to society in the abstract which may motivate even the statesman and the diplomat to be perfectly frank and aboveboard in their dealings with men and to consider always the public welfare first when it is in conflict with their own. This is civic loyalty and truthfulness. Perhaps their opposites, civic disloyalty and untruthfulness, are all too common and are sometimes extended to the point of actual and corrupt betrayal of the public interest.

A PARTIAL LIST OF ATTITUDES AND IDEALS, both primary and derivative, arranged in the order of their increasing derivativeness, will help us to form some notion of how the derivative ideals grow out of the primary and less derivative attitudes. It will also enable us to observe the increasing abstractness and intellectualization of the attitude as it becomes more and more derivative in character. The list is presented in two parallel columns, the expansive and positive attitudes and ideals on the left and the recessive and negative attitudes and ideals on the right. A horizontal line divides the personal and more primary attitudes and ideals from the social and more derivative. This line marks the hypothetical point at which the individual begins to expand his view and includes people in his attitudes and ideals beyond the range of his immediate contacts. But of course the dividing line can be drawn only approximately.

Positive Attitudes and Ideals	Negative Attitudes and Ideals
Seeking to possess	Repulsion
Love and liking	Dislike, disgust
Devotion	Hatred
Tenderness	Brusqueness
Kindness	Unkindness
Helpfulness	Hindrance
Loyalty	Disloyalty
Friendliness	Antagonism
Service	Destructiveness
Equality	Superiority (and inferiority)
Democracy	Privilege
Truthfulness	Untruthfulness
Fair play	Deceit and trickery
Justice	Injustice
Lawfulness	Unlawfulness

Group and class loyalty, clannishness

Patriotism

Internationalism

Humanitarianism for all mankind

(*Gregariousness*)

Hatred and disloyalty to other groups and classes (competition)

Treason

Anti-internationalism (sometimes a narrow nationalism)

Misanthropy

(*Recessiveness*)

Devotion to abstract principles of
   Truthfulness,
   Fair play,
   Justice,
   Law and order

(*Idealism*)

Repudiation of the principles of
   Truthfulness,
   Exploitation of others,
   Perversion of justice,
   Disorganization of relationships

(*Machiavellianism*)

Intellectualized or constructive attitude of service toward one's

Systematically seeking to exploit one's

Neighbor,
Group,
Class,
Country,
Nationality,
Race,
World as a whole (Mankind)
(*Altruism*)

Devotion to the abstract principles of science and the investigation of facts and the discovery of scientific principles, laws, and formulas.

Projection of constructive ideals for the realization of all of the desired social objectives mentioned above.

Neighbor,
Group,
Class,
Country,
Nationality,
Race,
World as a whole (Mankind)
(*Opportunism*)

Opposition to investigation, dependence upon fiat, tradition, prejudice, and ignorance as a means of escaping unsettlement of emotional attachments to the past and the perpetuation of privilege.

Opposition to idealistic movements, desire to keep the masses in a subordinate position and the world in ignorance, because of fear either of the supernatural or of social revolution, or because of distrust of the popular intelligence or emotional balance.

Other items which should be included in the lists will occur to readers, and critics will also observe here, as in the case of the list of groups in the preceding chapter, that the sequential relationship must vary according to circumstances and the problems of adjustment. In fact the list of attitudes above the horizontal line should perhaps be divided into three major sections or groups of attitudes representing as many general points of view. The possibility of such separation or subsidiary classification has been indicated by the device of wide spacing. The principle to be emphasized by this list is that attitudes and ideals have become increasingly abstract and derivative as our direct contacts with others have widened into indirect contacts. As a result mankind is now dominated largely by derivative ideals, both positive and negative.

THE EXPANSION OF RESTRICTIVE PRIMARY ATTITUDES INTO CONSTRUCTIVE DERIVATIVE IDEALS—Such great composite social ideals as democracy, internationalism, humanitarianism, or Christianity, Judaism, Buddhism, and the like, contain both primary and derivative elements. Originally the primary attitudes and ideals predominated in these great emotional and intellectual complexes. Democracy was a matter of brotherhood or equality of members of the same primary group. Humanitarianism was clannishness or tribalism or love for one's own. Internationalism was at first impossible, because there had been no analysis and recognition of collective behavior patterns or groups other than of one's own kind. Religion, like the patriotism which in all probability originally sprang from it, was the application of the primary attitudes and ideals mentioned above to the supernatural personality or personalities worshiped in common, and thence by induction to all of those who engaged in the common worship of the supernatural beings. Thus the group itself comes to be objectified as a spirit or as a quasi-personality which is worshiped or reverenced, and we come to conceive ourselves as having very great obligations to it which are expressed in the form of the primary attitudes. This is patriotism of the more primitive sort. It is indicated familiarly by such colloquial phrases as "Motherland," "Fatherland," "Uncle Sam," "John Bull," "La Belle France." It demands devotion to our town or tribe or country, right or wrong, and regardless of who rules it. The man and the state, like the gods, can do no wrong.

But modern patriotism and democracy and religion are much less concrete and emotional and are more abstractly constructive. They have been intellectualized, and derivative ideals are supplementing or replacing the primary attitudes. The true patriot in the modern sense may criticize his country if he thinks it is pursuing unethical or mistaken policies. He may seek to dispossess the dominant government, if he is sincere in offering a better one, although the persons in power or who profit from the situation which exists, however undesirable in general it may be, are certain to cast many unsavory epithets upon him, to call him traitor and perhaps attempt to defend their interests by discrediting him or even by doing him bodily or economic injury.

Likewise, every one who attempts to dispossess false gods and substitute more humane and rational religious controls is likely to be branded as infidel and punished as strongly as lies in the power of the "faithful." Every old religion based upon primary group or personality conceptions, which has now, like the Greek and Norse theologies, passed into the innocuous estheticism of mythology, has persecuted those philosophers who were trying to substitute a higher and more intellectual type of religious control. Religion has been increasingly intellectualized until abstract or derivative ideals of social welfare and public duty have come to supplement, and even to assume dominance and direction over, the more restrictive primary attitudes, especially of the more emotional sort, which formerly constituted its core. Every great evolving religion of which we have a record has advanced from magic and ritual toward rational social controls as guiding principles in just that degree to which intellectual analysis has taken the place of primary attitudes in the understanding of the explanatory content of these religions.

DEMOCRACY AS AN EXAMPLE—Democracy has also become largely intellectualized. Personal equality and a feeling of friendliness and of brotherhood are still important in democracy. But we no longer place the chief emphasis on these attitudes, important as they are. We recognize that we cannot have friendliness and brotherhood without equality of opportunity, and further that we cannot have either this equality of opportunity or the more personal amenities without first securing certain abstract and far-reaching types of social organization which stand back of and promote the democratic personal relationships. Hence the first consideration in modern democracy is the building up of derivative democratic ideals such as those of social service, intelligent discharge of citizenship duties, and the discomfiture of those politicians who prey upon the public, which will bring into existence protective social organization calculated to foster justice and friendliness in the wider social contacts. The rendering of justice itself is now an abstract as well as a concrete process, involving adjustments reaching very far afield beyond the borders of the primary group.

This necessity of first giving attention to the derivative or abstract overhead organization in order to secure democracy and justice has not always existed. In the early stages of social evolution, where the primary group dominated practically all collective and individual behavior, democracy and justice could be secured by means of the direct promulgation of primary attitudes and ideals. But now that the primary and less derivative groups are themselves dominated and shaped by the more abstract derivative group ideals, we must either look first after the more abstract ideals and adjustments or lose the fruits even of the primary democratic ideals. Social life has become highly abstract and intellectual, at least in the control centers. Just as industry has outgrown the empirical invention and demands the projected or logically synthetic invention, so also has society grown beyond the point where it can be successfully and properly controlled by primary emotional attitudes. There must be projective thinking—projective social invention—in the process of evolving modern democratic social controls. And back of this process of abstract projective social organization for the common welfare are the method inventions of social science as the intellectual materials out of which the new democratic order must be projected and fashioned. Primary emotional attitudes can be made to support this new abstract system, but they could never create it.

The Hygiene of Positive and Negative Attitudes and Ideals—From our discussion it will be apparent that both primary and derivative ideals may be bad or anti-social as well as good or socially approved. Aversion, hate, disloyalty, deceit, as primary attitudes, are bad only when they cause harm to the group or to individuals without protecting greater interests or larger numbers of individuals. We might well prefer to abolish these negative attitudes from our thoughts and behavior altogether as a protection against injustice or other evil, for it is not always easy to apply such weapons to the defense of positive ideals and efforts without harm. But so long as the world of collective behavior is subject to conflicts and to maladjustments, intended or unintended, this apparently is not possible. We sometimes regard it as a virtue to hate evil or even to deceive the deceivers and to betray those who work in unrighteous causes. Certainly as the world is organized it appears not infrequently to be good policy to do these things, and almost no one is averse to attacks upon the unesthetic and the immoral and the injurious.

But it is not so clear that we are justified in espousing the negative derivative ideals, at least in our own group, and possibly even in the world at large. It is a question whether we should ever hate a whole people, even our martial enemies or be disloyal to any social cause however doubtful its validity for which we profess loyalty, or deceive a whole people with regard to our attitudes regarding public policy. If the world were free from adverse and unjust compulsion by derivative group organizations we might lead the wholly positive idealistic life. As it is, perhaps we cannot. But that we are obligated not to entertain or promulgate any of the negative ideal against just and righteous social organization and primary group relationships is now clearly recognized. The only question is with reference to the criterion of righteousness and justice which we employ, and that changes from time to time and from place to place. The best rule to follow, perhaps, is to employ the positive ideals and attitudes where possible and to use the negative ones when necessary to defend the positive ideals, but to use them temperately and sparingly.

DERIVATIVE IDEALS MUST DOMINATE IN CASE OF CONFLICT—The derivative ideals are difficult to formulate. They are abstract and their statement is feasible only after an intellectual analysis of collective relationships and behavior has been made. They are dependent upon the mastery of abstract intellectual symbolism, or the conditioning of collective behavior to abstract symbolic stimuli. But the primary attitude and ideals grow directly out of elementary and largely emotional direct contact behavior itself. Hence they are easy to formulate, so much so in fact that most of them are objectified before the person has developed intellectual analyses of suff cient breadth or scope to test their validity. Since the derivative ideals grow up as extensions and as correctives or perversions of the primary attitudes and ideals in a complex and abstractly organized world, the two types of ideals often are in conflict. Love and loyalty, freedom and truthfulness, and the like, are now to be employed in the service of good causes, not merely on impulse, as formerly they often were. We no longer believe it wise to give money or sympathy to beggars regardless of circumstances, nor should we necessarily stand by friends or family contrary to the public interest. The narrower social relations must be organized within the wider social relationships, and we must see to it that the wider ones are just and helpful in order that the narrower may also be just and good. If the primary contacts are in opposition to a rational derivative social order and if our primary attitudes ignore just derivative ideals, the former in each case are anti-social and must give way to the latter.

MISUSE OF THE PRIMARY ATTITUDES—Sometimes designing persons are guilty of anti-social conduct in the more indirect and derivative relations of social life under the cover of approved primary attitudes and contacts. The corrupt politician or "boss" very frequently wins his way to popular favor by personal friendliness, generosity, and apparent sympathy for the poor, and intercession with judges and other officials in behalf of the criminal and unfortunate. At the same time he is perhaps filching the produce of their labor from these same poor and unfortunate through some form of public graft or corruption. The people whom he befriends, and most of the public at large perhaps, are not able to detect or understand and disapprove the significance of the latter behavior, but it is easy for them to see and approve the former. Such methods of blinding the popular intelligence by interposing the strong appeal of emotional primary attitudes before intellectual analysis have been in use from the earliest times of which we have a record. Such people may keep the letter of the law of righteousness (especially of the ancient law, developed in primary group relationships), but not the spirit of modern social righteousness. An industry may pay its employes well and still overcharge the public. A church may be generous with individuals and seek to save their souls and still cast its immense power against the realization of the great derivative ideals of social justice, democracy, and scientific truth and investigation. All too frequently the much abused word "fundamentalism" means a return to emotional judgments and prejudices instead of an advance forward toward fundamental intellectual analysis and derivative ideals.

Many people trained in primary attitudes and ideals, but ignorant of the wider derivative ideals, are often unwittingly guilty of great breaches in social morality. Ross calls the disregard of derivative ideals "sinning by syndicate." That is, men who are above reproach in primary contacts may still own unsanitary and condemned tenements. The men who act upon the principle "Let the public be damned" are very frequently kind and considerate in primary contacts. Neglect in inculcating derivative ideals and attitudes is dangerous to social welfare. That is, personality integration in our day must include an adequate emphasis upon derivative ideals as well as upon primary ones.

CONCLUSION—In our collective capacity we must learn to understand the derivative ideals and to make them effective as behavior patterns, if we wish to be truly good or socialized members of our groups. We live in larger and more abstract groups now and we must not ignore the needs of these overhead or derivative control organizations. If any institution is still organized primarily on the basis of a primitive interpretation of and loyalty to uncorrected primary attitudes and ideals which bring it in conflict with the intellectualized and socialized derivative ideals, that institution must be reorganized and put into line with modern derivative organization of thought and institutional behavior. This means that the members of such institutions must be taught to think in terms of abstract or derivative adjustments, made on the basis of scientific ideals of collective behavior, instead of on the basis of traditions and beliefs coming down unmodified from the primary group life and emotional behavior of primitive times. Our age is vastly complex and our contacts are indirect and derivative and our thinking must be more and more complex and intellectually constructive also. Because of this our form

ive institutions, especially the schools, must learn to teach
the young, and the old, to think abstractly and intelligently
about all phases of social behavior. They must teach us to
imitate or assimilate principles as well as personalities. Personal and primary ideals and behavior are not to be discarded,
but they must be made to conform to the scientifically projected
and organized derivative ideals and values by which collective
behavior must in the future be regulated.

MATERIALS FOR SUPPLEMENTARY READING

Blackmar and Gillin, *Outlines of Sociology,* Chs. XVII, XVIII, XXIII, XXIV, XXVII, XXVIII
Bogardus, E. S., *Fundamentals of Social Psychology,* Chs. VI, XX, XXI, XXVI, XXVIII
Carmichael, R. D., "The Need of an International Mind," *Sci. Mo.,* XIX: 47-52
Cooley, C. H., *Social Organization,* Chs. IV, V, XI
Ellwood, C. A., *The Psychology of Human Society,* Chs. X, XIII, XVI
Giddings, F. H., *Studies in the Theory of Human Society,* Ch. X
Howard, G. E., "Ideals as a Factor in the Future Control of International Society," *Pub. Amer. Sociological Society,* XII: 1-10
Pillsbury, W. B., *The Psychology of Nationalism and Internationalism,* Ch. VIII
Ross, E. A., *Principles of Sociology,* Chs. XLVI, XLVII
—, *Latter Day Saints and Sinners*
—, *Sin and Society*
—, *Social Control,* Chs. XVII, XVIII
Steiner, J. F., *Community Organization,* Ch. III

CHAPTER XXVIII

DIRECT CONTACT GROUPS: RATIONAL TYPES

We have already spoken of the influence of certain primary groups, especially of the family, the play group, and the neighborhood, on individual behavior. In this and the following chapter we shall describe the typical forms which direct contact or face-to-face groups take, and show how they are used to condition individual behavior in a collective situation.

TWO TYPES OF GROUPS—When collective behavior is organized around an interest common to a number of people, whether the interest and organization are permanent or only temporary, we have what may be called a group. The essential fact about the group is that a number of people are responding at approximately the same time to the same or similar or supplementary sets of stimuli. This statement includes, of course, also the reciprocal responses of members in the group. It is not necessary that all those responding shall behave in the same manner, but if the group is to possess the requisite unity there will be a large amount of uniformity in the responses to the common and reciprocal stimuli.

Also it is not necessary that the persons responding to common or reciprocal stimuli shall be in direct contact with one another, or that the group shall be of a face-to-face sort. Many groups are so spread abroad that their members have mainly or exclusively indirect contacts with one another. Stimuli come to them from the common source only by means of carriers, such as newspapers, telegraph, radio, and the like. But there is the same sort of uniformity of response, the same characteristics of permanency or temporariness, as in the face-to-face groups. Also, there may be present either emotional or intellectual qualities in the communication, or both.

The distinction between face-to-face contacts and non-face-to-face contacts in groups is fundamental since the psychology of these two types of contacts differs to a marked degree. In face-to-face contacts, all the kinesthetic and exteroceptive senses are active in receiving stimuli to facilitate responses. Direct contact is the medium par excellence for the communication of emotional behavior. Non-face-to-face or indirect contacts, on the other hand, must rely almost wholly upon verbal stimuli apprehended nearly exclusively through the ears and eyes. As a result, the content of indirect communication is usually intellectual, although it may also be emotional. Illiterate people are not reached by indirect stimuli without the intervention of literate persons, except through the radio and the phonograph. And even here the crowd setting as an accompaniment of the speaking voice, which greatly influences the emotional quality of communication, is absent.

PRIMARY AND DIRECT CONTACT GROUPS DISTINGUISHED—A distinction should also be drawn between direct contact groups in general and primary groups. Primary groups are those face-to-face or direct contact groups into which the child is born and which mold his behavior from the beginning of his self-active existence. Primary groups constitute a much less extensive category than the direct contact groups. The latter category includes the less formative and more purely administrative direct contact groups, even such derived ones as deliberative assemblies, which function primarily in the control of behavior already integrated as well as those primary groups which organize or integrate behavior or character, such as the family, play group, and neighborhood group.

TYPES OF DIRECT CONTACT GROUPS—The general distinction here made between direct and indirect contact groups is sometimes stated in terms of crowds and publics, the latter being the indirect contact groups. The term crowd, however, is not an equally happy term to cover all face-to-face or direct contact groups. It is associated in our minds with the quality of mobbishness. In fact, some writers, like Martin, use the term crowd to cover all types of irrational collective behavior, whether the participants have direct or indirect contacts with one another. Face-to-face groups vary all the way in rationality of behavior from the deliberative assembly, which is guided in its transactions by formal rules of order, to the mob, which is wholly under the influence of some leader or fixed idea which controls and directs the emotions of the members.

It is scarcely possible to classify direct contact groups according to any one set of traits or categories, because the same set of characteristics is not necessarily important in all groups. Consequently we shall present in the following pages those classes of direct contact groups which are most functional in modern society and state their most prominent psycho-social traits more or less regardless of whether these characteristics occur in other groups also. Certain characteristics, however, such as the ability of a group to survive and the type of psychic behavior involved in its organization, are important in all groups. Consequently the degree of permanency and of rationality obtaining in groups will be considered in the following classification. The order of direct contact groups, in the decreasing ratio of their permanency, and secondarily of the rationality of their behavior, is somewhat as follows: genetic groups, clubs and other direct contact purposive associations, deliberative assemblies, discussion groups and classes, audiences, informal clubs, ceremonials, rallies and demonstrations, involuntary crowds, mobs. This classification of groups is, of course, purely tentative and empirical. A more complete and accurate classification must await further research. There are, however, good grounds for using this classification. It is based mainly upon the psychological mechanisms employed rather than upon the aims or purposes of the members of the groups. All political, economic, religious, educational, fraternal, administrative, etc., groups, in their face-to-face aspects take on the guise of one or more of the forms described in this and the following chapters.

GENETIC GROUPS, which are primary groups in their simple forms, are perhaps the most permanent of all face-to-face associations, unless indeed we except corporations, which are only in part direct contact groups, and chartered or incorporated clubs. The membership changes but the groups continue and are located in the same areas and perform essentially the same functions for many generations. The best known ex

...mples of these genetic groups are perhaps the family, the neighborhood proper, the play group, and other neighborhood groups. But these neighborhood groups very quickly graduate from the category of genetic groups into clubs and purposive associations. Genetic groups are not always rational in their constitution, although they tend to become more nearly so with increasing culture. These groups, being very general and inclusive in character, employ the methods of organization and procedure which we find operative in the less general types of groups described in subsequent pages of this chapter.

CLUBS AND PURPOSIVE ASSOCIATIONS are the most permanent of all non-primary face-to-face or direct contact groups. They are also frequently rational, especially if they also partake of the nature of deliberative assemblies. There are many kinds of face-to-face associations, but the most numerous of these are the business associations and the multi-type organizations known as clubs. Of business, occupational, professional and other interest associations, such as corporations, firms of professional men, labor union locals, armies, etc., we need say but little. They are very common. They are also highly purposive in character. The behavior of their members is presumably controlled by highly rational considerations, and they make a considerable use of those aspects of science which apply most particularly to their objects in view. Most of such associations very easily expand into the category of indirect contact groups.

Clubs are also generally purposive in character. Some clubs, such as scientific societies, debating societies, professional groups, are frequently organized about more or less abstract and scientific interests. Other clubs, such as various local religious societies, political groups, and reform or law enforcement clubs, are presumably organized for the purpose of promoting the public welfare. Some societies of this general type, like lodges and local coöperative societies, are organized primarily for the mutual benefit of their members. Others still, and perhaps by far the largest number, find their reason for existence in amusement and recreation. Some of these may be fairly ephemeral, but clubs ordinarily and on the average have a considerable span of life. Both the club and the business and professional associations frequently overlap with deliberative assemblies. Clubs and associations also make use of the methods of procedure and organization employed by other direct contact groups described in this chapter.

The team constitutes one of the most highly integrated and purposive types of groups belonging to the general classification here under discussion. Because of its high degree of organization it usually represents the maximum of effectiveness in collective behavior. The organization and behavior of the team need not be democratic; ordinarily they are dictated for the chief objective of team work is coördination of effort and efficiency. We find teams in almost all aspects of collective behavior, ranging from manual labor and athletic activities to religious campaigns and scientific research.

RATIONAL VERSUS SUGGESTION CONTROL IN DIRECT CONTACT GROUPS—DELIBERATIVE ASSEMBLIES—The highest degree of rationality of organization in direct contact groups is to be found in the deliberative assembly. Here the common stimulus to which all of the members of the group respond is a common problem. The problem may be political, economic, legal, religious, ethical, esthetic, scientific, or of any character whatever. The essential general characteristic of the problem is that it shall be of significance to all of those who deliberate and exchange views regarding it. This deliberation may take place by means of indirect contacts, through the media of writing, print or otherwise, as well as through the direct contacts of oral speech. In such cases there is a deliberative public rather than a deliberative assembly. But the members of deliberative assemblies usually have been influenced by indirect contacts or public opinion before they come into the assembly. The different members will frequently have different interests at stake and therefore will support different views in the discussion. This is particularly true of representative deliberative assemblies, where representatives of diverse constituencies from various geographical sections, classes, nationalities, religions, etc., meet to iron out conflicts of interests and arrive at a compromise program. Such a representative assembly need not be political. It may be religious, industrial, or of any other character and complexion.

Where the deliberative assembly is local and the members of a group participate directly rather than through their representatives, there is still room for difference of opinion and conflict in the discussion, but such conflict is usually not so pronounced because of the greater homogeneity of the participating members and their interests. Where the deliberative assembly is made up of members with like interests, whether they be a board of directors of an industrial corporation, or direct participators, as in the case of a district school meeting or of the stockholders of a local coöperative society, there is also likely to be a considerable uniformity of response. But even in these cases there is room for much difference of opinion and deliberative discussion with regard to policies and aims and methods to be employed. Even in the meetings of scientific associations, where the data dealt with are most clearly subject to demonstration, discussion and conflict may be very considerable.

The function of the deliberative assembly is to give opportunity for the rational discussion and weighing of all aspects of questions which come before it. The normal result of such discussion is that all pertinent and available data are presented and considered impartially and as objectively as possible by all of those present. The assumption is, of course, that such rational and unbiased consideration of the data will lead to the selection of the most effective program for the conduct of the affairs of the groups. But such objectivity and complete rationality in the choice of a program is not possible of complete realization. In the first place it is not possible wholly to divorce one's judgments from his personal feelings and interests. And in the second place it is not possible to have all of the facts presented mean, even intellectually, the same thing to all the members, because their experiences have been different and their values vary accordingly. Consequently in almost all cases the formulation of group objectives and of programs to carry those objectives into execution is the result of compromise instead of the result of unity of opinion.

Rules and organization of the deliberative assembly—The deliberative assembly is bound by rules of order and very probably possesses a constitution and by-laws. National deliberative assemblies frequently develop elaborate rules for their guidance and employ a trained parliamentarian to interpret the rules in application to particular situations. They may even have a committee on rules which further assists in the parliamentary control of the body by bringing in new rules or modifications of old rules for the purpose of facilitating a particular procedure or of untangling some stubborn conflict of interests. Besides the presiding officer, the secretary, and the minutes or records of proceedings, which practically all deliberative assemblies possess, legislative assemblies usually have floor leaders or whips whose business it is to keep party discussion within the lines agreed upon in party caucus and to get out the vote for approved measures. Smaller and less representative assemblies, where there is less political maneuvering, may dispense with many of these parliamentary controls or employ them in a less rigorous and regiminal way.

The ostensible function of the parliamentary procedure rules, officers, records, etc., is the prevention of the use of force, intimidation and other non-rational controls in effecting collective judgments, decisions, and other behavior in the assembly. Freedom of speech on the floor, equality of opportunity in participation, and an adequate hearing for all members and interests are aimed at. Rules and records and a fair administration are supposed to insure these desirable ends. And in large measure they do achieve this result. But it is entirely possible for rules to be made in such a way, and for presiding officers, rules committees, parliamentarians, whips, caucuses, etc., to behave in such a manner, as to defeat these ends and give the advantage to some one faction or interest as over against other interests. This may occur even in those deliberative assemblies where the parliamentary precautions (or distortions) are most numerous. Committee appointments in political assemblies are uniformly made with such an end in view. The deliberate purpose of parliamentary procedure in such bodies often seems to be to enable the majority or some powerful and well organized minority to put through its program without allowing the opposition adequate means of expression and discussion. Yet parliamentary procedure cannot be dispensed with in such cases without r ducing the process of skillful maneuvering to disorder and chaos. The problem of the dominant group is to preserve sufficient respect for the parliamentary procedure among the opposition, while they accomplish their ends, that an open rebellion and disregard for the rules and authority by the opposition will not occur. In this objective the dominant faction is generally assisted by the strong respect which the constituents of the representatives in the deliberative assembly usually have for parliamentary practices and their prevailing ignorance regarding their abuse and perversion by parliamentarians.

In more local deliberative assemblies such abuses of the parliamentary procedures are usually avoided or mitigated by the direct participation of the members of the group and by the more frequent homogeneity of membership and interests involved. In those deliberative assemblies where the interests represented are subject to sudden or strong attack from without and frequently require immediate defense and vigorous policies of action, as in military and capitalistic enterprises, and in criminal organizations, the form of the control tends to pass from that of the deliberative assembly to the dictatorship, and parliamentary practice is modified or suspended accordingly.

Discussion and Committee Control—Also the methods of discussion used in deliberative assemblies are not always conducive to the formation of rational judgments, although the ostensible purpose of the discussion is such. Appeals to prejudice and other forms of suggestion may be substituted for the impartial statement of facts. Covert threats and other means of verbal intimidation are not infrequently employed on such occasions. In political representative assemblies frequently but little attention is given to the verbal arguments of the speaker by fellow members. During the period of speech making members are often absent from the chamber attending caucuses and committee meetings, or are engaged in other political or non-political activities. Questions are decided primarily in committee meetings and caucuses where adequate discussion may be had or where the vote is strictly along partisan lines. Speeches in the chamber of the political deliberative assembly of the representative type are primarily for the constituents of the speaker or the gallery rather than for the members of the deliberative body. In such cases as those here described the deliberative character of the assembly is largely lost, or it is to some extent transferred to the committee rooms. The real business of the assembly is transacted in the committees, which are always dominated by the majority party in the assembly, and almost always by the dominant faction in the majority party. Because of this committee domination there is little real opportunity for rational discussion to influence decisions in a deliberative assembly. In fact, domination of committees by the leading faction in the assembly turns it into a dictatorship instead of a truly deliberative assembly. The chamber itself serves primarily for final parliamentary skirmishes and for taking and recording the vote, and for oratory. But in non-representative political and in local and non-political assemblies deliberation may reach a high degree of development, with the result that public opinion is created and collective behavior is determined and initiated in a rational manner. Where parliamentary procedure is manipulated collective behavior is also determined and initiated, but not necessarily rationally.

DISCUSSION GROUPS—The discussion group is a modified deliberative assembly. It differs from the ordinary form of the latter, however, in a most important respect. Ordinarily it does not seek to direct collective behavior outside of the group. The function of the discussion group is to discuss. The subject matter of the discussion may be anything in which the members of the group are interested. Often it is political, economic, religious, educational, scientific. The interested people meet for the purpose of comparing views, exchanging facts, ascertaining the trends of opinion and of influencing them. A unity of opinion may be sought as the result of the discussion, or each one may be left to formulate his own conclusions. In the more highly developed and organized discussion groups there are likely to be committees for the purpose of presenting resolutions of findings, programs, declarations of principles, etc. These, if adopted as the unanimous or compromise opinion or "sense" of the whole group, may be presented to some administrative or legislative body with the request that they be put into effect or enacted into law, or sent to a newspaper for publication, thus attempting indirectly to control collective behavior at large. The more loosely organized discussion groups, such as discussion clubs, may be content merely with individual statements of opinions and supporting data without any attempt to influence deliberative assemblies or the public and administrative authorities in any informal way. Among primitive peoples and children consensus of opinion often develops as a result of discussion without any formal statement of such opinion. Debating societies usually appoint judges to render a decision and when the decision is reached the club or society takes no further action. Forums and social centers may follow either policy on occasion. Scientific societies practically never take a vote or offer resolutions, but remain content with hearing what each member has to say. Semi-propaganda societies, such as conferences on good government, social welfare, housing reform, public health, etc., usually combine with scientific discussion an attempt to influence public opinion and legislation or administration through resolutions or other pronouncements. However, some of these societies are very conservative in the matter of resolutions.

The Temper and Effects of Discussion Groups—The type of discussion groups may vary greatly, ranging from those that engage only in calm and unemotional straightforward presentations of data and individual or collective conclusions, to those that employ emotional oratory, suggestion in various forms, verbal intimidation, and other mob-like methods. In the latter types of discussion, of course, the character of the discussion groups proper is lost and a propaganda group or worse takes its place.

Whether there is any formal attempt to influence public opinion and public officials and representatives, or whether the discussion group is content with an interchange of facts and opinions, an effect is nevertheless usually exerted upon collective behavior. Discussion groups, especially if they publish their discussions in local newspapers or in regular proceedings, constitute one of the most effective means of influencing public opinion. So important are they that there has been in recent years a movement on foot to multiply the number of local forums or discussion groups, in clubs, social centers, and elsewhere, in order to secure that interchange of opinion and information which is believed to be so necessary in a democracy. Such discussion groups are all the more desirable now that the old neighborhood contacts have so largely disappeared and that so much manufactured and ill digested opinion obtains circulation through indirect means of communication, such as the newspaper, radio, movie, the paid propagandist, advertising, and the like.

CLASSES FOR INSTRUCTION play a much larger part in collective thinking and in the generation of collective behavior than they did in earlier times. The development of universal education, by which all the youth are subjected to class instruction, and the growth of university extension for adults, have extended the period of formal instruction for large numbers of people through at least the first half of the life period. The woman's club movement, which has an educational side, belongs more to the discussion group than to the class group phase of group organization. However, it has aspects of the latter phase also. The class differs from the discussion group in that the primary purpose of the former is learning rather than discussion, although discussion properly occurs as an aspect of the learning process. Also, there is much more previous preparation for the class by reading.

THE AUDIENCE ordinarily does not enter into discussion but gives its attention solely to the lecturer or performer. Usually also it requires no special preparation. The audience is still an important type of direct contact group, although it is less important than it was before the development of the movie. The old lecture audience, which had so much vogue in the nineteenth century, is now relatively unimportant. Vaudeville has cheapened it, although it still survives in something of the old form in the Chautauqua. Even the church audience has declined in quality and interest. The radio has extended and widened the audience to a remarkable degree and has brought the inclusion of serious up-to-date subjects within the mental purview of millions of people. The radio has expanded the audience from the exclusive category of direct contact groups

RATIONAL GROUPS

to that of the indirect contact groups also. The modern visual analogues of the audience are the groups attending the movies, mainly for amusement and other trivial purposes, and the newspaper and the magazine reading publics. These also illustrate the tendency of direct contact groups to expand into indirect contact groups.

RELATIVE PERMANENCY AND SERIOUSNESS OF PURPOSE OF THE GROUPS DISCUSSED—The adventitious character of these groups increases as we descend from the deliberative assembly to the audience, or (to adopt a cognate expression) the "visience" of the movies. The deliberative assembly always, and the discussion group generally, assemble for the express purpose of a collective examination of facts and opinions and for arriving at a collective outlook or program. There is also a large element of permanency in these groups. The membership changes fairly slowly and the forms and functions of the groups are likely to persist for a considerable length of time. But the class and the audience or "visience," especially the last, do not necessarily possess permanency of organization. The class may remain intact for a period of weeks or months, but it rarely persists beyond that time. The audience and "visience" are exceedingly temporary, having an existence of an hour or so only. In the case of the class and the audience, the interest which brings the members together is frequently confined to the immediate subject matter. This is especially true of the audience. Church audiences, which closely resemble classes or even clubs, are nearly permanent in character. The deliberative assembly may embrace a large number of interests which are common to the members, almost as many as are involved in life itself; or it may involve only one, as in financial bodies, or only a few. But these interests, whether few or many, are likely to be relatively permanent. The discussion group is also likely to grow up among people with a large number of persisting common interests and therefore to last, although there are exceptions to this statement. All of these groups may be equally concerned with abstract problems, although the groups last mentioned are least likely to be so concerned. The audience and the "visience" are particularly likely to find their interests, as a whole or in part, in the concrete sensorily based fields of experiences, such as are common to amusements.

MATERIALS FOR SUPPLEMENTARY READING

Allport, F. H., *Social Psychology*, Ch. XI
Beach, W. G., *An Introduction to Sociology and Social Problems*, Chs. XI, XII
Bogardus, E. S., *Fundamentals of Social Psychology*, Chs. XVII, XXIII, XXIV
Follett, M. P., *The New State*
Hartson, L. D., "The Psychology of the Club; A Study in Social Psychology," *Ped. Sem.*, XVIII: 353-414
LeBon, G., *The Crowd*, Book III, Chs. III, IV, V
———, *The Psychology of Revolution*, pp. 167-251
Lindeman, E. C., *The Community*
———, *Social Discovery*, Ch. V
McDougall, W., *The Group Mind*, Ch. III
Puffer, J. A., *The Boy and His Gang*
Ross, E. A., *Principles of Sociology*, Chs. XXIII, XXIV
———, *Social Psychology*, pp. 63-65
Russell and Rigby, *Working Lads' Clubs*
Webster, H., *Primitive Secret Societies*

CHAPTER XXIX

DIRECT CONTACT GROUPS: NON-RATIONAL TYPES

We have discussed very briefly the more or less rational types of direct contact groups. In this chapter those direct contact groups which change more rapidly and are ephemeral and which are organized on a suggestion or non-rational and irrational basis will be taken up. In this connection also will be considered oratory as a chief method of conveying suggestion in non-rational direct contact groups.

INFORMAL CLUBS, SOCIAL SETS, ETC.—There is a type of face-to-face group which resembles the club more closely than any other organization, but lacks the permanency and definiteness of integration of the club. Ordinarily groups of this type are wholly non-rational. In fact such groups are ordinarily very fluid, the membership changing constantly. Nor do all of the members often assemble at any one time or in any one place. The most common examples of this type of group are the social sets, such as the "four hundred," the cliques which organize themselves around a few striking personalities, the rings, etc. Every community possesses them. They lack any definite organization, but practically every one understands the essential facts about membership, leadership, the scope of their activities, etc. Their main interests almost invariably center in the ritual of polite social intercourse, amusements, fashion, eating, entertaining, and kindred activities. To many of the members the "proper" exercise of these functions, that is, their exercise according to the accepted rituals of their observance, is a sort of religion. Spencer recalls the case of a woman who said that being well dressed gave her a peace such as religion could not give. Somewhat like these informal groups, but even more ephemeral, although perhaps frequently possessing a more serious purpose, are the temporary bazaars, picnics, receptions, dinners, and like assemblages, designed either for pleasure or to raise money for some cause. Their very transitory assemblies are frequently, but not always, organized within a "set" or "clique."

CEREMONIALS claim a considerable amount of interest among modern peoples, as indeed they have always demanded, perhaps even more of primitive peoples who frequently have relatively fixed groups or "committees" assigned to the performance of particular ceremonies. Ceremonial performances have always, apparently, been used to commemorate and inculcate the most important truths or beliefs and experiences of peoples. Birth, puberty, marriage, death, and adventitious crises and discoveries have called forth this type of collective response among peoples of all ages. Even among highly literate and cultured peoples, who possess the power of preserving the memory and significance of events in more abstract and intellectual forms, ceremonials develop around the striking events of their history. We have our national holidays to commemorate the chief crises and achievements and personages in our history. Also we commemorate the most important achievements of our civilization, especially those connected with religion, in much the same way.

Ceremonials do not develop as a means of commemorating scientific achievement to the same extent as in religion and art, probably because the former is more easily communicated through intellectual symbols, while the latter still uses gesture language and other emotional communication symbols to a very considerable extent. Science perpetuates its meaning in literature, while religion, especially of the traditional type, is the chief cultivator of ritual and ceremonial. In this respect traditional religion has a close competitor as well as coadjutor, in the esthetic traditions and fine arts. In fact, art largely grew out of the ceremonial and other commemorative functions, including religious ceremonials.

The ceremonial, which becomes stereotyped and ossified in *ritual,* is primarily a type of gesture communication, but it also includes some elements of intellectual symbolization. It is much more primitive than the literary forms of collective expression and communication which have grown up to supplement it, and in some cases to supplant it, in the period of civilization. It finds its chief employment at present in the perpetuation of emotional values and in appeal to the young and the comparatively uneducated or those who have not been trained for the intellectual analysis of collective relationships and functions. Children, lower culture peoples, the uneducated, women, and men, is approximately the order in which ceremonials make an appeal to people in modern life. The more analytical and intellectual people become in their attitudes, the less likely they are to fall back upon ceremonial and ritual as a means of organizing their collective behavior.

THE DECLINE OF THE CEREMONIAL—Consequently, modern societies make comparatively less use of ceremonial and ritual than primitive societies. Puberty ceremonies have practically vanished from among us, although there are possibly certain remnants of them in the confirmation ceremonies of some of our more traditional religions. Birth and infant baptismal ceremonials have also diminished in importance. The marriage ceremonial has become as much or more an opportunity for the competitive display of wealth and station as originally it served the function of invoking the favor of the spirits or of palliating their vindictiveness with reference to the union. Death and burial are often treated by us with a degree of simplicity and lack of emotional outburst which would be regarded by the primitive man as sacrilegious and a direct challenge to the spirits to make reprisals.

The reason for this decline in the use of ceremonials with reference to the great individual events of our lives is undoubtedly to be found in the fact that our superior analysis of natural processes and causation has intellectualized our attitudes towards our lives. Perhaps also we see these outstanding events more as necessary parts or transition phases of the whole line of development. We no longer personify striking events or look for personality causes behind them. We analyze and intellectualize them. They do not mean less to us, but we see them more in perspective with the total development of life and of the whole of nature itself. Our methods of control over them, in so far as we are able to direct them, are now through science instead of through the magic and spirit control attempted by primitive peoples. Much ceremonial regarding the great crises in the lives of individuals, as it has come down to us, has been derived from magical practices, although the more obvious meaning of such ceremonial has usually been turned into merely esthetic and commemorative moral-emotional, or even competitive social, values in our time.

CEREMONIALS COMMEMORATING IMPORTANT SOCIAL EVENTS MORE RATIONAL—Ceremonial has always been a collective or group form of behavior. The interest, whether it centered in the welfare of the individual or in that of the group, was always based upon experiences which were common to all members of the group. Consequently ceremonials have at all times been largely public affairs, involving a collective response to an outside power or principle, or the mutual and reciprocal responses of members of the group to each other. Perhaps the latter, or mutual and reciprocal responses developed out of the collective response to the outside agency. Modern ceremonials, aside from the survivals, are particularly group products and group functions. They arise primarily in connection with events affecting the collective welfare. Early ceremonials took place wholly within the limits of face-to-face groups, but with the expansion of modern groups, as the result of the development of indirect media of communication, ceremonials now extend into distance contact relationships also. The collective behavior involved in the ceremonial is very little deliberative or abstract, although some of our patriotic ceremonials, like Fourth of July celebrations, the Colonial settlements pageants, Settlement of the West pageants, etc., and the Darwinian Centennial, the Shakespearean Centenary, etc., have attempted successfully to intellectualize the ceremonial procedure.

Discussion is at a minimum in ceremonial, but even here the concrete and formal and ritualistic tends to be crowded out by the analytical and the abstract. Ceremonials commemorating crises or other significant events in the lives of both individuals and society are, in spite of the magical survivals which often persist in them, important methods of teaching significant lessons. Usually ceremonials celebrating social crises contain fewer magical survivals than those commemorating individual life events, because they are ordinarily of more recent origin. Ceremonials celebrated by indirect contact communication are still less likely to carry magical survival practices, which are ordinarily concrete and direct in their methods of performance.

RALLIES AND DEMONSTRATIONS—Less intellectual and abstract than the behavior of audiences, but usually with more participant activity on the part of the members, is the behavior of groups engaged in rallies and demonstrations. If there is discussion in such groups the intellectual element is at a minimum and suggestion and the communication of emotional attitudes are primary. In the matter of the dominance of suggestion over intellectual analysis, rallies and demonstrations are similar to ceremonials, and all three differ in this respect very largely from the other types of direct contact groups already discussed. But unlike ceremonials, the dominating purpose of the rally is usually not commemoration but the support of some present faction or program by creating public opinion in its favor. Rallies and demonstrations can be organized about any personality, movement, or proposal, at any time, if these objects of attention are sufficiently spectacular or dramatic to secure the interest of the people. But they are rarely purely spontaneous collective phenomena; they are manipulated. Rallies and demonstrations require an active leader to a greater extent than any of the collective functions which we have previously considered. The group itself has been formed at the intance of the leaders for the specific purpose of behaving in a prearranged manner with reference to some object or value which they are supporting.

PURPOSES AND METHODS OF RALLIES AND DEMONSTRATIONS—Rallies and demonstrations are organized primarily in support of political and religious interests or beliefs and personalities. But excellent examples can also be found in connection with sports and amusements, particularly in college athletics, art, literature, community affairs, public health and sanitation, etc. The groups thus formed are but little intellectual. The object in organizing them is rarely to stimulate analysis of values and programs, but to create an emotional attachment for such programs, movements, or persons. Otherwise we should have discussion groups instead of rallies and demonstrations. The professional evangelist does not invite his audience to argue out the question of the advisability of seeking membership in his religion and denomination. On the contrary, he is as anxious as the stock salesman or the insurance agent to prevent intellectual analysis. He stigmatizes such analysis as stiff-necked and sinful defiance to his God and as the result of the promptings of the Evil One. He uses all of the arts of suggestion, verbal intimidation, and emotional appeal known to him to blind the auditor to the other side of the question and to influence him to see the truth as it is made manifest through the speaker. In this way professional revivals become demonstrations of religious emotionalism and rallies to the cause and dogmas of the particular religion or denomination which is being preached.

The control through suggestion of collective emotional expression in line with the preacher's purpose is very important in the manipulation of such group behavior. The evangelist has the auditors sing songs the words of which express the same meanings as his sermons, and thus they become participators emotionally instead of remaining indifferent or becoming antagonists. Other music, prayers, workers circulating through the audience, etc., also add to the suggestive stimuli and heighten the emotional condition of the auditor by multiplying stimuli through various sensory channels.

ILLUSTRATIONS—The political rally or demonstration is organized in a very similar manner. Here participation is also important as a means of conditioning the overt and emotional behavior of the voter to the candidate or issue as stimulus. Campaign songs are sung, torchlight processions and banner parades are engineered, and sometimes experience meetings are arranged at which the veteran faithful appear and voice their approval. Clever and suggestive campaign speakers are employed who, by painting rosy pictures of their side and dark pictures of the other side, and by the use of flattery, appeal to pride and fear, seek to win the audience which has already been prepared emotionally for the verbal appeal by participation exercises and stirring music. The use of stereotyped stimuli, of phrases such as "full dinner pail," or of stigmatizing epithets like "socialist," "hyphenated American," or "slave driving capitalist," are largely depended upon for results. Argument from the floor is hissed down, and the offender will be carried out by the police if he asks embarrassing questions or challenges arguments, if the meeting is politically "regular." Political campaigns are won primarily by emotional appeal and suggestion. If the previous experiences of the auditor or the record of the opposition has conditioned the responses of the auditor to pointed and effective suggestion stimuli, it should be easy enough to win him over to the cause on the basis of emotional appeal.

College rallies are just as carefully planned, ordinarily. The student body, already emotionally predisposed to the cause by their daily contacts on the campus, pour into the auditorium to the martial strains of the college band. They sit jammed together, arm to arm, in plain view of each other, so that all expressions of emotion are easily communicated from one to another. The speakers chosen are college favorites. The student body participates through college yells and singing led by the yell leaders. As the crowning act of the drama the team itself marches onto the stage and a bedlam of enthusiasm is released in the audience. No intellectual analysis or argument is necessary or would be tolerated. The whole process occurs on the basis of suggestion under skilled leadership.

EPHEMERALNESS OF RESULTS FROM SUCH METHODS—Such groups are ephemeral, lasting only until after the election or the game, or until the souls have been saved. The ease with which the revival convert backslides is proverbial. Since the behavior is manipulated and is the product of suggestion rather than of intellectual analysis it can be staged again upon occasion. Such methods are also used in behalf of more permanent ends and programs, such as public health and sanitation, community improvement, coöperative organization, good government, and the like. But they are useful primarily as a method of arousing interest. To be truly and permanently effective they should be followed up by a carefully arranged and executed educational program. If follow-up work is not done the rally or demonstration may result in more harm than good. For, while it orients people emotionally toward a common cause, emotional support is easily dissipated if it is not braced by intellectual convictions and deepened by continued achievement. An ineffective utilization of the emotions weakens emotional impulses and tends habitually to divorce emotional expression from achievement.

CROWDS AND MOBS are the lowest forms of human groups. They approximate most closely to the packs and herds of the lower animals. Crowds may be either voluntary or involuntary. That is, the members of the group may come together on purpose, or they may associate by accident, with all grades of aggregation and association between. It is usually some strong emotion or curiosity impulse which integrates a crowd. Emotion is especially dominant in the mob. Rallies and demonstrations are crowds, but usually they are carefully controlled and are not ordinarily allowed to become mobs.

Mobs are crowds in which the attention and emotions of the members become concentrated upon some object or activity with so much intensity that the members lose the power of rational inhibition. They carry out the suggestions given them or the impulses within them with reference to the object or behavior without restraint. They go mad temporarily, as in lynchings; and under the impetus of mutual and reciprocal stimulation by suggestion pouring in through almost every sense, especially the visual, auditory, and tactual senses, they perpetrate acts which as individuals they would not perform. Restraints and inhibitions from intellectual considerations being removed, suggestions are received uncritically from any source, so that the criminally minded, because of the greater strength of their lawless and uninhibited impulses, may easily dominate the mob. And good men may themselves become criminal under such conditions.

QUALITIES AND RESULTS OF CROWDS AND MOBS—Ross has characterized the mob very effectively, pointing out the weak or biased moral sense, the insincerity, fickleness, lack of intelligence, instability, ephemerality, credulity, simple-mindedness, and untruthfulness of its members. These traits appertain also to the members of a crowd, although in less degree. It is not possible to remove them from the crowd and mob without transforming these groups into other types of groups, such as discussion groups, or deliberative assemblies. This, however, is a difficult matter to achieve, because of the more or less adventitious character of crowds and the low intellectual and moral character of some of their members.

Crowds generally form in the streets or in public places. Their formation is often accidental or involuntary, the source of attraction frequently being as trivial as a street accident or fight, the trick of a publicity-seeking fakir, or a traffic jam. A street speaker may gather around him on a summer night scores of desultory wanderers, more or less disreputable in character and of low intellectual attainments. If he is a skillful orator he may be able to hold and augment his group and even throw them into the frenzy of a mob, inciting them to wreck buildings or other property. But if he tries to convert them to intellectual principles and win them to a long-time program of social reform, he will find that they lack the intellectual grasp and the moral continuity of purpose necessary to carry out such a program. Street converts made in a crowd are good for very little except immediate action. When used in revolutions, as they often have been in the past, they must be employed at once, while their enthusiasm is hot. If they are allowed to disperse the powerful suggestion which comes from mutual stimulation is lost and their ardor cools and each one goes his own way in search of work, adventure, or forgetfulness.

Modern Life and Crowd Behavior—Modern life has often been said to favor crowds and the mob spirit. It is doubtful if modern society can offer more striking examples of mob behavior than those to be found in primitive societies or in ancient history. But there are many things in modern life which favor the adventitious formation of crowds. The anonymity of our city life, while it decreases homogeneity, yet removes inhibitions and favors the mob spirit. The vast number of the idle and unrestrained, the multitude of stimuli and the high degree to which these stimuli are organized and even commercialized or manipulated, favor crowd organization. The fact that so much amusement is performed for the spectator and that he is not called upon for participation brings large masses of people together and places them in attitudes of receptivity to suggestion. Audiences of the amusement sort are merely crowds and the mob spirit can easily be released among them by the proper suggestions.

GOOD AND BAD RESULTS OF CROWDS—It must not be supposed, however, that all crowds are bad. Nevertheless, the crowd methods of organizing behavior are necessarily of a low order intellectually, and therefore relatively without moral discernment or standards. Occasionally crowds, or even mobs organized in support of high purposes rise to the level of heroism. The mob which destroyed the French Bastille in 1789 was apparently motivated by a high type of idealism. Mobs have often taken up the gauntlet against tyranny when individuals would not dare to protest. In fact mobs have perhaps in the past been the chief foils of tyrants. But mob action is an expensive and risky method of reform, and we are now developing more rational procedures through legislatures and other groups organized for more intellectual types of collective action. Crowds and mobs easily become the tools of designing and unscrupulous persons, and for every instance of good result achieved by them there are probably scores of questionable or positively harmful results.

ORATORY—Perhaps the chief technic factor in the control of the crowd and in the production of mobs is oratory. With the coming of the newspaper, oratory is not relatively so important as formerly, but it is still a powerful agent of collective control. There are many kinds of oratory, according to the form and length of the oration, the method of delivery, and the relative degrees of intellectuality and emotionality of the content. But oratory which manipulates the crowd and may transform it into a mob must depend on suggestion rather than on intellectual analysis. The orator must be skilled in his understanding of the signs of the emotions of his auditors, and he will be most effective if he has proper support from music, the surroundings, including the meeting place, the previous experiences and preconceptions of his auditors, and their participation in the exercises as described above. Under such favorable circumstances they will be highly susceptible to the orator's suggestions and he can come more directly to the point and make strong and powerful appeals for their support of the cause which he wishes to further. Figurative and strong emotional language is of course always more effective for brief appeals than intellectual analysis. The battle speeches of Napoleon are good examples of this sort of brief address. They are rivaled also by the few well chosen and well directed words of mob leaders at appropriate moments. Under favorable conditions a high grade crowd may even listen with interest to lengthy intellectual analyses and arguments on topics which they regard as of great importance.

An Illustration—But in the absence of such favorable conditions the skillful orator may win over his crowd audience and even be able at the end of his address to secure their willing attention to matters of considerable weight and of a character which they would not ordinarily accept. But this requires both skill and time, and probably also prestige. An illustration drawn from an actual case will make the matter clear. Several years ago a three-times unsuccessful candidate for the presidency came to speak to the people of a small southern university town. He was not very popular with most of the two thousand people who gathered to hear him, but in the hour and thirty minutes in which he spoke he won them over completely. The first fifteen minutes of his address he spent in compliments regarding their "beautiful little city," reviewing its show places, and in praise of the "splendid mothers and fathers" of that city, with their high ideals and their sacrifices for their children and community. Interest was intense and I saw a man in front of me nudge his companion and remark, "Pretty good!" With this preparation, aided by his melodious voice, the orator spent thirty minutes telling jokes on himself and his opponents. He spared neither himself nor his political enemies. All he said was in good humor, but with the grateful attitude of his hearers, aroused by the previous fifteen minutes of compliments, the political jokes on himself were turned into material for sympathy, and those on his rivals into mild ridicule, by the method of negative suggestion. The man in front of me said, "He certainly bears no grudge!" And seemingly that was the way all of the audience felt. His apparent objectivity won their hearty approval. The next thirty minutes were spent in trite and fulsome praise of American institutions, very melodiously spoken. He could make the most banal statement appear to be of the utmost importance by the way in which he said it. There were the usual remarks about the greatness of the founders of the republic, the wonderful document, our Constitution, which came inspired from their brains, the glorious devotion to democracy of the hero of the southern people, Jefferson, a hint at the sorrows for the "lost cause" now turned into an effort for achievement for the future, well chosen references to the blood shed on many battlefields in defense of the liberties of the American people, in which they had always done at least their share. Some of the women with memories were crying. The men looked self-conscious, stoical and proud of themselves. He had only been manipulating a common stock of suggestion stimuli, but he knew with the unerring skill of the practiced orator what responses were conditioned to these stimuli. He held that audience in the hollow of his hand and their beliefs on the tip of his tongue. And here, with his compliment to their martial defense of their liberties scarcely spoken, he turned to the fourth part of his oration and said, in the last fifteen minutes of his harangue, what he had come there to say. The hour and a quarter of flattery and sentimental truism had been only preparation. He assured them that a more insidious enemy than armies was invading their land and liberties, called upon them to protect the republic for their children against unscrupulous greed and conscienceless exploitation, and to choose Woodrow Wilson as the leader of their civic army to do battle with this modern monster. He sketched the aggression of monopolies and advocated governmental reforms and a progressive machinery of democracy. He left the audience enthusiastic for the very principles which most of them had previously opposed because he knew how to assimilate or condition his liberal program to their preconceived beliefs and emotions. It was a case of conditioning by analogy and similarity. It was characteristic of the most successful kind of oratory. The method here used is typical. Most of the time must be spent in telling the people what they know or believe already, with emphasis and approval, in order that they may be led to believe what before was foreign or unacceptable to them, by showing them analogies or similarities, mainly emotional and stereotyped, which they had not previously suspected. Or their beliefs may be changed merely by direct conditioning.

THE MIXED CHARACTER OF MOST GROUPS—It must not be supposed that there is a sharp line of demarcation between direct and indirect contact groups. Most modern groups are mixed or involve both direct and indirect contacts. Thus the nation, the state, even the city and the community, rural or urban, exhibit both direct and indirect contacts among their members. Except for the size of the indirect contact groups and the expanse of territory which they cover, they would be direct contact groups. But their overgrowth compels them to use indirect media for the consummation of their contacts, since all of the members of the group cannot ever be brought together in face-to-face association for any purpose at any one time. Business associations, scientific and art societies, and similar organizations, likewise possess a dual character, but with the emphasis upon the derivative or indirect contact aspect instead of upon the direct contact phase, as in the former case. In these types of groups the members ordinarily make their contacts through indirect media and resort to face-to-face contacts only on special occasions, such as at regular directors' or program meetings.

Mixed groups take three leading forms. These may be described as follows: *Associations,* in so far as they possess a face-to-face character instead of being based on indirect contacts, come under the categories of deliberative assemblies and discussion groups and classes. They are essentially purposive in character and constitute the highest form of mixed groups. *Societies,* an appellation sometimes used interchangeably with associations, are any sort of direct or indirect contact groups having a relatively permanent or at least a continuous existence covering a considerable period of time. The term is more inclusive than that of associations, which it embraces. We do not ordinarily speak of purely temporary groups possessing only an accidental or unconscious organization as societies. It is to these that we commonly apply the term crowd, or even mob, thereby indicating a greater degree of ephemeralness and a lower type of organization. *Institutions* are those associations and societies which possess a high degree both of permanency and of organization, although it is not necessary that this organization should have been achieved consciously or purposively. Institutions are also thought of as possessing a considerable degree of abstract content, in which symbolic contact mechanisms loom large. In modern society this abstract and invisible element in institutions practically always outweigh the concrete and local face-to-face extensions which almost all institutions possess. Thus the derivative aspects of the group now dominate the primary and face-to-face aspects in institutions. This is perhaps least true in the family institution and most largely the case in the institution of morals.

MATERIALS FOR SUPPLEMENTARY READING

Allport, F. H., *Social Psychology*, Ch. XII
Andrews, L. C., *Military Manpower*, pp. 175-185
Bogardus, E. S., *Fundamentals of Social Psychology*, Ch. XXII
Cooley, C. H., *Human Nature and the Social Order*, Ch. X
———, *Social Organization*, Ch. XIV
Dunlap, K., *Social Psychology*, pp. 215-220
Gardner, C. S., "Assemblies," *Amer. Jour. Sociology*, XIX: 537-555
Gault, R. H., *Social Psychology*, Ch. VII
Ginsberg, M., *The Psychology of Society*, Ch. IX
LeBon, G., *The Crowd*, Bk. I, Chs. I-IV; Bk. II, Chs. I, II, IV; Bk. III, Chs. I, II
McDougall, W., *The Group Mind*, Ch. II
Martin, E. D., *The Behavior of Crowds*
Park and Burgess, *Introduction to the Science of Sociology*, Ch. XIII
Ross, E. A., *Social Control*, Ch. XIX
———, *Social Psychology*, Chs. III, IV
Steiner, J. F., *Community Organization*, Ch. XXII
Wallas, G., *The Great Society*, Ch. VIII
Watts, F., *Abnormal Psychology and Education*, pp. 19-25

CHAPTER XXX

INDIRECT CONTACT GROUPS AND COMMUNICATION

WANING OF THE DOMINANCE OF DIRECT CONTACT GROUPS IN THE CONTROL OF COLLECTIVE BEHAVIOR—Powerful as are the direct contact groups which we have described in organizing public opinion and in initiating collective behavior types, their influence is being surpassed by that of the indirect contact groups to be described in Chapter XXXI. Communication is being constantly intellectualized, and even the emotions are being associated with and expressed through abstract symbols. Interests expand to embrace larger numbers of people spread abroad over wider ranges of territory. Communication of the whole of the content of our culture by means of direct contacts is becoming increasingly difficult or impossible. Hence the wider and more important interests are organizing groups on an abstract and derivative basis. The old primary groups remain and always will remain, but their function in promoting collective behavior is becoming supplementary to the work of the derivative groups instead of continuing to dominate the latter. Discussion is now largely through the printed page, and dialectic which held the stage as a method for the discovery of truth in the times of the great Greek philosophers takes diminished rank in comparison with the positive findings of the laboratory and statistical investigation. The appeal of oratory, although still heard and applauded, is of small volume in comparison with propaganda in print, which reaches—if less vivdly—to the minds of myriads instead of hundreds.

An indirect contact group is a derivative group which has lost its face-to-face character. When well integrated, it is the highest or most abstract form of the derivative group. Consequently it is the most widely and effectively functional of all modern groups. Because the contacts of its members are indirect it is organized upon the basis of public consciousness and public opinion. Without the operation of these types of functional consciousness in some degree, publics and indirect contact groups generally could scarcely be said to exist. These functional phases of consciousness which are at the basis of indirect contact groups are organized through communication. Communication and discussion are the matrix out of which associations, societies, and publics arise. Consequently this chapter will deal with communication. The following chapter will be concerned with the types and functions of indirect contact groups and especially of publics.

THE ORIGIN OF INDIRECT CONTACT GROUPS—Indirect contact groups and publics are a product of civilization and literacy. They began to have existence with the invention of oral language and the spread of the use of its symbols for purposes of communication beyond the limits of the horde and clan. But it can scarcely be said that the use of spoken or written language alone created derivative indirect contact groups, although such group organization was not possible without language. The underlying cause of the expansion of groups beyond the limitations of direct or face-to-face contacts was the growth of productive technique or inventions. These inventions enabled people over wide territories to make similar and coadaptive or coöperative adjustments to nature, and the rise of media and methods of exchange kept primary groups in functional contact with each other. Thus the surplus population of the primary groups did not split off and begin independent existence, but formed similar units, in the form of clans, phratries, and tribes, and later of nations, and kept up their contacts with the parent and sister groups on the basis of their similarity of productive technique and exchange relationships. Language was the communication technique by which these coöperative or coadaptive relationships were made possible.

But almost as important as language in binding these expanded populations together was the similarity of their social inventions, such as their beliefs, traditions, customs, conventions, and the functional organization of these, such as their religious, domestic, economic, and embryo political institutions. But the most important bond of all, because it was at once the medium of communication and the storehouse for those social inventions, was language. Language is the means or technique by which all of these other preliminaries to the derivative or indirect contact groups are realized or made effective. They grew up in the period of language and were not possible before them.

THE EXPANSION OF DIRECT INTO INDIRECT CONTACT GROUPS—While derivative groups were initiated in the period of oral language, such groups could not be much more than compound direct contact groups before the advent of written language. There was no such thing in primitive society as individuals or even families living as independent units, apart from a close immersion in face-to-face groups, while at the same time they were united in a larger and more abstract derivative group by indirect contacts. There was no adequate technique of communication for such abstract relationships.

Early man lived a more or less communistic life. With the methods of food getting which were at his disposal it was not possible for individuals or even families, except in unusual circumstances, to secure adequate and continued means of subsistence by their own unaided efforts and at the same time protect themselves from wild animals and other men. Life had to be coöperative. Because of the lack of abstract symbols of communication, which developed to any considerable extent only with the coming of written language and the storage of objectified neuro-psychic technique, the sole type of coöperation which could be developed effectively was communal or direct contact coöperation.

With the coming of written language and consequently more abstract and inclusive symbolization of relationships, coöperation over a wider range of contacts, including the indirect, became not only possible but also easy and is now the dominant relationship in our society. We still live in face-to-face groups. We are born and reared in such, and we work and amuse ourselves in them, but we are constantly becoming less dependent upon them, and even they are dominated and shaped by the indirect contact groups. Our modern world, especially the urban world, finds more and more of its essential contacts at a distance, and of an abstract character, while the less essential contacts of amusement and recreation, and the like, are more frequently reserved to the face-to-face groups. But even these less essential functions of life are coming to be engineered or organized and directed from above or through abstract and indirect contact channels.

CHANGES IN THE MEANS OF COMMUNICATION—DIRECT EXPRESSION—The growth of indirect contact groups depends, therefore, upon the expansion of the means of communication. The means of communication have undergone a development from the concrete and direct to the indirect and abstract, which corresponds to the development of groups from the face-to-face type to those with distance contacts. We have already noted the fact that early communication was by facial and bodily expression and gesture. Primitive man was comparatively more dependent than we are upon the emotional expressions of the face and the posture of the body and gestures. Yet with all his dependence upon such expressions as a means of communicating his attitudes, the content of such expression was in all probability not so rich then as now. The mobility of the modern face and the multifold expression of feature, of eye, and of posture, are remarkable. There is nothing in the expression of the savage which corresponds to it, just as there is nothing in his life and emotional experiences which adequately compares to the emotional richness of the modern man and woman. The actor in civilized society utilizes these forms of facial expression and gesture to indicate a refinement and elaboration of feeling which is largely foreign to the primitive man. And all people among us are in some degree amateur actors of the same kind.

The primitive man wears a mask in his ceremonials to symbolize in stereotyped form the expression of the spirit or personality or to represent the character of the power which he is impersonating. Modern man dispenses with masks and makes his face and body indicate the idea or attitude which he wishes to convey. Consequently modern expression is much more fluid and mobile and the content of such communication is vastly more subtle and intricate. Yet we must not suppose primitive man to have been expressionless. The very fixit and stoicalness of his expression when on parade or in the presence of strangers was a part of his aptitude at expression and served to indicate very well the attitude which he had at that moment. Other movements and attitudes, in which the stranger was not so likely to see him off his guard, were characterized by other and equally appropriate types of expression. The expression of the primitive man is inferior to our own as a means of communication, not so much because of any lack of adaptation of the form of the expression to the content or feeling, as because of the lack of richness and variety.

PRIMITIVE AND MODERN ART COMPARED—Art in its utilitarian aspects begins as the means of representing and preserving the direct expressions discussed above. Early art, as was shown in a previous chapter, is a form of writing serving the function of perpetuating the bodily attitudes of men and animals and the facial expression of men. It communicates from man to man and from group to group the perceptions and emotions of men. Gradually, on the one hand, it becomes abstracted and stereotyped into interchangeable word and idea symbols which form the basis and the early content of intellectual writing. On the other hand, it retains its flexible diverse form and concrete pictorial symbolization and is perfected as a means of emotional expression and communication. This is art proper, as distinguished from writing in the intellectual sense. Thus modern representative and plastic art—painting and sculpture—are vastly more expressive, or at least have a greater refinement of expression, than primitive art of the same general type.

Modern art has a greater expressiveness for two reasons. One is that modern life has vastly extended the range of experience and deepened it. The other is that man has become self-expressive, instead of trying merely to depict the forces, powers, and personalities which rule him. The widening of human experience has enabled man to perceive more in nature and in man, in human relationships, aims, fears, hopes, than could have been dreamed of by early man. Increase in experience, according to the principles of recognition and imitation which were presented in Part III, deepens the powers of perception and feeling. These two powers together increase the facilities of the individual for making projective elaborations which are the essence of artistic creation. Just as the life o modern man is richer, so is his power to understand other greater, and his power to communicate his attitudes and percep tions and ideals to others is correspondingly augmented. Thi accounts for the wealth of expression in modern plastic and pictorial art.

WHY ART BECOMES MORE INTELLECTUALIZED—But this in creased emotional expressiveness of modern art does not con tinue to grow unrestrainedly. Modern life becomes increas ingly intellectual and demands more and more that its mean of communication shall become intellectualized in order t carry the heavy load of ideas and principles which are neces sary to effective adjustment in our abstractly organized world Even plastic and pictorial art are affected by this demand fo intellectualization. This does not mean that art becomes les expressive. As a matter of fact, it becomes more expressive but its expressiveness is more under control. As said earlier modern symbolism in art is largely an attempt to intellectualiz it, to stereotype and conventionalize its forms in order to us them to communicate ideas and systems of thought in thought-heavy civilization. This fact explains the puzzling ol servation so often made by the archeologist to the effect th: the art which is so vigorous and responsive and flexible in th youth of a people often becomes so formal and stereotyped an unbending at just that point where apparently the wealth an culture of the people should have made it most live and vigor ous and emotionally creative. Their culture had by that tim become so intellectualized and the load of tradition and sup posedly valuable meaning which their culture carried so heav and the need for keeping this meaning intact apparently s great, that the attempt to carry it down to posterity and th wish to interpret it uncorrupted to the present and future ger erations through the channels of art forced them to systematiz and stereotype the communication symbols. This froze t the creative spirit in their art.

Perhaps the inferiority of the creative spirit in Roman ar as compared with Greek art, and of late Greek art as con pared with early Greek art, was not due wholly to the esthet and intellectual poverty of the latter peoples, but in part to their greater moral earnestness and deeper sense of the necessity of communicating the cultural values of their civilization and of losing none of it. Such a feeling is likely to arise in the moral and intellectual maturity of a people, especially if this maturity is reached in a declining age economically, as was the case with the Greeks, or in the midst of exacting external pressures, as was the situation with Rome. Such a people no longer feels free to live the life of easy, happy self-expression and experimentation. Their intellectuals and moralists, who may be found among even the artists, feel the necessity of making their productions carry some message. Thus this intellectual and moral weight calls for a formalization and standardization of the prevailing means of communication, especially of those that reach the masses who must be educated in the principles deemed most indispensable. That is why an ethical religion almost, if not quite, always formalizes art, in large degree sterilizes it emotionally by confining its expression in fairly definite channels, and intellectualizes it by causing it to communicate definite and well recognized concepts and values.

ART AS A REFLEX OF NATIONAL LIFE—Great national feeling will do the same for the art of the age. Periods of national integration are not periods of new ideas in art. Art becomes too self-conscious, is forced to assume too much of a message to posterity and to contemporaries. This is Vergil's great fault. He taught a lesson of loyalty and patriotism to the Roman people. Horace, the country gentleman and man of irresponsible pleasures, wrote better poetry although he did not teach better lessons. After the age of political experiments and of economic plenty in Medieval Italy, art lapsed as emotional creation and became didactic. It became representative of the mind seeking for effective adjustment to a narrowing or troublesome environment, and not of the creative joyous spirit of adventure made possible by the possession of economic plenty. Dante's works appeal to us more as a museum depicting his age or as a labored sermon than as a spontaneous expression of poetry. The great literature of Spain falls within the period of expansion and the fruits of victory, but after

Cervantes comes philosophy and didacticism. The eighteenth century in England, an age of political and economic trials, was also an age of decline in all forms of expressive art except character painting and that of the psychological novel, which arose and served as a means of making people more self-analytical to meet the needs of adjustment in their changing age. The bounty of the nineteenth century gave everywhere a new impetus to expressive and creative art. But to-day, with the tide turning towards an economic decline, we are beginning again to stereotype and intellectualize art. We call it modernism, a term which is by no means inappropriate, since the movement to which it applies is the outgrowth of the increasingly derivative and self and socially conscious character of our modern world. It does not matter that the artist does not himself realize the meaning of the new tendencies in his art. He would not be an artist, but a philosopher, if he did not respond readily and almost naïvely to the pressures of his environment, including the "spirit of the times."

SELF-ANALYSIS IN MODERN ART—In those ages in which the heavy demands of adjustment to environment force art into formal and intellectualized or at least into stereotyped and generalized forms of expression and communication, the self-expressive element in art tends to diminish or perish. There is no longer room for Pan and the dance of the dryads and the frolics of the satyr. Life has become a serious business and the weight of its problems turns emotional play into intellectual striving. Even self-expression becomes introspective and analytical. Omar reflects in beautiful numbers upon the meaning and uncertainty of existence. The problem of fate and the uncontrollable character of destiny appear in the Greek drama. Morality plays carry on the religious questionings of the Middle Ages and seek to turn the soul of man inside out. The psychological novel of Fielding, the psychological drama of Ibsen and the modern decadents, the morbid self-examining poetry of the Bohemians and Greenwich Villagers so self-conscious in their attempts to abandon themselves to living, the self-revealing, psychoanalytic novels of Zola and D. H. Lawrence and Theodore Dreiser, the emotional retrospections of William de Morgan, among a flood of other writings of this sort, reveal how uncertain of their behavior our brave protagonists of freedom are in reality in spite of all their redundant protestations. Such art only reveals the fact that the artist, and perhaps the rest of the world with him, no longer dares to respond freely to suggestion and to express himself upon impulse. It is the art of inhibition, not of freedom. It is the art of a struggling world, which finds difficulty in making its adjustments to nature and man, not the art of the care-free creator of types of beauty and will, which grow out of the abundance of free and uninhibited experience. This tendency toward inhibition has grown with numbers and complexity in our world. We are in a retrenching age morally and emotionally.

INTELLECTUAL COMMUNICATION is the latest form to develop. The intellectual symbols used in this type of communication developed through the abstracting and stereotyping of representative symbols used in art in the manner mentioned above. This gave rise to a new type of art, literary art, as distinguished from the old plastic and pictorial art. But literary art is an offshoot of pictorial art through the symbolization of communication terms. The manner in which literary art was developed and abstracted has been treated in a previous chapter.

As shown in Part III, gesture language symbolized emotional attitudinal experiences rather than intellectual ones. No considerable intellectual communication content ever could have been developed through the use of gesture symbols alone. The communication of intellectual content by means of deaf and dumb alphabets became possible only after verbal symbols of the oral or written type had been invented. The deaf and dumb language is a translation or transformation of the written language, just as writing is a translation of oral symbols and communication. But for many reasons the deaf and dumb manual translations are not so effective for communication purposes as is writing. In this age of distance contact groups, which must utilize indirect media of communication, written language is still the chief form employed, despite the appearance of the radio. It alone possesses all of the qualities, such as abstractness, precision, and durable and unchanging content, which enable it to serve the purpose of conveying meaning from persons or groups in one place to others at a great distance in space or time. Radio transmission has some, but not all, of these qualities.

THE DEVELOPMENT OF MECHANISMS OF INTELLECTUAL COMMUNICATION—We have seen how facial expression and gesture, although they probably served as the means of direct communication before the invention of oral language, were greatly developed, supplemented, and enriched by the appearance of verbal language or speech. Speech socialized life as nothing before it had been able to do. Ideas appeared, meanings developed rapidly, an understanding of the world, and a constancy of interpretation of nature unknown in the past, began to appear. Man was approaching to philosophy with the growth of speech. But above all, it permitted the interchange of attitudes, of impressions, fears, joys, information, finally, of abstract ideas and principles. Art was an attempt to objectify these impressions, feelings, attitudes, ideas. Art developed and became as richly expressive, as beautifully descriptive, and as idealistic, finally, as the nature of man became rich with experience, as his inner self developed and rose in organization from chaotic impulses, fears, and tumultuous emotions into an integrated, orderly and continuous personality. As ideas emerged from his emotional complexes and became fixed in his memory as definite norms of measurement or points of reference to which other impressions, impulses, or ideas were referred for comparison and testing, the intellectual content of his mental life appeared and developed.

These ideas also had to be symbolized and expressed or recorded objectively. Thus, as we have seen, picture writing, as the most flexible form of objective expression of mental content, appeared as a modification of primitive pictorial art. Pictographs were at first merely stereotyped ideographs or idea-graphs, so formalized that when once learned they could be recognized anywhere and at all times by those who had mastered them. These were further simplified and stereotyped into the alphabet, and synthetic integration of idea symbols began to be formed abstractly to supplement the concrete ideographs. The ideographs had themselves been objectified to symbolize things and to express action. Abstract qualities were included in the meaning of the ideograph by slight modification of its form. Thus, through the modification and stereotyping of its form, it came in time to express the whole content of spoken language in writing. But the synthetic formation of words on an alphabetical basis, the invention of composite and abstract (non-pictorial) ideographs, marked a great advance in variety of expression and hence of the elaboration of the written content of communication. With the invention of synthetic words it was no longer necessary to find a picture or pictograph for every idea. Writing was simplified in form and made more abstract in content at the same time, and the way was thus opened for the recording and storing and transmission of an illimitable volume of knowledge.

THE FUNCTION OF WRITING IN INTELLECTUAL COMMUNICATION—As man's thinking became more and more projected towards the future, as the result of his undertaking activities which could not be completed immediately, the value of writing as a means of recording plans and aims of behavior became much greater. It is here that the storage function of abstract language symbols became of most use. Not only did written language make it possible for human society to cease living on a hand-to-mouth basis, as it were, but it facilitated coöperation over very wide areas. In our day communication by means of abstract written symbols has made our civilization all but world wide, and we are attempting to build it with reference to future generations as well as our own. Modern science, which is the chief instrument of man in this two-fold aim of his to achieve a widespread and lasting culture, is possible only because we have an abstract written language in which we can express and store and communicate definite and quantitative meanings regarding people and things in such a way that the behavior of others towards these objects may be the same as or comparable to our own, even though these people may be separated from us by great distances of space and time. Only on such a basis of identical or similar responses of different people to the same behavior stimuli, made possible by an abstract and definite language symbolism which unifies space and time, is it possible to achieve that high degree of coöperation and continuity which is the essence of civilization.

THE DOMINANCE OF INDIRECT CONTACT GROUPS RESULTS FROM THE USE OF ABSTRACT AND INTELLECTUAL COMMUNICATION SYSTEMS—Everywhere in the world where this language and its resultant science have penetrated and become a familiar possession, the life of man has become organized into indirect contact or derivative groups. The primary and direct contact groups continue for the performance of certain necessary and valuable types of adjustment, but their character is modified, often even determined quite completely, by the requirements of the abstractly organized overhead or derivative groups. The abstract groups are dominant in modern life, and as long as we live by science and in a world of the widest possible coöperation this will continue to be so. Likewise our lives are molded, indirectly or directly, by the abstract derivative values, ideals and principles, which have grown up as the scientific formulations of projected forms of adjustment in modern society. This is a guarantee that we may live sanely, if not always intimately; although there is no reason why emotional and intimate contacts and attitudes may not also obtain as before, if they conform to the requirements of the more general and abstract principles and values governing collective existence on a wide scale. We can no longer live locally or clannishly and partisanly in a narrow way without danger of conflict with powers greater and more abstract and indomitable than ourselves and our clans. It is the abstract derivative group which rules modern life, and the language of communication which brings about relatively uniform and coöperative responses to the distant and often abstract stimuli which operate upon us collectively is the language of the printed page, the broadcast vocal language of the radio, and the reduplicated pictures or films of the movies. The lecturer also plays his part in carrying the abstract message, but his is a declining rôle. The movie works primarily on the emotions and unconscious behavior sets. It is powerful, perhaps the more so because it works mainly through unconscious emotional mechanisms. But the control of collective behavior of tomorrow lies primarily through the newspaper and the radio. The abstract or derivative groups which possess these mechanisms of communication as their mouthpieces will dominate our civilization. The problem of a democratic and scientifically organized society is the problem of how to socialize these instruments of communication.

SUMMARY AND CONCLUSIONS—Thus we find that indirect contact groups were made possible by new means of communication, especially through the use of abstract language symbols. The earliest language forms were facial and bodily expression, gesture, and vocal cries, words and holophrases. These types of language were used only for communication in the direct contact groups and were first developed in primary groups. But they also served as the bases for the development of language symbols which could be used for communication between members of indirect contact groups. Thus facial expression, posture, and gestures became the early symbols of plastic and pictorial art. And vocal symbols, transferred to written characters, later served for the development of communication in indirect contact groups through intellectual language.

We have described the development of these several forms of indirect communication in the preceding paragraphs of this chapter. As the technique of indirect communication developed and became successively more abstract and intellectual in content, the wider in extent and the more inclusive of numbers and of interests became the indirect contact groups or publics dependent upon these modes of communication. The most widespread publics were not possible before the appearance of writing or printing. And the great diversity of intellectual publics which characterizes modern life had to await the advent of an abundance of printed material. Just what will be the effect of the phonograph, the moving picture, and the radio upon the extent and number, as well as upon the intellectual character, of publics is still a matter of conjecture. But it seems to be a safe generalization to make that every increase in the extent and ease of indirect communication helps to hasten the approach of the fusion of all peoples and of all classes in one general cultural public. Whether the culture of this composite public will be of relatively a high or a low order will depend partly upon the means of communication used, partly upon the degree to which this communication is commercialized, and partly upon the native abilities of the members of this wider public, and their willingness to provide for specialization of function, and for freedom in planning and developing the future.

MATERIALS FOR SUPPLEMENTARY READING

Bogardus, E. S., *Fundamentals of Social Psychology*, Chs. VIII, X, XXIII, XXV
Cooley, C. H., *Social Organization*, Chs. VI, XVI, XVII
Edman, I., *Human Traits and Their Significance*, Ch. X
Ellwood, C. A., *The Psychology of Human Society*, Ch. VII
Ginsberg, M., *The Psychology of Society*, Ch. XI
Hirn, Y., *The Origins of Art*
Lippmann, W., *Public Opinion*, Chs. IV, V, XXI-XXIV
McDougall, W., *The Group Mind*, Ch. VIII
Park and Burgess, *Introduction to the Science of Sociology*, pp. 356-389
Ross, E. A., *Social Control*, Ch. XX

CHAPTER XXXI

TYPES AND FUNCTIONS OF INDIRECT CONTACT GROUPS

DIRECT AND INDIRECT CONTACT GROUPS RELATED—
We found that the direct contact groups fall into two major divisions, the primary and the secondary or derivative groups. The derivative groups furthermore extend beyond the limits of face-to-face associations into the field of indirect contact groups. These indirect contact groups embrace the mixed types referred to in the previous chapter—the associations, societies, and institutions—and a wholly indirect type of group, the public. The public is the psychic aspect of indirect group contacts and may be considered either as an indefinite separate group form, or as the medium in and through which the other indirect group contacts are integrated. Because of this peculiar relationship of publics to other group forms we shall devote most of this chapter to their consideration. Associations, societies, and institutions will here be considered wholly as indirect contact groups, although obviously they are not exclusively such.

There is no distinct dividing line between face-to-face and distance contacts in derivative groups of the simpler sort. The transition in such groups to indirect contacts of the members is a gradual one. Even in the case of the more abstract and far-reaching indirect contact groups—the publics and associations proper—there are upon occasion supplementary direct contacts. Representatives of the publics and associations come together for greater facility and freedom of discussion and for purposes of making quick decisions on some controversial issue. Governments of all types and sizes of territorial units afford good examples of this practice. The same sort of thing occurs in corporations, science, art, educational, reform and other indirect contact associations and publics. Perhaps the chief source of deliberative assemblies in our day is this occasional condensation of publics and associations for purposes of discussion. Deliberative assemblies are ordinarily made up of representatives of publics and associations, and they are formed for purposes of rational discussion. Hence the care generally used in elaborating for their guidance a complex system of rules and a large body of administrative officers. Although we placed the deliberative assembly third in our list of direct contact groups, it is the chief functional connecting link between direct contact groups and publics and associations.

THE CLASSIFICATION OF INDIRECT CONTACT GROUPS—We also found that the various types of direct contact groups already have well established names. We listed and described them without much attempt at classification. They might, however, be classified according to the degree of their permanency, stability, the methods of communication used in them, their size, the types of people included, their functions, the degree to which the members are aware of these functions, the degree of the functional unity among the members, and the degree of compactness and definiteness of organization. In listing and describing the major types of direct contact groups it was not possible to make any very large use of these criteria of classification, because the classifications overlap in such a way that they cannot be made to run parallel. In general, however, these types of groups were listed according to the relative degree of their permanency and the degree of definiteness of the organization, and especially of the rationality of purposes and methods employed.

We find also that publics and other indirect contact groups bear fairly well established class names. One convenient method of classifying them is to follow precedent and, as in the case of direct contact groups, to arrange them under the captions already applied to them by popular usage. But some criterion must be formed to determine the order in which they shall be listed. Indirect contact groups may be classified according to their function, the degree to which the members are aware of the organization and of the function, the degree to which they are organized in the pursuit of some purpose, the kinds of organization (political, economic, esthetic, etc.), the

INDIRECT CONTACT GROUPS 481

instruments by which they achieve their organization or communication of aims and contents, the extent of territory covered, the proportion by ages, sex, and classes of the demotic content included, the degree of compactness or looseness of organization, the kind of leadership accepted or adopted, the permanency, etc. Such classifications as these also overlap and it is not possible to arrange a list of indirect contact groups in such a way as to exemplify all of these classifications in any definite order of succession. Therefore, it will serve our purposes better to describe briefly a few of the more prominent associations and publics under the names popularly assigned to them and to indicate their classification when it seems important to do so.

ASSOCIATIONS of the indirect contact type are the inevitable result of modern life. Modern communication and transportation systems have made it increasingly easy for widely separated individuals to combine into associations for mutual benefit, and the needs of modern life have made it equally necessary. They are purposive and very definitely organized, usually with an elaborate constitution or set of rules. Cole defines an association as "any group of persons pursuing a common purpose or system or aggregation of purposes by a course of coöperative action extending beyond a single act, and, for this purpose, agreeing together upon certain methods of procedure, and laying down, in however rudimentary a form, rules for common action. At least two things are fundamentally necessary to any association—a common purpose or purposes and, to a certain extent, rules of common action."

Associations may be classified according to whether the members have direct or indirect contacts. They may further be classified according to their functions or purposes. Thus there are economic, political, religious, recreational, social reform, etc., associations. They may be grouped according to the nationality of the members into American, English, German, etc. There are various degrees of stability in associations; some are temporary, while others are more permanent. Cole has a two-fold classification, first according to the content of the interests and second according to the method of operation. Thus he divides associations according to the form they take into "political, the vocational and appetitive, the religious, th[e] provident, the philanthropic, the sociable, and the theoretic. On the basis of the method of operation, he distinguishes th[e] administrative and the propagandist. Associations may also b[e] divided into sub-groupings, either on the basis of territory o[r] on the basis of function. Thus there may be a national o[r] an international association with various sub-association[s]. Also there are economic associations with sub-groupings fo[r] philanthropic, political, or other action; or religious associa[-]tions with sub-divisions for philanthropic, educational, politica[l] or economic purposes; etc.

The members of associations are usually very conscious o[f] their membership in the organization. They feel bonds o[f] community with other members in carrying out the purposes o[f] the association. Thus in an economic association, such as [a] trade union, the members feel bound by ties of common inte[r]est, although in other fields, religious, political, or racial, the[y] may be more or less antagonistic to each other. Similarly me[n] may have religious interests in common if they belong to t[he] same religious association and still experience economic o[r] political antagonisms. This illustrates a very significant pri[n]ciple regarding indirect contact groups, especially of the ass[o]ciation type. They claim only a relatively small part of t[he] personality, not the whole of it. One can belong fully to on[ly] one family, one play group, or one neighborhood, and to on[ly] one face-to-face group of any kind at a time. He may belo[ng] to as many associations as he has diverse interests, and this [is] true in the main of other indirect contact groups also. T[he] attempts of radical labor leaders to make the workers "cla[ss] conscious" have often failed because all individuals have mo[re] than economic interests, and belong to other associations tha[n] merely the economic. The overlapping of associations, soc[i]eties, and institutions is possible because of the segregation [of] interests within the individual. He associates himself [in] indirect contact groups according to the various types [of] interests which he experiences. Sometimes these interests a[re] based on his organic drives. In other cases they are the res[ult] of his acquired behavior patterns. Frequently they rest up[on] both types of impulses. But on the whole there is perha[ps] some tendency for indirect contact associations to be built primarily upon acquired interests, while the native drives more frequently find direct expression through face-to-face group contacts. There are more acquired interests in modern life than in primitive, consequently there are more associations and other types of indirect contact groups.

The association cuts across publics, although for certain purposes it constitutes a public in itself. It also crosses the boundaries of societies, although perhaps less frequently. Associations cut across each other also, since individuals may belong to several different associations. Economic associations are perhaps the most far-reaching in crossing the boundaries of other indirect contact groups because in cases of acute conflict within the individual the sustenance interests will usually win out. Political and religious associations also are far-reaching.

Most associations of any degree of permanency or importance have some organ of communication, such as a magazine, newspaper, advertising, radio, etc.

SOCIETIES—The concept of society is not at all clear-cut and precise, but indicates rather the fact of reciprocal and coöperative relations of human beings as they function in primary groups, associations, publics, institutions, etc. We frequently speak of all mankind or of a nation as a whole as society by which we mean, as Park and Burgess indicate, "a constellation of other smaller societies, that is to say, races, peoples, parties, factions, cliques, clubs, etc." As Cole states it, society in general is "a resultant of the interaction and complementary character of the various functional associations and institutions. Its concern is solely with the organized coöperation of human beings." It is readily seen, therefore, that all the groups we have discussed, primary and derivative, of the direct or indirect contact type, together or any combination of them, constitute a society. In fact any group whatever may be called a society, although such usage is indefinite and of doubtful value. In primitive society, past and present, the direct contact groups predominate, but in modern society, as we have already emphasized, the tendency is for the derivative groups to dominate the whole. Thus publics and associations come to be more important in determining policies than the family, the neighborhood, or the local community. A comparison of modern and medieval European societies illustrates clearly this tendency. Modern democratic societies, as contrasted with feudal societies, are likewise illustrative of this principle. The loyalties of the individual in a feudal society are chiefly to the local primary group or community and secondarily to the king or chief who symbolizes the whole organization. In modern democratic societies, one's first allegiance is to the abstract society as a whole, and secondarily to his state, his city, or his community. If there is a conflict of interests, the good of the larger society is ordinarily conceived to come first. If we accept Giddings' classification of societies into sympathetic, congenial, approbational, despotic, authoritative, conspiral, contractual, and idealistic, we may still observe this principle working in view of the fact that modern societies are more and more of the idealistic type which generally involve indirect rather than direct association.

TYPES OF PUBLICS—NATIONALITIES—Perhaps the widest reaching publics possessing any considerable degree of consciousness of kind or of similarity of purpose of the members are nationalities. Nationalities are also societies. We have already mentioned the functional types of consciousness which help to integrate nationalities. Each of these factors also serves as the basis for the integration of publics of greater or less extent than nationalities. Thus we have language publics, religious publics, and various groups centering about all sorts of customs, traditions, conventions, beliefs, folkways, mores, etc., such as may be integrated into publics.

LANGUAGE PUBLICS—Since indirect contact groups or publics are formed and held together by means of communication, language is naturally the most important of all of the factors integrating publics. Language similarity merely provides the mechanism for the integration of the public. Of itself it is not determinative of the degree of compactness or of consciousness of a common purpose or of the type of organization and leadership of the public. These must depend primarily on other factors, such as similarity of the people included and of their needs, the geographic setting in which they are located, the technique at their disposal for making a common language effective in communication, the degree and kinds of concerted opposition to their functional unity and culture which they encounter from without, the kinds and efficiency of their educational systems, and the degree and quality of their culture. Publics always tend to be as widespread as the common language, but this correspondence of territory with language may be prevented especially by conflict in national or economic or religious interests, by distance, or by differences in degrees of culture. Radical differences in culture may amount almost to a difference in languages, because of the differences in terminology and subtlety of meaning involved in expression. Dialects also correspond pretty closely to grades in culture.

Some publics transcend the barriers of language differences, especially when economic, geographic, religious, or political, and even cultural interests are widespread. Thus there is developing a sort of vague world-wide public consciousness as the result of international trade and finance. The great world religions reach across language barriers, modern empires include many tongues, and the scientific public is truly international. But all publics which extend beyond uniform language areas are ordinarily not highly conscious of their similarity of mind and of purpose. They are easily broken up when smaller and more highly unified other publics come in conflict with them. The pages of history are filled with attempts to expand and integrate public opinion over wide areas, including many languages, peoples, economic interests, and diverse customs and beliefs, in the support of political units and powers. The failures are almost as numerous as the attempts. Success is, however, more marked in our day than at any previous time in history, because with the growth in means of communication there has been a parallel expansion of economic interests and enterprises and of culture. The radical dissimilarity of peoples tends to disappear, religions become more tolerant of each other, and customs and beliefs tend to be adjusted throughout the world. An international language would be of the very greatest service in furthering these uniformizing tendencies and in the production of more widespread publics.

SOCIAL AND ECONOMIC CLASSES AS PUBLICS—The variou[s] industrial and occupational and social class publics perhap[s] come next after language in the matter of extent. Moder[n] states tend somewhat to be integrated about unity of economi[c] opportunity, natural resources and other economico-geographi[c] factors. Unity of public consciousness and of public opinio[n] usually follow in the wake of political integration, or perhap[s] as often produce political integration, if not prevented b[y] other interrupting factors. Those of the same occupationa[l] professional, and social class interests throughout the worl[d] also tend to become aware of their common interests and c[f] the advisability of coöperating. Socialist leaders boasted be[-] fore the Great War that the working classes of the world we[re] a brotherhood, of which the red flag (symbolizing communit[y] of blood) was the symbol, and that no more wars could occu[r] because the workers of the nations would not fight against eac[h] other. Likewise, when the Great War had progressed fo[r] about three years and there was apparent danger that its gre[at] destructiveness of life and property and the burden of de[bt] which it was piling up might induce the revolt of the workir[g] classes after it closed, Lord Lansdowne appealed to the rulin[g] classes of all countries to stop the war in their common interes[t.] When republics were new in the eighteenth and early nin[e-] teenth centuries, the titled and privileged classes of all countri[es] made common war upon them. This was particularly true [in] the case of the French Revolution. The Holy Alliance is a[n] other example of this tendency. To-day the prevailing publ[ic] opinion of the world seems to be directed against the sovi[et] republic of Russia.

This coöperative or public consciousness of classes, based [on] class interests, appears to be growing everywhere througho[ut] the world. Long ago it had developed within national a[nd] local territorial units. It has always been the chief line [of] cleavage between political parties, as earlier it was the chi[ef] basis of the distinction between rulers and ruled. The chi[ef] psycho-social significance of political parties is that the fo[r-] merly unrecognized and unintegrated classes have develop[ed] sufficient public consciousness to organize as indirect conta[ct] groups or associations and publics and to substitute parliame[nt] tary and publicity methods of promoting their interests for the old practices of intermittent and sporadic revolt through violence.

RELIGION AND SCIENCE AS BASES OF PUBLICS—Religions were formerly, and still are, powerful integrations of public opinion. At certain periods of history they have overshadowed or dominated the organization of practically all other types of publics. This was because the content of their religious public consciousness appeared to men to be the most important for the control of human relationships. The beliefs of religion, touching as they did all aspects of man's most fundamental relations and obligations, dominated his hygiene, diet, ethical values, reproductive and domestic contacts, social obligations, esthetic attitudes and opinions, even his economic and political practices. No public or association could be formed which was not acceptable to the dominant religion. Tolerance of different religious beliefs was impossible. But with the development of a wider range of contacts made possible by the growth of better facilities for communication, which have brought all the peoples of the world and their practices and beliefs into contact with each other, a larger degree of tolerance has developed. Still perhaps this tolerance is in some religions more the result of a truce or compromise than of a decrease in the dogmatism of religious beliefs or faith in the special efficacy of particular rituals and magic.

But even religious dogmatism has gradually been diminished by the development of a secular philosophy, as earlier described, and the growth of demonstrated scientific data and principles. The spreading abroad of new knowledge has tended to weaken the grasp of religious tradition upon the control of human conduct and to deritualize adaptive behavior and to advance religion to the function of a social and supernatural sanction of the practices approved by science. The old religious dogmas and rituals were usually based upon what appeared to be the best procedures men had discovered at the time the beliefs and practices were reduced to dogmas and ritual. The effect of the new learning of science is to advance the beliefs and practices of religion to the level of a saner scientific knowledge and practice. Because religion has often opposed this rational modernization it has lost caste with many, and science has correspondingly gained. As a consequence the power and scope of the religious publics have declined, while those of science and of philosophic opinion, sound and unsound, have greatly increased. The number of publics or of integrations of public opinion about all sorts of beliefs and isms in our day is astounding. But the contents of these are gradually being tested by the standards of science and order is being brought out of this chaotic condition.

ART PUBLICS, ETC.—Other important publics are being organized around fashions, fads, crazes, and conventional beliefs of all sorts. These are discussed in the chapter on non-institutional controls and need not be dealt with here. Artistic or esthetic publics also constitute a considerable phase of the organized behavior of man. Perhaps enough has been said in Part IV about the communicative function of art in society to indicate the social importance of art publics. One additional remark is perhaps appropriate. The substitution of esthetic standards of measurement of the value of individual and collective behavior for scientifically tested utilitarian values may have a very unfavorable effect upon social organization and survival. Esthetic standards are almost wholly subjective and the amount of correction which they receive from the uniformizing effect of public opinion in the field of art—if this public opinion is the product of esthetic rather than of scientific and utilitarian judgment—will not serve to render them truly objective. Since art, like religion, is so largely concerned with emotional attitudes and values, the artist classes, like the priestly, are always in danger of pronouncing judgment upon behavior from the standpoint of esthetic or feeling criteria. This must be corrected by an appeal to the sciences, especially to the social sciences.

INSTITUTIONAL PUBLICS—Publics also grow up about all sorts of local and national interests. We have not space to deal with these individually. But the major interests of mankind tend to organize for their satisfaction vast systems of technique, of beliefs and procedure, which remain relatively constant, at least in form, over long periods of time. These relatively stable integrations of adjustment technique are institutions. The technique is held together functionally by the unified approval of the group which constitutes the personality content of the institution. Each institution has its public, whether it be religious, political, domestic, economic, artistic, or any type whatever. Each institution is, in a sense, a public. The nature and functions of institutions will be discussed in a separate chapter.

In this discussion we have given most of our attention to the relative extent and functional solidarity of publics, which enable them to survive in competition with other publics. Also our discussion has not attempted to show the effects of different degrees of compactness of organization and of consciousness of purpose in the members of publics upon the functioning of those publics. This is an important phase of a complete treatment of the subject of publics. Some implications regarding this matter will develop incidentally in connection with the discussion of non-institutional and institutional controls. There is not space for a more detailed analysis of publics, and such is not necessary in a general treatise on the principles of social psychology. A detailed application of our classification to the problems of social organization and control would more properly come in separate treatises on those subjects.

EFFECTS OF THE WIDER CONTACTS OF INDIRECT CONTACT GROUPS—SYMPATHY AND TOLERANCE—The expansion of groups and the development of contacts have had many important effects upon the life and attitudes of modern populations. One of the most obvious of these is the broadening of the sympathies of modern cultured peoples. The increase of our indirect contacts, if not direct ones, through increased travel has brought us into quasi-contact with the most distant peoples. We have learned facts regarding the more intimate aspects of their lives—their struggles, fears, hopes, aims, fortitude, sincerity, and many other qualities. We have found them, although in different clothes and with various customs and languages, surprisingly like ourselves in the fundamental aims and relationships of life. Their sorrows and joys, amusements and sense of responsibility, their needs and efforts at their satisfaction, loyalties and affections, are of a pattern with our own, although their religious beliefs may be different, their governments undemocratic or even unintelligent, and their languages "sound like some meaningless jargon." Human nature, like human problems, is not so different in all parts of the world, although it may be expressed through different forms of behavior and different symbols, and be manifested in different degrees. As a result of these indirect contacts through the press, the stories of missionaries, traders, returned travelers, and pictures, we have come to understand the fundamental aspects of peoples under the superficial covering of dissimilarity of dress, beliefs, and mannerisms. Our humanitarianism has broadened. The old classification of the world into Greeks and barbarians, Jews and Gentiles, or kindred terms of contrast, has all but disappeared. We still recognize, to be sure, differences in the degrees of achievement of civilization and in the fitness of men by training and outlook to carry on the work of science and culture. But we no longer tolerate to the same extent acts of cruelty to and oppression of the weak by the powerful, of the ignorant by the sophisticated, merely because the former classes are far away and speak a different language, worship strange gods and wear "absurd" clothes. We have come in some degree to grasp the relativity of things social. We recognize, at least to some extent, that nothing in the matter of clothing could be more absurd than our fashions. Contacts with many peoples and philosophies have shown the more intellectual among us that practically all peoples have believed themselves to possess revealed and infallible religions. Tolerance and a growing sense of a world-wide brotherhood of purpose, if not of race, are the chief fruits of our wider, derivative contacts.

LIMITATIONS UPON TOLERANCE AND SYMPATHY—But we should not deceive ourselves into believing that this tolerance and sympathy are fully achieved and that all men adopt them fully. Although the range of sympathy has vastly increased, even as the range of our indirect contacts has grown, sympathy and tolerance for things unlike what we know are still very superficial and thin. We accept the peoples of a different color, religion, dress, or philosophy into the general fold of our humanity only if they do not come into conflict with us economically and politically. We have learned through the development of scientific standards of social behavior and a comparative study of the mores and folkways of all peoples the relativity of beliefs based on tradition rather than knowledge, of color, of the cut of clothes, of customs and conventions of social intercourse. But our economic interests and the political interests which support these come nearer home to us and we are less tolerant of any differences in the behavior of others which lead to conflict regarding these fundamental interests. We would no longer fight an international war because of differences in religion or of dress or of customs and beliefs about magic or philosophy, as our predecessors living in an age less enlightened by intimate knowledge of other peoples are supposed to have done, but we do go to war over disputes regarding territory, the non-payment of debts, the exploitation of natural resources, and the like. Tolerance of the economic conflicts of interest can be achieved only with the greatest difficulty. The better policy is to cause such conflicts to disappear through some form of coöperation which makes for a greater uniformity of economic interest over the world as a whole.

DISTANCE CONTACT SYMPATHIES WEAKER—The newer and wider-spread sympathies are also less intense than the old ones which grew up in the primary and face-to-face groups because of the difference in the ways in which the two types of sympathy and understanding are built up in us. The sympathies and loyalties of the direct contact groups are largely concretely emotional, being the product quite as much of sensory contacts and impressions as of an intellectual understanding. But we must rely in the main upon indirect and non-sensory contacts, or the mediation of intellectual symbols, for our understanding of superficially unlike peoples at a distance. Emotional attitudes towards such people can be aroused only through the translation of these intellectual symbols and concepts into the language of the senses and emotions. Also our contacts with those nearest us, and in face-to-face relations with us, are much more numerous than those with people at a distance. Hence, concreteness, volume, and persistency of contacts all operate in favor of the greater sympathy for those near us and condition our impulses to a stronger emotional response in their behalf. We ordinarily still think more of members of our immediate family than of any one else in the world, more of our kin than of acquaintances, of friends than of strangers, of fellow nationals than of members of other nationalities within the same race, and of members of our own race than of other races. But this is not necessarily true of those who have developed strongly the intellectual methods of understanding and have subjected themselves rigorously to abstract controls over behavior.

THE EFFECT UPON PERSONALITY—This expansion of contacts to the indirect and derivative sphere, and of our sympathies and understanding to include all men, has had a marked effect upon the personalities of the modern cultivated man and woman. They have become more cosmopolitan, urbane, and complete or well rounded. They are perhaps less intense and impulsive, but they are also less bigoted. The behavior of such personalities is sure to be more rational and tolerant. It is the ignorant person, whether ignorant of human nature at home or abroad, who resorts most easily to force in minor maladjustments with companions or nations. The cosmopolitan personality can see things from many angles and distinguish fundamental conflicts from the incidental and temporary. The intellectualized and cosmopolitan personality does not really lose force of character, although at first glance it may seem to do so. The bigoted or ignorant man may be the first to take direct and overt action, because he has only one resource in solving his problem—the one which is most obvious and direct. But the intellectual personality, whose sympathies and understanding are broader, usually gains accuracy and effectiveness through his apparent delay in action. He transfers his behavior from the overt to the internal sphere and works out a "solution." He is ruled by intellect rather than by emotions. In the end his solution is best and will endure longest. If all past religious disputes and conflicts of cultures and races, of mores and of beliefs, could have been settled by the method of the cosmopolitan character instead of by that of the bigot of the narrow view, the world would be richer and happier now. Even in the twentieth century we need nothing else so much as tolerance produced by a wider understanding of men and institutions everywhere, and a final resort to the arbitra-

INDIRECT CONTACT GROUPS

tion of science instead of to that of force in the settlement of disputes and conflicts of interest.

THE DEVELOPMENT AND UTILIZATION OF SOCIAL SCIENCE AS A RESULT—Social science is the crowning achievement of this intellectualization of the means of communication which has arisen as the result of the expansion of group contacts and of the use of abstract symbols as the media of language. As the substitution of vocal symbols for gestures and of writing for pictures in communication brought language from an emotional to an intellectual plane, so has the invention of quantitative symbols and logic within language given rise to science. Gradually the emotional content in language gives way to the intellectual and the indefinite and ambiguous in communication are replaced by the accurate and the quantitative. The result is that our understanding of our world, near and far, is greatly increased and made more definite and dependable. The life of emotion does not disappear with the intellectualization of language and the scientific testing of hypotheses, beliefs, and behavior. It is only controlled and made effectively functional in adjustment situations by the application of scientific tests and direction to it. The human spirit is set free from prejudice, narrowness, and bigotry by this intellectual and scientific dominance, and a wider range of coöperation and a more effective type of collective behavior are made possible.

MOB-MINDEDNESS AND MISREPRESENTATION IN INDIRECT CONTACT GROUPS—But it must not be supposed that the advent of science and the intellectualization of our contacts has freed us entirely from the dangers of the mob spirit and rule by suggestion in the interests of prejudiced or corrupt factions such as we found to obtain so easily in the direct contact groups. Mob-mindedness does exist in the public as well as in the crowd, as may be illustrated by the panic and the boom and in war time. It may be carried by the newspaper, radio, moving picture, propagandist orator, bigoted preacher, or any other agency of indirect communication which is operative in the derivative group. Abstract words after all have their emotional associations and may condition irrational responses. And much of our language is still largely emotional in its content. The range of epithets which may be employed by the propagandist and partisan to produce almost exclusively emotional and irrational responses is very wide. Figures of speech with emotional connotations, an emotional style, scores of methods of appealing to prejudice and bigotry rather than to reason, to fear instead of to confidence and constructive tolerance, may be employed by writers for the daily paper as well as by the orator. Incendiary and bigoted writings and speeches broadcast by radio are altogether too prevalent to-day for the good of our civilization. The movies, with their more direct and immediate appeal to emotion through the depicting of gesture and facial expression, can be and too frequently are made powerful instruments of partisan propaganda. We have discovered the language of science, but it is still too frequently neglected in organizing the public opinion and collective behavior of mankind to have dissipated the mob spirit entirely.

OVERCOMING OBSTACLES TO RATIONAL CONTROL IN INDIRECT CONTACT GROUPS—And yet we have made important advances in the direction of the substitution of the language of science and of scientific thinking for emotional appeal and behavior. We have achieved the method by which collective behavior may be reorganized and rationally controlled in the interest of a truly coöperative and democratic social order. There are yet some obstacles to putting this method completely into practice. One is that we have not yet been able, in spite of the rapid extension of our educational system, to bring the majority of mankind within a reasonable distance intellectually of our leading scientific thinkers. The data and principles of science must be made as nearly universal possessions as possible. The church must become a coöperator with the school in this respect, in order that true knowledge and a true religion may develop together and that there shall not be a fundamental opposition between the two greatest interests of mankind. Another difficulty is that we have not yet learned how to make the dissemination of knowledge and the creation of public opinion a function of the total social interest instead of partisanship and prejudice. Unification of beliefs and dictation of opinion by some official bureau or agency are not desirable, at least under present conditions. But there is the greatest need for some method of checking willful misrepresentation through press, radio, movie, and the speeches of propagandists wherever such misrepresentation exists and in whatever cause. Scientific accuracy of statement of fact, or the statement of opinion as opinion and not as fact, are the ends to be desired. Just how these ends are to be attained is not yet clear, but they are probably not impossible of achievement. A reasonably proper functioning of derivative group contacts and controls and the normal existence of derivative groups are not possible without them.

Nor need we despair of achieving such ends. We saw in the preceding chapters that whenever human beings are in face-to-face relationships, their behavior tends to become emotional. We saw that, in order to curb this tendency, elaborate rules, codes, parliamentary procedure, detailed administrative laws, and other technique were developed. The best illustration of this attempt at rational control of face-to-face contacts is the deliberative assembly. A description of its method of operation, its weaknesses as well as its strong points, was included in Chapter XXVIII. Etiquette, manners, "good form" in general, are other less rational attempts to prevent human contacts from becoming too uncontrolled. If such controls could be achieved in the more emotional face-to-face contacts, it should be possible for the human mind to devise equally efficient controls to prevent non-face-to-face contacts from being perverted by mob-mindedness.

MATERIALS FOR SUPPLEMENTARY READING

Bogardus, E. S., *Fundamentals of Social Psychology,* Chs. XVII, XXIV
Cole, G. D. H., *Social Theory*
Cooley, C. H., *Social Organization,* Ch. VIII
—, *Social Process,* Ch. XXIV
Ellwood, C. A., "Intolerance," *Pub. Amer. Sociological Soc.,* XIX: 1-14
Ginsberg, M., *The Psychology of Society,* Ch. X
Harris and Hooke, *The Community Newspaper*
Irwin, W., "The American Newspaper," *Colliers,* XLVI and XLVII. (A series of fifteen articles running from January 21 to July 29)
Le Bon, G., *The Psychology of Peoples*
Lippmann, W., *Liberty and the News*
McDougall, W., *The Group Mind,* Chs. V-VII, X
Park, R. E., *The Immigrant Press and Its Control*
Pillsbury, W. B., *The Psychology of Nationalism and Internationalism,* Chs. VI, VII
Ross, E. A., *Principles of Sociology,* Ch. XLIV
Yarros, V. S., "Journalism, Ethics and Common Sense," *International Jour. Ethics,* XXXII: 410-419

CHAPTER XXXII

THE INFLUENCE OF CONTACTS UPON INDIVIDUAL AND COLLECTIVE BEHAVIOR

In the preceding six chapters of Part IV we have bee[n] concerned with the classification and analysis of group form[s] and the attitudes of people within these groups. In this an[d] the four subsequent chapters we shall discuss the influence [of] group contacts upon individual and collective behavior. Th[e] theme will be discussed generally in this chapter and applic[a]tions of these processes to special problems of control will [be] taken up in the four following chapters. Thus, Chapte[rs] XXXIII and XXXIV will consider the question of leadersh[ip] and individual response to leadership. Chapters XXXV an[d] XXXVI will give an introductory analysis of non-institution[al] and institutional controls and the question of social change [in] a controlled situation.

THE INDIVIDUAL AND THE GROUP—Psychologically the i[n]dividual is human by virtue of belonging to a group. W[e] cannot even conceive of a human being apart from groups. [A] person who had never known group contacts would have bee[n] deprived of parents from infancy. He would know no gover[n]ment and experience no personal ties. He would produ[ce] everything he consumed. He would speak a unique languag[e] or rather none at all, for there would be no adequate relatio[n]ships to condition in him language responses. Finally, th[is] hypothetical person, like the animals, would have no self-co[n]sciousness, for self-consciousness arises only as the other p[ole] to social consciousness, and this also would be wanting to hi[m].

It is evident that an individual apart from a group wou[ld] certainly be far less than human. Descriptions of individua[ls] brought up with a minimum of human contacts make this clea[r]. The very fact of being human implies ties with other hum[ans] beings. Feral men do not walk or talk or think, or even perceive things, the way we do. This is what we would expect from our analysis in Part III where we saw that other personalities are indispensable in developing our own. But even after the human personality is adequately developed for functioning, the group has an important conditioning effect upon his responses. He is always a member of many groups, face-to-face and non-face-to-face, primary and derivative. But different types of group contacts produce different types of behavior. We will outline these differences very briefly.

I. INTELLECTUAL REACTIONS—*Coöperative Contacts*—We have already seen that the individual is likely to do abstract thinking in terms of verbal symbols, or even in the form of a conversation with either himself or a hypothetical companion. This is, as Cooley says, because "The impulse to communicate is not so much a result of thought as it is an inseparable part of it." In cases where our companions are imaginary, however, there is no necessity for "thinking a thing through," for the hypothetical person will certainly not be offended or mind greatly if we suddenly switch our train of thought from one thing to another without making it clear. And when we are thinking to ourselves, this is very likely to happen. Most of us when alone, with the exception of trained thinkers like Spencer, who could not stop thinking until he had solved the problem, dismiss an intellectual difficulty when it becomes too intense, if indeed we attempt to think about it at all. We are easily distracted, and extraneous stimuli can deflect the logical continuity of our thinking.

But when another person is actually present, we cannot be so flighty in our thinking. The necessity for communicating our thoughts overtly is a great stimulus to clarify our own ideas. We cannot jump dizzily from one idea to another according to the more or less random association of solitary thinking. The other individual holds us down to some sort of logical continuity and clarity. Furthermore, he adds a different viewpoint or additional data and thus fertilizes our own intellectual processes. In a friendly discussion, the give and take increase the efficiency of thinking far beyond its usual effectiveness. Many people think only under the stimulus of another personality. Two heads are indeed better than one in solving intellectual problems. Intellectual team work is as significant as other types of coöperation.

The introduction of a third person does not add so much relatively to efficiency in thinking as does the second. We might say that the additional persons usher in a condition of diminishing returns in thinking. Each individual is under less necessity of thinking out every point advanced by the others and he has less opportunity. He can relax more intellectually for if he does not carry on, the others will, until the discussion again turns towards matters with which he is already familiar or until he can "make a point." He does not have to parry the intellectual thrusts with so much acumen or receive them with so much understanding. Usually there is an alignment of two or more against one, or a larger group "lines up" on issues or takes sides. Thus one individual must carry the whole burden of his side whereas the other parties are sharing the other point of view. In cases of lining up by sides the intellectual fire is likely to become extremely desultory and the marshaling of ideas is likely to become lax and inefficient. Or the whole matter may degenerate into display of argumentative or forensic talents, or "showing off."

If, on the other hand, all are equally stimulated, the struggle to get a hearing often becomes quite intense. All speak at once and the tendency is for the group to become excited and emotional rather than to remain intellectual. Intense group discussion is usually lacking in intellectual generalship. But if the group becomes materially larger there results either the discussion group or the deliberative assembly, or possibly a mob. If the orderly type of group prevails, the discussion is likely to become a debate, and teams appear. At any rate, rules of order must be invoked to keep the atmosphere rational, for the tendency toward emotionality is greatly intensified. The debate is a well recognized form of the discussion group, usually with the addition of an audience. Thinking in such a group may be highly effective, but here we are dealing largely with the effects of an audience, and we may now turn to this topic.

Non-coöperative contacts: the effects of an audience—In case the other individuals are added, not coöperatively, but s an audience, the effects of their presence may be somehat different. When the others are our intellectual equals, whether they are sympathetic or critical listeners, the fact of their presence may stimulate us in much the same manner as though they actually participated in the thinking. We feel ourselves under the necessity of making a good showing before our friends or enemies and of meeting the arguments which we assume they would be likely to oppose to us if they were taking part in the discussion. On the other hand, an audience, even of one unfamiliar or unfriendly individual, may completely disorganize our thinking, and reduce us to an emotional state. This occurs in the case of the child who knows his lesson perfectly, but when he comes to recite it to his teacher, forgets it entirely, because of anticipated criticism. In a large audience, the result may be the same, and we call it "stage fright." In such cases the mere presence of so many unfamiliar faces causes us to assume that they will be critical or even unfriendly. The addition of a great many persons, however, may cause the individual personalities to drop out, and the emotional disturbance may thus, in the absence of any unfriendly demonstration, be minimized.

Experiments seem to indicate that as a rule the audience has a stimulating effect upon individuals, especially in familiar situations. The effect, moreover, is most marked in the case of slow thinkers or workers. Dress rehearsals are notoriously poor, even when the preparation is excellent, as actual performance later on before an audience demonstrates. It has often been said with more truth than is at first apparent that one of the chief functions of a class is to make the instructor think. We may even learn more by teaching than by being taught. The stimulating effect of the audience may operate even when the audience is not actually present, as in the case of the author in his study, the radio performer, the phonograph artist, the moving picture actor, the student preparing a lesson. In such cases the individual responds to his audience projectively. In any case, unless the behavior is reduced to an emotional reaction, the audience is likely to improve the quality of the response, particularly if it is appreciative. The great achievements of great artists before adoring audiences are not wholly subjective to the audiences. According to the theory of feeling set forth in Part II, it is precisely under such conditions of approval that the technic responses are least inhibited and performance is freest. This is a fact which all good teachers appreciate.

Effects of the presence of co-workers—When others are added not as audience, nor yet as competitors or coöperators, but as co-workers, the results are slightly different. In such cases, comparisons are made between the work of individuals done alone and that done in the presence of others. Results of tests as given by Allport and others seem to show an increase in speed and quantity of performance but a decrease in quality or accuracy. The presence of others stimulates motor responses but lowers the mental or logical efficiency of the individual, perhaps largely because the responses are speeded and because the rate of reaction is made too uniform. Also interrupting stimuli intrude and the worker does not have a chance to solve his problem in his own way. It is more difficult to think to ourselves in a group than when alone, but it is easier to do things overtly. The effect of others upon judgment is in the direction of moderation. Allport makes the following generalization from results of experiments: "There is a tendency toward moderation in judgments made in concert with others, the individual avoiding those extreme judgments at either end of the scale which he does not hesitate to make when judging alone. . . . To think and to judge with others is to submit one's self unconsciously to their standards. We may call this the attitude of social conformity."

Competitive contacts—Allport summarizes the results of tests on the effects of rivalry and competition. The effect of rivalry "is that of emotional reënforcement. . . . It improves the speed and quantity rather than the quality of the work in which it is operative. Rivalry, like social facilitation, varies with age, sex, and personality. . . . When rivalry produces a social increment in a group there is a tendency for the performances of the individuals to approach a common level."

Hostile contacts—If the other individuals added are antagonistic, the situation becomes emotional rather than intellectual, since the other individuals produce an interference behavior. There is no gain in the accuracy of behavior, there is usually a loss. A conflict of behavior patterns arises which inhibits or blocks the response and interferes with the technique. The effect upon personality is to make us more stubborn and set in our opinions. Experiments on the results of razzing show a loss in efficiency under the stimulus of a hostile environment. This is a fact very well known to the "rooters" of rival athletic teams, who sometimes use the method to the extent of completely demoralizing the weaker or less aggressive team. Some individuals, however, seem to thrive on opposition. They need the extra stimulus to put them in fighting trim. But their resulting efforts are more likely to be characterized by increased drive than by greater accuracy or insight. Ajax and Hercules fought with most energy, if somewhat blindly, when completely aroused. Other personalities, especially those who have been unfortunately repressed or dominated in childhood, are likely to collapse under opposition. Here, as in the case of the effects of rivalry, individual differences enter in.

II. EMOTIONAL REACTIONS—*Effects of Isolation*—The emotional results of isolation are perhaps greater than the intellectual, and more serious. We are accustomed to think of the solitary individual as more rational and less emotional than the individual in a group. This may sometimes be the case, but it is not necessarily so. Other personalities are the most fertile sources of stimulation, and therefore there is likely to be a great deal of neural interference or synthesis in the presence of others, and a consequent heightened emotional state. The result is somewhat the same if our contact with the other personalities is indirect or through symbolic media, such as books. But continued isolation is likely to produce equally intense emotional reactions. Ross cites the results of solitary confinement on prisoners. At the end of one year of solitary confinement in Auburn prison in 1821, five prisoners were dead, one had killed himself, another was mad, and the rest were melancholy." In another case at Mountjoy, "nearly one-half went mad before their release and many others died soon afterward." "Victims of long-enforced solitude generally become the prey of melancholia, delusions, and hallucinations. They cease to have emotions, shrink from the sight of others, an[d] perhaps return voluntarily to their cell as to a grateful shelter. Even the normal individual who is cut off from contacts be[-]comes "queer," "uncouth," "self-centered," "morbid," whe[n] not definitely pathological. Dementia præcox is described b[y] some psychiatrists as a "shutting in" of the personality. [It] requires the stimulating effect of the presence of others t[o] bring out the full force of the positive personality traits. Th[e] wisdom of the hermit has perhaps been overestimated. Ce[r]tainly his outlook has traditionally been a recessive, not a[n] aggressive, one. He would solve problems by retiring fro[m] them, not by grappling with them.

Isolation need not, of course, be physical. In many cases [it] is psychic only. It is axiomatic that one may be more alone i[n] a city than in the country. G. Stanley Hall said that the sadde[st] thing in his life was his isolation. Great men are usual[ly] isolated, for there are few who can understand them adequatel[y]. But even in these cases, they are likely to find emotional com[-]pensation through their symbolic contacts with the great me[n] of history. On the other hand, people often voluntarily see[k] isolation by withdrawing from too stimulating contacts [in] order that they may preserve their strength and maintain the[ir] emotional balance, or to regain them when temporarily d[e]pleted.

Coöperative or sympathetic contacts—The individual wh[o] is full of emotion—joy or sorrow or worry, for examp[le] —feels better if he can unload it or share it with others. W[e] often speak of "unburdening ourselves," and it is axiomat[ic] that "confession is good for the soul." Some psychologis[ts] claim that the chief therapeutic value of psychoanalysis resul[ts] from the fact that the neurotic individual gains a sympathe[tic] listener in the psychoanalyst. The theory of transference seem[s] to bear this out. The necessity for communicating emotion[al] attitudes seems to be even greater than for intellectual r[e]sponses. In the case of the joyous emotions, those which i[n]volve neural synthesis and incrementation, this may be due [to] the fact that inner activity is becoming so intense that unle[ss] overt activity can be substituted, blocking will occur. Or [it] may represent the seeking of further stimulation and reë[n-] forcement from the individual who shares our emotion. In the case of the unpleasant emotions, confessing or unburdening our souls objectifies the conflict and thus makes it easier for us to handle it. We may feel relieved, on the other hand, when we communicate our secret sins because of the sympathy, real or anticipated, of the other individual. Whatever the reason, it is a fact that most people experience a fundamental need for emotional communication.

Even when the emotional attitude is not intense, and where no intellectual problem is involved, the desire for emotional response is frequently great. People like to sit and gossip or chat regarding inconsequential matters merely for the sake of the warmth of human contacts. We like to describe our adventures, or feats and exploits. It is a method of preserving and enhancing our self-feeling. On the playground, at the party, on the bathing beach, or in the parade and in "Peacock Alley" it finds cruder expression in deliberate showing off. The intense and persistent addiction to fashion and strutting generally discloses the strong predilection of young and old, and particularly of youth who are brought into close assimilative relationships with members of the opposite sex, to exploit their personalities and physical extensions of them to the utmost. Age and culture ordinarily tone down the strutting habit, but they almost never eliminate it. This type of contact is characteristic of the informal club, social set, clique, ring, gang, etc., which exist largely to serve this special function.

When a number of people are sharing the same emotion the usual result is a crowd or mob. Thus the crowd and mob are the emotional analogues of the deliberative assembly or the discussion group. It is not only that crowds and mobs are emotional; but they are crowds and mobs because they are emotional. The stimulation works both ways.

Competitive contacts—All competition is emotional and it may be intellectual. Rallies, demonstrations, ceremonials, crowds, mobs, are often composed of individuals who are competing in emotional expression. Each tries to show greater patriotism, greater loyalty, greater enthusiasm, greater piety, than the others. Each strives to outdo the others. There is a consequent excessive emotional stimulation. It is analogous to an auction. The most emotional individuals set the pace, and the others attempt to overtake or to outdo them. The emotions thus expressed act as a spur and stimulus and as a challenge to the rest to equal the mark. This competition may develop so far as to create a craze. A marked example of this sort of emotional competition occurred in the winter of 1923-24 when "Marathon" dancers all over the country strove to outdo one another by dancing for three days or more in a single effort.

Most games between competing teams involve emotional competition, but since the activity takes place overtly and completely without inhibition it is not so apparent at a distance. Yet the tenseness of muscles and fixity of expression of the players disclose to the practiced observer how great is the emotional strain. The team which is habitually defeated or the one which invariably wins develops strong emotional attitudes and self-feeling, positive and negative. In either case the emotional disturbance may be so intense that there is a temporary disorganization of personality or loss of morale.

Hostile contacts are particularly emotional. The emotions which are most common in such relationships are irritation, anger, hate, and fear. These may occasionally arise in any type of face-to-face group, but they are particularly likely to be manifest in crowds and mobs. Mobs are especially prone to the expression of the most malevolent of the primary emotions because hostility can so easily arise in such collective situations. The lynching mob is an excellent example of this type. The anger of a group of men, aroused to white heat by reciprocal stimulation and strong suggestion and directed towards some suspect, especially of another race or nationality (in which case suggestion ordinarily works readily because of strong previous conditioning), knows no bounds until its fury has spent itself. Only those who have witnessed such demonstrations can actually realize the strength of such hostile emotions.

THE PSYCHOLOGY OF RADICALISM—Root has given an excellent picture of the mind of the radical or the one who finds himself out of agreement with the prevailing processes and ideas of society. Psychologically radicalism is unpleasant because it disrupts well-established habits. We saw in Chapter XI that interference with behavior systems produces unpleasant feeling tone. The status quo, which the radical attacks, is constituted of a vast system of customs and traditions, mores, folkways, etc. These are in the last analysis collective habits relatively uniform throughout the group. Thus the radical is attacking the habits of millions of men, and the reaction against him is proportionately strong when his attacks are recognized as such.

Root distinguishes two general types of radicals, the emotional and the intellectual or scientific. The emotional radical may be definitely psychopathic. In such a case he may have real gifts and ability, or he may be a fanatic, harnessing his drive to inconsequential and trivial movements. Many of the great leaders in religion and social reform apparently have been emotional radicals with psychopathic tendencies. In many cases, however, the emotional radical is naturally normal, but under the pressure of misfortune, failure, social disapproval, distress, or other hostile environmental conditions, he develops neurotic and hysterical symptoms. Few men possess the strength of character to undergo constant criticism and strong opposition from the public without developing compensating mechanisms. Under such pressure and the necessity of defending his position, the radical is likely to find himself pushed into a much more radical position than he at first contemplated. Thus Luther was driven into complete revolt and the Wesleys were forced to found a new denomination in opposition to the one they originally intended only to reform. Likewise, Ingersoll, who began with a protest against bigotry, was forced into "infidelity." How else can we explain the excesses of such social theorists as the philosophic anarchists than in terms of this development of a "defense mechanism," which looks for ever more exaggerated examples of social maladjustment to justify the attitude of protest? Finally they build up a radical "complex" which sets them over against society as it exists and thenceforward they become moral or emotional outlaws, against whom the emotions of every conservative or average man are turned. The radical complex, as Root says, leads the radical "to see in every act of society, in every move of every antagonist, a deep ulterior purpose." He assigns motives where none exist. Possibly he shows marked paranoiac tendencies.

Defenders of the established order, in their duel with the emotional radical, are at a great advantage, for they can seize upon the pathological exaggerations of the emotional radical, and with apparent calm and rationality which is in decided contrast to the excitability of the radical, win public confidence and approval. They can afford to make more gracious appeals. Conservatism is esthetically more attractive and pleasant, for it supplements established habits rather than interferes with them.

Root points out another interesting fact about the emotional radical, namely, his superiority-inferiority complex. He believes himself to be superior to his opponents, and yet his position and his status are inferior. The results are, "first, an aggressive and egotistical intellectual assertiveness which invites opposition," and, "an attitude toward tradition that is sweeping and illogical. Anything old is bad, anything new is good."

The philosophic or scientific radical is far more important, although the popular mind rarely realizes it. Root lists as the most profoundly radical critical tools, those of scientific doubt, the concept of cause and effect, the highly detached, impersonal attitude, the concept of degrees of truth, the pragmatic attitude, the discounting of ideas relating to the ego and the emotions, and creative thinking. The intellectual radical may be a great asset to social progress. In fact, so hard and fast does custom become that it is not possible to revise collective social adjustments effectively without some degree of critical intellectual analysis of our social system, and such analysis is the essential characteristic of intellectual radicalism.

COLLECTIVE BEHAVIOR under contact stimulation is more or less analogous to individual behavior under similar conditions. Collective behavior is, of course, the individual behavior of a number of persons responding with greater or less uniformity to the same or similar stimuli. We shall consider this collective or multiple behavior under two general headings, that of conflict and coöperation. Collective conflict itself implies coöperation. It is not possible for groups to engage in conflict with one another unless there is solidarity of individuals within. The individual tends to identify himself very closely with the groups to which he belongs. This is really another way of stating the fact, earlier emphasized, to the effect that the self-consciousness of the individual extends even to objects and people apart from himself. Thus the boy whose school wins a game feels superior to the boy whose team loses; the person from a large city feels superior to the person from a small town; the degenerate branches of distinguished families sometimes have more family pride than the more deserving ones. The grief of the Southerner over the "lost cause," the migration of the "German '48ers" to America to escape the shame and disappointment of the failure of their revolution, the regret of Jesus that Jerusalem would not hearken to his message, are examples which may illustrate the negative aspect of the same principle. The identification of feeling among members of a family or of a persecuted or unconventional religious sect, political faction, class, or race may be particularly strong. This is because the interests of the members are so closely similar within the group organization and so much in conflict with people outside that if one member suffers the others do also. In such cases one may be objective, rational and moral about all matters not affecting his group, but utterly without conscience or sense of obligation towards persons outside of his own group, when they are in conflict with his own fellows.

CONFLICT is both individual and collective. In fact, we may speak of three types of conflict altogether: (1) that within the individual's own personality, (2) that between individuals in the same or in different groups, and (3) that between groups.

Conflict within the individual personality arises from two sources. On the one hand the conflict may be between two or more organic drives and acquired dispositions integrated around these, or between acquired sets or values on a largely intellectual basis. The internal conflict is likely to be much stronger in the former case than in the latter, as was indicated in Chapter XIII. The several types of interests within the individual are frequently in conflict one with another for the dominance of the organism. This inner conflict of interests of course may also reflect itself in the conflict of the groups of which the individuals are members. But, on the other hand, conflicts between groups also reflect themselves within the individuals within rival face-to-face or indirect contact groups. Conflicts of loyalties to different interests or personalities and aggregations arise in this way because the same people are so often members of different associations, institutions, societies, publics.

Conflicts between individuals within the same group are usually the result of competition among them to profit in unequal degrees from the benefits of the group. Less frequently they are the result of the rivalry of different individuals attempting to outdo each other in making contributions to the group welfare. More frequently this conflict may be of the character of rivalry in self-improvement. Not infrequently there is conflict between members of groups as a result of an effort to mold the policies of the group in such ways as to represent more effectively the rival interests of the competing members. Sometimes, also, the conflicting loyalty of one party in the conflict owed to another group enters into the situation and gives direction or character to the struggle of personalities. Thus frequently the divided loyalties of immigrants in a new country render it impossible for them to coöperate fully with individuals of their adopted country in times of crises. At other times, or when the interests of the mother country are not involved, coöperation rather than conflict may be the regular procedure.

Conflict between members of competing groups arises easily when the groups are rivals. Frequently, however, the fact of membership in rival groups shields the members in some degree from conflicting relationships as individuals. Their groups undertake to carry on the conflict without subjecting the members to the strain individually. But such isolation of the individual in conflicting groups is more likely to occur in indirect contact groups than in face-to-face groups, and in highly organized than in loosely organized groups. In loosely organized face-to-face groups in which there is a good deal of feeling of solidarity, individuals frequently bear the brunt of the conflict. They are like pickets or advance guards who sustain the first shock of the enemy's fire and then perhaps fall back for the protection and support of their main bodies. Where conflict between members of rival groups is planted in earnest over group issues it is likely to be extremely bitter. In such cases it is reënforced by all of the ardor of loyalty to the group which arises from that identification with the fortunes of the group mentioned above, and it is also reënforced by the participation of other members of the rival groups, until finally it may become a general struggle between the two rival groups as wholes. This sort of struggle is well illustrated by the blood feuds of primitive people and of the Kentucky mountaineers. In these feuds the struggle is at first between two individuals, but it soon expands to involve the whole of the kin on both sides and it usually grows intense in proportion to the numbers involved.

THE CONFLICT OF GROUPS, like that of individuals, arises over interests. Long established interests of individuals nearly always manifest themselves by group cleavages, and in our highly derivative social organization these cleavages come to be more and more between indirect contact groups. Some of these conflicts we will now examine.

Rivalry and competition—Local or face-to-face groups still have their conflicts, especially in the field of rivalry, which sometimes become malicious rather than emulative. Athletic contests and business competition offer the most common examples of local group rivalries. Occupational and cultural groups, clubs, teams, etc., also frequently engage in rivalry. Where rivalry is with regard to excellence in skill of production, as in boys' and girls' agricultural and home economics clubs, or in art, literary, and educational achievement, it has a most valuable stimulating effect. It increases morale and stimulates to a further analysis of the technique and its improvement. The West Virginia community scoring plan is a good example of the effect which a device for increasing friendly rivalry in local group excellence may have upon the self and social consciousness of individuals in a group. The management of industrial concerns also frequently seeks to arouse company pride in their employés and to stimulate rivalry with reference to other firms as a method of securing better and more willing service. Occasionally a city or a whole state may adopt a similar program with good results. But it is ordinarily easier to stimulate a smaller group, such as a school, an athletic team, or a debating society to such emulative rivalry than a whole city or state, because suggestion works more concretely in the face-to-face group and it is easier for an individual to visualize his own function in a small compact group than in a large dispersed one.

As Ross has shown with excellent discrimination, rivalry and competition, when kept on a constructive plane, offer most excellent incentives to achievement. But they may also be very destructive when they have as their major or only objectives exploitation rather than the creation of values. It is very easy for competition or struggle for one's just share of wealth, honor, privilege, or what not, to pass the bounds of justice and conventionality and become positively immoral or criminal. There is almost universal disapproval of the person who is grasping or uses unfair methods or downright deception and violence in taking a disproportionate share of any good, material or immaterial. And there is almost equally universal approval of those who engage in creative rivalry and competition and thus leave the world richer for their striving. These attitudes apply to groups as well as to individuals, although we are more prone to condone an exploiting attitude in groups than in individuals and perhaps less ready to reward their efforts through constructive rivalry. This is because they are less concrete than individuals, and it is correspondingly difficult to assess praise or blame.

The conflict of derivative groups is much more frequently of an exploitive character. The relations of associations, societies, institutions, and publics are still more frequently negative than positive. This is probably because they are so universally organized around highly conscious derivative interests. This is particularly true of associations, which have come into existence for the specific purpose of promoting some particular collective interest or concern. Consequently, they are frequently fighting as well as constructive or creative groups.

Business and political associations illustrate this principle of strenuous competition quite well, as any student of economics or of politics well knows. Societies, because they are ordinarily more loosely organized, are less highly competitive. Their struggle is more likely to take the form of mild rivalry, although at times, as in the case of nationalities, art societies, or even philanthropic agencies, their competition may become sufficiently acrimonious. But in such cases we really have to do with associations as well as with the rather indefinite category of societies. Although conflicts are prone to arise out of the struggle of associations, especially economic associations, for control over markets or other national and international advantages, such struggles are very likely in the end to involve whole societies. This sort of competition is one of the most fruitful sources of modern warfare on an imperialistic basis.

Institutions, like associations, are usually highly integrated. The fact that they ordinarily embody a vested interest with all of the emotional attachments which this fact implies, renders the conflict between institutions relatively strong, although usually more or less formal. The church and the state, the school and the church, business and politics, or business and ethics, practically always manifest some degree of antagonism, which is constantly becoming concrete and aggressive through the local or face-to-face group extensions of these institutions. Institutions usually attempt, with more or less success, to solve their conflict difficulties by subordinating rival institutions. Thus in any large society, such as a nationality, there is frequently a hierarchy of institutions, at the head of which ordinarily stands the state. Subsidiary institutions, like the church and the school, may be more or less coördinate.

Publics, in the sense of psychic organizations or public opinion, serve largely to define the limits of inter-institutional conflicts. Associations also develop public opinion within their membership, and sometimes outside of it, for purposes of propaganda. Societies ordinarily are integrated by public opinion. Institutions in the less tangible sense, as distinguished from associations, objectify themselves almost completely through public opinion and their projections of written materials or codes. Associations always have administrative organizations, through which most of their competitive conflicts are carried on, but they also make copious appeals to public opinion, which they frequently attempt with more or less success to control. Publics, therefore, are strong factors in the conflicts of indirect contact groups. This conflict of publics may remain mild, or it may become intense and rancorous, as in the case of the contests of political parties, the feeling between denominational publics, or between fundamentalists and modernists, or even different nationalities and races. Conflicts between classes, religions, nationalities and races still frequently develop to the point of open violence and sometimes result even in warfare. The most effective remedy for such irrational conflicts, as already has been suggested, is more knowledge or the inculcation of science.

REVOLUTION is a special type of group conflict which arises between classes. It occurs when a dominant class controls the associations and institutions, and molds public opinion, in such a way that other classes are not able to benefit from them as largely as they feel they should.

Factional struggles—This control of associations or institutions may consist simply of the control of the patronage of these institutions. Most of the revolutions in Central America, for example, appear to have been the result of this sort of class discrimination. In such cases the revolutionary struggle is nearly always largely of the nature of a political uprising. Force instead of ballots is used, primarily because intimidation, bribery, patronage, etc., prevent a free exercise of the ballot. The objective in such a revolution is ordinarily the capture of the government, and consequently the patronage. This is revolution for the conquest of associations, and illustrates particularly well Martin's theory of revolutions, which maintains that revolutionary struggle is the result of the attempt of one group or crowd or class to replace another and that it changes little except the personnel of the associations and the patronage.

Institutional revolutions—There is, however, another type of revolution in which the objectives are much more fundamental and deep seated than in the case of conflict of classes over the control of associations, which may upon occasion degenerate into mere riots. These are the institutional revolutions, a type which has been emphasized in fact, if not in name, by Ellwood. Institutional revolutions vary in objectives from the concreteness and immediacy of struggles for governmental control, or mere political and industrial uprisings, on the one hand to the abstractness of struggle over principles on the other hand. As Martin and LeBon have demonstrated, all revolutions, whether of the associational or of the institutional type, justify themselves by an appeal to principles. Since such appeal is designed primarily to captivate public opinion, the appeal is likely to be the more fulsome the less sure the leaders are of the rightness of their cause in the eyes of the world. Some of the most hysterical appeals to principles have been made by mere political opportunists. But Martin and LeBon perhaps underestimate the objective sincerity of other types of institutional revolutionists, especially in the case of those more silent conflicts over the reorganization of relatively non-political and non-economic institutions like religion, if religious revolutions ever are detachable from economic and political motives. Such revolutions are caused primarily by the hardening of the custom and a sort of stasis in the codes of the institution. This sort of conservatism and blocking of progressive reorganization of the content and functions of institutions may occur either because the institutions are dominated by a privileged group within or by a privileged group without. Usually both causes operate, with the result that there is a sort of protective alliance between an economic or dynastic hierarchy which profits from the institutional stasis and the hierarchy of the institution itself. In such cases the objective of the revolutionists is to overthrow the hierarchies in order to make revision of their customs, creeds, and codes possible. Such revolutions are accomplished by silent methods where possible, but in other cases they may resort more or less to violence, especially in such cases as the French and American political revolutions of 1789 and 1776. But even in such types of revolution the struggle is largely economic, even if it is not of the crude nature of a factional fight for the control of the patronage.

Social revolutions—Yet another type of revolution is almost imperceptible in its operation. It is unplanned, and usually unnoticed until long after its effects have become quite marked. The commercial and industrial revolutions are typical of this form. The psychological aspects of this kind of revolution are to be noted in the changes in customs, traditions, mores, folkways, and other elements in the psycho-social environment produced by far-reaching technic and economic changes. We have already described the effect upon group organization of this type of revolution. Usually, as Ogburn has pointed out, the change in customs, traditions, and in the psycho-social environment generally, is slow, and there is a lag until the maladjustment becomes so acute as to force the readjustment. If the changes are rapid, the revolution may manifest itself in the conflict of the older and the younger generations. In such cases the old customs, traditions, etc., as embodied in the older members of society, have become obsolete for purposes of adjustment to new conditions. New psycho-social controls, however, have not as yet been perfected to take the place of the old, so that there is an apparent demoralization of society until the younger group evolves new and better fitting standards. This kind of revolution is really evolution, although it is more or less irregular in the form of its occurrence. It does not ordinarily involve violence, except occasionally where the struggle becomes by induction economic or political. However, this third form of revolution has more profound and far-reaching social effects than either of the other two types.

COÖPERATION—The tendency is for conflict to end in coöperation for self-defense. Thus the movies appoint a czar, baseball does the same, competing firms organize into trusts, and nations into a League of Nations. The normal collective attitude is not one of conflict, in spite of the emphasis given to social conflict by such social theorists as Gumplowicz, Ratzenhofer, Gobineau, and Novicow. Group conflict is inevitable, because individual interests clash and individuals tend to coöperate in groups. Thus group conflict is essentially an extension of coöperation through collective behavior or groups, and it must be explained on this basis. This fact also makes clear why there is ordinarily more conflict between derivative than between primary groups, and between indirect contact than between direct contact groups. The local and direct contact groups are now learning to coöperate within the organization of indirect contact groups very much as individuals have learned earlier to coöperate within the primary and face-to-face groups. Families coöperate in the community, communities in the state, local church societies within the larger denomination, political clubs within the political party, etc. More and more the local units, like individuals, delegate their conflicts to the overhead organization just as they also increasingly empower them to promote a large share of their coöperative behavior or enterprise. This movement of conflicts toward the periphery of social organization is a part of the tendency, which we have already so frequently emphasized, for the control of social contacts to become more and more indirect and derivative. It grows out of the extension and multiplication of distance contacts in modern complex life. The overhead organizations, whose function it is primarily to organize and correlate the interests of their constituent organizations and individuals, are too busy promoting coöperation within to turn to coöperation to any considerable extent with their competitors. Before there can be any large degree of coöperation between indirect contact groups there must develop a community of interests between their members and a reënforcing public opinion. There is, of course, a tendency for such publics to become ever more extensive and inclusive.

Not all coöperation between groups is necessarily purposive, or even conscious coöperation. The modern economic system involves the coöperation of groups the world over. As soon as any group ceases to be self-sufficing, as soon as exchange relationships are established, or as soon as any division of labor takes place, coöperation of either a purposive or of a non-purposive type enters in. The institution of slavery in the South was a form of racial coöperation, although it was not voluntary on both sides. The racial heterogeneity within the national unity of the United States illustrates this type of coöperation. Historically, the hostile invasion and conquest of one group by another has resulted in social realignment and coöperation, perhaps enforced by the stronger group. Migrations of peoples in the past resulting in the cross fertilization of cultures also illustrate non-purposive coöperation. Each race gave to the other various elements in its culture which it might never have produced by itself. This process of adjustment is sometimes called accommodation.

Since this volume is concerned so largely with the integration of personality in individuals as the result of selection by social stimuli, on the one hand, and with the integration of collective behavior patterns, on the other hand, it is not necessary to discuss the social psychology of coöperation further at this point. The psychology of concrete coöperative organizations as such falls in the field of social organization.

MATERIALS FOR SUPPLEMENTARY READING

Allport, F. H., *Social Psychology*, Chs. VII, XI, XII, XIV, pp. 234-239
Bartlett, F. C., *Psychology and Primitive Culture*, Chs. IV, V
Beach, W. G., *An Introduction to Sociology and Social Problems*, Chs. IX, XV, XVI, XVII, XVIII
Burnham, W. H., *The Normal Mind*, Chs. XV, XVI
Cooley, C. H., *Human Nature and the Social Order*, Chs. I, III, IV, VII, VIII
———, *Social Organization*, Ch. XXVII
———, *Social Process*, Chs. XII, XIII, XXII, XXIII
Edman, I., *Human Traits and Their Significance*, Ch. V
Ellwood, C. A., *The Psychology of Human Society*, Chs. VII, VIII
Groves, E. R., *Personality and Social Adjustment*, Ch. V
Lindeman, E. C., *Social Discovery*, Ch. VI
Park and Burgess, *Introduction to the Science of Sociology*, pp. 233-269, 288-293, 579-594
Root, W. T., "The Psychology of Radicalism," *Jour. Ab. Psy. and Soc. Psy.*, XIX: 341-356
Ross, E. A., *Principles of Sociology*, Chs. X-XIX, XXI-XXIV, XLIV
———, *Social Control*, Chs. II-V
———, *Social Psychology*, Chs. XVII-XIX, XXI
Small, M. H., "On Some Psychical Relations of Society and Solitude," *Ped. Sem.*, VII: 13-69
Williams, J. M., *Principles of Social Psychology*, Chs. II, V-XXX
———, *Our Rural Heritage*, Chs. XXII, XXIII

CHAPTER XXXIII

COLLECTIVE RESPONSES AND LEADERSHIP

THE ENVIRONMENTS CONDITION COLLECTIVE RESPONSES—
The stimuli which condition responses collectively and thus produce collective behavior must of course, like all other stimuli, have their source. This source is not infrequently some natural object or process. Geography and climate have been historically two of the main natural factors which have conditioned collective responses of a large degree of uniformity and have therefore created groups as defined above. Peoples living in a river valley, on a seacoast, or at a break in transportation, tend to be welded into a unified group economically, politically, and culturally. Areas of uniform rainfall as contrasted with other areas, dry, wet, cold, warm and temperate climatic regions, severally condition characteristic uniform responses in practically all of the inhabitants. The same is true of a distinctive type of fauna or flora, which will determine characteristic and fairly uniform methods of food getting and food consumption, property regulations, housing, clothing, leisure, recreation, religion, and even magic. Outstanding inventions, or physico-social environment, domesticated animals and plants in large numbers, or bio-social environment, may exercise an even greater influence over the collective responses of men through determining their occupations and habits of consumption, and even the occurrence and extent of their periods of leisure. The industrial revolution, which has been dependent primarily upon physico-social environment or physical inventions, is a good illustration of this type of influence.

THE PSYCHO-SOCIAL ENVIRONMENT AND COLLECTIVE RESPONSES—But the best example of the way in which some environmental fact or process conditions collective responses is to be found in the psycho-social environment. Man creates ideas, customs, traditions, conventions, mores, folkways, beliefs, codes, institutions—all sorts of psycho-social projected entities—which, in so far as they achieve objective integration, function as stimuli sources to both the individuals of the generation which have created them and to succeeding generations who will be molded by them and will in turn transform and transmit them. Every student of society knows that the personalities of the members of society are molded and fixed, in so far as they are fixed, by these psycho-social processes or uniformities of behavior. Institutions and customs, beliefs and traditions, the mores and the folkways, are reaching out with their objectively integrated stimuli on every hand to take hold of all persons who come within their reach or shadow to mold them into conformity, and no one escapes domination by some sort of psycho-social process and organization. The psycho-social environment is everywhere and all-compelling. This environment is not apart from us or external to men, except as it has been objectified and stored in symbols and structures which in turn serve as stimuli to the reproduction of the types of behavior which they symbolize and embody. But the environment is carried within us in the form of our daily behavior and thinking. Our conduct, when viewed objectively and collectively, is custom and tradition, institution, mores, beliefs. We cannot escape them, first, because they are rooted in our behavior, and second, because they are rooted in the behavior of other persons with whom we come in contact and to whom we adjust ourselves in collective behavior.

TOTAL SUMMATION OF STIMULI IN SYMBOLS AND IN PERSONALITIES—But of course we must not suppose that we always respond to the institutions, customs, traditions, conventions, beliefs, and other elements of the psycho-social environments as collective entities or integrations. Such a response is possible only when these processes of the psycho-social environment have become integrated and objectified from the behavior of the individuals whose symbolic behavior constitutes only a portion of these psycho-social processes into some symbolic or concrete representative system. We can, for instance, imitate or respond by suggestion to the psycho-social content of the institution of the church, or of the state, or of any other derivative institution, only when the essential beliefs, practices, teachings, etc., of these institutions have been embodied in print or other language symbols, or in the symbolic behavior or speech of some representative individual, which is less likely to occur. There are therefore two great channels through which the integrated and objectified content of a complex psycho-social process or institution may be brought to bear upon an individual: the printed treatise or some other non-personal system of objective symbols, and individual personalities who embody or represent the institution as a whole. Where the individual performs this mediating function and conditions the whole or a part of the content of the institution to others he may be called a leader.

The instances in which the complex psycho-social processes, such as institutions, operate as wholes upon the individual are of course exceptional. Not many of us take the trouble or have the capacity to master the significance and content of institutions and other psycho-social processes as wholes. Nor do many of us read books about institutions. The more common method of being influenced by psycho-social processes is by coming in contact in our daily behavior with persons whose behavior embodies some portion of the totality of the psycho-social processes, or institutions. These daily informal contacts do more in the aggregate than the relatively formal ones first mentioned to shape our responses to the psycho-social stimuli and to produce conformity to the psycho-social behavior patterns, although we are not ordinarily aware of the social function which such contacts serve. Thus we integrate our behavior in response to institutional and other psycho-social stimuli through our adjustments to a great many individual members of institutions and participants in other psycho-social processes. This piece-meal adjustment to the collective behavior forms accounts for the variety and the individual differences, as well as for the conformity, of our adjustments. Whether the persons we copy are leaders or not depends primarily on what relations they have with us.

PARTIAL SUMMATION OF STIMULI IN INDIVIDUALS—Whether we acquire the psycho-social processes or collective behavior patterns formally and largely consciously, or informally and incidentally and mainly unconsciously, this acquisition is for the most part accomplished through the direct imitation of persons. Only the more literate and abstractly thinking persons get any very considerable share of their behavior patterns through literature. But even these imitate or otherwise respond to persons indirectly, to those persons who produced the literature and who may not be very much hidden behind the printed page. This is particularly true in the case of the newspaper and the journal of opinion. The lighter kinds of literature which deal with concrete processes rather than abstractions—especially fiction, which is the most read, and drama—also pictorial art and sculpture, condition personality in individuals in much the same way as personal contacts with other persons condition it. The chief difference in habit formation under the dominance of representative art from habit formation as the result of direct personal contacts is that the personalities in the one case are ideal or fictitious and the sensory processes involved in conditioning responses are mainly visual, while in the other case the personalities which serve as models or as stimuli sources are actual and we apprehend them largely through auditory as well as visual channels. Also, in the former case we are dependent for the most part upon our imaginations for any stimuli which we may receive from the overt behavior of the fictional personalities, while we can actually see the real persons acting, observe their gestures, postures, and facial expression.

LEADERS AND LEADERSHIP—Thus direct stimulation by persons in face-to-face contacts with us is much more concrete and powerful. It embodies a multitude of reënforcing factors, such as tone of voice, the perception of facial and bodily expression and attitudes, gesture, etc., in addition to the more abstract word symbols which serve to direct us. The direct exercise of such concrete stimuli, verbal or otherwise, in influencing the behavior of others we call personal leadership. Where such influence is exerted through art, literature, or other persons or groups it is impersonal leadership.

Any person who is more than ordinarily efficient in carrying psycho-social stimuli to others and is thus effective in conditioning collective responses may be called a leader. It is not necessary that he should serve in this capacity of presenting stimuli for collective response on purpose. He may be an involuntary and unconscious leader perhaps even more frequently than a conscious and intentional leader. In fact, it is very probable that most leaders first learn to assume the rôle of leadership through discovering themselves operating unintentionally in that capacity. But of course the most effective type of leader is almost always the one who is conscious of his leadership, has a purpose in view, and studies the technique of leading successfully. Leadership is most conspicuous and most direct in the direct contact group and it is here that most leaders are trained. But leadership may also be indirect and may accordingly be carried on through printed symbols, through radio, moving pictures, or any other indirect contact stimuli. Such leadership may make the leader conspicuous, if he reveals his personality in connection with his leadership technique, or he may remain in the background, even to the point of being generally unknown.

Personal and Impersonal Leadership—In some causes anonymous leadership is the more effective, especially if the leader is unpopular or if the disclosure of his identity would lead to questions as to his motives. Also, it is sometimes true that a cause succeeds best if it is made to rely for its popular appeal upon its intrinsic merits and is not confused with the claims of personalities.

Ordinarily, however, the proper revealing of a personality behind the principle or the stimulus renders the cause the more effective. The warmth of personality makes a powerful appeal to most people and they judge causes or behavior primarily by the personalities to whom they are attached. Abstract causes and principles, which are oftenest communicated through literature or art, can dispense with the aid of the personality of the leader more effectively than can concrete and immediate ends. For the best control of the ordinary everyday responses to psycho-social stimuli, which do most to condition our collective behavior, the personality of the leader or stimulus source is essential. In such contacts we are very little sensible of the meaning of either the stimuli or of our responses. Our attention is centered primarily on the personality contacts through which the stimuli and responses are organized. The personality is merely the cue.

PROFESSIONAL AND AMATEUR LEADERSHIP—Leadership may furthermore be professional or amateur. Most leadership as it actually occurs in the unconscious direct contact situations is actually of the latter type. All of us practically are leaders with relation to some matters and on certain occasions. We play the rôle through the force of circumstances which have made us focal in the situation, without any choice or intention on our part. But there are also large numbers of semi-professional and professional leaders, some of whom perform the function for hire and others who do it for the pleasure or profit which it brings them. Being the focus of attention of many followers is an experience which makes a powerful appeal to most persons who have had it. The knowledge that others are taking our behavior as a cue or model after which they mold their own offers a thrill of excitement and pleasure which to most persons is irresistible.

Not infrequently, for both the amateur and the professional leader, there is another motive involved in leadership than merely that of the pleasure of the sense of power. Self-interest is a frequent incentive to the undertaking of leadership. One may hire out his talents as leader in the service of others or he may seek a following from the people as a method of promoting some cause of his own. The greatest rewards within the gifts of his fellows go to the successful leader. Whether he seeks wealth, power, or reputation of any sort it may be had by the successful leader who knows how to shape the behavior of others according to the stimuli which he offers them.

THE SUCCESSFUL LEADER MUST POSSESS PRESTIGE—The elements of prestige have already been discussed in the chapter on suggestion. The leader must be both a model to be imitated and a source from which suggestion radiates, each according to the type of leader he is and the function which he seeks to perform. The moral leader especially, the one who seeks to produce a desirable change in collective behavior, should be a model as well as a source of suggestion. He should, in so far as possible, serve as a model to illustrate the behavior which he is seeking to establish. Moral leaders are expected by their followers to exemplify the principles and beliefs which they expound, because the strongest appeal of the leader is directly to imitative behavior. He may offer principles and concepts for imitation, as the more valuable and stable and farther reaching. But the followers find it easier to understand and imitate a personality, and since he is the center of their attention they insist that he serve as their model. This is true both in reform and in war. The leader who is always at the front of the battle and who does what he preaches will, other things being equal, win most victories.

But the leader who is merely seeking some advantage for himself or for some faction which he represents—selfish leadership it may be termed as distinguished from social or positively idealistic leadership—may rely on indirect suggestion, innuendo, and similar methods of touching off the unconscious complexes and prejudices of his followers. Here success is more often attained negatively than in the former case. Here the imitation of a model is less important, while the use of suggestion takes the lead. This method may even consist of setting off responses of which the follower is not aware. A great deal of wit and sarcasm, of ridicule and malice, will be employed in such leadership. The opposition is painted darkly and as dangerous. Fear rather than love is appealed to. The motives are competitive rather than constructive. Of course both imitation and suggestion may be used in both the social or positively idealistic and self-seeking types of leadership, but ordinarily there is some sort of segregation or preponderance of methods such as that here indicated. In both types of leadership prestige is essential to the success of the leader.

METHODS OF APPEAL IN LEADERSHIP—Whether the leader makes use of direct or indirect contact methods, whether he visits people in person, speaks to them in groups, addresses them through the fictitious characters of novels and plays, paints idealistic scenes, presents his arguments in essays and treatises, or acts through organizations and administrative machinery which he has created, will depend mainly upon the circumstances, such as the size of the group he wishes to reach, the nature of the proposition or behavior for which he seeks a following, the time at his disposal, the kind of people with whom he must deal, the financial means and personal assistance at his disposal, and his own previous experience and training. For a relatively simple proposal, such as the success of a candidate, or of a fund to be collected, where personality counts a great deal and where there is only a limited number of people to be seen and sufficient time for the number of workers employed to see all persons concerned, the personal canvass is best. But where the cause is more or less abstract but can obtain a hearing through print, where there are many people widely scattered to be reached and there are not sufficient workers or leaders to reach them individually, and funds are scarce, a direct appeal through print, cartoon, picture, or mass meetings may be effective. Ordinarily the larger the amounts of well adapted literature and speakers which can be used the more successful will be the result. But care must always be taken not to tire those who are to be reached, for a surfeit of appeal may cause a temporary revulsion as pronounced as it is irrational. The minds of the masses are not capable of indefinite and continuous employment in the analysis of an abstract proposition. Intellectual indigestion is as certain to produce nausea and regurgitation as is physiological indigestion. Where there is an abundance of time and the people to be reached are widespread or in more or less segregated groups, and when the propaganda has to be handled with considerable care because on first impression it is unacceptable to those who are to receive it, the method of suggestion through art in the wider sense is probably the best one to follow. Fiction, drama, poetry, songs, pictures and paintings, cartoons, and even Chautauqua lectures, radio, and moving pictures, may accomplish in time, through indirect suggestion, a complete reversal of public opinion on any question, where direct methods might only antagonize.

INTELLECTUAL LEADERS AND LEADERS OF ACTION—Leaders may also be distinguished as intellectual leaders and leaders of action. Either type may function in either direct or indirect contact groups. But ordinarily the leader of action will be found operating primarily in face-to-face groups, while the intellectual leader will work most effectively, other things being equal, in indirect contact groups or in intelligent publics. The best type of leader for general purposes is unquestionably one which embodies both the capacity for intellectual leadership and the attributes which make for successful appeals to action. In direct contact groups, especially in the deliberative assembly, discussion group, class, and audience, the intellectual appeal may be quite efficacious. But in those face-to-face groups where the intellectual factor is less in evidence, the emotional appeals are stronger and the personality which can stimulate action is most in demand. Appeals to action are also important in indirect contact groups, especially for certain purposes. Such appeals are most effectively made through pictures, movie films, radio, and emotional or semi-emotional writing.

PROPAGANDA is a term which may be applied to professional leadership in the support of some cause, particularly when the methods employed to secure a following are those of indirect suggestion. The term has come among us to have somewhat of a sinister meaning, because it is so often a paid and a more or less concealed service in the interest of a selfish or partisan cause. There is no reason other than this why the term should not be applied also to the promotion of useful and unselfish or public causes. But considered in the less reputable sense there is now a vast amount of propaganda, especially through the indirect contact media of communication. Advertising, both in periodicals and on billboards, may properly be included under this category, in spite of the fact that some advertising serves most useful social purposes. With a largely partisan press the opportunity for propaganda may easily pervert both the editorial and the news columns of our daily papers, although some newspapers attempt to prevent this. There have been signs even of a tendency for propaganda to get a foothold in the magazines of fiction, in plays, in novels, in art, and in the movies. How far this tendency will go unchecked will depend upon the machinery which can be made available for a scientific control of communication in the indirect contact groups as suggested in the preceding chapter.

LEADERSHIP AS A FORM OF CONTROL—Environmental pressures operate for the most part along more or less conventional lines or in certain fairly specific forms of behavior. This is true partly because as our habits become fixed we are susceptible only to certain types of stimuli or to stimuli which have already conditioned our responses. Also, the psycho-social environmental pressures, which constitute most of the stimuli complexes which control or direct us, are themselves organized out of the collective behavior, and this behavior which constitutes psycho-social environmental pressures and serves as stimuli to our own imitative or suggested behavior is cast in definite, often stereotyped, forms. Leaders who seek to control or influence the behavior of others succeed best if they pay adequate attention to these facts. They are not able readily to control responses if they attempt to use behavior patterns or symbols as stimuli which have not become readily associated with the desired responses.

The leader must know what stimuli will condition adequate responses for his purposes and develop a technique for presenting these stimuli. These stimuli are his controls and they are to be found primarily as typical behavior patterns which may be spoken of collectively as certain uniformities of behavior or as verbal or other more or less abstract symbols of such behavior. The leader manipulates these behavior and symbolic controls in such ways as to produce like responses in others through the mechanism of concrete imitation by copying or of abstract imitation by interpretation of the symbols. Or the leader may use certain symbolic stimuli to release desired behavior without imitation, that is, through suggestion, where the desired response has become sufficiently conditioned by or associated with a particular cue or stimulus.

Leadership in such cases becomes largely a matter of the knowledge of conditioned responses and of the power to condition desired responses to the stimuli available, and finally of the manipulation of stereotyped conditioned stimuli, which is the method of suggestion. This is a relatively easy form of leadership which directs behavior along comparatively conventional paths. Leadership which produces more marked changes and breaks out new paths of policy or performance makes a larger use of the mechanism of imitation. Hence, it manipulates stimuli to the types of behavior which are desired in the collective responses of those who follow. The leader in a complex and abstractly organized society of derivative groups, in which the members respond to abstract verbal communication symbols, does not usually present the behavior pattern in concrete form, such as in gesture, mimicry, or pantomime. He uses instead the shorter cut method of verbal symbols or descriptions, to which the followers have already learned to condition the responses desired or to which he must teach them to condition their responses. This is, in its more conscious form, abstract imitation; in its less conscious and unelaborated forms, suggestion.

MATERIALS FOR SUPPLEMENTARY READING
(See end of Chapter XXXIV)

CHAPTER XXXIV

THE QUALITIES OF LEADERS

THE SOCIAL PSYCHOLOGY OF LEADERSHIP—The chief essential to leadership is always to be able to focus the attention of a group of people upon a common object of interest to them or to attach their interest, by a process of conditioning, to something which previously did not appeal to them. Sometimes the task is to make them realize or believe that they have this interest with regard to some form of behavior or object of attention and at other times it is the problem of getting them to respond effectively to that interest as a stimulus. Or it may be both. This focusing of the attention of individuals upon a single common object of interest may thus involve the creation of a new group, or it may merely call for the concentration of the behavior of an existing group upon some common interest in the most economical manner possible to produce the most favorable results in the light of the end set up.

TWO METHODS OF APPEAL—In performing this function the leader may find it advantageous either to concentrate the attention of the group upon himself and his behavior or upon some behavior objective or abstract value outside of himself. Which plan he should follow will depend largely upon his purpose or aim and the quality of his followers. If personal advancement is his motive, or if the intellectual quality of the members of the group averages low, or if the results sought can best be attained by emotional appeal without burdening the followers with too detailed an intellectual analysis of the aims and objectives of the movement, it is usually advisable to appeal to the trust and confidence of the group in the prowess, power, capacity, or good intentions of the leader and thus secure the support and personal loyalty of his followers to himself. This loyalty and support he can usually transfer with little difficulty to the end which he has caused to be associated in their minds with his own personality. But the higher the intellectual and moral grade of those who are to be directed by the leader and the less he aims at self-advancement and the more he seeks the promotion of some important cause or movement worthy of support in itself, the more likely the leader is to make himself merely tangential to the cause he represents. He will keep the realization of the objective set constantly in their view by all the devices of which he is master, bringing himself into the situation only when he finds that some dramatic element or appeal to personal loyalty will be more effective for the time being. Between these two extremes of leadership there are many gradations, and it is in the intervening ground that most leadership practice naturally falls. But leadership of crowds and direct contact groups is most likely to involve the former methods, while leadership of publics or of indirect contact groups may frequently employ the latter procedures.

THE TASK OF THE LEADER IS COMPLEX—In exercising the function of leadership it is not necessary always to secure uniformity of response of all of the followers to the same stimuli. It is not even necessary that all should respond equally or at all to the same stimuli. Only in the simpler tasks of collective behavior and achievement is the situation likely to have that degree of unity which will call forth the same type of response from every one to the same stimuli. This sort of uniform collective response might possibly occur in a small band hunting under a leader or in loading a heavy piece of machinery on a truck or in defending some limited position against an enemy group. But it will readily be seen that even in such simple instances some differentiation of effort will be necessary in order to perform the collective task efficiently. Even in simple cases where a leader seeks to get a group to vote as a unit for the same candidate, which is essentially a uniform type of response, stimuli must be varied in order to reach different types of people who have different experiences and therefore different preconceptions and values.

In the more complex tasks and in the larger and more populous groups, especially in the indirect contact groups where there is a maximum of opportunity for differences of experience and attitude and of technique on the part of the members of the group, it will be necessary for the leader to stimulate and organize very different behavior reactions with regard to both the same sets of stimuli and to different sets. It is also necessary for him to manipulate a variety of stimuli, sometimes a very great variety, in order to bring about the proper organization of behavior on the part of the members of the group. The more complex and abstract and extensive the objective, ordinarily the greater will be the variety of stimuli presented, and the more diverse the responses which it will be necessary to have organized into some sort of unity.

The task of the leader of complex movements in indirect contact groups becomes very heavy indeed. Not only does he have the problem of finding the right stimuli for each type of persons with whom he deals and likewise the problem of organizing a great variety of behavior responses to these stimuli, but he must also secure the harmonious and coöperative operation of the distance contact machinery of communication which is necessary for the carrying out of his plans. Complex leadership of this type involves the most consummate generalship and the highest type of intellect and statesmanship. The leader must know his people accurately, and this is not always an easy task in indirect contact groups covering wide areas. He must also know well the principles of social organization and how the operation of these may be affected by human nature and various environmental circumstances. In addition, he must have a good understanding of the machinery of communication and of its limitations and possibilities.

THE TRAINING OF THE LEADER—Leadership of such expertness is relatively rare. The task of leadership in any situation will of course vary in difficulty according to the means of communication and stimulation at the disposal of the leader on the one hand and of the degree to which the followers feel the need for leadership and are prepared to understand it and follow it on the other hand. But under the most favorable circumstances the difficulty of successful leadership in complex situations and for abstract ends is very great. Such leaders are not born, as some poetic temperaments have maintained, but they must be trained, either formally or in the hard school of experience. However, some elements of inherited equipment, as will appear later on, may be of great value as a general background to the achievement of successful leadership. Leaders of important movements must be trained, and this training will not come solely from the reading of books on sociology and psychology or from classroom lectures, valuable as a theoretical knowledge of human nature and of social organization is for the leader. The most effective training for leadership must be found in the practice of leadership, supported by natural ability and theoretical training. And the practice of leadership itself consists not alone in the art and practice of making appeals to persons directly or through the indirect media of communication, but it is also to be had largely in the intelligent performance of a variety of everyday collective functions which bring one into contact with his fellows. It is from these contacts that the observant person may learn how people are manipulated by stimuli, and thus in the practice of leadership and in intelligent following he may gain confidence in his own technique and powers.

QUALITIES AND EQUIPMENT OF THE LEADER—IN FACE-TO-FACE GROUPS—Leaders are likely to be found in all groups, even in deliberative assemblies, but the leaders in groups concerned primarily with intellectual analysis and discussion serve more as foci of attention than directors of thought. In classes and audiences the leader becomes more dominant and he may even by the use of well directed verbal stimuli dictate the collective behavior which obtains in the group, although such dictation is not essential to the successful functioning of the groups. In the case of the rally or demonstration, however, the leader or leaders must direct the collective behavior of the group.

Perhaps the simplest and most elementary item of equipment of the personal leader is the possession of a striking physical personality. Size, good looks, the appearance of strength of body and of character are invaluable assets for the leader who must come in personal contact with people who are moved more by emotional stimuli to the senses than by rational considerations. But even among people of intellectual trends the striking physical personality may exert a powerful influence. From childhood one is conditioned by his experiences to respect size and the evidences of physical prowess. To have these and other advantageous personal qualities gives the possessor a feeling of self-confidence which is of great value in personal leadership in crowds. Add to these physical qualities the power of ready speech and the oratorical gift of emotional appeal, and a certain readiness in repartee which enables the leader to extricate himself from otherwise embarrassing logical situations, and his equipment for direct contact leadership has a very powerful foundation.

IN INDIRECT CONTACT GROUPS—These personal qualities are not of so much importance for leadership in indirect contact groups. Size, good looks, the self-confident manner, readiness of speech and repartee, the poses of the practiced orator, are not so easily conveyed to the members of the public who dwell at a distance from the speaker or writer. Most of his contacts will be made through written language, which does not reveal the concrete personality of the writer directly to the senses of the reader, or through the radio, which has the important advantage of revealing the concrete appeal of the voice in whatever degree it exists. However, the voice is primarily an asset in personal appeal in the degree to which it is made to function in connection with appeals to the visual sense and to the extent the responses of both senses can be integrated in a unitary response. Aside from the vocal content of the stimuli presented by the leader, the appeal which he makes to the visual sense, and through it to the kinesthetic senses, is more important than his appeal to the auditory sense. Something of the visual appeal can be accomplished even through indirect contact media by means of pictures. Movies, especially news reels, newspaper illustrations and illustrated supplements, magazines, and picture posters carry pictorial representations of importance as agents of concrete sensory appeal at a distance. These are rendered all the more important when supplemented and reënforced by anecdotes and descriptive material in print which serve to illustrate the concrete personal characteristics of the leader.

THE IMPORTANCE OF SYMPATHY IN LEADERS—Another important, perhaps the most indispensable, quality for success in personal leadership is an attitude of sympathy and understanding on the part of the leader. This is important also in indirect contact leadership, but it is not so easy to make it manifest through the more abstract agencies of communication as through those of direct contact. However, the properly worded printed speech, supplemented by anecdote and perhaps life history, and especially the more direct contact of the radio, or pictures of the leader in sympathetic and friendly poses, are valuable means of making people understand that the leader possesses this quality of sympathy and good fellowship. Political leaders especially are likely to be extensive "joiners," partly because they fear to deny their favors to solicitors and partly because they know the value of having many contacts of good fellowship. In the more personal types of leadership in direct contact groups the chief cause of the popularity of the leader is his readiness of sympathetic response to human need or appeal. Some of the most corrupt of our political bosses have had very strong and genuine sympathies and were so kindly and helpful to their relatively ignorant constituents that they were retained in office in spite of their notorious records for public incompetency and graft.

Many years ago the writer asked a physician in a certain district in Chicago why that district defended a certain malodorous politician after his crimes against the public had been publicly exposed and he had been dismissed from office. My companion informed me that it was because Mr. —— was always ready to help any family in need, to pay the rent overdue, to bear the expense of a funeral for the poor, to send food or coal, or to intercede with landlords, policemen, inspectors and judges. His constituents understood these virtues or primary attitudes, whereas they knew little or nothing of the theory and practice of American political institutions in the abstract, that is, of derivative ideals. Consequently they dubbed him "The Little Father" and did his bidding and enjoyed his bounty, which in turn he took from the public treasury. The cold and intellectual personality has little chance of successful leadership unless it hides behind the screen of indirect communication and even then a press agent is needed to give the proper touches of ordinary humanity through anecdotes and the like. Even Napoleon was the idol of his army largely because of his impassioned appeals to their more concrete interests and desires, and because merit or devotion were always likely to attract his attention and secure a reward.

JUSTICE AND HUMANITARIANISM IN LEADERS—A strong sense of justice, especially if seasoned by sympathy, is also a strong asset in successful leadership. The more personal the practice of justice is the greater will be its appeal. Abstract justice has its value, even before the scattered public which makes its contacts indirectly, but most people like the justice of their leaders to be warm blooded, and by no means wholly blind. Closely allied to the sense of justice in the leader is the humanitarian attitude. It also should be warm and direct. Abstract benevolence never has appealed to a great many people. The philanthropist who bestows alms is much more acceptable as a leader than the philanthropist and reformer who merely establish public welfare organizations, organize reform associations, or make gifts for scientific social research. But leaders who can talk affectingly in a philanthropic vein, provided they identify themselves with the people and do not behave condescendingly, may often secure a better following than those who actually accomplish great transformations in social organization in a quiet and unostentatious manner. The demagogue who preaches equality, fraternity, and liberty, but never gets beyond the use of the terms as shibboleths with which to win votes, may, unless he is detected in his hypocrisy, secure a better following than the statesman who says little and accomplishes more in legislative reform. The latter type of men may become the heroes of the next generation, but they are not likely to be lionized in their own.

HONESTY AND GOOD FAITH IN LEADERS—The crowd or the public must also believe the leader to be honest or faithful and devoted to their cause if he is to secure their support. As between general honesty and identification with their cause personally, if a choice must be made, the group will nearly always choose the latter attitude in a leader. Few people are capable of objectifying their judgments to the degree that they can prefer a good quality in its abstract application to society as a whole to its concrete application to themselves in particular.

When we say a leader must be honest to be successful, we mean that he must keep faith with those who follow him, or they will repudiate him. He must not even acknowledge a higher good or an allegiance to a greater cause than their own. Such "traitors" have been persecuted in all ages. But the difficulty here is not so much that people are inherently dishonest or selfish, but that they find it very difficult to see truth and duty in the abstract or in any way except from the personal viewpoint. The leader must be loyal to the things to which his group is loyal, but by skillful manipulation he may be able, at least in some degree, to change their loyalties.

THE LEADER MUST HAVE INSIGHT—The leader must know human nature in general and he must know his people in particular. The naïve person who does not readily sense attitudes and changes of emotion in his crowd or public, or who has an absolutistic faith in human nature which renders him impervious to the worst of which people are capable collectively and individually and which makes him a simpering sentimental optimist about human beings and human institutions, cannot achieve and maintain successful leadership under complex and changing conditions. Yet neither can the chronic pessimist or the cynic be successful as a leader. The leader must know that anything can happen, no matter how bad or how good, when collective conditions are ripe for it. It is his business to understand conditions of all sorts, to detect them and impending changes before others are aware of them, and to estimate the ways in which the people he leads will probably respond to these conditions. The leader, if he is to secure the best results, therefore, must be a good judge of character, be without prejudices regarding the limits or forms of collective and individual behavior in crucial situations, be an intelligent student of social organization and tendencies, and be possessed of astuteness, resourcefulness, and patience in dealing with people and situations. Some of these qualities are perhaps more difficult to exercise successfully amid the rapid changes of attitude of direct contact groups than in the more leisurely movements of distributed public opinion. But, on the other hand, it usually requires more astuteness of judgment to estimate character, tendencies, and possible reactions in indirect contact groups than in those of the face-to-face type. In the one case courage and persistence, and in the other clarity of judgment and capacity to take risks, are necessary to avoid mistakes and failures in leadership.

COURAGE AND PERSISTENCE IN LEADERS—Thus courage and persistence are always essential to successful leadership. Opposition will at times become very strenuous and upon occasion even violent. Under such circumstances the man who lacks the courage of his convictions has no business in the rôle of leadership. Failure under such circumstances is the most irretrievable type of failure. Here also independence of judgment is necessary. A weak personality will become convinced that he is wrong or that his cause is unworthy or that his chances of success are poor, in the face of opposition. In most men such intellectual and emotional responses are conditioned to strenuous opposition. The leader of independent judgment will make up his mind for himself and will discount all suggestions to the contrary. The able leader will hold on as long as there is a fair chance of success and thus pilot his cause through many a storm which would have shipwrecked the plans of a less resolute leader. The value of tenacity of purpose or persistence therefore can scarcely be overestimated. Yet, on the other hand, the leader must not be so dogged and uncompromising that he is unable to perceive when a cause is defunct. To be the leader of a lost cause may be romantic, but it does not spell success.

Good natural ability, originality, initiative, good intellectual training, soundness of judgment, mental flexibility, forethought, etc., are assocated qualities, all of which are essential to the highest form of leadership. They perhaps count for most in leadership in indirect contact groups, where the problem of successfully initiating and guiding collective behavior is usually greatest. Often leaders, who themselves lack either the natural ability or the training to initiate successful programs, do very well in subordinate positions. Originality in leadership is the quality of uniqueness of character and thought which enables one to plan something which appeals to others or to use methods of execution which will attract attention. But originality may be a detriment instead of an asset unless one is able to temper it with good judgment and inspirit it with initiative. The original person without initiative is only a dreamer, and the dreamer may have admirers but few followers. To be original without sound judgment is to be a freak or a crank. Self-confidence should also be coupled with originality and initiative to enable the independent leader to take the full measure of responsibility for his ideas or program.

Mental flexibility is another trait which is very important for the leader in a dominant position. He needs to be able to change his plans or tactics without hesitation the moment that he sees the old methods are not working well. To hesitate, to fumble, to be doubtful, may easily be fatal in critical situations. The effective leader should be clear-headed and self-confident, sure of himself but always ready to learn and sensitive to the least need of change and on the lookout for the best new methods. Yet he should seek to avoid the necessity for an undue amount of change by painstaking forethought which will enable him to plan far ahead into the future. When once his plan is decided upon he should administer it with concentrated effort and energy. Great energy of body and of mind and high power of concentration are requisite to leadership of the very highest class.

OTHER MORAL QUALITIES OF LEADERS—Certain moral or moral-social and moral-psychic qualities are also essential to successful leadership. The best type of leader should have both intellectual and moral vision. He should know society and the possibilities and limitations of programs for its betterment. He should be able to foresee opportunities for progress before they are generally apparent. He should also have positive idealism. The purely selfish, scheming sort of personality who seeks always to better his own condition at the expense of others, instead of along with the improvement of others, is likely sooner or later to fail. Some men do succeed at the expense of almost everybody else, but such men occupy more nearly the rôle of social buccaneers than that of leaders. They and a chosen crew take advantage of a disorganized or of an as yet incompletely organized condition of society to carry out their schemes regardless of either the wishes or the interests of others.

The highest type of moral leadership is of course that in which the leader is willing to sacrifice himself for the success of a principle or a cause, and to find his own greater self-realization in the triumph of the cause with which he has identified himself, or to go down with it in defeat. There have not been a great many truly great leaders of this type in the history of the world, but mankind is not likely to forget those it has once recognized and understood. The next highest type of leader is the one who is willing to sacrifice self and others for a great and worthy cause. Other moral qualities essential to a high degree of success in leadership are power of inhibition and of self-discipline. Headstrongness and strong convictions are often necessary to success in leadership, but these qualities must not be unrestrained. Unchecked they produce in the end bigots and social wreckers rather than effective leaders. Even the leader, perhaps the leader more than most men, should develop a power of sane and just self-examination and should be able to say to his impulses and enthusiasms, however strong, "no," or, "with moderation."

OTHER QUALITIES OF LEADERS—If the leader possesses all of the qualities here claimed for him he should yet display a cheerful and even temper and be able to take success and temporary setbacks, or even failure, with poise and to renew his attack undaunted. The leader who becomes irritable or sour or loses his nerve has already lost much, perhaps most, of the battle. He should also have had experience which gives a sureness of touch and fineness of technique which are indispensable in delicate causes. These, together with self-confidence, inspire the confidence of others and bring to him a reputation for achieving success. If in addition to these qualities he also possesses organizing and executive ability and a knowledge of human nature and of society, and is free from unreasonable restraints imposed by custom or prejudice or superstition or an arbitrary power, and if his project is one which in its nature is capable of success, the way should be open for the accomplishment of his ends. Of course but few leaders ever possess all of the psychic and psycho-social qualifications and conditions here outlined. But there are also but few truly great leaders.

THE ART OF BEING LED is a factor among the conditions of success in leadership which is sometimes overlooked. Yet it is scarcely second in importance to the qualities themselves which are necessary to successful leadership. Every sincere and idealistic leader has sooner or later reached the limits to which he could carry his scheme, not alone because his own powers failed, but because he could no longer count on the knowledge, idealism, courage, concentration, and singleness of purpose of a sufficient number of his followers to make further advance possible. Some leaders have taken these limitations as a matter of course, while others have encountered them with surprise and grief and cynicism. This has been particularly the case in our country with those who have sought to establish a true democracy of the people. There are few who are now as sanguine regarding possibilities in this connection as were some of our idealistic forefathers. Likewise the indefinite perfectibility of mankind which appeared so self-evident in theory and so certain of achievement in practice to the intellectual leaders of the late eighteenth century is now known to be a myth. But much more can be accomplished in preparing the masses to be led effectively for the establishment of a better social order than has yet been done. A more nearly universal education in the principles and data of science, especially of the social sciences, training in respect for proved facts and in the factual discrediting of superstition, magic, and merely mystical daydreaming and escape-from-reality philosophies, and finally training in loyalty to the best social order and types of personality which scientific method can project, will set free a vast volume of the energies of men now unused or inhibited, to be applied to constructive purposes through intelligent social and personal leadership.

MATERIALS FOR SUPPLEMENTARY READING

Allport, F. H., *Social Psychology*, pp. 419-424
Andrews, L. C., *Manpower*
Bogardus, E. S., *Fundamentals of Social Psychology*, Chs. XXXII, XXXIII, XXXV, XXXVI, XXXVIII-XL
Cooley, C. H., *Human Nature and the Social Order*, Ch. IX

PSYCHO-SOCIAL ENVIRONMENT

Dunlap, K., *Social Psychology*, Ch. VIII
Ellwood, C. A., *The Psychology of Human Society*, Chs. VII, X
Gault, R. H., *Social Psychology*, Ch. IX
Hocking, W. E., "Leaders and Led," *Yale Review*, XIII: 625-641
Lumley, F. E., *Means of Social Control*, Ch. VIII
LeBon, G., *The Crowd*, Book III, Ch. III
Lippmann, W., *Public Opinion*, Chs. XIII, XIV, XV
McDougall, W., *The Group Mind*, Ch. IX
Miller, A. H., *Leadership*
Mumford, E., *The Origins of Leadership*
Strong, E. K., Jr., "Control of Propaganda as a Psychological Problem," *Sci. Mo.*, XIV: 234-252
Williams, J. M., *Principles of Social Psychology*, Chs. VIII, XIV

CHAPTER XXXV

NON-INSTITUTIONAL CONTROLS

THE NATURE AND KINDS OF CONTROLS—A control is any stimulus or complex of stimuli which calls forth a response. Thus all stimuli are controls. Controls may be of many different categories, such as physical, including geographical, climatic, temperature, humidity, etc.; biological, including plant and animal life of various forms and in various combinations; and social controls, including those of physico-social, bio-social, and psycho-social environments in their manifold forms. These classes of controls are all of the objective or environmental kind, and all controls exist fundamentally and ultimately in the environment. There are also individual and personal controls, as distinguished from social controls. But these have been fixed in the individual personality either through the ontogenetic influence of environmental pressures or through the phylogenetic influence of environment in selecting the forms of inheritance. There can be no subjective controls which have not been derived at some time, in the individual or in the race, from the environmental pressures.

In this book we are not particularly concerned with the physical and biological and the physico-social and lower bio-social environmental controls as they operate in the organization of collective responses. They are of importance primarily to the sociologists and other social scientists rather than to the social psychologists. Our concern in this and the following chapter is mainly, but not exclusively, with those controls which are to be found in the psycho-social and human bio-social environments. They are by far the most numerous in modern life and they dominate our responses much more directly and intimately, and for the most part, in much greater detail, than do the controls of the natural and the lower social environments.

The Types of Psycho-social Controls—In general we may distinguish two types of psycho-social controls, the non-institutional and the institutional. The non-institutional psycho-social controls are those which are relatively ephemeral in form, unstandardized, and changing readily and rapidly, as compared with the institutional controls. These non-institutional controls are constituted of behavior patterns which are relatively loosely organized collectively. They are typified particularly by fads, fashions, crazes, and transient conventional beliefs and attitudes of all kinds. The institutional controls are those types of behavior organization which are relatively permanent. Although they change, they do so more slowly and thus retain their organization although their content may be gradually transformed. The forms of psycho-social behavior which are included under the institutional controls are of two general types, the subjective or relatively immaterial and intangible, which are carried only in the individual behavior, and the objective or material and tangible, which have externalized existence. Under the subjective aspects may be included conventions, traditions, and customs, which tend to become integrated symbolically in ritual. The objective institutional social controls are codes, administrative organizations, and physical extensions. In the objective social controls the bio-social and the physico-social elements often outweigh the psycho-social, especially in the administrative organization and physical extensions. In the codes, however, the written symbolical or externalized neuro-psychic content of the psycho-social environmental controls predominates. Beliefs, mores, folkways, etc., are other terms which may, under certain circumstances, be applied to the less objective aspects of institutions.

The Psycho-social Controls Are Dominant—Of course, as was intimated above, the institutional controls are not exclusively psycho-social. They make use of bio-social, physico-social, and even to some extent of natural environmental factors in the integration of their relatively stable and continuous organizations and structures. But, like the non-institutional social controls, they are primarily psycho-social. It is the psycho-social elements in both the institutional and the non-institutional social controls which dominate their organization

NON-INSTITUTIONAL CONTROLS 543

and give direction and effectiveness to their functions as controls. There are, of course, non-institutional controls which are also non-social. This is the case, for example, with the physico-geographic, climatic, natural resources, and altitude controls. They produce effects transitory as well as permanent upon social organization, mainly indirectly, by means of conditioning the collective living processes, but they are not themselves social. It is the physical and social inventions and the method or scientific inventions which man produces to help him in his collective adjustments to these non-social controls which become his social controls and dominate most intimately and directly his collective life processes. Most natural environmental controls become institutionalized, that is, produce relatively permanent or institutionalized responses instead of ephemeral and non-institutional responses.

In this chapter we shall consider the leading non-institutional controls, giving particular attention to the psycho-social phenomena of fads, fashions, and crazes. But we shall also include in our discussion some account of rumor, and the more ephemeral aspects of conventions, beliefs, public opinion, and even of science. These latter psycho-social processes in their more permanent forms overlap with, or are also included in, the institutional controls.

FADS: THEIR NATURE AND FUNCTION—Fads, like all other non-institutional or unstable social controls, may consist of either overt or inner behavior. They may be habits of action or of thought. A fad is some form of behavior which does not secure universal or continuous acceptance by the group, but is taken up by only a portion of the group and dies out in the course of a relatively short period of time because of lack of support. A fad usually lasts for only a season or a portion of a season. Its chief appeal is in its novelty and its function seems to be that of calling attention to the one who adopts it. Thus, it is a sort of consciously or unconsciously used advertising device. Some people adopt fads quite consciously for the sake of the temporary prestige which they will gain thereby or for the sake of being in the limelight, or in some other light brighter than that at the periphery of the group's attention. Others adopt fads more or less unconsciously. They have no adequate realization of their significance for themselves as means of advertising, but they experience a heightened emotional sense of well-being when they are following the lead of those who have obtained attention by espousing the fad. Their choices are made largely in the realm of the emotional consciousness and subconsciousness rather than intellectually.

Still others invent the fads, accidentally or purposively. Frequently comes the news from Atlantic City or Palm Beach that some one has designed and wears a striking bathing suit, or that some one at Newport has a new doll, or that another person, who cannot achieve distinction for the profundity of his thought, maintains a reputation for eccentricity by frequently enunciating some new or fantastic theory about almost anything of which he has some glimmering of knowledge. There are people who thus make a business of the art of securing the attention of their companions or contemporaries and enjoy immensely being for the time the center of interest, however trivial the interest manifested in them or their behavior may be.

In contrast with such people—the faddists—are those persons who are interested in true achievement of a fundamental character. Their interest is so strongly centered in their work or the objects or ideas they have created that they are very little conscious of themselves as creators. Instead of seeking to be the center of attention they are frequently shy and embarrassed when attention is drawn to them by their behavior or ideas. They, rather than the faddists, are the more likely to produce behavior or objects worthy of survival.

FADS ARE EVERYWHERE—Fads are to be found in practically every phase of behavior. They occur most frequently, perhaps, in the realms of clothing, recreation, and in the intercourse of leisured groups. These fields of behavior are still most experimental and no adequately standardized tests have been worked out for their control. In the matter of clothing the fad is usually in the nature of an unusually extreme interpretation or variation of the prevailing fashions. Thus the hat may be exceptionally large or small, or high or low, or the ornamentation may be especially striking or it may be particularly plain. The faddish skirt may be especially full or tight, or slit unusually high, or the wrap dress may be worn without sufficient underclothing, so as to reveal more or less of the body. The handkerchief may be noticeably plain or colored, the stockings may run to excessive shades or designs, the cut of the neck may be especially low, or the heels may be very high or very low. In the matter of recreation a group may take up a game not hitherto very popular and concentrate on that. Or they may turn to walking with a vengeance, or to dry bathing, skiing, fancy dancing, ukulele playing, petting, etc. Many varieties of handshakes, lifting of the hat, bowing, verbal greetings, and leave takings become the fads of the day in the polite intercourse of a single generation. One form succeeds another quite rapidly among those who endeavor to keep up to date or lead in the trivial. It is their main source of excitement and means of distinction.

Fads are also to be found in the more serious aspects of life. Diet, which should normally be a matter of some forethought, is often made the vehicle of faddism. Our beliefs about art, literature, morals, and social questions are also subject to waves of faddism. Bizarre or eccentric views on questions of religion, politics, or economic and social welfare may pass current in certain circles for a time and then give way to others, perhaps equally unwarranted or unusual. Even the field of science is not free from faddist notions. A new method of brushing the teeth, a much recommended "psychic" or "hygienic" treatment for indigestion or colds or various other ills, may gain a good deal of currency before its uselessness is discovered. Certain authors and forms of art become "the rage." Some years ago every one was reading historical romances. Later it was the "problem" novel. Recently the small town novel held sway. Cubism had its day; also free verse. Formerly dentists did much more indiscriminate toothdrawing than is at present the case. There is almost an established rhythm of advice which emphasizes alternately the use of a tooth powder and of a tooth paste. At one time we are told not to drink water with our meals and at another we are told to do so. During the late war it became quite common for people to believe in spirit communications. The various types of breakfast foods have all had their morning. The raw-food eaters succeeded the vegetarians. Now come the vitaminists, often finding vitamins everywhere except where they exist. Some fads have a substratum of scientific fact, but it is the nature of the fad to exaggerate practice based on this element of fact and thus, through pushing it to extremes, to discredit it with thinking people.

How Fads May Grow into Fashions or Conventional Practices—While fads are usually merely extreme interpretations of practices of existing fashions or other more institutionalized behavior, and as a consequence disappear after they have served their function of advertising their followers, they may however be endowed with a longer life or receive more general acceptance. Thus the fad may become a fashion by appealing to such large numbers as to become the general rather than the exceptional practice or trend of thinking. The slit skirt which is extreme one season may become the fashionable or average standard of the next. The dress that comes to the knees is a fad at one time, but it may be a fashion at another. Carrying lizards or other animals chained to the neck or collar may or may not go beyond the stage of faddism. Likewise, an extreme interpretation in medicine or ethics, or social work, or even in history, may at one period be accounted only a fad, while further research or practice may confirm it and raise it to the dignity of permanent fact and procedure. Thus, at one time mental healing and osteopathy were regarded by the conservative medical profession as wholly faddistic. Now, some of these practices have been adopted by the medical practitioners as sound in certain types of cases.

Fads and Fashions Compared—Fashions belong to the same order of instability and irrationality as fads, but their instability and ephemerality are not so marked. Ordinarily they persist for a longer period of time and appeal to larger numbers of people. Fads and fashions are to be distinguished primarily on the basis of differences in the degree of their universality, intensity, and duration which exist between these two categories of behavior. Fashions ordinarily persist for a longer period, because their irrationality is either not so great or not so apparent as that of fads. Yet a fashion does not persist, without serious modification, beyond what may be termed its conventional season. Changes in the fashions of clothes occur usually each climatic season, or rather considerably in advance of the seasons. Changes in the fashions of social intercourse may persist for a longer period, or until the followers catch up with the initiators in the race for distinction or attention. Fashions in sports also change with the climatic seasons, although they may recur the corresponding season of the year following. Fashions in clothing do not recur in following seasons, because such recurrence would cut down the profits of the fashion makers and would rob the devotees of fashion of much of their chance for distinction. The extent of the fashion is usually much greater than that of the fad. Only the more daring, or reckless, or thoughtless follow the fad. The more conservative middle-grounders make the fashion practically universal in the course of time. The greater degree of universality of the fashion may be manifest in either of two ways. The fashion may cover a larger territory or it may appeal to more people in the same territory. Where a fad becomes practically universal within a limited territory it remains a fad rather than a fashion, because on the basis of a wider comparison it lacks universality. The fact that the fad is usually an extreme form of the fashion has already been illustrated.

CLOTHING THE CHIEF BASIS OF FASHION—Fashions, like fads, are most common in the matter of clothing, amusement and recreation, and polite intercourse, but are to be found everywhere. Both fads and fashions are means of advertising the personality of the person who adopts them. Quite frequently they constitute in large measure the content of the personality. The people who follow fads and fashions are ordinarily not those who possess the most profound types or richest content of personality. Their personalities, like the fashions and fads they adopt, are superficial, transitory, and often of unsound mental, moral, and social value. They build up their personalities in large measure out of the shifting content of this fashionable and faddist behavior and consequently do not anchor themselves morally anywhere in particular. Fashions and fads are means of competition. Their followers, not having founded their characters on the firmer foundations of devotion to a program of tested achievement values, constantly and restlessly flounder around in the sea of unsettled emotions and experiences catching at every floating practice or belief which offers any support to their disintegrating and evaporating personalities.

FASHION LEADERS AND PRESTIGE—The leaders of fashions are those who invent or first adopt new behavior patterns and exploit these as long as they give them distinction from the common herd. But as the multitudes begin to adopt the same practices and threaten them with the oblivion of anonymity because of the increasing numbers of devotees, the leaders abandon the old fashions and adopt new ones, thus seeking to perpetuate their distinction and leadership of attention.

The method by which the leaders secure a supply of new fashions is an interesting and instructive lesson in social psychology. They may accomplish this end by individual invention. That is, some leader, perceiving her prestige to be in danger of submergence by the rising tide of the mass of imitators, may launch out upon a search for variations. Thus she may create fads and these fads may become new fashions. Every leader in fashions needs followers, for without followers there can be no fashions, although there may be fads. A fad may occasionally remain individual behavior, but a fashion is always collective behavior on a considerable, almost a universal, scale. So long as those who adopt the new fashion are following the leader her prestige is secure, but when they begin merely to imitate the fashion regardless of the leader it is time for her to seek to initiate a new fashion, for the old fashion has become a folkway rather than a matter of consciously "follow the leader."

THE PROFESSIONAL FASHION EXPERT—Most fashions are no longer invented by the one who introduces them. Modern professional leaders of fashion—if the term professional may be properly applied to those who make it the main concern of their lives to lead in the fashions—are little more than promoters, sometimes movie actresses or only manikins. The rate of change in fashions is too great for the leaders to invent a considerable number of the fashions which they introduce. Consequently the competition between leaders of fashion is not so much to invent as to introduce new fashions, although there may be competition in the former matter also. Competition in fashion is keenest in the matter of clothing. This is because clothing is the most external of all the forms of borrowed behavior, while sports and forms of social intercourse follow closely after. All of this illustrates the principle that we perceive and imitate most easily visible forms of behavior. It is in this field of the visible and overt behavior fashions, especially that of clothing, that the expert or specialist inventor and purveyor have been most developed in the service of fashion. We have here the expert designer who produces new "creations" which the promoters of fashion purchase at prices which pay the designers handsome commissions for their risk and ingenuity. Likewise, the expert caterer, decorator, amusement providers, and a host of other aids to the leisured, are constantly inventing new methods of appealing to their clients and patrons, who are seeking to maintain or increase their prestige by presenting themselves before the public in something new. The desire to lead in the fashions is very similar to the almost universal desire of amateurs, and of professionals, to star, or at least to participate, in a play or a pageant or a folk dance. The chances for self-advertisement are excellent.

Leading in fashions may have little intellectual responsibility attached to it. If one possesses sufficient wealth he can hire or purchase the plans for the competitive display as well as the objects of display themselves. Wealth is the primary necessity to modern leadership in fashion. There are no longer many bargains in self-display.

FASHION COMPETITION AND WEALTH—The very success with which the fashion promoters secure a following makes it inevitable that the more highly competitive fashions, especially those in clothes, should have short lives. The ease with which fashion news circulates and designs can be copied, the machine processes by which styles in clothing and weaves in fabrics, ideas, materials, procedure of all kinds, can be duplicated almost everywhere makes it certain that very soon all of those who measure success in life by the degree to which they approach their leaders in dress, manners, standards of living, in conduct, and in their ideas will soon have produced pretty good imitations. Thus they make themselves like the personalities of the leaders of fashion, however superficial the content of these personalities may be. This wholesale copying brings about a tremendous uniformity or rhythm of change. Everybody becomes much like everybody else, but unlike himself of yesterday. A premium is placed upon the mere fact of change regardless of its more ultimate and long-time adjustment values. From this situation of mob uniformity the leaders or promoters of fashion wish to escape. Consequently they patronize the new designs and precipitate other changes. And this goes on continuously and endlessly. The result is that fashion becomes highly commercialized where it is most competitive and leadership in fashion does not depend on brains—or at least not on the brains of the leaders—but on the possession of the money with which to purchase the new designs. This money is not earned by the leaders of the fashions, but in most cases by some one else. Consequently competition in modern fashion has reduced itself primarily to the unintellectual basis of a competition in the spending of money which some one else provides. The moral and social effects of this tendency are interesting, but not particularly pertinent to the present treatment.

TENDENCIES IN FASHIONS COMPARED—There are of course fashions in the less competitive fields—in the semi-intellectual, esthetic, literary, artistic, and other phases of life—which are not so strongly subject to this rapid rate of change. Here leadership is less likely to depend on ability to spend and more likely to rest upon individual ingenuity and intellectual capacity or some other higher quality of personality in the fashion leader. Fashions in clothing and entertainment are the lowest form of fashions from the standpoint of the personality qualities demanded of their leaders and therefore the types most universally exploited. These fashions are so highly competitive because they are so superficial and objective, so easily perceived and understood and imitated. To follow them requires little or no intelligence beyond the ordinary, because others can be hired to do the planning and work. They are almost external to one's personality. But even in these there is some degree of variation. While every one attempts to conform to the general pattern, individual initiative, or more likely the inventiveness of the designers, will produce a great many variations which will conform to individual taste or personality. Consequently in highly competitive fashions there are two types of endeavor. One is imitation of the main patterns of dress, entertainment, behavior, thought, while the other is competitive and differentiating within the larger trend, the striving for a minor note of uniqueness within the larger whole of conformity. Both tendencies are highly profitable to the commercial caterers of fashion.

LEADERS AND FOLLOWERS OF FASHION—While the general purpose of the leader and follower of fashion is the same—the acquirement of distinction—the methods used are very different. The one promotes the new and invites a following up to a certain point of success, but thereafter fears it and seeks to escape from the sameness which her success in leadership has created. This success in leadership depends largely upon her prestige, and particularly perhaps upon the judgment or luck she has in choosing her designer or caterer. It is up to him to offer new wares which will enable her to hold her place of leadership. Sooner or later almost all leaders go down in this competition, for the high financial rewards to the caterers stimulate the strongest competition among them for new "ideas." Even the prestige of certain sources of fashion, like Paris or London, or in such a name as Poiret, does not always suffice to give a monopoly against new designs or plans and new designers.

On the other hand, the people who follow the fashions seek to borrow reflected distinction by conformity to the leader. As it were, the followers steal the virtue or magical power of those who are ahead of them in the game and force the leaders into new modes to escape contamination from the mob. At the bottom of this competitive fashion process imitation of the fashions is mainly negative in motive. Those who are interested primarily in other and more fundamental values of life conform more or less tardily to the changes of fashions and then only to escape the unpleasant and eliminative effects of being too different from others. There is a strong antipathy among the conventional and the dogmatic, who are usually the more ignorant and fear ridden, to people who look different from the ordinary run of people. The demand for conformity is very strong among us. The strongest weapon which could be used against excess of fashion would be the inoculation of tolerance.

THE CRAZE is less rational than either fad or fashion and may grow out of either. Ordinarily crazes develop slowly, gradually gaining momentum in the emotions and practices of men and women. In these early stages they are fads or fashions, but finally the mutual and reciprocal suggestion of the adherents of the fads or fashions begins to work rapidly and the movement gains momentum quickly and becomes a craze. It sweeps over great numbers of people at large, or most or all of the members in a selected group, with magnetic power. Under the influence of this strong interstimulation a high degree of irrational excitement and faith in the virtues of the plan or object of the behavior is generated and the craze is followed madly until it results either in success or in a logical contradiction and absurdity.

Crazes, like the other forms of unstable, non-institutional social controls considered in this chapter, may be either in the nature of overt behavior or of the character of internal behavior or ideas and emotions. All crazes have some emotional content and not infrequently they partake of the nature of ideals. The idealism of crazes is often extremely strong, although it may employ unsound procedure and be very irrational. Many crazes are based on almost purely physical overt behavior, such as dancing, athletic exercises, fashions in clothes and entertainment. Others involve a certain type of intellectual activity, mainly of a perceptual order, such as card games, mah jong, doing cross word puzzles, solving rebuses and conundrums. Such crazes often develop to a violent intensity, involving a large portion of the population and consuming much or most of the free energies of people which should be devoted to more original thinking on the adjustment problems of life. Other crazes fall into the category of beliefs, and are borne along by public opinion. These are especially likely to be found in the fields of politics, religion, art, and even pseudo science. The most nonsensical views about the coming of the world to an end or the will and ability of a certain man to save civilization, if elected to office, or the "divine" mission of a certain school of art or a new religion may be entertained with the strongest conviction by people who mutually stimulate each other to such absurdities. Sometimes, of course, a craze may be based on valid principles and be the result merely of very great enthusiasm for the cause. Quick and violent revolutions rightly or wrongly undertaken are merely crazes. We have a craze wherever there is highly intense collective activity with a large degree of mob-mindedness manifest.

CRAZES AND SUGGESTION—Suggestion is the chief psycho-social process involved in the craze. The fad and fashion may develop along the leisurely pathway of imitation. It is not until the responses are well conditioned to the stimuli by means of imitation that the fad and the fashion turn into the craze. For it is not until then that suggestion can operate readily and freely. Once the conditioning of responses is sufficiently complete the multiplication of stimuli resulting from constant interstimulation of the group produces, in the absence of rational or irrational inhibitions, that multiplication and concentration of uniform collective responses which we call a craze. The fact that not all fads and fashions become crazes when the conditioning of responses has been sufficiently established through imitation is due to the existence of inhibitions. Sometimes these are positive ones in the nature of rational judgments which restrain the behavior from excess. In the other cases the inhibitions are negative and are of the nature of financial inability or of religious or domestic or other conventional restraints which prevent the responses from operating with full strength.

INTOLERANCE AND THE DEFLATION OF CRAZES—Crazes which win general approval are not regarded as irrational, but are accounted as praiseworthy enthusiasm, sometimes even as inspired. Revolutions which succeed are always right, no matter how much suffering they may cause. Religious revivalists and political campaigners and art enthusiasts are very self-congratulatory over the degree of mob excitement which they have stimulated. The dogmatists and servants of darkness and ignorance are always self-styled servants of the Lord or "defenders of religion" or "knights of civilization." No other people are so incapable of therapeutic introspection as the crazed. It is when the people tire of the continued enthusiasm or monotony of activity required of them or when they find that their assumptions were incorrect that the craze loses its drawing power. In such cases the craze deflates rapidly, sometimes within a few hours or days, although it may have been growing for months, occasionally for years. Marathon dancing increased in wildness for weeks in 1923-1924, but quite suddenly collapsed as soon as the limits of competitive endurance were reached and the newspapers, considering that there was no longer sufficient news material in those extravagances, ceased to stimulate them by their sensational accounts. Many a revolution or riot has collapsed from fatigue due to too greatly sustained excitement or even from such a mechanical cause as the turning of a fire hose upon a mob. The cold water turns the behavior in other directions and the interstimulation ceases, consequently the responses no longer work to perpetuate the craze. Likewise, when the midnight hour appears and the end of the world has not come, the watchers begin to go home and the realization of the fact that they have followed a false prophet inhibits their ardor for a year or a decade or a generation. Even the religious zealots who murder with fire, sword, and gun, and behave irreligiously and maliciously towards others with different beliefs, in the name of their gods, lose their convictions or grow fatigued from the monotony of their responses in the course of time and desist from their intolerant and nefarious practices. Their enthusiasm for "righteousness" collapses and cannot be revived, even by their medicine men and priesthood.

IGNORANCE AND REPRESSION AND CRAZES—Since crazes operate primarily through suggestion they are most likely to occur among the ignorant and those of lower intelligence levels. But, as Ross has pointed out, even the intelligent may be drawn into the maelstrom of a craze if its volume and intensity become sufficiently great. This is the more likely to occur when there are insufficient data or a lack of distributed information with which to test the validity of the assumptions of the craze. The very intensity of the craze itself may come in time to inhibit judgment and leave the normally intelligent exposed to its suggestions. Ross has also shown that one craze is frequently succeeded by another, exciting and arousing emotions of a different character. One set of reactions may become fatigued or the unsoundness of the craze may become manifest; yet there may be a large fund of excitement and undirected energy available when the old craze collapses. This favors the promotion of a new craze if the responses of the people are properly conditioned to any set of stimuli prevalent in the group. Finally, not only is an ignorant society or group more likely to be the victim of crazes, but any active or dynamic society suffers from the same disadvantage because of the large amount of physical and mental energies which it releases in relatively uncontrolled or non-stereotyped responses. The best way to prevent crazes is to make people intelligent and to give them an abundance of functional outlets for their energies and complete freedom of thought. Enforced homogeneity of thought or behavior will not prevent crazes, but may confine them to the lines of interest which are dominant in the group. If the causes of homogeneity also make for repression, crazes are almost certain to break out as exaggerations of some of the accepted practices or beliefs. The repressed energies demand some sort of escape and they find it through the paths of least resistance.

Although crazes tend to be organized as excessive exploitations of fads, fashions, and conventions, they may arise synthetically and apparently spontaneously out of materials of thought or action which are common to the group but were not previously organized into collective responses. The conditioning of responses to stimuli which exist in the group is basic to the craze in such cases. It is necessary merely to organize these stimuli in the thinking or overt behavior of the group to have them operate as sources of suggestion. If there are not adequate inhibitions present the collective responses may become a craze. But this source of the craze is relatively rare, although it may reënforce the craze arising from other sources.

THE PSYCHOLOGICAL BASES OF FADS, FASHIONS, AND CRAZES are rather deep seated. When responses have become so automatic that they can be made unconsciously, the individual turns to various other activities, sometimes of doubtful value. The child in his search for new experiences is manifesting the same behavior. The human mechanism is so constructed that it economizes energies by relegating much-repeated behavior to automatic levels. But human beings cannot live entirely on an unconscious or a simple perceptual level. As a result they must seek effective outlets for their energies. This is especially true of people who live routine lives. The desire for distinction is also very deeply rooted in human nature. It is an almost inevitable product of the early care of the child. Being the center of attention is usually conditioned to pleasant associations, and the desire to be in the limelight is a logical outcome. Finally, the desire to be like others in our group is another strongly conditioned trait of human beings. Wide divergences from the standards of the group are weeded out by negative conditioning. These are the psychological bases which give rise to extreme forms of non-institutional controls, namely, the desire for new experiences, the desire for distinction, and the desire to be like others.

PROPHYLACTICS FOR NON-INSTITUTIONAL CONTROLS—Professor Ross has discussed the prophylactics for "mob-mindedness" at some length. We may summarize them generally in the light of our discussion of their psychological causes. Since much of the adaptive behavior in modern times has become routine and capable of being handled more or less automatically, we must furnish other useful outlets for organic energies. A more socialized type of education and a more rational control over the aims and methods of all of our directive institutions would help here. There should also be opportunity for distinction in rational fields. The scientist who is working on a problem and the artist who expresses himself fundamentally in his work are rarely followers of fads. If we could give all people equally engrossing forms of self-expression and distinction, they would be less susceptible to fads. If they cannot gain distinction in socially acceptable fields, they will try to get it in those which are socially less valuable. If they cannot have fame they will seek notoriety.

OTHER CONVENTIONS—A convention is any contemporary practice or belief which occurs collectively or in reduplication.

According to this definition we should include fads, fashions, and crazes among the conventions. But there are also other conventional or contemporary practices and beliefs which scarcely reach the degrees of universality of collective acceptance and of irrationality and instability which are ordinarily attributed to fads, fashions, and crazes. They are more irregular in their appearance or continuance, or they are more firmly established in fact and therefore not susceptible to the laws of the more irrational or pervasive conventions. In this classification we may list rumors, beliefs, public opinion, and scientific data and principles. To be sure rumors and beliefs may at any time become the subject matter of fads, fashions, or crazes, and public opinion may carry either an irrational or a rational and scientific content, or both together. But there is yet a distinction in practice, however difficult it is to define schematically and verbally, which appears to justify relatively separate categories for these types of conventions last mentioned. One basis of distinction is, perhaps, to be found in the fact that they may, with the exception of rumor, have a history which extends far back into the past from which they have been derived with little or no change of form or content. Also, they are likely to extend into the future without losing their identity. This latter fact is particularly true of science. Beliefs and public opinion are more fluid and are constantly merging with fads, fashions, and crazes. Rumor is particularly ephemeral and fluid, only now and then being stabilized or crystallized into beliefs, public opinion, or scientific fact. Also, these four secondary types of conventions are wholly in the field of mental or internal instead of overt behavior.

RUMOR travels from mouth to ear, from mind to mind. It is irresponsible. Hence it suffers constantly from elaboration and is transformed and augmented by the daydreams and wishes, the envies and jealousies, of the minds through which it passes. Wise people give little attention to rumors, at most merely taking a hint from them for further investigation. Yet, because of the multitudinous minds through which rumors have passed and in which they have undergone elaboration, it is practically impossible to verify or disprove a rumor by the method of tracing it to its source. Rumors are not recorded, hence their instability. Rumor, because it is verbal and irresponsible and therefore meets the need of the average mind for an outlet for repressed wishes through elaboration, constitutes a large part of the collective mental content. But there is a growing tendency to test rumors by subjecting them to a comparison with known facts, a sort of test in the light of their inherent probability. The fact that we are aware of the tendency of the human mind to elaborate statements as a subjective relief from repression helps us to discount many rumors which we might otherwise be tempted to believe. Of course, back of rumors there is some sort of truth, but its nature is always very difficult or impossible to unravel. Frequently the background of fact in a rumor is as much or more in the behavior of the elaborators to whom it has served as a release for repressed desires than in that of the person to whom the rumor is attached. Jung has given an excellent example of this. Gossips are almost universally people who do, or are restrained only by fear from doing, the things they retail with so much avidity. On the other hand, people who are morally incapable of doing what is recounted are, in the vast majority of cases, also incapable of recounting it. But in spite of the fact that we know these things in the abstract, we are very much influenced in the concrete by rumors in making our judgments. Because of their anonymity it is usually difficult to identify rumors as such.

BELIEFS may arise out of rumors, facts, or inferences from observations, or they may come down to us from the past as traditions. They may be clearly defined in our consciousness, or they may be so hazy and indefinite as to be in the category of emotional attitudes. They may be reduced to printed or written form, and thus serve collectively as declarations of principles or as creeds. They may float about, so to speak, in the public opinion of the time, in the form of proverbs, axioms, platitudes, aphorisms, adages, wise sayings, maxims, and the like, and thus be the property of everybody implicitly, but of nobody by avowal. There is among us a sort of cavalier method of treating proverbs which professes a half scorn for them as merely folk beliefs but nevertheless makes use of them by innuendo and specific citation in an argument or when we wish to support a cause. The creeds likewise have our nominal acceptance rather than our overt or conscious espousal. Often we adhere nominally or perfunctorily to creeds and declarations of principles without actually knowing their content. We profess this acceptance through our adherence to some organization which espouses these principles as its guiding code. But here we are getting into the realm of institutional controls which at this point are difficult to separate from the non-institutional. Beliefs vary greatly in fluidity, from an instability approaching that of rumors at one extreme to that of printed declarations of principles and even established facts at the other extreme. A very large portion of the content of the collective mental behavior falls under the category of beliefs.

PUBLIC OPINION is any fairly uniform collective expression of mental or inner behavior reactions. Its content may be that of rumors, beliefs, facts, principles, or of fads, fashions, and crazes in their psychic aspects. It is a collective phenomenon which is also a composite fact. Public opinion is what the members of any indirect contact group or public think or feel about anything and everything. Ordinarily we insist that these opinions and attitudes of the members of the group shall have sufficient uniformity to insure a unity of definition of the content of public opinion. But some writers use the concept much more loosely and include the most diverse opinions and attitudes under the general term public opinion. It would seem better, however, to speak in such cases of public opinions, reserving the term public opinion for uniform mental reactions to stimuli.

Public opinion is very powerful in modern society. One cannot live in the midst of views and attitudes, if expressed with any degree of vigor, without being influenced by them. The great volume of public opinion which is generated in the modern world through conversation, press, theater, telephone, telegraph, radio, lectures, preaching, and other agencies, is especially favorable to the production of uniform responses, particularly among those who are but poorly informed in matters of fact.

Public opinion may arise out of a contemporary situation,

or it may descend from the past as tradition and thus have an institutional aspect. While public opinion is never free from institutional determination and from some degree of control from the past, it is constantly undergoing revision in the present. This fluidity is due in part to the highly dynamic character of modern society and in part to the fact that scientific data and principles are gradually entering into the content of public opinion and are transforming it.

SCIENCE—Experimental methods in the laboratory and careful observation and statistical generalization of phenomena are constantly producing a mass of tested data and principles in every field of interest. The highest grade of mental content is tested knowledge or facts. These are accepted by most people as the standards by which all other behavior, mental or overt, should be tested. Thus science becomes the arbiter of all truth or harmony of collective behavior. In each field of interest we build up collections of tested and harmonized data and principles and call these collective organizations the science of that particular field. All of the sciences of the several fields together are found to harmonize among themselves and they are spoken of collectively simply as *science*.

Science may be institutional or non-institutional. All of the institutions are slowly transforming the inner and overt behavior content of their members in harmony with the findings of science. Highly competitive institutions, like the economic and to some extent the political and educational, undergo this reorganization fairly readily and willingly. The less competitive institutions, such as the theological and esthetic, make the transformation with much difficulty and delay. But since science is nothing but tested knowledge or behavior and since tested knowledge and behavior are better than untested, the transformation to conform to the findings of science must inevitably occur everywhere, unless our culture is to deteriorate and our civilization to decay.

Science is also entering into and transforming beliefs and public opinion as rapidly as we are able to make it available for these modes of psychic behavior. Gradually it drives rumor into the periphery of our consciousness, and fads, fashions, and crazes recede before its bright light of investigation. Ultimately these great irrational collective forms of conduct will have to justify themselves on the basis of collective utility and scientific fact and principle, or disappear.

How the Non-institutional Controls Work—As was said above, these controls operate to make uniform our behavior in the group. This uniformization takes place both through imitation and suggestion. New conditionings of responses to stimuli which have been perceived or recognized are accomplished through the process which we defined above as imitation. Collective behavior on an imitative basis is therefore a growth. It proceeds only as rapidly as the individuals of the group can perceive the stimuli and make them effective by conditioning their responses to them. But once these responses are thus conditioned suggestion becomes the dominant means of behavior control. Thus in a completely uniformized society people would be completely controlled, at least after maturity of behavior had been reached, through suggestion. Such a situation we actually find existent in many primitive peoples who have long been isolated from disturbing contacts with other cultures and who have made no dynamic inventions of their own. They have little analytical awareness of their institutions and can give only perfunctory, if any, reasons for their practices. Even an advanced society which became highly institutionalized and ossified would behave in much the same manner, as was the case with most advanced oriental cultures until recently.

But where new advances in science are constantly being made, as among ourselves, and where economic resources are being exploited as a result, and where new means of communication and transportation, new industrial organizations, changes in the plane of living, and the like, are constantly being introduced, the collective mental and overt behavior will be highly dynamic. The people will be highly conscious and analytical and critical of their institutions. Institutional behavior will in large measure give place to non-institutional behavior. But in a highly developed society the institutions do not of course disappear. They become much more flexible and submit to revision the better to fit themselves as controls for the functional adjustment of their members, or they resist changes altogether. This growth of the non-institutional controls, especially of the fads, fashions, and crazes, is therefore a function primarily of a dynamic or transitional phase of social development. It necessarily involves much incomplete adjustment or maladjustment while the readjustment is taking place. This produces much waste, but the ultimate adjustment is usually so much more to be desired that it justifies any incidental waste.

It is at this point that science becomes a corrective as well as a cause of maladjustment. While in modern society science is often at the basis of the disorganization which arises in a transition period, it also becomes the chief means by which waste and maladjustment can be reduced to a minimum in the transition process. It becomes the critic and corrective of the extravagances of fads, fashions, crazes, rumors, beliefs, and public opinion in their revolt against institutions. Its greatest service will be found in making the transition process orderly and conformable to the requirements of economy of thought and action. It is possible that we shall always in the future have a highly dynamic world and therefore a dynamic society. It will be the task of science to discover the most economical and efficient methods by which necessary changes and readjustments can be brought about in such a world. It is in response to this need that the social sciences are now being developed and extended into many practical applications.

MATERIALS FOR SUPPLEMENTARY READING

Blackmar and Gillin, *Outlines of Sociology,* Ch. XXII
Bogardus, E. S., *Fundamentals of Social Psychology,* Chs. XIII, XXIX, XXX, XXXI
Case, C. M., *Outlines of Introductory Sociology,* Ch. XXIX
Ellwood, C. A., *The Psychology of Human Society,* Chs. VIII, X, XI
Gault, R. H., *Social Psychology,* Ch. VIII
Godkin, E. L., *Unforeseen Tendencies of Democracy*
Jung, C. G., *Analytical Psychology,* Ch. IV
Langenhove, F. van, *The Growth of a Legend*
Lumley, F. E., *Means of Social Control,* Ch. IX
Park and Burgess, *Introduction to the Science of Sociology,* pp. 816-841
Ross, E. A., *Principles of Sociology,* Chs. XXXIV, XXXV

——, *Social Control,* Chs. X, XII
——, *Social Psychology,* Chs. V-XV, XXII
Simmel, G., *Philosophie der Mode*
Sully, J., *An Essay on Laughter,* pp. 273-281
Sumner, W. G., *Folkways,* Chs. I, II, V, XVII
Tarde, G., *Laws of Imitation,* Ch. VII
——, *L'Opinion et la foule*
Veblen, T. B., *The Theory of the Leisure Class,* Ch. VII

CHAPTER XXXVI

INSTITUTIONAL CONTROLS

This chapter will discuss the institution as a control agency only in the larger aspects. We are interested primarily in the psycho-social processes which are common to all institutions and only to a minor degree in the workings of particular institutions. Social psychology is concerned with the psycho-social processes of institutions, but much less with the total functioning of specific institutions as adjustment agencies. This subject belongs rather to sociology, political science, and economics, which rest largely upon social psychology. Consequently we shall not attempt at this point any classification of institutions or analysis of their several specific functions, but confine our treatment to the operation of the psycho-social processes involved in them.

THE CONTENT OF INSTITUTIONS—Institutions are primarily, but not wholly, psycho-social phenomena. They are organized out of conventions, traditions, customs, codes, and other uniformities of psychic behavior common to the group. But they also contain as their biological and physical structures or skeletons certain administrative organizations and physical extensions. The former represent social inventions of a bio-social type and the latter are the inventions of physico-social technique, such as offices and buildings, apparatus for communication and transportation, the machinery of production, laboratories, printing equipment, and the like, which are necessary for broadcasting as effectively as possible the psycho-social content of the institutions. Customs themselves are, as we saw in Chapter VI, largely human bio-social environmental processes. The psycho-social content of institutions is of course their most important aspect, but it is able to propagate itself among the members of the group and become uniform collective behavior only by the aid of certain bio-social and physico-social structures and processes. Hence, the administrative organization and physico-social technique are indispensable parts of the institutions themselves. Because they are the most readily perceived aspects of the institutions they are sometimes mistaken for the whole content, and by a sort of metonymy we commonly characterize institutions in terms of these objective and material forms of organization. The subjective and objective aspects of institutions have already been outlined in Chapter XXXV.

THE NATURE OF INSTITUTIONS—Institutions are of course not external to people, as the man on the street so frequently assumes. They are simply the relatively permanent and formal ways in which people behave or act in making their collective adjustments to nature and to others of their kind. Institutions are relatively permanent, but not unchanging. They are in large degree the product of the stable and fixed needs of individuals and of groups, but they also modify and mold the permanent characters of individuals and groups. The institution is a coöperative method of meeting some fundamental needs of men which can be most effectively met through a fairly stable form of collective endeavor or social organization. Consequently the great social institutions relate themselves to family life, the production and distribution of food and other physical necessities of man, protection against seen and unseen or imagined enemies, associational and recreational (gregarious) contacts, the increase of individual efficiency along economic and spiritual lines, the promotion of the material and spiritual welfare of the group as a whole. The earliest institutions were the product of the more organic needs. The more spiritual and idealistic institutions have developed only as man's nature has been developed and refined to such a degree that he has become able to experience such needs and organize collectively for their promotion.

THE INSTITUTION AS A CONTROL AGENCY—These coöperative or collective ways of satisfying human wants or needs function as social controls in two ways. In the first place they serve as rules of the game and provide machinery for the coöperation of the members of the group in performing collective functions. In the second place, they are relatively permanent ways of acting, changing so slowly that they do not lose their identity in one or many generations. Thus they serve as social mechanisms to induct each succeeding generation into the practices of the preceding generations. In this way collective life is made continuous in time as well as in space. Of course it is the individual, and not the institution, which the child imitates, but the behavior of the parent or teacher is standardized and uniformized by that coöperative interchange of contacts, functions, and services which we objectify and symbolize as the institution. The institution has primarily a conceptual and abstract, rather than a perceptual and concrete existence. But its function in social control is none the less definite and important for that. Its objective existence is in the behavior of men and in its codes, administrative organization and physical extensions which serve largely to integrate the behavior of men.

TRENDS IN INSTITUTIONS—The institution itself changes just as the needs and methods of collective or coöperative endeavor change. The early institutions were built up about organic needs, and these institutions continue, although their content and functions have been greatly modified by the passage of time. For example, the family is no longer just a breeding and child-rearing coöperative organization or institution, although these functions still persist in most families and occupy a portion of their time. Nor is it any longer largely a productive unit economically. The family has now become a coöperative form of behavior involving much wider and more spiritual interests, in which a man and a woman, and through a portion of their lives, the children, join their efforts for the purpose of living an all round normal, healthful, and emotionally and intellectually satisfying life. Not all families have attained this ideal, but this is the tendency, while the reproductive and child-rearing, and perhaps the economically productive, functions of the family tend to become secondary in successful family life.

This same tendency toward a growing emphasis upon the spiritual and idealistic or constructive function is manifest in practically all institutions. Even the economic institutions have their constructive and spiritual aspects, as well as their

INSTITUTIONAL CONTROLS

physical and biological. Religion, which began apparently as a method of protective magic employed against unfriendly or evil spirits and as a control over the services of those more favorably inclined spirits, has become a means to the cultivation of the finer emotions and ideals of men and to the promotion of constructive and altruistic social contacts. Government was at first almost wholly negatively protective against enemies from without and against the revolt of the exploited classes from within. It is now the chief agency for constructive social welfare. Also idealistic institutions have arisen on top of the old institutions devised to serve the primitive organic and emotional needs of man. Thus we have educational, ethical, and esthetic institutions, which are largely, although not wholly, the product of the cultural rather than of the instinctive needs of man. As we refine our individual characters through multiplication of contacts and adjustments, we build up coöperative or collective methods of satisfying these refined needs, and thus perpetuate these changes in our characters in the form of coöperative behavior which we objectify as institutions.

THE DEVELOPMENT OF OBJECTIVE CONTENT IN INSTITUTIONS—The early institutions were very largely subjective in content. There were no written rules of procedure, the administrative organization was very slight, and the physico-social or bio-social technique was but little developed. The primitive family or the collective food-getting endeavors of the group were largely spontaneous. Buildings, tools, apparatus of all sorts, were scanty. Agreement on plans and their coöperative execution were accomplished through the communication of verbal or gesture symbols instead of through written rules. Formal decisions as a result of such informal discussion were the exception rather than the rule among early peoples.

Even the subjective or immaterial aspects of these institutions were not particularly well developed. There were few spoken conventions and traditions in the early stages of the development of institutions. Custom was negative rather than positive. That is, the member of the group was conscious of it in the breach rather than in the practice. Behavior was largely spontaneous and the result of biological needs, but where modified by the pressures of collective contacts, patterns of behavior were imitated or conditioned largely unconsciously rather than purposively. Hence early man was not particularly aware of his institutional controls, although he was dominated by them. He did not learn to conceptualize and objectify them until within the period of recorded human history. This conceptualization and symbolic objectification once accomplished, it was much easier for him to modify and perfect his institutions consciously and to develop them with foresight in constructive directions.

The major growth and service of institutions as intelligent social controls has come since man has been able to objectify them symbolically, and therefore to analyze and evaluate and reconstruct them. With the development of the social sciences he has acquired a technology for the intelligent reconstruction and invention of institutions. He is now endeavoring to build and rebuild his institutions according to his perceived needs. He is utilizing science in his own collective control. This is one of the causes which has produced the large degree of social disorganization in our day. It is necessary to replace much that is merely traditional or customary in our institutions by organization, objectives, and ideals which are scientifically tested, and to build up efficient administrative organizations and technique for carrying these into effect.

CUSTOMS are the least psychic of the subjective or nonmaterial forms of institutional controls. They consist of the standardized overt behavior of individuals which has descended by pattern from the past. But, of course, they have their basic internal mechanisms, which are usually unconscious or on the lowest level of consciousness. Customs are habits of overt response which come down to us from preceding generations. They may be somewhat modified in the process of transmission, but such modification is not great enough ordinarily to cause them to lose their identity. A large part of our daily behavior is of this customary character and ordinarily we are not strikingly self-conscious about such behavior. The things we do almost automatically from day to day are only in the periphery of our consciousness. They become focal only when we modify them. We acquire such behavior patterns ordinarily without bringing the learning process above the automatic level of response. Or, if the learning is more highly conscious, the behavior soon lapses into a lower level of consciousness or into unconsciousness. For the most part only the learning process itself is conscious, and there is no particular awareness or appreciation of the significance of the behavior for the adjustment either of the individual or of the group. While each customary act is habitual for the individual, it is the collective character of the behavior pattern and the fact that it is transmitted from one person to another in consecutive time periods which render it custom. Ordinarily we do not reflect that our behavior, even our conscious behavior, is largely customary activity.

The Revision and Testing of Customary Behavior Patterns—But people in more advanced groups are more likely to become aware of the consecutive or historical origin of much of their behavior. Especially is this true in periods of transition. They recognize that the chief sanction for this behavior which they have imitated from parents and others of the community is the prestige of the persons who served as models for them and who in a manner forced it upon them. Ordinarily they had no other models whom they could imitate, and therefore little choice with regard to the selection of their behavior. Realizing these facts, people in an age of science and of transition—which means an age of competing models and of data for judgment of relative values—frequently raise the question of the validity of the customary behavior which they have copied. They wish to test it, and for this purpose they use two types of tests. One is that of subjective or personal hedonic appeal. If the behavior is pleasurable they accept it, but if it is unpleasant they reject it. This criterion of valuation is uncertain and often erroneous. The better test is the objective one of science. The question here raised and answered is, What will be the objective result of the behavior, the effect upon the self and others concerned? This test, in so far as it can be applied, is valid and effective and should be final. It becomes more feasible as we develop the social sciences in greater detail and apply them to the organization and control of collective contacts and relationships. Revisions of habits based on customary models should, in so far as possible, be made with the assistance of scientific data and principles.

COMPARISON OF CUSTOMARY AND RATIONAL CONTENT IN INSTITUTIONS—The older institutions, such as the family, collective economic behavior, government, art, and religion, normally would carry the larger weight of custom, while the newer institutions, such as education, law, and ethics, would be expected to be less dominated by customs. But this is not always the case. If an old institution has been much revised recently in order to make it a successful collective adjustment mechanism, the relative amount of custom in it may be smaller than that in a newer institution. Thus economic and political institutions have relatively small amounts of custom, because they have been constantly reorganized and reëvaluated in this age of industry and democracy. Institutions which are open to tests of efficiency change more rapidly than those not open to such tests. On the other hand, the family and religion are still largely ruled by custom and each succeeding generation makes its adjustment within these institutions largely on a customary basis. Art and the esthetic also carry heavy loads of custom control or domination, although these institutions were relatively later in development. The same is true to a less degree of ethics. Law is one of the newer institutions, as distinguished from mere custom, but it still carries a very heavy load of custom and tradition from the past. It is very difficult to bring law up to that degree of modernity and rationality which would make it a successful means of collective adjustment or adaptation. Education, however, has recently thrown off a great burden of custom domination and is now rapidly revising its institutional organization and procedure on the basis of the findings of a new science of education. New social and mental sciences covering all of these institutions are arising and transforming them in a rational manner. This is particularly true of the sciences of economics, politics, sociology, anthropology, ethics and esthetics.

THE VALUE OF CUSTOMARY BEHAVIOR—Custom, however, has validity, and it also possesses utility. Because a form of behavior has descended from the past is not sufficient warrant for condemning it as irrational or anti-social or obstructive, any more than it would justify us, as some seem to think, in giving it our approval. It is perfectly fitting that all customs should be analyzed and tested for their validity and utility in the light of present needs by means of scientific facts and principles where these are available. And those customs which are no longer useful, or are harmful, should logically be set aside in favor of others which are more serviceable in collective adjustments. But a valid custom has a certain advantage in its stability. It occupies a strategic position in collective behavior. Collective behavior falls naturally into the mold of custom, through the process of mutual interstimulation and imitation. Custom we shall always have with us, and our problem is not to extirpate it, but to test it continually by means of the science which applies to that field of behavior and to revise it when necessary, and to use it effectively for control purposes when it meets the tests. To attempt to do the work of the world on the basis of fully conscious behavior would be to undertake a load which it would be impossible to carry.

THE NATURE AND VALIDITY OF TRADITIONS—Traditions are the conscious equivalents of habits derived from customs. In individuals the tradition takes the form of a belief about some particular practice which is reputed to have occurred at an earlier date. This belief in the past occurrence of some event is also usually associated with the belief that the practice was enjoined upon later generations or that its success in the past implies that it would be a successful and proper practice with us. Traditions are a higher order of collective behavior patterns than are most customs, because they are conscious. They contain a certain amount of rational or pseudorational sanction in that they involve some examination of the past event which serves as a model and sanction for the habit which is being built up in the individual in the present. But there is no certainty that the tradition is valid, either with respect to the authenticity of the traditional event or as a sanction for present behavior. The folk, through their exercise of wish elaboration, are constantly creating myths regarding supposed events in the past which are intended to serve, or at least do serve, as sanctions for present behavior. Likewise an event which may have been proper and advisable under the circumstances and in the light of the limitations to knowledge and the preconceptions of the past would not necessarily be good procedure in the present.

THE TESTING OF TRADITIONS—As a consequence, there must be constant testing and revision of traditions just as of customs. Historical research, now that it is developing scientific methods, is constantly testing the authenticity of traditional events, the accounts of which come down to us from the past. This historical examination and testing is going on in all fields of knowledge, but it has attracted most attention perhaps in connection with religion and politics, because these fields formerly depended so much upon traditions to justify their creeds and principles and doctrines or dogmas. In the field of religion this method of testing traditions has been called the Higher Criticism. It is no longer so extensively used in connection with politics, because most of the old traditional political dogmas, such as those of the divine right of kings, of the theocratic origin of the state, the inferiority of the people, and the political and social incompetence of women, have been exploded in so far as any traditional basis or sanction is concerned. At present there is an active dispute between theology and the critical historians in western countries over the factual validity of many of the traditions of the founding of the religions and denominations current there. Those who accept the finding of the critical historians call themselves Modernists, while those who reject these findings and cling to their traditions are sometimes termed Fundamentalists.

TRADITION AND WRITTEN RECORDS—Traditions were more valuable as institutional controls before the advent of literature than they are at present. A tradition is a belief held collectively and transmitted from the past, sometimes from the very remote past before written history began. Traditions may undergo considerable modification in this process of transmission, as may be seen from an examination of the several stories of early patriarchs current in the different religions which have a Semitic origin and therefore perhaps a common early history. It is to be expected, in the light of what we know about the selective influence of environmental stimuli, that traditions as well as customs would be modified to fit the circumstances and the control and adjustment needs of the peoples among whom they are repeated and preserved. Among a preliterate people tradition is the chief method of preserving the accumulated wisdom and beliefs of the people and of handing them on to future generations. But with the advent of a literature the vocal recounting of the deeds and thoughts of the past gives way to written records which are much more accurate as to form. However, the early written records are themselves largely traditional, representing merely the transference of vocal traditions to the relatively fixed and permanent form of writing. The written form is no guarantee of the accuracy of the content, but it is a protection against easy modification. But before the printing of books, modifications even of written records or traditions were fairly frequent because of the interpolations often made by copyists. The only sure guarantee of authenticity of the content of written records and statements is to be found in its source. If it is the product of tested and repeated observation or of the laboratory it may be regarded as fairly authentic. Repetition of hearsay or the reduction of folk rumors and beliefs to writing has but little value in itself and must be supported by corroborative evidence or must fall clearly within the limits of probability before it can be accepted as precedent or model for behavior.

CONVENTIONS serve about the same function in institutional as in non-institutional controls. But the conventions of institutional controls are much more stable and constant and continuous in their existence and operation. As a consequence the conventional institutional controls are somewhat different from the non-institutional conventional controls. They are very largely the present aspects of customs and traditions. While a convention is a form of contemporaneous action or thought, it may nevertheless have originated in the past and have come down to us as a modified or unmodified form of a custom or of a tradition. On the other hand, the convention may have originated in the present. In the latter case it would not be an institutional control, although it might be in the process of becoming such by being adopted into a revised institutional organization. Conventions, whether originating in the present or derived from the past, may have both the inner or mental and the overt or muscular behavior aspects.

THE FORMS OF CONVENTIONAL INSTITUTIONAL CONTROLS—For the most part, we may say, the institutional conventional control is the present aspect of a tradition or a custom. This fact would appear to eliminate rumor from among the institutional controls. It is too variable and ephemeral to be counted among the permanent forms of behavior which constitute the institutions. Beliefs, as the present aspects of traditions and as the result of scientific investigation, are among the most common institutional contents. Public opinion sometimes has the stability essential to an institutional process. This is true especially in a relatively static society largely controlled by custom and tradition, but it is not so frequently the case in modern dynamic societies. In such societies public opinion is likely to represent the more ephemeral collective responses of the masses to the questions of the hour and is largely based upon the propaganda, often highly prejudiced, of those interests which have mouthpieces in the form of newspapers, radio, or other types of rapid and voluminous communication. The findings of scientific investigators are the most trustworthy conventional content of the institutional controls. Gradually, as scientific data and principles accumulate, they are substituted for what is untrustworthy in the traditional content of institutions, and thus the institutions are revised on a tested knowledge basis. The administrative procedure in the institution is also revised to conform to the scientifically amended theory of its organization.

THE REVISION OF INSTITUTIONS THROUGH SCIENCE—This process of revision of institutions on the basis of scientific knowledge goes on slowly as yet, but it is the most hopeful fact in the modern social control situation. Through this means we may expect ultimately to secure a fairly rational organization of society, which will select the habits of its members into an economical and efficient and normal coöperative or collective plan of life. At present the loss of time and energy and the injury to the individual through unwise inhibitions upon his powers and the repression of his emotions and impulses resulting from an irrational institutional organization are appalling. We have begun to reorganize institutions on a rational basis through revising first the institutions of industry, government, and education. There are also indications that the process of revision and reorganization is going on within the other less competitive institutions, although more slowly and with more strongly expressed opposition. The great prerequisite to making this rational reorganization effective is an ever increasing fund of scientific knowledge covering all of the fields of human relationships. If the organization of institutions is made rational or scientific the problem of securing a rational non-institutional social organization will in part solve itself, since the substitute operation of non-institutional social controls is in considerable measure due to the ineffective functioning of institutional controls. However, the problem of technique in securing a scientific determination of the non-institutional controls is essentially the same as that in the case of the institutional controls.

THE OBJECTIVE INSTITUTIONAL CONTROLS are of less importance from the standpoint of social psychology than are the subjective or relatively non-material institutional processes. They are constructed and standardized for the purpose of rendering the subjective and non-material processes relatively permanent in their forms and functions. The necessity for standardization and the stereotyping of the subjective processes was not so great in primitive societies because collective behavior was not so complex. Where exact reproduction or repetition of behavior was desirable it was possible to secure this uniformity in a local face-to-face group through ritualization. The ritual reduced the whole group to something like an administrative organization. But for the most part life was still largely experimental and social organization had not proceeded very far or become particularly complicated. Also the chances for distortion of subjective control processes, such as traditions, conventions, and customs, by passing through many minds and being subjected to revision from many viewpoints, were not then so marked. Nor were the results of such distortion so serious as now. Groups were small and distance contacts were fewer and all of the members of the group were more likely to react coördinately or coadaptively to the same original stimulus. But in modern society distance or indirect contacts are so numerous and so many of the subjective institutional control processes are liable to be distorted by verbal communication that it has been necessary to reduce them to fixed and verifiable forms. Also, modern social organization, especially industrial and political organization, is so delicately and quantitatively adjusted that it is necessary to guard against undue distortion of meaning or of behavior by having the subjective controls accurately defined and interpreted. This need, which was beginning to be apparent long ago, perfected writing and later printing as the repository of the subjective institutional controls.

CODES AND RITUALS—Code is the general term which we apply to any traditional or conventional control in a literate society when it is being standardized or stereotyped so as to prevent too rapid and irrational or irresponsible change. It performs the stereotyping function served by the ritual in earlier times, but much more clearly because in a much more intellectual manner. The ritual belongs primarily to the preliterate society and marks an attempt to make definite through gesture and vocal language the essential dogmas or beliefs of the institution before it is possible to reduce them to writing. It tends to give way to the code among literate and intellectual peoples. The code is a written or printed set of rules of procedure, or "of the game," and its content may be viewed by any one and from it always the same meaning is to be drawn, if the reader has the power to interpret the symbols. The code contains the most important content of the theory of the institution, or that part of it which is regarded as most important and which the members of the institution desire to make definite and keep intact. However, not all of the theory of any institution is reduced to written or codal form. Even in the state and in financial and public service corporations, which have reason to make their codes as definite and specific as possible, some parts of the theory of the institution are unavoidably left to custom, tradition, and convention, especially as they appear in the ritual. But as these non-written aspects of the theory or regulative processes of the institution grow in volume they are likely to be reduced to written or codal form.

INSTITUTIONAL CONTROLS

CODES HAVE VARIOUS FORMS—In various institutions the code or written theory takes on various forms and is called by various names. In the corporation the code is usually the charter under which it does business, the various general legislative enactments of governmental bodies which cover such lines of business, and the rules made by the particular business itself to cover its procedure. In the state there are usually several elements or sections to the code. In the United States, for example, there are our federal constitution, the state constitutions, the treaties with foreign countries, the enactments of the federal congress and the state legislatures, the ordinances of city councils, the court decisions and the formal administrative rules and regulations of the numerous administrative bodies which have jurisdiction over us, and the common law which we have inherited from England. In the church the code is the promulgated creed and other legislative enactments, decrees of councils, bulls, declarations, general letters, etc., of ecclesiastical dignitaries with jurisdiction and the written rules and regulations of local congregations, where they exist.

SOME INSTITUTIONS POSSESS BUT SLIGHT CODES OF THEIR OWN—Some of the newer and accessory institutions, like education, have little in the way of an independent codal enactment of their own. This is because they are so dependent upon the state, if they are public schools, or upon the church, if they are parochial schools, for their support and for the enforcement of needed regulations. Therefore, their codes are to a large degree enacted into the codes of the overhead organization upon which they are dependent. The same is true of public and ecclesiastical charities, of recreation, esthetics, and morals. However, all of these, except morals, may have some sort of definite or written regulations of their own which might be called codes, even if they are only local administrative rules. The peculiar case of morals will be discussed later.

ADMINISTRATIVE ORGANIZATION is not primarily a psychosocial phenomenon and will not be discussed in detail here. Consideration of it belongs primarily under sociology and political science. However, the type of administrative organization which any institution develops for the purpose of exercising its control function to the best advantage will depend primarily upon the code and the subjective processes of that institution. In a complex modern institution the code usually gives considerable space to defining and specifying the nature and functions and powers and limitations of the administrative organization. In the more loosely organized and less stereotyped institutions the administrative organization is more or less indefinite, its powers and limitations poorly defined, and its functions ordinarily quite flexible. In such cases the administrative organization may come to dominate the institution and to dictate its subjective as well as its objective process content. This it does the more easily because the institution lacks definite objective rules or principles with which adequately to control the administrative organization which may itself be self-constituted. The character of the administrative organization necessarily exercises the greatest influence upon the quality and direction of the functioning of the institution as a social control agency.

THE MATERIAL EXTENSIONS of institutions are even less a phase of the subject matter of social psychology, but belong primarily to the field of social technology and to the art of government. However, the social institution will be effective in proportion as it develops both a good administrative organization and an efficient physico-social apparatus for carrying its controls into effect. The more functional an institution is in the social life or collective adjustment process, the more necessary is an effective equipment with which to work.

SOME DIFFERENTIAL TRAITS OF INSTITUTIONS—HIGHLY OBJECTIFIED FUNCTIONAL TYPES—It was noted in the discussion above that different institutions undergo different degrees of objectification. The highly competitive and highly functional adjustment institutions especially are likely to develop primarily in the direction of codes, administrative organization, and physico-social and bio-social equipment and technique. This is likely to happen to any institution which is being perfected rapidly and used constantly for control purposes in a highly complex society. It is truer of growing institutions than of those declining in power. The state and economic institutions are examples preëminently of this tendency. Business handles the most immediately vital, the subsistence, interests of the community. And the state is rapidly coming to be the great deciding and administrative agency of the public in all of its most vital concerns. In fact, the state has taken the place of the religious institution as the chief and final authority in handling matters of public concern. This is because the people consider it to be based on sounder principles of practical social adjustment and to be more amenable to the findings of science.

DECADENT TYPES—On the other hand, there are certain other institutions which are still largely or even primarily dominated by custom and tradition. This dominance may be due to a number of causes. The institution may be in a declining and recessive condition, so that it lacks sufficient hold upon the confidence of the people to establish a conspicuous objective aspect or organization. It may not be able to maintain or find employment for a large administrative organization, and its services to the public may not call for an elaborate and up-to-date physical equipment. On the other hand, however, such a declining institution may seek to check its decline by an elaborate and showy formulation of its principles in the form of a code. It may even become very dogmatic in its insistence upon at least verbal conformity to the principles of the code and attribute its growing weakness to the lack of respect of the masses for "the law" instead of to its own failure to serve the legitimate interests of the people. In such effete and declining institutions the administrative officials may increase unwarrantably in numbers and they may use their positions to exploit the popular respect for the institution or the fears which it inculcates for their own selfish ends, including the collection of revenues for the support of the faction in power. Thus the physical extensions or technique are developed and utilized primarily in the service of this same exploiting group rather than of the people as a whole. The traits here described have not infrequently been characteristic of decaying governments and religious hierarchies before their fall. Such a condition in an institution produces a remarkable effect upon it. It becomes recessive and its teachings become subjective and introvert instead of objective and extrovert. Unable to control the external adjustments of men or to play a considerable rôle in worldly affairs, it places emphasis upon self-examination and verbal and internal conformity to the principles of the code. It deals with beliefs rather than with practice, and its practice is likely to be in the nature of ceremonial and ritual rather than of functional objective adjustments to the practical requirements of life. Such institutions, whether political, religious, or esthetic, are in advanced stages of decay.

CONTROLS IN SUBJECTIVE INSTITUTIONS—In another type of institutions the subjective processes predominate because they are primarily subjective institutions. That is, their problems are problems of judgment rather than of administration. This is particularly true of morals, although it is also to some extent the case with esthetics and religion. Ethical judgments are preëminently the result of a comparison of the utilities of conflicting or competing processes of behavior in any field of conduct whatever. It is not the business of ethics to enforce, except in so far as our sense of the right is compulsory. In the same way the sense of the fitting may also be compulsory in esthetics, or the sense of obligation to the superior or to the brother may be coercive in religion. But ethics is merely a court of appeal from the crude and automatic practice of life, and any question may be referred to it from any situation. It operates most effectively when there is the largest possible body of scientific data regarding consequences and of principles for guidance. It leaves enforcement to the institutions within whose jurisdictions the problems arise, or to the state and the church, the two great general agents of adjustment and justice of mankind. Therefore, it has no written code of its own, nor any administrative organization or physical technique and apparatus. These it borrows from other more objective institutions, or it turns its decisions over to them for their action. The general body of scientific knowledge is gradually becoming the accepted code of a developing rational ethics.

THE PROBLEM OF FLEXIBILITY—Some are inclined to deprecate the growing objectification of institutions, even of the state, and to see in it a new menace of rigidity similar to that exercised by custom and tradition and the ritual in the older subjective or less tangible institutions. The fear is that constitutions, written creeds, charters, and the like, although at first a protection because they make definite the functions and powers of the institution and the rights of the people who function within the institution, may become the bulwark of the conservatives and of those profiting from special interests. A written document may be so hemmed about by restrictions that it is extremely difficult to amend it when it no longer provides for the needs of the people concerned. We have seen examples of such difficulty in political constitutions and religious creeds. Consequently liberals often prefer unwritten constitutions, like that of Great Britain, or highly flexible and traditional creeds, or no creeds at all, as in the case of the Unitarian church.

The problem of securing flexibility of institutions along with sufficient definiteness of regulatory content to make for efficiency is unquestionably an important one. It seems scarcely likely that we can dispense with written documents or codes in the great regulatory or control institutions, because of the necessity for definiteness and quantitative efficiency already mentioned. But for the sake of a reasonable measure of individual liberty and of social progress and to prevent exploitation it appears to be equally evident that the codes shall be made capable of reasonably easy modification. It must be possible to keep them up with the times in order that they may regulate the control services of the institution in a truly functional manner.

Flexibility of codes and of institutions generally is not so dangerous in an age of science as it was in the age of the dominance of tradition and custom. If we can only make sure that changes are sanctioned by scientific fact there is no danger whatever in flexibility, but on the contrary a very great gain for efficient social adjustment. Clearly, therefore, on the social control side the great psycho-social need is for the development and application of science, and especially of the social sciences, to the problems of collective adjustment.

MATERIALS FOR SUPPLEMENTARY READING

Baldwin, J. M., *The Individual and Society,* Ch. IV
Bartlett, F. C., *Psychology and Primitive Culture,* Ch. III
Bogardus, E. S., *The Fundamentals of Social Psychology,* Chs. XIV, XV, XXX, XXXI

Case, C. M., *Outlines of Introductory Sociology,* Ch. III
Cooley, C. H., *Social Organization,* Part V
Coolidge, M. R., *Why Women Are So*
Dewey, J., *Human Nature and Conduct,* Part I, Sections IV, V
Dunlap, K., *Social Psychology,* Chs. III, IV
Edman, I., *Human Traits and Their Significance,* Ch. XI
Ellwood, C. A., *The Psychology of Human Society,* Chs. VI, X, XIII
Gault, R. H., *Social Psychology,* Ch. VIII
Ginsberg, M., *The Psychology of Society,* Chs. VII, VIII
Judd, C. H., "The Psychology of Social Institutions," *Jour. Ab. and Soc. Psy.,* XX: 151-156
Ogburn, W. F., *Social Change*
Park and Burgess, *Introduction to the Science of Sociology,* pp. 841-848
Ross, E. A., *Principles of Sociology,* Chs. XXXIV, XL, XLII, XLV, XLIX-LIII
———, *Social Control,* Chs. XI, XV, XVI, XXVIII-XXXIII
———, *Social Psychology,* Ch. XXIII
Sumner, W. G., *Folkways*

CHAPTER XXXVII

SUMMARY AND CONCLUSIONS

We have now completed the main argument of the book. We may, therefore, restate very briefly the chief themes of the several parts and relate all of these functionally in a final statement. In Part I the contention was that science is (1) an analysis, preferably quantitative, primarily of an object of study and secondarily of its environment, (2) a statement of the relationship which the object studied bears to its environment, and (3) an analysis of the effects produced in this object by its contacts with its environment. In the physical sciences both the environment and the objects studied are essentially of the same general order of phenomena. Consequently these sciences consist of an analysis of physical and chemical relationships, terrestrial or cosmic. In the biological sciences, however, there is a large differentiation between the object studied and its environment, hence a more considerable emphasis, first, upon the relationship between the organism and its environment and, second, the consequent determination of organic types by their environmental pressures. In the social sciences the distinction between environment and the collective behavior of organisms studied is most marked. It became necessary, therefore, in Part II to point out in some detail the inherited and acquired behavior patterns which ordinarily have been established in the human organism as the result of its contacts with its environments past and present. These are the foundational processes of behavior with which the social scientist must start in building up his account of the integration of the forms of collective behavior which constitutes the subject matter of his special science.

Our concern was with social psychology rather than with the other social sciences or with social science in general. Consequently, it was necessary in Part I to define the relationship of social psychology to the other social sciences and especially to give an account of the several types of social psychology. In the light of our earlier definitions and distinctions it seems essential to characterize social psychology as the science which studies the development of collective or social adjustment patterns in the individual as the result of his contacts with his various environments, especially with the most important of all of these environments, the psycho-social. This viewpoint in social psychology recognizes all three of the phases of science which we have isolated or defined and which were stated in the preceding paragraph.

Social psychology is interested in the analysis of the collective or general psycho-social environment. In this treatise Part IV is devoted to this phase of the subject. Social psychology is also concerned with the relationships between the environment and the individual living in a social situation. Parts III and IV attempt to give a detailed account of the processes involved here. The social behavior of the organism in cross section was studied in Part II. Here we started with those organic behavior patterns which had been integrated apparently phylogenetically by environmental pressures and traced the growth of neuro-psychic technique, including and particularly emphasizing the acquired behavior patterns and their symbolic objectifications in language, art, literature, and science, with especial reference to their contributions to the integration of personality. With the completion of Part II a brief outline of the behavior equipment of the socially functioning individual at our stage of social development had been presented. The technique of the operation of environmental stimuli upon the individual through immediate selection, was presented in Part III and Part IV.

It may appear to some readers and critics that the scope of our treatment is too narrow or too broad, or in some respects both too narrow and too broad. Undoubtedly some will deplore the lack of applications of the principles of social psychology to some of the more pressing problems of social adjustment or collective adaptation in society as it exists. Our purpose in writing this treatise has been to present the principles, not the applications, of social psychology. The applica-

SUMMARY AND CONCLUSIONS 585

tions should be set forth in general and special treatises in the fields of social organization, social control, and social ethics. Others, who believe that the subject matter of social psychology falls wholly within the field of psycho-social contacts, or of coadaptive psychic relationships between individuals in a collective situation, will probably doubt the advisability of the inclusion of most of Part II and perhaps the whole of Part III. To this objection we would answer that the content of Part II must be presented, either formally or informally, in any treatise on social psychology, for the data are indispensable to the discussion of psychic relationships of individuals in a social situation. It has seemed to fit in more logically with our analysis of the subject matter of social psychology to present this material separately and as a unit which would serve as a point of departure for the discussion in the subsequent parts. Certain of the more restrictive social psychologists will also object to the presentation of Part IV, on the ground that it is really psychological sociology rather than psychology, of which social psychology is a phase. Our viewpoint is that social psychology is an outgrowth of both psychology and sociology and overlaps both fields. Others still will see no valid justification for the inclusion of Part III, believing that it belongs to educational rather than to social psychology. Our answer to this view is that an analysis of the methods of integrating the personality is as fundamental to social psychology as it is to educational psychology, which in fact has been largely specialized off from social psychology and individual psychology for a specific function and in a particular field.

These anticipated methodological criticisms are evidences of the partial development of social psychology at the present time and of the conflicting views regarding its subject matter held by the various types of social psychologists. The method of treatment followed in this volume has been largely synthetic. Except for the exaggerations of instinct by one school of social psychologists, and the uncritical use of the concepts of imitation and suggestion by another school, all of the more general viewpoints in social psychology previously set forth by writers in the field have been largely sound as far as they went. The more recent writings in the field have attempted more or less to bridge the gaps in the older treatises. The present work, in bringing together and harmonizing and relating the partial treatments of other previous writers, is merely following out the principles set forth in our definition of science. The school of Tarde and Ross emphasized primarily the dynamic aspects of the psycho-social environment, although it did not define or classify environments. The school of Cooley has developed the relationship of the environment to the individual and the consequent changes in the individual, without treating either process in a wholly concrete and detailed manner. McDougall's school has attempted to account for changes occurring in the individual on the basis of their derivation from within rather than as the result of the reaction of the organism to selecting stimuli from without. This school does not deny the operation of external pressures, but in practice it assigns but little importance to them and offers no account of their operation. The work of Child and Herrick has justified the present writer in his earlier emphasis upon the selective function of environment and has provided him with a concrete method of accounting for organic and neural changes in the individual behavior in response to environment, while the theory of the conditioning of responses through positive association and the inhibitions of protopathic stimuli has given the basis for an account of the mechanisms of acquiring those behavior patterns of a higher neuro-psychic order which function in civilization. The chief additional contribution made to the subject of social psychology by the present work has been in the application of data known analytically by the psychologists to a detailed synthetic account of the ways in which the individual actually acquires his adjustment behavior patterns or habits of adaptation and control in a collective or social situation and thus comes to integrate his personality.

Our discussion of the conditioning of responses brought us to a consideration of the constructive integration of personality in ourselves through imitation. Some writers and teachers will be unfriendly to this apparent attempt of ours to revive the somewhat waning concept of imitation. The present author's work in this connection is not dictated by any sentimental partisanship for the term imitation. He sincerely be-

SUMMARY AND CONCLUSIONS

lieves that the concept has a valid and perhaps an indispensable place in social psychology and sociology, although probably not in individual psychology as such. It is true that the whole process of imitation can be described in terms of the conditioning of responses. Imitation is merely a short cut symbol, like many other such, with a definite meaning of its own. Because it is a short cut symbol for an involved social-psychological process it is valuable in the theory of sociology and the other social sciences which deal with psycho-social processes in the large and do not enter into detailed psychological analyses of these processes. It has seemed to the author that the proper place to present this analysis is in social psychology, which overlaps with both psychology and sociology.

The author also believes that some advance has been made in this volume in the psychological analysis of the social-psychological mechanism of suggestion, and especially in the account of its operation in collective behavior situations. Response by suggestion is one of the most persistent and common forms of behavior in collective relationships. It is almost the whole content of much of our institutional and non-institutional behavior. In the past social psychologists have too frequently treated suggestion, either by implication or expressly, as the *cause* of response or behavior rather than as a *method* of response. Neither imitation nor suggestion is the ultimate explanation of any form of behavior, as was assumed when it was commonly believed that there was an instinct to imitate and an instinct of suggestibility. To characterize an act as imitated or as suggested is merely to classify it preparatory to further investigation into the circumstances under which it was conditioned to its stimulus on the one hand or to state it as an objective behavior process on the other hand.

This brings us, finally, to the question of the relationship of social psychology to the other social sciences, a subject we are now better equipped to discuss than we were at the beginning of the volume. Some sociologists many years ago looked upon sociology as primarily an application of psychology to the theory of the organization of collective contacts, and recently there has been a strong movement to make analogous statements regarding economics. Doubtless we shall in time observe similar tendencies with respect to political science and history, as these subjects develop beyond the empirical stage into that of a constructive elaboration of theory. But sociology, or any other social science, is not social psychology. As we explained in Part I, social psychology arose to meet the demands of the social sciences upon psychology for principles and concepts which would aid in the explanation of social adjustments. Since modern social contacts are primarily psychic, the social sciences are very largely dependent upon social psychology for methods of interpretation of the collective behavior with which the social sciences are concerned. Some of the social sciences have been regrettably slow in recognizing this fact. But dependence upon social psychology for aid in the interpretation of collective phenomena is far different from an identity between the social sciences and social psychology.

All of the sciences are related more or less directly or indirectly. The data of all of the sciences must be used by each of the sciences in some way to explain the phenomena of its own problems. Sociology, for example, is not wholly foreign even to physics and chemistry, nor to astronomy and mathematics. The social sciences are especially closely related to psychology and biology. Social psychology is therefore one of the chief intellectual handmaidens to all of the social sciences. They use her data and principles of the explanation of behavior. But they are separate sciences by virtue of the separateness of their problems. A science is organized about its problems, and all of the other sciences are called upon to aid in providing a theoretical solution of those problems in so far as they can contribute explanatory data. The problems of sociology have to do with the origin, organization, maintenance, transformation, functioning, and decay of groups of all kinds. Political science is concerned with the same problems, but especially with reference to groups of one specific kind—the political. Economics has a like set of problems centering in economic, or production, distribution and consumption, behavior. History deals with the past functioning of individuals and groups in these same types of relationships. In order to state and solve their problems theoretically these several social disciplines must make very extensive application of the data of social psychology. But in less degree they must employ for like purposes the data and principles of biology, and even of chemistry and of physics. Yet we should not identify the social sciences with biology or chemistry, however much the former may be indebted to the latter for an explanation of their problems.

The problem of social psychology is as distinct as that of any other social science. It is to find out how men behave in groups, or, in other words, to study the reactions of individuals to the psycho-social environment and the consequent building up of collective adjustment behavior patterns in the individuals in response to social stimuli. In order to answer these questions it is necessary, on the one hand, for the science of social psychology to have an analysis of the psycho-social environment in terms of the processes operating to provide stimuli to the responding individual, and, on the other hand, to understand the organization of behavior patterns in the individual himself. With these two backgrounds it is possible to give an account of the further integration of behavior patterns of individuals responding individually or collectively to psycho-social stimuli. It is such materials as these that we have attempted to present in outline, without more than merely illustrative applications, in the volume which is now closed.

GENERAL BIBLIOGRAPHY

KEY:—In order to save space the following abbreviations have been used for magazines occurring frequently in the bibliography: *A. J. Psy.*—American Journal of Psychology; *A.J.S.*—American Journal of Sociology; *Br. J. Psy.*—British Journal of Psychology; *Educa.*—Education; *Ed. Rev.*—Educational Review; *I.J.E.*—International Journal of Ethics; *J.A.P.*—Journal of Abnormal Psychology; *J.A.P.S.P.*—Journal of Abnormal Psychology and Social Psychology; *J.A.S.P.*—Journal of Abnormal and Social Psychology; *J. Ap. Psy.*—Journal of Applied Psychology; *J. Ap. Soc.*—Journal of Applied Sociology; *J.P.P.S.M.*—Journal of Philosophy, Psychology and Scientific Methods; *J.S.F.*—Journal of Social Forces; *Ped. Sem.*—Pedagogical Seminary and Journal of Genetic Psychology; *P-A. Rev.*—Psycho-analytic Review; *Psy. Mon.*—Psychological Monographs; *Psy. Rev.*—Psychological Review; *Sci. Mo.*—Scientific Monthly; *S.F.*—Social Forces.

Repetitions of bibliographical items are avoided by indicating the previous chapter in which the full citation occurs by Roman numerals in parentheses.

CHAPTER I. SCIENCE AND THE ENVIRONMENT

Bernard, L. L., "The Objective Viewpoint in Sociology," *A.J.S.*, XXV:298-325; Blackmar and Gillin, *Outlines of Sociology*, Ch. XXI; Bushee, F. A., *Principles of Sociology*, Chs. I, XXX; Case, C. M., *Outlines of Introductory Sociology*, pp. xv-xxxvi; Child, C. M., *Physiological Foundations of Behavior*, Chs. I, II; Curtis, W. C., *Science and Human Affairs;* Dealey, J. Q., *Sociology; Its Development and Applications;* Edman, I., *Human Traits and Their Significance*, Ch. XIV; Ellwood, C. A., "Objectivism in Sociology," *A.J.S.*, XXII:289-305; Ellwood, C. A., *Sociology in Its Psychological Aspects*, Ch. III; Fisher, A., "Soziologie, Sozialwissenschaften, Sozialpsychologie," *Archiv f. d. ges. Psychol.*, XLIV:132-171; Giddings, F. H., *The Scientific Study of Human Society;* Gillette, J. M., "Boundary Lines of Social Phenomena," *A.J.S.*, XXX:585-93; Hayes, E. C., *Introduction to the Study of Sociology*, Chs. I, II; Lindeman, E. C., *Social Discovery*, Part I; Maciver, R. M., *Community*, pp. 45-52; Millikan, R. A., "Science and Human Affairs," *Amer. Education*, XXVI:60-68; Moore, H. R., "The Unity of Science; An Outline," *Monist*, XXX:481-512; Park and Burgess, *Introduction to the Science of Sociology*, Ch. I; Pearson, Karl, *The Grammar of Science;* Poincaré, Henri, *The Foundations of Science;*

Ross, E. A., *The Foundations of Sociology;* Thomas and Znanieki, *The Polish Peasant,* I: 1-86; Znanieki, Florian, *The Laws of Social Psychology.*

CHAPTER II. THE SCOPE AND RELATIONS OF SOCIAL PSYCHOLOGY

Allport, F. H., "The Psychological Bases of Social Science," *Psy. Bul.,* XXII: 561-574; Allport, F. H., "Social Psychology" (a review), *Psy. Bul.,* XVII: 85-94; Dunlap, K., "The Foundations of Social Psychology," *Psy. Rev.,* XXX: 81-102; Duprat, G. L., "L'orientation actuelle de la sociologie en France," *Rev. Int. de Soc.,* XXX: 464-481; Editors: "The Field of Social Psychology and Its Relation to Abnormal Psychology," *J.A.P.S.P.,* XVI: 3-7; Ellwood, C. A., "Prolegomena to Social Psychology," *A.J.S.,* IV: 656-665, 807-822, V: 98-109, 220-7; Ellwood, C. A., "The Psychological View of Society," *A.J.S.,* XV: 596-610; Ellwood, C. A., "The Relations of Sociology and Social Psychology," *J.A.P.S.P.,* XIX: 3-12; Ellwood, C. A., "Social Psychology and the Social Sciences," *Psy. Bul.,* XVIII: 203-10; Fisher, A., *Arch. f. d. ges. Psychol.,* XLIV: 132-171 (I); Gault, R. H., "Psychology in Social Relations," *A.J.S.,* XXII: 734-48; Gault, R. H., "The Standpoint of Social Psychology," *J.A.P.S.P.,* XVI: 41-6; Hall, G. S., "Social Phases of Psychology," *A.J.S.,* XVIII: 613-21; Kantor, J. R., "How Is a Science of Social Psychology Possible?", *J.A.P.S.P.,* XVII: 62-78; Kantor, J. R., "What Are the Data and Problems of Social Psychology?", *J.P.P.S.M.,* XX: 421-33, 449-57; Leuba, J. H., "Methods and Principles in Social Psychology," *Psy. Bul.,* XIV: 367-78; Leuba, J. H., "Sociology and Psychology," *A.J.S.,* XIX: 323-42; Lowie, R. H., "Psychology and Sociology," *A.J.S.,* XXI: 217-29; Maciver, R. M., "What Is Social Psychology?", *Sociol. Rev.,* VI: 147-60; Mead, G. H., "Social Psychology as Counterpart to Physiological Psychology," *Psy. Bul.,* VI: 401-8; Park, R. E., "The Group Concept and Social Research," *A.J.S.,* XXVII: 169-83; Park, R. E., "The Social Organism and the Collective Mind," *A.J.S.,* XXVII: 1-21; Ross, E. A., "The Present Problems of Social Psychology," *Proc. St. Louis Cong. of Arts and Science,* V: 869-82; Rivers, W. H. R., "Sociology and Psychology," *Sociol. Rev.,* IX: 1-13; Sieber, A. S., "Masse und Personlichkeit," *Grenzboten,* LXXX: 1-3; Suttie, I. O., "'Social' and 'Individual' Psychology," *J. Ment. Sci.,* LXIX: 180-2; Thomas, W. I., "The Province of Social Psychology," *Proc. St. Louis Cong. of Arts and Science,* V: 860-8; Thomas, W. I., "Scope and Method of Folk Psychology," *A.J.S.,* I: 434-45; Tosti, G., "Social Psychology and Sociology," *Psy. Rev.,* V: 348-61; Wallis, W. D., "The Independence of Social Psychology," *J.A.S.P.,* XX: 147-50.

CHAPTER III. PHASES OF THE SUBJECT

Allport, F. H., "The Group Fallacy in Relation to Social Science," *J.A.P.S.P.*, XIX: 60-73; Ayres, C. E., "The Epistemological Significance of Social Psychology," *J.P.P.S.M.*, XV: 35-44; Bagehot, W., *Physics and Politics;* Baldwin, J. M., *Social and Ethical Interpretations;* Barnes, H. E., "Some Typical Contributions of English Sociology to Political Theory," *A.J.S.*, XXVII: 573-87, 737-757; Burnham, W., *The Normal Mind;* Cooley, C. H., *Human Nature and the Social Order;* Davenport, C. B., "Chromosomes, Endocrines and Heredity," *Sci. Mo.*, XX: 491-98; Davy, G., "Problemes de Psychologie Sociale," *J. de Psy.*, XX: 734-55; Dunlap, K., "The Applications of Psychology to Social Problems," *Ped. Sem.*, XXX: 523-49; Dunlap, K., *Psy. Rev.*, XXX: 81-102 (II); Duprat, G. L., *La Psychologie Sociale;* Freud, S., *Group Psychology and the Analysis of the Ego*, Chs. II, III; Goldenweiser, A. A., "Psychology and Culture," *Pub. Amer. Sociological Soc.*, XIX: 15-23; Hocking, W. E., "Instinct in Social Philosophy," *J.A.P.S.P.*, XVIII: 153-66; James, W., "Great Men, Great Thoughts, and the Environment," *Atl. Mo.*, XLVI: 441-59; Jennings, H. S., "Heredity and Environment," *Sci. Mo.*, XIX: 225-38; Judd, C. H., "The Psychology of Social Institutions," *J.A.S.P.*, XX: 151-156; Kantor, J. R., "An Essay toward an Institutional Conception of Social Psychology," *A.J.S.*, XXVII: 611-27, 758-79; Kantor, J. R., "Concerning Some Faulty Conceptions of Social Psychology," *J.P.P.S.M.*, XX: 421-33, 449-57; Kantor, J. R., "The Institutional Foundation of a Scientific Social Psychology," *J.A.P.S.P.*, XIX: 46-56; Kantor, J. R., "Problem of Instincts and Their Relation to Social Psychology," *J.A.P.S.P.*, XVIII: 50-77; Kirkpatrick, E. A., *Fundamentals of Child Study;* LeBon, G., *The Crowd;* Lippmann, W., *Public Opinion;* Maciver, R. M., (I); McDougall, W., "Can Sociology and Social Psychology Dispense with Instincts?", *A.J.S.*, XXIX: 657-70; McDougall, W., *The Group Mind;* Newman, H. H., *Outlines of General Zoölogy;* Ross, E. A., *Social Psychology;* Sighele, S., *La Foule Criminelle;* Sighele, S., *Psychologie des Sectes;* Smith, A., *Theory of Moral Sentiments;* Sumner, W. G., *Folkways;* Tarde, G., *Laws of Imitation;* Tarde, G., *La Logique Sociale;* Tarde, G., *L'Opposition Universelle;* Trotter, W., *Instincts of the Herd in Peace and War;* Veblen, T., *The Theory of the Leisure Class;* Wallas, G., *The Great Society;* Wallas, G., *Human Nature and Politics;* Wells, W. R., "The Value for Social Psychology of the Concept of Instinct," *J.A.P.S.P.*, XVI: 334-43.

CHAPTER IV. METHOD OF THE PRESENT TREATMENT

Allport, F. H., *J.A.P.S.P.*, XIX: 60-73 (III); Allport, F. H., *Social Psychology*, Ch. I; Bernard, L. L., *Instinct: A Study in Social Psychology;* Cooley, C. H., *Human Nature and the Social Order;* Cooley, C. H., *Social Organization;* McDougall, W., *An Introduction to Social Psychology;* Watson, J. B., *Behavior: An Introduction to Comparative Psychology,* Ch. I; Watson, J. B., *Psychology from the Standpoint of a Behaviorist,* Ch. I; Williams, J. T., "Education in Recent Sociology," *Educa.*, April, 1921.

CHAPTER V. THE ORGANIC BASES OF BEHAVIOR

Alexander, F. M., *Man's Supreme Inheritance;* Bawden, H. H., "The Evolution of Behavior," *Psy. Rev.*, XXVI: 247-76; Bayliss, W., *Principles of General Physiology* (2d ed.), Chs. XIII, XV, XVI; Cannon, W. B., *Bodily Changes in Pain, Hunger, Fear and Rage,* Ch. II; Child, C. M., *The Origin and Development of the Nervous System;* Dana, C. L., "The Anatomic Seat of the Emotions," *Archiv. Neu. and Psychiatry,* VI: 634-9; Dunlap, K., *Elements of Scientific Psychology,* Chs. II-VII, IX; Dunn, H. L., "The Growth of the Central Nervous System in the Human Fetus as Expressed by Graphic Analysis and Empirical Formulæ," *J. Compar. Neurol.*, XXXIII: 405-92; Ferris, H. B., "The Neurone," *Psy. Bul.*, XV: 257-63; Ellwood, C. A., *The Psychology of Human Society,* Ch. II; Ellwood, C. A., "Is Society a Psychical Unity?", *A.J.S.*, X: 666-71; Herrick, C. J., "The Evolution of Intelligence and Its Organs," *Science*, N.S., XXXI: 7-18; Herrick, C. J., "Some Reflections on the Origin and Significance of the Cerebral Cortex," *J. Animal Behav.*, III: 222-36; Herrick, C. J., "A Sketch of the Origin of the Cerebral Hemispheres," *J. Compar. Neurol.*, XXXII: 429-54; Hunter, W. S., *General Psychology,* Pt. II, Ch. II; Holt, E. B., "Reflex Mechanisms and the Physiology of Nerve and Muscle," *Psy. Bul.*, XV: 263-72; Johnson, G. T., "A Survey of the Physiology of Cerebration," *J.A.P.S.P.*, XVI: 115-36; Judd, C. H., *Psychology* (2d ed.), Chs. II, III, VI; Kempf, E. J., *The Autonomic Functions and the Personality;* Kuntz, A., "The Development of the Sympathetic Nervous System in Man," *J. Compar. Neurol.*, XXXII: 173-230; Lashley, K. S., "Studies of Cerebral Function in Learning," *J. Compar. Psychol.*, I: 453-68; Lashley, K. S., "Studies of Cerebral Function in Learning," *Psy. Rev.*, XXXI: 369-75; Lickley, J. D., *The Nervous System;* Lillie, R. S., *Protoplasmic Action and Nervous Action;* Lucas, K., *The Conduction of the Nervous Impulse;* Mursell,

J. L., "The Stimulus-Response Relation," *Psy. Rev.*, XXIX: 146-62; Parker, G. H., *The Elementary Nervous System*; Russell, S. B., "Advance Adaptation in Behavior," *Psy. Rev.*, XXIV: 413-25; Russell, S. B., "The Evolution of Nerve Muscle Mechanism," *J. Compar. Psy.*, I: 395-412; Sapir, E., "Do We Need a 'Superorganic'?" *Amer. Anthrop.*, XIX: 441-9; Seashore, C. E., *Introduction to Psychology*, Ch. XIII; Starbuck, E. D., "The Intimate Senses as Sources of Wisdom," *J. Relig.*, I: 129-45; Thurstone, L. L., "The Stimulus-Response Fallacy in Psychology," *Psy. Rev.*, XXX: 354-69; Troland, L. T., "The Physical Basis of Nerve Functions," *Psy. Rev.*, XXVII: 323-50; Warren, H. C., *Elements of Human Psychology*, Chs. II, III; Warren, H. C., "Psychology and the Central Nervous System," *Psy. Rev.*, XXVIII: 249-69; Warren, H. C., "The Significance of Neural Adjustment," *Psy. Rev.*, XXIX: 481-9; Weiss, A. P., "Behavior and the Central Nervous System," *Psy. Rev.*, XXIX: 329-43.

CHAPTER VI. THE ENVIRONMENTAL BASES OF BEHAVIOR

Abbot, E. S., "The Biological Point of View in Psychology and Psychiatry," *Psy. Rev.*, XXIII: 117-28; Alexander, H. B., "A Comparison of the Ranks of American States in Army Alpha and in Social-Economic Status," *School and Soc.*, XVI: 388-92; Bawden, H. H., *Psy. Rev.*, XXVI: 247-76 (V); Bernard, L. L., "The Significance of Environment as a Social Factor," *Pub. Amer. Sociological Soc.*, XVI: 84-112; Boas, F., "The Growth of Children as Influenced by Environmental and Hereditary Conditions," *School and Soc.*, XVII: 305-8; Boodin, J. E., "The Existence of Social Minds," *A.J.S.*, XIX: 1-47; Brimhall, D. R., "Family Resemblances Among American Men of Science," *Am. Naturalist*, LVI: 504-47, LVII: 74-88, 137-52; Bruce, H. A., *Handicaps of Childhood*; Claghorn, K. H., "Methods of Evaluating Our Immigrant Peoples," *Mental Hyg.*, VII: 20-31; Davies, G. R., *Social Environment*; Davies, G. R., "A Statistical Study in the Influence of the Environment," *Quart. J. North Dak.*, April, 1924; Ellwood, C. A., "Mental Patterns in Social Evolution," *Pub. Amer. Sociological Soc.*, XVII: 88-100; Huxley, J., "Biology and Sociology," *Monist*, XXXIII: 364-89; Koller, A. H., *The Theory of Environment*; Kroeber, A. L., *Amer. Anthrop.*, XIX: 163-213 (V); Nice, M. M., "The Development of a Child's Vocabulary in Relation to Environment," *Ped. Sem.*, XXII: 35-64; Patten, S. N., "The Genesis of Personal Traits," *Pop. Sci. Mo.*, LXXXIII: 149-57; Patten, S. N., "The Laws of Environmental Influence," *Pop. Sci. Mo.*, LXXIX: 396-402; Pearse, A. S., "The Effects of Environment on Animals," *Am. Naturalist*, LVI: 144-58;

Pound, A., *The Iron Man in Industry;* Pressey, L. W., "The Influence of (a) Inadequate Schooling and (b) Poor Environment upon Results with Tests of Intelligence," *J. Ap. Psy.,* IV: 91-6; Sapir, E., "Culture, Genuine and Spurious," *A.J.S.,* XXIX: 401-29; Schlapp, M. G., "Causes of Defective Children," *J. Hered.,* XIV: 387-97; Smith, J. R., "The Elements of Geography and the Geographic Unit," *School and Soc.,* XVII: 617-28; Smith, W. R., "The Rôle of Social Heredity in Education," *A.J.S.,* XXIV: 566-80; Sumner, F. B., "The Organism and Its Environment," *Sci. Mo.,* XIV: 223-33; Visher, S. S., "A Study of the Place of Birth and of the Occupation of Fathers of Subjects in 'Who's Who in America,'" *A.J.S.,* XXX: 551-7; Visher, S. S., and Haverstock, G., "'Who's Who' Among American Women," *Sci. Mo.,* XV: 443-7; Wientrob, J. and R., "The Influence of Environment on Mental Ability," *J. Ed. Psy.,* III: 577-586; Wissler, C., "The Psychological Aspects of the Culture-Environment Relation," *Amer. Anthrop.,* XIV: 217-25; Wissler, C., "The Relation of Culture to Environment from the Standpoint of Invention," *Pop. Sci. Mo.,* LXXXIII: 164-8; Young, S. A., "A Study in Children's Social Environment," *Studies in Ed.,* II: 123-40.

CHAPTER VII. THE INHERITED AND ACQUIRED EQUIPMENT OF MAN

Balk, L., "The Endocrine Glands in the Evolution of Man," *Lancet,* CCI: 588-92; Bernard, L. L., "A Criticism of the Psychoanalysts' Theory of the Libido," *Monist,* XXXIII: 240-71; Blackmar, F. W., "Hereditary Traits as Factors in Human Progress," *Pub. Amer. Sociological Soc.,* XVI: 154-65; Boas, F., "Changes in the Bodily Form of Descendants of Immigrants," *Amer. Anthrop.* (N.S.), XIV: 530-62; Bruce, H. A., *Handicaps of Childhood;* Carmichael, L., "The Development of Behavior in Vertebrates Experimentally Removed from the Influence of External Stimulation," *Psy. Rev.,* XXXII: 51-58; Case, I., and Lewis, K., "Environment as a Factor in Feeblemindedness," *A.J.S.,* XXIII: 661-9; Chase, H. W., "On the Inheritance of Acquired Modifications of Behavior," *A. J. Psy.,* XXVIII: 175-90; Dawson, G. E., "A Characterization of the Prevailing Defects in Backward Children and a Method of Studying Them," *Ped. Sem.,* XVI: 429-36; Dumas, D., "Un Nouveau Chapitre de Psychologie," *Rev. Philos.,* XLVIII: 161-99; Gates, A. I., "The Inheritance of Mental Traits," *Psy. Bul.,* XVIII: 358-65; Herrick, C. J., *Neurological Foundations of Animal Behavior;* Holmes, A., *Principles of Character Making,* Ch. III; Howerth, I. W., "Universal Education and the Increase of Genius," *Ed. Rev.,* LXIII: 50-56; Hunter, W. S., and Sommermier, E., "The Relation of Degree of Indian Blood to Score on the Otis Intelligence Test," *J. Compar.*

Psy., II: 257-77; Jennings, H. S., *Sci. Mo.,* XIX: 225-38 (III); Jennings, H. S., "The Origin of Variations," *Am. Naturalist,* LVI: 5-15; Jordan, D. S., "The Inbred Descendants of Charlemagne," *Sci. Mo.,* XIII: 481-92; Kammerer, P. R. P., *The Inheritance of Acquired Characteristics;* Kroeber, A. L., *Amer. Anthrop.,* XIX: 163-213 (V); Kuo, Z. Y., "A Psychology without Heredity," *Psy. Rev.,* XXXI: 427-48; Lewis, F. T. A., "A Note on Symmetry as a Factor in the Evolution of Plants and Animals," *Am. Naturalist,* LVII: 5-41; MacPhail, A. H., "Tonsils and Adenoids," *Ped. Sem.,* XXVII: 188-94; Moorrees, V., "The Immediate Heredity of Primary Aments Committed to a Public Institution," *J. Ap. Psy.,* VIII: 89-127; Myers, G. C., "Intelligence of Troops Infected with Hookworm versus Those Not Infected," *Ped. Sem.,* XXVII: 211-42; Naccarati, S., "The Morphologic Aspect of Intelligence," *Columbia University Contr. to Phil. and Psy.,* XXVII, No. II (1921); Naccarati, S., and Garrett, H. E., "The Influence of Constitutional Factors on Behavior," *J. Exper. Psy.,* VI: 455-65; Naccarati, S., and Lewy-Guinzburg, R. L., "Hormones and Intelligence," *J. Ap. Psy.,* VI: 221-34; Norsworthy and Whitley, *Psychology of Childhood,* Ch. I; Patten, S. N., *Pop. Sci. Mo.,* LXXXIII: 149-57 (VI); Potter, H. W., and Viers, R. S., "Hereditary and Nonhereditary Mental Defects," *Archiv. Neu. and Psychiatry,* IX: 339-46; Pound, A., "The Iron Man and the Mind," *Atl. Mo.,* CXXIX: 179-89; Strecker, E. A., "Physical Factors in Mental Retardation," *J. Amer. Med. Assn.,* LXXV: 659-61; Strong, E. K., Jr., *Effects of Hookworm Disease on Mental and Physical Development of Children;* Suttie, I. D., "Some Aspects of Sociology and Their Psychiatrical Application. I. Culture and Endowment," *J. Ment. Sci.,* LXIX: 49-51; Tanberg, A., "Internal Secretions between Mother and Child," *Acta Med. Scand.,* LVI: 33-51; Wallin, J. E. W., "An Investigation of the Sex, Relationship, Marriage, Delinquency and Truancy of Children Assigned to Special Public School Classes," *J.A.P.S.P.,* XVII: 19-34; Wallin, J. E. W., "A Study of the Industrial Record of Children Assigned to Public School Classes for Mental Defectives, Etc.," *J.A.P.S.P.,* XVII: 120-31; Wells, W. R., "The Meaning of Inherited and Acquired in Reference to Instinct," *J.A.P.S.P.,* XVII: 153-61.

CHAPTER VIII. BEHAVIOR PATTERNS: THEIR NATURE AND DEVELOPMENT

Beach, W. G., *An Introduction to Sociology and Social Problems,* Chs. IV, VI; Blanton, M. G., "The Behavior of the Human Infant During the First Thirty Days of Life," *Psy. Rev.,* XXIV: 456-83; Bogardus, E. S., "The Principle of Group Priority," *J. Ap. Soc.,* XI: 784-7; Burnham, W. H., "Mental Hygiene and the Conditioned

Reflex," *Ped. Sem.*, XXIV: 449-88; Burnham, W. H., "Metabolism in Childhood," *Ped. Sem.*, XXVII: 303-23; Cason, H., "General Aspects of the Conditioned Response," *Psy. Rev.*, XXXII: 298-316; Cason, H., "The Physical Basis of the Conditioned Response," *A. J. Psy.*, XXXVI: 371-93; Child, C. M. (I); Craig, W., "Tropisms and Instinctive Activities," *Psy. Bul.*, XVI: 151-9, XVII: 169-78; Drummond, M., *The Dawn of Mind*, Ch. III; Dunlap, K., "The Identity of Instinct and Habit," *J.P.P.S.M.*, XIX: 85-93; Edman, I., *Human Traits*, Chs. I-VII; Frank, L. K., "Suggestions for a Theory of Learning," *Psy. Rev.*, XXX: 145-8; Ginsberg, M., *The Psychology of Society*, Ch. I; Groves, E. R., *Personality and Social Adjustment*, Chs. III, IV; Holmes, A. (VII), Ch. VI; Holmes, S. J., "A Tentative Classification of the Forms of Animal Behavior," *J. Compar. Psy.*, II: 173-90; Holt, E. B., "Reflex Mechanisms and the Physiology of Nerve and Muscle," *Psy. Bul.*, XV: 263-72; Humphrey, G., "The Conditioned Reflex and the Elementary Social Reaction," *J.A.P.S.P.*, XVII: 113-19; Humphrey, G., "Is the Conditioned Reflex the Unit of Habit?", *J.A.P.S.P.*, XX: 10-16; Hunter, W. S. (V), Pt. II, Ch. III; Hunter, W. S., "The Modification of Instinct," *J.P.P.S.M.*, XIX: 98-101; Hunter, W. S., "The Modification of Instinct from the Standpoint of Social Psychology," *Psy. Rev.*, XXVII: 247-69; James, W., *Principles of Psychology*, Vol. II, Ch. XXIV; Johnson, G. T., *J.A.P.S.P.*, XVI: 115-36 (V); Judd, C. H., *Psychology*, Ch. IX; Kantor, J. R., "The Integrative Character of Habits," *J. Compar. Psy.*, II: 195-226; Kantor, J. R., "How Do We Acquire Our Basic Reactions?", *Psy. Rev.*, XXVIII: 385-424; Kantor, J. R., "The Psychology of Reflex Action," *A. J. Psy.*, XXXIII: 19-42; Kempf, E. J. (V); Koffka, K., *The Growth of the Mind*, Ch. III; Kuo, Z. Y., "How Are Our Instincts Acquired?", *Psy. Rev.*, XXIX: 344-65; Kuo, Z. Y., "A Psychology without Heredity," *Psy. Rev.*, XXXI: 427-48; McDougall, W., (IV), Chs. II, III, IV; Morgan, L., *Habit and Instinct*; Maupin, O., "Habit Formation in Animals," *Psy. Bul.*, XVIII: 573-620; Meyer, M. F., "Some Nonsense about the 'Common Path,'" *Psy. Rev.*, XXXII: 431-42; Mursell, J. L., "The Ontogenetic Significance of Instinct, Habit, and Intelligence," *Psy. Rev.*, XXIX: 163-79; Parmelee, M., *The Science of Human Behavior*, Ch. XIII; Robinson and Robinson, *Readings in General Psychology*, Chs. IV, V; Rivers, W. H. R., *Instinct and the Unconscious*; Rivers, W. H. R., *Psychology and Politics*, Ch. II; Seashore, C. E., *Introduction to Psychology*, Chs. XV, XVI; Shepard, J. F., "Habit Formation and Higher Mental Capacities in Animals," *Psy. Bul.*, XVII: 187-97; Shinn, M. W., *Biography of a Baby*, Ch. II; Tarde, G., *Etudes de psychologie sociale*, pp. 279-86; Thorndike, E. L., *Educational Psychology* (Briefer Course), Pt. I; Thorndike, E. L., *Original Nature of Man*; Tolman, E. C., "The Nature of Instinct," *Psy. Bul.*, XX: 200-18; Wallas, G., *The Great Society*, Chs. III, V;

Warren, H. C., "A Classification of Reflexes, Instincts, and Emotional Phenomena," *Psy. Rev.*, XXVI: 197-203; Warren, H. C., *Elements of Human Psychology;* Warren, H. C., *Human Psychology*, Chs. VI, VII; Washburn, M. F., "Tropisms and Instinctive Activities," *Psy. Bul.*, XV: 273-80; Watson, J. B., "The Place of the Conditioned Reflex in Psychology," *Psy. Rev.*, XXIII: 89-115; Watson, J. B., "Practical and Theoretical Problems in Instinct and Habit," in *Suggestions of Modern Science Concerning Education;* Williams, J. M., *Principles of Social Psychology*, Ch. I; Woodworth, R. S., *Dynamic Psychology*, Chs. III-V; Zigler, M. J., "Instinct and Psychological Viewpoint," *Psy. Rev.*, XXX: 447-60.

CHAPTER IX. MISUSE OF THE CONCEPT OF INSTINCT

Ayres, C. E., "Instinct and Capacity," *J.P.P.S.M.*, XVIII: 561-66, 600-606; Bernard, L. L., "Discussion of Professor McDougall's Paper," *J.A.P.S.P.*, XIX: 42-5; Bernard, L. L., "Instincts and the Psychoanalysts," *J.A.P.S.P.*, XVII: 350-66; Bernard, L. L., "The Misuse of Instinct in the Social Sciences," *Psy. Rev.*, XXVIII: 96-119; Colvin, S. S., *The Learning Process;* Colvin and Bagley, *Human Behavior;* Cason, H., "Gregariousness Considered as a Common Habit," *J.A.P.S.P.*, XIX: 96-105; Dunlap, K., *J.P.P.S.M.*, XIX: 85-93 (VIII); Dunlap, K., "Are There Any Instincts?", *J.A.P.*, XIV: 307-11; Eldridge, S., "Instinct, Habit, and Intelligence in Social Life," *J.A.P.S.P.*, XIX: 142-54; Ellwood, C. A., "The Instincts in Social Psychology," *Psy. Bul.*, XVI: 71-5; Faris, E., "Are Instincts Data or Hypotheses?", *A.J.S.*, XXVII: 184-96; Geiger, J. R., "Concerning Instincts," *J.P.P.S.M.*, XX: 57-68; Geiger, J. R., "Must We Give Up Instincts in Psychology?", *J.P.P.S.M.*, XIX: 94-7; Hocking, W. E., "Instinct in Social Philosophy," *J.A.P.S.P.*, XVIII: 153-66; Hunter, W. S., *J.P.P.S.M.*, XIX: 96-100 (VIII); Hunter, W. S., *Psy. Rev.*, XXVII: 247-69 (VIII); James, W., (VIII); Kantor, J. R., "The Problem of Instinct and Its Relation to Social Psychology," *J.A.P.S.P.*, XVIII: 50-77; Kuo, Z. Y., "Giving Up Instincts in Psychology," *J.P.P.S.M.*, XVIII: 645-64; Kuo, Z. Y., *Psy. Rev.*, XXIX: 344-65 (VIII); Kirkpatrick, E. A., *The Fundamentals of Child Study;* Laing, B. M., "The Contemporary Theory of Instinct," *Monist*, XXXV: 49-69; McDougall, W. (IV), Chs. III, IV; McDougall, W., *Outline of Psychology*, Ch. V; McDougall, W., *J.A.P.S.P.*, XIX: 13-41 (III); McDougall, W., "The Use and Abuse of Instinct in Social Psychology," *J.A.P.S.P.*, XVI: 285-333; Perry, W. J., "Pugnacity," *Monist*, XXXIII: 116-38; Suttie, J. D., "Critique of the Theory of Herd Instinct," *J. Ment. Sci.*, LXVIII, 245-54; Tead, O., *Instincts in Industry;* Tolman, E.

C., "Can Instincts Be Given Up in Psychology?", *J.A.P.S.P.*, XVII: 139-52; Tolman, E. C., *Psy. Bul.*, XX: 200-18 (VIII); Warren, H. C., *Human Psychology;* Watson, J. B., *Behavior, an Introduction to Comparative Psychology,* Ch. IV; Watson, J. B., "What the Nursery Has to Say about Instincts," *Ped. Sem.*, XXXII: 293-326; Woodworth, R. S., *Psychology,* Ch. VIII.

CHAPTER X. HABIT MECHANISMS AND THE ADJUSTMENT PROCESS

Barnes, E., "How Words Get Content," *Stud. Ed.*, II: 43-61; Bartlett, F. C., et. al., "Is Thinking Merely the Action of Language Mechanisms?" (Symposium), *Br. J. Psy.*, XI: 55-104; Bawden, H. H., *Psy. Rev.*, XXVI: 247-76 (V); Bode, B. H., "Intelligence and Behavior," *J.P.P.S.M.*, Jan. 6, 1921; Bohn, W. E., "First Steps in Verbal Expression," *Ped. Sem.*, XXI: 578-95; Chamberlain, A. F., "Acquisition of Written Language of Primitive People," *A. J. Psy.*, XVII: 69-80; Chamberlain, A. F., *The Child: A Study in the Evolution of Man,* Ch. V; Chambers, W. G., "How Words Get Meaning," *Ped. Sem.*, XI: 30-50; Clark, R. S., "An Experimental Study of Silent Thinking," *Archiv. Psy.*, 1922; Coleman, L. V., "Museums—Educational Storage Batteries," *J.S.F.*, II: 721-3; Conradi, E., "Children's Interests in Words, Slang, Stories, Etc.," *Ped. Sem.*, X: 359-404; Conradi, E., "Psychology and Pathology of Speech Development in the Child," *Ped. Psy.*, XI: 328-80; Dashiell, J. F., "Is the Cerebrum the Seat of Thinking?", *Psy. Rev.*, XXXII: 13-29; Delacroix, H., "Les Conditions psychologiques du langage," *Rev. Philos.*, XCVII: 28-66; Dewey, J., "Knowledge and Speech Reactions," *J.P.P.S.M.*, XIX: 561-70; Esper, E. A., "The Psychology of Language," *Psy. Bul.*, XVIII: 490-6; Faris, E., "Preliterate Peoples: Proposing a New Term," *A.J.S.*, XXX: 710-12; Grant, J. R., "A Child's Vocabulary and Its Growth," *Ped. Sem.*, XXII: 183-203; Guillet, C., "The Growth of a Child's Concepts," *Ped. Sem.*, XXIV: 81-96; Hall, G. S., "Gesture, Mimesis, Types of Temperament, and Movie Pedagogy," *Ped. Sem.*, XXVIII: 171-201; Hinckley, O. C., "A Case of Retarded Speech Development," *Ped. Sem.*, XXII: 21-46; Hollingworth, L. S., Burke, A., and Garrison, C. G., "The Psychology of a Prodigious Child," *J. Ap. Psy.*, I: 101-10; Hunter, W. S., *The Delayed Reaction in Animals and Children;* Hunter, W. S., "The Delayed Reaction in a Child," *Psy. Rev.*, XXIV: 74-87; Hunter, W. S., "The Symbolic Process," *Psy. Rev.*, XXXI: 478-97; Huxley, J. S., *Monist,* XXXIII: 364-89 (VI); Kantor, J. R., "An Analysis of Psychological Language Data," *Psy. Rev.*, XXIX: 267-309; Kantor, J. R., *J. Compar. Psy.*, II: 195-206 (VIII); Kantor, J. R., "An Objective Interpretation of Meanings," *A. J. Psy.*, XXXII:

231-248; Keyser, C. J., "The Nature of Man," *Hib. J.,* XX: 324-34; Kroeber, A. L., *Amer. Anthrop.,* XIX: 163-213 (V); Lashley, K. S., "The Neural Mechanism of Voluntary Movements," *Psy. Bul.,* XXI: 94-5; Lukens, H. T., "Preliminary Note on the Learning of Language," *Ped. Sem.,* III: 424-60; Marett, R. R., *Anthropology,* Ch. V; Markey, J., "The Place of Language Habits in a Behavioristic Explanation of Consciousness," *Psy. Rev.,* XXXII: 384-401; Mead, G. H., "A Behavioristic Account of the Significant Symbol," *J.P.P.S.M.,* XIX: 157-63; Nice, M. M., "Speech Development of a Child from Eighteen Months to Six Years," *Ped. Sem.,* XXIV: 204-43; Nice, M. M., *Ped. Sem.,* XXII: 35-64 (VI); Otis, A. S., "Do We Think in Words?", *Psy. Rev.,* XXVII: 399-419; Pelsma, J. R., "A Child's Vocabulary and Its Development," *Ped. Sem.,* XVII: 328-69; Pollack, F., "An Infant's Progress in Language," *Mind,* III: 392-401; Rasmussen, V., *Child Psychology,* Vol. I, Ch. XIII; Reed, H. B., "The Existence and Function of Inner Speech in Thought Processes," *J. Exper. Psy.,* I: 365-92; Reymert, M. L., "The Development of a Verbal Concept of Relationship in Early Childhood," *Scand. Sci. Rev.;* Saer, D. J., "The Effect of Bilingualism on Intelligence," *Br. J. Psy.,* XIV: 24-38; Santayana, G., "Literal and Symbolic Knowledge," *J.P.P.S.M.,* XV: 421-44; Santayana, G., "Living Without Thinking," *Forum,* LXVIII: 731-5; Sapir, E., *Language: An Introduction to the Study of Speech;* Smith, F., "Bilingualism and Mental Development," *Br. J. Psy.,* XIII: 271-82; Smith, M. K., "The Psychological and Pedagogical Aspect of Language," *Ped. Sem.,* X: 438-58; Stoner, W. S., *Natural Education,* Ch. III; Swift, E. J., "Language, Thought and Instincts," *J.P.P.S.M.,* XX: 365-72; Thorson, A. M., "The Relation of Tongue Movements to Internal Speech," *J. Exper. Psy.,* VIII: 1-32; Watson, J. B., "The Place of Kinæsthetic, Visceral and Laryngeal Organization in Thinking," *Psy. Rev.,* XXXI: 339-47; Weiss, A. P., *Psy. Rev.,* XXIX: 329-43 (V); Wheeler, R. H., and Cutsforth, T. D., "Synæsthesia in the Development of the Concept," *J. Exper. Psy.,* VIII: 149-59; Wilson, W. R., "Selection in 'Trial and Error' Learning," *Psy. Rev.,* XXXI: 150-60; Wyczoikowska, A., "Theoretical and Experimental Studies in the Mechanism of Speech," *Psy. Rev.,* XX: 448-58.

CHAPTER XI. THE FUNCTIONAL ORGANIZATION OF CONSCIOUSNESS—THE FORMS OF CONSCIOUSNESS

Allport, F. H., "A Physiological-Genetic Theory of Feeling and Emotion," *Psy. Rev.,* XXIX: 132-9; Bartlett, F. C., "Feeling, Imaging and Thinking," *Br. J. Psy.,* XVI: 16-28; Bernard, L. L., *Transition to an Objective Standard of Social Control,* Chs. II, III; Boodin, J. E., "Cognition and Social Interpretation," *A.J.S.,*

XX: 181-219; Boodin, J. E., "Sensation, Imagination and Consciousness," *Psy. Rev.*, XXVIII: 425-52; Columbia Associates in Philosophy, *An Introduction to Reflective Thinking;* Dashiell, J. F., "A Physiological-Behavioristic Description of Thinking," *Psy. Rev.*, XXXII: 54-73; Davis, W. M., "The Reasonableness of Science," *Sci. Mo.*, XV: 193-214; Dewey, J., "The Naturalistic Theory of Perception by the Senses," *J.P.P.S.M.*, XXII: 596-605; Dewey, J., "The Theory of Emotion," *Psy. Rev.*, I: 553-69; Dunlap, K., *Elements of Scientific Psychology*, Chs. VIII, X; Dunlap, K., "Thought-Content and Feeling," *Psy. Rev.*, XXIII: 49-70; Fisher, S. C., "The Process of Generalizing Abstraction; and Its Product, the General Concept," *Psy. Mon.*, XXI: No. II (whole No. 90); Follett, M. P., *Creative Experience*, Chs. V, VIII; Frost, E. P., "Cannot Psychology Dispense with Consciousness?", *Psy. Rev.*, XXI: 204-11; Gilchrist, O., "A New View of Mental Development," *Psy. Rev.*, XXXI: 297-310; Ginsberg, M., (VIII), Chs. III-V; Griffiths, C. H., "Results of Some Experiments on Affection, Etc.," *J. Exper. Psy.*, III: 447-64; Hayes, E. C., "La Raison et le progrès moral," *Rev. de l'Inst. de Sociol.*, July, 1920; Helson, H., "The Psychology of Gestalt," *A. J. Psy.*, XXXVI: 342-70; Hollingworth, H. L., *The Definition of Judgment;* Hunter, W. S., (V), Pt. II, Chs. 5-7; Hunter, W. S., "The Problem of Consciousness," *Psy. Rev.*, XXXI: 1-31; Johnson, W. F., "Analysis of Thinking," *Mind* (N.S.), XXVII: 1-21; Judd, C. H., *Psychology*, Chs. IV, V, XII, XV; Kantor, J. R., "An Objective Analysis of Volitional Behavior," *Psy. Rev.*, XXX: 116-44; Kantor, J. R., "An Attempt toward a Naturalistic Description of Emotions," *Psy. Rev.*, XXVIII: 19-42, 120-40; Kantor, J. R., *Principles of Psychology*, Chs. XII-XIV; Kantor, J. R., "The Psychology of Feeling or Affective Reactions," *A. J. Psy.*, XXXIV: 433-63; Kantor, J. R., "Suggestions toward a Scientific Interpretation of Perception," *Psy. Rev.*, XXVII: 191-216; Kempf, E. J., (V), 17-90; Kenagy, H. G., "The Theory of Social Forces," *Psy. Rev.*, XXIV: 376-90; Koffka, K., (VIII), Ch. III; Koffka, K., "Perception: An Introduction to the Gestalt-Theorie," *Psy. Bul.*, XIX: 531-85; Köhler, W., "An Aspect of Gestalt Psychology," *Ped. Sem.*, XXXII: 691-723; Köhler, W., "The Problem of Form in Perception," *Br. J. Psy.*, XIV: 262-8; Libby, W., "Conceptual Thinking," *Sci. Mo.*, XV: 435-42; Libby, W., "The Scientific Imagination," *Sci. Mo.*, XV: 263-70; MacCurdy, J. T., *Psychology of Emotion;* Mach, E., *The Analysis of Sensations;* Mach, E., "On the Part Played by Accident in Invention and Discovery," *Monist*, VI: 161-175; Mason, O. T., *Origins of Invention;* Melrose, J. A., "The Organic Setting of the Problem of Thinking," *Psy. Rev.*, XXX: 370-9; Melrose, J. A., "The Structure of Animal Learning," *Psy. Rev.*, XXVIII: 189-221; Meyer, M. F., "The Nervous Correlate of Pleasantness and Unpleasantness," *Psy. Rev.*, XV: 201-16, 292-322; Monakow, C. v., *The Emotions, Morality and the Brain;* Moore, D. T. V., *Dynamic Psychology,* Pts. II, III, VI; Moore, D. T. V., "Image and Meaning in Memory and Perception," *Psy. Mon.,* XXVII:69-296; Mursell, J. L., "The Concept of Sensation," *J.P.P.S.M.,* XIX:684-90; Norsworthy and Whitley, (VII), Ch. VII; Ogden, R. M., "Are There Any Sensations?", *A. J. Psy.,* XXXIII:247-254; Parmelee, M., "Recent Advances in the Psychology of Behavior," *Sociol. Rev.,* XI:21-27; Parmelee, M., (VIII), Chs. XIV-XVI; Paton, S., *Human Behavior,* Ch. VII; Paulhan, F., *Psychologie de l'invention;* Perry, R. B., "The Appeal to Reason," *Phil. Rev.,* Mar., 1921; Picard, M., "The Coördinate Character of Feeling and Cognition," *J.P.P.S.M.,* XVIII:288-295; Reid, L. A., "Instinct, Emotion, and the Higher Life," *Br. J. Psy.,* XIV:78-93; Reiser, A. L., "The Structure of Thought," *Psy. Rev.,* XXXI:51-73; Rignano, E., *Psychologie du Raisonnement;* Roback, A. A., "The Interference of Will Impulses," *Psy. Mon.,* XXV: No. 5 (whole No. 111); Robinson and Robinson, (VIII), Chs. VI, XI, XIV, XVI, XVIII; Rosenow, C., "Behavior and Conscious Behavior," *Psy. Rev.,* XXX:192-216; Ruediger, W. C., "Memory, Thought, and Logic," *Psy. Bul.,* XVII:254-6; Seashore, C. E., (VIII), Chs. XX, XXI; Shand, A., *The Foundations of Character,* Bk. I, Chs. IV, V, XI, XII, XIV, XV; Spearman, C., *The Nature of Intelligence and the Principles of Cognition;* Taylor, A. R., *The Study of the Child,* Chs. IX, X; Thorndike, E. L., "The Effect of Changed Data upon Reasoning," *J. Ex. Psy.,* V:33-8; Thurstone, L. L., "The Stimulus-Response Fallacy in Psychology," *Psy. Rev.,* XXX:354-69; Tolman, E. C., "A Behavioristic Account of the Emotions," *Psy. Rev.,* XXX:217-27; Tolman, E. C., "Nerve Processes and Cognition," *Psy. Rev.,* XXV: 423-42; Turner, J. E., "Freedom of Will and Action," *I.J.E.,* XXX: 231-40; Warren, H. C., *Psy. Rev.,* XXVI:197-203 (VIII); Warren, H. C., *Elements of Human Psychology,* Chs. V, VI; Warren, H. C., *Human Psychology,* Chs. VII-X, XIV, XV; Warren, H. C., *Psy. Rev.,* XXIX:481-9 (V); Washburn, M. F., *The Animal Mind;* Watson, J. B., "Experimental Studies on the Growth of the Emotions," *Ped. Sem.,* XXXII:327-48; Watson, J. B., "Recent Experiments on How We Lose and Change Our Emotional Equipment," *Ped. Sem.,* XXXII:349-71; Watson, J. B., "A Schematic Outline of the Emotions," *Psy. Rev.,* XXVI:165-96; Watson, J. B., and R. R., "Studies in Infant Psychology," *Sci. Mo.,* XIII:493-515; Wechsler, D., "What Constitutes an Emotion?", *Psy. Rev.,* XXXII:235-40; Weiss, A. P., *Psy. Rev.,* XXIX:329-43 (V); Wheeler, R. H., "An Experimental Investigation of the Process of Choosing," *Univ. of Oregon Pub.,* I: No. II, 1920; Wohlgemuth, A., "The Coexistence and Localization of Feeling," *Br. J. Psy.,* XVI:116-22; Wohlgemuth, A., "The Influence of Feeling on Memory," *Br. J. Psy.,* XIII:405-16; Woolbert, C. H., "A Behavioristic Account of Intellect and Emotions," *Psy. Rev.,* XXI:265-72; Young, P. T., "Pleasantness and

Unpleasantness in Relation to Organic Response," *A. J. Psy.*, XXXII: 38-54.

CHAPTER XII. THE FUNCTIONAL ORGANIZATION OF CONSCIOUSNESS—THE OBJECTS OF CONSCIOUSNESS

Allport, F. H., "The Group Fallacy in Relation to Culture," *J.A.P.S.P.*, XIX: 185-91; Allport, F. H., *J.A.P.S.P.*, XIX: 60-73 (III); Ames, E. S., "Religion in Terms of Social Consciousness," *J. Relig.*, I: 264-70; Baldwin, J. M., "The Genesis of Social 'Interests,'" *Monist*, VII: 340-57; Bernays, E. L., *Crystallizing Public Opinion*, Pt. II, Ch. V; Bodenhafer, W. B., "The Comparative Rôle of the Group Concept in Ward's *Dynamic Sociology* and Contemporary Sociology," *A.J.S.*, XXVI: 273-314, 425-74, 588-600, 716-43; Boland, G., "Taking a Dare," *Ped. Sem.*, XVII: 510-24; Boodin, J. E., *A.J.S.*, XIX: 1-47 (VI); Burnham, W. H., "The Normal Mind," *Ped. Sem.*, XXIX: 383-99; Burr, A. R., *The Autobiography;* Cooley, C. H., et al., "Social Consciousness," *A.J.S.*, XII: 675-94; Creighton, J. E., "The Social Nature of Thinking," *Phil. Rev.*, XXVII: 274-95; Ellwood, C. A., *J.A.P.S.P.*, XIX: 3-12 (II); Gault, R. H., "The Sense of Social Unity," in *Studies in Psychology in Honor of E. B. Titchener*, 121-7; Hall, G. S., and Smith, T. L., "Showing Off and Bashfulness as Phases of Self-Consciousness," *Ped. Sem.*, X: 159-99; Holmes, A. (VII), Ch. IX; James, W. (VIII), Ch. X.; Kline, L. W., and France, C. J., "The Psychology of Ownership," *Ped. Sem.*, VI: 421-70; Krueger, E. T., "Personality and Life-History Documents," *Pub. Amer. Sociological Soc.*, XIX: 176-80; Laird, J., "The Group Mind and the General Will," *Monist*, XXXIII: 453-72; de Lanessan, J. L., "Race, Nationality, and Mentality," *Rev. Int. de Soc.*, June, 1917; Libby, W., et al., "The Contents of Children's Minds," *Ped. Sem.*, XVII: 242-72; Lippmann, W., *Public Opinion;* Lowell, A. L., *Public Opinion and Popular Government;* Lutoslawski, W., "La Conscience national," *La Paix par le droit*, Sept., 1916; MacDougall, R., "The Self and Mental Phenomena," *Psy. Rev.*, XXIII: 1-29; McDougall, W., (III), pp. 41-55; Mead, G. H., "Social Consciousness and the Consciousness of Meaning," *Psy. Bul.*, VII: 397-405; Mead, G. H., "Psychology of Social Consciousness Implied in Instruction," *Science*, N.S., XXI: 688-93; Morse, R. M., "The Development of Social Consciousness in the Sunday School," *Ped. Sem.*, XVI: 523-9; Perry, R. B., "Is There a Social Mind?", *A.J.S.*, XXVII: 561-72, 721-36; Rogers, A. K., "Class-Consciousness," *I.J.E.*, April, 1917; Royce, J., "The External World and the Social Consciousness," *Phil. Rev.*, III: 513-45; Royce, J., "Self-Consciousness, Social Consciousness and Nature," *Phil. Rev.*, IV: 465-85, 577-602; Sharp, F. C., "Some Problems in the Psychology of Egoism and

Altruism," *J.P.P.S.M.*, XX: 85-104; Shepard, W. J., "Public Opinion," *A.J.S.*, XV: 32-60; Swett, H. P., "Her Little Girl," *Ped. Sem.*, XVII: 104-10; Taylor, A. R., *The Study of the Child*, Ch. XVII; Willey, M. W., and N. B., "The •Conditioned Response and Consciousness of Kind," *A.J.S.*, XXX: 22-28.

CHAPTER XIII. PATHOLOGICAL FORMS OF CONSCIOUSNESS

Adler, A., *The Neurotic Constitution;* Allport, F. H., "Timidity and the Selling Personality," *The Eastern Underwriter*, XXI: 15-17; Bagley, E., "The Etiology of Phobias," *J.A.P.S.P.*, XVII: 16-18; Bagley, E., "The Inferiority Reaction," *J.A.P.S.P.*, XVIII: 269-73; Binet, A., *Alterations of Personality;* Brink, L., "How the Concept of the Unconscious is Serviceable," *J.A.P.S.M.*, XV: 405-14; Chase, H. W., "Psychoanalysis and the Unconscious," *Ped. Sem.*, XVII: 281-327; Craig, M., "Some Aspects of Education and Training in Relation to Mental Disorder," *J. Ment. Sci.*, LXVIII: 209-28; Drever, J., "'Conscious' and 'Unconscious' in Psychology," *J.A.P.S.P.*, XIX: 327-32; Editors, "The Activity and Nature of Subconscious Processes," *J.A.P.S.P.*, XIX: 129-31; Eisler, E. R., "The Religious Factor in Mental Disorder," *J.A.P.S.P.*, XIX: 85-95; Freud, S., *General Introduction to Psychoanalysis;* Freud, S., *Psychopathology of Everyday Life;* Harrison, M., "Mental Instability as a Factor in Progress," *Monist*, XXXII: 189-99; Humphrey, G., "The Child's Unconscious Mind," *J.A.P.S.P.*, XV: 387-402; Humphrey, G., "Education and Freudianism," *J.A.P.S.P.*, XV: 350-86; Janet, P., "The Fear of Action," *J.A.P.S.P.*, XVI: 150-60; Janet, P., *The Major Symptoms of Hysteria;* Jones, E., *Papers on Psychoanalysis;* Jung, C. G., *Analytical Psychology;* Jung, C. G., "La Structure de l'inconscient," *Archiv. de Psy.*, Dec., 1916; Kantor, J. R., "Human Personality and Its Pathology," *J.P.P.S.M.*, XVI: 236-46; Kempf, E. J., (V); Kraepelin, E., *Psychiatrie;* Leonard, E. A., "A Parents' Study of Children's Lies," *Ped. Sem.*, XXVII: 105-36; Lodge, O., "Testimony to a Child's Impression of Fairies," *J. Soc. Psychical Research*, XX: 63-70; Martin, L. J., "An Experimental Contribution to the Investigation of the Subconscious," *Psy. Rev.*, XX: 251-8; Mercier, C. A., *Conduct and Its Disorders Biologically Considered;* Moore, D. T. V., *Dynamic Psychology*, Pts. IV, V; Mühl, A. M., "Automatic Writing Combined with Crystal Gazing as a Means of Recalling Forgotten Incidents," *J.A.P.S.P.*, XIX: 264-73; Mühl, A. M., "Automatic Writing as an Indicator of the Fundamental Factors Underlying the Personality," *J.A.P.S.P.*, XVII: 162-83; Mühl, A. M., "The Use of Automatic Writing in Determining Conflicts and Early Childhood Impressions," *J.A.P.S.P.*, XVIII: 1-31; Mursell, J. L.,

"Repression, Release and Normality," *Psy. Rev.*, XXX: 1-19; Mursell, J. L., "Sublimation and the Ideal of Education," *Ped. Sem.*, XXX: 24-30; Ogburn, W. F., "Bias, Psychoanalysis, and the Subjective in Relation to the Social Sciences," *Pub. Amer. Sociological Soc.*, XVII: 62-74; Partridge, G. E., "Reverie," *Ped. Sem.*, V: 445-74; Poffenberger, A. T., "The Subconscious—What Is It?", *Sci. Mo.*, XIV: 379-90; Prince, M., "A Critique of Psychoanalysis," *Archiv. Neu. and Psychiatry*, VI: 610-33; Prince, M., *The Unconscious;* Pruette, L., "Some Applications of the Inferiority Complex to Pluralistic Behavior," *P-A. Rev.*, IX: 28-39; Reed, E. F., "Psychic Mechanisms and Social Radicalism," *J.S.F.*, II: 36-40; Ribot, T. A., *Diseases of Personality;* Rinaldo, J., *Psychoanalysis of the "Reformer";* Robinson, E. S., "A Concept of Compensation and Its Psychological Setting," *J.A.P.S.P.*, XVII: 383-94; Sands, I. J., and Blanchard, P., "Some of the Psychological Mechanisms of Human Conduct," *Mental Hyg.*, VI: 498-521; Smith, M. H., *The Psychology of the Criminal;* Stratton, G. M., *Experimental Psychology, Etc.*, Chs. V-VII; Tanner, A., "Adler's Theory of *Minderwertigkeit*," *Ped. Sem.*, XXII: 204-17; Taylor, W. S., "Rationalization and Its Social Significance," *J.A.P.S.P.*, XVII: 410-18; Townsend, H. G., "The Concept of Inferiority," *School and Soc.*, XV: 134-8; Tridon, A., *Psychoanalysis and Behavior;* Watson, J. B., "The Psychology of Wish-Fulfillment," *Sci. Mo.*, Nov., 1916; Watson, J. B., "The Unverbalized in Human Behavior," *Psy. Rev.*, XXXI: 273-80; Williams, T. A., "Prevalent Misunderstanding Concerning Unconscious Mind," *J.A.P.S.P.*, XIX: 77-84; Young, K., "The Integration of the Personality," *Ped. Sem.*, XXX: 264-85.

CHAPTER XIV. GENERAL SETS, POWERS, AND INTELLIGENCE

Baldwin, B. T., "Factors Influencing Mental Development," *Psy. Bul.*, XX: 671-4; Baldwin, B. T., "The Relation between Mental and Physical Growth," *J. Ed. Psy.*, XIII: 193-203; Bernard, L. L., "A Criticism of the Psychoanalysts' Theory of the Libido," *Monist*, XXXIII: 240-71; Bishop, O., "What Is Measured by Intelligence Tests?", *J. Ed. Research*, IX: 29-38; Boring, E. G., "Intelligence as the Tests Test It," *New Repub.*, XXXV: 35-7; Bosner, F. G., "A Study of the Relations between Mental Activity and the Circulation of the Blood," *Psy. Rev.*, X: 120-38; Burk, F., "From Fundamental to Accessory in the Development of the Nervous System and of Movements," *Ped. Sem.*, VI: 5-64; Burt, C., *Mental and Scholastic Tests;* Byrd, H., "A Case of Phenomenal Memorizing by a Feeble-Minded Negro," *J. Ap. Psy.*, IV: 202-6; Chapman, J. C., "Persistence, Success and Speed in a Mental Task," *Ped. Sem.*, XXXI: 276-84; Colvin, S. S., "The Present Status of Mental Testing," *Ed. Rev.*,

LXVI: 320-37; Dearborn, G. V. N., "Movement, Cenesthesia, and the Mind," *Psy. Rev.*, XXIII: 190-207; Dickenson, Z. C., *Economic Motives;* Doll, E. A., "Improper Use of the Intelligence Quotient," *J. Delinquency*, May, 1920; English, H. B., "Dynamic Psychology and the Problem of Motivation," *Psy. Rev.*, XXVIII: 239-48; Fernald, W. E., "The Diagnosis of the Higher Grades of Mental Defect," *Amer. J. Insanity*, LXX: 253-64; Fernald, W. E., "Standardized Fields of Inquiry for Studies of Defectives," *Mental Hyg.*, I: 211-34; Freeman, F. N., "Mental Tests," *Psy. Bul.*, XVII: 353-62; Freeman, F. N., "Tests," *Psy. Bul.*, XVI: 374-81; Fukuda, T., "A Survey of the Intelligence and Environment of School Children," *A. J. Psy.*, XXXVI: 124-39; Fuller, R. G., "Child Labor and Mental Age," *Ped. Sem.*, XXIX: 64-71; Hamid, S. A., "Some Factors of Effectiveness in Mental ('Intelligence') Tests," *Br. J. Psy.*, XVI: 100-15; Hines, H. C., *Measuring Intelligence;* Hollingworth, L. S., "Differential Action Upon the Sexes of Forces Which Tend to Segregate the Feebleminded," *J.A.P.S.P.*, XVII: 35-57; Hollingworth, L. S., Burke, A., Garrison, C. G., *J. Ap. Psy.*, I: 101-10 (X); Hollingworth, L. S., et al., "Subsequent History of E—; Five Years After the Initial Report," *J. Ap. Psy.*, VI: 205-10; Holmes, S. J., *The Trend of the Race*, Ch. III; Hurlock, E. B., "The Effect of Incentives Upon the Constancy of the I. Q.," *Ped. Sem.*, XXXII: 422-34; Ide, G. G., "The Increase of the I. Q. Through Training," *Psy. Clinic*, XIV: 159-63; "Intelligence and Its Measurement" (Symposium and Discussions), *J. Ed. Psy.*, XII: 123-44, 148-54, 155-58, 195-212, 270-5, 315-41, 401-7, 439-44; Jordan, A. M., "The Validation of Intelligence Tests," *J. Ed. Psy.*, XIV: 348-72, 414-28; Knight, F. B., and Remmers, H. H., "Fluctuations in Mental Production When Motivation Is the Main Variable," *J. Ap. Psy.*, VII: 209-23; Lashley, K. S., "Contributions of Freudianism to Psychology: Physiological Analysis of the Libido," *Psy. Rev.*, XXXI: 192-202; Lincoln, E. A., "The Constancy of Intelligence Quotients," *J. Ed. Psy.*, XIII: 484-95; Lowell, F., and Woodrow, H., "Some Data on Anatomical Age and Its Relation to Intelligence," *Ped. Sem.*, XXIX: 1-15; Maher, E. A., "Moral and Social Development of the Six Year Old Child," *Ped. Sem.*, XXXI: 268-75; *Memoirs of the National Academy of Sciences*, XV, Pt. III, Chs. VIII, XI, XIII; Minogue, B. M., "A Case of Secondary Mental Deficiency with Musical Talent," *J. Ap. Psy.*, VII: 349-52; Moss, F. A., "Study of Animal Drives," *J. Exper. Psy.*, VII: 165-85; Mursell, J. L., "Hunger and Appetite," *Psy. Rev.*, XXXII: 317-33; Naccarati, S., and Lewy-Guinzberg, R. L., "Hormones and Intelligence," *J. Ap. Psy.*, VI: 221-34; Peckstein, L. A., "The Definition of Intelligence," *Psy. Mon.*, XXX; Perrin, F. A. C., "The Psychology of Motivation," *Psy. Rev.*, XXX: 176-91; Peterson, J., "Intelligence Conceived as a Mechanism," *Psy. Rev.*, XXXI: 281-7; Peterson, J., "Intelligence and Learning,"

Psy. Rev., XXIX: 366-89; Pintner, R., *Intelligence Testing, Methods and Results;* Poffenberger, A. T., and Carpenter, F. L., "Character Traits in School Success," *J. Exper. Psy.*, VII: 67-74; Pohlman, A. G., "The Heredity of the Upright Position and Some of Its Disadvantages," *Monist,* XVII: 570-82; Reed, H. B., "The Effect of Training on Individual Differences," *J. Exper. Psy.*, VII: 186-200; Révész, G., *The Psychology of a Musical Prodigy;* Ruml, B., "Reconstruction in Mental Tests," *J.P.P.S.M.*, XVIII: 181-5; Schmitt, C., "The Binet Simon Tests of Mental Ability. Discussion and Criticism," *Ped. Sem.*, XIX: 186-200; Sears, C. H., "Home and School Punishment," *Ped. Sem.*, VI: 159-85; Spearman, C., (XI); Starr, A. S., "An Analytic Study of the Intelligence of a Group of Adolescent Delinquent Girls," *Psy. Clinic,* XIV: 143-54; Stern, W., *The Psychological Methods of Testing Intelligence;* Stone, C. P., "A Comparative Study of the Intelligence of 399 Inmates of the Indiana Reformatory and 653 Men of the United States Army," *J. Crim. Law and Criminology,* XII: 237-57; Teagarten, F. M., "'The Constancy of the I. Q.' Again," *J. Ed. Psy.*, XIII: 366-72; Terman, L. M., "A New Approach to the Study of Genius," *Psy. Rev.*, XXIX: 310-18; Terman, L. M., "An Experiment in Infant Education," *J. Ap. Psy.*, V: 219-28; Terman, L. M., *The Measurement of Intelligence;* Terman, L. M., "The Mental Test as a Psychological Method," *Psy. Rev.*, XXXI: 93-117; Thomson, G. H., Claparède, E., and Thurstone, L. L., "The Nature of General Intelligence and Ability," *Br. J. Psy.*, XIV: 229-47; Thorndike, E. L., "A Constant Error in Psychological Ratings," *J. Ap. Psy.*, IV: 25-29; Thorndike, E. L., "Measurement of Intelligence," *Psy. Rev.*, XXXI: 219-52; Thurstone, L. L., *The Nature of Intelligence;* Toops, H. A., and Symonds, P. M., "What Shall We Expect of the A. Q.?", *J. Ed. Psy.*, XIII: 513-28; Wallin, J. E. W., *Causative Factors of Mental Inferiority and the Prevention of Degeneracy;* Wallis, W. D., "The Development of the Human Chin," *Anatom. Rec.*, XII: 315-28; Warren, H. C., *Elements of Human Psychology,* Chs. XV, XVI; Warren, H. C., *Human Psychology,* Chs. XVII-XIX; Wells, W. R., "Natural Checks on Human Progress," *Monist,* XXXI: 121-32; Wheeler, R. H., "A Psychological Description of Intelligence," *Psy. Rev.*, XXXI: 161-74; Whipple, G. M., "The Intelligence Testing Program and Its Objectors—Conscientious and Otherwise," *School and Soc.*, XVII: 561-8, 596-604; Whipple, G. M., *Manual of Mental and Physical Tests;* Whitely, P. L., "The Dependence of Learning and Recall upon Prior Mental and Physical Conditions," *J. Exper. Psy.*, VII: 420-8; Witmer, L., "Intelligence—A Definition," *Psy. Clinic,* XIV: 65-7; Witmer, L., "What Is Intelligence and Who Has It?", *Sci. Mo.*, XV: 57-67; Young, K., "The History of Mental Testing," *Ped. Sem.*, XXXI: 1-48; Young, P. T., "The Phenomenon of Organic Set," *Psy. Rev.*, XXXII: 472-8.

CHAPTER XV. RACE, NATIONALITY, CLASS

Arlitt, A. H., "On the Need for Caution in Establishing Race Norms," *J. Ap. Psy.*, V: 179-83; Arlitt, A. H., "The Relation of Intelligence to Age in Negro Children," *J. Ap. Psy.*, VI: 378-84; Bagley, W. C., "The Army Tests and the Pro-Nordic Propaganda," *Ed. Rev.*, LXVII: 179-87; Baldwin, B. T., "Individual and Racial Differences," *Psy. Bul.*, XX: 674-77; Bassett, P. M., and Porteus, S. D., "Sex Differences in Porteus Maze Test Performance," *Training Sch. Bul.*, XVII: 105-20; Bevis, W. M., "Psychological Traits of the Southern Negro with Observations as to Some of His Psychoses," *A. J. Psychiatry*, I: 69-78; Boas, F., *Amer. Anthrop.* (N. S.), XIV: 530-62 (VII); Boas, F., "Human Faculty as Determined by Race," *Proc. Amer. Assn. for the Advancement of Sci.*, XLIII: 301-27; Boas, F., "The Problem of the American Negro," *Yale Rev.*, Jan., 1921; Boas, F., "What Is Race?", *Nation*, CXX: 89-91; Bousfield, P., *Sex and Civilization;* Brandenburg, G. C., "Psychological Aspects of Language," *J. Ed. Psy.*, IX: 313-32; Bridges, W. J., and Coler, L. E., "The Relation of Intelligence to Social Status," *Psy. Rev.*, XXIV: 1-31; Brigham, C. C., *A Study of American Intelligence;* Bruner, F. C., "Hearing of Primitive Peoples," *Archiv. Psy.*, No. XI; Burnham, W. H., "Sex Differences in Mental Ability," *Ed. Rev.*, LXII: 273-84; Burtt, H. E., "Sex Differences in the Effect of Discussion," *J. Ex. Psy.*, III: 390-5; Chapman, I. C., "The Relation of Family Size to Intelligence of Offspring and Socio-Economic Status of Family," *Ped. Sem.*, XXXII: 414-21; Clark, W. W., "Birth Rate and Native Intelligence," *Psy. Clin.*, XIV: 111-15; Clark, W. W., "Home Conditions and Native Intelligence," *J. Delin.*, VII: 17-23; Cobb, M. V., "The Limits Set to Educational Achievement by Limited Intelligence," *J. Ed. Psy.*, XIII: 449-66; Colvin, S. S., and Allen, R. D., "Mental Tests and Linguistic Ability," *J. Ed. Psy.*, XIV: 1-20; Cooper, R. W., and Cooper, H., *Negro School Attendance in Delaware;* Cornell, E. L., and Lowden, G. L., "A Comparison of the Stanford and Porteus Tests in Several Types of Social Inadequacy," *J.A.P.S.P.*, XVIII: 33-42; Crafts, L. W., "Bibliography of Feeble-Mindedness in Relation to Juvenile Delinquency," *J. Delinquency*, I: 195-208; Davenport, C. B., "Comparative Social Traits of Various Races," *School and Soc.*, XIV: 344-8; Davenport, C. B., and Crayton, L. C., "Comparative Social Traits of Various Races," *J. Ap. Psy.*, VII: 127-34; Davidson, P. E., "The Social Significance of the Army Intelligence Findings," *Sci. Mo.*, XVI: 184-94; Derrick, S. M., "A Comparative Study of the Intelligence of Seventy-five White and Fifty-five Colored College Students by the Stanford Revision of the Binet-Simon Scale," *J. Ap. Psy.*, IV: 316-29; Dexter, E. S., "The Relation between Occupation of Parent and Intelligence of Children,"

School and Soc., XVII: 613-4; Duff, J. F., and Thomson, G. H., "The Social and Geographical Distribution of Intelligence in Northumberland," *Br. J. Psy.*, XIV: 192-8; Ellis, H., *Man and Woman;* Ellis, H., "The Mind of Woman," *Atl. Mo.*, Sept., 1916; English, H. B., "An Experimental Study of Mental Capacities of School Children, Correlated with Social Status," *Psy. Mon.*, XXIII: 266-331; Faris, E., "The Mental Capacity of Savages," *A.J.S.*, XXIII: 603-19; Feingold, G. A., "Intelligence of the First Generation of Immigrant Groups," *J. Ed. Psy.*, XV: 65-82; Ferguson, G. O., "Mental Status of the American Negro," *Sci. Mo.*, XII: 533-43; Fukuda, T., "A Survey of the Intelligence and Environment of School Children," *A. J. Psy.*, XXXVI: 124-39; Fuller, B., "Race and Nationality," *Contemp. Rev.*, CXX: 337-45; Garth, T. R., "A Comparison of the Intelligence of Mexican and Mixed and Full Blood Indian Children," *Psy. Rev.*, XXX: 388-401; Garth, T. R., "A Comparison of Mental Abilities of Mixed and Full Blood Indians on a Basis of Education," *Psy. Rev.*, XXIX: 221-36; Garth, T. R., "The Psychology of the American Indian," *Indian Sch. J.*, June, 1920; Garth, T. R., "Racial Differences in Mental Fatigue," *J. Ap. Psy.*, IV: 235-44; Garth, T. R., "The Results of Some Tests on Mixed and Full Blood Indians," *J. Ap. Psy.*, Dec., 1921; Garth, T. R., "A Review of Racial Psychology," *Psy. Bul.*, XXII: 343-64; Gates, A. I., "Experiments of the Relative Efficiency of Men and Women in Memory and Reasoning," *Psy. Rev.*, XXIV: 139-46; Geddes, P., and Thomson, J. A., *The Evolution of Sex;* Grigg, J. E., "The Comparison of Races," *Sci. Mo.*, XX: 248-54; Hall, G. S., "The Dangerous Age," *Ped. Sem.*, XXVIII: 276-94; Hankins, F. H., "Individual Differences and the Democratic Theory," *Pol. Sci. Quart.*, XXXVIII: 388-412; Hankins, F. H., "Individual Differences and Their Significance for Social Theory," *Pub. Amer. Sociological Soc.*, XVII: 27-39; Hart, H., "Familial Differential Fecundity," *J. Amer. Stat. Assn.* (N. S.), XXX: 25-30; Hart, H., "Occupational Differential Fecundity," *Sci. Mo.*, XIX: 527-32; Hart, H., "Socialization Test," *J. Ap. Soc.*, VII: 163-6; Herskovits, M. J., "Brains and the Immigrant," *Nation*, CXX: 139-41; Hollingworth, L. S., "Comparison of the Sexes in Mental Traits," *Psy. Bul.*, XVI: 371-3; Hollingworth, L., "Variability as Related to Sex Differences in Achievement," *A.J.S.*, XIX: 510-30; Hinds, J. H., "A Comparison of the Brightness of Country and City High School Children," *J. Ed. Psy.*, Feb., 1922; Howard, J. H., "Psychological Differences between Children and Adults," *Ped. Sem.*, XX: 236-53; Huntington, E., "The Factor of Health in Mexican Character," *J. Internat'l Relations*, Oct., 1920; Huntington, E., "The Relation of Health to Racial Capacity," *Geog. Rev.*, Apr., 1921; Ide, G. G., "The Increase of the Intelligence Quotient Through Training," *Psy. Clinic*, XIV: 159-62; Jordan, A. M., "Notes on Racial Differences," *School and Soc.*, XVI: 503-4; Kornhauser, A. W., "The Economic Standing of Parents and the Intelligence of Children," *J. Ed. Psy.*, IX: 159-164; LeBon, G., *The Psychology of Peoples;* Lowie, R. H., "Psychology, Anthropology, and Race," *Amer. Anthrop.*, XXV: 291-303; Luckey, B. M., "Racial Differences in Mental Ability," *Sci. Mo.*, XX: 245-8; MacDonald, H., "The Social Distribution of Intelligence in the Isle of Wight," *Br. J. Psy.*, XVI: 123-29; McFadden, J. H., and Dashiell, J. F., "Racial Differences as Measured by the Downey Will-Temperament Test," *J. Ap. Psy.*, VII: 30-53; Mayo, M. J., "The Mental Capacity of the Negro," *Archiv. Psy.*, No. XXVIII; Miner, J. B., "Deficiency and Delinquency: An Interpretation of Mental Testing," *Ed. Psy. Monogr.*, No. XXI; Montague, H., and Hollingworth, L. S., "The Comparative Variability of the Sexes at Birth," *A.J.S.*, XX: 335-70; Moore, H. T., "Further Data Concerning Sex Differences," *J.A.P.S.P.*, XVII: 210-14; Morse, J., "A Comparison of White and Colored Children Measured by the Binet-Simon Scale of Intelligence," *Pop. Sci. Mo.*, LXXXIV: 75-79; Murchison, C., "The Intelligence of White Foreign Born Criminals," *Ped. Sem.*, XXXI: 297-307; Murchison, C., and Burfield, H., "Geographical Concomitants of Negro Criminal Intelligence," *Ped. Sem.*, XXXII: 26-44; Murchison, C., and Burfield, H., "Types of Crime and Intelligence of Negro Criminals," *Ped. Sem.*, XXXII: 239-47; Murchison, C., and Nafe, R., "Intelligence of Negro Criminal Recidivists," Ped. Sem., XXXII: 248-56; Odum, H. W., "Negro Children in the Public Schools of Philadelphia," *An. Amer. Acad.*, XLIX: 86-208; Pearson, P. H., "Physical and Intellectual Traits and Social Orders," *Ped. Sem.*, XXX: 152-5; Peterson, J., "The Comparative Abilities of White and Negro Children," *Comp. Psy. Mon.*, I: No. 5; Peterson, J., "Comparison of White and Negro Children in Multiple Choice Learning," *Proc. Amer. Psy. Assn.*, 1921; Phillips, B. A., "The Binet Tests Applied to Colored Children," *Psy. Clinic*, VIII: 190-6; Pintner, R., "Comparison of American and Foreign Children on Intelligence Tests," *J. Ed. Psy.*, XIV: 292-5; Pintner, R., "One Hundred Juvenile Delinquents Tested by the Binet Scale," *Ped. Sem.*, XXI: 523-31; Pintner, R., and Keller, R., "Intelligence Tests of Foreign Children," *J. Ed. Psy.*, XIII: 214-22; Porteus, S. D., "Mental Tests with Delinquents and Australian Aboriginal Children," *Psy. Rev.*, XXIV: 32-42; Pressey, L. W., *J. Ap. Psy.*, IV: 91-96 (VI); Pressey, L. W., and Pressey, S. L., "Further Data with Regard to Sex Differences," *J. Ap. Psy.*, V: 78-84; Pressey, L. W., and Ralston, R., "The Relation of the General Intelligence of School Children to the Occupation of Their Fathers," *J. Ap. Psy.*, III: 366-73; Pressey, L. W., and Teter, G. F., "A Comparison of Colored and White Children by Means of a Group Scale of Intelligence," *J. Ap. Psy.*, III: 277-82; Pressey, L. W., and Thomas, J. B., "A Study of Country Children in (1) a Good and (2) a Poor Farming District by Means of a Group Scale of Intelligence," *J. Ap. Psy.*, III: 283-6; Pyle, W. H., "The Mind of the Negro Child," *School* and Soc., I: 357-60; Reuter, E. B., "The Superiority of the Mulatto," A.J.S., XXIII: 83-106; Rowe, E. C., "Five Hundred Forty-seven White and Two Hundred Sixty-eight Indian Children Tested by the Binet-Simon Tests," Ped. Sem., XXI: 454-68; Sangren, P. V., "Social Rating of Best and Poorest High School Students," J. Ed. Psy., XIV: 209-14; Sheldon, W. H., "The Intelligence of Mexican Children," School and Soc., XIX: 139-42; Snow, A. J., "Labor Turnover and Mental Alertness Test Scores," J. Ap. Psy., VII: 285-90; Stearns, A. W., and Chapman, J. V., "The Kind of Men in State Prison," J.A.P., XV: 335-49; Strong, A. C., "Three Hundred Fifty White and Colored Children Measured by the Binet-Simon Measuring Scale of Intelligence," Ped. Sem., XX: 485-515; Strong, E. K., Jr., "An Interesting Sex Difference," Ped. Sem., XXII: 521-8; Sunne, D., "A Comparative Study of White and Negro Children," J. Ap. Psy., I: 71-83; Symonds, P. M., "A Second Approximation to the Curve of the Distribution of Intelligence of the Population of the United States, Etc.," J. Ed. Psy., XIV: 65-81; Thomas, I. W., "Race Psychology with Particular Reference to the Immigrant and the Negro," A.J.S., XVII: 725-75; Thomas, W. I., Sex and Society; Thorndike, E. L., Educational Psychology, III: 206-24; Thorndike, E. L., "Intelligence Scores of Colored Pupils in High Schools," School and Soc., XVIII: 569-70; Vaerting, M., "Psychotechnische Kampfmethoden gegen das weibliche Geschlecht," Die Neue Generation, XVII: 245-50; Van Wagenen, M. J., and Kelley, F. E., "Language Abilities and Their Relations to College Marks," J. Ed. Psy., XI: 459-73; Voigtländer, E., "Zur Problematik der Geschlechtesunterschiede," Ztschr. f. Sexualwiss., X: 89-99; Washburn, M. F., "A Questionary Study of Certain National Differences in Emotional Traits," J. Compar. Psy., III: 412-30; Watson, H. K., "Causes of Delinquency Among Fifty Negro Boys," Stud. in Sociol., U. of Southern Calif.; Watts, F., Abnormal Psychology and Education, Ch. IV; Waugh, K. T., "A Comparison of Oriental and American Student Intelligence," Proc. Amer. Psy. Assn., XXIX; Wells, G. R., "The Application of the Binet-Simon Tests to Groups of White and Colored School Children," Psy. Mon., XXXII: 52-8; Willis, C. B., "The Effects of Primogeniture on Intellectual Capacity," J.A.P.S.P., XVIII: 375-7; Woodworth, R. S., "Comparative Psychology of the Races," Psy. Bul., XIII: 388-96; Woodworth, R. S., "Racial Differences in Mental Traits," Science (N. S.), XXI: 171-86; Yates, D. H., "A Study of Twenty High School Seniors of Superior Intelligence," J. Ed. Psy., XI: 264-274; Young, K., "Intelligence Tests of Certain Immigrant Groups," Sci. Mo., XV: 417-34.

CHAPTER XVI: THE ATTITUDES AND PERSONALITY

Allport, F. H., and G. W., "Personality Traits: Their Classification and Measurement," *J.A.P.S.P.*, XVI: 1-40; Allport, G. W., "Personality and Character," *Psy. Bul.*, XVIII: 441-55; Allport, G. W., "The Study of the Undivided Personality," *J.A.P.S.P.*, XIX: 132-41; Bain, A., *On the Study of Character;* Balkin, *The New Science of Analyzing Character;* Berman, L., *The Glands Regulating Personality;* Bernard, L. L., "A Theory of Rural Attitudes," *A.J.S.*, XXII: 630-49; Blackford, M. H., *Analyzing Character;* Brandenberg, G. C., "Analyzing Personality," *J. Ap. Psy.*, IX: 139-55, 281-92; Bridges, J. W., "Theories of Temperament: An Attempt at Reconciliation," *Psy. Rev.*, XXX: 36-44; Burgess, E. W., "The Study of the Delinquent as a Person," *A.J.S.*, XXVIII: 657-80; Case, C. M., *Outlines of Introductory Sociology*, Ch. IV; Chambers, O. R., "A Method of Measuring the Emotional Maturity of Children," *Ped. Sem.*, XXXII: 637-47; Cleeton, G., and Knight, F. B., "Validity of Character Judgments Based on External Criteria," *J. Ap. Psy.*, VIII: 215-31; Collins, M., "Character and Temperament Tests," *Br. J. Psy.*, XVI: 89-99; Conklin, E. S., "The Definition of Introversion, Extroversion and Allied Concepts," *J.A.P.S.P.*, XVII: 367-82; Conklin, E. S., "A Genetic Scheme for the Classification of Personalities," *Ped. Sem.*, XXXI: 316-32; Cory, C. E., "The Problem of the Individual," *J.A.P.S.P.*, XVI: 374-83; Coudenhove, H., "The African Folk," *Atl. Mo.*, CXXVIII: 463-73; Davenport, C. B., "The Trait Book," *Eugenics Record Office Bul.*, No. VI (1912); Dewey, J., *Human Nature and Conduct*, Pt. I, Sec. III; Downey, J. E., "Character and Handwriting," *Psy. Bul.*, XVI: 28-31; Downey, J. E., "Jung's 'Psychological Types' and Will-Temperament Patterns," *J.A.P.S.P.*, XVIII: 345-49; Dugas, L., "Le Soupçon," *J. de Psy.*, XX: 636-50; Dunlap, K., "Fact and Fable in Character Analysis," *An. Amer. Acad.*, CX: 13-21; Dunlap, K., "Instinct and Desire," *J.A.S.P.*, XX: 170-3; Dunlap, K., "The Reading of Character from External Signs," *Sci. Mo.*, XV: 153-65; Edman, I., *Human Traits and Their Significance*, Chs. V-VII; Faris, E., "The Concept of Social Attitudes," *J. Ap. Soc.*, IX: 404-9; Fernald, G. G., "Character as an Integral Mentality Function," *Mental Hyg.*, II: 448-62; Fernald, G. G., "Character *versus* Intelligence in Personality Studies," *J.A.P.*, XV: 1-10; Filter, R. O., "A Practical Definition of Character," *Psy. Rev.*, XXIX: 319-24; Filter, R. O., "An Experimental Study of Character Traits," *J. Ap. Psy.*, V: 297-317; Folsom, J. K., "A Statistical Study of Character," *Ped. Sem.*, XXIV: 399-440; Fosbroke, G. E., *Character Analysis Through Analysis of Features;* Fouillée, A., *Tempérament et caractère selon les individus, les sexes et les races;* Fowler, J. A., *Character Analysis;* Freyd, M., "Introverts and Extroverts," *Psy. Rev.*, XXI: 74-87; Goring, C., *The English Convict;* Gosline, "Personality from the Introspective Viewpoint," *J.A.P.*, XV: 36-44; Groves, E. R., *Personality and Social Adjustment;* Hall, G. S., *Ped. Sem.*, XXVIII: 171-201 (X); Hammett, F. S., "Temperament and Bodily Constitution," *J. Compar. Psy.*, I: 489-94; Hart, H., "A Socialization Test," *Survey*, XLVII: 249; Heaton, W., *Temperament and Sex;* Herd, H., "The Element of Character in Mental Deficiency," *School Hygiene*, XII: 173-82; Hinkle, B. M., "A Study of Psychological Types," *P.-A. Rev.*, IX: 107-97; Hoch, A., and Amsden, G. S., "A Guide to the Descriptive Study of Personality," *Rev. Neurol. and Psychiatry* (1913), pp. 577-87; Hoffman, G. L., "An Experiment in Self-Estimation," *J.A.P.S.P.*, XVIII: 43-49; Holt, E. B., *The Freudian Wish and Its Place in Ethics;* Hull, C. L., and Montgomery, R. B., "An Experimental Investigation of Certain Alleged Relations between Character and Handwriting," *Psy. Rev.*, XXVI: 63-74; Ikin, A. G., "The Ontogenesis of Introvert and Extrovert Tendencies," *Brit. J. Med. Psy.*, III: 81-94; James, W., (VIII), Vol. II, Ch. XXVI; Jung, C. G., *Analytical Psychology*, Ch. XI; Jung, C. G., *Psychological Types;* Knight, F. B., and Franzen, R. H., "Pitfalls in Rating Schemes," *J. Ed. Psy.*, XIII: 204-13; Kohs, S. C., "An Ethical Discrimination Test," *J. Delinquency*, XI: 1-15; "Lens," "Introverts and Extroverts," *New Statesman*, XVIII: 697-8; Lombroso, C., *The Man of Genius;* McDougall, W., (IX), Ch. XIII; Moore, H. T., and Gilliland, A. R., "The Measurement of Aggressiveness," *J. Ap. Psy.*, V: 97-118; Myerson, A., *The Foundations of Personality;* Naccarati, S., and Garrett, H. E., "The Relation of Morphology to Temperament," *J.A.P.S.P.*, XIX: 254-63; Norsworthy, N., "The Validity of Judgments of Character," *Essays in Honor of William James* (2d ed.), pp. 542-52; Pagnier, A., *Le vagabond;* Park and Burgess, (I), pp. 108-125, 451-490; Partridge, G. E., *An Outline of Individual Study;* Paterson, D. G., "The Graphic Rating Scale," *J. Personnel Research*, I: 361-76; Paton, S., (XI), Chs. IV, VI, X, XII; Poffenberger, A. T., and Carpenter, F. L., *J. Exper. Psy.*, VII: 67-74 (XI); Porteus, S. D., "Temperament and Mentality in Maturity, Sex and Race," *J. Ap. Psy.*, VIII: 57-74; Pillsbury, W. B., *Essentials of Psychology* (revised ed.), Ch. XVI; Potter, H. W., "Personality in the Mental-Defective," *Mental Hyg.*, I: 487-97; Pressey, S. L., "A Group Scale for Investigating the Emotions," *J.A.P.S.P.*, XVI: 55-64; Pressey, S. L., and Chambers, O. R., "First Revision of a Group Scale for Investigating the Emotions," *J. Ap. Psy.*, IV: 97-104; Prince, M., "The Problem of Personality: How Many Selves Have We?", *Ped. Sem.*, XXXII: 266-92; Prince, M., "The Structure and Dynamic Elements of Human Personality," *J.A.P.*, XV: 403-13; Rayner, H., "Temperament," *J. Ment. Sci.*, LXVII: 151-162; Ream, M. J., "A Social Relations Test," *J. Ap. Psy.*, VI: 69-73; Ream, M. J., "Temperament in Harmonious Human

Relationships," *J.A.P.S.P.*, XVII: 58-61; Reuter, E. B., "The Social Attitude," *J. Ap. Psy.*, VIII: 97-101; Rosanoff, A. J., "A Theory of Personality Based Mainly on Psychiatric Experience," *Psy. Bul.*, XVII: 281-99; Rugg, H., "Is the Rating of Human Character Practicable?", *J. Ed. Psy.*, XII: 425-38, 485-501, and XIII: 30-42, 81-93; Russell, B., "Some Traits of the Chinese Character," *Atl. Mo.*, CXXVIII: 771-7; Small, A. W., *General Sociology*, Chs. XXVII, XXXI; Smith, W. W., *The Measurement of Emotion*; Snow, A. J., "An Experiment in the Validity of Judging Human Ability," *J. Ap. Psy.*, VIII: 339-46; Spaulding, E. R., "Imbalance in the Development of the Personality as a Cause of Mental Ill Health," *Mental Hyg.*, IV: 897-910; Spaulding, E. R., "The Rôle of Personality Development in the Reconstruction of the Delinquent," *J.A.P.S.P.*, XVI: 97-114; Sunne, D., "Personality Tests: White and Negro Adolescents," *J. Ap. Psy.*, IX: 256-80; Thomas, W. I., and Znanieki, F., (I); Travis, L. E., "The Measurement of Fundamental Character Traits by a New Diagnostic Test," *J.A.P.S.P.*, XIX: 400-20; Warren, H. C., *Human Psychology*, Chs. XVIII, XIX; Washburn, M. F., and Stepanova, V., "Absolute Judgments of Character Traits, Etc.," *A. J. Psy.*, XXXIV: 96-9; Webb, E., "Character and Intelligence," *Br. J. Psy. Monogr.*, No. III, 1915, 1-99; Wells, F. L., "The Systematic Observation of the Personality in Its Relation to the Hygiene of the Mind," *Psy. Rev.*, XXI: 295-333; White, W. A., *Mechanisms of Character Making*, Ch. X; Wooley, H. T., "Personality Studies of Three-Year-Olds," *J. Exper. Psy.*, V: 381-91; Yerkes, R. M., and LaRue, D. W., *Outline of Study of the Self*.

CHAPTER XVIII. THE INTEGRATION OF PERSONALITY IN THE SOCIAL ENVIRONMENT

Adams, H. F., "The Formation of Associations," *Psy. Rev.*, XXXI: 376-96; Blackmar and Gillin, *Outlines of Sociology*, Ch. XXVI; Burgess, E. W., *The Function of Socialization in Social Evolution*; Burnham, W. H., "The Hygiene and Pedagogy of Habit," *Amer. J. School Hyg.*, I: 137-51; Burnham, W. H., "Mental Hygiene and the Conditioned Reflex," *Ped. Sem.*, XXIV: 449-88; Burnham, W. H., "Mental Hygiene and Habits of Thinking," *Ped. Sem.*, XXX: 105-126; Burnham, W. H., "The Significance of the Conditioned Reflex in Mental Hygiene," *Mental Hyg.*, V: 673-706; Cason, H., *Psy. Rev.*, XXXII: 298-316 (VIII); Crosland, H. R., "Conscious Analysis in Learning," *Psy. Rev.*, XXIX: 75-87; Gleason, J., "Learning," *Psy. Bul.*, XVI: 339-44; Hamel, I. A., "A Study and Analysis of the Conditioned Reflex," *Psy. Mon.*, XXVII: 1-65; Hunter, W. S., *Psy. Rev.*, XXXI: 478-97 (X); Koffka, K., "Mental Development," *Ped. Sem.*, XXXII: 659-73; Maher, E. A., *Ped. Sem.*, XXXI: 268-75

(XIV); Marett, R. R., (X); Moss, F. A., "Note on Building Likes and Dislikes in Children," *J. Exper. Psy.*, VII:475-8; Mursell, J. L., "The Principle of Integration in Objective Psychology," *A. J. Psy.*, XXXV:1-15; Perrin, F. A. C., "Learning," *Psy. Bul.*, XV:346-56; Rowe, S. H., *Habit Formation and the Science of Teaching;* Shepard, J. F., "Habit Formation and Higher Mental Capacities in Animals," *Psy. Bul.*, XVI:164-77; Strong, E. K., Jr., "The Learning Process," *Psy. Bul.*, XV:328-43; Watson, J. B., and R. R., "Conditioned Emotional Reactions," *J. Exper. Psy.*, III:1-14; Woods, E. L., "An Experimental Analysis of the Process of Recognizing," *A. J. Psy.*, XXVI:313-87; Young, K., *Ped. Sem.*, XXX:265-85 (XVI).

CHAPTER XIX. SUGGESTION AND PERSONALITY DEVELOPMENT

Archer, R. L., "What Is Suggestion?", *J. Exper. Ped.*, V:7-17; Bennett, R. A., *Suggestion and Common Sense;* Bergson, H. L., *Laughter;* Bechterew, W. v., *Die Bedeutung der Suggestion im Sozialen Leben;* Binet, A., *La Suggestibilité;* Brown, W., *Suggestion and Mental Analysis;* Burtt, H. E., and Clark, J. C., "Facial Expression in Advertisements," *J. Ap. Psy.*, VII:114-26; Carpenter, R., "Laughter, a Glory in Sanity," *A. J. Psy.*, XXXIII:419-22; Colvin, S. S., "The Educational Value of Humor," *Ped. Sem.*, XIV:517-24; Coriot, I. H., "Suggestion as a Form of Medical Magic," *J.A.P.S.P.*, XVIII:258-68; Drummond, M., (VIII), Ch. VII; Eastman, G. R., *Psychology for Business Efficiency;* Eastman, M., *The Sense of Humor;* Fenton, F., *The Influence of Newspaper Presentations Upon the Growth of Crime and Other Anti-Social Activity;* Flower, J. C., "Suggestion," *Brit. J. Med. Psy.*, III:39-50; Freud, S., (III), Ch. IV; Freud, S., *Wit and Its Relation to the Unconscious;* Gault, R. H., "Suggestion and Suggestibility," *A.J.S.*, XXV:185-94; Gregory, J. C., *The Nature of Laughter;* Greig, J. Y. T., "Freud's Theory of Wit," *Brit. J. Med. Psy.*, III:51-58; Greig, J. Y. T., *The Psychology of Laughter and Comedy;* Hall, G. S., and Allin, A., "The Psychology of Tickling, Laughing, and the Comic," *A. J. Psy.*, IX:1-41; Hamill, R. C., "The Rôle of the Risqué Story," *J.A.P.S.P.*, XVI:269-73; Jastrow, J., "The Psychology of Conviction," *Sci. Mo.*, Dec., 1917; Johnson, E., "Christian Science," *Open Court*, XXXVII:78-87; Jones, E., "The Nature of Auto-Suggestion," *Brit. J. Med. Psy.*, III:194-212; Jones, M. C., "The Elimination of Children's Fears," *J. Exper. Psy.*, VII:382-90; Keatinge, M. W., *Suggestion in Education;* Laird, D. A., "Critique of the Association Test as Applied to Advertising," *J. Exper. Psy.*, VI:357-65; Leuba, J. H., "Religious and Other Ecstasies," *J. Relig.*, I:391-403; McComas, H. C., "The Origin of Laughter," *Psy. Rev.*, XXX:45-55; McDougall, W., "A

New Theory of Laughter," *Psyche,* II: 292-303; McDougall, W., "Why Do We Laugh?", *Scribners,* LXXI: 359-63; Meredith, G., *An Essay on Comedy;* Mode, P. G., "Revivalism as a Phase of Frontier Life," *J. Relig.,* I: 337-54; Morgan, J. J. B., "The Nature of Suggestibility," *Psy. Rev.,* XXXI: 463-77; Meyers, G. C., "The Control of Conduct by Suggestion," *J. Ap. Psy.,* V: 26-31; Münsterberg, H., *On the Witness Stand;* Pintner, R., "Community of Ideas," *Psy. Rev.,* XXV: 402-10; Poffenberger, A. T., "The Conditions of Belief in Advertising," *J. Ap. Psy.,* VII: 1-9; Prideau, E., "Suggestion and Suggestibility," *Brit. J. Psy.,* X: 228-41, *Brain,* XLII: 291-303; Reed, H. B., "Associative Aids," *Psy. Rev.,* XXV: 128-155, 257-85, 378-401; Root, W. T., "The Psychology of Radicalism," *J.A.P.S.P.,* XIX: 341-56; Sidis, B., *The Psychology of Laughter;* Strong, E. K., Jr., "Control of Propaganda as a Psychological Problem," *Sci. Mo.,* XIV: 234-52; Sully, J., *An Essay on Laughter;* Town, C. H., "Suggestion," *Psy., Bul.,* XVIII: 366-75; Travis, L. E., "Suggestibility and Negativism as Measured by Auditory Threshold During Reverie," *J.A.P.S.P.,* XVIII: 350-68; Veblen, T., (III); Wallas, G., *Human Nature in Politics,* Ch. II; Wallis, W. D., "Why Do We Laugh?", *Sci. Mo.,* XV: 343-8; Washburn, M. F., "An Instance of the Effect of Verbal Suggestion on Tactual Space Perception," *A. J. Psy.,* XX: 447-8; Weeks, A. D., "The Mind of the Citizen," *A.J.S.,* XXI: 382-98; Winch, W. H., *Children's Perceptions,* pp. 188-93.

CHAPTER XX. THE CONDITIONS OF SUGGESTIBILITY

Adams, H. F., *Advertising and Its Mental Laws;* Aveling, F., and Hargreaves, H. L., "Suggestibility With and Without Prestige in Children," *Br. J. Psy.,* XII: 53-75; Bernheim, H., *Hypnotisme, Suggestion, Psychothérapie;* Beyer, A., *Religion und Suggestion;* Binet, A., (XIX); Binet, A., et Henri, V., "De la Suggestibilité naturelle chez les enfants," *Rev. Phil.,* XXXVIII: 337-47; Blanchard, F. L., *The Essentials of Advertising;* Brown, W., "Individual and Sex Differences in Suggestibility," *Univ. Calif. Pub. in Psy.,* II: 291-430; Coleman, W. M., "The Psychological Significance of Bodily Rhythms," *J. Compar. Psy.,* I: 213-20; Duprat, G. L., "Psycho-Pathologie individuelle et sociale," *Rev. Int. de Soc.,* July-Aug., 1920; Fenton, F., (XIX); Foster, H., *Advertising and Its Mental Laws;* Franken, R. B., "Advertising Appeals Selected by the Method of Direct Impression," *J. Ap. Psy.,* VIII: 232-44; Gault, R. H., *A.J.S.,* XXV: 185-94 (XIX); Isaacs, E., "The Nature of the Rhythm Experience," *Psy. Rev.,* XXVII: 270-99; Kaiser, I. R., "The Psychology of the Thrill," *Ped. Sem.,* XXVII: 243-80; Kitson, H. D., and Campbell, J. J., "The Package as a Feature in Magazine Advertising,"

J. Ap. Psy., VIII: 444-5; Kitson, H. D., and Morgan, H. K., "Ratio Between Size of Type in Headline and Size of Advertisement," *J. Ap. Psy.*, VIII: 446-9; Köhler, W., *The Mentality of Apes;* Laslett, H. R., "The Value of Relevancy in Advertisement Illustrations," *J. Ap. Psy.*, V: 270-9; Luckiesh, M., *Light and Color in Advertising and Merchandising;* McGeoch, J. A., "The Relationship between Suggestibility and Intelligence in Delinquents," *Psy. Clinic*, XVI: 133-4; Meyer, A., "Shall Couéism Spell Progress or Retrogression?", *Open Court*, XXXVII: 473-7; Morgan, J. J. B., *Psy. Rev.*, XXXI: 463-77 (XIX); Moore, H. T., "The Comparative Influence of Majority and Expert Opinion," *A. J. Psy.*, XXI: 16-20; Münsterberg, H., *Psychotherapy*, Ch. V; Nixon, H. K., "Two Studies of Attention to Advertisements," *J. Ap. Psy.*, IX: 281-92; Poffenberger, A. T., *J. Ap. Psy.*, VII: 1-9 (XIX); Poffenberger, A. T., "Motion Pictures and Crime," *Sci. Mo.*, XII: 336-9; Prideau, E., *Br. J. Psy.*, X: 228-41, *Brain*, XL: 291-303 (XIX); Small, M. H., "The Suggestibility of Children," *Ped. Sem.*, IV: 176-220; Stoll, O., *Suggestion und Hypnotismus;* Strong, E. K., Jr., "The Effect of Size of Advertisements and Frequency of Their Presentation," *Psy. Rev.*, XXI: 136-52; Strong, E. K., Jr., "Theories of Selling," *J. Ap. Psy.*, IX: 75-86; Sutherland, E. H., "Public Opinion as a Cause of Crime," *J. Ap. S.*, IX: 51-6; Travis, L. E., *J.A.P.S.P.*, XVIII: 350-68 (XIX); Travis, L. E., "Studies in Dissociation," *J. Exper. Psy.*, V: 338-46; Underhill, E., "Suggestion and Religious Experience," *Fortn. Rev.*, CXI: 410-21; Wells, W. R., "Experiments in Waking Hypnosis for Instructional Purposes," *J.A.P.S.P.*, XVIII: 389-404.

CHAPTER XXI. IMITATION AND PERSONALITY DEVELOPMENT

Compayré, G., *Development of the Child in Later Infancy*, Ch. I; Dashiell, J. F., *Psy. Bul.*, XVIII: 395; Dewey, J., "Imitation in Education," *Cyclopedia of Education*, III: 389-90; Dresslar, F. B., "A Morning's Observation of a Baby," *Ped. Sem.*, VIII: 469-81; Dunlap, K., *Social Psychology*, pp. 204-5; Frear, C., "Imitation," *Ped. Sem.*, IV: 382-6; Haskell, E. M., "Imitation in Children," *Ped. Sem.*, III: 30-47; Henderson, E. N., *A Text-Book in the Principles of Education*, Ch. XI; Koffka, K., (VIII), pp. 306-19; Tarde, G., *The Laws of Imitation;* Taylor, A. R., *The Study of the Child*, Preface; Thorndike, E. L., *Educational Psychology*, Vol. I, Ch. VIII.

CHAPTER XXII. PERSONALITY DEVELOPMENT THROUGH THE DIRECT IMITATION OF PERSONS

Barnes, E., "Children's Ideals," *Ped. Sem.*, VII: 3-12; Barnes, E., "Type Study on Ideals. VII. Application," *Studies in Ed.*, II: 277-80; Bell, S., "A Study of the Teacher's Influence," *Ped. Sem.*, VII: 492-525; Bernheimer and Cohen, *Boys' Clubs;* Björkman, E., *The Soul of a Child;* Bohannon, E. W., "The Only Child in the Family," *Ped. Sem.*, V: 475-96; Book, W. F., "The High School Teacher from the Pupil's Point of View," *Ped. Sem.*, XII: 239-88; Brill, A. A., *Psychoanalysis,* pp. 253-65; Brown, H. W., "The Deforming Influence of the Home," *J.A.P.*, XII: 49-57; Browne, T. J., "The Clan or Gang Instinct in Boys," *Association Outlook,* IX, No. 8; Buck, W., *Boys' Self-Governing Clubs;* Cameron, E. H., "Psychology of the Pre-School Child," *Proc. Amer. Child Hyg. Assn.*, XII: 137-44; Campbell, C. M., "The Experiences of the Child, How They Affect Character," *Mental Hyg.*, IV: 312-19; Chadwick, M., "The Misunderstood Child," *Family,* XIII: 264-6; Chambers, W. G., "The Evolution of Ideals," *Ped. Sem.*, X: 101-43; Chun, C., "Social Factors in My Education," *School and Soc.*, XIII: 372-8; Criswell, W. S., "The Challenge of the Underprivileged Boy," *J.S.F.*, I: 270-2; Croswell, T. R., "Amusements of Worcester School Children," *Ped. Sem.*, VI: 314-71; Darrah, E. M., "A Study of Children's Ideals," *Pop. Sci. Mo.*, LIII: 88-98; Dealy, C. E., "Problem Children in the Early School Grades," *J.A.P.S.P.*, XVIII: 125-36; Dodd, C. I., "School Children's Ideals," *Nat'l Rev.*, XXIV: 875-89; Doeblin, M. I., "Recreation versus Delinquency," *School and Soc.*, XII: 478-87; Evans, E., *The Problem of the Nervous Child;* Forbush, W. B., "Boy's Clubs," *Ped. Sem.*, XVI: 337-43; Forbush, W. B., "The Social Pedagogy of Boyhood," *Ped. Sem.*, VII: 307-46; Gulick, L. H., "Psychological, Pedagogical and Religious Aspects of Group Games," *Ped. Sem.*, VI: 135-51; Hall, G. S., *Ped. Sem.*, XXVIII: 171-201 (X); Hall, G. S., "Some Fundamental Principles of Sunday School and Bible Teaching," *Ped. Sem.*, VIII: 439-68; Hamilton, A. E., "Camping versus the Gang," *Ped. Sem.*, XXX: 1-15; Hartson, L. D., "The Psychology of the Club; A Study in Social Psychology," *Ped. Sem.*, XVIII: 353-414; Johnson, J. H., "Rudimentary Society Among Boys," *Johns Hopkins Hist. and Pol. Studies,* 1884; Johnson, M., "Home Life for the Child," *Playground,* XVIII: 590-2; Kantor, J. R., *Psy. Rev.*, XXVIII: 328-55 (VIII); Kline, L. W., "Truancy as Related to the Migrating Instinct," *Ped. Sem.*, V: 381-420; Kratz, H. F., "Characteristics of the Best Teacher as Recognized by Children," *Ped. Sem.*, III: 413-418; Maner, H., *Kinderideale;* Martin, L. J., *Mental Training for the Pre-School Child;* Mitchell, L. S., *Here and*

Now Story Book, Introduction; Monroe, W. S., "The Social Sense in Childhood," *Child Study Mo.,* III: 624-7; Neter, E., *Das einzige Kind und seine Erziehung;* Perez, B., *La Psychologie de l'enfant de trois á sept ans,* Ch. VII; Poffenberger, A. T., *Sci. Mo.,* XII: 336-9 (XX); Puffer, J. A., "Boys' Gangs," *Ped. Sem.,* XII: 175-212; Richards, A., "School Adjustment and the Psychic Environment," *Ped. Sem.,* XXVII: 178-87; Rogers, A. L., "The Relation of an Inventory of Habits to Character Development," *Kindgtn. and First Grade,* VII: 309-15; Sadler, M. E. (Ed.), *Moral Instruction and Training in Schools,* Vols. I, II; Scott, C. A., "The Influence of Kindergarten Methods on the Socialization of the School," *Ped. Sem.,* XVI: 550-6; Smith, S. R., "Report of the Committee on the Influence of Fraternities in Secondary Schools," *School Rev.,* XIII: 1-10; Sneath, E. H., Hodges, G., and Tweedy, H. H., *Religious Training in the School and Home,* Chs. IX, XI, XII; Street, J. R., "A Study in Moral Education," *Ped. Sem.,* V: 5-40; Taft, J., "Mental Hygiene Problems of Normal Adolescence," *Mental Hyg.,* V: 741-51; Taylor, C. K., *Character Development;* Taylor, J. P., "Children's Hopes," *Annual Report of the Superintendent of Public Instruction for New York,* 1895-96; Taylor, J. S., "Some Practical Aspects of Interest," *Ped. Sem.,* V: 497-511; Warner, M. L., "Influence of Mental Level in the Formation of Boys' Gangs," *J. Ap. Psy.,* VII: 224-36; Whitcomb, C. T. C., "Report on Organizations Among High School Students," *69th Mass. Report of Education,* 180-9; White, W. A., *The Mental Hygiene of Childhood,* Chs. V, IX; Williams, P. F., "A Study of Adolescent Friendships," *Ped. Sem.,* XXX: 342-6; Wooley, H. T., *J. Exper. Psy.,* V: 381-91 (XVI); Wyckoff, A. E., "Children's Ideals," *Ped. Sem.,* VIII: 482-94.

CHAPTER XXIII. PERSONALITY DEVELOPMENT THROUGH THE INDIRECT IMITATION OF IDEAL PERSONS

Adler, F., *The Moral Instruction of Children,* Chs. VI-X; Allen, E., "The Pedagogy of Myth in the Grades," *Ped. Sem.,* VIII: 258-77; Anderson, R. E., "A Preliminary Study of the Reading Tastes of High School Pupils," *Ped. Sem.,* XIX: 438-60; Anthony, K., *Margaret Fuller: A Psychological Biography;* Barnes, E., *Ped. Sem.,* VII: 3-12 (XXII); Barnes, E., *Stud. Ed.,* II: 277-80 (XXII); Björkman, E., *Gates of Life;* Brown, D. D., "Young People's Ideas of the Value of Bible Study," *Ped. Sem.,* XVII: 370-86; Chamberlain, A. F., "Recent German Discussions on Folk-Lore in the School," *Ped. Sem.,* VII: 347-56; Chambers, W. G., *Ped. Sem.,* X: 101-43 (XXII); Chandler, E. H., "How Much Children Attend the Theatre, the Quality of the Entertainment They Choose and Its Effect Upon

Them," *Ped. Sem.*, XVI: 367-71; Chrisman, O., "How a Story Affected a Child," *Child Study Mo.*, II: 650-61; Chun, C., *School and Soc.*, XIII: 372-8 (XXII); Coe, G. A., "A Study in Civic Training," *Ped. Sem.*, XXIX: 205-31; Comstock, A., "The Work of New York City for the Prevention of Vice, and Its Bearing on the Morals of the Young," *Ped. Sem.*, XVI: 403-20; Conradi, E., *Ped. Sem.*, X: 359-404 (X); Crumly, C. W., "The Movies—Bane or Blessing?", *Educa.*, Dec., 1919; Darrah, E. M., *Pop. Sci. Mo.*, LIII: 88-98 (XXII); Dawson, G. E., "Children's Interest in the Bible," *Ped. Sem.*, VII: 151-78; Dawson, N. P., "The American Age of Ego," *Forum*, LXVII: 95-104; Dodd, C. I., *Nat'l Rev.*, XXIV: 875-89 (XXII); Ellis, A. C., "Sunday School Work and Bible Study in the Light of Modern Pedagogy," *Ped. Sem.*, III: 363-412; Emerson, R. W., *Essay on Art;* Fenton, F., (XIX); Fleming, P. J., "Moving Pictures as a Factor in Education," *Ped. Sem.*, XVIII: 336-52; Forbush, W. B., *The Boy Problem;* Fowler, R. B., "Motion Picture Shows and School Girls," *J. Ap. S.*, VII: 76-83; Gilbert, K. E., "The Mind and Its Discipline," *Phil. Rev.*, XXVII: 413-27; Gilliland, A. R., and Moore, H. T., "The Immediate and Long Time Effects of Classical and Popular Phonograph Selections," *J. Ap. Psy.*, VIII: 309-23; Goddard, H. H., "Negative Ideals," *Studies in Ed.*, II: 392-8; Gray, P. L., "Children and Cinema," *J. Exper. Psy.*, V: 194-8; Green, J. L., "What Children Read for Fun," *School and Soc.*, XVII: 390-2; Gruenberg, S. M., *Your Child Today and Tomorrow*, Chs. X-XI; Hall, G. S., *Ped. Sem.*, XXVIII: 171-201 (X); Hall, G. S., *Ped. Sem.*, VIII: 439-68 (XXII); Hall, G. S., "Psychology of Childhood as Related to Reading and the Public Library," *Ped. Sem.*, XV: 105-15; Hauri, N. von, *Das Märchen und die Kindesseele;* Heniger, A. M. H., *The Kingdom of the Child;* Heniger, A. M. H., "The Spoken Drama versus 'The Movies' for Children," *Ped. Sem.*, XXXI: 388-98; Hewins, C. M., "Reading Clubs for Older Boys and Girls," *Ped. Sem.*, XVI: 325-30; Irving, A. P., "Home Reading of School Children," *Ped. Sem.*, VII: 138-40; Jones, M. C., "The Elimination of Children's Fears," *J. Exper. Psy.*, VII: 382-90; Jordan, A. M., "Children's Interests in Books and Magazines," *Ped. Sem.*, XXXII: 455-69; Köhler, A., "How Children Judge Character," *Studies in Ed.*, I: 94-7; Lalo, C., "L'Art et la vie," *J. de Psy.*, XVIII: 408-17; Lashley, K. S., and Watson, J. B., "A Psychological Study of Motion Pictures in Relation to Venereal Disease Campaigns," *Social Hyg.*, VII: 181-219; Lawrence, I., "Children's Interest in Literature," *Proc. N. E. A.*, 1899, 1044-51; Lee, E. A., "The Motion Picture as a Factor in Public Education," *Ele. Sch. J.*, XXIV: 184-90; Maner, H., (XXII); Moss, F. A., *J. Exper. Psy.*, VII: 475-78 (XVIII); Pintner, R., "Æsthetics," *Psy. Bul.*, XVII: 331-5; Report of the National Board of Review of Motion Pictures, 1920, "Motion Pictures Not Guilty"; Robinson, E. S., "The Compensatory Function of Make-Believe Play," *Psy. Rev.*, XXVII: 429-39; Robin, R. W., and Briggs, T. H., "Intelligence and Literature," *School and Soc.*, XVIII: 508-10; Sadler, M. E., (XXII); Science Service, "Educational Value of the Movies," *School and Soc.*, XVII: 586-587; Smith, F. P., "Pupil's Voluntary Reading," *Ped. Sem.*, XIV: 208-22; Snedden, D., "The Future of Musical Education in Public Schools," *School and Soc.*, XVII: 589-96; Snow, A. J., "A Psychological Basis for the Origin of Religion," *J.A.P.S.P.*, XVII: 254-60; Thurber, C. H., "The Relation of Child Study to Sunday School Work," *N-W. Mo.*, VIII: 137-41; Vostrovsky, C., "A Study of Children's Reading Tastes," *Ped. Sem.*, VI: 523-35; Vostrovsky, C., "What Determines Leadership in Children's Plays," *Studies in Ed.*, I: 295-7; Wallin, J. E. W., "The Moving Picture in Relation to Education, Etc.," *Ped. Sem.*, XVII: 129-42; Weigall, A., "The Influence of the Kinematograph Upon National Life," *Nineteenth Cent.*, April, 1921; Wissler, C., "The Interests of Children in the Reading Work of the Elementary Schools," *Ped. Sem.*, V: 523-40.

CHAPTER XXIV. PERSONALITY DEVELOPMENT THROUGH THE PROJECTIVE IMITATION AND ASSIMILATION OF PRINCIPLES AND CONCEPTS

Adler, F., (XXIII), Chs. XI-XVII; Albee, E., "Philosophy and Literature," *Phil. Rev.*, XXVII: 343-55; Barnes, E., "The Development of the Historical Sense in Children," *Studies in Ed.*, I: 43-52, 83-93; Bennett, C. A., "Art as an Antidote for Morality," *I.J.E.*, XXX: 160-171; Bennion, M., "Character Education," *School and Soc.*, XVII: 720-3; Boensch, O., "Kunst und Gefühl," *Logos*, XII: 1-28; Burrow, T., "Social Images versus Reality," *J.A.P.S.P.*, XIX: 230-5; Chun, C., *School and Soc.*, XIII: 372-8 (XXII); Colvin, S. S., "The Source of Educational Objectives," *School and Soc.*, XVII: 505-13; Deonna, W., "Prototypes de quelques motifs dans l'art barbare," *Rev. de l'hist. des relig.*, Mar.-Apr., 1916; Eaton, T. H., "The Development of Moral Character in the Public School System," *School and Soc.*, XV: 99-103; Forbush, W. B., (XXIII); Gale, H., "Musical Education," *Ped. Sem.*, XXIV: 503-14; Gilliland, A. R., and Moore, H. T., *J. Ap. Psy.*, VIII: 309-23 (XXIII); Gould, F. J., *Moral Instruction;* Hall, G. S., *Morale;* Hilmer, H., "The Outlook for Civilization," *Ped. Sem.*, XXXI: 247-67; Hughesdon, P. J., "The Relation Between Art and Science," *Mind* (N. S.), XXVII: 55-76; Lalo, C., *J. de Psy.*, XVIII: 408-17 (XXIII); Macaulay, T. B., *Essay on Milton;* Morgan, A. E., "The Advancement of Latent Human Powers," *School and Soc.*, XV: 80-7; Oppenheim, N., *Development of the Child*, Ch. VI; Otto, M. C., "The Moral Education of Youth," *I.J.E.*, XXXII: 52-67; Prall, D. W., "Concerning the Nature of

Philosophy," *J.P.P.S.M.*, XV: 127-30; Rigg, J. B., "Science and Liberal Education," *School and Soc.*, XVII: 477-85; Rogers, A. K., "Principles of Moral Legislation," *I.J.E.*, XXIX: 466-80; Rugh, C. E., *Moral Training in the Public Schools;* Rynearson, E., "Essentials of a High-School Vocational Guidance Program," *School and Soc.*, XVII: 10-17; Sadler, M. E. (Ed.), (XXII); Sargeaunt, G. M., "Two Studies in Plato's *Laws:* 1. 'Song and Dance' as a Function of the State," *Hib. J.*, XXI: 493-502; Simons, S. E., "Imitative Writing in the High School," *Ped. Sem.*, XVII: 451-79; Snedden, D., "The Waning Powers of Art," *A.J.S.*, XX: 801-21; Soal, C. W., "The Mechanism of Cultural Variations," *Sociol. Rev.*, XV: 173-9; Taylor, C. K., (XXII); Yarros, V. S., "Remaking of Minds and Morals," *Open Court*, XXXVI: 332-6; Young, S., "Social Science and Culture," *New Repub.*, XVI: 68-71.

CHAPTER XXVI. PRIMARY AND DERIVATIVE GROUPS

Baker, P. J. N., "The Growth of International Societies," *Economica*, XII: 262-71; Beach, W. G., *An Introduction to Sociology and Social Problems*, pp. 91-2; Bernays, E. L., (XII), Pt. II, Chs. VI, VII, Pt. III, Ch. II; Bernheimer and Cohen (XXII); Bohn, F., "The Ku Klux Klan Interpreted," *A.J.S.*, XXX: 385-407; Boodin, J. E., "The Unit of Civilization," *I.J.E.*, XXX: 142-59; Bowman, L., "Social Workers Broaden Their Conception of Community," *S.F.*, IV: 103-4; Bücher, K., "Mittelalterliche Handwerkverbände," *Ztschr. f. d. ges. Staatswiss.*, LXXVII: 295-327; Burns, A. T., "Effect of Modern Industry on Community Life," *Nat'l Conf. Soc. Work*, XLIX: 77-82; Calhoun, A. W., *A Social History of the American Family from Colonial Times to the Present;* Chapin, F. S., "Some Thoughts on Our Social Machinery," *Survey*, LIII: 322-3; Clow, F. R., "Cooley's Doctrine of Primary Groups," *A.J.S.*, XXV: 326-47; Douglass, H. P., *The Little Town;* Durkheim, E., "La Famille conjugale," *Rev. Phil.*, Jan.-Feb., 1921; Edlund, R. C., "Community Solidarity: The Small Town," *Nat'l Conf. Soc. Work*, XLIX: 335-40; Ferris, H. J., *Girls' Clubs;* Follett, M. P., "Community Is a Process," *Phil. Rev.*, Nov., 1919; Fry, H. P., *The Modern Ku Klux Klan;* Giddings, F. H., "Stimulation Ranges and Reaction Areas," *Psy. Rev.*, XXXI: 449-55; Gilbert, M., "Les Institutions des vallées d'Andorre," *Rev. Internationale*, XXXII: 350-70; Goodsell, W., *A History of the Family as a Social and Educational Institution;* Harper, J. W., "Industrial Unrest: A Plea for National Guilds," *Hib. J.*, Oct., 1919; Hartson, L. D., *Ped. Sem.*, XVIII: 353-414 (XXII); Hughan, J. W., *A Study of International Government;* Johnson, J. H., *Johns Hopkins Univ. Studies*, XI, 2d Series, 1884 (XXII); Kelwey, V., "If a Chinese Leaves His Village," *Asia*, XXIV: 463-7; Kolb, J. H.,

"A Study in Rural Community Organization," *A.J.S.*, XXIX: 34-41; Lee, J., "The Community, Maker of Men," *Survey*, XLIX: 576-9, 598-99; Lee, J., "Play and the Ultimates," *Education*, May, 1921; Lindeman, E. C., "The Place of the Social Community in Organized Society," *Nat'l Conf. Soc. Work*, XLIX: 67-77; McKenzie, R. D., "Community Forces," *J.S.F.*, II: 560-8; McKenzie, R. D., *The Neighborhood: A Study of Local Life in the City of Columbus, Ohio;* Melvin, B. L., "Social Possibilities of the Village," *J. Ap. S.*, VII: 302-8; Merz, C., "The Passing of the Poolroom," *New Repub.*, XXXV: 15-17; Naylor, E. H., *Trade Associations;* Pangburn, W., "The War and the Community Movement," *A.J.S.*, XXVI: 82-95; Park, R. E., "Racial Assimilation in Secondary Groups," *A.J.S.*, XIX: 606-23; Pillai, P. P., "The Economic Life of India," *Sociol. Rev.*, XVI: 322-35; Puffer, J. A., (XXII); Purdy, L., "The Breakdown of City Government Due to Greater Cost and New Functions," *Nat'l Munic. Rev.*, XII: 223-5; Queen, S. A., "What Is a Community?", *J.S.F.*, I: 375-82; Queen, C. N., and Queen, S. A., "Some Obstacles to Community Organization," *J. Ap. Sociol.*, VIII: 283-8; Sanderson, D., "Changes in the Rural Family," *Relig. Ed.*, XIX: 22-32; Sanderson, D., *The Farmer and His Community;* Scelle, G., "Philosophie de la quatrième assemblée de la Société des Nations," *Rev. Econ. Internat'l*, XCVII: 220-240; Schalling, E., "Den Svenska Förvaltningens Rötter," *Statsvetenvskaplig Tidskrift*, XXVI: 1-18; Snedden, D., "Communities, Associate and Federate," *A.J.S.*, XXVIII: 681-93; Taylor, C. C., "Organizing Farmers for Economic and Political Action," *Pub. Amer. Sociological Soc.*, XVII: 194-9; Taylor, G. R. S., "The Reconsideration of the Middle Ages," *Nineteenth Cent.*, XC: 650-60; Thomas, W. I., and Znanieki, F., (I), Vol. I, 87-524, Vol. II; Todd, A. J., "The Family as a Factor in Social Evolution," *Nat'l Conf. Soc. Work*, XLIX: 13-21; Tönnies, F., "Die grosse Menge und das Volk," *Schmollers Jahrbuch*, XLIV: 317-45; Tufts, J. H., "The Community and Economic Groups," *Phil. Rev.*, Nov., 1919; Vanderbyll, H., "The Great Teacher," *Open Court*, XXXIX: 43-64; Wallace, W. K., "The Passing of Politics," *North Amer. Rev.*, CCXIX: 783-92; Waters, M. van, "What's Wrong With the Home?", *New Repub.*, XLI: 277-80; Warner, F. L., "Groups," *Atl. Mo.*, CXXXII: 72-6; Weber, M., "The City. A Sociological Study," *Archiv f. Sozialwiss. u. Sozialpol.*, XLVII: 621-72; Williams, J. M., *An American Town;* Woodburn, A. S., "Can India's Caste System Survive in Modern Life?", *J. Relig.*, II: 525-37; Woods, R. A., *The Neighborhood in Nation Building;* Woods, R. A., "The Neighborhood in Social Reconstruction," *A.J.S.*, XIX: 577-91; Yarros, V. S., "What Shall We Do With the State?", *A.J.S.*, XXV: 572-83, XXVI: 60-72.

CHAPTER XXVII. PRIMARY AND DERIVATIVE ATTITUDES AND IDEALS

Barnes, E., *Ped. Sem.*, VII: 3-12 (XXII); Barnes, H. E., "The Evolution of American Jurisprudence as Illustrated in the Criminal Code of Pennsylvania," *Open Court*, XXVII: 321-38; Bernard, L. L., "Religion and Theology," *Monist*, XXXII: 61-88; Bernays, E. L., (XII), Pt. III, Ch. III; Blau, J., "The Cry of the Modern Pharisee," *Atl. Mo.*, CXXIX: 1-13; Bogardus, E. S., "The World as a Group Concept," *J. Ap. Sociol.*, VII: 31-8; Bohn, F., *A.J.S.*, XXX: 385-407 (XXVI); Boutroux, E., "Morality and Democracy," *North Amer. Rev.*, CCXIV: 166-76; Carter, C. S., "Puritanism: Its History, Spirit, and Influence," *London Quart. Rev.*, CCLXXXIII: 79-90; Case, C. M., "Instinctive and Cultural Factors in Group Conflicts," *A.J.S.*, XXVIII: 1-20; Case, C. M., *Non-Violent Coercion;* Cronbach, A., "Family-Life Ideals in Traditional Judaism and Today," *Relig. Ed.*, XIX: 5-14; Dennet, T., "New Codes for Old," *J. Amer. Asiatic Assn.*, Aug., 1918; Duguit, L., *Law in the Modern State;* Ellwood, C. A., "The New Sociology and the Old Gospel," *Christ'n Cent.*, XXXIX: 151-4; Friedman, E. M., "The Jewish Mind in the Making," *Mental Hyg.*, VII: 345-56; Fischer, L., "New Morals for Old: Communist Puritans," *Nation*, CXIX: 235-6; Gandhi, M., *Young India. 1919-1922;* Goddard, H. H., *Studies in Ed.*, II: 392-8 (XXIII); Grabo, C. H., "The Sentiment of Patriotism," *World Tomorrow*, VII: 37-9; Graham, K., "Ideals," *Fortn. Rev.*, CXII: 1001-11; Graves, W. B., "A Code of Ethics for Business and Commercial Organizations," *I.J.E.*, Oct., 1924, 41-59; Handman, M. S., "The Sentiment of Nationalism," *Pol. Sci. Quart.*, Mar., 1921; Harada, H., "The Spirit of Modern Japan," *Jap. Rev.*, Feb., 1920; Hay, E. E., "Family Folkways and Mores," *J. Relig.*, Mar., 1921; Hayes, A. G., "New Morals for Old: Modern Marriage and Ancient Laws," *Nation*, CXIX: 187-9; Hinkle, B., "Women and the New Morality," *Nation*, CXIX: 541-3; Howerth, I. W., "The Teaching of Patriotism," *Ed. Rev.*, LXVII: 135-40; Lazaron, M. S., "The American Jew: His Problems and His Psychology," *J. Relig.*, I: 378-90; Lloyd, A. H., "The Duplicity of Democracy," *A.J.S.*, XXI: 1-14; Lloyd, A. H., *Leadership and Progress*, Pt. II; Loisy, A., "La Société des Nations et la religion de l'humanité," *La paix par le droit*, Mar.-Apr., 1920; Maciver, R. M., (I), Bk. III, Ch. VI; Mathews, S., *The Validity of American Ideals;* Mecklin, J. M., "The Challenge of Fundamentalism," *Amer. Rev.*, II: 478-85; Mecklin, J. M., "The International Conscience," *I.J.E.*, Apr., 1919; Mecklin, J. M., "The Passing of the Saint," *A.J.S.*, XXIV: 353-72; Miller, H. A., "Patriotism and Internationalism," *Pub. Amer. Sociological Soc.*, XVI: 135-44; Muntz, E. E., "Civilization and Its Effect on Indian Character," *S.F.*, IV: 131-6; Morgan,

J. V., "Industrialism in Wales," *Edinburgh Rev.*, Jan., 1920; Naylor, E. H., (XXVI); Parmelee, M., "The Rise of Modern Humanitarianism," *A.J.S.*, XXI: 345-59; Parsons, E. C., "New Morals for Old: Change in Sex Relations," *Nation*, CXVIII: 551-3; Patrick, G. T. W., "Can the Sentiment of Patriotism be Refunded?", *A.J.S.*, XXX: 569-84; Robinson, J. H., *The Mind in the Making;* Sheldon, W. H., "Social Tyranny," *Phil. Rev.*, March, 1920; Sneath, E. H., Hodges, G., and Tweedy, H. H., (XXII), Chs. VII, VIII, X, XII, XIV, XV; Stern, E., "Die Jüngste Entwicklung der Jugenbewegung," *Ztschr. f. angewdete. Psy.*, XXII: 442-55; Sterry, N., "Social Attitudes of Chinese Immigrants," *J. Ap. Psy.*, VII: 325-33; Stewart, H. L., "Is Patriotism Immoral?", *A.J.S.*, XXII: 616-29; Stoddard, L., "Social Unrest and Bolshevism in the Islamic World," *Scribners*, LXX: 161-9; Thilly, F., "Sociological Jurisprudence," *Phil. Rev.*, XXXII: 373-84; Thomas, W. I., "The Persistence of Primary-Group Norms in Present-day Society and Their Influence in Our Educational System," in *Suggestions of Modern Science Concerning Education*, Ch. IV; Thomas, W. I., and Znanieki, F., (I), Vols. IV, V; Tönnies, F., *Schmollers Jahrbuch*, XLIV: 317-45 (XXVI); Tönnies, F., "Zur Soziologie des Demokratischen Staates," *Weltwirtsch. Archiv*, XIX: 540-84; Tyne, C. H. van, "The Indian Ferment," *Atl. Mo.*, CXXX: 401-13; Voelker, P. F., *The Function of Ideals and Attitudes in Social Education;* Ward, H. F., "Social Science and Religion," *J. Relig.*, I: 476-89; Wesep, N. B. van, *The Control of Ideals: A Contribution to the Study of Ethics;* Wieman, H. N., "Objectives versus Ideals," *I.J.E.*, XXXV: 299-307; Williams, J. M., (XXVI); Willis, W. C., "The Measure of Social Attitudes," *J. Ap. Soc.*, VIII: 345-54; Wolfe, A. B., "Individualism and Democracy," *I.J.E.*, XXXIII: 398-415; Yarros, V. S., "Civilization, Science and Inspiring Ideals," *Open Court*, XXXVII: 15-23; Yarros, V. S., "Social Ideals and Human Nature," *Open Court*, XXXVI: 586-93; Yule, E., "Japan's New Woman," *Scribners*, LXX: 349-61.

CHAPTER XXVIII. DIRECT CONTACT GROUPS: RATIONAL TYPES

Bentham, J., *Essay on Political Tactics;* Bentley, M., "A Preface to Social Psychology," *Psy. Mon.*, XXI: 1-25; Boas, F., "The Social Organization and the Secret Societies of the Kwakiutl Indians," *U. S. Nat. Mus., An. Report*, 1895, 311-78; Botsford, G. W., *The Roman Assemblies;* Conradi, E., "Learned Societies and Academies in Early Times," *Ped. Sem.*, XII: 384-426; Durkheim, E., *Rev. Phil.*, XCI: 1-14 (XXVI); Ginsberg, M., *The Psychology of Society*, Ch. XI; Griffith, C. R., "A Comment Upon the Psychology of the Audience," *Psy. Mon.*, XXX: 36-47; Hartson, L. D., "A Study of Voluntary Associations, Educational and Social, in Europe During the Period 1100-1700," *Ped. Sem.*, XVIII: 10-30; Heckethorn, C. W., *The Secret Societies of All Ages and Countries;* Howard, G. E., "Social Psychology of the Spectator," *A.J.S.*, XVIII: 33-50; Jephson, H., *The Platform;* Johnson, J. H., *Johns Hopkins Hist. and Pol. Studies,* 1884 (XXII); La Hodde, L. de, *The Cradle of Rebellions;* Lee, G. S., *Crowds;* Lindeman, E. C., "Some Sociological Implications of the Farm Bureau Movement," *Pub. Amer. Sociological Soc.*, XVIII: 183-9; Meyer, B. F., "Fraternal Beneficiary Societies," *A.J.S.*, VI: 645-61; Palanti, G., "L'Esprit de corps," *Rev. Phil.*, XLVIII: 135-45; Sheldon, H. D., *Student Life and Customs;* Simmel, G., "The Sociology of Secrecy and of Secret Societies," *A.J.S.*, XI: 441-98; Steiner, J. F., *Community Organization;* Steiner, J. F., "A Critique of the Community Movement," *J. Ap. Soc.*, IX: 108-14; Williams, J. M., (XXVI); Woolbert, C. H., "The Audience," *Psy. Mon.*, XXI: 37-54.

CHAPTER XXIX. DIRECT CONTACT GROUPS: NON-RATIONAL TYPES

Addison, J. T., "The Modern Chinese Cult of Ancestors," *J. Relig.*, IV: 492-503; Bentley, M., *Psy. Mon.*, XXI: 1-25 (XXVIII); Bois, H., *Le Réveil au pays de Galles;* Burns, J., *Revivals, Their Laws and Leaders;* Christenson, A., *Politics and Crowd-Morality;* Clark, H., "The Crowd," *Psy. Mon.*, XXI: 26-36; Collins, J., "Revivals Past and Present," *Harpers Mo.*, Nov., 1917; Conway, M., *The Crowd in Peace and War;* Davenport, F. M., *Primitive Traits in Religious Revivals;* Frachtenberg, L. J., "The Ceremonial Societies of the Quileute Indians," *Amer. Anthrop.*, XXIII: 320-52; Hartson, L. D., *Ped. Sem.*, XVIII: 10-30 (XXVIII); Haynes, G. E., "Race Riots in Relation to Democracy," *Survey*, Aug. 9, 1919, 697-99; James, E. O., *Primitive Ritual and Belief;* MacKay, C., *Memoirs of Extraordinary Popular Delusions and the Madness of Crowds;* Martin, E. D., "Some Mechanisms Which Distinguish the Crowd from Other Forms of Social Behavior," *J.A.P.S.P.*, XVIII: 187-203; Miceli, V., "La Psicologia della folla," *Revist. Ital di Soc.*, III: 166-95; Moxon, C., "Is the Practice of Fellowship a Narcotic Indulgence?", *Open Court*, XXXIX: 21-7; Needham, M. W., *Folk Festivals, Their Growth and How to Give Them;* Park, R. E., *Masse und Publikum;* Parsons, E. C., "Ceremonial Impatience," *J.P.P.S.M.*, XV: 157-64; Pillsbury, W. B., *The Psychology of Nationalism and Internationalism*, Chs. III, VI, VII; Rossi, P., *Le suggesteur et la foule;* Schroeder, T., "Revivals, Sex and Holy Ghost," *J.A.P.*, XIV: 34-47; Shepard, W. T., "A Study of the Methods of Revivalists," *J.A.P.S.P.*, XVI: 137-43; Sighele, S., (III); Spicer, D. G.,

Folk Festivals and the Foreign Community; Stalker, J., "Revivals of Religion," *Enc. Relig. Ethics,* X: 753-7; Tarde, G., *L'Opinion et la foule;* Talley, T. H., "Garvey's Empire of Ethiopia," *World's Work,* XLI: 264-70; Tawney, G. A., "The Nature of Crowds," *Psy. Bul.,* II: 329-33; Tylor, E. B., *Primitive Culture,* Ch. XVIII; Vleugels, W., "Wesen und Eigenschaften der Masse," *Koelner Vierteljh. f. Sozialwiss.,* II: 71-80; Wieser, F., 'Machtpsychologie," *Ztschr. f. Volkwirtsch. u. Sozialpol.* (N. F.), III: 1-30; Willey, M. M., and Rice, S. A., "William Jennings Bryan as a Social Force," *J.S.F.,* II: 338-44; Wissler, C. (Ed.), "Societies of the Plains Indians," *Anthrop. Papers of the Amer. Mus. Nat. Hist.,* XI, Pts. I-XIII.

CHAPTER XXX. INDIRECT CONTACT GROUPS AND COMMUNICATION

Abercrombie, L., "Communication versus Expression in Art," *Br. J. Psy.,* XIV: 68-77; Arnold, M., "Communication on the Roads," *World Tomorrow,* VI: 271-2; Bentley, M., *Psy. Mon.,* XXI: 1-25 (XXVIII); Bernays, E. L., (XII), Pt. II, Chs. I-IV, Pt. III, Ch. I, Pt. IV, Ch. I; Bloomfield, L., *An Introduction to the Study of Language;* Burns, C. D., "The Old Religion and the New," *I.J.E.,* Oct., 1924, 82-93; Buch, M. A., "Culture Transition in India," *Indian J. Sociol.,* II: 107-20; Chamberlain, A. F., *A. J. Psy.,* XVII: 69-80 (X); Crumley, C. W., *Educa.,* Dec., 1919 (XXIII); Didan, M., "Remarques sur l'art préhistorique et l'art negre," *Rev. Anthrop.,* XXXIV: 369-73; Ellis, H., "The Philosophy of Dancing," *Atl. Mo.,* CXIII: 197-207; Faris, E., *A.J.S.,* XXX: 710-12 (X); Grosse, E., *The Beginnings of Art;* Hall, G. S., *Ped. Sem.,* XXVIII: 171-201 (X); Hadley, A. T., *Undercurrents in American Politics;* Haydon, A. E., "Modernism as a World-Wide Movement," *J. Relig.,* V: 1-13; Jesperson, O., *Language, Its Nature, Development and Origin;* Judd, C. H., (X); LeBon, G., *The World in Revolt. A Psychological Study of Our Times;* Lindeman, E. C., "Religion and Rural Culture," *Survey,* LIII: 511-12; Lofthouse, W. F., "Art Among the Cavemen," *London Quart. Rev.,* Jan., 1922, 147-60; Mallery, G., "Sign Language Among North American Indians Compared With That Among Other Peoples and Deaf Mutes," *U. S. Bur. Amer. Ethnology, First Annual Report;* Marouzeau, J., "Langage affectif et langage intellectuel," *J. de Psy.,* XX: 560-78; Mason, W. A., *A History of the Art of Writing;* Nichols, R. H., "Fundamentalism in the Presbyterian Church," *J. Relig.,* V: 14-36; Park, R. E., "The Concept of Social Distance," *J. Ap. Soc.,* VIII: 339-44; Rainwater, C., "Socialized Leisure," *J. Ap. Soc.,* VII: 255-9; Russell, B., "The Effect of Science on Social Institutions," *Survey,* LII: 5-11; Sapir, E., "Language and Environment," *Amer. Anthrop.,* XIV: 226-42;

Sutherland, E. H., "The Isolated Family," *Relig. Ed.*, XIX: 32-6; Traquair, R., "Man's Share in Civilization," *Atl. Mo.*, CXXXIV: 502-8; Walleschek, R., *Primitive Music;* Waters, M. van, *New Repub.*, XLI: 277-80 (XXVI); Wesep, H. B. van, (XXVII); West, C. A., "The New Scientific Religion, Etc.," *London Quart. Rev.*, CCLXXXIII: 29-39; Wright, H. W., "The Basis of Human Association," *J.P.P.S.M.*, July 29, 1920.

CHAPTER XXXI. TYPES AND FUNCTIONS OF INDIRECT CONTACT GROUPS

Allen, F. L., "Newspapers and the Truth," *Atl. Mo.*, CXXIX: 44-54; Alvord, M. V., *The Country Newspaper;* Ambedkar, B. R., "Castes in India," *Indian Antiquary*, May, 1917; Anderson, N., "Trial by Newspaper," in *The Child, the Clinic and the Court*, pp. 108-119; Atkins, G. G., *Modern Religious Cults and Movements;* Bellows, H. A., "The Politics of Wheat," *Forum*, LXXII: 497-504; Benevenisti, J. L., "Rural Germany and the Towns," *Contemp. Rev.*, CXXV: 600-606; Bentley, M., *Psy. Mon.*, XXI: 1-25 (XXVIII); Bernays, E. L., (XII), Pt. II, Chs. I-IV, Pt. V, Ch. I; Bertrand, L., "La Révolution espagnole," *Rev. de Deux Mondes*, XCIII: 274-89; Booth, M., "The German Movement," *Hib. J.*, XXII: 468-78; Boothe, V. B., *The Political Party as a Social Process;* Bourgoing, P. de, *Les Guerres d'idiome et de nationalité;* Braun, A., "Geschäfts und Partiepresse (eine Untersuchung)," *Archiv f. Sozialwiss. u. Sozialpol.*, L: 204-21; Brown, H. C., "Social Psychology and the Problem of a Higher Nationality," *I.J.E.*, XXVIII: 19-30; Bryan, W. J., "A National Bulletin," *Forum*, April, 1921; Buch, M. A., *Ind. J. S.*, II: 107-20 (XXX); Bücher, K., "Zur Frage der Pressereform," *Zeitschr. f. d. ges. Staatswiss.*, LXXVI: 296-331; Buck, O. M., "Some Backgrounds of Indian Nationalism," *Methodist Rev.*, CVIII: 57-73; Buonaiuti, E., "Religion and Culture in Italy," *Hib. J.*, XIX: 636-43; Cell, G. C., "The Decay of Religion," *Methodist Rev.*, CVII: 64-78; Coleman, G. W., "The Contribution of the Open Forum to Democracy in Religion," *J. Relig.*, II: 1-15; Crawshay-Williams, E., "The International Idea," *I.J.E.*, April, 1917; Crumly, C. W., *Educa.*, Dec., 1919 (XXIII); Dashiell, J. F., "Some Psychological Phases of Internationalism," *A.J.S.*, XXV: 757-68; Detweiller, F. S., *The Negro Press in the United States;* Dewey, J., "If War Were Outlawed," *New Repub.*, XXXIV: 234-5; Dibblee, G. B., *The Newspaper;* Duguit, L. (XXVII); Eliot, T. D., "A Psychoanalytic Interpretation of Group Formation and Behavior," *A.J.S.*, XXVI: 333-52; Field, G. C., "The Influence of Race in History and Politics," *Hib. J.*, XXI: 287-300; Fouillée, A., *Equisse psychologique des peuples européens;* Gennep, A. van, "Classe Rivale, Noblesse et Nationalité," *Rev. de l'Inst. de Soc.*, II: 201-22; Giddings, F. H., *Descriptive and Historical Sociology*, Bk. I, Chs. II, III; Gillette, J. M., "Agrarian Political Movements with Special Reference to the Non-Partisan League," *Pub. Amer. Sociological Soc.*, XVIII: 194-8; Goldstein, J., "Die Presse," *Archiv f. Sozialwiss. u. Sozialpol.*, LI: 362-81; Groves, E. R., "Government by Group Pressure," *North Amer. Rev.*, CCXVIII: 477-83; Hall, G. S., "Can the Masses Rule the World?", *Sci. Mo.*, XVIII: 456-66; Harger, C. M., "The Changing Country Press," *Scribners*, LXXV: 446-450; Hauser, H., "De l'Américanisme et de ses Variétés," *Rev. Int. de Soc.*, XXXII: 1-6; Hauser, H., "Le Principe des nationalités," *Le Rev. Polit. Internat.*, Mar.-Apr., 1916; Haydon, A. E., *J. Relig.*, V: 1-13 (XXX); Kawabé, K., *The Press and Politics in Japan;* Kurihara, M., "Moral Problems of Young Japan," *Hib. J.*, XXII: 103-12; Lee, P. R., "Changes in Social Thought and Standards Which Affect the Family," *Family*, IV: 103-11; Lloyd, A. H., "Newspaper Conscience—A Study in Half-Truths," *A.J.S.*, XXVII: 197-210; Meader, J. R., "Religious Sects," *Enc. Amer.*, XXIII: 355-61; Mecklin, J. M., *I.J.E.*, Apr., 1919 (XXVII); Meillet, A., "Les Langues et les Nationalités," *Scientia*, XVIII: 192-201; Miller, H. A., "Nationalism and the Jews," *World Tomorrow*, VI: 8-10; Mombert, P., "Zur Frage der Klassenbildung," *Koelner Vierteljh. f. Sozialwiss.*, I: 40-45; Moore, H. M., "Our Complex Civilization and the Genius of Its Youth," *School Rev.*, XXIX: 617-29; Newbigin, M. I., "Race and Nationality," *Geog. J.*, Nov., 1917; Nichols, R. H., *J. Relig.*, V: 14-36; Odum, H. W., "The Duel to the Death," *S.F.*, IV: 189-94; Odum, H. W., "Fundamental Principles Underlying Interracial Co-operation," *J.S.F.*, I: 282-9; Otlet, P., "La Société intellectuelle des nations," *Scientia*, Jan., 1919; Park, R. E., "The Natural History of the Newspaper," *A.J.S.*, XXIX: 273-89; Park and Burgess, (I), Ch. III, 311-27; Partridge, G. E., *The Psychology of Nations;* Payne, G. H., *History of Journalism in the United States;* Perry, W. J., "The Relation of Class Divisions to Social Conduct," *Hib. J.*, XX: 507-523; Platt, C., "Class Consciousness," *A.J.S.*, XXX: 558-68; Pound, A., "The Iron Man in International Politics," *Atl. Mo.*, CXXVIII: 611-18; Pratt, J. B., "Religion and the Younger Generation," *Yale Rev.*, XII: 594-613; Probst, J., "L'Esprit de Clan, Etc.," *Rev. Int. de Soc.*, XXXII: 15-21; Rachfahl, F., "Der Weltkrieg und die Nationalitäten Europas," *Weltwirtsch. Archiv*, XX: 92-101; Saunders, K., "Glimpses of the Religious Life of New Japan," *J. Relig.*, II: 70-80; Schay, R., "Die Jüdischen Intellektuellen," *Koelner Vierteljh. f. Sozialwiss.*, III: 124-32; Sheldon, C. M., "The Experiment of a Christian Daily," *Atl. Mo.*, CXXXIV: 624-33; Sheldon, W. H., "Social Tyranny," *Phil. Rev.*, Mar., 1920; Singh, St. N., "Caste and the New Indian Constitution," *London Quart. Rev.*, July, 1919; Small, A. W., "The Bonds of Nationality," *A.J.S.*, XX: 629-83; Small, A. W., "Schmoller on

Class Conflicts in General," *A.J.S.*, XX: 504-31; Sorabji, C., "Women in India: Some Problems," *Fortn. Rev.*, CXV: 661-73; Stead, W. T., "Government by Journalism," *Contemp. Rev.*, XLIX: 653-74; Steiner, J. F., "Community Disorganization," *J.S.F.*, II: 177-87; Stern, E., *Ztschr. f. ang. Psy.*, XXII: 442-55 (XXVII); Strong, E. K., Jr., *Sci. Mo.*, XIV: 234-52 (XIX); Taylor, C. C., *Pub. Amer. Sociological Soc.*, XVII: 194-9 (XXVI); Traquair, R., "The Caste System in North America," *Atl. Mo.*, CXXXI: 417-23; Tyau, M. T. Z., "The Moving of the Waters in China," *Contemp. Rev.*, CXX: 354-61; Ward, H. F., "Repression of Civil Liberties in the United States," *Pub. Amer. Sociological Soc.*, XVIII: 127-46; Wash, H. E., "The Nationalist Movement in Asia and the Future of Missions," *Methodist Rev.*, CVIII: 108-15; White, N. I., "Racial Feeling in Negro Poetry," *S. Atl. Quart.*, XXI: 14-29; Wolfe, A. B., "Emotion, Blame, and the Scientific Attitude in Relation to Radical Leadership and Method," *I.J.E.*, XXXII: 142-59; Yarros, V. S., "Isolation and Social Conflicts," *A.J.S.*, XXVII: 211-21; Yarros, V. S., "The Press and Public Opinion," *A.J.S.*, V: 372-82.

CHAPTER XXXII. THE INFLUENCE OF CONTACTS UPON INDIVIDUAL AND COLLECTIVE BEHAVIOR

Allport, F. H., "The Influence of the Group Upon Association and Thought," *J. Exper. Psy.*, III: 159-82; Allport, F. H., "Social Change," *J.S.F.*, II: 671-6; Baldwin, J. M., "Rivalry," *Dict. Phil. and Psy.*, II: 476-8; Bernhard, E., "Die gesellshaftlichen Mächte in der französischen Kultur," *Logos*, II: 71-85; Boland, G., "Taking a Dare," *Ped. Sem.*, XVII: 510-24; Bonnaterre, J. P., *Notice historique sur le sauvage de l'Aveyron, et sur quelques autres individus qu'on a trouvés dans les forêts à différentes epoques;* Brill, A. A., (XXII); Burk, F. L., "Teasing and Bullying," *Ped. Sem.*, IV: 336-71; Burnham, W. H., "The Group as a Stimulus to Mental Activity," *Science* (N. S.), XXXI: 761-7; Cooley, C. H., "Personal Competition: Its Place in the Social Order, Etc.," *Ec. Stud.*, IV, No. II; Feuerbach, P. J. A. von, *Caspar Hauser;* Gates, G. S., "The Effect of an Audience Upon Performance," *J.A.P.S.P.*, XVIII: 334-44; Gates, G. S., and Rissland, L. Q., "The Effect of Encouragement and of Discouragement Upon Performance," *J. Ed. Psy.*, XIV: 21-6; Hall, G. S., and Smith, T. L., *Ped. Sem.*, X: 159-99 (XII); Hartson, L. D., *Ped. Sem.*, XVIII: 353-414 (XXII); Hoch, A., "On Some of the Mental Mechanisms in Dementia Præcox," *J.A.P.*, V: 255-73; Howard, G. E., *A.J.S.*, XVIII: 33-50 (XXVIII); Itard, J. E. M. G., *De l'education d'un homme sauvage, et des premiers developpements physiques et moraux du jeune sauvage de l'Aveyron,* pp. 45-6; Kingsley, C., *The Hermits;* Laird, D. A., "Changes in Motor Control and

Individual Variation Under the Influence of Razzing," *J. Exper. Psy.*, VI: 236-46; LeBon, G., *The Psychology of Revolution;* McKenzie, R. D., "Community Forces, Etc.," *J.S.F.*, II: 415-21; Martin, E. D., *The Behavior of Crowds;* Mayer, A., "Ueber Einzel- und Gesamtleistung des Schulkindes," *Archiv f. d. ges. Psychol.*, I: 276-416; Meumann, E., *Haus- und Schularbeit;* Moede, W., "Der Wetteifer, seine Struktur und sein Ausmass," *Ztschr. f. Ped. Psy.*, XV: 353-68; Münsterberg, H., *Psychology, General and Applied*, Ch. XX; Münsterberg, H., *Psychology and Social Sanity*, pp. 181-202; Novicow, J., "The Mechanism and Limits of Human Association, Etc.," *A.J.S.*, XXIII: 289-349; Ogburn, W. F., *Social Change;* Ordahl, G., "Rivalry," *Ped. Sem.*, XV: 492-549; Parsons, E. C., *Social Freedom;* Peterson, J., "The Functioning of Ideas in Social Groups," *Psy. Rev.*, XXV: 214-26; Rauber, A., *Homo Sapiens Ferus;* Ravitch, J. S., "Relative Rate of Change in Customs and Beliefs of Modern Jews," *Pub. Amer. Sociological Soc.*, XIX: 171-6; Raphaelson, R., "The Hedonism of Disillusionment in the Younger Generation," *I.J.E.*, XXXII: 379-97; Rogers, A. K., *I.J.E.*, Apr., 1917 (XII); Small, A. W., *A.J.S.*, XX: 504-31 (XXXI); Spargo, J., *The Psychology of Bolshevism;* Swett, H. P., "Her Little Girl," *Ped. Sem.*, XVII: 104-10; Travis, L. E., "The Effect of a Small Audience Upon Eye-Hand Coördination," *J.A.S.P.*, XX: 142-6; Triplett, N., "The Dynamogenic Factors in Pace-Making and Competition," *A. J. Psy.*, IX: 507-32; Ueda, T., "The Psychology of Justice," *Ped. Sem.*, XIX: 297-349; Vierkandt, A., "Zur Theorie der Revolution," *Schmollers Jahrbuch*, XLVI: 19-42; Vincent, G. E., "The Rivalry of Social Groups," *A.J.S.*, XVI: 496-84; Whittemore, I. C., "The Competitive Consciousness," *J.A.S.P.*, XX: 17-33; Whittemore, I. C., "The Influence of Competition on Performance," *J.A.P.S.P.*, XIX: 236-53; Wolfe, A. B., *I.J.E.*, XXXII: 142-59 (XXXI); Wolfe, A. B., "The Motivation of Radicalism," *Psy. Rev.*, XXVIII: 280-300; Woolbert, C. H., "Conviction and Persuasion: Some Considerations of Theory," *Quart. J. Pub. Speaking*, III: 250-64; Zimmermann, J. G., *Solitude*.

CHAPTER XXXIII. COLLECTIVE RESPONSES AND LEADERSHIP

Bentley, M., *Psy. Mon.*, XXI: 1-25 (XXVIII); Bernays, E. L., (XII), Pt. I, Ch. I, Pt. III, Ch. III, Pt. IV, Ch. II; Bogardus, E. S., "Implications of Democratic Leadership," *J. Ap. Soc.*, VIII: 108-15; Brent, C. H., *Leadership;* Chafee, Z., *Freedom of Speech;* Chapin, F. S., "Leadership and Group Activity," *J.S.F.*, III: 141-5; Chapin, F. S., "Socialized Leadership," *J.S.F.*, III: 57-60; Clayton, J., *Leaders of the People;* Davies, G. R., *Social Environment*, pp. 135-7; Dodge, R., "The Psychology of Propaganda," *Relig. Ed.*, XV:

241-52; Dixon, R. B., "Some Aspects of the American Shaman," *J. Amer. Folk-Lore*, XXI: 1-12; Ellwood, C. A., "The Principles in Accordance With Which Public Opinion Can Be Formed by the Church Democratically and Effectively," *Relig. Ed.*, April, 1920; Ely, R. T., *The World War and Leadership in a Democracy;* Fiske, G. W., "The Development of Rural Leadership," *Pub. Amer. Sociological Soc.*, XI: 54-81; Fustel de Coulanges, *The Ancient City,* Bk. III, Ch. IX; Gowin, E. B., *The Executive and His Control of Men;* Graves, W. B., *I.J.E.*, Oct., 1924, pp. 41-59 (XXVII); Irwin, W., "Raw News and Peace Views," *World Tomorrow*, VII: 40-1; Keirstead, W. C., "The Leadership of the Ministry in Industrial and Social Life," *J. Relig.*, II: 44-57; Kohler, J., *Evolution of Law*, II: 96-103; Larrabee, H. A., "The Formation of Public Opinion Through Motion Pictures," *Educa.*, June, 1920; Lindeman, E. C., *Survey*, LIII: 511-14 (XXX); Lloyd, A. H., *A.J.S.*, XXI: 1-14 (XXVII); McKenzie, R. D., "Community Forces," *J.S.F.*, II: 266-73; Mehles, G., "Die Beziehung zwischen Einzelmensch und Gemeinschaft," *Logos*, II: 31-70; Morgan, E. L., "The Professional Training of Rural Leaders," *Pub. Amer. Sociological Soc.*, XVII: 185-194; Nash, J. V., "The Anatomy of Democracy," *Open Court*, XXXVII: 449-62; Odin, A., *Genèse des grands hommes, gens de lettres français modernes;* Smith, J. M. P., *The Prophet and His Problems;* Vostrovsky, C., "What Determines Leadership in Children's Plays," *Studies in Ed.*, I: 295-7; Vierkandt, A., "Führende Individuen bei den Naturvölkern," *Ztschr. f. Sozialwiss.*, XI: 542-53, 623-39; White, R. C., "The City-Drift of Population in Relation to Social Efficiency," *J.S.F.*, II: 17-23; Willey, M. W., and Rice, S., *J.S.F.*, II: 338-44 (XXIX); Woods, F. A., *The Influence of Monarchs;* Yarros, V. S., *A.J.S.*, V: 372-82 (XXX); Yarros, V. S., "Representation and Leadership in Democracies," *A.J.S.*, XXIII: 390-402.

CHAPTER XXXIV. THE QUALITIES OF LEADERS

Almack, J. C., "The Influence of Intelligence on the Selection of Associates," *School and Soc.*, XVI: 529-30; Andrews, L. C., *Military Manpower;* Brent, C. H., (XXXIII); Case, C. M., "Gandhi and the Indian National Mind," *J. Ap. Soc.*, VII: 293-301; Chapin, F. S., *J.S.F.*, III: 57-60, 141-5 (XXXIII); Clayton, J., (XXXIII); Dodge, R., "The Conditions of Effective Human Action," *Psy. Bul.*, XV: 137-147; Eager, G. B., "Luther as a Social Influence," *Review and Expositor*, Oct., 1917; Ely, R. T., (XXXIII); Gowin, E. B., (XXXIII); Grabo, C. H., "Education for Democratic Leadership," *A.J.S.*, XXIII: 763-8; Hankins, F. H., *Pol. Sci. Quart.*, XXXVIII: 388-412 (XIV); Ikin, A. G., "The Qualities Desirable in a Foreman," *J. Nat'l Institute Indus. Psy.*, II: 13-17; Knight, F. B., "Qualities Related to Success in Teaching," *Columbia University Contr. to Ed.*, No. CXX; Leopold, L., *Prestige: A Psychological Study of Social Estimates;* Morgan, E. L., "Training for Rural Leadership," *J.S.F.*, II: 41-2; Myers, G. C., "Training for Leadership," *School and Soc.*, XVII: 437-9; Nutting, L. R., "The Characteristics of Leaders," *School and Soc.*, XVIII: 387-90; Peterson, J., and Quentin, D. J., *The Psychology of Handling Men in the Army;* Sanders, W. B., "Training for Rural Leadership," *J.S.F.*, II: 42-5; Schwarz, O. L., *General Types of Superior Men;* Simpson, R. M., "Creative Imagination," *A. J. Psy.*, XXIII: 234-43; Smith, J. M. P., (XXXIII); Terman, L. M., "A Preliminary Study in the Psychology and Pedagogy of Leadership," *Ped. Sem.*, XI: 413-51; Terman, L. M., and Chase, J. M., "The Psychology, Biology and Pedagogy of Genius," *Psy. Bul.*, XVII: 397-409; Willey, M. M., and Rice, S. A., *J.S.F.*, II: 338-44 (XXIX); Williams, P. E., *Ped. Sem.*, XXX: 342-46 (XXII).

CHAPTER XXXV. NON-INSTITUTIONAL CONTROLS

Allport, F. H., *J.A.P.S.P.*, XIX: 185-91 (XII); Allport, F. H., *J.A.P.S.P.*, XIX: 60-73 (III); Aria, E., "Fashion, Its Survivals and Revivals," *Fortn. Rev.*, CIV: 930-7; Arthur, G., "Eliminating First Grade Failure Through the Control of Intellectual, Physical and Emotional Factors," *School and Soc.*, XV: 474-84; Bigg, A. H., "What Is 'Fashion'?", *Nineteenth Cent.*, XXXIII: 235-48; Boas, F., "The Development of Folk-Tales and Myths," *Sci. Mo.*, III: 335-43; Clerget, P., "The Economic and Social Rôle of Fashion," *Am. Rep. Smithsonian Inst.*, 1913, 755-65; Cobb, F. I., "Public Opinion," *Senate Document,* No. 175; d'Avenal, G., "Du Superflu au nécessaire," *Rev. de Deux Mondes*, XV: 384-401; Dicey, A. V., *Lectures on the Relation between Law and Public Opinion in England during the Nineteenth Century;* Dufaux, M., "Une Forme de l'automatisme sociale: la convention," *Rev. Phil.*, Mar., 1916; Foley, C. A., "Fashion," *Econ. Jour.*, III: 458-74; Gennep, A. van, *La Formation des légendes;* Gould, R. L., "Superstitions Among Scottish College Girls," *Ped. Sem.*, XXVIII: 203-48; Harding, T. S., "The Greatest Faith of All," *Open Court*, XXXVI: 230-42; Hart, J. K., "New Folkways," *Survey*, LIII: 341-2; Hocart, A. M., "The Common-Sense of Myths," *Amer. Anthrop.*, July-Sept., 1916; Hollingworth, L. S., "Social Devices for Impelling Women to Bear and Rear Children," *A.J.S.*, XXII: 19-29; Interchurch World Movement, *Public Opinion and the Steel Strike of 1919;* Kauffmann, F., "Zur Theorie des Mythos," *Archiv f. d. ges. Psychol.*, XLVI: 61-9; Kroeber, A., L., "On the Principle of Order in Civilization as Exemplified by Changes of Fashion," *Amer. Anthrop.* (N. S.), XXI: 235-63; LeBon,

G., *Les Opinions et les croyances;* Linton, E. L., "The Tyranny of Fashion," *Forum,* III: 59-68; Lloyd, J. H., "Mental Contagion and Popular Crazes," *Scribners,* Feb., 1921; Lowell, A. L., (XII); Martin, E. D., *J.A.P.S.P.,* XVIII: 187-203 (XXIX); Mead, G. H., "The Psychology of Punitive Justice," *A.J.S.,* XXIII: 577-602; Oertal, H., "Psychic Epidemics," *Can. J. Mental Hyg.,* III: 1-10; Parsons, E. C., "Avoidance," *A.J.S.,* XIX: 480-4; Parsons, E. C., *Fear and Conventionality;* Parsons, E. C., "Nursery and Savagery," *Ped. Sem.,* XXII: 296-9; Patrick, G. T. W., "The Psychology of Crazes," *Pop. Sci. Mo.,* LVII: 285-94; Peters, I. L., "A Questionnaire Study of Some of the Effects of Social Restrictions on the American Girl," *Ped. Sem.,* XXIII: 550-69; Peters, I. L., "Superstitions Among American Girls," *Ped. Sem.,* XXIII: 445-51; Ravitch, J. S., *Pub. Amer. Sociological Soc.,* XIX: 171-6 (XXXII); Repplier, A., "Are Americans a Timid People?", *Yale Rev.,* XIII: 1-13; Sageret, J., "L'Opinion," *Rev. Phil.,* LXXXVI: 19-38; Schmalhausen, S. D., "Our Tainted Ethics," *P-A. Rev.,* VIII: 382-406; Shaler, N. S., "The Law of Fashion," *Atl. Mo.,* LXI: 386-98; Shepard, W. J., *A.J.S.,* XV: 32-60 (XII); Simmel, G., "The Attraction of Fashion," *Internat'l Quart.,* X: 130-55; Sombart, W., "Wirtschaft und Mode," *Grenzf. des Nerven- und Seelenlebens;* Spencer, H., *Principles of Sociology,* Pt. IV, Ch. XI; Taft, D. R., "History Textbooks and International Differences," *Pub. Amer. Sociological Soc.,* XIX: 180-3; Teslaar, J. S. van, "The Death of Pan, Etc.," *P-A. Rev.,* VIII: 180-3; Thomas, W. I., "The Psychology of Woman's Dress," *Amer. Mag.,* LXVII: 66-72; Vostrovsky, C., "A Study of Children's Superstitions," *Studies in Ed.,* I: 123-43; Waugh, W. T., "The Causes of War in Current Tradition," *Br. J. Psy.,* XI: 159-63; Yarros, V. S., *A.J.S.,* V: 372-82 (XXXI).

CHAPTER XXXVI. INSTITUTIONAL CONTROLS

Allport, F. H., *J.S.F.,* II: 671-6 (XXXII); Belloc, H., "Factors of Historical Change in Society," *Sociol. Rev.,* XV: 1-6; Bernard, L. L., "The Conditions of Social Progress," *A.J.S.,* XXVIII: 21-48; Bosanquet, H., "The Psychology of Social Progress," *I.J.E.,* VII: 265-81; Dinsmore, C. A., "The Influence of Science on Modern Religious Thought," *J.S.F.,* II: 239-44; Discussion, "The Control of Public Opinion in the United States," *School and Soc.,* XV: 421-3; Duguit, L., *Law in the Modern State;* Eleutheropulos, A., "Gesellschaft und Staat," *Ztschr. f. d. ges. Staatswiss.,* LXXVI: 169-78; Ellwood, C. A., "Modifiability of Human Nature and Human Institutions," *J. Ap. Soc.,* VII: 229-37; Ellwood, C. A., "Religion and Social Control," *Sci. Mo.,* Oct., 1918; Ellwood, C. A., "The Religious Revolution," *Christ. Cent.,* XXXIX: 138-42; Faris, E., *A.J.S.,* XXX: 710-12

(X); Geiger, J. R., "Religious Worship and Social Control," *I.J.E.*, XXIX: 88-97; Givler, R. C., *The Ethics of Hercules;* Goldenweiser, A. A., "Magic and Religion," *Psy. Bul.*, XVI: 82-90; Guérard, A. C., *Reflections on the Napoleonic Legend;* Haydon, A. E., "Why Do Religions Die?", *J. Relig.*, March, 1921; Herskovits, M. J., "Social Pattern," *S.F.*, IV: 57-69; Huxley, J., "Progress: Biological and Other," *Hib. J.*, XXI: 436-60; Jenness, D., "The Cultural Transformation of the Copper Eskimo," *Geo. Rev.*, XI: 541-50; Kantor, J. R., *J.A.P.S.P.*, XIX: 46-56 (III); Kern, R. R., "The Supervision of the Social Order," *A.J.S.*, XXIV: 260-88, 423-53; Kokaurek, A., and Wigmore, J. H., *Evolution of Law;* Maciver, R. M., Bk. II, Ch. IV (I); Maine, H. S., *Ancient Law;* Molan, G. H. T., "The Behavioristic Bases of the Science of Law," *Amer. Bar Assn. J.*, VIII: 737-62; Mathews, S., "Theology from the Point of View of Social Psychology," *J. Relig.*, III: 337-52; Odum, H. W., "Dependable Theory and Social Change," *J.S.F.*, II: 282-6; Opie, T. F., "The Place of the Church Among Social Forces," *J.S.F.*, I: 581-4; Pound, R., "Law and Morals," *J.S.F.*, I: 350-359, 528-37; Ravitch, J. S., *Pub. Amer. Sociological Soc.*, XIX: 171-6 (XXXII); Root, W. T., *J.A.P.S.P.*, XIX: 341-56 (XXXII); Schmalhausen, S. D., *P-A. Rev.*, VIII: 382-46 (XXXV); Snedden, D., "Education for Citizenship," *I.J.E.*, XXX: 1-15; Soal, C. W., "On the Mechanism of Cultural Variations," *Sociol. Rev.*, XV: 313-20; Tsu, Y. Y., "Present Tendencies in Chinese Buddhism," *J. Relig.*, I: 497-512; Wallis, W. D., "Mental Patterns in Relation to Culture," *J.A.P.S.P.*, XIX: 179-84.

INDEX

Abbreviated conditioning of responses, 286
Abilities, 206 ff.; special, 219, 220
Abstract character of classes, 244
Abstract imitation, 330, 332, 385
Acquired behavior patterns, 118, 143, 247; non-overt, 121, 143, 145-156; sources of, 119; acquired character of thinking, 149; acquired characteristics, inheritance of, 102; and thought, 149, 163; acquired elements in personality, 257; in suggestion, 285; acquired factors in class, 243; acquired skills, 216, 218, 222
Acquiring habits, 120, 143
Action, automatic, 34; by choice, 34; by impact, 34; three types of, 33
Adams, H., 182
Adaptation to environment, 118, 142; of instincts in man, 117
Addams, J., 127, 359, 381, 402
Adjustment, 53, 142 ff.; and art, 401; and attitudes, 246; complexity of, 54; and conflict, 189 ff.; human, 53, 62; and imitation, 322; and intelligence, 212; internal, 142 ff., 158 ff.; through language, 144, 147-156; as life, 247; to models, 343 ff.; neuro-psychic, 143, 147-156, 393; overt, 143; and philosophy, 401; and protoplasm, 53; reciprocal processes of, 270; and science, 395; and speech, 150; through symbols, 145, 152, 393; through trial and error, 143
Adler, A., 194
Æschylus, 397
Age and intelligence, 233
Allport, F. H., 13, 16, 17, 19, 21, 24, 29-32, 37, 45, 68, 122, 141, 156, 171, 185, 255-257, 261, 280, 284, 299, 341, 450, 464, 500, 516, 539
Americans, intelligence of, 226
Andrews, L. C., 464, 539

Appeal of leaders, 523, 528
Apprehension of behavior, degrees of ease of, 168
Aristophanes, 397
Aristotle, 71, 72, 74, 396
Art and adjustment, 401; and censorship, 379; and the curriculum, 400; educative significance of, 377; intellectualization of, 470; modern, 469; and national life, 471; and personality, 375-381; and philosophy, 397, 400; primitive, 469; primitive appeal in, 378; and public opinion, 488; and recreation, 380; and science, 376, 389, 394; and self-analysis, 472; and suggestion, 375
Art of being led, 539
Associations, 463, 481, 510; classifications of, 481; group, 411; overlapping of, 482; and publics, 483; purposive, 441
Attitudes, 425 ff.; and adjustment, 246; acquired, 248; classifications of, 250; communication of, 249, 333; as conditioned responses, 248; derivative, 427, 430; emotional, 247; imitative, 322 ff.; inherited, 248; integration of, 249; intellectual, 247; nature of, 246; permanent, 251; and personality, 255; physical, 247; primary, 426, 429; and social psychology, 248; and symbolic expression, 248; and temperament, 251; typical, 249
Attitudinal behavior, 122, 143, 248
Audience, 448; effects of, on behavior, 498
Autobiography, 372
Autonomic system, 61
Auto-suggestion, 292-295
Average man, 260

Bacon, R., 397
Bagehot, W., 26, 27, 72
Bagley, W. C., 131, 223

Bain, A., 28
Baldwin, J. M., 24, 27, 29, 31, 32, 105, 156, 171, 185, 223, 280, 299, 341, 581
Bartlett, F. C., 516, 581
Baudouin, C., 299
Bawden, H. H., 223
Beach, W. G., 450, 516
Beers, C. W., 205
Behavior, affective, 159; apprehension of, 168; and art, 375, 389, 397, 470; attitudinal, 122, 246 ff.; and the audience, 478; automatic, 34, 36, 127; cause of, 73; collective, 87, 88, 235, 335, 385, 395, 465, 496, 506, 517; competitive, 502; continuous, 247; control of, 67, 465; coöperative, 497, 502, 514; of crowds, 459; customary, 565; emotional, 160, 247, 501; environmental bases of, 69 ff., 143; and the environments, 272; fixity of, and instinct, 125; functional, 158 ff.; and generalization, 388; and groups, 411, 437, 451, 465; habitual, 36, 120, 142 ff.; hostile, 500, 504, 507; human, 109; imitative, 322, 343, 361, 383; impulsive, 127; individual, 87, 89; instinctive, 36; institutional, 564; intellectual, 497; internal, 144, 147, 248; and isolation, 501; and language, 82, 144-156, 388; of leaders, 517, 528; limitations of, due to inheritance, 139; and literature, 372, 392; and lower social environments, 79; and natural law, 73; non-overt, 121, 143, 248; objectified, 272; organic bases of, 51 ff., 206 ff.; of the organism, 39; overt, 143, 144; pathological, 187; pattern, 59, 95, 107 ff., 118, 123, 142, 144, 152, 323, 343, 569; and personality, 255, 273-275, 322, 343, 361, 383; and philosophy, 395; psychic, 121, 143, 149-155, 389; psycho-social, 22, 23, 144-156; and psycho-social environment, 83; of radicals, 505; random, 111; rational, 34, 147, 163, 283, 388, 570; revolutionary, 512; and science, 395; and social psychology, 107; suggested, 283, 286, 373; and superpersonality, 73; symbolic, 142, 147-156, 388; sympathetic, 502; and temperament, 252; and thought, 149, 163; trial and error, 143, 144; tropistic, 109; unconscious, 35, 187, 189, 283; units of, 107; unpremeditated, 127; vague, 127
Behavior patterns, acquired, 118, 142, 143; customary, 568; instinctive, 36; modification of, 95, 144, 569; source of, 119, 142, 147, 152-155; traditional, 571
Beliefs, 558
Bentley, M., 24
Bernard, L. L., 37, 68, 89, 105, 122, 132, 141, 156, 171, 205, 223
Bernheim, 36
Biography, grading of, 370; and personality, 368
Biological environments, 75; dominance of, 124; biological viewpoint, 37
Bio-social environments, 75, 79, 81, 270
Blackmar, F. W., 437, 562
Boas, F., 105, 226, 245
Bodin, 71, 72, 74
Bogardus, E. S., 14, 16, 27, 29, 30, 105, 122, 171, 185, 299, 341, 424, 437, 450, 464, 478, 495, 539, 562, 581
Bonser, F. G., 359
Boys' gangs, 357
Brain organization, 208
Brothers and sisters as models, 353
Buckle, T. H., 71
Bunyan, J., 392
Burgess, E. W., 122, 245, 299, 341, 464, 478, 516, 562, 582
Burnham, W. H., 30, 105, 122, 185, 218, 223, 261, 280, 516
Bushee, F. A., 245

Carmichael, R. D., 437
Case, C. M., 89, 157, 245, 402, 562, 582
Cause of behavior, 73
Cells, reproductive, 90; somatic, 90

Censor, escape from, 201, 373, 380
Censorship, 191; of art, 379; of wishes, 191
Cerebral cortex supreme, 62, 209
Ceremonials, 452; commemorative, 454; decline of, 453
Cervantes, 472
Character, 254; and models, 343 ff.; and play, 356; and the school, 353
Characteristics, acquired, 102
Charcot, 36
Child, C. M., 11, 37, 52, 68, 89, 93, 94, 96, 98, 103, 106, 112, 117, 208, 264, 265, 586
Child's admiration for father, 346; attachment to mother, 345, 349
Complexity of environments, 70
Composite environments, 76, 84
Concept of instinct, confusions, 127, 133; literary usage of, 126; misuse of, 123, 126; origins of, 123
Conceptual distinctions, artificial character of, 23; conceptual terms mistaken for instincts, 135; conceptual thinking, 133
Conditioned response, abbreviated, 286; and attitudes, 248, 249; and environment, 517, 526; and imitation, 270; and leadership, 528; negative, 120; positive, 120; significance of, 275; and social control, 276; in suggested behavior, 286; symbolic, 286-289
Conditioners of behavior, environmental, 517, 526; language, 145, 147 ff.; symbols, 144, 147, 152, 286-289; verbal, 137 ff.
Conditioning stimuli, 120, 248, 270, 526
Conflict, 189; and censorship, 191; and coöperation, 507; of derivative groups, 510; and distortion, 200; of factions, 512; of groups, 509; within the group, 508; between individuals, 508; origin of, 202; and personality, 507; and repression, 190, 507; revolutionary, 512
Conklin, E. G., 106
Conn, H. W., 264
Consciousness, cognitive, 162; collective, 183; emotional, 160; feeling, 159; forms of, 158 ff.; functional organization of, 158 ff., 172 ff.; objects of, 172 ff.; pathological forms of, 187 ff., 204; public, 173, 179, 183; rational, 163; of self, 174, 176, 181; social, 173, 177, 182, 271; types of, 172, 173
Contacts, competitive, 500, 503; coöperative, 497, 502; with coworkers, 500; in derivative groups, 423, 489; distance, 491; face-to-face, 439; hostile, 500, 504; indirect, 439; through language, 147, 151; non-coöperative, 498; in primary groups, 413; symbolic, 145, 153, 270, 390, 424; sympathetic, 502
Continuity of meaning and stereotyped symbols, 288
Contrasuggestion, 289
Control, of behavior, 67, 276, 398; by committees, 445; of derivative attitudes, 431-434; of derivative groups, 417, 465; environments, 76, 119; through institutions, 565; by leaders, 525; rational, 388, 442, 494; through suggestion, 320, 442
Controls, institutional, 504, 574, 575, 580; kinds of, 541; nature of, 541; non-institutional, 541, 556, 561; psycho-social, 542
Conventions, 81, 514, 518, 546, 556, 573
Cooley, C. H., 25, 29-32, 40, 172, 177, 185, 248, 280, 299, 412, 424, 437, 464, 478, 495, 497, 516, 539, 582, 586
Coolidge, M. R., 582
Coöperation, 497, 502, 514
Cope, H. F., 402
Cortex, 55, 59
Cortical dominance, 62, 144, 209, 225; through language, 144, 145, 152; social results of, 63; cortical selection, 64
Co-workers, 500
Crazes, 552; deflation of, 553; and ideals, 552; and ignorance, 554; and intolerance, 553; psychology

of, 555; and repression, 554; and suggestion, 553
Criticisms, anticipated, 42
Crowds, 458; and modern life, 459; results of, 460
Cultural lag, 514
Culture, 207 ff., 514; and environment, 65; and language, 144 ff.; and organism, 207; and postnatal environment, 100; and suggestibility, 309
Curriculum, and art, 400; and philosophy, 400; and science, 399
Custom, 514, 518, 568; revision of, 569; testing of, 569; value of, 570

Dante, 471
Darwin, C., 102, 105, 182
Dashiell, J. F., 323
Davenport, C. B., 37
Davenport, F. M., 321
Davies, G. R., 106
Daydreaming, 198
Deliberative assemblies, 442; discussion in, 445; function of, 443; organization of, 443; parliamentary procedure in, 444
Dementia præcox, 199, 502
Democracy, 432
Democratic societies, 484
Demonstrations, 455
DeMorgan, W., 472
Derivative attitudes, 429; derivative control environments, 76, 84, 119; derivative groups, causes of growth of, 420; conflict of, 510; contacts in, 423; dominance of, 417; examples of, 419; necessity for, 422; derivative ideals, examples of, 429; must dominate in conflict, 434
Determination by environment, 75 ff.; method of, 93; determination of inheritance, 92
Devine, E. T., 127
Dewey, J., 24, 30, 89, 122, 141, 157, 171, 185, 280, 359, 402, 582
Differentiation of environments, 70
Direct contact groups, 439, 451; expansion of, 467; leadership in, 531; rational control in, 442; suggestion control in, 442; types of, 439; waning of control by, 417, 420, 465
Direct suggestion, 295
Discipline and primary group, 414
Discussion, and committee control, 445, in deliberative assemblies, 445
Discussion groups, 446; effects of, 447; temper of, 447
Disintegration of instincts in man, 117
Disposition, 254
Dispositions, acquired, 118, 142 ff., 216; fundamental, 218; inherited, 107 ff.
Dissimilarity of responses, 88
Dissociation, of personality, 203 ff.; and suggestibility, 310
Distortion, of nationalities, 192; of personalities, 192, 200, 203, 365-368; schizophrenic, 198
Division of personality, 203
Dominance, of acquired technique, 142; cortical, 62, 63, 144; of derivative attitudes and ideals, 431, 434; of derivative groups, 417, 465; of environment, 45, 66, 138, 145, 152; of inherited technique, 142; of instincts, 137; of language controls, 144-154; of neural protoplasm, 52; of neuro-psychic patterns, 144; of psycho-social controls, 542; of psycho-social environment, 21, 135, 145-156, 518; of symbolic controls, 66, 135, 144, 147, 152-156, 476
Down, Langdon, 220
Downey, J., 261
Drama, 395
Dreiser, T., 472
Drever, W., 28
Drives and intelligence, 212
Dunlap, K., 15, 17, 24, 68, 106, 245, 424, 464, 540, 582
Duprat, C., 27
Duration of stimulus in suggestion, 301

Economic classes, 486
Edman, I., 157, 171, 185, 223, 245, 261, 478, 516, 582

INDEX

Education, and art, 377, 400; and imitation, 332; and leadership, 530; and philosophy, 400; and science, 399
Effective systems, 56
Ellwood, C. A., 14, 16, 24, 27, 29, 30, 89, 122, 141, 171, 223, 245, 341, 424, 437, 478, 495, 513, 516, 540, 562, 582
Emotion, 160; composite nature of, 161; and feeling, 160
Emotional attitudes, 247; reactions, 501
Emotions, derivative, 161; primary, 161
End organs, 57, 58
Environment, 11, 21, 23, 29; and behavior, 272; and class, 242; dominance of, 45, 138, 144, 271; emphasis upon, 586; and the individual, 39, 270; and language, 63, 82, 144, 271; and nationality, 241; neglect of, 72; and the organism, 43, 94; organization of, 69 ff., 144; psychic, 70; psychosocial, 21, 23, 80 ff., 145-156, 270, 514; and race, 228; and science, 11; significance of, 69, 586; social, 65, 70, 189; study of, 70
Environmental cause, 73; controls, 145, 147, 213; determination, 93, 138, 145, 518, 586; pressures, 44, 60, 145, 206, 249, 251, 271, 518, 525; selection of traits, 104, 143; theory, 74, 272, 586; transmission of traits, 101, 145, 152-156, 270
Environments, biological, 75; biosocial, 75, 270, 272; classification of, 75; complexity of, 70; composite, 76; condition collective responses, 517; derivative, 76; differentiation of, 70; institutionalized, 76; natural, 76; organic, 75; physical, 75; physico-social, 75, 272; psycho-social, 76, 152-156, 270, 272; social, 75, 189
Epic poetry, 395
Escape, from censor, 201; from reality, 194, 364
Ethical standards, and philosophy, 398; and science, 398

Euripides, 397
Expression, symbolic, 248
External storage of symbols, 152; and a closed system, 155; and the expert, 153; increasing volume of, 153
Exteroceptive senses, 57

Factional struggles, 512
Faculty concept, 158
Fads, and fashions, 546; function of, 543; nature of, 543; psychological bases of, 555; universality of, 544
Fairy stories, 365
Fashions, 546; in clothing, 547; competition in, 549; and fads, 546; expert in, 548; followers of, 551; leaders of, 548, 551; psychological bases of, 555; tendencies in, 550; variety of, 547
Father model, 345; incompleteness of, 350; necessity of, 347; unavailability of, 350; value of, 346
Feeble-mindedness, 218; and race, 232; and suggestibility, 306
Feeling, 159; and emotion, 160; not perceptual, 159; pleasant, 159; tones of, 160; unpleasant, 159
Feldman, W. M., 106
Ferris, H. J., 359
Fiction, and distortion of personality, 364; as model, 365, 372; as release for wishes, 373; serious, 374; social effects of, 374; and suggestion, 372
Fielding, H., 391, 472
Finot, J., 245
Fishberg, M., 245
Fixed ideas, 200, 314
Folkways, 518
Follett, M. P., 280, 299, 341, 424, 450
Followers, 539, 551
Forbush, W. B., 360
Forel, A., 127
Forms of consciousness, 158 ff.
Frear, C., 360
Free will, 168
Freud, S., 129
Freudian hypothesis, 200

Froebel, F., 381
Functional behavior concept, 158 ff.; functional organization of consciousness, 158 ff., 172 ff.; illustrations of, 181
Fundamental dispositions, 107 ff., 142 ff.; early origin of, 218

Gang, 356; boys', 356; decay of, 362; girls', 357; leader of, 358; and its successors, 359
Gardner, C. S., 464
Gault, R. H., 15, 16, 24, 30, 106, 122, 185, 223, 226, 245, 299, 321, 464, 540, 562, 582
Geiger, J. R., 381
General sets, 206 ff.
Generalization, in art, 390, 394, 397; and ethical standards, 398; in literary arts, 392; nature of, 389; in philosophy, 389, 392, 395, 397; projective, 393; reaction against, 392; social, 399; and social behavior, 395; and socialization, 388
Genetic groups, 440
Gestalt theory, 82
Gesture language, 148, 150
Giddings, F. H., 186, 437, 484
Gillin, J. L., 437, 562
Ginsberg, M., 24, 37, 186, 245, 464, 478, 495, 582
Girls' gangs, 357
Givler, R. C., 131
Gladden, W., 126
Gobineau, C., 514
Godkin, E. L., 562
Godwin, W., 26
Goldenweiser, A. A., 89, 245
Gradients, 52, 112
Great men and isolation, 502
Griggs, E. H., 382, 402
Group contacts, 416
Groups, 411; conflict of, 509; direct contact, 439, 451; derivative, 417; discussion, 446; genetic, 440; indirect contact, 420, 465; and individual, 496; mixed character of, 463; non-rational, 451-464; permanency of, 449; primary, 412-417, 439; rational, 438-450; types of, 411, 438

Gumplowicz, L., 514
Groves, E. R., 186, 205, 516
Guyer, M. F., 103

Habit, 29, 36; and emotions, 151; function of, 143; and language, 144, 145, 147-155; mechanisms, 142 ff.; and thought, 149; and trial and error, 143, 144
Habit technique, 142 ff.; stairway of, 143
Habits, acquiring, 120; inner, 143, 144; and instincts, 137; mistaken for instincts, 128; overt, 143, 144
Hall, G. S., 360, 402, 502
Hamilton, G. V., 205
Hands, 208
Harris and Hooke, 495
Hart, B., 205
Hart, H., 237
Hartley, D., 28
Hartson, L. D., 450
Healy, W., 205, 281, 360
Helvetius, 28, 29
Hereditary transmission of traits, 101
Heredity, 90 ff.; and class, 243; diagram of, 91; and intelligence, 215, 221; and maladjustment, 244; Mendelian theory of, 90; and race, 228
Herodotus, 397
Herrick, C. J., 37, 56-58, 61, 68, 98, 107, 122, 171, 264, 265, 586
Herskovitz, M. J., 230
Hetero-suggestion, 294
Hirn, Y., 478
Historical abstraction, 387; historical movements, identification with, 388; historical personalities as models, 366; limitations upon use of, 384
History and personality, 367
Hocking, W. E., 321, 540
Hollingworth, H. L., 261, 321
Holmes, S. J., 220
Homer, 397
Hostile contacts, 500, 504
Howard, G. E., 437
Human adjustment, 53, 62; human behavior, 107 ff.; and tropisms,

INDEX

109; human structural organizations, 207
Hume, D., 28, 29
Humor, 292
Humphrey, G., 341
Hunter, W. S., 24
Huntington, E., 71
Hutcheson, 28
Hygiene, mental, 204; of positive and negative attitudes, 433; social, 204
Hypothesis, Freudian, 200
Hypnotism, 316-320; success in, 317
Hysteria, 194

Ibsen, 472
Ideal personalities as models, 363
Ideals, 425, 429; constructive, 431; and crazes, 553; and democracy, 432; derivative, 427, 431; hygiene of, 433
Ideas, 517; fixed, 314
Imitation, 269 ff., 587; abstract, 330, 332, 385; accidental, 324; acquired basis of, 328; and age, 340, 343; automatic, 323; through biography, 368, 384; of brothers and sisters, 354; cause of, 329; in children, 277; and classes, 339; and collective behavior, 345, 385; concrete, 332; controversy regarding, 322, 587; direct, 279, 343, 383; of distant persons, 365; of the father, 345; through fiction, 372; in the gang, 356; through history, 367, 384; of ideal persons, 361; indirect, 279, 361, 385; and language, 277; and leadership, 526; through literature, 365, 385; mechanism of, 323; of the mother, 342; nature of, 322; neural basis of, 328; non-personal, 331; overt, 279; personal, 330, 383; and personality development, 322, 342, 361, 383; of persons outside the home, 351; and play, 356; of playmates, 354; projective, 324, 325, 383; psychic, 328, 330; purposive, 324; recognitive basis of, 325; rhythms of, 337; in the school, 352; and sex, 355; suggestion, 323; symbolic, 279, 330; by trial and error, 324; as vicarious integration of personality, 333

Imitative conditioning of responses, 270; thinking, 336

Impulses, 144; acquired, 120, 143; to identification with historical movements, 387; to overt behavior, 147; random, 110

Indians, intelligence of, 228

Indirect contact groups, 420, 479; classification of, 480; effects of, 489; increasing importance of, 465, 467; leadership in, 532; and mob-mindedness, 493; origin of, 466; and personality, 492; and rational control, 494; and social science, 493; and sympathy, 490; and tolerance, 490

Indirect suggestion, 295; dangers of, 297; examples of, 296; methods of, 296; superiority of, 296

Individual behavior, 87, 89, 107, 123, 142; and the group, 496

Individual and environment, 40, 78, 145, 272

Inferiority, compensation for, 196; feeling, 196

Inheritance, of acquired characteristics, 102; and class, 243; concept of, 73; determination of, 92; and intelligence, 215-218; and limitations upon behavior, 139; Mendelian theory of, 90; and race, 228

Inherited attitudes, 247; inherited equipment of man, 90 ff., 215; inherited traits, 107 ff.; and intelligence, 215; and personality, 257; source of, 103; structural, 221

Inner behavior, 143, 147; and attitudes, 247 ff.; and language, 144, 147-156; and thought, 149

Innuendo, 298

Insinuation, 298

Instinct, 28, 36, 114, 117 ff.; definition, 114, 134; and emotions, 151; erroneous view of, 116, 127; literary usage of, 126; not physiological need, 140

Instinct, concept of, 114, 117 ff.;

confusions, 127; criticism of, 133; misuse of, 123 ff., 126; origins of, 123; widespread use of, 123
Instinctive attitudes, 247; elements in suggestion, 285
Instincts, and adaptation, 117; classifications of, 129, 134; not conceptual, 134, 135; delayed, 118; disintegration of, in man, 117; do they dominate habits, 137; examples of, 130; do they exist in man, 136; and habits, 128; not purposive, 115; are structural, 134
Institutional controls, 574; environments, 76; publics, 488; revolutions, 512
Institutions, 81, 86, 464, 489, 511, 518; and codes, 577; composite character of, 86; content of, 564, 570; as control agency, 565; decadent, 579; and derivative ideals, 436; extensions of, 578; flexibility of, 580; modification of, 574; nature of, 565; objective content in, 564; subjective, 580; traits of, 578; trends in, 566
Integration of behavior, 249, 273, 333; of personality, 256, 273-275, 333, 413
Intellectual attitudes, 247; reactions, 497
Intelligence, 209; and acquired skills, 216-219, 222; and adjustment, 212; and brain, 212; and city, 236; and classes, 243; and country, 236; drives and, 212; factors in, 211; forms of, 211; and inheritance, 215; and language, 210, 216, 230; limitations upon, 216; measurement of, 214-218; and motivation, 213; and nationality, 240; nature of, 210; and occupation, 237; and personality, 256; quotient, 216, 218; and race, 226 ff.; and sex, 239; special, 219; and structure, 208, 221; and temperament, 213, 251
Interests, conflict of, 507, 509; theory of, 250
Internal behavior, 144-156, 248
Intolerance, 493; and crazes, 553

Invention, 165; degrees of abstractness of, 166; types of, 165
Inventions, as environment, 78, 79; influence of, 71
Investigation, 165
Irwin, W., 495
Isolation, 502; effects of, 501; and great men, 502
Italians, 230; compared with native Americans, 231; intelligence of, 230

James, W., 28, 29, 131
Jastrow, J., 261
Jennings, H. S., 37, 107, 122, 143
Josey, C. C., 141
Judd, C. H., 157, 186, 205, 582
Judgment, 164
Jung, C. G., 129, 558, 562
Justice and leadership, 534

Kammerer, P., 103
Kant, E., 28
Kantor, J. R., 122
Keller, A. G., 89
Khaldun, I., 71, 74
Kidd, B., 126, 129
King, I., 341
Kirkpatrick, E. A., 29, 131
Kitson, H. D., 321
Köhler, W., 171, 329, 341
Kræpelin, E., 36
Kretschmer, E., 223, 261
Kroeber, A. L., 24, 68

Lamarck, 102
Langenhove, F. van, 562
Language, as environment, 62 ff., 82, 145; forms of, 149; gesture, 148, 150; and imitation, 277; and inner behavior, 144-149; and intelligence, 210, 231; and mental tests, 214; publics, 484; and race, 231; rapid change of, 271; speech, 150; symbolic, 147-156; verbal, 147-154; written, 151-156
Language forms and environmental controls, 145; language symbols, function of, 144, 147-156
Lappin, Mrs., 228
Lawrence, D. H., 472

Leaders, 520; of action, 524; equipment of, 531; of fashion, 548, 551; intellectual, 524; personality of, 531; qualities of, 528, 531, 537; successful, 522; task of, 529; training of, 530

Leadership, amateur, 522; appeal, 523, 528; and collective responses, 517; and control, 525; and courage, 536; in the gang, 358; and good faith, 534; and honesty, 534; and humanitarianism, 534; impersonal, 521; and insight, 535; and justice, 534; moral, 538; and persistence, 536; personal, 521; and prestige, 522, 548; professional, 522; qualities of, 358; and social psychology, 528; and sympathy, 532

LeBon, G., 27, 127, 450, 464, 495, 513, 540

Lee, J., 128

Leopold, L., 321

LePlay, 397

Levels of control of behavior, 67; of personality, 196, 258, 277; of suggested responses, 278

Lewis, S., 374

Life as adjustment, 247

Lindeman, E. C., 424, 450, 516

Lippmann, W., 27, 478, 495, 540

Literature and personality, 365

Literary arts and generalization, 392

Locke, J., 29

Loeb, J., 108, 122

Logic, 164

Long, E. H., 230

Lower social environments, 78

Luckey, G. W. A., 382

Lumley, F. E., 299, 540, 562

MacCunn, J., 360, 382, 402

MacCurdy, J. T., 205

MacDonald, H., 237

Maciver, R. M., 24, 424

McDougall, W., 13, 14, 16, 17, 24, 25, 28-30, 32, 36, 37, 39, 129, 130, 171, 186, 253, 254, 261, 299, 321, 324, 341, 424, 450, 464, 478, 495, 540, 586

McMillan, M., 382

Maladjusted classes, 244

Manias, 200, 314

Marett, R. R., 126

Martin, E. D., 30, 32, 299, 439, 464, 513

Marvin, F. S., 126

Mead, G. H., 30

Mead, M., 230, 231

Mechanisms of adjustment, compensatory, 194; habitual, 118, 142 ff.; imitative, 323; instinctive, 114, 123 ff.; mechanisms of behavior, 107, 123, 142, 187; neuropsychic, 328; organic, 209; verbal, 145, 152, 210, 286, 328; mechanisms of communication, 474

Mendelian theory, 73, 90, 93, 103, 217

Mental defect, and environment, 218; and race, 232; mental hygiene, 204; mental tests, 214; and acquired skills, 216; and intelligence, 215; and language, 214; types of, 215.

Meyer, M. F., 157, 159

Mill, J. S., 28

Miller, A. H., 540

Miller, I. E., 171

Miller, K., 245

Misrepresentation and distance, 495

Misuse of concept of instinct, 123 ff., 133, 135

Mob-mindedness in indirect contact groups, 493

Mobs, 458

Models for imitation, 342, 363; in art, 375; in biography, 368; brothers and sisters, 353; in fairy stories, 364; father, 345-348; the gang, 356; in history, 367, 384; ideal, 363 ff.; inadequacy of, 361; in literature, 365, 372, 385; mother, 342-346; outside adults, 351; playmates, 354; school children, 352

Modification of behavior patterns, 95, 96, 143, 144

Moll, A., 321

Monotony in stimuli, 300

Montesquieu, 71, 72, 74

Morality plays, 472

Mores, 518

Mother model, 342; dominance of, 348; importance of, 344
Motility and personality, 256
Motivation, 213
Movements, random, 110
Movies, 476, 494
Mumford, E., 540
Münsterberg, H., 299, 382
Music, 376

National life and art, 471
Nationalities, 484
Nationality, distortion of, 192; elements of, 240; nature of, 240; unity of, 241
Natural environments, 76
Natural law and behavior, 73
Negative suggestion, 290
Neglect of environment, 72
Negro race, 226 ff.; and environment, 228-232; intelligence of, 226-234; and white race, 226
Neighborhood, 420, 484
Neural dominance, 62, 208, 209; protoplasm, 52, 53
Neuro-muscular behavior, 143
Neuro-psychic behavior, 121, 143 ff., 248, 283; mechanisms, 143, 273, 328; technique, 62 ff., 81, 143-155
Neurons, 59, 206
Neurosis, 202, 204
Newman, H. H., 37
Nietzsche, F., 127
Non-institutional controls, 541; how they work, 561; prophylactics against, 556
Norsworthy, N., 122, 205
Novel, 391
Novicow, J., 514

Objects of consciousness, 172
Occupation and intelligence, 237; and race, 229-232; and sex, 236
Odum, H. W., 232, 233, 245
Ogburn, W. F., 582
Omar, 472
Opinion, public, 183, 485, 511, 559
Oratory, 460
Organic bases of maladjustment, 244; bases of temperament, 252; environments, 75; structures, 206-209
Organism, behavior of, 39; and environment, 43, 94; inheritance of, 92; nature of, 51; and self-consciousness, 175
Organization, of consciousness, 158 ff., 172 ff.; cortical, 66, 143; degrees of, 85; functional, of consciousness, 163; human structural, 207; internal, 144-156; overt, 143; psycho-social, 41; of thought, 164-167
Organs, sense, 57
Overcompensation, 196
Overt behavior, and language, 144; mechanisms, 143, 144

Paranoia, 199
Park, R. E., 122, 245, 299, 341, 464, 478, 495, 516, 562, 582
Parmelee, M., 68
Partial suggestion, 290
Paton, S., 68, 122, 223, 281
Pathological forms of behavior, 187 ff.; significance of, 204
Patrick, G. T. W., 299, 321
Patterns, acquired, 118, 144; attitudinal, 250; behavior, 59, 95, 107 ff., 118, 123 ff., 142 ff., 269 ff., 322 ff.; conceptual, 135, 145; habitual, 144 ff.; imitative, 322 ff.; instinctive, 130; modification of, 95; source of, 119
Perception, and feeling, 159; relative ease of, 168
Permanent attitudes, 251
Personality, 255; and abstract principles, 385; acquired, 257; analysis of, 256; and art, 375; and average man, 260; and behavior, 270, 273; and biography, 368, 385; classification of, 259; development of, 273, 282, 343, 361; distortion of, 192, 200, 367; division of, 203; and environment, 270; extensions of, 257; extrovert, 258; and history, 367, 384-388; ideal, 364; and imitation, 322 ff., 333, 343 ff.; and indirect contact groups, 492; inheritance of, 257; integration of,

273-275, 333, 413; and intelligence, 256; introvert, 259; and leadership, 518 ff., 531; and literature, 372; and motility, 256; and self-expression, 256; and sociality, 256; socialization of, 388; sources of, 273; and temperament, 256

Personality levels, 196, 258 ff.; and imitation, 277; and language, 277

Persons, ideal, 361

Peters, C. C., 261

Peterson, J., 341

Phantasy, 197; forms of, 198

Philosophy, and adjustment, 401; and art, 397, 399; displaced by science, 398; and ethical standards, 398; and generalization, 389, 392, 395, 397; and science, 395, 398

Phobias, 314

Physical environments, 75

Physico-social environment, 75, 79, 81

Physiological need not instinct, 140

Pillsbury, W. B., 245, 437, 495

Plato, 396

Play, and art, 380; and character, 356

Playmates as models, 354

Poetry, 395

Poffenberger, A. T., 382

Postnatal development, 98, 100, 144

Powers, 206 ff.

Preconceptual development, 100; influences, 100

Prejudices, 315

Prenatal development, 99

Pressey, L. W., 237

Pressures, environmental, 44, 60, 206

Prestige, and fashion, 548; and leadership, 522; and suggestibility, 295, 303

Preyer, 28

Price, 28

Primary attitudes, 426; misuse of, 435

Primary groups, declining importance of, 415, 417; definition of, 412; and discipline, 414; examples of, 418; and personality integration, 413; preservative function of, 415; and production, 416; transmissive function of, 415

Primitive elements in art, 378

Prince, M., 203, 205

Processes, behavior, 107 ff.; cognitive, 162; emotional, 160; feeling, 159; habitual, 118, 142 ff.; historical, 367, 387; instinctive, 114, 123 ff.; mental, 158 ff.; psychosocial, 19, 144-156; rationality, 163; reciprocal, of adjustment, 270; stimulus-response, 53-62, 107 ff., 158 ff.; unconscious, 187

Progress, why difficult, 170

Projective generalization, in art, 394; and control, 393; in science, 394

Projective imitation, 324, 388

Propaganda, 493-495, 511, 525

Prophylactics against non-institutional controls, 556

Proprioceptive senses, 57

Protoplasm, 51 ff., 90 ff., 206; characteristics of, 52; neural, 52, 53

Pseudo feeble-mindedness, 218

Psychic behavior, 121, 143, 272; environment, 70; imitation, 330

Psychoanalysis, 502

Psychoanalysts, 187

Psychology, 19; and attitudes, 249; biological viewpoint in, 37; of coöperation, 516; of crazes, 555; of fads, 555; of fashions, 555; of radicalism, 504; social, 7, 10 ff.; and social psychology, 191; and temperament, 254

Psychoses, 199, 202, 204

Psycho-social, 20 ff.; behavior, 22, 143; controls, 66, 145, 147, 152, 518, 542; dominance of, 542; function of, 543; nature of, 543; environment, 21, 76, 80 ff., 145, 147, 152, 213, 517; and institutions, 86; processes, 20 ff., 142 ff., 147, 152

Public consciousness, 179, 486; aspects of, 180

Public opinion, 183, 485, 511, 559; and art, 488; and classes, 486; and collective consciousness, 185; and institutions, 488; and language,

485; and nationality, 484; and religion, 487; and science, 487; types of, 184
Publics, 486, 512; and art, 488; and classes, 486; and institutions, 488; and language, 484; and nationality, 484; and religion, 487; and science, 487; types of, 484
Puffer, J. A., 360, 450
Purposive associations, 441; imitation, 324
Pyle, W. H., 29, 227, 228, 233, 234, 236, 237, 239, 245

Qualities of leaders, 528, 531, 537
Quetelet, 397

Race, 224; an abstraction, 235; characteristics of, 225; colored, 226; and environment, 225, 228-232; fact versus concept of, 226; and heredity, 228; and intelligence, 226-234; and language, 229-231; and mental defect, 232; white, 226
Race traits, anatomical, 225; physiological, 225; psychological, 225; social, 225
Radicalism, psychology of, 504; types of, 506
Rallies, 455
Random behavior, 111; impulses, 110; movements, 110; and reflexes, 114
Rasmussen, W., 360
Rational behavior, 163, 283
Rationality processes, 163
Rationalization, 191
Ratzel, F., 71
Ratzenhofer, G., 250, 514
Reason, 163
Receptor systems, 56
Reciprocal process of adjustment of individual and society, 270
Recreation and art, 380
Reflex arc, 112, 113
Reflexes, 112; function of, 113; origins of, 112; and random movements, 114
Reid, T., 28
Release of wishes, 194, 373, 380, 554
Religion and public opinion, 487

Repetition of stimulus, 301
Repression, 190; and conflict, 190, 191, 373; and crazes, 554; origins of, 202; and race, 230
Reproductive cells, 90
Responses, to art, 375; and behavior, 88; collective, 517; and competition, 510; conditioned, 120, 248, 270, 275, 278, 286-289; coöperative, 497; and co-workers, 500; emotional, 501; to fiction, 372; in groups, 496 ff.; to ideal personalities, 363; imitative, 322, 333; intellectual, 497; to leaders, 518, 528; noncoöperative, 498; stereotyped, 283, 287; suggested, 278, 283, 286
Reuter, E. B., 245
Revision of institutions, 569, 574
Revolution, 512; factional, 512; institutional, 512; social, 513; types of, 512
Rhythm in stimuli, 300
Rhythms of imitation, 337
Rituals, 576
Rivalry, 509
Robinson, E. S., 68, 157, 261
Robinson, F. R., 68, 157, 261
Root, W. T., 505, 506, 516
Ross, E. A., 15-17, 21, 24, 25, 27, 30, 72, 89, 128, 171, 186, 281, 299, 321, 332, 341, 373, 402, 424, 437, 450, 464, 478, 495, 501, 516, 554, 556, 562, 582, 586
Rumor, 557
Rural environment, and intelligence, 236; and race, 232
Russell and Rigby, 450

Schaupp, Z., 37
Schizophrenic distortions, 198
Schneider, 28
School, and character, 353; and imitation, 352
Schools of social psychology, 25 ff.; environmentalist school, 29; instinctivist school, 28; planes and currents school, 26; synthetic, 30
Science, 3, 560; and art, 376, 389, 394; and custom, 569; displaces philosophy, 398; and education,

INDEX

399; and environment, 11; and ethical standards, 398; function of, 8; and generalization, 389, 394, 399; and institutions, 574; nature of, 3; and philosophy, 395, 398; and public opinion, 488; social, 7; and social behavior, 395

Sciences, applied, 3; basic, 3; classification of, 3; general, 3; organization of, 7; origin of, 6; social, 9; special, 3; unity of, 5

Scientific analysis and environmental theory, 74

Selection, cortical, 64

Self, 175 ff.; self-analysis in modern art, 472; self-expression and personality, 256

Self-consciousness, 174; abstract, 176; attitudinal, 176; in the child, 174; extension of, to external objects, 175; illustrations of, 181; inner, 176; organic, 174; sensory and perceptual, 175

Sense organs, 57

Sentiments, 162

Sets, neural, 206; social, 451

Sex, and imitation, 355; and intelligence, 239; and race, 234; and suggestibility, 309

Shaftesbury, 28

Sharp, F. C., 360, 382, 402

Sherrington, C. S., 59, 68

Shinn, M. W., 341

Sidis, B., 299, 321

Sighele, S., 27

Simmel, G., 563

Skills, acquired, 216, 222; manual, 208; neuro-psychic, 213; special, 220; vocal, 208

Small, A. W., 127, 250

Small, M. H., 516

Smith, A., 28, 29

Social adjustment, 10; factors in, 10; and generalization, 385; and language, 144; and trial and error, 144

Social classes, 241, 486

Social consciousness, 173, 177; abstract, 179; examples of, 182; phases of, 177; symbolic, 179

Social control and the conditioned response, 276

Social environment, 65, 70, 75, 142-156; dominance of, 65, 145, 152-156, 271; and the individual, 270; as objectified behavior, 272

Social environments, and behavior, 79, 145-156, 213, 269 ff.; lower, 78

Social hygiene, 204

Social organization, and derivative groups, 420; and primary groups, 417

Social psychology, and attitudes, 248; and behavior, 107; of co-operation, 516; criticisms of, 42; definitions of, 13 ff., 584; departures in, 41; field of, 17, 248, 249; and forms of consciousness, 173; kinds of, 25 ff.; problem of, 589; and psychology, 19, 44; relationships of, 587; and sociology, 20, 44, 124, 588; synthetic treatment of, 38; Tardean, 269

Social science, 9; early intellectualism of, 32; field of, 17; functions of, 9; and indirect contact groups, 498

Social sets, 451

Sociality and personality, 256

Socialization, 388

Societies, 463, 483, 511; democratic, 484

Society, 8, 9; and language, 145

Sociology, 20 ff., 588; and social psychology, 20, 44, 124

Somatic cells, 90

Sophists, 26, 74

Sophocles, 397

Special abilities, 220-223

Speech, 151; preliminary to adjustment, 150

Spencer, H., 28, 182

Stages of development, 98; postnatal, 98, 100; preconceptual, 100; prenatal, 99

Starch, D., 29, 321

Steiner, J. F., 424, 437, 464

Stephen, L., 28

Stereotyped responses, 283, 287-289

Stern, W., 157, 171, 186, 205, 299

Stewart, D., 28
Stimulation, threshold of, 313
Stimuli, in art, 375, 380; in collective behavior, 385; duration of, 301; environmental, 269 ff.; in fiction, 372; and imitation, 323; in leaders, 518, 526; and models, 343 ff.; monotony of, 300; repetition of, 301; rhythm in, 300; in science, 376; volume of, 302
Stimulus-response processes, 53, 107 ff., 157, 270, 300
Stoner, W. S., 360, 382
Storage of symbols, external, 152-156, 272; increasing volume of, 153
Story-telling, 198, 365
Stratton, G. M., 261, 321
Strong, A. C., 229
Strong, E. K., Jr., 540
Structures, organic, 206-209; underlying intelligence, 221
Struggles, factional, 512
Study of environment, 71
Subconsciousness, 188
Sublimation and cortical selection, 64
Suggested behavior, 278, 283, 286
Suggestibility, 300 ff.; and abnormality, 313; and dissociation, 310; and duration of stimulus, 301; and education, 308; and experience, 308; external conditions of, 300; and fasting, 311; and fatigue, 311; and feeble-mindedness, 306; and fixed ideas, 314; and hypnotism, 316; and hysteria, 314; internal conditions of, 304; and intoxication, 311; and lower animals, 306; and manias, 314; and monotony, 300; and phobias, 314; and prejudices, 315; and prestige, 303; and repetition, 301; and rhythm, '300; and sex, 309; and threshold of stimulation, 313; and the unfilled mind, 305; and volume of stimuli, 302; and the young, 307
Suggestion, 269; acquired elements in, 285; and art, 375; aspects of, 284; auto-, 292, 294; and conditioned responses, 286-289; contra-, 289; and crazes, 553; definition of, 282; direct, 295; and fiction, 372; hetero-, 294; and hypnotism, 316; indirect, 295; instinctive elements in, 285; and leadership, 526; by negation, 290; partial, 290; and prestige, 295, 303; types of, 318; ubiquitousness of, 320
Suggestion imitation, 323
Sully, J., 563
Summary, general, 583-589; Part II, 262-265; Part III, 403-407
Sumner, W. G., 27, 321, 563, 582
Superpersonality and behavior, 73
Swift, E. J., 360
Symbolic communication, 476; conditioning of responses, 286; controls, 66, 135, 144, 145, 147-156, 391; expression, 248; generalization, 385 ff.; imitation, 279, 330
Symbolism, 199
Symbols, external storage of, 152; increasing volume of, 153; psychosocial, 145, 270, 390; stereotyped, 287-289, 468; verbal, 144, 152, 210, 391
Sympathy, 489; and coöperation, 502; and distance, 491; and leadership, 532; limitations to, 490
Synapses, 60

Tarde, G., 26, 27, 72, 563, 586
Taylor, M., 360
Teams, 442
Technique, habit, 153; language, 144-152; manual, 208; neuromuscular, 143; neuro-psychic, 143, 152, 213; verbal, 145, 152; vocal, 209
Temperament, 251; as behavior, 252; classification, 252; organic bases of, 252; and personality, 256
Terman, L. M., 214
Terminology, 141
Tests, Alpha, 215; army, 215; mental, 214; and race, 224; special, 219
Theory, environmental, 74; of inheritance, 90; Mendelian, 90
Thinking, acquired in character, 149; imitative, 336; and invention,

INDEX

165; and investigation, 165; and language, 147-149; and logic, 164; original, 336; and reason, 163
Thomas, F., 89
Thomas, J. B., 237
Thomas, W. I., 30, 245, 250, 261
Thompson, H. P., 239
Thorndike, E. L., 131, 132, 134
Threshold of stimulation, 313
Thucydides, 397
Tolerance, 489; limitations to, 490
Traditions, 518; nature of, 571; testing of, 572; validity of, 571
Traits, acquired, 97, 101; environmentally selected, 104; inherited, 90, 101, 103; racial, 225
Transition to psycho-social environment, 80
Transmission of traits, environmental, 101, 145; hereditary, 101, 142
Trial and error, internal, 143, 144; overt, 143, 144
Tropisms, 107; and human behavior, 109
Trotter, W., 28

Unconscious, the, 187; types of, 189
Unconscious behavior and suggestion, 283
Understanding the world at a distance, 179
Upright position, 207
Urban environment, and intelligence, 236; and race, 232
Usage of concept of instinct, 123, 126; criticism of, 133; statistical analysis of, 132
Utilitarianism, 28, 33

Varendonck, J., 205
Veblen, T. B., 27, 563
Verbal symbols, 144, 152, 210; conditioners of inner behavior, 147
Viewpoint of this book, 38, 47
Vincent, G. E., 127

Visceral senses, 58
Vocal equipment of man, 208
Volume of stimuli and suggestibility, 302

Wallas, G., 24, 27, 29, 30, 89, 171, 464
Ward, L. F., 106
Warren, H. C., 24, 68, 131
Watson, J. B., 31, 44, 68, 122, 132, 157, 171, 261
Watts, F., 205, 215, 223, 261, 414
Webster, H., 450
Weismann, A., 102
White, W. A., 205
White race, 226
Whitley, M. T., 122, 205
Whitman, W., 378
Wieman, H. W., 424
Williams, J. M., 14, 16, 24, 89, 261, 424, 516, 540
Wishes, and compensation, 194; and crazes, 554; release through art, 380; release through fiction, 373; theory of, 250
Wissler, C., 89
Wit, 292
Wohlgemuth, A., 205
Woodworth, R. M., 31, 122, 131, 171, 211, 216, 223, 253, 261, 281
Wooley, H. P. T., 239
Words as conditioners of responses, 148
World, understanding the, 179
Written language, 151-155; and intellectual communication, 475

Xenophon, 397

Yarros, V. S., 402, 495
Yerkes, R. M., 215, 223
Yoakum, C. S., 223
Youth and suggestibility, 307

Znanieki, F., 245
Zola, 472

14849